# The Routledge Companion to Air Transport Management

*The Routledge Companion to Air Transport Management* provides a comprehensive, up-to-date review of air transport management research and literature. This exciting new handbook provides a unique repository of current knowledge and critical debate with an international focus, considering both developed and emerging markets, and covering key sectors of the air transport industry.

The companion consists of 25 chapters that are written by 39 leading researchers, scholars and industry experts based at universities, research institutes, and air transport companies and organisations in 12 different countries in Africa, Asia-Pacific, Europe and North America to provide a definitive, trustworthy resource. The international team of contributors have proven experience of research and publication in their specialist areas, and contribute to this companion by drawing upon research published mainly in academic, industry and government sources.

This seminal companion is a vital resource for researchers, scholars and students of air transport management. It is organised into three parts: current state of the air transport sectors (Part I); application of management disciplines to airlines and airports (Part II); and key selected themes (Part III).

**Nigel Halpern** is Associate Professor in Air Transport and Tourism at Kristiania University College, Norway. Nigel is also Visiting Research Fellow with the School of Aviation at the University of New South Wales, Australia. He has previously worked at Molde University College, Norway; the Centre for Civil Aviation at London Metropolitan University, UK; the UK Department for Transport, Local Government and the Regions; the UK Civil Aviation Authority; and PGL Travel in the UK, France and Spain. Nigel teaches and conducts research and consultancy in air transport and tourism. He is co-author of the Routledge book *Airport Marketing* (2013).

**Anne Graham** is Professor of Air Transport and Tourism Management at the University of Westminster, UK. Anne has been involved in air transport and tourism teaching, research and consultancy for over 30 years. She has a particular interest in airport management, economics and regulation, and air travel and tourism demand analysis. In addition to previously being Editor in Chief of the *Journal of Air Transport Management* for a number of years, Anne has published extensively in the field of air transport and tourism. She is author of the Routledge book *Managing Airports: An International Perspective* (4th edition, 2014) and co-author of *Airport Marketing* (2013) and *Airport Finance and Investment in the Global Economy* (2017).

# Routledge Companions in Business, Management and Accounting

Routledge Companions in Business, Management and Accounting are prestige reference works providing an overview of a whole subject area or sub-discipline. These books survey the state of the discipline including emerging and cutting edge areas. Providing a comprehensive, up to date, definitive work of reference, Routledge Companions can be cited as an authoritative source on the subject.

A key aspect of these Routledge Companions is their international scope and relevance. Edited by an array of highly regarded scholars, these volumes also benefit from teams of contributors which reflect an international range of perspectives.

Individually, Routledge Companions in Business, Management and Accounting provide an impactful one-stop-shop resource for each theme covered. Collectively, they represent a comprehensive learning and research resource for researchers, postgraduate students and practitioners.

Published titles in this series include:

*The Routledge Companion to Performance Management and Control*
Edited by Elaine Harris

*The Routledge Companion to Management Information Systems*
Edited by Robert D. Galliers and Mari-Klara Stein

*The Routledge Companion to Critical Accounting*
Edited by Robin Roslender

*The Routledge Companion to Trust*
Edited by Rosalind Searle, Ann-Marie Nienaber and Sim Sitkin

*The Routledge Companion to Tax Avoidance Research*
Edited by Nigar Hashimzade and Yuliya Epifantseva

*The Routledge Companion to Intellectual Capital*
Edited by James Guthrie, John Dumay, Federica Ricceri
and Christian Neilsen

*The Routledge Companion to Behavioural Accounting Research*
Edited by Theresa Libby and Linda Thorne

*The Routledge Companion to Accounting Information Systems*
Edited by Martin Quinn and Erik Strauss

*The Routledge Companion to Air Transport Management*
Edited by Nigel Halpern and Anne Graham

# The Routledge Companion to Air Transport Management

*Edited by Nigel Halpern and Anne Graham*

LONDON AND NEW YORK

First published 2018
by Routledge

2 Park Square, Milton Park, Abingdon, Oxfordshire OX14 4RN

52 Vanderbilt Avenue, New York, NY 10017

*Routledge is an imprint of the Taylor & Francis Group, an informa business*

First issued in paperback 2020

*British Library Cataloguing in Publication Data*
A catalogue record for this book is available from the British Library

*Library of Congress Cataloging-in-Publication Data*
Names: Halpern, Nigel, author. | Graham, Anne, 1958- author.
Title: The Routledge companion to air transport management /
    Nigel Halpern and Anne Graham.
Description: 1 Edition. | New York : Routledge, 2018. | Series: Routledge
    companions in business, management and accounting | Includes
    bibliographical references and index.
Identifiers: LCCN 2017037177 (print) | LCCN 2017058496 (ebook) |
    ISBN 9781315630540 (eBook) | ISBN 9781138641372
    (hardback : alk. paper)
Subjects: LCSH: Airlines—Management. | Airports—Management. |
    Aeronautics, Commercial—Economic aspects. | Social responsibility
    of business.
Classification: LCC HE9780 (ebook) | LCC HE9780 .H35 2018 (print) |
    DDC 387.7068—dc23
LC record available at https://lccn.loc.gov/2017037177


ISBN: 978-1-138-64137-2 (hbk)
ISBN: 978-0-367-65614-0 (pbk)


Typeset in Bembo
by Swales & Willis Ltd, Exeter, Devon, UK

# Contents

List of figures  *viii*

List of tables  *x*

Notes on contributors  *xii*

Acknowledgements  *xx*

List of abbreviations and acronyms  *xxi*

Introduction to *The Routledge Companion to Air Transport Management*  1
*Nigel Halpern and Anne Graham*

**PART I**

**Current state of the air transport sectors**  **9**

1 The global airline industry  11
*John F. O'Connell*

2 The air cargo industry  29
*Rico Merkert and David Alexander*

3 The airport industry  48
*Lucy Budd and Stephen Ison*

4 Air traffic management and air navigation service providers  60
*Marc Bourgois, Eduardo García and Peter Hullah*

5 The commercial aerospace industry  81
*Fariba E. Alamdari, Jan Hogrefe and Wendy R. Sowers*

6 Impacts of liberalisation in global mature markets  93
*David Gillen*

Contents

7  Liberalisation developments in key selected emerging markets      108
   *Eric T. Njoya and David Warnock-Smith*

8  Evolving airline and airport business models      122
   *Marina Efthymiou and Andreas Papatheodorou*

**PART II**
**Application of management disciplines to airlines and airports      137**

9  Airline business strategy      139
   *Gui Lohmann and Bojana Spasojevic*

10  Airport business strategy      154
    *Nigel Halpern*

11  Airline economics and finance      171
    *Anming Zhang and Yahua Zhang*

12  Airport economics and finance      189
    *Anne Graham*

13  Airline marketing      206
    *Blaise P. Waguespack*

14  Airport marketing      220
    *Nigel Halpern*

15  Airline capacity planning and management      238
    *Cheng-Lung Wu and Stephen J. Maher*

16  Airport capacity planning and management      259
    *Dieter Wilken*

17  Airline sustainability and corporate social responsibility      277
    *Robert Mayer*

18  Airport sustainability and corporate social responsibility      297
    *Christopher Paling and Callum Thomas*

**PART III**
**Key selected themes      311**

19  Patterns and drivers of demand for air transport      313
    *Xingwu Zheng and Anne Graham*

20  The role of technology in airline management and operations          331
    *Berendien Lubbe and Theunis Potgieter*

21  Key aspects in aviation security          344
    *William G. Morrison and Kathleen Rodenburg*

22  Airline service quality and the consumer experience          362
    *Dawna L. Rhoades*

23  Consumer protection regimes and passenger complaints          373
    *Paul Hooper*

24  Low cost carrier implications for human resource management          392
    *Geraint Harvey and Peter Turnbull*

25  Air transport and climate change          402
    *Stefan Gössling*

*Index*          417

# Figures

1.1   Number of passengers carried worldwide, 1991 to 2015                     12
1.2   Revenues and profitability for the world's commercial airlines,
      1978 to 2015                                                              15
2.1   Significant air freight markets and key trade lanes, 2014                 32
2.2   Industry air cargo indices (tonnage, revenue and FTK), 2005 to 2016       36
2.3   Global economic growth and air freight, 2005 to 2015                      37
2.4   Growth of air cargo trade (FTK), year-on-year, August 2016               38
2.5   Cargolux weekly scheduled freighter network, December 2016               39
2.6   Traditional air cargo supply chain versus integrator                      41
3.1   Proportion of world's airports/airfields with paved runways by world
      region, 2013                                                             49
4.1   FABs and participating states                                            64
4.2   Scope of ATM/ANS                                                         65
4.3   Expected implementation of FRA in European airspace                      72
4.4   Evolution of ATFM delay, 2006 to 2015                                    73
4.5   A sustainable flightpath towards reducing emissions                      75
5.1   Commercial aircraft deliveries, 1960 to 2016                             83
5.2   Regional fleet composition by aircraft type, 2015 and 2035               84
5.3   Aircraft fleet evolution, 2015 to 2035                                   85
5.4   Aircraft retention, replacement and growth, 2015 to 2035                 87
9.1   The Ansoff Matrix                                                       144
9.2   Middle East carriers' annual ASKs, 2006 to 2016                        148
13.1  Airline distribution channels                                          212
15.1  An example airline network                                             239
15.2  Example of propagated delay                                            249
16.1  Air traffic distribution in the global airport network, 2014           260
16.2  Cumulative distribution of air traffic in the global airport
      network, 2014                                                          261
16.3  Layout of Munich Airport                                               268
16.4  Biannual slot coordination cycle                                       271
16.5  Development of average aircraft size (seats per flight) and aircraft
      movements in the global airport network, 2006 to 2014                  273

17.1   GRI Airline Framework                                              288
20.1   Holistic view of the airline business                             334
20.2   Advanced technologies in terminal handling                        342
25.1   Emerging environmental issues in the context of aviation          404
25.2   ICAO's 'timeline of inaction'                                     408

# Tables

| | | |
|---|---|---|
| 1.1 | Passenger traffic by region, 2000 versus 2015 | 13 |
| 2.1 | SWOT analysis of the air cargo industry | 33 |
| 2.2 | Interregional air cargo movements, 2014 | 34 |
| 2.3 | Country pairs with high freight load factors (in excess of 5,000 tonnes of air cargo), 2014 | 35 |
| 2.4 | Airline business models and corporate objectives | 42 |
| 2.5 | Top 20 air cargo carriers, 2015 | 44 |
| 2.6 | Top 10 freight forwarders (by air traffic), 2015 | 44 |
| 3.1 | The 10 countries with the most airports/airfields and most airports/airfields with paved runways, 2013 | 50 |
| 3.2 | Types of airport privatisation | 55 |
| 3.3 | The changing nature of private airport investors in the UK, 1980s to 2010s | 56 |
| 4.1 | Evolution of the regulatory and standardisation roles in ATM | 62 |
| 4.2 | FABs and participating states | 64 |
| 4.3 | Benefits of full SES/SESAR implementation by 2030 | 67 |
| 4.4 | Schema of regulatory principles for RPAS | 70 |
| 6.1 | Foreign ownership restrictions on airlines for selected countries | 97 |
| 6.2 | Financials of three global alliances | 98 |
| 6.3 | Alliance networks weekly schedule operations | 98 |
| 6.4 | Cross-regional ownership | 99 |
| 6.5 | HHI by region based on share of seats | 104 |
| 7.1 | Domestic air transport markets in Brazil and Russia, January 2016 versus 2015 | 110 |
| 7.2 | GDP and air passenger indicators for Kenya and JKIA, 2010 to 2015 | 111 |
| 7.3 | LCCs based in Kenya | 112 |
| 7.4 | GDP and air passenger indicators for Mexico, 2010 to 2015 | 113 |
| 7.5 | GDP and air passenger indicators for Indonesia, 2010 to 2015 | 115 |
| 7.6 | GDP and air traffic indicators for Saudi Arabia and GACA airports, 2010 to 2015 | 118 |
| 9.1 | Averaged benchmarked values for the six indices, 2008 to 2009 | 142 |
| 10.1 | Strategies for accomplishing long-term objectives | 161 |
| 13.1 | Types of airline pricing | 211 |

| 13.2 | The five biggest spenders among the US airlines for sponsorships, 2015 | 215 |
|---|---|---|
| 13.3 | Sponsorship activation methods | 216 |
| 14.1 | Main stages in the airport route development process | 222 |
| 14.2 | Activities used in airport route development | 223 |
| 16.1 | Separation minima in ATS surveillance systems | 264 |
| 16.2 | Declared capacities of selected airports by runway capacity class, 2016 | 266 |
| 17.1 | ISO 26000 core subjects of JAL Group | 289 |
| 19.1 | Global scheduled air transport demand, 1990 to 2015 | 314 |
| 19.2 | Regional distribution of scheduled air transport demand, 1990 to 2015 | 314 |
| 19.3 | Emerging markets by different sources | 320 |
| 19.4 | Economic and air transport performance of selected emerging markets | 321 |
| 19.5 | Average annual growth rates of selected emerging markets, 1990 to 2015 | 321 |
| 19.6 | Domestic demand shares of selected emerging markets, 1990 and 2015 | 322 |
| 19.7 | Examples of demand elasticities estimated for the selected emerging markets | 323 |
| 19.8 | The estimation results for RPKs | 325 |
| 19.9 | The estimation results for DRPKs | 326 |
| 19.10 | The estimation results for FTKs | 326 |
| 21.1 | Comparison of various biometric technologies | 355 |
| 22.1 | Popular press quality awards | 364 |
| 22.2 | Service quality studies using SERVQUAL/SERVPERF | 365 |
| 22.3 | Other primary data service quality studies | 366 |
| 22.4 | Service quality studies using secondary data | 367 |
| 23.1 | Complaints (per million enplanements) received by the DOT, 2000 to 2015 | 378 |
| 25.1 | Environmental impacts of aviation | 403 |
| 25.2 | Contribution of aviation to changes in atmosphere physics and chemistry | 404 |

# Contributors

**Fariba E. Alamdari** is Vice President, Marketing at Boeing Commercial Airplanes. Her team of world-class technical marketing experts partner with the Boeing sales and product strategy team, forecast demand for aircraft and related services, and evaluate market risks and opportunities. In 2006, she joined Boeing from Cranfield University in the UK, where she served as Chair of the university's Department of Air Transport, Professor of Air Transport Management and Dean of the Faculty of Engineering, Manufacturing and Science. In addition to publishing more than 70 articles and reports on aviation-related issues, Alamdari has chaired and spoken at many international conferences. She is a Fellow of the Royal Aeronautical Society, and recipient of several awards, including: Woman of the Year by Air Transport News in 2016 Ellis Island Medal of Honor from the National Ethnic Coalition of Organisations (NECO) in 2016 (presented each year on historic Ellis Island in the US to a select group of individuals for their accomplishments in their field), the Leadership Award from the Centre for Women & Democracy in 2015, the Professional Award from Career Communication Group, Inc in 2011 and the Professional Practice Recognition Award from State University of New York Institute of Technology, School of Business in 2010. Alamdari received a PhD and a master's degree from Cranfield University, UK. She also received an honorary Doctor of Science from Cranfield in 2017.

**David Alexander**'s pathway in transport and logistics has encompassed over 15 years of industrial experience, primarily at Asia-Pacific's largest privately owned 3PL Linfox. While undertaking an engagement in a front-line management role overseeing transport operations across the Greater Sydney Metropolitan Area, he completed a Bachelor of Business and Commerce, specialising in logistics and operations management. Accentuating his knowledge of aviation, shipping, transport and logistics further, David graduated with master's degrees in Transport Management and Logistics Management at the Institute of Transport and Logistics Studies (ITLS). He is currently undertaking the final stages of a PhD project in aviation management at ITLS.

**Marc Bourgois** holds an MSc in Engineering and in Artificial Intelligence from the Katholieke Universiteit Leuven, Belgium. For the last 10 years, he has been managing innovative research activities for Air Traffic Management at the EUROCONTROL Experimental Centre near Paris, and is currently the coordinator for exploratory research activities in the SESAR and Research division of EUROCONTROL, responsible for growing its network, participation and capabilities for performing long-term research. He is also involved in strategic activities such as the Advisory Council for Aeronautical Research in Europe (ACARE), and he serves regularly on programme committees and project selection boards. Previously,

Marc had a career in computer science research, starting in factory automation at Siemens Corporate Research in Bruges, followed by contributions to high-level distributed programming languages at the European Computer Industry Research Centre in Munich and systems architecture at EUROCONTROL Headquarters in Brussels.

**Lucy Budd** is Reader in Air Transport and Programme Director of the MSc in Air Transport Management in the School of Civil and Building Engineering at Loughborough University, UK. Dr Budd has extensive experience of teaching air transport at both undergraduate and postgraduate level, and she has published widely in the area of air transport operations and aviation management. She is co-editor of the Routledge book *Air Transport Management: An International Perspective* (2016).

**Marina Efthymiou** is Assistant Professor in Aviation Management at Dublin City University Business School, Ireland. In the past, she held posts at the University of West London, UK and EUROCONTROL, the international organisation for the safety of air navigation in Europe, based in Brussels. Dr Efthymiou's research interests focus on the business economics of air navigation service providers, air traffic management and policy issues, aviation governance and performance regulation, as well as the implications of aviation for the environment in a sustainable context.

**David Gillen** holds the Vancouver International Airport Professorship in Transportation Policy & Management in the Sauder School of Business and is Director, Centre for Transportation Studies, University of British Columbia, Canada. He is Editor of *Journal of Transport Economics and Policy*, former Associate Editor of *Transportation Research E: Logistics & Transportation Review* and is on the Editorial Boards of a number of other transportation and logistics-related journals. He has published numerous articles and books covering transportation economics, management and policy. His current research includes examining the role of transportation in the supply chain and studying the linkages between transportation investments and productivity in the economy. His most recent project is measuring productivity in supply chains, introducing quality into productivity metrics and empirically measuring how delays are propagated through supply chains.

**Eduardo García** is the CANSO Manager European ATM Coordination and Safety. He coordinates CANSO's positions on topics covering technical, operations and safety measures. He has received the SESAR Distinguished Service Award for sustained outstanding performance in the HALA! (Higher Automation Levels in ATM) Research Network by the SESAR Scientific Committee, and was also awarded the Derek George Astridge Safety in Aerospace Award and the Safety Award in Mechanical Engineering by the Institution of Mechanical Engineers, UK.

**Stefan Gössling** is a Professor at the Department of Service Management and Service Studies, Lund University, as well as the School of Business and Economics, Linnaeus University, both in Sweden. He is also the Research Coordinator at the Centre for Tourism Studies at the Western Norway Research Institute. His research focuses on the sustainability of transportation and tourism.

**Anne Graham** is Professor of Air Transport and Tourism Management at the University of Westminster, UK. Anne has been involved in air transport and tourism teaching, research and consultancy for over 30 years. She has a particular interest in airport management, economics and regulation, and air travel and tourism demand analysis. In addition to previously being

Editor in Chief of the *Journal of Air Transport Management* for a number of years, Anne has published extensively in the field of air transport and tourism. She is author of the Routledge book *Managing Airports: An International Perspective* (4th edition, 2014) and co-author of *Airport Marketing* (2013) and *Airport Finance and Investment in the Global Economy* (2017).

**Nigel Halpern** is Associate Professor in Air Transport and Tourism at Kristiania University College, Norway. Nigel is also Visiting Research Fellow with the School of Aviation at the University of New South Wales, Australia. He has previously worked at Molde University College, Norway; the Centre for Civil Aviation at London Metropolitan University, UK; the UK Department for Transport, Local Government and the Regions; the UK Civil Aviation Authority; and PGL Travel in the UK, France and Spain. Nigel currently teaches and conducts research and consultancy in air transport and tourism. He is co-author of the Routledge book *Airport Marketing* (2013).

**Geraint Harvey** is a Senior Lecturer in Industrial Relations and HRM at Birmingham Business School, University of Birmingham, UK. His research has focused on change in employee and industrial relations, the role of trade unions within the high-performance paradigm, and employee voice in firm ethics and corporate social responsibility. He has published research in a range of journals such as *Work, Employment and Society, Human Resource Management Journal, European Journal of Industrial Relations, Journal of Business Ethics* and *International Journal of Human Resource Management*, while his PhD thesis was published as a book, *Management in the Airline Industry*. He has been commissioned to conduct research on employment relations in the civil aviation industry for the International Labour Organisation, International Transport Workers Federation and European Transport Workers Federation.

**Jan Hogrefe** is Chief Economist for Boeing Commercial Airplanes (BCA). In this role, he leads analyses of global macroeconomic developments for BCA. He works with BCA leaders and customers on identifying and assessing the economic trends that shape the global aviation industry. Prior to joining Boeing in 2014, he worked at the Centre for European Economic Research (ZEW) in Germany, leading economic policy consulting projects for governmental and private institutions from across Europe – mostly with a focus on issues regarding macroeconomics and international trade. Jan holds a doctorate degree in Economics from the University of Tuebingen, Germany, has published several articles in international scientific journals, and frequently speaks at various economic conferences and industry events.

**Paul Hooper**'s career spans more than four decades in government, ICAO, consulting and universities, and he has served in numerous countries throughout Asia and the Pacific, as well as in Canada and the United Arab Emirates. As a consultant, Paul has advised governments, aid agencies, airports, airlines and other private sector entities on initiatives involving institutional strengthening, aviation policy and regulations, consumer protection, privatisation, economic analyses and strategic planning. Paul is also a highly respected educator and researcher. He is currently a freelance consultant while also maintaining an association with the School of Aviation at the University of New South Wales, Australia as an adjunct faculty member.

**Peter Hullah**, originally a mathematician, has been working at the EUROCONTROL Experimental Centre, near Paris, France for over 34 years. He has spent the last 17 of these working in areas related to aircraft impacts on the environment, managing EUROCONTROL's contributions to such EU-sponsored projects as Sourdine II (advanced continuous decent approaches), Imagine (noise modelling), HISAC (supersonic business jets), MIME (noise trading), REACT4C (climate-optimised aircraft trajectories) and in the X-Noise network. He is a member of the joint programming committee of the biennial Aircraft Noise and Emission Reduction Symposium (ANERS). He is EUROCONTROL's focal point for WG3 – Environment and Energy – in the Advisory Council for Aeronautical Research in Europe (ACARE) and took part in the production of the EC's Strategic Transport Research and Innovation Agenda. He is currently researching the present and future impact of drones, and especially future autonomous drones, both on air traffic management and on society, as well as investigating mobility as part of the team for the DATASET2050 project looking at the background to the ACARE 90% four-hour door-to-door target.

**Stephen Ison** is Professor of Transport Policy and Programme Director of the BSc degrees in Air Transport Management and Transport and Business Management in the School of Civil and Building Engineering at Loughborough University, UK. Professor Ison has taught transport economics and policy for over 30 years, and has written and edited nine books in the areas of aviation, business and economics. He is co-editor of the Routledge book *Air Transport Management: An International Perspective* (2016).

**Gui Lohmann** is Associate Professor in Aviation Management and Head of the Aviation Discipline at Griffith University, Australia. He has authored several books, including *Tourism Theories: Concepts, Models and Systems*, published by CAB International, and peer-reviewed journal articles in English, Spanish and Portuguese on transport- and tourism-related topics. He has worked as a consultant for the Brazilian Ministry of Tourism, the World Tourism Organisation and the United Nations Environment Programme, in addition to providing consulting to Adelaide Airport, Brisbane Airport Corporation and Queensland Airport Ltd. Gui is the founder and previous executive director of ABRATUR, the International Academy for the Development of Tourism Research in Brazil.

**Berendien Lubbe** holds a PhD in Communication Management and is currently Head of the Tourism Management Division in the Faculty of Economic and Management Sciences at the University of Pretoria in South Africa. Her research focuses on the role of air transport in tourism, tourism distribution, corporate travel and tourism competitiveness. She has published in numerous journals, and her books *Tourism Distribution: Managing the Travel Intermediary* and *Tourism Management in South Africa* have been widely prescribed. She is a recipient of the Laureate Award from the University of Pretoria for her contribution to educational innovation and is a past board member of the International Federation for Information Technologies in Travel and Tourism (IFITT).

**Stephen J. Maher** is a Research Fellow at the University of Lancaster, UK. He was awarded a postdoctoral fellowship from the EPSRC in 2017. His current research involves the development of solution algorithms for large-scale optimisation problems arising from airport capacity management. Stephen received his PhD in Mathematics from UNSW Sydney, Australia in 2014. In 2012, Stephen was awarded the Anna Valicek medal for the paper 'The recoverable robust tail assignment problem'. His doctoral thesis was awarded the dissertation prize from the Aviation Applications Section of INFORMS.

**Robert Mayer** is a Course Director and Lecturer in the Centre of Air Transport Management at Cranfield University, UK. He previously worked for the University of Huddersfield and

Austrian Airlines. Robert's main areas of expertise and research interests are in airline and environmental marketing, airline economics, and air cargo. He has a PhD in Airline Marketing from Loughborough University, UK, an MSc in Air Transport Management from Cranfield University and a degree in European Economics and Business Management from the University of Applied Sciences BFI Vienna.

**Rico Merkert** is Professor in Transport and Supply Chain Management and Deputy Director of the Institute of Transport and Logistics Studies at the University of Sydney, Australia. Rico is Editor in Chief of the *Journal of Air Transport Management* and an appointed member of various US Transportation Research Board (TRB) Standing Committees on Aviation Economics and Air Cargo. He has been involved in a number of projects on benchmarking, transport economics, strategy, policy and management for a range of clients such as the European Commission and a number of major airlines. Most of his recent projects focus on the efficient management of various elements of the aviation supply chain both in the global and regional context.

**William G. Morrison** is an Associate Professor of Economics in the Lazaridis School of Business and Economics at Wilfrid Laurier University, Canada. From 2008 to 2014, he served as Director of the Laurier Centre for Economic Research and Policy Analysis. Bill's research expertise includes applied transportation economics, game theory, and strategy and behavioural economics. He is Associate Editor for the *Journal of Air Transport Management*, a Research Fellow with the Centre for Transportation Research at the University of British Columbia, Canada and a member of the Advisory Committee for the European Aviation Conference. His research in air transportation focuses on airline competition; airport operations, financing, performance and strategies; economic aspects of aviation security; and aviation policy. Bill's published research includes both peer-reviewed (academic) publishing and consulting or technical reports for governments and private organisations. He holds an Honours BA in Economics from the University of Stirling, UK, an MA in Economics from Carleton University, Canada and a PhD in Economics from Simon Fraser University, Canada.

**Eric T. Njoya** is a Senior Lecturer in the Department of Logistics, Operations, Hospitality and Marketing at Huddersfield University, UK. He holds a PhD from the Karlsruhe Institute of Technology, Germany. His current research focuses on the tourism benefits of air transport liberalisation and the role of air transport in achieving regional economic growth.

**John F. O'Connell** completed an MSc in Air Transport Management from Cranfield University, UK and an MBA (Aviation) from Embry-Riddle Aeronautical University, USA, later returning to Cranfield to complete a PhD in Airline Strategy. He also holds a pilot's licence. He is currently a Senior Lecturer in Airline Management at the Air Transport Department at Cranfield University. He specifically lectures in Airline Strategy and also covers areas such as deregulation, ancillary revenues, emerging aviation markets and the exponentially growing Arabian Gulf aviation market. He conducts an annual airline management course for Singapore Airlines and Turkish Airlines on-site. He has produced over 40 academic journal papers as well as a popular book entitled *Air Transport in the 21st Century*. Previously, 'Frankie' worked for the Boeing commercial aircraft company as an analyst for a number of years, and then for Embry-Riddle Aeronautical University (extended campus in California) as an airline lecturer for a further five years. While at Embry-Riddle, he regularly lectured at the NASA Ames research facility at Moffett Field. He is also a regular speaker at international commercial conferences discussing the ongoing trending events in the airline industry.

**Christopher Paling** is a Senior Lecturer and Researcher at Manchester Metropolitan University, UK, working within the University's Centre for Aviation, Transport and the Environment (CATE). He returned to academia in 2012 after 11 years working for the Manchester Airports Group as an environmental manager. His research and teaching is focused on the environmental sustainability of air transport and the implications of a changing climate upon aviation. Recent research has included the carbon impact of increased runway capacity at airports, categorising scope 3 emissions at airports, and the implications of a changing climate for an aircraft manufacturer.

**Andreas Papatheodorou** is currently Professor in Industrial and Spatial Economics with emphasis on Tourism at the University of the Aegean, Greece. He is also an Adjunct Professor at the University of New South Wales, Australia. An Oxford University graduate, Professor Papatheodorou served in the past as Dean of the London College of Hospitality and Tourism at the University of West London, UK. He is a prolific academic researcher and industry advisor in areas related to air transport and tourism economics. His work has received wide recognition at an international level, with over 2,600 citations on Google Scholar.

**Theunis Potgieter** holds a master's degree in International Business from UOWD Dubai and runs his own travel distribution and aviation consulting firm. He is a seasoned aviation executive and has held senior commercial roles with Emirates, South African Airways, Qatar Airways and start-up carriers. His specific interest is in the economic optimisation of aviation distribution systems with the development of new travel distribution technology.

**Dawna L. Rhoades** received her PhD in Management from the University of Houston, USA. She is a Professor of Management and Chair of the Department of Management, Marketing, and Operations in the College of Business at Embry-Riddle Aeronautical University in Daytona Beach, Florida, USA, where she teaches international business, strategic management, and international aviation management at both the undergraduate and graduate level. Her research interests include strategic alliances, regional carrier strategy, and service and safety quality at airlines and airports, and intermodal transportation. Her work has appeared in such journals as the *Journal of Air Transport Management*, *Journal of Air Transport World Wide*, *Journal of Transportation Management*, *Journal of Managerial Issues*, *Managing Service Quality*, *World Review of Science, Technology, and Sustainable Development* and the *Handbook of Airline Strategy*. She is the author of a recently published book entitled *Evolution of International Aviation: Phoenix Rising* and the editor of the *World Review of Intermodal Transportation Research* (WRITR).

**Kathleen Rodenburg** has a Bachelor of Commerce degree, an MA and PhD in Economics from the University of Guelph, Canada and an MBA from Wilfrid Laurier University, Canada. She has 15 years of business and industry experience, holding senior management positions at a Tier I organisation in the areas of marketing, sales, supply chain management and finance. Currently, Kathleen is an Assistant Professor in the College of Business and Economics at the University of Guelph. Her research interests include game theory, decision theory and teaching pedagogies for business students. Additionally, she has worked on research in conjunction with William G. Morrison in the area of aviation security.

**Wendy R. Sowers** leads Boeing Commercial Airplanes' (BCA) analysis of the airline industry. In her current role, she directs the development of Boeing's annual *Current Market Outlook* – a 20-year global forecast for air traffic and airplane demand – as well as near- and mid-term market and product analysis supporting BCA's business and strategic planning. Over the last 20 years, Wendy has held a variety of positions at BCA, including product marketing, competitor analysis and strategy, and supply chain management. She holds a Bachelor of Arts degree in Economics and English from the College of William and Mary, USA and a Master of Business Administration from the University of Washington, USA.

**Bojana Spasojevic** is a Lecturer in Aviation Management at Griffith University, Australia with a particular interest in the field of air transport and tourism. Her PhD topic focuses on leadership and stakeholder engagement during the process of air route development. She uses innovative teaching in her courses, including the use of the Airline Online simulation as well as the AirportIS database. She has worked on consulting projects for Brisbane Airport Corporation and Adelaide Airport Ltd in Australia.

**Callum Thomas** is Chair of Sustainable Aviation at Manchester Metropolitan University, UK. He returned to academia in 1998 after 13 years in the aviation industry. He is internationally known within the industry and has been an advisor to the UK government and the EU on aviation and the environment and sustainability issues. He was responsible for establishing Manchester Airport's Bird Control Unit and Environment Department. His expertise involves the sustainable development of aviation, environmental constraints upon airport growth and the impact of airport operations on local communities.

**Peter Turnbull** is Professor of Management at the School of Economics, Finance & Management, University of Bristol, UK. He was previously an Academic Fellow at the International Labour Organisation (ILO) and has produced several reports for the ILO, European Commission, International Transport Workers' Federation, European Transport Workers' Federation and European Cockpit Association. His current research focuses on new business strategies, atypical forms of employment, and 'social dumping' in the European transport sector (specifically, civil aviation, road and ports/maritime). He is an Academic Fellow of the Chartered Institute of Personnel and Development (CIPD) and a member of the Advisory, Conciliation and Arbitration Service (ACAS) arbitration panel.

**Blaise P. Waguespack** graduated from the University of North Texas, USA with a PhD in Marketing and is a Professor of Marketing in the College of Business at Embry-Riddle Aeronautical University in Daytona Beach, Florida, USA. Dr Waguespack co-authored a chapter in *Handbook of Airline Strategy* and has publications appearing in journals such as *Managing Service Quality*, *Journal of Transportation Management*, *Journal of Air Transportation World Wide*, *Journal of Air Transport Management* and other international and national conference proceedings. Aviation industry firms Dr Waguespack has worked with include Bombardier Aerospace, United, Allied Signal and American Express.

**David Warnock-Smith** is Director of Aviation, Events & Tourism at Buckinghamshire New University, UK. He holds a PhD from Cranfield University, UK. His current research focuses on air transport strategies in deregulated markets.

**Dieter Wilken** founded an air transport research group in the German Aerospace Centre (DLR) in 1976 and has since been Member of the Scientific Staff and Deputy Director of the DLR Institute of Air Transport and Airport Research. He holds degrees from the Technical

University of Munich, Germany and the University of California, Berkeley, USA in Transport Engineering. His prime involvement has been in studies on analysing and forecasting air transport demand and supply in Germany, Europe and worldwide. For estimating the effect of capacity constraints, he developed functional tools to describe the capacity and capacity utilisation of airports worldwide. As a national delegate, he participated in several studies and expert groups of the EU, ECAC, COST, EUROCONTROL and ICAO-CAEP. He has authored and co-authored numerous scientific reports, contributions to books and journal articles.

**Cheng-Lung Wu** is an Associate Professor in the School of Aviation in UNSW Sydney, Australia. Dr Wu specialises in solving operations and scheduling problems of airlines and airports. Many of his past projects helped industry partners save millions of dollars in operating costs or enhance product sales and revenues. He joined UNSW in 2002 after his PhD from Loughborough University in the UK and had spent time both in the public and private sector. Dr Wu also provides consulting services to airlines, airports and investment firms, and has been a certified professional training instructor for IATA since 2010.

**Anming Zhang** is a Full Professor of Operations and Logistics and holds the Vancouver International Airport Authority Chair Professor in Air Transportation at Sauder School of Business, University of British Columbia (UBC), Canada. He served as the Chair of the Operations and Logistics Division at Sauder School of Business (2003–2005), and as the Director of UBC's Centre for Transport Studies (2003–2004). He has been the Vice President (Academic & Program) for the World Air Transport Research Society since 2006. Professor Zhang is the recipient of the WCTR-Society Prize, awarded to the overall best paper of the 8th World Conference on Transportation Research in Antwerp, Belgium, in 1998. In June 2014, he won the Best Overall Paper Prize at the annual conference of the International Transport Economics Association, Toulouse School of Economics, France. He has published about 150 refereed journal papers in the areas of transportation, logistics, industrial organisation and the Chinese economy.

**Yahua Zhang** is a Senior Lecturer in the School of Commerce, University of Southern Queensland, Australia. He conducts research in the economics of transport, and particularly aviation, the economics of regulation, competition and market structures, and the behaviour of markets and the participants. He also has strong interests in the areas of cold chain logistics and agricultural value chains.

**Xingwu Zheng** is a Professor at the Civil Aviation University of China. His research focuses on air transportation economics and policy. He has managed research projects on the international air transportation market and policy for CAAC. Also as an expert of CAAC, he took part in the WTO's second review of the Annex on Air Transport Services of GATS from 2005 to 2007 and the Doha Round of trade negotiation in air transportation services. In 2011, he joined the ICAO MBM expert group and GMTF expert group to draft the $CO_2$ reduction market-based measures scheme for international air transportation. Zheng holds a PhD in International Economics from Nankai University, China.

# Acknowledgements

The editors would like to thank everyone that has been involved in producing *The Routledge Companion to Air Transport Management*. We would like to thank the contributors of each chapter, which includes 39 air transport experts from around the world that have supported this companion, devoted precious time to it, and responded to our requests for information and editorial suggestions in a timely and enthusiastic manner. We would like to thank the publisher Routledge (and especially Laura Hussey and Amy Laurens) for inviting us to put this companion together and for providing support and encouragement along the way. We would like to thank the many students and practitioners that we have encountered over the years that have contributed to our knowledge and understanding of the air transport industry. Last but not least, we would like to thank family and friends for their never-ending support, especially those who have had to put up with the disruption to their lives while we have been editing this book. In particular, we would like to thank Anne-Merete, Leo, Felix, Mia, Grete, Tore, Bridget, David, Ian, Lorna, Callum and Ewan.

Anming Zhang and Yahua Zhang (authors of Chapter 11, 'Airline economics and finance') would like to thank Nigel Halpern and Qiwei Hu for helpful comments, and Will Zhang for his research assistance with part of the literature review.

William G. Morrison and Kathleen Rodenburg (authors of Chapter 21, 'Key aspects in aviation security') would like to acknowledge that funding for their research was provided by the Federal Government of Canada through the Kanishka Project Contribution Program. The Kanishka Project was initiated through the efforts of victim families of the Air India bombing of 1985 in which 329 innocent people lost their lives.

# Abbreviations and acronyms

| | |
|---|---|
| A4A | Airlines for America |
| AACO | Arab Air Carriers Organisation |
| AAPA | Association of Asia Pacific Airlines |
| ABAS | aircraft-based augmentation system |
| ACAC | Arab Civil Aviation Commission |
| ACARE | Advisory Council for Aeronautical Research in Europe |
| ACAS | Advisory, Concilation and Arbitration Service |
| ACC3 | Air Cargo or Mail Carrier Certificate |
| ACI | Airports Council International |
| ACMI | aircraft, crew, maintenance and insurance |
| ACRP | Airport Cooperative Research Program |
| ADS-B | automatic dependent surveillance-broadcast |
| AEA | Association of European Airlines |
| AENA | Spanish Airports and Air Navigation |
| AIAS | Alaska International Airport System |
| AIS | aeronautical information system |
| ALI | Air Liberalisation Index |
| AMC | acceptable means of compliance |
| ANERS | Aircraft Noise and Emission Reduction Symposium |
| ANS | air navigation services |
| ANSP | air navigation service provider |
| AOC | air operator certificate |
| APV | approach procedures with vertical guidance |
| AQR | Airline Quality Rating |
| ARIMA | autoregressive integrated moving average |
| ARM | aircraft routing model |
| ARR | accounting rate of return |
| ARS | airline reservation system |
| ART | advanced remote tower |
| ASA | air service agreement |
| ASAP | Air Service Agreements Projector |
| ASD | AeroSpace and Defence Industries Association of Europe |
| ASEAN | Association of Southeast Asian Nations |
| ASK | available seat kilometre |
| ATA | Air Transport Association of America |
| ATAG | Air Transport Action Group |

| | |
|---|---|
| ATC | air traffic control |
| ATFM | air traffic flow management |
| ATM | air traffic management |
| ATM MP | air traffic management master plan |
| ATRS | Air Transport Research Society |
| ATS | air traffic service |
| ATS | air transport system |
| ATSEP | Air Traffic Safety Electronic Personnel |
| ATW | Air Transport World |
| BAA | British Airports Authority |
| BALPA | British Airline Pilots Association |
| Baro-VNAV | barometric vertical navigation |
| BASA | bilateral air services agreement |
| BASSA | British Airlines Stewards and Stewardesses Association |
| BCA | Boeing Commercial Airplanes |
| BDO | behaviour detection officer |
| BEMOSA | Behavioural Modelling for Security in Airports |
| BIMP/EAGA | Brunei-Daressalam-Indonesia-Malaysia-Philippines East ASEAN Growth Area |
| BRIC | Brazil, Russia, India and China |
| CAA | Civil Aviation Authority |
| CAG | Changi Airport Group |
| CAM | Contract Air Mail |
| CAN | Committee on Aircraft Noise |
| CANSO | Civil Air Navigation Services Organisation |
| CAPA | Centre for Aviation |
| CAPPSII | Computer-Assisted Passenger Prescreening System |
| CARATS | Collaborative Action for Renovation of Air Transport Systems |
| CATE | Centre for Aviation, Transport and the Environment |
| CATSA | Canadian Air Transport Security Authority |
| CCC | Committee on Climate Change |
| CCO | continuous climb operation |
| CDO | continuous descent operation |
| CEN | European Committee for Standardisation |
| CENELEC | European Committee for Electrotechnical Standardisation |
| CFMU | central flow management unit |
| $CH_4$ | methane |
| CIA | Central Intelligence Agency |
| CIPD | Chartered Institute of Personnel and Development |
| CJEU | Court of Justice of the European Union |
| CNS | communications, navigation and surveillance |
| CO | carbon monoxide |
| $CO_2$ | carbon dioxide |
| CoC | Crews of Convenience |
| COFECE | Mexican Competition Commission |
| COMAC | China's Commercial Aircraft Corporation |

| COOPANS | An international partnership between the ANSPs of Austria (Austro Control), Croatia (Croatia Control), Denmark (Naviair), Ireland (Irish Aviation Authority) and Sweden (LFV), with Thales as the chosen industry supplier |
| CORSIA | Carbon Offsetting and Reduction Scheme for International Aviation |
| CPM | crew pairing model |
| CRM | customer relationship management |
| CRS | computer reservation system |
| CS | corporate sustainability |
| CSM | corporate societal marketing |
| CSR | corporate social responsibility |
| CUI | capacity utilisation index |
| CWC | carrier within a carrier |
| $D^3$ | demand-driven dispatch |
| DATAS | Delta Automated Travel Account System |
| dB | decibels |
| DCF | discount cash flow |
| DEA | data envelopment analysis |
| DEFRA | Department for Environment, Food and Rural Affairs |
| DFNI | Duty Free News International |
| DFW | Dallas/Fort Worth |
| DG MOVE | (EC) Directorate-General for Mobility and Transport |
| DLR | German Aerospace Centre |
| DMAN | departure management |
| DOT | Department of Transportation |
| DRPK | domestic revenue passenger kilometre |
| DRS | decreasing returns to scale |
| DVL | German Institute for Experimental Aviation |
| EAA | European Aviation Agency |
| EAC | East African Community |
| EACCC | European Aviation Crisis Coordination Cell |
| EAD | European aeronautical information system database |
| EASA | European Aviation Safety Agency |
| EASCG | European Air Traffic Management Standards Coordination Group |
| EATCHIP | European Air Traffic Control Harmonisation and Integration Programme |
| EC | European Commission |
| ECAA | European Common Aviation Area |
| ECCSA | European Centre for Cyber Security in Aviation |
| EDA | European Defence Agency |
| EDS | explosion detection systems |
| EEA | European Economic Area |
| EEC | European Economic Community |
| EFB | electronic flight bag |
| EFQM | European Federation of Quality Management |
| EMGP | Emerging Market Global Players |

| ERAA | European Regional Airlines Association |
|------|----------------------------------------|
| ETD | explosion trace detection systems |
| ETS | Emissions Trading Scheme |
| ETSI | European Telecommunications Standards Institute |
| EU | European Union |
| EUROCAE | European Organisation for Civil Aviation Equipment |
| EUROCONTROL | European Organisation for the Safety of Air Navigation |
| FA | fleet assignment |
| FAA | Federal Aviation Administration |
| FAB | Functional Airspace Block |
| FAK | freight all kinds |
| FAM | fleet assignment model |
| FDI | foreign direct investment |
| FFP | frequent flyer programme |
| FGLS | feasible generalised least square |
| FME–CWM | Dutch Employers' Organisation and Trade Association for the Technological-Industrial Sector |
| FoC | Flags of Convenience |
| FP6 | sixth framework programme |
| FRA | free route airspace |
| FSNC | full service network carrier |
| FTC | Federal Trade Commission |
| FTK | freight tonne kilometre |
| FTSE | Financial Times Stock Exchange |
| G20 | Group of Twenty – Forum for the Governments and Central Bank Governors from 20 major economies |
| GACA | General Authority of Civil Aviation |
| GANP | Global Air Navigation Plan |
| GAO | Government Accountability Office |
| GBAS | ground-based augmentation system |
| GCC | Gulf Cooperation Council |
| GDP | gross domestic product |
| GDS | global distribution system |
| GFAM | generic fleet assignment model |
| GFC | global financial crisis |
| GIACC | Group on International Aviation and Climate Change |
| GIP | Global Investment Partners |
| GLONASS | Globalnaya Navigazionnaya Sputnikovaya Sistema (Russia's GPS) |
| GM | guidance material |
| GMBM | global market-based measure |
| GNSS | Global Navigation Satellite System |
| GPS | Global Positioning System |
| GRI | Global Reporting Initiative |
| GVC | global value chain |
| $H_2O$ | dihydrogen monoxide (water) |
| HC | hydrocarbons |
| HFC | hydrofluorocarbon |
| HHI | Herfindahl-Hirschman Index |

| | |
|---|---|
| HR | human resources |
| HRM | human resource management |
| HSR | high-speed rail |
| IAG | International Airlines Group |
| IATA | International Air Transport Association |
| IBE | Internet booking engine |
| IBM | International Business Machines Corporation |
| ICAO | International Civil Aviation Organisation |
| ICPEN | International Consumer Protection Enforcement Network |
| ICT | information and communication technology |
| IFAM | itinerary-based fleet assignment model |
| IFC | International Finance Corporation |
| IFE | in-flight entertainment |
| IFITT | International Federation for Information Technologies in Travel and Tourism |
| IFR | instrument flight rules |
| ILO | International Labour Organisation |
| ILS | instrument landing system |
| IMF | International Monetary Fund |
| IMT-GT | Indonesia-Malaysia-Thailand Growth Triangle |
| IoT | Internet of Things |
| IP | industrial partnership |
| IPCC | Intergovernmental Panel on Climate Change |
| IPO | initial public offering |
| IRS | increasing returns to scale |
| ISO | International Organisation for Standardisation |
| IT | information technology |
| ITLS | Institute of Transport and Logistics Studies |
| JARUS | Joint Authorities for Rulemaking on Unmanned Systems |
| JATM | *Journal of Air Transport Management* |
| JIT | just in time |
| JKIA | Jomo Kenyatta International Airport |
| JV | joint venture |
| KAA | Kenya Airport Authority |
| kt | kilotonnes |
| LAPA | Líneas Aéreas Privadas Argentinas |
| LCC | low cost carrier |
| LCLH | low cost long haul |
| LCT | low cost terminal |
| LEO | low earth orbit |
| LFA | low fare airline |
| LFAM | leg-based fleet assignment model |
| LGBT | lesbian, gay, bisexual and transgender |
| LSA | latent semantic analysis |
| MAG | Manchester Airports Group |
| MALIAT | Multilateral Agreement on the Liberalisation of International Air Transportation |
| MAS | Tourism Information and Research Centre |

| | |
|---|---|
| MATSE | meetings of European air transport ministers |
| MC99 | Montreal Convention of 1999 |
| MNJV | metal neutral joint venture |
| MoT | Ministry of Transport |
| Mt | million tonnes |
| MTOM | maximum take-off mass |
| $N_2O$ | nitrous oxide |
| NDC | New Distribution Capability |
| NEB | national enforcement body |
| NECO | National Ethnic Coalition of Organisations |
| NextGen | Next Generation Air Transportation System |
| Next Eleven | Bangladesh, Egypt, Indonesia, Iran, Mexico, Nigeria, Pakistan, the Philippines, Turkey, South Korea and Vietnam |
| NGO | non-governmental organisation |
| NM | nautical mile |
| NM IR | Network Manager Implementing Rule |
| NOP | Network Operations Plan |
| $NO_x$ | nitrogen oxides |
| NPV | net present value |
| NSA | national supervisory authority |
| $O_3$ | trioxygen or ozone |
| OBC | online brand community |
| OCA | Office of Consumer Affairs |
| OD | origin-destination |
| ODFAM | origin-destination fleet assignment model |
| OECD | Organisation for Economic Co-operation and Development |
| OEM | original equipment manufacturer |
| ONS | Office for National Statistics |
| OPEC | Organisation of the Petroleum Exporting Countries |
| OTA | online travel agency |
| OTPP | Ontario Teachers' Pension Plan |
| PANS | Procedures for Air Navigation Services |
| PARS | Programmed Airline Reservation System |
| pax | passengers |
| PBN | performance-based navigation |
| PCP | pilot common project |
| PFC | perfluorocarbon |
| PFM | passenger flow model |
| PKM | passenger kilometre |
| PMM | passenger mix model |
| POD | Post Office Department |
| PPP | public–private partnership |
| PRB | performance review body |
| PwC | PricewaterhouseCoopers |
| QR | quick release |
| RDF | Route Development Fund |
| re-FA | re-fleeting |
| RF | radiative forcing |

| | |
|---|---|
| RFID | radio frequency identification |
| RFS | Road Feeder Services |
| RM | revenue management |
| RMP | restricted master problem |
| RNP | required navigational performance |
| ROIC | return on invested capital |
| ROR | rate of return |
| RPAS | remotely piloted aircraft system |
| RPK | revenue passenger kilometre |
| RPM | revenue passenger mile |
| RTCA | Radio Technical Commission for Aeronautics |
| RTK | revenue tonne kilometre |
| RVSM | reduced vertical separation minima |
| SABRE | Semi-Automatic Business Research Environment |
| SAM | single aviation market |
| SAS | Scandinavian Airlines |
| SATCOM | satellite communication |
| SBAS | satellite-based augmentation system |
| SDM | SESAR Deployment Manager |
| SDR | Special Drawing Right |
| SES | Single European Sky |
| SESAR | Single European Sky ATM Research |
| SESAR JU | Single European Sky ATM Research Joint Undertaking |
| $SF_6$ | sulphur hexafluoride |
| SFAM | subnetwork fleet assignment model |
| SG | schedule generation |
| SID | standard instrument departure |
| SJU | SESAR Joint Undertaking |
| $SO_2$ | sulphur dioxide |
| $SO_x$ | sulphur oxides |
| SST | self-service technology |
| STAR | standard arrival route |
| SWIM | system-wide information management |
| SWOT | strengths, weaknesses, opportunities and threats |
| TCA | terminal control airspace |
| TEU | twenty-foot equivalent unit |
| TFP | total factor productivity |
| TIP | threat image projection |
| TMC | travel management company |
| TQM | total quality management |
| TRB | Transportation Research Board of the National Academies |
| TSA | Transportation Security Administration |
| TTP | trusted traveller programme |
| UAC | United Aircraft Corporation |
| UAS | Unmanned Aircraft System |
| UBC | University of British Columbia |
| UHC | unburned hydrocarbons |
| UK | United Kingdom |

## Abbreviations and acronyms

| | |
|---|---|
| ULD | unit load device |
| UN | United Nations |
| UNCATD | United Nations Conference on Trade and Development |
| UNEP | United Nations Environment Programme |
| UNFCCC | United Nations Framework Convention on Climate Change |
| UNWTO | United Nations World Tourism Organisation |
| UPR | user-preferred route |
| US | United States |
| USA | United States of America |
| UTM | Unmanned Aircraft System traffic management |
| VFR | visiting friends and relatives |
| VFR | visual flight rules |
| VOR | VHF omnidirectional range |
| VTTS | value of travel time savings |
| WACC | weighted average cost of capital |
| WBCSD | World Business Council for Sustainable Development |
| WCED | World Commission on Environment and Development |
| WMO | World Meteorological Organisation |
| WOM | word of mouth |
| WRAP | Waste and Resources Action Programme |
| WRITR | *World Review of Intermodal Transportation Research* |
| WTO | World Trade Organisation |
| ZEW | Centre for European Economic Research |

# Introduction to
# *The Routledge Companion to Air Transport Management*

*Nigel Halpern and Anne Graham*

Routledge companions are prestige reference works that provide an overview of a whole subject area, and review the state of the discipline, including emerging and cutting-edge issues. This companion is on air transport management, a subject area that has developed, alongside growth and developments in the air transport industry, as a discipline of its own during the latter stages of the twentieth century, and is a flourishing area of interest to researchers, scholars and students in the twenty-first century.

## From early pioneers to a major industry

People have long been attracted to air transport as a field of research, with one of the most famous pioneers being the Italian Renaissance polymath Leonardo da Vinci, who produced some of the earliest known designs of flying machines during the 1480s. Other early pioneers include the Montgolfier brothers, who invented the hot air balloon during the 1780s, Sir George Cayley, who developed an understanding of the underlying principles and forces of flight from the 1790s, Otto Lilienthal, who developed an understanding of control in flight with his glider flights in the 1890s, and Samuel Langley, who attempted to invent working piloted heavier-than-air aircraft during the 1890s. The early focus of research was understandably on aeronautical science, and several societies were established, for instance, in France, Germany, the United States (US) and the United Kingdom (UK) during the late nineteenth century to support the development of the field of aeronautical science (Brata and Neves, 2011). One example is the UK's Royal Aeronautical Society (originally called the Aeronautical Society of Great Britain) that was founded in London in 1866.

As will be mentioned in the early chapters of this companion, the Wright brothers are generally credited as being the first to successfully invent, build and fly a heavier-than-air aircraft on 17 December 1903 in Kitty Hawk, North Carolina in the US when they flew 37 metres in 12 seconds. The first air cargo flight took place in the US on 7 November 1910 between Dayton and Columbus in Ohio, carrying 88 kilogrammes of silk over a distance of 105 kilometres, while the first scheduled passenger flight, also in the US, commenced on 1 January 1914 between St Petersburg and Tampa in Florida (approximately 30 kilometres). Many universities established aeronautical science programmes around this time; for instance, the Graduate School of

Aerospace and Mechanical Engineering in Paris in 1909, the German Institute for Experimental Aviation (DVL) in Berlin in 1912, the aeronautics programme at the University of Michigan in 1915, and the establishment of what later became Embry-Riddle Aeronautical University in 1925 (Brata and Neves, 2011).

The air transport industry has come a long way since the first flight in 1903. As of 2014, the industry had 1,402 commercial airlines operating 26,065 aircraft with 32.8 million flights supported by 173 air navigation service providers and 3,883 airports (IATA, 2015). Every day, 104,000 flights carry 9.8 million passengers and US$17.5 billion worth of goods (ATAG, 2016). As the air transport industry has grown and developed, so too have the employment needs of the industry. Almost 10 million jobs worldwide are directly associated with airlines, airports, air navigation service providers, civil aerospace (aircraft systems, frames and engines) and other on-airport positions (ATAG, 2016). There are many additional jobs in other sectors that are linked to air transport such as the jobs of those working in air transport-related areas of education, research, consultancy, government departments and agencies, non-governmental organisations, financial institutions, the media and tourism.

The air transport industry has also undergone something of a transformation over the years from being an industry characterised by extensive regulation and government ownership and control to one that is increasingly deregulated and liberalised, and therefore exposed to competitive forces. There has also been greater commercialisation of publicly owned and operated companies that in many cases are now fully privatised. This has had important implications for how the industry is managed, for instance, with a greater focus on maximising profits (e.g. by reducing costs and improving efficiency). This means that now, more than ever before, air transport managers need to fully appreciate the linkages and relationships between the different sectors of the industry, the regulatory environment within which they operate, and the different business models that have evolved. Crucially, they also need to understand and be knowledgeable of the modern-day role played by different management disciplines, such as business strategy, economics and finance, marketing, capacity planning and management, sustainability and corporate social responsibility, in achieving success in the industry. Furthermore, this now rapidly changing and dynamic industry requires an insightful and informed awareness of key themes related to issues such as security, service quality, consumer protection, human resource management and climate change.

Many universities and colleges have responded to these diverse and wide-ranging needs of the industry and have established air transport management programmes. For instance, the MSc in Air Transport Management at Cranfield University in the UK, which is still offered today, was established in 1964 (Cranfield University, 2017), while the Transport Studies Group was established at the co-editor's institution, the University of Westminster in the UK, by Professor Rigas Doganis (distinguished aviation academic, consultant and advisor). The University of Westminster's association with aviation goes back to when it was founded in 1838 by the previously mentioned pioneer of underlying principles and forces of flight, Sir George Cayley.

There are now hundreds of higher education institutes worldwide offering degree programmes from undergraduate to postgraduate and PhD for students in air transport management, along with research centres and institutes focused on various aspects of air transport management. A growing number of researchers, scholars and students are active in the field either as air transport specialists or as specialists from other disciplines, applying their work or studies to air transport management.

## Key sources of literature

Air transport management has therefore developed as an area for researchers, scholars and students, and is increasingly recognised as an academic discipline of its own. There is now a substantial and growing body of literature on the subject. This includes literature from academic sources (i.e. in journals, books or theses published by academic or commercial publishers) and so-called grey literature from research institutes, private companies, consultancies, government departments and agencies, and non-governmental organisations (i.e. in research reports, annual reports, government documents and industry reports).

In terms of academic literature, the *Journal of Air Transport Management* (published since 1994) is generally considered to be the leading academic journal devoted to "economic, management and policy issues facing the air transport industry today" (JATM, 2017). It is the most cited journal and source of literature in this companion – cited almost 200 times. Air transport is a multi-sector, multidisciplinary area, so literature is also published in other journals that are not only focused specifically on air transport management. For instance, *Transportation Research* (published since 1967) is cited almost 100 times in this companion. Other popular journals cited in this companion are the *Journal of Transport Geography, Tourism Management, Journal of Airport Management, Journal of Transport Economics and Policy, Transport Policy* and *Research in Transportation Business & Management*.

There is also a growing number of books devoted to the study of air transport management. For instance, as of June 2017, Routledge lists 42 books in its aerospace and air transport industries product range (in their economics, business, finance and industries subject area). The books cover various facets of aerospace and air transport – some of them focusing specifically on air transport management (e.g. Budd and Ison, 2016; Wensveen, 2015). Routledge books on air transport management-related subjects (including those previously published by Ashgate, which is now a part of Routledge) are cited over 60 times in this companion.

In terms of grey literature, the main sources of interest in this companion are documents (e.g. relating to policy and legislation) published by specialised agencies (such as the International Civil Aviation Organisation – a specialised agency of the United Nations), political and economic unions (such as the European Union [EU] and its European Commission [EC]), government departments (such as national transport departments) or agencies (such as national civil aviation authorities or federal aviation administrations), or national research councils (such as the US Transportation Research Board). Such sources are cited over 100 times in this companion.

There are then publications from industry associations such as the International Air Transport Association, Airports Council International and the Air Transport Action Group. Publications from these three associations alone are cited over 60 times in this companion. Other popular sources of grey literature are annual reports (e.g. of airlines and airports) or market forecasts (such as from Boeing or Airbus) that are cited almost 50 times in this companion, and reports or articles published by research institutes, consultancies and the media, especially those dedicated to air transport such as the Centre for Aviation (CAPA), Flight Airline Business and Airport World – these three alone are cited about 50 times in this companion.

## Aim and structure of this companion

Aiming to complement existing textbooks on air transport management, this companion provides a comprehensive, up-to-date review of air transport management research and literature. It provides a unique repository of current knowledge and critical debate with an international focus, considering both developed and emerging markets, and covering key sectors of the air transport industry. It presents a balanced and critical overview of current knowledge and explores key issues and debates. There are a total of 25 chapters in this companion that are written by a team of 39 leading researchers, scholars and industry experts based at universities, research institutes, and air transport companies and organisations in 12 different countries in Africa, Asia-Pacific, Europe and the US to provide a definitive, trustworthy resource. The international team of contributors have proven experience of research and publication in their specialist areas, and contribute to this companion by drawing upon research published mainly in academic, industry and government sources. This seminal companion intends to act as a touchstone for researchers, scholars and students of air transport management.

While this companion aims to be as comprehensive as possible, areas of interest are, like the air transport industry itself, very diverse, and it is impossible to cover everything. Focused on the needs of the modern-day air transport manager as discussed above, this book is therefore organised into three parts: current state of the air transport sectors (Part I); application of management disciplines to airlines and airports (Part II); and key selected themes (Part III).

## Part I. Current state of the air transport sectors: Chapters 1–8

Part I considers the main air transport sectors (passenger airlines, air cargo, airports, air traffic management and air navigation service providers, and commercial aerospace). Part I also examines the changing business environment within which air transport companies operate (in terms of liberalisation and competition in both mature and emerging markets), and how airline and airport business models are subsequently evolving. Each chapter identifies important themes for each sector, many of which are developed further in Parts II and III. Part I consists of eight chapters.

Chapter 1, 'The global airline industry', by John F. O'Connell (Cranfield University, UK), looks at the paradox of sustained long-term growth and only marginal profitability in the global airline industry. It briefly investigates the growth, dispersion and segmentation of passenger traffic, and the profitability of the global airline industry, before focusing on the profitability of airlines domiciled in three main geographical areas: the US, Europe and Asia.

Chapter 2, 'The air cargo industry', by Rico Merkert and David Alexander (University of Sydney, Australia), explores four key themes associated with the air cargo industry: dynamics of the air cargo industry from historical perspectives to the current paradigm shift of 'final mile' delivery systems; impacts of macroeconomic and microeconomic factors for air cargo; relationships between air cargo industry participants, air cargo business models and management strategies; and regulation of the air cargo industry and the impact that antitrust determinations can have on the high-risk, low-return airline industry.

Chapter 3, 'The airport industry', by Lucy Budd and Stephen Ison (Loughborough University, UK), describes the contemporary scale and scope of global airport provision, and charts the historical evolution of the airport as a site of aeronautical activity into increasingly diverse commercial enterprises that must meet the challenging needs of a wide range of users. It then documents the reasons for, and implications of, changes in patterns of airport ownership and management structures, using the UK as an example, before discussing the main challenges and opportunities facing the commercial airport industry.

Chapter 4, 'Air traffic management and air navigation service providers', by Marc Bourgois (EUROCONTROL, Belgium), Eduardo García (CANSO, Belgium) and Peter Hullah (EUROCONTROL, Belgium), focuses on the major legal, technical and transversal aspects of modern air traffic management (ATM). It begins with a discussion of the applicable regulatory, organisational and business frameworks. This is followed by a description of the new technical developments designed to equip ATM for the twenty-first century. The transversal aspects of network management, the environment and safety are then expounded. The chapter focuses on the European situation but also has relevance to other dense air traffic areas such as the US, and to areas experiencing rapid air traffic growth such as from the Middle East through to South East Asia and China.

Chapter 5, 'The commercial aerospace industry', by Fariba E. Alamdari, Jan Hogrefe and Wendy R. Sowers (Boeing Commercial Airplanes, USA), looks at the size of the global fleet and its geographical distribution. Trends in aircraft development are discussed against the backdrop of demand and strategy considerations. In a discussion about today's commercial aerospace industry, supplier relations are highlighted, as are freighter aircraft. Given the size and reach of the commercial aerospace industry, the chapter contains a brief discussion on the economic importance of the industry and on a key future challenge – environmental sustainability. The chapter concludes with an outlook for the near and far future of the industry.

Chapter 6, 'Impacts of liberalisation in global mature markets', by David Gillen (University of British Columbia, Canada), traces the factors that led to deregulation and how deregulation in air transport may or may not be tied to other trade initiatives. It looks at the evolution of the industry, the growth of airline alliances, the introduction of joint ventures and the recent development of metal neutral joint ventures. The consequences of this evolution for competition and the benefits of liberalised markets are considered. The chapter finishes with a discussion of where to next for these markets and the key forces at work.

Chapter 7, 'Liberalisation developments in key selected emerging markets', by Eric T. Njoya (Huddersfield University, UK) and David Warnock-Smith (Buckingham New University, UK), examines the degree of air transport liberalisation in emerging economies and its effect on the state and intensity of competition. It provides a brief overview of the bilateral and multilateral policies used by emerging markets to expand their air services. The chapter then reviews the literature on air transport liberalisation and competition in emerging economies and their role in facilitating this growth, and presents four case studies in which air policy and the structure of the airline industry are analysed in detail. The chapter also considers the need for further liberalisation and competition policies to safeguard consumer interests.

Chapter 8, 'Evolving airline and airport business models', by Marina Efthymiou (Dublin City University, Ireland) and Andreas Papatheodorou (University of the Aegean, Greece), highlights the business environment for airlines and airports before the opening up of the airline market. Then, it presents major developments in the post-liberalisation period, essentially focusing on airline and airport business model specialisation. Subsequently, the chapter analyses the issue of convergence at both airline and airport business models, and continues by elaborating on the role of airport cities and the triangular relationship between airlines, airports, and local community and destination authorities.

### Part II. Application of management disciplines to airlines and airports: Chapters 9–18

Part II demonstrates how academic disciplines of business strategy, economics and finance, marketing, capacity planning and management, and sustainability and corporate social responsibility have been applied to the study of air transport. The focus is on the two key industry sectors, namely airlines and airports. Part II consists of 10 chapters.

Chapter 9, 'Airline business strategy', by Gui Lohmann and Bojana Spasojevic (Griffith University, Australia), is structured into four main sections. The first section provides some generic strategies. The second section focuses on airline differentiation strategies and niche products, mainly charter and leisure carriers. The third section tackles growth strategies, examining the four distinct strategies proposed by Ansoff's Matrix: market penetration, product development, market development and diversification. The fourth section considers different strategic growth methods, including organic growth, mergers and acquisitions, industry cooperation and franchising. To conclude, the chapter considers future trends in the airline industry.

Chapter 10, 'Airport business strategy' by Nigel Halpern (Kristiania University College, Norway), concentrates on the formulation of airport business strategy. The chapter consists of four main sections. The first section considers the competitive landscape. The next two sections focus on strategic decisions within the context of generic and growth strategy frameworks. The final section summarises key points from the chapter and identifies opportunities for future research.

Chapter 11, 'Airline economics and finance', by Anming Zhang (University of British Columbia, Canada) and Yahua Zhang (University of Southern Queensland, Australia), surveys topics in the field of airline economics. The first two sections of the chapter centre on key issues and debates relating to cost and demand analysis. The core financial issues an airline faces are then discussed, followed by a review of the analysis of airline profitability and its determinants. The last section contains concluding remarks, including a brief discussion about some under-researched areas where definitive answers to some interesting issues are still lacking.

Chapter 12, 'Airport economics and finance', by Anne Graham (University of Westminster, UK), provides a comprehensive assessment of current issues and challenges in airport economics and finance. The chapter considers pricing and explores the airport–airline relationship. This leads on to economic regulation and aeronautical revenues. Attention is then given to non-aeronautical or commercial revenues, which is an increasingly important aspect of the airport business. An assessment of arguably the most popular area of research, namely efficiency and economic performance, then follows before conclusions are drawn and key avenues for future research are identified.

Chapter 13, 'Airline marketing', by Blaise P. Waguespack (Embry-Riddle Aeronautical University, USA), utilises a classic four P's approach to airline marketing, considering the airline product, place (distribution), promotion and price, while reviewing some of the possible legal and regulatory concerns that impact how airline marketing is addressed today. The conclusion recognises the task of meeting the basic needs of passengers in a constantly changing technological and world marketplace, and identifies subsequent needs for future research.

Chapter 14, 'Airport marketing', by Nigel Halpern (Kristiania University College, Norway), considers literature on three main areas of airport marketing: aviation marketing to airlines and trade, especially the airport route development process; marketing to commercial business partners such as retailers; and the marketing of airports to consumers – with a focus on airport marketing communications and branding. The conclusion summarises key areas of interest and gaps in the literature.

Chapter 15, 'Airline capacity planning and management', by Cheng-Lung Wu (University of New South Wales, Australia) and Stephen J. Maher (University of Lancaster, UK), focuses on capacity planning and operational management for airlines. Two main issues are considered: fleet assignment during schedule planning, and disruption management during operations. The conclusion identifies directions for future research.

Chapter 16, 'Airport capacity planning and management', by Dieter Wilken (German Aerospace Centre – DLR, Germany), describes the capacity situation at airports, deals with the capacity relevant components of airports, and states some capacity estimates of major airport elements. The main features and drawbacks of slot coordination are then described in the context of efficient usage of slot capacity. Finally, the capacity management means of public authorities, airlines, airports and air navigation service providers to cope with capacity constraints are discussed.

Chapter 17, 'Airline sustainability and corporate social responsibility', by Robert Mayer (Cranfield University, UK), defines sustainability and corporate social responsibility from an airline perspective and discusses the developments, communication strategies and reporting standards in airline sustainability and corporate social responsibility. It takes a global approach, providing examples of developments in industry practice and latest research from around the world.

Chapter 18, 'Airport sustainability and corporate social responsibility', by Christopher Paling and Callum Thomas (Manchester Metropolitan University, UK), considers the concept of sustainability and corporate social responsibility as it applies to airports from a largely United Kingdom or European perspective. It describes the variety of environmental issues arising from airport operations, and management approaches, including the role of engagement with the environmental agenda as a matter of commercial self-interest, but also as a matter of sustainability and corporate social responsibility.

## Part III. Key selected themes: Chapters 19–25

Part III applies a multi-sector and multidisciplinary approach that to some extent reflects on debates in the first two sections. Insights are offered into how the sectors and application of academic disciplines is changing, and what key trends and developments are likely to drive change in the future. Key selected themes are patterns and drivers of demand for air transport, the role of technology in airline management and operations, key aspects in aviation security, airline service quality and the consumer experience, consumer protection regimes and passenger complaints, low cost carrier implications for human resource management, and air transport and climate change.

Chapter 19, 'Patterns and drivers of demand for air transport', by Xingwu Zheng (Civil Aviation University of China, China) and Anne Graham (University of Westminster, UK), begins by considering general growth patterns and characteristics of demand. This leads on to an assessment of the drivers of demand and associated elasticity estimates, and an examination of a number of demand models and forecasts. This is followed by a specific analysis of demand in emerging markets, through selecting a mix of eight very different countries, with the chapter concluding by looking to the future and identifying demand issues that need further research.

Chapter 20, 'The role of technology in airline management and operations', by Berendien Lubbe (University of Pretoria, South Africa) and Theunis Potgieter (Independent Consultant, South Africa), begins with a brief historical overview of the most important developments. A discussion follows on the role of technology in supporting the various management and operational functions of an airline, especially airline distribution and e-commerce. The chapter ends with a look at some of the challenges and what the future may hold for airlines when it comes to information and communications technology.

Chapter 21, 'Key aspects in aviation security', by William G. Morrison (Wilfrid Laurier University, Canada) and Kathleen Rodenburg (University of Guelph, Canada), reviews economic and related research on key aspects of aviation security. The chapter focuses on seven main areas: the extent to which aviation security is a private or public good; the cost–benefit approach to evaluating aviation security; efficient and risk-based approaches to aviation security; the human factor in aviation security; the role of new technology; layered screening and pre-emption in airport screening; and non-passenger screening and security. A conclusion briefly considers directions for future research.

Chapter 22, 'Airline service quality and the consumer experience', by Dawna L. Rhoades (Embry-Riddle Aeronautical University, USA), explores the concept of service quality and the past two decades of research on the topic to help understand the relationship between the research and its findings, the future of airline service quality, and the approaches that management might take to address these issues.

Chapter 23, 'Consumer protection regimes and passenger complaints', by Paul Hooper (University of New South Wales, Australia), discusses the consumerism movement and its implications for regulation and management, the scope of passenger protection and its treatment in the US and the EU, passenger complaints, including statistical evidence and published research into causes and consequences of passenger dissatisfaction, and how to manage complaints and how to turn a dissatisfied passenger into a customer who has a long-term commitment to the brand.

Chapter 24, 'Low cost carrier implications for human resource management', by Geraint Harvey (University of Birmingham, UK) and Peter Turnbull (University of Bristol, UK), discusses the human resource practices associated with the low cost model and the impact of competition from these airlines on the human resource management strategies of traditional full service or legacy carriers. The chapter considers the influence of industry crises, the terrorist attacks in the US on 11 September 2001 and the global financial crisis. Recent human resource management initiatives are documented, and the chapter ends with a discussion of what is the most enduring, distinctive and arguably the most successful human resource management strategy in civil aviation.

Chapter 25, 'Air transport and climate change', by Stefan Gössling (Lund University, Sweden), provides a brief overview of the sector's environmental impacts, though its main focus is a discussion of air travel's contribution to emissions of greenhouse gases and policy responses to address the situation.

## References

ATAG (Air Transport Action Group) (2016). *Aviation: Benefits Beyond Borders*, Geneva, ATAG.

Brata, J.M.M. and Neves, F.M.S.P. (2011). *The history of aviation education and training*. Online. Available at: http://enu.kz/repository/2011/AIAA-2011-407.pdf (accessed 21 June 2017).

Budd, L. and Ison, S. (2016). *Air Transport Management: An International Perspective*, London, Routledge.

Cranfield University (2017). *Air transport management*. Online. Available at: www.cranfield.ac.uk/courses/taught/air-transport-management (accessed 25 June 2017).

IATA (International Air Transport Association) (2015). *Fact sheet: economic and social benefits of air transport*. Online. Available at: www.iata.org/pressroom/facts_figures/fact_sheets/Documents/fact-sheet-economic-and-social-benefits-of-air-transport.pdf (accessed 21 June 2017).

JATM (Journal of Air Transport Management) (2017). *Journal of Air Transport Management*. Online. Available at: www.journals.elsevier.com/journal-of-air-transport-management/ (accessed 10 October 2017).

Wensveen, J.G. (2015). *Air Transportation: A Management Perspective*, 8th edition, London, Routledge.

# Part I

# Current state of the air transport sectors

# 1

# The global airline industry

*John F. O'Connell*

## Introduction

Over the past century, commercial aviation has shaped the world by growing economic prosperity, stimulating trade, and cultivating tourism development, while its relative affordability in more recent times has allowed it to become an integral part of many people's lifestyles. Every day throughout the world, over 9 million passengers travel on 104,000 flights over a network of 51,000 routes, while US$17.5 billion worth of goods are transported to industry and homes. Aviation's global economic impact (direct, indirect, induced and tourism catalytic) is estimated at US$2.7 trillion, equivalent to 3.5 per cent of world gross domestic product (GDP) (ATAG, 2016; IATA, 2016a). The airline industry is characterised by sustained long-term growth in demand for air services. Yet the industry, consisting of around 1,400 airlines globally in 2015 with a combined fleet of over 23,151 aircraft (ATAG, 2016; IATA, 2016a), remains in a financially challenging state, returning only marginal profitability down through the decades. The paradox of sustained long-term growth and only marginal profitability forms the basis for this chapter, which consists of six main sections. The first section briefly investigates the growth, dispersion and segmentation of passenger traffic (the air cargo industry is covered in detail in Chapter 2). The chapter then investigates the profitability of the global airline industry before focusing on the profitability of airlines (see also Chapter 11) domiciled in three main geographical areas: the United States (US), Europe and Asia. The final section provides a conclusion to the chapter.

## Growth, dispersion and segmentation of passenger traffic

ICAO (2016a) reported that world passenger traffic grew by 6.8 per cent in 2015, 1 per cent higher than in the previous year. This is the highest recorded growth since the post-recession rebound in 2010. The air transport industry is at the epicentre of a wide and far-reaching value chain that encapsulates many industries. For instance, tourism is an important catalytic enterprise in which aviation plays a key role. There were approximately 1.2 billion international tourists in 2015, 54 per cent of whom arrived by air, and this segment of tourists spent US$620 billion on travel, accommodation, food, entertainment and tourist amenities, which have a multiplier catalytic effect into the global economy. Thirty years earlier, only one-third of tourists travelled by

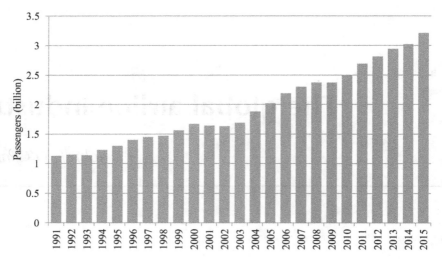

*Figure 1.1*   Number of passengers carried worldwide, 1991 to 2015

*Source*: Author analysis from ICAO, IATA, AEA, ATA, AAPA, AACO and LCC databases.

air, which highlights the growing interdependency between aviation and tourism that is becoming more and more interwoven (UNWTO, 2016). Figure 1.1 shows that 3.2 billion passengers travelled by air worldwide in 2015 – double the number of passengers since the early 2000s. The expansion of overall global passenger travel during the last 15–20 years is largely attributed to a number of factors, including deregulation (see Chapters 6 and 7), low entry barriers, strengthening global economies, increased disposable income, the ascent of the global middle class, falling fares, the rise of low cost carriers (LCCs), tourism development, including overseas holidaying, and increased international trade, which encourages business travel. Airlines worldwide reacted by adding large amounts of capacity (i.e. seats) in order to capture the increasing passenger traffic.

Table 1.1 illustrates the geographical dispersion of these 3.2 billion passengers, with North America recording 924 million passengers, which comprises both domestic and international travellers; however, this market increased by just 27 per cent over the 15-year period from 2000 to 2015. Meanwhile, Europe witnessed the doubling of its traffic over the same time frame, which is attributable to the open sky bloc that was extended to several Eastern European states, thereby removing all restrictions regarding designation, market access and capacity. It liberalised the licensing of carriers, the routes they fly and the prices they can impose, while opening up cross-border and domestic markets (including cabotage) and also removing national ownership restrictions. As a consequence, traffic surged between Eastern and Western Europe. Meanwhile, Asia's traffic almost tripled from 378 million passengers in 2000 to over 1 billion by 2015, while also accounting for around 40 per cent of the global cargo tonnage. The region is home to 56 per cent of the world's population, which generates 31 per cent of global GDP. Asia is immersed in economic prosperity, a rapidly rising middle class and populations that are steadily moving into cities. Asia-Pacific nations have been one of the most dynamic tourism markets over the past decade and have become the world's second most important region in terms of international tourist arrivals (AAPA, 2016; IMF, 2016a).

Many different categories of passenger travel by air today, and their characteristics and needs are very different from each other. Passenger segmentation data captured by the UNWTO in 2015 found that 53 per cent of passenger boardings were for leisure, recreation and holiday

*Table 1.1* Passenger traffic by region (millions), 2000 versus 2015

|  | 2000 | 2015 | % change 2000–2015 |
|---|---|---|---|
| North America | 726 | 924 | 27 |
| Europe | 420 | 868 | 107 |
| Asia-Pacific | 378 | 1,035 | 174 |
| Central/South America | 82 | 181 | 121 |
| Middle East | 44 | 173 | 293 |
| Africa | 29 | 34 | 17 |
| Total | 11,679 | 3,215 | 92 |

*Source*: Author analysis from ICAO, IATA, AEA, ATA, AAPA, AACO and LCC databases.

purposes, while 27 per cent were visiting friends and relatives (VFR) or travelling for health and religious purposes, 14 per cent were for business and professional purposes, and the travel purposes of the remaining 6 per cent were not specified (UNWTO, 2016). This varies significantly, however, from region to region and from country to country. For instance, a United Kingdom (UK) international passenger survey in 2015 indicates that 58 per cent of UK residents' travel abroad by air was for holiday purposes, 21 per cent VFR and 10 per cent business, with other categories constituting the remaining 11 per cent (ONS, 2016).

The underpinning criteria that prompt passengers to take a flight form an imperative and crucial layer of airline research. The International Air Transport Association's (IATA) global passenger survey report (IATA, 2015a) sampled 7,250 respondents across 140 countries and revealed that the overall top five influences when purchasing a ticket were price (43 per cent), followed by schedule/most convenient flight times (21 per cent), frequent flyer programme (FFP) (13 per cent), global network (9 per cent) and on-time performance (6 per cent). The high proportion of passengers attracted by price is indicative of the rapid rise of LCCs. It is worth noting that when business and leisure passengers were further segmented, the results change considerably. Business passengers' top five influences were price (36 per cent), schedule (25 per cent), FFP (10 per cent), global network (10 per cent) and on-time performance (11 per cent). Meanwhile, leisure passengers' top five influences were price (52 per cent), schedule (19 per cent), FFP (8 per cent), global network (8 per cent) and on-time performance (4 per cent) (IATA, 2015b).

Air travel has a bright future ahead of it, with passenger traffic predicted to double over the next 20 years, growing by 4.5 per cent per annum (Airbus, 2016a; IATA, 2016b). In fact, over the last 100 years since the first commercial passenger service in 1914, 65 billion passengers have flown. IATA now expects the next 65 billion will travel in a much shorter time frame in just the next 20 years (IATA, 2014).

These forecasts are endorsed by the significant backlog orders at the three main aircraft manufacturers amounting to 12,884 aircraft by late 2016 comprising 6,749 Airbus aircraft (Airbus, 2016b), 5,635 Boeing aircraft (Boeing, 2016a) and 500 Embraer aircraft (Embraer, 2016) (see Chapter 5). The underpinning drivers for this traffic augmentation include the positive world GDP projections of 2.4 per cent annually over the next 20 years (World Bank, 2016), population expansion, and the inexorable rise of an increasingly affluent middle class and a surge in travel from emerging markets, as 75 per cent of these citizens are forecast to take an air trip by 2035, up from 25 per cent who travelled by air in 2016. Meanwhile, the world's population is increasingly migrating towards capital cities, where almost two-thirds are projected to reside by 2035 – inhabitants from developed metropolitan cities now treat air travel as a lifestyle.

Asia-Pacific is singled out as being the source for more than half of the new passengers over the next 20 years, where it will feature in more than half of the top 20 global traffic growth flows. Meanwhile, China will displace the US as the world's largest aviation market (defined by traffic to/from and within the country), while India will displace the UK for third place by around 2025. Boeing (2016b) envisions that more than 100 million new passengers are projected to board aircraft for the first time in Asia-Pacific, and this will be replicated each year over the coming decades. This is becoming ever more evident as the traffic at Thailand's 38 airports, for example, has doubled in just six years, and one-third of all traffic from Thailand now goes to China (Airports of Thailand, 2016).

## The profitability of the global airline industry

Global airline traffic has been doubling every 15 years since the early 1970s despite the fact that it is fully exposed to many external forces that cause its growth to widely fluctuate. Events such as wars, terrorism, diseases, natural catastrophes, recessions, credit tightening, high inflation and rising oil prices force downward pressure on economic activity, while the opposite occurs for prolonged stock market gains, rising house prices, high employment and so forth. These characteristics all contribute to the cyclical nature of economic activity, which is intrinsically linked to the demand for air travel. From the 1970s to the present day, there has been a number of major cataclysmic events that have adversely affected economic prosperity, and these include the oil crises of the 1970s and late 1980s, the Gulf War in the early 1990s, the Asian financial crisis, SARS, 9/11, the Iraq War, and the severe recession that followed in 2008. In the case of 9/11, for instance, Ito and Lee (2005) found that it led to an ongoing downward shift in demand for commercial air services in the US of roughly 7.4 per cent, after accounting for factors such as trend, seasonality and general macroeconomic conditions.

The full repercussions of Brexit (the UK's decision to leave the European Union [EU]), will remain unknown over the coming years, but problems are escalating, with Sterling reaching a 31-year low, equivalent to where it traded in March 1985, causing major concerns for UK-domiciled airlines[1] that are now exposed to escalating procurement costs (e.g. for fuel, aircraft, and airport fees) that are sourced in foreign currencies. The UK faces a trade-off between accessing the European single aviation market and having the policy freedom to set its own regulations. Taken as a whole, the EU is easily the single biggest destination market from the UK, accounting for 49 per cent of passengers and 54 per cent of scheduled commercial flights according to the author's estimates. In between these global cataclysmic events, global economies recover, but the cycle of boom years followed by recession is becoming a permanent fixture in the global economic landscape.

Consequently, the demand for air transport is also cyclical in nature as it is synchronised with the economic cycles. Many academics have identified a direct correlation between real GDP (inflation adjusted) and the demand for air travel (see Chapter 19), and this interlink contributes to the cyclical financial performance of the industry. The literature is replete with research inferring to the correlated relationship between air transport developments and economic prosperity from which the financial performance of the world's airlines show a pendulum-like motion of profit and loss making swings that are directly correlated to global GDP, where air traffic growth is 1.5 to 2 times that of the rate of growth of the economy (e.g. Brueckner, 2003; Button and Taylor, 2000; Chi and Baek, 2013; Chin and Tay, 2001; Debbage and Delk, 2001; Dobruszkes et al., 2011; Doganis, 2010; Marazzo et al., 2010; O'Connell, 2011; Profillidis and Botzoris, 2015; Yao and Yang, 2012).

Figure 1.2 shows this oscillating spectrum of profits and losses for the global airline industry from 1978 to 2015. From the inception of the industry in the 1920s to recent years, the sum

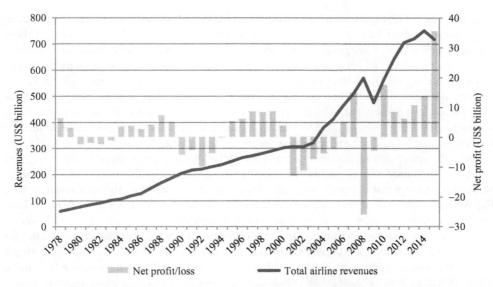

*Figure 1.2* Revenues and profitability for the world's commercial airlines, 1978 to 2015

*Source*: Data from ICAO and IATA databases.

of aggregated profits balanced out the sum of the aggregate losses, and in more recent years the industry only produced very small operating margins in the low digits, normally just hovering at around 3 to 4 per cent for full service carriers, even during good economic times. However, there was an evident upsurge in profitability for 2015, as shown in Figure 1.2, with the world's airlines generating net profits of over US$35 billion[2] on revenues of around US$751 billion, producing a margin of almost 5 per cent.

The positive financial results have further ripple effects because for the first time the global industry has produced higher return on invested capital (ROIC) when compared to the cost of capital, which is the return required by investors, or the return that investors could expect to achieve by investing their capital in other industries with a similar risk profile. This accolade has now been achieved for two consecutive years. IATA (2016b) reported that global airlines generated an ROIC of 9.8 per cent, which adequately rewards equity shareholders. Qantas Group (2016), for example, reported an ROIC of 16 per cent for 2015. However, the cumulative net profit of US$35 billion that the industry aggregated is determined by the performance of a relatively small number of large airlines as almost 60 per cent of this global profit was generated by the four major US airlines, while the large airline groups such as Emirates, Lufthansa Group, International Airlines Group (IAG) and Ryanair each produced over US$1.65 billion in net profits in 2015.

Unquestionably, the principal contributor for the surge in global profitability for 2015 has been the sharp fall in oil prices, which aggregated into substantial financial benefits for the world's carriers as the price of crude oil fell from US$110 per barrel in early 2014 to less than US$40 per barrel 24 months later, while it climbed to over US$52 per barrel by late 2016. In 2016, the global airlines were estimated to have spent US$127 billion on fuel, which is 44 per cent less than in 2014 – few predicted the pace and depth of the decline in fuel prices, and carriers who had hedged[3] fuel at high prices were disadvantaged. In Europe, airlines tend to hedge higher shares of their fuel than elsewhere in the world, with easyJet hedging 87 per cent of their

15

requirements at US$81 per barrel for 2016, while IAG and Ryanair fixed 81 and 95 per cent, respectively, of their fuel uplift at just over US$62 per barrel. Meanwhile, American Airlines pursues a policy of not hedging, thereby procuring fuel at current market rates, which allows it to capitalise when fuel prices are low – notably, it was the world's most profitable airline in 2015, producing US$7.6 billion in net profits. Hedging when fuel prices are high can have a severely damaging impact when it retracts. This effect was evident when Cathay Pacific, for example, hedged 62 per cent of its fuel requirements at US$85 a barrel, and as a consequence it posted fuel hedging losses of US$580 million for the first six months of 2016, and was forecast to incur similar losses for the remaining six months (Bloomberg, 2016a).

New disruptive airlines continue to enter the global marketplace equipped with leaner cost structures, high productivity mandates and best practice efficiencies that trigger structural shifts within the industry that distinctly impact the legacy incumbent airlines. Ambitious carriers from the Arabian Gulf fit into this category as Emirates, Qatar Airways and Etihad Airways have moved the tectonic plates of the aviation world, having changed the global traffic flows by carving new traffic corridors from the Indian subcontinent to North America via Gulf hubs, for example. These carriers have capitalised on their geocentric location, which encapsulates 80 per cent of the world's population residing within an eight-hour flight radius from the Gulf hubs. Their aspiration is to become super connectors by using sixth freedom traffic rights to aggregate passenger volumes from the multiple spokes to their hubs for onward redistribution. Their reward is apparent, as there are unprecedented increases in passenger traffic year over year navigating through their respective hubs. Their ambition is evident when considering that 20 per cent of the wide-body aircraft backlog at Boeing and Airbus is destined for these three carriers.

There will now be an examination of the profitability generated by the airlines domiciled in the world's three largest air transport markets that encompass the large geopolitical powerhouses of the US, Europe and Asia. These markets are assessed in detail to uncover the underlying principles that are shaping their airline business models.

## The challenges facing US airlines in generating profitability

In the early 2000s, the US majors were facing multiple problems, including the 9/11 attacks, the sudden decline of the dot-com industry (a critical component of their business-class passenger revenues),[4] high operating unit costs,[5] delays, increasing debt, poor airport and navigational infrastructure, many large-sized competitors that were adding capacity, falling yields, and the threat posed by the LCCs, which were increasingly encroaching on domestic markets. Subsequently, from 2001 to 2009, the US carriers posted net losses of around US$65 billion (A4A, 2016a). Fast-forwarding 10 years, the commercial landscape is virtually unrecognisable as the US airline industry has become the world's most profitable, generating almost US$20 billion in net profits in 2015, which represents over 60 per cent of the world's profits. Seven key elements that underpin the foundations for this turnaround have been identified.

First, the US carriers have endeavoured to successfully control capacity in their biggest market – the domestic market. They have retained a disciplined approach as capacity has only increased by 2 per cent per annum since 2010, which has subsequently helped to record the world's highest load factor in 2015, averaging 83.5 per cent (US DOT, 2016). Meanwhile, ATW (2016a) reported that Delta, American and United are all expected to increase capacity growth by just 1 per cent in 2017.

Second, consolidation has been one of the primary drivers of profitability as it has reduced the number of major US airlines from eight to four[6] from 2009 to 2013. This resulted in a more comprehensive route network with less duplication, albeit with improved operational efficiency, while they have also leveraged their large-scale conglomerate positioning to accrue deeper discounts. By 2016, these four US majors now control around 80 per cent of the capacity in the US domestic market – Delta Air Lines, for example, generated over 68.5 per cent of its passenger revenues (US$23.8 billion) from its domestic market in 2015 (Delta Air Lines, 2016).

Third, there has been debt reduction. A4A (2016a) reported that from 2010 to 2015, the industry reduced debt by US$54.3 billion. Chapter 11 bankruptcy has expedited the debt reduction process and it has been circulating in the US landscape for decades. It has been used as a mechanism to rightsize the carrier by restructuring leases, labour and pension obligations and to reorganise its capital structure.

Fourth, US carriers increased labour and asset productivity while expanding route networks and increasing frequency, and they also optimised their hubs to accommodate increased transfer traffic. The US also imposes tight restrictions in foreign ownership, constraining it to 25 per cent, which serves as a barrier to entry.

Fifth, the US carriers have been leaders in inducing new revenue mechanisms through innovative ancillary revenue streams by unbundling the products normally bolted to the fare and charging for baggage, reservation changes, assigned seating, extra leg room, lounge access and so on. However, a significant chunk of the non-ticket revenue is now being generated from the co-branded credit card arrangements with large banks that issue frequent flyer miles as a reward mechanism for using their credit card. Ideaworks (2016) established that United Airlines generated US$3 billion from its banking partnership with credit cards in 2015, while Delta Air Lines earned US$2.4 billion. In addition, the three US majors have optimised the financial tools of their FFP by switching from a mileage-based method of reward to a revenue-based platform to reward the most lucrative travellers. Ancillary revenue has become a large-scale enterprise that is being vigorously pursued by the US carriers. United Airlines generated 16.4 per cent of its total passenger revenues from ancillary revenues in 2015, with American 11.5 per cent, Southwest 10.7 per cent, Delta 9.3 per cent and Alaska 19.5 per cent, while ultra LCC Allegiant Airlines produced 37.6 per cent of its total revenues from ancillaries (Ideaworks, 2016).

Sixth, US carriers pumped almost US$69 billion over the last five years into product enhancements such as acquiring new aircraft, refurbishing older aircraft, installing lie-flat beds, debuting premium economy class, Wi-Fi, improved lounges, baggage systems, check-in procedures, initiated mobile phone platforms and enhanced IT tools (A4A, 2016b).

Lastly, and very importantly, the international market is largely capacity-controlled through a tripartite ensemble of alliances, joint ventures (JVs) and antitrust immunity. The US majors are the founding fathers of alliance[7] partnerships, which allow member carriers to feed traffic to each other's hubs in different continents, creating a vast network of interlinking routes supported by reciprocal FFPs. These alliances have created powerful and dominant hub linkages between carriers aligned to the same alliance. On the North Atlantic corridor, for example, the Star Alliance has 100 per cent of the direct market between Frankfurt and the following US cities that have a United Airlines hub: Newark (New York), Washington, Chicago, Los Angeles and San Francisco. Meanwhile, the SkyTeam members have a monopoly of the market between Amsterdam and Delta's hubs at New York JFK, Los Angeles, Detroit, Atlanta and Minneapolis. In addition, the Oneworld members have 100 per cent of the market between Madrid and American Airlines hubs at Chicago, Los Angeles and Philadelphia, while Oneworld's American and British Airways has a JV monopoly between Heathrow and Dallas.

The three alliances accounted for around 73 per cent of seat capacity[8] on the North Atlantic in 2016. Many of these alliance partners have evolved the partnership into deeper JVs in the form of antitrust immunity that allows the carriers to collaborate with each other by setting fares and determining schedules together. It creates a metal neutrality mechanism whereby it becomes effectively indifferent as to which aircraft or metal carries a passenger. It also accommodates the sharing of revenues and profits/losses generated by the parties on the JV routes. This powerful tool expands the scope of traffic as 86 per cent of the traffic on the North Atlantic is now in the form of JVs – carriers outside of the alliance, such as Virgin Atlantic, also perform JV activity with Delta, which creates a cartel-like situation. Hawaiian Airlines researched the impact of air fares as a result of these JVs and established that fares on the North Atlantic increased by 22 per cent from 2000 to 2014 (CAPA, 2016). The significance of such JVs is very apparent because in 2014, the three big US majors generated around US$3.4 billion in operating profits from their international operations, while 91 per cent (US$3.1 billion) was generated from their North Atlantic operations (American Airlines, 2015; Delta Air Lines, 2015; United Airlines, 2015).

Overall, these seven categories have produced a very significant impact on the US airline industry, as they contributed in amassing almost US$56 billion in net profits from 2010 through to June 2016.

## The challenges facing European airlines in generating profitability

There are 9.6 million flights a year in European airspace carrying 868 million passengers and 7.5 million tonnes of freight. Europe is connected to 160 countries worldwide, and aviation contributes €452 billion each year to European GDP, demonstrating that the aviation sector acts as a catalytic multiplier of economic prosperity (ATAG, 2016; EUROCONTROL, 2016; ICAO, 2016a). In total, there are 116 air operator certificate (AOC) holders in the EU. The US$6.9 billion profits generated by the European airlines for 2015 dwarfed that of the US carriers, but there are huge challenges confronting the sector. Seven key elements that underpin the challenges facing the European airline industry have been identified.

First, the market is much more fragmented when compared to the US situation, as the five largest airlines, which include Lufthansa Group, Air France-KLM and IAG, have all consolidated through mergers,[9] and, together with Ryanair and easyJet, they control 55 per cent of the intra-European market, while the remaining 111 smaller carriers account for the rest. Capacity on intra-European markets is continuously added, dampening yields.

Second, LCCs are pushing into primary airports and realigning their distribution channels to incorporate global distribution systems (GDSs) in order to penetrate into the higher-value business travel segment. They have also adapted their product offerings; Ryanair, for example, promotes a campaign entitled 'always getting better'.[10] This puts severe structural pressure on the legacy full service airlines that have relied on the business traveller as a primary source of their income. Meanwhile, long-haul LCCs are now beginning to gain traction, with Norwegian operating from six EU states to the US, with ambitions to carve more intercontinental city pairs.

Third, there is escalating competition emanating from the Gulf carriers and Turkish Airlines, which continue to record the world's fastest growth at 10+ per cent year on year. Traditionally, European carriers would connect sixth freedom traffic through their respective hubs and then redistribute this traffic eastwards. However, the Gulf and Istanbul hubs have engineered their bases to become important transfer points for passengers who are beginning to redirect and reshape the traditional traffic flows (Hooper et al., 2011; Murel and O'Connell, 2011; O'Connell, 2006; Vespermann et al., 2008). Turkish Airlines is quickly becoming a formidable force whose Istanbul hub is on the crossroads of Europe, Asia, the Middle East and Africa. Analysis from OAG data revealed that it served 2,406 flights per week to Europe from Istanbul Atatürk Airport in the summer of 2016. It has consistently increased the number of passengers transferring from one international to another international flight by 34 per cent per annum, from 1.13 million in 2005 to 18.38 million by 2015 (Turkish Airlines, 2015). Like the Gulf carriers, Turkish Airlines has big ambitions as it aims to have a fleet of 427 aircraft by 2022, and to accommodate this expansion a new airport is being constructed with a passenger throughput of 150 million passengers costing US$29 billion – making it the world's second largest airport after Dubai World Central (Flightglobal, 2013).

Fourth, the European airlines are also challenged by currency devaluations as the euro dropped significantly in value against all the main currencies in 2015. According to the IMF (2016b), the average euro exchange rate against the US dollar was 16.4 per cent lower in 2015 than in the previous year's average. Many EU-domiciled airlines pay a large chunk of their expenses in US dollars[11] (e.g. fuel and aircraft financing), and when the US dollar appreciates in value, it increases the cost burden for airlines that operate outside the US.

Fifth, the continent is being plagued by labour unrest (see Chapter 24). PwC (2016) found that there were 95 air traffic control (ATC) strikes across 10 EU countries, encompassing 176 days of strike activity between 2010 and 2015. French air traffic controllers alone accounted for 95 days of strikes, forcing millions of passengers to be disrupted. These strikes reduced EU GDP by €10.4 billion, mostly from reduced tourism spending, while airline revenues were reduced by €636 million. Similarly, labour unrest is infiltrating through the airline boardrooms as flight crews demand improved remuneration packages. Lufthansa's annual report for 2015 mentioned the word strike 44 times – 8,125 flights were cancelled while 1.1 million passengers were affected during 2015. There were 30 days of strikes in 2014 and 2015, costing Lufthansa €500 million (ATW, 2015; Lufthansa, 2015). During 2016, there were multiple strikes, costing the carrier around €10 million per day, instigated by pilots, yet *The New York Times* (2016) reported that Lufthansa's pilots earn about 30+ per cent above the global average, with the highest-ranked captains earning €250,000 per year. The same rhetoric echoes at the Air France-KLM Group, which also has high labour costs[12] (labour represents 29 per cent of revenues versus 15 per cent at Turkish Airlines) but low productivity in terms of revenue generated per employee. Dell'Oro (2015) reports that Air France pilots are paid on average 37 per cent more than its competitors. Yet a two-week pilot strike at Air France in September 2014 cost the group €425 million (Air France-KLM, 2015b).

Sixth, there are severe infrastructure constraints at airports (see Chapter 16) and with air traffic management (ATM) systems (see Chapter 4). There are imminent shortfalls when expanding airport infrastructure (new runways and terminal development) as it is falling behind the capacity growth of Europe's airlines. As a consequence, there are 101 slot-controlled airports in Europe, out of a total 168 slot-controlled airports worldwide. Subsequently, airport charges are escalating. A research report by Aviation Economics (2016) cites that charges at the largest 21 European airports have increased by 80 per cent between 2005 and 2014. Individual countries such as Spain, Italy and the UK, for example, have witnessed increases of 255, 141 and 120 per cent, respectively, from 2005 to 2014, while the UK and Switzerland have become the most expensive countries to operate to, commanding an average charge of €43.63 and €38.24 per passenger, respectively, which were inclusive of all charges (e.g. landing, air bridges and passenger charges).

Another large infrastructure bottleneck is the airspace that is approaching the limit of what the navigational systems can manage, which is currently at 26,000 aircraft movements a day (EUROCONTROL, 2016). Currently, aircraft must operate through a network of 67 individually controlled airspace blocks whose inefficiencies are apparent as aircraft must circumnavigate through the multiple air corridors. Lufthansa's CEO Carsten Spohr highlights the disorganisation by stating that the current ATM system adds 10 per cent to airlines' fuel bills, equating to 64 of Lufthansa's 640 aircraft operating and burning fuel each year because of the inadequate infrastructure (ATW, 2016b). However, a proposed solution termed the Single European Sky project that aims to integrate these 67 blocks into nine Functional Airspace Blocks has been ongoing since 1999 with little movement. Schulte-Strathaus (2009) indicated that airlines could save up to €5 billion annually if the proposal was enacted.

Lastly, European airlines also face challenges in relation to Regulation EC No 261/2004, which facilitates passengers in the case of cancellations, rerouting, delays and denied boarding, and legislates that financial compensation[13] applies; for example, when flights are delayed on arrival by three hours or more than the scheduled time of arrival, then passengers may be entitled to compensation (see Chapter 23).

Overall, these seven categories have constrained the European airlines from generating large profits. More consolidation needs to take place, infrastructural improvements of airports and ATM systems need to be urgently concluded, while a remedy for the festering roots of disgruntled employees must be sought. Network carriers in particular need to produce value-added and consumer-driven product differentiation beyond the basics of the LCC product. The excessive competition has triggered the yields of EU legacy airlines to fall from around 13 cents per revenue passenger kilometre (RPK) in 1991 to around 6.7 cents per RPK by 2015 (AEA, 2016).

## The challenges facing Asian-based airlines in generating profitability

Asia-Pacific is home to 4 billion people and its air transport sector is rapidly expanding, with seat capacity for the region growing by around 9 per cent in 2015. Meanwhile, Asia's share of global traffic (RPK) is forecast to increase from 29 per cent in 2015 to 36 per cent by 2034. Its air transport industry contributes US$626 billion to the region's GDP each year (AAPA, 2016; ATAG, 2016). According to IATA (2016c), the world's 10 busiest domestic and international routes are all in Asia. Yet the Asian carriers only recorded profits of US$5.8 billion in 2015, equating to US$4.89 per passenger, which is a large improvement over the US$1.81 per passenger in 2013 (IATA, 2016b). The Asian carriers are also facing mounting challenges associated with seven key areas.

First, major structural changes are taking place in the Asian aviation landscape as the region is beginning to loosen its regulatory shackles and embrace liberalisation. This has the effect of inducing competition but has also depressed yields. These two colliding effects are evident when assessing the liberalisation of the Singapore-Kuala Lumpur city pair. Hanaoka et al. (2014) uncovered that the 34-year-old air service agreement (ASA) between Singapore and Kuala Lumpur was a duopoly for decades, served solely by the respective flag carriers. The restrictive legislation was enacted by the Malaysian government to protect Malaysian Airlines. However, since the city pair was deregulated, the number of flights had doubled by 2016, when compared to 2000 levels.[14] Bowen (2016) highlights the yield impact from deregulation by citing that average fares on the Singapore-Kuala Lumpur city pair were US$150 when the competition was restricted to a duopoly. Yet within a few months of the city pair being deregulated, the average fare fell to US$80. Similarly, Boeing (2014) affirms that the open skies agreement between Japan and Taiwan facilitated a doubling in the number of destinations between these two countries from 2011 to 2013.

Historically, air transport in South East Asia was regulated on the basis of bilateral agreements, which impose restrictions in operations in the region. South East Asia established an aviation block known as the ASEAN[15] single aviation market that came into effect on 1 January 2015. It removed the frequency and capacity constraints existing in bilateral ASAs between member states endorsing third, fourth and fifth freedom traffic rights. However, there are many issues restraining the full integration of the ASEAN open sky pact as seventh freedom and domestic operations by foreign carriers have yet to be constituted, while the jurisdiction on ownership laws still restricts foreign ownership to 49 per cent. In preparation for the open skies legislation, Asia's LCCs have been ramping up their order books for short-haul aircraft, with Lion Air ordering 440 aircraft, AirAsia 400 and VietJet 199, while the flag carriers have relatively few on order. This impinges huge concerns for the future of the region's flag carriers. Merrill Lynch (2016) also reported that ticket prices fell in the Asia-Pacific zone by an average 9 per cent in 2015.

Second, severe infrastructural constraints at key Asian airports have become a major obstacle. Jakarta, for example, has a metropolitan population of around 10 million that consists of the largest middle-class catchment area in the country. Jakarta is the most economically important city in Indonesia as it is the epicentre of political and business activity. Yet Jakarta's Soekarno Hatta Airport only has a design capacity of 38 million passengers, but had to handle 52 million passengers in 2015. The airport accounts for 35 per cent of Indonesia's total traffic and is the world's main gateway into Indonesia. Similarly, Manila's Ninoy Aquino International Airport has a design capacity of 28 million passengers but handled 36.6 million passengers in 2015. While its two runways can only accommodate an average of 36 take-offs and landings per hour, the peak-hour demand far exceeds this capacity limit, resulting in congested runways that cause flight delays and cancellations. Many other airports across Asia-Pacific resonate the same frustration, which limits the opportunity for full service airlines to take advantage of the regulatory freedoms. Infrastructure constraints in India plus the weak balance sheets of Indian carriers are preventing Mumbai and Delhi from developing into major hubs. This, to an extent, undermines the international growth prospects of Indian full service airlines and has allowed Dubai to grow as an offshore hub serving the subcontinent.

Third, Asian carriers tend to focus on air cargo operations. Airlines based in the Asia-Pacific region fly almost two-fifths of total international freight tonne kilometres (FTKs), which represents around 40 million in metric tonnes each year. Revenues from the carriage of cargo amount to over US$21 billion per year, making freight an integral component of the business model of Asian-domiciled full service airlines (AAPA, 2016; ACI, 2016; IATA, 2016d). Demand for air cargo remains suppressed given that major Asian economies such as China are slowing, while Europe remains stagnated and the US is taking longer than expected to recover. However, the industry continues to add capacity, which materialises from the reactivation of dedicated freighters that were previously grounded due to high fuel costs and from the entrance of belly-hold capacity belonging to wide-body passenger aircraft. Cathay Pacific, for example, had one A350 entering service every month during 2016 providing 20 tons of belly-hold capacity.

Asian-based long-haul LCCs are also moving into this territory as AirAsia X transports belly-hold cargo that contributed around US$25 million to its ancillary revenues in 2015 (AirAsia X, 2016). However, the load factors pursuant to Asian air cargo only reached around 57 per cent in the summer of 2016, contributing to the ongoing financial stresses. Merrill Lynch (2016) reported that air cargo yields in Asia were down 25 per cent when comparing 2016 levels to that of 2012, and warned that pricing is unlikely to improve unless there is a sustained recovery in world trade. This significantly influences the bottom line as cargo makes up 25 per cent of Cathay Pacific's total revenues, while for Korean Air, Thai Airways and Singapore Airlines it comprises 23, 14 and 12 per cent, respectively. Meanwhile, Garuda has diversified away from cargo as it only reaps 5 per cent of its revenues from cargo (mainly domestic).

Fourth, safety issues are of major concern to the regulatory authorities, as traffic in the region is growing exponentially, and ICAO stated that one-third of aircraft accidents in Asia-Pacific over the years 2008 to 2012 involved deficiencies in regulatory oversight, while another 27 per cent involved deficiencies in safety management (*The Japan Times*, 2015). Annual audits by ICAO are lagging in eight essential safety categories that include: legislation; organisation;

licensing; operations; airworthiness; accident investigation; air navigational services; and aerodromes. Indonesia,[16] which was previously banned from operating to Europe and to the US, failed almost every function, attaining a safety compliance of just 47.23 per cent, well below the global average of 64.76 per cent. Meanwhile Thailand's compliance rating of 31.03 per cent was more distressing, and ICAO stated that the government was not providing sufficient safety oversights to ensure the effective implementation of applicable ICAO standards (ICAO, 2016b). However, Singapore recorded a very high compliance safety rating of 98.62 per cent.

Fifth, Asian carriers are also faced with comparable challenges to that of their European counterparts in relation to currency volatility, relentless competition and cost pressures. The strengthening of the US dollar against many Asian currencies has affected the financial performance of nearly all Asian-domiciled airlines. Cebu Pacific, for example, has 60 per cent of its expenses in US dollars coupled with 100 per cent of its debt. Garuda's seat capacity is heavily skewed towards its domestic market, while only 45 per cent of its revenues are earned in foreign currency, making it very financially exposed, as the US dollar appreciated by 66 per cent in value against the Indonesian rupiah from early 2012 to late 2015 according to XE.com. The range of fuel hedging rates between Asian carriers is considerable, with the AirAsia group hedged at 75 per cent, while Japan Air Lines registers just 5 per cent. After the 2008 financial crash, the Chinese airlines suffered big losses after the value of their crude oil futures collapsed, and from the aftermath the Chinese government barred airlines from buying crude future contracts, from which they are now reaping the benefits. In addition, many Asia-Pacific-based airlines (AirAsia, Cathay Pacific, Cebu Pacific, Malaysia Airlines, Thai Airways) have removed their fuel surcharge, which was an embedded incremental cost that was passed on to the passenger for many years (Flightglobal, 2016). No doubt, this will benefit the consumer, but ultimately it will deflate yields further.

Sixth, Asia-Pacific will experience the greatest global demand for flight crews and technicians over the next 20 years. In fact, the region comprises 40 per cent of the global requirement due to the backlog of single-aisle aircraft earmarked for Asia, mostly driven by LCCs. Boeing (2016b) estimates that Asia-Pacific will require 248,000 new pilots and 268,000 technicians over the next 20 years, compared to 104,000 pilots and 118,000 technicians for Europe. Bloomberg (2016b) reports that China alone needs to hire 100 pilots a week for the next 20 years to meet demand. This human resource shortfall is damaging the region and is slowing growth, as two Japanese carriers, for example, recently trimmed the number of flights due to pilot shortages, while Jetstar held off on expansion (Flightglobal, 2016).

Lastly, the Chinese market continues to outshine its neighbours. The big three megacarriers that include Air China, China Eastern and China Southern made net profits of US$1.1 billion, US$820 million and US$766 million, respectively, in 2015 (Flightglobal, 2016). According to OAG/MIDT data, there are 202 commercial airports in China and 31 Chinese airlines, which transported 356 million domestic and 35 million international passengers in 2014. They have demonstrated exceptional double-digit annualised growth over 2010 to 2014. China now absorbs 200 new passenger aircraft every year. IMF (2016a) shows that China's economy is slowing, but it continues to grow, registering 6.6 per cent in 2016, while the combination of trade and tourism is spurring Chinese carriers to expand aggressively. Air China, for example, opened 29 new international routes in 2015 and now serves 111 such destinations, while China Eastern added 49 long-haul aircraft to increase its international capacity by 30 per cent in 2016. However, the enlargement of its international footprint is pressurising the profitability of other North Asian carriers, such as Korean Air, Asiana, JAL and ANA, that have long relied on using their sixth freedom traffic rights to carry traffic from mainland China to the US[17] via their respective hubs. Analysis from MIDT data reveals that Korean Air transported

234,418 passengers in 2015 (10 per cent less than in 2014) from mainland China (excluding Hong Kong) to North America via Seoul's Inchon International Airport, generating US$245.3 million, while its Korean rival, Asiana, carried 118,550 passengers (7 per cent less than in 2014), making around US$100 million. The Japanese incumbents had also capitalised as All Nippon Airways uplifted 73,370 passengers in 2015 (61 per cent decrease over 2014) from mainland China via Tokyo's Narita/Haneda to North America, making US$89 million, while JAL transported around 35,000 travellers (28 per cent less than in 2014), which netted US$38.6 million. As Chinese carriers continue to grow their international services, the network airlines of neighbouring countries such as Korea and Japan are witnessing reductions in the volume of Chinese traffic being fed into their long-haul networks. This is particularly affecting the Korean network airlines – Korean Air and Asiana returned aggregated net losses of US$482 million in 2015. The scenario may well reverse over the coming years, with Chinese airlines redirecting traffic flows between North America and North Asia via Chinese hubs, which would trigger a paradigm shift in global traffic flows, similar to what is currently unfolding through the Arabian Gulf hubs.

## Conclusion

It is clearly evident that there are numerous challenges facing the airline industry and that there are many micro- and macro-level forces interplaying that inevitably are shaping the industry. It appears to be in near constant turbulence and in perpetual change. Airlines must prepare well in advance for the impending cyclicality of downward macroeconomic forces that regularly hit the industry. They must remain armed with agile and responsive strategies to challenge competitive threats. Carriers must decide if their core competencies are pivoted on differentiation or low cost, as it is extremely difficult to integrate both elements successfully – being 'stuck in the middle' positions the carrier towards mediocracy and structural weakness. Full service airlines should rely on producing added value and consumer-driven product differentiation beyond the basics of the LCC product. Airlines need to build up a large cash balance as it has become an essential element in defying the gravitational pull towards bankruptcy. All carriers must continue their resolve to tighten cost and become better negotiators as each link in the supply chain (e.g. aircraft manufacturers and airports) generates higher margins than the airline industry.

Airline management must reconcile with militant unions and harness wasteful discourses into solvable issues where both parties are appeased. The proliferation of new growth opportunities emanating from hatching new open skies policies should dominate the global debate stage, as connectivity will be the catalyst to global trade and tourism prosperity. Consolidation has occurred in the US and to a lesser extent in Europe, but it is a platform to reduce capacity and streamline competition and must be widely embraced going forward. This upscaling strategy tightens the collective bargaining power to obtain higher discounts and creates a formidable force. Circumnavigating this entity is also ongoing with JVs through an antitrust immunity mechanism whereby it becomes effectively indifferent as to which aircraft or metal carries a passenger. Equity partnerships are proliferating across the globe, with Etihad Airways, Delta Air Lines and Qatar Airways leading the charge, and they have the potential to fracture alliances that have unsecured relationships among its members.

Incremental cost efficiencies will be driven by technological developments (see Chapter 20) and carriers must adopt IT applications that peel away cost and drive value – airlines must become innovators and not followers. Check-in procedures are a prime example of how the industry has rapidly evolved in a very short time frame, moving from the traditional mechanism of checking in by agent, to kiosk, to web, to mobile phone, with each pulse point removing cost while adding value. Airlines must mastermind the science of fuel and currency hedging, because these practices inflict large collateral damage to profits when mismanaged. Marketing through social media sites provides an instant and fertile platform to launch a promotional sales campaign (see Chapter 13). Presently, such sites are lifestyle tools for the younger generation, and they will become a platform from where airline brands will become indoctrinated into the mindset from a young age. They have the potential to become another distribution channel posing challenges for online travel agents and GDSs. Creating additional revenue streams inside the framework of the conventional business model will be the next game changer, as airline products become unbolted from the fare and sold off as separate entities, while cross-selling third-party commission-based travel by-products such as hotels and car rentals will reform the mechanism of regenerating profitability. The industry must continue to innovate with a commercial mandate as the analogy pertaining to FFPs identified an opportunity to transform them from an expense item to a welcome recipient of revenue as airlines are generating billions of dollars by being affiliated with co-branded credit cards.

This 100-year-old industry continues to prosper as the macro- and micro-forces continue to shape it. It will remain a sustainable entity that will propel trade, tourism and become an integral part of people's lifestyles – for sure, it will still be around in another 100 years, but what will it look like then?

## Notes

1 UK seat capacity for the following airlines shows their exposure to Brexit in 2016. easyJet has 57 per cent of its seats that touch the UK, IAG 48 per cent, Ryanair 37 per cent, Wizz Air 29 per cent, Norwegian 16 per cent and Air France-KLM 8 per cent (author's own analysis from OAG data).
2 The North American carriers made US$22.48 profit per passenger in 2015. Meanwhile, the European carriers made US$7.55, and the Asian carriers made US$4.89 (IATA, 2015b).
3 In order to protect against fluctuating fuel prices and to give visibility in cost control, airlines hedge fuel to minimise their exposure to adverse price movements based on expected future price levels.
4 IBM, for example, spent nearly US$340 million on domestic US air travel in 2001 (IBM, 2003).
5 The break-even load factor of US network scheduled airlines was over 85 per cent from late 2001 to late 2002.
6 The following US majors merged from 2009 to 2013: Northwest with Delta in 2009; United with Continental in 2010; AirTran with Southwest in 2011; and American with US Airways in 2013. Meanwhile, two smaller carriers (Alaska and Virgin America) domiciled on the US West Coast merged in 2016, and the Virgin America brand will be retired in 2019.
7 There are three global airline alliances, Oneworld, SkyTeam and Star, which collectively carried around 2 billion passengers in 2015, serving some 3,240 destinations and collectively generating US$470 billion worth of revenues in 2015 (Oneworld Alliance, 2016; SkyTeam Alliance, 2016; Star Alliance, 2016).
8 Market share in terms of seats offered on the North Atlantic for summer 2016 are as follows: Oneworld (British Airways 10.4 per cent, American Airlines 9.8 per cent, Iberia 1.6 per cent, Finnair 0.3 per cent); SkyTeam (Delta 12.0 per cent, Air France 5.8 per cent, KLM 3.3 per cent, Alitalia 1.6 per cent); Star Alliance (United 10.6 per cent, Lufthansa 8.6 per cent, Air Canada 6.1 per cent, Swiss 1.8 per cent, Austrian 0.9 per cent, Brussels Airlines 0.3 per cent). The next top carriers outside of the alliances are Virgin Atlantic 5.6 per cent, Air Transat 2.8 per cent, Turkish 2.2 per cent, Aer Lingus 1.9 per cent, and Icelandair 1.5 per cent (author's own analysis using OAG data).
9 KLM and Air France merged in 2004. IAG includes British Airways and Iberia from 2009, Vueling from 2013 and Aer Lingus from 2015. Lufthansa Group includes Swiss from 2008, Austrian Airlines from 2009 and Brussels Airlines (45 per cent equity from 2008 and 100 per cent from 2017).
10 Ryanair aims to improve all aspects of the customer experience, through service, digital and in-flight developments. For business travellers, the ultra LCC now bundles the following entities at a premium price: security fast-track; priority boarding; premium allocated seat; +2/-2 day flexibility on ticket changes (as well as on the day of travel); dedicated business plus desk; free airport check-in. Over 25 per cent of Ryanair customers now travel for business purposes (Ryanair, 2016).
11 The expenses incurred in US dollar denominations for the following EU airlines in 2015 was Ryanair 48 per cent, IAG 45 per cent, Air France-KLM 42 per cent, Norwegian 35 per cent, Lufthansa

35 per cent, easyJet 34 per cent (Air France-KLM, 2015a; easyJet, 2015; IAG, 2015; Lufthansa, 2015; Norwegian, 2015; Ryanair, 2015).

12 Labour cost per available seat kilometre (ASK) in 2015 is: Lufthansa 2.8 cents; Air France-KLM 2.7 cents; IAG 2.4 cents; and easyJet 1.85 cents (author's calculations based on annual accounts).

13 The amounts of compensation payable are distance-related: €250 for all flights of 1,500 kilometres or less; €400 for flights between 1,500 and 3,500 kilometres; and €600 for flights over 3,500 kilometres.

14 In 2000, Singapore Airlines operated 63 flights a week between Kuala Lumpur and Singapore, while Malaysian Airlines had 83 services a week totalling 146 flights per week. However, by 2016, the landscape had completely changed as there were 298 services per week between Kuala Lumpur and Singapore, with the following breakdown: Singapore Airlines Group operated 89 flights per week; AirAsia 73; Malaysian Airlines 68; Jetstar Asia 29; and Malindi Airways 28, with others operating an additional 11 flights per week (analysis from OAG – data taken for the first week in August 2000 and August 2016).

15 ASEAN countries consist of Brunei, Cambodia, Indonesia, Lao PDR, Malaysia, Myanmar, Philippines, Singapore, Thailand and Vietnam.

16 Indonesian airlines had been banned from European airports since 2007, the same year that the US Federal Aviation Administration (FAA) downgraded the country's aviation safety to Category 2, stating that the country lacked regulations necessary to oversee air carriers in accordance with minimum international safety standards. There have been 13 accidents involving loss of life with Indonesian-registered aircraft from 2004 to 2015 (Indonesia Investments, 2016). Subsequently, the state has been upgraded to Category 1 safety status again after many years. India and the Philippines were also returned to Category 1 status in recent years after making improvements. Meanwhile, Thailand was downgraded to Category 2 in December 2015 by the FAA, which found that Thailand did not comply with ICAO's safety standards, and it still remains in this situation up until this book went to press (*The Jakarta Post*, 2016).

17 In 2000, Chinese carriers (excluding Cathay Pacific) operated just 20 flights per week from China to the US. However, by 2016, Chinese carriers were operating 164 weekly flights to the US (analysis of OAG data by the author).

# References

A4A (Airlines for America) (2016a). *Airlines for America projects summer air travel to hit all-time high*. Online. Available at: http://airlines.org/news/airlines-for-america-projects-summer-air-travel-to-hit-all-time-high/ (accessed 9 August 2016).

A4A (Airlines for America) (2016b). *US airlines: allocating capital to benefit customers, employees and investors*. Online. Available at: http://airlines.org/data/a4a-presentation-industry-review-and-outlook/ (accessed 12 November 2016).

AAPA (Association of Asia Pacific Airlines) (2016). *Asia Pacific airlines full year 2015 traffic results*. Online. Available at: www.aapairlines.org/resource_centre/AAPA_PR_Issue03_DecTraffic Results_27Jan16.pdf (accessed 10 October 2017).

ACI (Airports Council International) (2016). *ACI data & statistics*. Online. Available at: www.aci.aero/Data-Centre (accessed 28 September 2016).

AEA (Association of European Airlines) (2016). *AEA publications, S.T.A.R. 2016 ED*. Online. Available at: www.aea.be/ (accessed 2 November 2016).

AirAsia X (2016). *Annual report 2015*. Online. Available at: www.airasiax.com/ (accessed 1 November 2016).

Airbus (2016a). *Global Market Forecast 2016–2035*, Blagnac, Airbus.

Airbus (2016b). *Orders and deliveries*. Online. Available at: www.airbus.com/company/market/orders-deliveries/ (accessed 16 October 2016).

Air France-KLM (2015a). *Consolidated financial statement*. Online. Available at: www.airfranceklm.com/sites/default/files/communiques/consolidated_financial_statements_2015.pdf (accessed 19 November 2016).

Air France-KLM (2015b). *Annual Financial Report 2014*, Paris, Air France-KLM.

Airports of Thailand (2016). *Traffic data*. Online. Available at: www.airportthai.co.th/main/en (accessed 26 October 2016).

American Airlines (2015). *Annual report 2015 form 10-K*. Online. Available at: http://phx.corporate-ir.net/phoenix.zhtml?c=117098&p=irol-reportsannual (accessed 13 September 2016).

ATAG (Air Transport Action Group) (2016). *Aviation Benefits Beyond Borders*, Geneva, ATAG.

ATW (Air Transport World) (2015). *Spohr: Lufthansa strikes cost US$543 million over 2 years.* Online. Available at: http://atwonline.com/labor/spohr-lufthansa-strikes-cost-543-million-over-2-years (accessed 29 July 2016).

ATW (Air Transport World) (2016a). *Three reasons why major US airlines are not planning to grow in 2017.* Online. Available at: http://atwonline.com/blog/three-reasons-why-major-us-airlines-are-not-planning-grow-2017 (accessed 27 October 2016).

ATW (Air Transport World) (2016b). *A crazy business.* Online. Available at: http://atwonline.com/airlines/crazy-business (accessed 23 November 2016).

Aviation Economics (2016). *Analysis of airport charges: Airlines 4 Europe, version 1.4, January.* Online. Available at: http://a4e.eu/wp-content/uploads/2015/02/AvEc-Airport-Charge-Analysis-v1.5.pdf (accessed 6 November 2016).

Bloomberg (2016a). *Cathay shares drop as profit slumps 82% on fuel hedge losses.* Online. Available at: www.bloomberg.com/news/articles/2016-08-17/cathay-pacific-first-half-profit-slumps-lags-behind-estimates (accessed 26 August 2016).

Bloomberg (2016b). *Chinese airlines wave wads of cash to lure foreign pilots.* Online. Available at: www.bloomberg.com/news/articles/2016-08-17/chinese-airlines-lure-expat-pilots-with-lucrative-pay-perks (accessed 22 November 2016).

Boeing (2014). *Current Market Outlook 2014–2033*, Seattle, WA, Boeing.

Boeing (2016a). *Orders and deliveries.* Online. Available at: www.boeing.com/commercial/#/orders-deliveries (accessed 5 November 2016).

Boeing (2016b). *Global markets.* Online. Available at: www.boeing.com/resources/boeingdotcom/commercial/about-our-market/assets/downloads/cmo_print_2016_final_ updated.pdf (accessed 12 November 2016).

Bowen, J. (2016). Now everyone can fly? Scheduled airline services to secondary cities in Southeast Asia, *Journal of Air Transport Management*, 53, 94–104.

Brueckner, J.K. (2003). Airline traffic and urban economic development, *Urban Studies*, 40, 1455–1469.

Button, K. and Taylor, S. (2000). International air transportation and economic development, *Journal of Air Transport Management*, 6, 209–222.

CAPA (Centre for Aviation) (2016). *After the White Paper: time for the US major airlines and Gulf carriers to kiss and make up.* Online. Available at: http://centreforaviation.com/analysis/iata-after-the-white-paper-time-for-the-us-major-airlines-and-gulf-carriers-to-kiss-and-make-up-282419 (accessed 23 November 2016).

Chi, J. and Baek, J. (2013). Dynamic relationship between air transport demand and economic growth in the United States: a new look, *Transport Policy*, 29, 257–260.

Chin, A. and Tay, J. (2001). Developments in air transport: implications on investment decisions, profitability and survival of Asian airlines, *Journal of Air Transport Management*, 7(5), 319–330.

Debbage, K.G. and Delk, D. (2001). The geography of air passenger volume and local employment patterns by US metropolitan core area: 1973–1996, *Journal of Air Transport Management*, 7, 159–167.

Dell'Oro, J. (2015). *Les pilots d'Air France toujours trop chers*, Paris, Challenges.

Delta Air Lines (2015). *Investor relations.* Online. Available at: http://ir.delta.com/ (accessed 3 September 2016).

Delta Air Lines (2016). *SEC filings, 10-K annual report.* Online. Available at: http://ir.delta.com/stock-and-financial/sec-filings/default.aspx (accessed 2 December 2016).

Dobruszkes, F., Lennert, M. and Van Hamme, G. (2011). An analysis of the determinants of air traffic volume for European metropolitan areas, *Journal of Transport Geography*, 19, 755–762.

Doganis, R. (2010). *Flying Off Course: Airline Economics and Marketing*, 4th edition, London, Routledge.

easyJet (2015). *Annual report 2015.* Online. Available at: http://corporate.easyjet.com/investors.aspx (accessed 1 November 2016).

Embraer (2016). *Embraer releases second quarter 2016 results.* Online. Available at: www.embraer.com/Documents/noticias/Release%20US%202Q16_FINAL.pdf (accessed 28 September 2016).

EUROCONTROL (2016). *Single European Sky.* Online. Available at: www.eurocontrol.int/dossiers/single-european-sky (accessed 14 May 2017).

Flightglobal (2013). *Turkish consortium wins new Istanbul airport project.* Online. Available at: www.flightglobal.com/ (accessed 29 November 2016).

Flightglobal (2016). *Paid subscription flight information database.* Online. Available at: www.flightglobal.com/ (accessed 8 August 2016).

Hanaoka, S., Takebayashi, M., Ishikura, T. and Saraswati, B. (2014). Low-cost carriers versus full service carriers in ASEAN: the impact of liberalisation policy on competition, *Journal of Air Transport Management*, 40, 96–105.

Hooper, P., Walker, S., Moore, C. and Al Zubaidi, Z. (2011). The development of the Gulf region's air transport networks: the first century, *Journal of Air Transport Management*, 17(6), 325–332.

IAG (International Airlines Group) (2015). *Annual reports and accounts 2015*. Online. Available at: www.iagshares.com/phoenix.zhtml?c=240949&p=irol-reportsannual (accessed 1 December 2016).

IATA (International Air Transport Association) (2014). *New IATA passenger forecast reveals fast-growing markets of the future*. Online. Available at: www.iata.org/pressroom/pr/Pages/2014-10-16-01.aspx (accessed 28 July 2016).

IATA (International Air Transport Association) (2015a). *Global Passenger Survey Report*, 2015 edition, Material No. 8232–03, Montreal, IATA.

IATA (International Air Transport Association) (2015b). *Airlines continue to improve profitability 5.1% net profit margin for 2016*. Online. Available at: www.iata.org/pressroom/pr/Pages/2015-12-10-01.aspx (accessed 28 September 2016).

IATA (International Air Transport Association) (2016a). *Annual review 2016*. Online. Available at: www.iata.org/publications/Documents/iata-annual-review-2016.pdf (accessed 10 October 2017).

IATA (International Air Transport Association) (2016b). *IATA forecasts passenger demand to double over 20 years*. Online. Available at: www.iata.org/pressroom/pr/Pages/2016-10-18-02.aspx (accessed 9 November 2016).

IATA (International Air Transport Association) (2016c). *World Air Transport Statistics*, 60th edition, Geneva, IATA.

IATA (International Air Transport Association) (2016d). *Air freight market analysis*. Online. Available at: www.iata.org/Whatwedo/Documents/economics/freight-analysis-jul-2016.pdf (accessed 17 November 2017).

IBM (International Business Machines Corporation) (2003). *Driving an operational model that integrates customer segmentation with customer management*. Online. Available at: www.03.ibm.com/industries/automotive/doc/content/bin/auto_driving_operational.pdf (accessed 12 June 2016).

ICAO (International Civil Aviation Organisation) (2016a). *Economic development 2015, air transport yearly monitor*. Online. Available at: www.icao.int/sustainability/Documents/Yearly%20Monitor/yearly_monitor_2015.pdf (accessed 13 November 2016).

ICAO (International Civil Aviation Organisation) (2016b). *Safety audit information*. Online. Available at: www.icao.int/safety/pages/USOAP-Results.aspx (accessed 29 August 2016).

Ideaworks (2016). *Ancillary revenue report series for 2016*. Online. Available at: www.ideaworkscompany.com/wp-content/uploads/2016/09/2016-Ancillary-Revenue-Yearbook-R.pdf (accessed 21 November 2016).

IMF (International Monetary Fund) (2016a). *IMF sees subdued global growth, warns economic stagnation could fuel protectionist calls*. Online. Available at: www.imf.org/en/News/Articles/2016/10/03/AM2016-NA100416-WEO (accessed 22 November 2016).

IMF (International Monetary Fund) (2016b). *Exchange rate archives by month*. Online. Available at: www.imf.org/external/np/fin/data/param_rms_mth.aspx (accessed 15 September 2016).

Indonesia Investments (2016). *Ban on Indonesia's airlines entering US airspace lifted*. Online. Available at: www.indonesia-investments.com/news/news-columns/ban-on-indonesia-s-airlines-entering-us-airspace-lifted/item7102? (accessed 9 September 2016).

Ito, H. and Lee, D. (2005). Assessing the impact of the September 11 terrorist attacks on U.S. airline demand, *Journal of Economics and Business*, 57, 75–95.

Lufthansa (2015). *Annual Financial Report 2015*, Cologne, Lufthansa Group.

Marazzo, M., Scherre, R. and Fernandes, E. (2010). Air transport demand and economic growth in Brazil: a time series analysis, *Transportation Research Part E: Logistics and Transportation Review*, 46(2), 261–269.

Merrill Lynch (2016). *Airlines: Asia-Pacific, Focus Switches to Capacity Growth as Oil Impact Fades*, New York, Merrill Lynch.

Murel, M. and O'Connell, J.F. (2011). Potential for Abu Dhabi, Doha and Dubai Airports to reach their traffic objectives, *Research in Transportation Business & Management*, 1(1), 36–46.

Norwegian (2015). *Annual Report 2015*, Fornebu, Norwegian.

O'Connell, J.F. (2006). The changing dynamics of the Arab Gulf based airlines and an investigation into the strategies that are making Emirates into a global challenger, *World Review of Intermodal Transportation Research*, 1(1), 94–114.

O'Connell, J.F. (2011). The rise of the Arabian Gulf carriers: an insight into the business model of Emirates Airline, *Journal of Air Transport Management*, 17(6), 339–346.

Oneworld Alliance (2016). *News and information*. Online. Available at: www.oneworld.com/member-airlines/overview (accessed 3 December 2016).

ONS (Office for National Statistics) (2016). *Travel trends: 2015*. Online. Available at: www.ons.gov.uk/peoplepopulationandcommunity/leisureandtourism/articles/traveltrends/2015#uk-residents-visits-abroad (accessed 23 November 2016).

Profillidis, V. and Botzoris, G. (2015). Air passenger transport and economic activity, *Journal of Air Transport Management*, 49, 23–27.

PwC (PricewaterhouseCoopers) (2016). *Economic impact of air traffic control strikes in Europe*. Online. Available at: https://a4e.eu/wp-content/uploads/2016/10/A4E-Economic-Impact-ATC-Strikes-Final-Report_160929-vf.pdf (accessed 17 September 2016).

Qantas Group (2016). *Qantas 2016 Annual Report*, Sydney, Qantas Group.

Ryanair (2015). *Annual Report 2015*, Dublin, Ryanair.

Ryanair (2016). *Ryanair launches new leisure plus fares and improved business plus offering*. Online. Available at: http://corporate.ryanair.com/news/news/160616-ryanair-launches-new-leisure-plus-fare-improved-business-plus-offering/?market=en (accessed 2 December 2016).

Schulte-Strathaus, U. (2009). *For the airlines, the Single Sky cannot come a moment too soon*. Online. Available at: www.eurocontrol.int/sites/default/files/article/attachments/schulte-strathaus-skyway52.pdf (accessed 16 September 2016).

SkyTeam Alliance (2016). *SkyTeam facts and figures*. Online. Available at: www.skyteam.com (accessed 29 July 2016).

Star Alliance (2016). *Media resources*. Online. Available at: www.staralliance.com (accessed 29 July 2016).

*The Jakarta Post* (2016). *Indonesian airlines can fly to US as FAA upgrades safety rating*. Online. Available at: www.thejakartapost.com/news/2016/08/16/indonesian-airlines-can-fly-to-us-as-faa-upgrades-safety-rating.html?fb_comment_id=1035899383196035_1036011229851517#f305d5cbf8769a8 (accessed 17 November 2016).

*The Japan Times* (2015). *In wake of accidents, safety issues challenge fast-growing Asian aviation market*. Online. Available at: www.japantimes.co.jp/news/2015/04/07/business/wake-accidents-safety-issues-challenge-fast-growing-asian-aviation-market/#.WB5sbph77L8 (accessed 22 September 2016).

*The New York Times* (2016). *Lufthansa joins Germany's list of companies in distress*. Online. Available at: www.nytimes.com/2016/11/30/world/europe/lufthansa-pilots-strike-germany.html?_r=0 (accessed 12 November 2016).

Turkish Airlines (2015). *Turkish Airlines Annual Report 2015*, Istanbul, Turkish Airlines.

United Airlines (2015). *United Airlines SEC filings*. Online. Available at: http://ir.united.com/financial-performance/sec-filings (accessed 22 July 2016).

UNWTO (United Nations World Tourism Organisation) (2016). *UNWTO Tourism Highlights*, Madrid, UNWTO.

US DOT (United States Department of Transportation) (2016). *Bureau of transportation statistics*. Online. Available at: www.rita.dot.gov/bts/sites/rita.dot.gov.bts/files/subject_areas/airline_information/index.html (accessed 16 July 2016).

Vespermann, J., Wald, A. and Gleich, R. (2008). Aviation growth in the Middle East: impacts on incumbent players and potential strategic reactions, *Journal of Transport Geography*, 16(6), 388–394.

World Bank (2016). *Global Economic Prospects*, Washington, DC, World Bank.

Yao, S. and Yang, X. (2012). Air transport and regional economic growth in China, Asia-Pacific, *Journal of Accounting Economics*, 19, 318–329.

# 2

# The air cargo industry

*Rico Merkert and David Alexander*

## Introduction

The air cargo industry has significantly changed since the introduction of aircraft in the early twentieth century. Air cargo, especially air mail, dominated the early commercial activities of airlines until the development of aircraft such as the DC-3 and the economics of air passenger travel took over. The Second World War saw a resurgence in air cargo, with military airlifts and post-war humanitarian operations (e.g. the Berlin Airlift). Despite facing two international oil crises in 1973 and 1978, the 1970s saw further development of the air cargo industry, with the birth of FedEx (a few years after DHL) and liberalisation of domestic air cargo markets in the United States (US) in 1977. In the last decade, the air cargo industry has been embroiled in antitrust behaviour by airlines, felt a significant drop in demand during the global financial crisis (GFC), and subdued growth during a period of high oil prices (above US$100 per barrel). Nonetheless, the global air cargo industry continues to play an essential role in international trade, annually shipping US$5.6 trillion of goods, over 52 million tonnes of freight, worth 35 per cent of all merchandise import value (Shepherd et al., 2016). The relationship between the air cargo industry and economic prosperity cannot be easily dismissed.

This chapter explores four key themes associated with the air cargo industry: dynamics of the air cargo industry; impacts of macroeconomic and microeconomic factors for air cargo; relationships between air cargo industry participants, air cargo business models and management strategies; and regulation of the air cargo industry. To explore the dynamics of the air cargo industry, the first section of this chapter reflects on the history of air cargo over the last century, including the current paradigm shift of 'final mile' delivery systems conducted by air. Macroeconomic factors for air cargo are provided in the market analysis (section 2), current state of the air cargo industry (section 3) and growth potential for air cargo (section 4). Air cargo products (section 5) and provision of air cargo services (section 6) represent microeconomic market factors. Relationships between air cargo participants, air cargo business models and management strategies are covered within section 7 on current actors and air cargo business models. The final section of this chapter provides an overview of the regulation governing the air cargo industry and the impact that antitrust determinations can have on the high-risk, low-return airline industry.

## Development of the air cargo industry

Within seven years of the Wright brothers' historic aerial flight in 1903, the first commercial cargo carried by aircraft, 88 kilogrammes of silk, took off from Dayton, Ohio in the US, to land in nearby Columbus for delivery to the Home Dry Goods Store (Allaz, 2004). Shortly thereafter, the first official air mail flight occurred in India in February 1911 (Allaz, 2004). The newspaper industry became enthralled, with the speed of air transport providing a boon to the time-sensitivity of the freshly printed news. The delivery of the Berlin-based newspaper *Berliner Morgenpost* by air to Frankfurt in 1911 became the first instalment of the German air cargo industry (Lufthansa Group, 2016). Concurrently, air mail and air cargo services were developing operations in South America (Colombia), Asia-Pacific (Japan, Australia), Europe (England, France, Italy and others) and Africa (Congo and South Africa) (Allaz, 2004).

Evidence of military applications for air mail commenced prior to the First World War, with regional conflicts between Italy and the Ottoman Empire, as well as between Mexico and the US, providing an opportunity to test the shipment of urgent communications by air (Allaz, 2004). During the First World War, military air mail routes were developed in Germany between Berlin, Hanover and Cologne in 1917, and the Allies developed air mail routes between England and northern France (Allaz, 2004). At the conclusion of the First World War, the first humanitarian air cargo movements were organised, providing emergency supplies to war-ravaged regions, including the first cargo drops by parachute (Allaz, 2004). Parachutes allow cargo shipments to be deployed from the skies practically anywhere, without the need for runway infrastructure for a supply aircraft to land, conserving fuel and reducing risk to life and property within heavily contested conflict zones.

The success of aircraft during the First World War enhanced the case for the provision of regular, scheduled air transport services put forward by the US Post Office Department (POD). With a grant provided by Congress, the US POD commenced operation of the first regular, scheduled air mail services between the US capital Washington, DC, and the major cities New York and Philadelphia (ACI, 2013). The US POD would soon establish a national air network, following the extensive rail system from New York to San Francisco. Under the Kelly Act in 1925, the US Congress voted for outsourcing the provision of these air transport services to private interests (USPS, 2006). Controversy erupted in the provision of tenders in 1930, and new legislation was formalised by Senators Black and McKellar in the Air Mail Act of 1934 (US Senate, 2016).

The automotive and air cargo industries also formed a relationship in the 1920s, with the great entrepreneur Henry Ford and the Ford Motor Company expressing interest in air transport. With the success of the Ford Trimotor aircraft – nicknamed the Tin Goose – and the formation of Ford Airlines (Ford Motor Company, 2010), the air cargo industry would continue to advance. Ford Airlines shipped more than 1,000 tonnes of freight, primarily automotive parts, in 1926, in addition to servicing Contract Air Mail (CAM) services to and from Detroit on behalf of the US POD (Ford Motor Company, 2010). Simultaneously, in Europe, the formation of Deutsche Luft Hansa (now known simply as Lufthansa) led to further development of German air cargo transport, with 258 tonnes of air cargo shipped in 1926 (Lufthansa Group, 2016). Advancements in aircraft technology, especially extending operational range, soon provided for transatlantic services between North and South America and Europe (Allaz, 2004).

The Second World War (1939–1945) truly tested the capabilities of the air cargo industry. Improvements in aircraft technology, including reliability, speed, navigation and other factors, played an integral part to the haulage of air cargo during this time. Between 1942 and 1945, over 650,000 tonnes were shipped by air between India and southern China (ACI, 2013). This was soon eclipsed by the Berlin Airlift post-Second World War, with humanitarian aid in excess of 2.2 million tonnes shipped by US and United Kingdom (UK) forces from 1948 to 1949 (Morrell, 2011). Humanitarian aid missions to remote areas damaged by natural disasters and regional conflicts have continued to expand under the United Nations (UN), formed after the Second World War in 1945, including the transport of vehicles and supplies for the provision of multinational peacekeeping missions.

The introduction of the jet engine, another aircraft technology developed initially for military purposes during the Second World War, significantly enhanced the civilian air transport industry from the 1950s. Instrumental to the development of air mail and air cargo services, and still as relevant today, is the factor of speed (Doganis, 2010) that an aircraft can provide over other transport modes. Air cargo services for time-sensitive and highly perishable goods, such as premium seafood, agricultural products, flowers and pharmaceuticals (Morrell, 2011), could be shipped to broader markets as fresh produce (rather than frozen). Moreover, speed is also considered a favoured quality for just-in-time (JIT) global value chains (GVCs) that manufacture products ranging from as small as the Apple iPhone (and other consumer electronics) to sections of aircraft such as the Boeing 787 Dreamliner (Gates, 2005).

Commercial air cargo would be further boosted in the 1970s, despite being an era of two global oil crises (1973 and 1978). During this time, door-to-door express delivery providers DHL (1969) and FedEx (1973) were born (ACI, 2013); airlines such as Lufthansa had developed significant international air cargo networks utilising dedicated freighters such as the Boeing 747F and wide-bodied jet aircraft with sizeable belly-holds (Lufthansa Group, 2016); and deregulation of air transport (see Chapters 6 and 7) commenced with air cargo reform in the US with the passing of the Air Cargo Act in 1977 (Morrell, 2011), a year prior to the Airline Deregulation Act. Liberalisation of air cargo in the European Union (EU) also preceded the Third Package of air transport reforms and development of the Single European Sky (Morrell, 2011).

The onset of the first Gulf War in 1991 introduced yet another technology to benefit the air transport industry, the Global Positioning System (GPS). GPS has provided enhancements in navigation, especially with airspace restrictions due to bilateral agreements or war zones. Combined with reliable wireless communication networks, GPS has led to the development of remotely operated unmanned drone aircraft, initially for military use in surveillance and bombing missions. Small-scale, commercially available drones are developing a niche market for air cargo, providing short-range shipments that can effectively compete with surface transport. Domino's now offers pizza delivery utilising autonomous drones to New Zealand customers (McFarland, 2016a). Amazon Prime Air commenced a trial delivery in the UK (McFarland, 2016b). Drones have also been used by individuals for collection of goods, despite air safety regulations (Farquhar, 2016). Effective regulation of airways for the growth of commercial and civilian use of drones remains a notable challenge for authorities.

## Air cargo market analysis

Air cargo can be characterised as one of three distinct markets: express, general air freight and air mail services (for a good overview of the latest developments in the air cargo market, see Merkert et al., 2017). Express air cargo is notably time-sensitive products that are either highly perishable, prone to obsolescence and/or of significant value, attracting a premium pricing over general air freight. General air freight includes container shipments (unit load devices, ULDs) that may be consolidated by shippers, freight forwarders or other cargo agents, or packages and other large items that benefit from the speed of air transport (Wensveen and Merkert, 2015), without the critical priority factor of express air cargo. General air freight may be trucked for long distances before being flown, or transported under a multimodal supply chain (such as air-sea and air-rail transport). Air mail consists of the carriage of envelopes, letters and documents on aircraft, traditionally stamped 'par avion' (carriage by air).

The air cargo industry comprises significant international trade flows, primarily in the northern hemisphere between North America, Europe and Asia, as depicted in Figure 2.1. The US, the world's largest economy, remains a large air cargo market both domestically and with trade to Asia, Europe and South America. In Asia-Pacific, the air cargo industry is of relatively high significance, led by China (including Hong Kong), Japan, Korea, Taiwan and Singapore with export of products such as consumer electronics, textiles, clothing and footwear to 'Western' markets. Latin America, Africa, the Middle East and South Asia are developing market share in air cargo, increasing trade activity to the major economic blocs in Europe and Asia as well as the US. Notably, the domestic air cargo market share in large land mass regions such as the US, China, Russia and Europe is also highly significant, as well as in Indonesia, the world's largest chain of islands, where domestic air cargo traffic amounts to 57 per cent of the total national air cargo task (Alexander and Merkert, 2017). Finally, airports in the Middle East, in particular Dubai, have been growing as a global epicentre for air transport.

As previously discussed, one of the key factors that differentiates the air cargo industry over other modes is speed (Doganis, 2010). Other strengths of this industry include safety (low number of accidents per million freight tonne kilometres (FTKs) compared to other modes), reliability (minimal service cancellations or rescheduling) and security (restricted airport zones for handling cargo). These strengths represent part of the value proposition of air cargo, and are critical to ongoing success. Air cargo also holds some market power for long-haul, high-value commodities, as there simply is no other method to transport these high-security, time-sensitive items. Table 2.1 provides a strengths, weaknesses, opportunities and threats (SWOT) analysis as developed by IATA (2015) on the air cargo industry.

Omitted from IATA's 2015 analysis, and an important strength to be recognised, is the flexibility of air cargo services. Air cargo can be carried by a wide variety of dedicated freighter aircraft or in the belly-hold of wide-bodied passenger aircraft, flown overnight or by day,

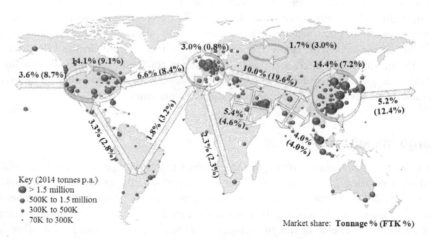

*Figure 2.1*   Significant air freight markets and key trade lanes, 2014

*Source*: Compiled using data from CAPA (2015) and Boeing (2014).

Table 2.1 SWOT analysis of the air cargo industry

| Strengths | Weaknesses |
|---|---|
| • Speed (relative to other modes)<br>• Security<br>• Reliability<br>• Safety<br>• No path congestion<br>• Low land occupancy<br>• Best mode for landlocked countries<br>• No modal competition for high-value goods on long-haul transport | • Overcapacity<br>• Misunderstood value proposition<br>• Weak economics of most carriers<br>• Perceived as not 'green'<br>• Complex operating environment<br>• Security compliance issues<br>• Misperceptions on price competitiveness<br>• Lack of transparency and communication between stakeholders<br>• Lack of investments to modernise and innovate |
| Opportunities | Threats |
| • Liberalisation of the market<br>• Growth in economy and trade<br>• Globalisation of supply chains<br>• Urbanisation and development of megacities<br>• Capacity increase in extra-European airports<br>• Expedited customs clearance<br>• E-commerce growth supported with express delivery solutions | • In-flight cargo fires<br>• Trade protectionism<br>• Increased regulatory oversight on aircraft loading<br>• Under-representation of cargo sector in policymaking<br>• Increase in onshoring and nearshoring<br>• Unregulated supply chain participants<br>• Limitations on ground infrastructure availability and investment<br>• Airport congestion<br>• Airport operating hours restrictions (night curfews)<br>• Fuel cost fluctuations<br>• Terrorist threats and inadequate security screening<br>• Increasing competition with other modes<br>• External shocks |

Source: Adapted from IATA (2015).

transported on point-to-point services (where economies of scale and density are present) or shipped on the hub-and-spoke network of carriers (Morrell, 2011). Air cargo can be carried by dedicated cargo airlines, integrators, passenger and cargo airlines or cargo alliances, including charter services. Charter aircraft provide additional capacity for seasonal events, such as during the retail build-up for the Christmas holidays, as a contingency measure to operational issues (i.e. grounding of regular aircraft for maintenance and/or servicing), or as provision of service for a one-off event (i.e. Formula One consignments) (Gibson Freight, 2016), all potentially at short notice.

A primary weakness of the air cargo industry, as indicated by IATA (2015), is overcapacity. Overcapacity can be measured in several ways, geographically system-wide, regional or national coverage, or by city and/or route (airport pair), or operationally by alliance, airline business and aircraft. System-wide or alliance measures incorporate aggregate statistics, including the number of dedicated freighters currently parked (or grounded) and average daily operating hours (which has dropped from 13.5 hours in 2007 to 10.5 hours) (IATA, 2016a). Moreover, average load factors of just 42.4 per cent (IATA, 2016b) provide a measure on the efficiency of capacity utilisation within the system, including belly-hold capacity of passenger wide-bodied aircraft. Load factors between major international regions for air cargo range between 8 and 88 per cent on minor routes and 24 to 59 per cent on major routes (ICAO, 2014), as provided in Table 2.2.

*Table 2.2* Interregional air cargo movements, 2014

| From region | To region | Freight tonne kilometre performed (000) | Mail tonne kilometre performed (000) | Freight load factor |
|---|---|---|---|---|
| Asia-Pacific | North America | 12,532,288 | 535,200 | 58.8% |
| Asia-Pacific | Europe | 12,523,815 | 454,301 | 51.0% |
| Europe | Asia-Pacific | 11,392,745 | 425,790 | 45.0% |
| Europe | North America | 8,469,582 | 268,333 | 38.4% |
| North America | Asia-Pacific | 7,097,351 | 330,063 | 36.5% |
| North America | Europe | 7,057,168 | 375,741 | 30.6% |
| Latin America/Caribbean | North America | 2,695,524 | 7,771 | 28.2% |
| North America | Latin America/Caribbean | 2,368,276 | 96,755 | 24.2% |
| Europe | Africa | 2,126,107 | 41,191 | 31.5% |
| Europe | Latin America/Caribbean | 2,105,193 | 61,921 | 29.7% |
| Africa | Europe | 2,069,531 | 12,481 | 30.9% |
| Latin America/Caribbean | Europe | 1,911,559 | 26,515 | 25.1% |
| Europe | Middle East | 1,182,631 | 29,857 | 30.9% |
| Asia-Pacific | Middle East | 886,149 | 30,347 | 36.2% |
| Middle East | Europe | 817,307 | 34,783 | 24.6% |
| Asia-Pacific | Africa | 607,562 | 5,744 | 29.9% |
| North America | Middle East | 405,356 | 24,007 | 30.9% |
| Middle East | Asia-Pacific | 369,033 | 18,810 | 14.3% |
| Middle East | North America | 338,634 | 14,244 | 33.9% |
| North America | Africa | 216,411 | 8,433 | 16.1% |
| Africa | Asia-Pacific | 182,738 | 9,933 | 9.2% |
| Africa | Middle East | 182,471 | 2,394 | 17.2% |
| Africa | North America | 126,493 | 3,403 | 11.5% |
| Africa | Latin America/Caribbean | 122,648 | 2,218 | 31.1% |
| Middle East | Africa | 84,955 | 854 | 8.0% |
| Latin America/Caribbean | Africa | 77,613 | 527 | 22.2% |
| Latin America/Caribbean | Asia-Pacific | 22,403 | 43 | 13.4% |
| Asia-Pacific | Latin America/Caribbean | 20,210 | 487 | 10.3% |
| Latin America/Caribbean | Middle East | 2,676 | 0 | 87.7% |

*Source*: Data from ICAO (2014).

Notably, load factor measures are typically based on weight capacities (tonnage) and not necessarily indicative of volumetric (m$^3$) load factors (i.e. cubing out of cargo holds) (Morrell, 2011). Trade between South, Central and North America, by weight, appears more balanced, although differentials between commodities (high-density capital goods and high-value consumer electronics versus low-density agricultural products) would indicate an imbalance based on cubic measures. Of final note in regional trade is the volume of cargo hauled between Africa and South/Central America. These two regions mostly compete in similar air transport markets (i.e. floriculture), and are considered developing nations, yet freight occupancy factors are not dissimilar to more established trade routes. Freight occupancy on selective nation pairs in Table 2.3 can easily exceed 80 per cent (e.g. links to South Korea).

Misconceptions of the value proposition of air cargo, and thus understanding of price competitiveness, are a significant market challenge. Transport costs alone do not provide an accurate comparison of mode choice. The speed of air transport also provides for shortened product development across GVCs. The development of agile supply chains leveraging shortened lead times for delivery and increased turnover of inventory has improved the cash-to-cash cycle for

*Table 2.3* Country pairs with high freight load factors (in excess of 5,000 tonnes of air cargo), 2014

| From | To | Freight revenue traffic (tonnes) | Mail revenue traffic (tonnes) | Total capacity including pax (tonnes) | Freight occupancy[1] |
|------|-----|-----|-----|-----|-----|
| Norway | Rep. of Korea | 15,709 | 5 | 16,610 | 94.6% |
| Spain | Uzbekistan | 10,386 | 1 | 11,106 | 93.5% |
| Sweden | Rep. of Korea | 9,782 | 0 | 10,949 | 89.3% |
| Taiwan | United States | 55,077 | 0 | 73,391 | 83.9% |
| Rep. of Korea | Austria | 33,506 | 103 | 44,556 | 82.1% |
| China | Netherlands | 169,802 | 2,488 | 276,902 | 80.9% |
| Germany | Senegal | 16,649 | 240 | 21,025 | 80.1% |
| Rep. of Korea | Netherlands | 23,126 | 804 | 40,115 | 79.9% |
| Norway | Thailand | 8,429 | 64 | 17,786 | 79.9% |
| Vietnam | Australia | 33,259 | 0 | 64,568 | 78.1% |

*Source*: Data from ICAO (2015).

*Note*:
1 Measured on total filled hold capacity (freighter and wide-bodied aircraft) and excludes passengers.

savvy business managers, and is a key to the success of clothing and accessories retailer Zara (Ferdows et al., 2003). Global collaboration in the manufacture of the Boeing 787 Dreamliner results in a new aircraft produced every two to three days (Gates, 2005). Additionally, the argument that air cargo is often not considered as environmentally friendly, based on the contribution of carbon emissions by air transport, needs to be weighed against factors of surface transport carriage of freight, such as road congestion, as well as the marginal costs associated with carriage of cargo on a route that will be serviced by a scheduled passenger wide-bodied aircraft (Alexander and Merkert, 2017; Merkert and Ploix, 2014).

Premium pricing of air cargo services by airlines and freight forwarders, as evidenced by Alexander and Merkert (2017), is another concern. Premiums are often used strategically to deter certain fringe markets; moreover, excessive pricing may result in the loss of a broader general market for air cargo services, and thus undermine growth in air freight volumes (possibly resulting in lower overall yields, a critical aspect of profitability for an industry that is known for bankruptcies). Conversely, undercutting of air cargo rates may result in a growth in business (cargo hauled and FTK), but may also result in operating losses, or even worse is matched by larger competitors that can leverage economies of scale. Price-fixing of air cargo rates and fuel surcharges by competitors has also led to substantial antitrust action (EC, 2010).

## Current state of the air cargo industry

In 2015, the air cargo industry shipped 52.2 million tonnes of products, generating revenues totalling US$52.8 billion (IATA, 2016c). In total, the air cargo industry provided some 188 billion FTKs (World Bank, 2015) at an average cost of US$0.28 per FTK. Average stage length for every tonne of cargo moved exceeded 3,500 kilometres. Industry revenues have fallen since the GFC recovery of 2010, while cargo tonnage has creeped upwards. Measured in FTKs, the two largest integrated service providers, FedEx and UPS, are currently ranked first and third, respectively, in the provision of air freight movements globally (DHL is of comparable size as Deutsche Post owns five airline subsidiaries operating for DHL Express), with the airline Emirates filling second place (Air Cargo News, 2016a). Moreover, air mail services, once such a dominant factor for air transport a century ago, accounted for just 2.6 billion FTKs (ICAO, 2015), or 1.4 per cent of all air cargo by this measure.

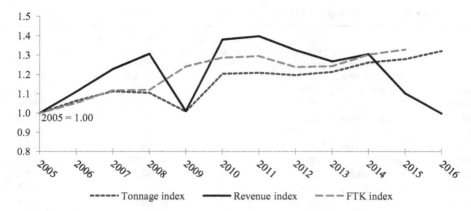

*Figure 2.2* Industry air cargo indices (tonnage, revenue and FTK), 2005 to 2016

*Source*: Calculated from data compiled from IATA (2016c) and World Bank (2015).

Events over the last decade have had a profound and significant impact on the air cargo industry. From mid-2008 to late 2008, mortgage foreclosures and tightening of credit impaired retail consumer confidence, leading to the GFC and a dramatic fall in international trade. GVCs of products such as consumer electronics (semiconductors, a sensitive air freight market, have been included in IATA's *Cargo Chartbook* since commencement in 2008) were notably disrupted by events of the GFC. Inventory levels of discretionary products declined, and global air freight volumes, by tonnage, decreased from 45.4 million tonnes in 2007 to 41.1 million tonnes in 2009, before recovering in 2010 (IATA, 2016c). Figure 2.2 indicates the changes to tonnage, revenue (excluding inflation) and industry FTKs for air cargo from 2005. Yields, measured either as US$ per kilogramme (IATA, 2016d) or US$ per FTK, continue to decline in an industry facing declining revenues and increasing demand, with the freight task increasing in both tonnage and distance.

A significant contribution to the decline of air cargo during the GFC involved international air freight between the US and the rest of the world, which fell from 8.6 million tonnes in 2006 to just 7 million tonnes in 2009 (Alexander and Merkert, 2016). The downturn in air cargo volume, and reduced profitability during this period, forced bankruptcies of cargo airlines, such as Gemini Air Cargo (Doganis, 2010), which was provided finance by the insolvent Lehmann Brothers. While a bailout of the financial services industry in the US economy avoided significant impacts brought on by the GFC, key trading partners in the UK and South Korea were not as fortunate during this period (Alexander and Merkert, 2016). Moreover, the impacts of the GFC may have been worse if China did not rise as an economic superpower during this period. China, with the world's second largest air transport market, underwent economic growth of more than 8 per cent for several years, with gross domestic product (GDP) rising from US$2.7 trillion in 2006 to over US$10 trillion in 2014.

Post-GFC, the air transport industry experienced several years of high oil prices, subduing any recovery in air cargo markets. With Brent crude reaching over US$100 per barrel from 2010 to 2014, and pricing in jet fuel refining margins over 10 per cent, growth in air cargo remained stagnant over several years (IATA, 2016a). With the price of oil receding to around US$50 per barrel more recently, the Organisation of the Petroleum Exporting Countries (OPEC) has recently called for a cut in oil production (Razzouk et al., 2016), potentially contributing to higher prices, and flowing through to higher operating costs for airlines. Fuel surcharges associated with higher oil prices have noticeably been relaxed, resulting in lower air cargo revenues and attracting more marginally viable air cargo markets, leading to increased growth.

## Growth potential for the air cargo industry

The air cargo market is currently measured by tonnage (especially handled at airports) and FTKs (the freight task conducted by airlines). Based on tonnage handled at airports, ACI (2015) has predicted a 2.3 per cent growth in volume over the long term (25 years). The two major aircraft manufacturers, Boeing and Airbus, have long-term 20-year forecasts for air cargo growth of between 4.0 and 4.2 per cent, as measured in FTK (Airbus, 2016a; Boeing, 2016). Growth in air cargo is expected in key geographical markets such as the Asia-Pacific region (consisting of major air cargo markets in China, including Hong Kong, Japan, Korea, Taiwan and Singapore). Increases in online shopping (e-commerce) and increased demand of products produced in international supply chains under traditional manufacturing methods will provide the impetus for some of this growth (Boeing, 2016). However, increases in digital purchases (e-books and other non-physical products) and continued advancements in 3D printing techniques may off-set, and potentially lead to a decline in, the demand for future air cargo services.

The close relationship between air cargo and GDP has been long established in the air freight industry (Airbus 2016a; Boeing, 2016; Hakim and Merkert, 2016; Morrell, 2011). Moreover, key indicators to trade such as manufacturing (Otto, 2008), a component of GDP, and merchandise exports impact freight demand for all modes (including by air). Manufacturing employment and contributions are considered key factors by Alexander and Merkert (2017), Lakew and Tok (2014) and Shepherd et al. (2016) for air freight market development. Figure 2.3 provides an indication of the relationship between global GDP, global manufacturing, global exports and air freight (as measured in both tonnes and FTKs) for the period 2005–2014. The impact of the GFC on economic growth, world trade and air freight is clearly noticeable in 2009.

A key area of growth in air cargo traffic is transhipment (transportation of air cargo from one airport to another via an intermediate airport hub), and several major airport hubs have

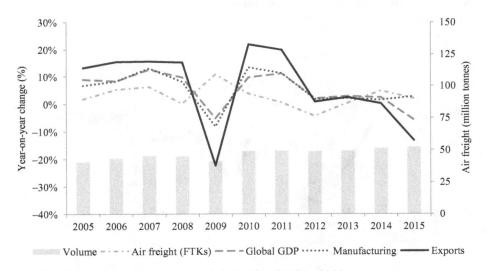

*Figure 2.3* Global economic growth and air freight, 2005 to 2015

*Source*: Data from IATA (2016c) and World Bank (2015).

developed significant volumes of air cargo traffic through transhipments. As previously stated, the Asia-Pacific region is an important centre for air cargo, transhipments included, with Incheon International Airport in Seoul attracting approximately 1 million tonnes, 46 per cent of total air cargo (Lee, 2015), and Singapore Changi Airport attracting 900,000 tonnes, 50 per cent of total air cargo (Changi Airport, 2016) via transhipment. Ted Stevens Anchorage International Airport, as a trans-Pacific gateway between Asia and North America, handles over 70 per cent of cargo traffic as transhipments (AIAS, 2016). London Heathrow Airport, a transatlantic hub and gateway for Britain, is home to transhipments in the order of about 600,000 tonnes (45 per cent of air cargo) (Air Cargo News, 2016b). Transhipments are also a significant focus for the recent development of Dubai World Centre, with links to North America, Asia-Pacific, Europe, South America and African markets provided by Emirates, the world's second largest carrier of air cargo by FTKs. Movement of air cargo through these major gateways can leverage significantly from the growth in air cargo along major trade routes, as indicated in Figure 2.4.

In addition to the importance of freight hub airports, the largest cargo airline networks operate on a truly global scale. Figure 2.5 provides an indication to the extent of the Cargolux network (Cargolux, 2016). This network utilises a traditional hub-and-spoke system, with a key hub in Luxembourg (and secondary hub in Milan), incorporates schedules using multi-leg trips and a rotating pattern for airports in close proximity (such as Singapore/Kuala Lumpur, Istanbul, as well as Dubai and surrounding Gulf nations in the Middle East). Notably, air traffic between Asia and Europe is fed through a combination of direct and hub services, with no dominant airport for this activity (unlike, for instance, Asia/North America traffic routing through Anchorage).

Political factors, such as the UK's Brexit vote in June 2016 (IATA, 2016a), which has seen a remarkable devaluation of the British pound against major currencies, and the transition in the US to the Trump Administration in early 2017, supported by both a Republican Congress and House, will most likely have a significant impact on trade and economic growth, and air cargo demand as a result. Unfavourable foreign policy fuelled by renewed patriotic views such as a move away from free trade agreements and globalisation, as well as the strategic decision of businesses to return to domestic supply chains (onshoring), could negatively impact the air cargo industry.

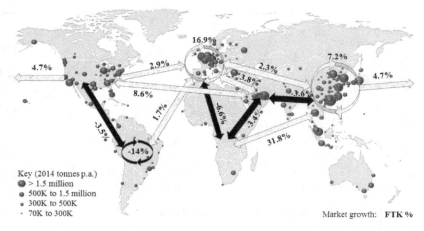

*Figure 2.4*  Growth of air cargo trade (FTK), year-on-year, August 2016

*Source*: Compiled using data from IATA (2016d).

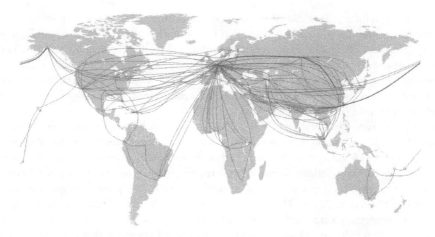

*Figure 2.5*   Cargolux weekly scheduled freighter network, December 2016

*Source*: Author supplied image developed by open-source data from Cargolux (2016).

## Categories of air cargo goods

The carriage of air cargo is primarily subject to time, cost and quality decisions made by shippers (Morrell, 2011) as part of a transport solution. Shippers utilising air cargo services are typically businesses or government departments with a specific requirement that cannot be met by other transport services. Businesses, as shippers, include primary producers (agricultural products), manufacturers (from consumer electronics to pharmaceutical products) or aggregators such as import/export brokers, freight forwarders and third-party logistics providers. Consignees include multinational corporations, retail companies (including e-commerce shopping), government/postal departments and other buyers of air cargo services.

Time-sensitive characteristics of goods shipped by air include perishability, obsolescence and priority service demand (Wensveen and Merkert, 2015). These products can include aquacultural, horticultural and floricultural goods (such as premium seafood, cherries and red roses), live animals (from racehorses to family pets) and printed material (such as newspapers, express air mail and documents). The premium attribute of speed (Doganis, 2010) provided by air transport over surface transport modes (sea, rail and road) enables movement of time-sensitive goods to much broader markets. JIT supply chains typically involve scheduled delivery of products to optimise the total production cost profile (between labour and capital factors), and air transport provides for fast service.

Air cargo, carried on a premium mode of transport, is often charged at a much higher rate to equivalent surface transportation (Wensveen and Merkert, 2015). Operational charges quoted to shippers remain a significant factor influencing modal choice (Morrell, 2011), as well as competitive offerings between air carriers. Service rates are based on a variety of factors – general or specific commodity, ULD/container, class of product (i.e. requiring special handling), freight all kinds (FAK), volume contracts and premium product requirements (such as time-definitive) (Morrell, 2011; Wensveen and Merkert, 2015). The potential lack of availability in cargo hold capacity (i.e. at Christmas) may also attract a premium or increase lead times for delivery.

Air cargo goods can be divided into four primary classes: supply chain cargo, project cargo, perishable cargo and contingency cargo. Supply chain cargo shipped by air includes automotive parts, electronic semiconductors and other semi-finished or finished products. Allaz (2004) includes these products as two distinct groups, although these items have very similar qualities when transported by air, either as part of a JIT manufacturing process or urgently required inventory (Doganis, 2010). JIT shipments are planned and regular, leveraging volume discounts in collaboration with key airlines. JIT also benefits from lower inventory holding costs, shrinkage rates and improved turnover, enhancing business cash flows. Zara, the international clothing chain, has developed an air cargo supply chain to produce fast fashion distributing to stores throughout the world (Ferdows et al., 2003).

Project cargo typically involves capital equipment and machinery, such as the transport of Formula One vehicles, and is more sporadic in demand (Gibson Freight, 2016). Project cargo can also include the movement of ultra-high-value products, such as artwork, gold, jewellery and precious stones, requiring stricter security measures provided by air transport (see Chapter 21). Perishable cargo includes items with a short shelf life or that are prone to rapid obsolescence (Wensveen and Merkert, 2015). This includes seasonal produce for North–South transport, or vice versa. Contingency cargo, unplanned and irregular in demand, such as for humanitarian needs, is most often met with charter or temporarily parked aircraft at short notice.

Microeconomic factors, such as the shutdown of West Coast maritime ports in the US in 2015, and the collapse of Hanjin Shipping Company, have increased demand for air cargo services, albeit on a temporary basis (IATA, 2016b). Air cargo handles 35 per cent of the value of merchandise trade (exports), which translates into less than 1 per cent of total international freight by weight, with the global maritime fleet carrying the bulk of trade along major shipping lanes (IATA, 2015). Businesses that initially used air transport for rapid deployment of products (such as the new iPhone) often switched to sea transport for bulk shipments to minimise costs, but were once again reliant on air transport as a stopgap measure to avoid inventory stock-outs.

## Provision of air cargo services

Currently, air transport acts in competition with maritime, rail and road transport for the carriage of freight, offering a premium product due to speed (especially on long-haul routes) within a logistical supply chain, but limited in provision of the 'final mile' of delivery. As a result, air transport is often linked with road, with deliveries and collections made by truck to airport loading facilities. Air transport also combines with maritime (air-sea) and rail (air-rail) as part of a multimodal transport solution (Morrell, 2011). Moreover, business models focused on the provision of surface transport only (road, rail, sea or combinations thereof) compete with marginal air cargo markets, adopting 'reefer' container technology (environmentally controlled containment) to provide additional lifespan to perishable goods during transport (Morrell, 2011).

Air cargo, excluding the most time-sensitive products, can be shipped across Road Feeder Services (RFS) for up to 800 kilometres, or 12 hours by road, before arriving at an airport, as reported by the EC (2008), providing a significant competitive hinterland for air cargo. Regions with multi-airport systems (such as Belgium, the Netherlands and Luxembourg – known collectively as Benelux) are becoming more evident in the movement of air cargo, especially with airport/airline choice modellers. Dependent upon other factors (such as total cost of service and flight frequency), air cargo can then be routed across a multitude of air stages or delayed at hub airports awaiting consolidation with air freight from other origin points, provided the consignment arrives at the destination within the often generous delivery window schedule provided to the consumer (i.e. 6–8 days for delivery on long haul compared to ~24 hours of actual flight time).

Major airlines (such as Lufthansa and Cathay Pacific), dedicated cargo carriers (Cargolux and Polar Air Cargo) and integrators (FedEx, UPS and DHL) provide a variety of air cargo services that support global supply chains and international trade. Regular scheduled services are augmented by charter operations and vary based on seasonal demand (especially the lead-up to the festive season in December). Textile, manufacturing (such as Boeing, Apple and Samsung) and newspaper industries, retailers, postal services, military operations and providers of humanitarian aid (among others) have all derived benefits from the transport utility provided by aircraft.

Several aircraft types are available for the provision of air cargo services, including passenger aircraft (belly-hold cargo), passenger aircraft (main deck cargo), convertible (or quick-change), converted dedicated freighters and factory-built freighters. Most common are the passenger aircraft with belly-holds with high (wide-bodied aircraft) and low capacity (single-aisle or narrow-bodied aircraft). The cargo potential for these aircraft ranges from less than 1 tonne to over 20 tonnes (e.g. Airbus 350) (Airbus, 2016b). Routes with higher freight volumes initially employ passenger aircraft with main deck cargo (a partition is erected between the passenger seating area and cargo zone), increasing payload capability.

Convertibles and quick-change aircraft can be changed between passenger and freight carriage at short notice (typically between day and night or weekday and weekend services). Converted freighters are ex-passenger aircraft (typically Boeing 747s) refurbished for freight (typically after the major overhaul known as the D service maintenance check). Factory built freighters are new aircraft, typically designated as Airbus 330F or similar. The global fleet of aircraft total over 1,500 dedicated freighters (Boeing, 2016), with payload capacities ranging from 1 tonne to over 80 tonnes.

Meanwhile, Boeing (2016) and Airbus (2016a) continue to forecast increased aircraft requirements, including dedicated freighters, to cater for expected growth in air transport across the next 20 years. New aircraft, composed of lighter composite materials and more efficient engine systems, provide improved fuel consumption and lower operating costs as a result (albeit at a high capital cost, with some aircraft listed at over US$250 million). Future conversion of today's new aircraft, likely at the time of major overhaul (the first or second maintenance D check carried out every 4–5 years), will offset some of the capital expense required for growing the dedicated freighter fleet. Conversion of aircraft is also known to extend the effective lifespan of the asset, an important consideration for financial companies involved in purchasing and leasing aircraft to airlines.

## Current actors and air cargo business models

Traditional air cargo supply chains typically suffer from structural weaknesses. Several steps are involved in the shipment process, package loading, counting, storage and documentation from origin to destination, as indicated in Figure 2.6. Time wastage, duplication of processes and documentation, leading to inefficiencies, which, combined with disadvantages in terms of risk management, supply chain visibility and joint profit management, have provided integrators (door-to-door express companies such as FedEx) with a competitive advantage in recent years.

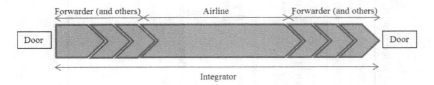

*Figure 2.6* Traditional air cargo supply chain versus integrator

*Source*: Authors.

Table 2.4 Airline business models and corporate objectives

| Corporate objectives | Passenger/cargo operations | | Cargo operations | | |
|---|---|---|---|---|---|
| Cargo strategy | Belly | Belly flex/combination | All-cargo | ACMI/charter | Integrated |
| Customer marketing strategy | Value cargo as an important by-product of the core passenger business. | View freighters to capture high market shares of core routes, leveraging belly-hold network. | Airport-to-airport transport of cargo is the primary business task. | Airport-to-airport demand (and matching supply) is the primary business task. | Primarily provide express network capacity for premium air cargo products. |
| Network design strategy | Freight forwarders, some shippers, government mail contracts. | Freight forwarders, shippers, government, other airlines and integrators. | Freight forwarders, shippers, government, other airlines and integrators. | Some freight forwarders, government, other airlines and integrators. | Mainly direct shippers. |
| Capacity management strategy | Centred on passenger gateway airports, mix of long-, medium- and short-haul routes. Typically a member of an airline alliance. | Similar to belly carriers, use of freighters as supplement on high-density routes. Some cargo-only destinations. | Cargo-focused, including multi-leg or asymmetrical stages. | No network. Routings are determined by clients. | Hub-and-spoke, with distribution centres for sortation and processing. |
| | Residual belly-hold capacity. | Combination of passenger and freighter aircraft. | Dedicated freighter fleet. | Leasing of aircraft on short- and long-term basis. | Cargo aircraft as a link in door-to-door services. |

Source: We acknowledge the input of Frederic Horst in the production of this table.

Airlines and air cargo providers offer a degree of flexibility for customer-specific solutions and compete for business from freight forwarders and surface transport providers. Several airline business models (see Chapter 8) have been developed for the provision of air cargo services. These include the belly-hold carrier and belly flex/combination carrier, primarily airlines that incorporate passenger and cargo operations, then dedicated cargo services such as all-cargo airlines, aircraft, crew, maintenance and insurance (ACMI)/charter services, and integrated providers (as detailed in Table 2.4).

The belly-hold carrier has a very limited dedicated freighter fleet for air cargo, focusing primarily on passenger markets and utilising excess capacity from wide-bodied aircraft to market the cargo business. Delta, American, Virgin, United and Continental are major airlines that fit within this group. Some airlines have identified opportunities for establishing dedicated freighter networks as an operating division, such as Korean Air, Lufthansa, Singapore Airlines, Air France-KLM, Emirates, Etihad and Qantas, and fit within the belly flex/combination model (Merkert and Alexander, 2016).

All-cargo airlines, such as Cargolux and Polar Air Cargo, focus strategically on air cargo markets, purchasing and converting aircraft for cargo handling across a broad network. ACMI operators act to lease aircraft to other airlines based on market demand, supplementing major airline operations, or acting as a financial investor for smaller operators with limited capital expenditure provisions. Finally, integrated logistics organisations (such as FedEx, UPS and DHL) have developed air networks to provide express package service delivery, and can leverage these networks for general air cargo to compete with airlines.

With various business strategies, airlines involved in the air cargo industry have several methods of cost allocation. Airline management can consider air cargo to be a by-product of the passenger business and use revenues to break even, including marginal increases. Cargo capacity can be considered a joint product, with pricing based on factors such as weight, volume, zone, revenue and profit contribution. Finally, setting an indicative profit margin, thus profit is proportional to revenue, is a pricing strategy that airlines can use.

Key to developing economies of scale is vertical integration (via mergers and acquisitions) or strategic partnerships (see Chapter 9) with key customers, such as between Qantas and Australia Post (Qantas, 2016). The top 20 air cargo carriers provided in Table 2.5 notably include integrators (FedEx, UPS), all-cargo airlines (Cargolux, Polar Air Cargo, AirBridgeCargo) and combination carriers.

An important factor to air cargo carriers is the business of freight forwarders (as indicated in Table 2.6) – agents involved in the brokering of air cargo to consumers, and consolidators of cargo volumes, as well as managing sea freight (the major modal competitor to air cargo). DHL leads the freight forwarding business, and is not included in Table 2.5, as the parent company, Deutsche Post, operates several airlines in different jurisdictions (Europe and Asia).

Consolidation of the air cargo industry is most apparent with the purchase of TNT by FedEx in 2015 (the former was unsuccessfully pursued by both UPS and DHL). FedEx, primarily based in the US (along with UPS), has been expanding into providing global integrated transport solutions. TNT's European presence (and competition to incumbent DHL) notably attracted FedEx and UPS, with the view to increasing network reach and market share (with improving economies of scale and density for air cargo movements, especially premium express packages). In Asia, DHL, FedEx and UPS are developing hub-and-spoke networks with local air cargo market participants, due primarily to regulatory obstacles. The Asian market, as a result, remains fragmented, in particular with the development of air cargo businesses of Chinese airlines (China Southern, Air China, China Eastern and China Airlines) and regional neighbours (Cathay Pacific, Korean Air and Singapore Airlines).

*Table 2.5* Top 20 air cargo carriers, 2015

| Rank | Airline (or airline group) | Scheduled cargo traffic (FTKs mn) | Tonnage (000) |
|------|---------------------------|-----------------------------------|---------------|
| 1 | FedEx | 15,799 | 7,087 |
| 2 | Emirates | 12,157 | 2,454 |
| 3 | UPS Airlines | 10,807 | 4,482 |
| 4 | Cathay Pacific Group | 9,935 | 1,558 |
| 5 | Korean Air | 7,761 | 1,533 |
| 6 | Qatar Airways | 7,660 | 1,466 |
| 7 | Lufthansa | 6,888 | 950 |
| 8 | Cargolux | 6,309 | 757 |
| 9 | Singapore Airlines | 6,083 | 1,084 |
| 10 | Air China | 5,718 | 1,256 |
| 11 | China Southern Airlines | 5,355 | 1,389 |
| 12 | China Airlines | 5,343 | 1,306 |
| 13 | China Eastern Airlines | 4,542 | 1,255 |
| 14 | Etihad Airways | 4,400 | 904 |
| 15 | Polar Air Cargo | 4,186 | 685 |
| 16 | AirBridgeCargo Airlines | 4,069 | 615 |
| 17 | British Airways | 4,055 | 606 |
| 18 | All Nippon Airways | 3,840 | 1,165 |
| 19 | EVA Air | 3,757 | 624 |
| 20 | Asiana Airlines | 3,595 | 856 |

*Source*: Data from Air Cargo News (2016a).

*Note*: The combined DHL activities would rank it in the top five, as Deutsche Post owns five airline subsidiaries operating for DHL Express.

*Table 2.6* Top 10 freight forwarders (by air traffic), 2015

| Freight forwarder | Gross revenue (US$ mn) | Air freight (tonnes) | Ocean freight (TEU) |
|-------------------|------------------------|----------------------|---------------------|
| DHL Supply Chain & Global | 29,562 | 2,109,000 | 2,930,000 |
| Kuehne + Nagel | 21,100 | 1,250,000 | 3,820,000 |
| DB Schenker | 17,160 | 1,128,000 | 1,942,000 |
| UPS Supply Chain Solutions | 8,215 | 935,300 | 615,000 |
| Expeditors | 6,617 | 872,480 | 1,043,880 |
| Panalpina | 6,091 | 836,200 | 1,593,900 |
| Nippon Express | 15,822 | 711,354 | 855,002 |
| Bolloré Logistics | 4,998 | 580,000 | 844,000 |
| Hellmann Worldwide Logistics | 3,987 | 561,240 | 888,284 |
| Sinotrans | 7,314 | 522,600 | 2,801,300 |

*Source*: Data from Armstrong & Associates (2016).

*Note*: TEU is an abbreviation for twenty-foot equivalent unit.

## Regulatory obstacles to the growth of air cargo

Scheduled international air cargo transport is regulated by the nine freedoms of the air, used in the formation of bilateral, multilateral and open skies agreements between nations (Chapters 6 and 7 discuss these freedoms in relation to the passenger market). As mentioned previously, deregulation or liberalisation of air cargo (in the US and Europe) has preceded that of air passenger transport. Moreover, only 85 of the 120 international open skies partners with the

US provide all-cargo carriers with seventh freedom rights (Bureau of Public Affairs, 2016). Countries located in North Asia, namely Japan, Korea and Taiwan, do not provide all-cargo carriers from the US with open skies freedoms (and vice versa), and there is no US/China open skies agreement currently in place. Integrators such as FedEx and UPS are required to develop partnerships with local businesses to provide door-to-door services. Partnerships are not new to the air transport industry, as they were originally developed to circumvent restrictions in bilateral agreements (such as code-sharing of flights).

Airport ownership and operation (see Chapter 3), despite privatisation within the UK, Australia and other progressive nations, remains typically in control of local port authorities or provincial governments, such as in the US or most of Asia (Graham, 2011). Capital investment in airport expansion, in particular to handle cargo such as customs clearance and quarantine facilities, is often consolidated to a major hub (such as JFK in New York). Surface infrastructure (such as roads) is similarly provisioned to a major airport. This effectively develops a barrier for cargo airlines, as infrastructure is an important factor of airport choice (and impairs the potential of open skies). Some major airports operate under a curfew, restricting night flights (Doganis, 2010), another deterrent to efficient air cargo movements.

Regulation of the operation of dedicated freighters, as evidenced at slot-constrained London Heathrow Airport (Airports Commission, 2013), while constraining activities of all-cargo airlines, does result in enhanced utilisation of belly-holds of wide-bodied aircraft for the shipment of cargo. Another high-volume cargo airport, ranked third by tonnage after Hong Kong and Memphis (ACI, 2016), Shanghai Pudong receives no dedicated freighters according to CAPA (2015). While Heathrow and Pudong support high-volume cargo along with passenger movements, airports that focus on cargo (such as Anchorage, Alaska and Luxembourg) typically enjoy high freighter capacity utilisation.

As with all competitive markets, the regulation of the air cargo industry is subject to antitrust and anticompetitive behaviour proceedings. While more than 200 airlines are involved in air freight (CAPA, 2014), cartel activities have taken place recently into price-fixing by major airlines (Department of Justice, 2007) such as British Airways, Air France-KLM and Singapore Airlines (members of rival airline alliances, Oneworld, SkyTeam and Star Alliance, respectively) with participation from major freight forwarders Kuehne + Nagel International, Panalpina and DB Schenker (Department of Justice, 2010). The air cargo industry was impacted by the coordinated setting of fuel surcharges and security rates over several years from 2000 to 2006. Criminal and civil litigation has resulted in penalties in excess of US$3 billion in the US alone (Air Cargo News, 2016c), although initial EU rulings of €799 million in fines have been overturned (Oliver, 2015). In an industry that earned only US$52 billion in revenues in 2015 (and continuing to soften in 2016), with cargo divisions reporting operational losses, the antitrust proceedings reinforce the generally high-risk, low-return business environment of air transport.

## Conclusion

The air cargo industry undoubtedly remains a challenge to policymakers, airport and airline management, and other market participants. With an environment consisting of ever-declining yields, low load factors (under 50 per cent of capacity), cargo hold oversupply (primarily due to matching air passenger demand to aircraft frequencies) and modal competition (by road and sea on key routes), the air cargo industry faces many challenges. Liberalisation of air cargo, in particular domestic cabotage, remains an ever-increasing challenge at the regional level, evidenced by the dominance of FedEx and UPS in the US market (and DHL in Europe), as well as the restrictive operations of these companies on foreign soil. The Asia-Pacific market, already the most significant market for air cargo, faces consolidation challenges as it continues to grow. Technological innovation (e-commerce, automated drones) provides opportunities for air cargo market participants, while disruptive technologies (3D printing, reefer containers) may extinguish others. The future of air cargo, as always, remains within its core values – providing fast, secure, reliable, safe and flexible transport solutions.

## References

ACI (Airports Council International) (2013). *Air cargo guide. Chapter 1: a historical perspective*. Online. Available at: www.aci-na.org/content/air-cargo-guide (accessed 23 January 2017).
ACI (Airports Council International) (2015). *World Airport Traffic Forecasts 2016*, Montreal, ACI.
ACI (Airports Council International) (2016). *Freight summary: cargo traffic for past 12 months ending December 2015*. Online. Available at: www.aci.aero/Data-Centre/Monthly-Traffic-Data/Freight-Summary/12-months (accessed 23 January 2017).
AIAS (Alaska International Airport System) (2016). *Historical Activity Summary Report, Fiscal Year 2010–2015*, Alaska, AIAS.
Airbus (2016a). *Global Market Forecast Mapping Demand 2016–35*, Blagnac, Airbus.
Airbus (2016b). *Aircraft families A350 dimensions & key data*. Online. Available at: www.airbus.com/aircraftfamilies/passengeraircraft/a350xwbfamily/a350-1000/specifications/ (accessed 23 January 2017).
Air Cargo News (2016a). Top 25 air cargo carriers: FedEx maintains top spot, *Air Cargo News*, 5 July.
Air Cargo News (2016b). The ACN interview: Heathrow's man with a plan, *Air Cargo News*, 31 May.
Air Cargo News (2016c). Air cargo antitrust settlements totalling $1.2bn granted final approval in the US, *Air Cargo News*, 10 October.
Airports Commission (2013). *Comments on Published Short and Medium Term Proposals*, Heathrow Airport, Heathrow Airport Limited.
Alexander, D. and Merkert, R. (2016). Evaluation of US international air freight markets post-GFC. In *Proceedings of the 20th Air Transport Research Society World Conference*, Rhodes, Air Transport Research Society.
Alexander, D. and Merkert, R. (2017). Challenges to domestic air freight in Australia: evaluating air traffic markets with gravity modelling, *Journal of Air Transport Management*, 61, 41–52.
Allaz, C. (2004). *The History of Air Cargo and Air Mail from the 18th Century*, London, Christopher Foyle Publishing.
Armstrong & Associates (2016). *A&A's top 25 global freight forwarders list*. Online. Available at: www.3plogistics.com/3pl-market-info-resources/3pl-market-information/aas-top-25-global-freight-forwarders-list/ (accessed 23 January 2017).
Boeing (2014). *World Air Cargo Forecast 2014–2033*, Seattle, WA, Boeing.
Boeing (2016). *World Air Cargo Forecast 2016–2035*, Seattle, WA, Boeing.
Bureau of Public Affairs (2016). *Full List of Open Skies Partners*, Washington, DC, Department of State.
CAPA (Centre for Aviation) (2014). *Airline Statistics*, Sydney, CAPA.
CAPA (Centre for Aviation) (2015). *Airport Statistics*, Sydney, CAPA.
Cargolux (2016). *Flight schedule*. Online. Available at: www.virtualcargolux.org/home/flight-schedule/ (accessed 14 December 2016).
Changi Airport (2016). *Global air cargo hub*. Online. Available at: www.changiairport.com/corporate/partner-us/cargo.html (accessed 23 January 2017).
Department of Justice (2007). *United States of America v. British Airways PLC*. Online. Available at: www.justice.gov/atr/case-document/file/489846/download (accessed 23 January 2017).
Department of Justice (2010). *Six International Freight Forwarding Companies Agree to Plead Guilty to Criminal Price-Fixing Charges*, 30 September, Washington, DC, Department of Justice.
Doganis, R. (2010). *Flying Off Course: Airline Economics and Marketing*, 4th edition, New York, Routledge.
EC (European Commission) (2008). *Commission Decision, COMP/M.5141-KLM/Martinair, 17/12/2008*, Brussels, EC.
EC (European Commission) (2010). *Antitrust: Commission fines 11 air cargo carriers €799 million in price fixing cartel*. Online. Available at: http://europa.eu/rapid/press-release_IP-10-1487_en.htm (accessed 23 January 2017).
Farquhar, P. (2016). This man faces a $9000 fine after using a drone to buy a sausage from Bunnings, *Business Insider Australia*, 9 November.

Ferdows, K., Lewis, M. and Machuca, J.A.D. (2003). Zara case study, *Supply Chain Forum: An International Journal*, 4(2), 62–67.

Ford Motor Company (2010). *Henry Ford helps start commercial aviation in the United States*. Online. Available at: http://ophelia.sdsu.edu:8080/ford/12-10-2010/about-ford/heritage/milestones/trimotorairplanes/678-tri-motor-airplanes.html (accessed 23 January 2017).

Gates, D. (2005). Boeing 787: parts from around the world will be swiftly integrated, *The Seattle Times*, 11 September.

Gibson Freight (2016). *Case studies: Formula One and Moto GP*. Online. Available at: http://gibsonfreight.com.au/case-studies/#f1 (accessed 23 January 2017).

Graham, A. (2011). *Managing Airports: An International Perspective*, 4th edition, Abingdon, Routledge.

Hakim, M.M. and Merkert, R. (2016). The causal relationship between air transport and economic growth: empirical evidence from South Asia, *Journal of Transport Geography*, 56, 120–127.

IATA (International Air Transport Association) (2015). *IATA Cargo Strategy 2015–2020*, Montreal, IATA.

IATA (International Air Transport Association) (2016a). *IATA Cargo Chartbook, Q2 2016*, Montreal, IATA.

IATA (International Air Transport Association) (2016b). *Air Freight Market Analysis: October 2016*, Montreal, IATA.

IATA (International Air Transport Association) (2016c). *Economic Performance of the Airline Industry Tables, December 2016*, Montreal, IATA.

IATA (International Air Transport Association) (2016d). *IATA Cargo Chartbook, Q3 2016*, Montreal, IATA.

ICAO (International Civil Aviation Organisation) (2014). *Traffic by Flight Stage Statistics 2014*, Montreal, ICAO.

ICAO (International Civil Aviation Organisation) (2015). *Traffic by Flight Stage Statistics 2015*, Montreal, ICAO.

Lakew, P.A. and Tok, Y.C.A. (2014). *Determinants of Air Cargo Traffic in California, UCI-ITS-WP-13-7*, Irvine, CA, University of California.

Lee, J. (2015). Korea looks to strong 2015, *Asia Cargo News*, 25 March.

Lufthansa Group (2016). *Airfreight in Germany*. Online. Available at: www.lufthansagroup.com/en/company/themen/100-years-of-airfreight/history.html (accessed 23 January 2017).

McFarland, M. (2016a). Domino's delivers pizza by drone in New Zealand, *CNNTech*, 26 August.

McFarland, M. (2016b) Amazon makes its first drone delivery in the UK, *CNNTech*, 14 December.

Merkert, R. and Alexander, D.W. (2016). Managing freight operations chains of passenger airlines at international airports. In: J.D. Bitzan, J.H. Peoples and W.W. Wilson (eds). *Book Series: Advances in Airline Economics. Volume 5 – Airline Efficiencies*, Bingley, Emerald.

Merkert, R. and Ploix, B. (2014). The impact of terminal re-organisation on belly-hold freight operation chains at airports, *Journal of Air Transport Management*, 36, 78–84.

Merkert, R., Van de Voorde, E. and de Wit, J. (2017). Making or breaking: key success factors in the air cargo market, *Journal of Air Transport Management*, 61, 1–5.

Morrell, P.S. (2011). *Moving Boxes by Air: The Economics of International Air Cargo*, Aldershot, Ashgate.

Oliver, C. (2015). EU court overturns €790m air cargo cartel fines, *Financial Times*, 17 December.

Otto, A. (2008). Reflecting the prospects of an air cargo carrier. In: S. Albers, H. Baum, S. Auerbach and W. Delfmann (eds). *Strategic Management in the Aviation Industry*, Aldershot, Ashgate.

Qantas (2016). *Qantas freight is now operating two domestic freighter networks*. Online. Available at: www.qantas.com.au/qfreight/qfe/operational-notices-archive/au/en (accessed 23 January 2017).

Razzouk, N., Rascouet, A. and Motevalli, G. (2016). OPEC confounds skeptics, agrees to first oil cuts in 8 years, *Bloomberg*, 1 December.

Shepherd, B., Shingal, A. and Raj, A. (2016). *Value of Air Cargo: Air Transport and Global Value Chains*, Montreal, IATA.

US Senate (2016). *Special committee to investigate air mail and ocean mail contracts*. Online. Available at: www.senate.gov/artandhistory/history/common/investigations/MailContracts.htm (accessed 23 January 2017).

USPS (United States Postal Service) (2006). *The history of the United States Postal Service: air mail*. Online. Available at: https://about.usps.com/publications/pub100/pub100_026.htm (accessed 23 January 2017).

Wensveen, J.G. and Merkert, R. (2015). Air cargo. In: J.G. Wensveen. *Air Transportation: A Management Perspective*, 8th edition, Aldershot, Ashgate.

World Bank (2015). *Air transport, freight (million ton-km)*. Online. Available at: http://data.worldbank.org/indicator/IS.AIR.GOOD.MT.K1 (accessed 23 January 2017).

# 3

# The airport industry

*Lucy Budd and Stephen Ison*

## Introduction

Airports, those familiar and often much-maligned interfaces between ground and sky, are vital nodes in the modern world economy. Every year, the world's airports collectively facilitate the safe aerial movement of over 34.8 million flights, 3.57 billion passengers and over 50 million tonnes of valuable air freight (ATAG, 2016) and the prevalence and socio-economic significance of aviation is such that every nation worldwide, bar the European microstates of Andorra, Liechtenstein, Monaco, San Marino and the Vatican City, and some remote oceanic islands, has within its territory at least one airport capable of handling fixed-wing commercial aircraft. These facilities vary in size from profitable mega-aviation cities that handle tens of millions of passengers every year and boast attractions and facilities ranging from a 23-feet-high bronze sculpture of a teddy bear (Hamad International Airport, Doha) to butterfly and cactus gardens (Singapore Changi Airport), nature trails (Zurich Airport in Switzerland), a dental surgery (Sao Paulo Guarulhos International Airport in Brazil), saltwater aquaria (Vancouver International Airport in Canada) and an in-house brewery (Munich Airport in Germany), to loss-making, predominantly publicly owned remote landing strips that offer few, if any, concessions to passenger comfort.

According to the United States (US) Central Intelligence Agency (CIA), 41,789 airports or airfields (including closed or abandoned facilities) across all seven continents were visible from the air in 2013, of which 14,143 (34 per cent) had paved runways (CIA, 2016a, 2016b). Of the 34,022 active facilities, most serve the needs of the world's military and general aviation users (ATAG, 2016). In 2014, only 3,883 airports (9 per cent of the world total and 28 per cent of the paved total) handled scheduled commercial flights (ATAG, 2016). However, it is these airports, together with the passengers they serve and the wider aviation industry that they support, that are the focus of this chapter.

This chapter will show how innovations in aeronautical technology and aircraft design, combined with decades of geopolitical intervention, regulatory reform and the emergence of neo-liberal ideologies, has resulted in the formation of a diverse and highly complex global airport industry that serves the needs of diverse and increasingly discerning customers and clients. The chapter begins by describing the contemporary scale and scope of global provision. It then charts the historical evolution of the airport as a site of aeronautical activity into increasingly diverse commercial enterprises that have to meet the challenging needs of a wide range of users. It then documents the reasons for, and implications of, changes in patterns of airport ownership and management structures, using the United Kingdom (UK) as an example, and concludes by discussing the main challenges and opportunities facing the world's commercial airport industry.

## The world's commercial airports

The near 3,900 commercial airports worldwide that handle scheduled commercial air services (defined here as revenue-generating flights that operate to a published timetable) delineate a world in perpetual (albeit unevenly spatially distributed) motion. Airports permit passengers to complete long-distance journeys, which would once have taken many days or months by land or sea, in a matter of hours by air, and enable personal and professional relationships to be conducted at a distance and across multiple time zones. Yet despite commercial aviation's apparently international scope, airport provision and access is geographically uneven both between and within states. North America, for example, contains almost 36 per cent of the world's airports and airfields, while Africa contains 8 per cent and Oceania 1 per cent (see Figure 3.1).

The majority of the world's airports are located in countries that either have large and geographically widely distributed populations, mature or rapidly growing economies, challenging topography, large land areas, and/or in states that have historically had a large military (see Table 3.1). The US alone has 13,513 airports or airfields (32 per cent of the world total), of which 5,054 (36 per cent of the world total) have paved runways (CIA, 2016a, 2016b). In stark contrast, there are 27 countries or dependencies that only have one airport/airfield within their territory.

However, irrespective of location, most airports are small and high traffic volumes are disproportionately concentrated at a relatively small number of sites. These hubs, which include sites at Atlanta, Beijing and Dubai, not only act as the command and control posts of global

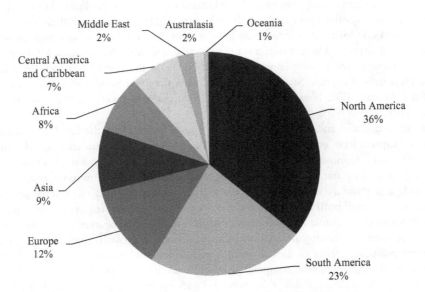

*Figure 3.1* Proportion of world's airports/airfields with paved runways by world region, 2013

*Source*: Data derived from CIA (2016a).

*Table 3.1* The 10 countries with the most airports/airfields and most airports/airfields with paved runways, 2013

| Total number of airports/airfields | | | Number of airports/airfields with paved runways | | |
|---|---|---|---|---|---|
| Rank | Country | Number | Rank | Country | Number |
| 1 | US | 13,513 | 1 | US | 5,054 |
| 2 | Brazil | 4,093 | 2 | Brazil | 698 |
| 3 | Mexico | 1,714 | 3 | Russia | 592 |
| 4 | Canada | 1,467 | 4 | Canada | 523 |
| 5 | Russia | 1,218 | 5 | China | 463 |
| 6 | Argentina | 1,138 | 6 | Australia | 349 |
| 7 | Bolivia | 855 | 7 | Germany | 318 |
| 8 | Colombia | 836 | 8 | France | 294 |
| 9 | Paraguay | 799 | 9 | UK | 271 |
| 10 | Indonesia | 673 | 10 | India | 253 |

*Source*: Data from CIA (2016a, 2016b).

air travel, but also have become major commercial enterprises in their own right. Airbus, the European aircraft manufacturer, defines an 'aviation megacity' as an airport that handles at least 10,000 long-haul passengers a day. In 2015, there were 42, and by 2033 it is estimated there will be 91 (ACI, 2015). Yet 91 still only represents 0.6 per cent of all the airports with paved runways and only 2.3 per cent of all the airports that handled commercial flights in 2014. Far more numerous than these major gateway international airports are secondary and/or regional facilities that either serve the mobility needs of distinct passenger segments (such as charter or low cost traffic, which does not use the expensive and often congested hubs), or parts of a country or region that is not geographically proximate to the main airport, which is usually, but in the case of the US particularly, not exclusively located in/near the capital city. These airports are typically smaller and offer fewer facilities than the major hubs, but are nevertheless vital income generators and employment centres in their own right. Some cities and city regions may also support several airports. These 'multi-airport regions' are usually characterised by the provision of three or more major airports (Bonnefoy et al., 2008). In the case of London, these facilities include Heathrow, Gatwick, Stansted, Luton, London City and Southend, while on the other side of the Atlantic, JFK, Newark/Liberty and LaGuardia collectively serve the aviation needs of New York.

This uneven global and regional distribution is significant. Over the last 100 years, a small number of airports have evolved from being rudimentary sites of aeronautical activity into key drivers of national economic growth, social opportunity and cultural exchange. These attributes are keenly desired by states whose economies are predicated on unfettered access to international trade and mobility and who value the global connectivity and rapid aerial mobility air travel affords. Indeed, both developed and developing nations have integrated air connectivity into their national economic development strategies and it is the apparent economic rationality (or the perceived inevitability of aviation-induced economic growth) that underpins much of the current political support for global airport development and expansion.

Certainly, the figures appear compelling. Worldwide, it is estimated that airports contribute to an industry whose direct, indirect, induced and wider economic (or catalytic) impact is in the region of US$2.7 trillion a year (ATAG, 2016), and airport industry revenues alone now exceed US$142.5 billion annually (ACI, 2016). However, as mentioned in more detail in Chapter 10, airports are operating in an increasingly challenging and competitive marketplace. In Europe and other key world markets, reduced government spending, more restrictive rules on permissible levels of state aid, and the growing trend towards airport privatisation mean that many facilities are no longer supported or financed by government investment, and so must attract investment and generate revenue from alternative sources. When this is coupled with increased controversy and political contestation concerning aircraft noise, local air quality, climate change and the effects of expansion on local communities (see Chapters 18 and 25), the challenges facing airport operators are considerable.

Although all commercial airports offer the same basic built infrastructure, including runways, air traffic control terminals, passenger terminals and cargo sheds that enable aircraft to safely land, take off and be serviced between flights and facilities in which passengers, baggage and cargo can be processed in accordance with strict (inter)national regulations governing safety, security, customs and immigration, every airport is unique. Each facility differs in terms of its geographic site and situation, the provision and extent of its air and landside facilities, its traffic mix, catchment area, population demographics, operating characteristics, volumes and seasonality of passengers and cargo, extent of competition with neighbouring facilities, ground access provision, commercial priorities, marketing attributes and ownership structure. Indeed, the last 100 years have seen airports evolve from privately owned flying fields, which afforded few if any concessions to passenger comfort, into state- or local authority-operated facilities run for the benefit of the region or nation. Some of these facilities have subsequently been sold to the private sector and transformed into part- or fully privatised commercial enterprises (see discussion below) that support a diverse range of aeronautical and non-aeronautical activities. In the European Union (EU) alone, the level of private investment in airports has risen from 23 per cent in 2010 to over 50 per cent by 2016 (ACI Europe, 2016), and even those that remain in public ownership have been forced to diversify their product offering and generate new sources of income from assets such as property, car parking, retail and external consultancy.

As a consequence, airports are now more than just transport nodes. They are complex international businesses that operate in highly defined yet dynamic regulatory, financial and operational environments that are, in turn, directly influenced by changes in the wider social, geopolitical and economic environments of the countries, regions and markets in which they operate and serve. The global airport industry as a whole now includes public institutions and private businesses that own and/or operate airports, as well as third-party providers that deliver services as diverse as refuelling, catering, ground handling, air traffic control, security and air cargo/logistics. Having described the scope of the global airport network, the following sections describe the evolution of airport operations and ownership from the origins of powered flight to the present day.

## From airfields to airports: the growth of the global airport industry

Investigations and experiments by pioneering scientists, engineers and philosophers into the possibility of heavier-than-air human flights, which began in ancient antiquity and culminated with the successful first flight of the Wright brothers' Flyer in December 1903, demanded the creation of a new transportation facility that would permit the safe transition of these new flying machines between land and sky. In order to help generate sufficient lift, the sites that were chosen for the earliest flights were exposed, windswept areas of flat land that were free from local obstructions and hazards such as telegraph poles, chimneys, residential areas and trees that would endanger aircraft. Racecourses, playing fields, agricultural land and municipal parks often provided ideal conditions, and many were temporarily reappropriated for the purposes of flight. By 1908, the Wright brothers had concentrated their activities at a site known locally as Huffman Prairie in Ohio in the US and constructed buildings adjacent to the flying area in which they could store and maintain their machines. Interestingly, it is claimed that the word 'hanger' comes from the French word for a hay barn.

These early flying fields were primarily designed for experimentation and initially did not feature demarcated runways. Pilots would merely point their aircraft into the wind and take off, regardless of the direction it was blowing from. However, despite the enthusiasm of these pioneers, designing aircraft was expensive, and to generate much-needed capital, many engineers and aviators staged air shows for the education and entertainment of the paying public. For reasons of safety and efficiency, these events necessitated the physical separation of publicly accessible landside areas from the technical airside areas where aircraft and their pilots were prepared for flight, and this early demarcation endures to this day.

The outbreak of the First World War prompted significant advances in aircraft design and technology. The new aircraft were larger and heavier than the early designs and required packed earth runways to support their weight. After the war ended, demobbed pilots were keen to use their new-found aeronautical prowess for peaceful purposes and began to form small private companies to operate air mail services and passenger flights. Following a short-lived but nonetheless pioneering passenger service across Tampa Bay in Florida in 1914, the world's first scheduled international service commenced between Hounslow Heath aerodrome, west of London, and Paris's Le Bourget airfield in August 1919. Despite only carrying one passenger and assorted high-value and perishable cargo (which reportedly included a brace of grouse and a pot of Devonshire cream), the inaugural flight proved the utility of employing aircraft for commercial purposes. By the mid-1920s, national governments in Europe and North America were actively promoting the development of municipal air facilities in major towns. In Great Britain, for example, Alan Cobham, Britain's self-appointed Air Ambassador, flew around the country advocating the formation of an aerodrome in every city as part of his Municipal Aerodrome Campaign, while in the US local corporations sought to finance and develop their own air facilities as statements of municipal pride and prestige. The frenzy of airfield construction that resulted led to a proliferation of airfields at a density that would far exceed future commercial requirements.

The introduction of regular international services from the 1920s onwards required the intervention of customs and immigration facilities, and a new word – 'airport' – was adopted to describe these new inland ports of the air. The development of progressively larger and heavier aircraft demanded the construction of more durable landing areas that could support the weight of the larger aircraft that were being introduced, and the first paved (as opposed to packed earth or grass) runway was reportedly constructed in Leipzig, Germany, in 1926. Despite their clear operational advantages and superior strength and drainage characteristics, then, as now, paved runways were expensive assets to construct and maintain (indeed, estimates of cost of constructing a third runway at London Heathrow Airport currently range from £16 billion to £19 billion), and a decision had to be taken regarding their siting and orientation to ensure that they were aligned as far as possible with the prevailing wind direction to ensure maximum usability.

As well as considering the operational requirements of the aircraft, attention was also given to the evolving needs of passengers. In the 1920s and 1930s, commercial flying remained an expensive and dangerous activity, and the early airlines had to persuade potential passengers that flying was not only safe and comfortable, but that it afforded distinct advantages over competing land-based modes of transport. At the time, only society's most affluent members could afford to fly and the airlines had to convince potential passengers to abandon the relative comfort and safety of steamships, private motor cars and railway carriages and take to the air. For example, at Croydon and Liverpool Speke airports in the UK, dedicated passenger terminals were constructed.

These buildings contained not only airline offices and air traffic control facilities, but also waiting areas, restaurants, newsagents, post offices, viewing facilities and customs posts for the convenience and comfort of the travelling public. One of the defining features of air travel was the length of time it took to process passengers and baggage. On arrival at the airport, individual travellers and their luggage were weighed and passengers were obliged to physically present themselves at a check-in desk at least an hour before take-off. Restaurants, shops and viewing areas were thus provided to make productive use of this 'dwell time' and perhaps distract passengers from the reality of the journey they were about to undertake. To permit operations during the hours of darkness and poor visibility, powerful searchlights were installed on the top of the buildings, and in time radio communication towers constructed to enable ground staff to speak directly to departing and arriving pilots.

The use of aircraft during the Second World War again stimulated advances in aeronautical design and technology. New navigation, communication and surveillance technologies were developed, mass aircraft production became the norm, and a new form of aircraft propulsion – the jet engine – was developed and utilised. These new aircraft required longer and stronger runways, and hundreds of new military airfields were constructed in the Allied and Axis nations to accommodate the new aerial squadrons. For example, in the UK, both the new and the hastily upgraded military airfields were taken over by central government and were generally provided with three paved intersecting runways. A small proportion of these sites would ultimately be redeveloped into commercial airports.

## From public to private: a UK example of the changing pattern of airport ownership

Following the end of the Second World War, the provision of airfields in Great Britain changed rapidly. London Airport (which was renamed Heathrow in 1966) opened to commercial flights in 1946, and by 2016 had developed into Europe's busiest airport, handling over 72 million passengers a year. The British government, keen to ensure the orderly development of post-war commercial flying in the country, enacted a National Airports Plan in 1947, under which strategically important airfields would be acquired for public ownership and developed for civilian use. The need for a national plan was based on the fact that airports are capital- and land-use-intensive infrastructure assets that require considered allocation of scare financial resources, as operating costs are high and few airports make a profit. In the 1966–1967 financial year, for example, the three Midlands airports made a cumulative loss of £390,000 after meeting their capital charges (Sealy, 1976).

In 1961, a British government White Paper had emphasised the importance of towns and cities getting directly involved in the provision and operation of local airports. The document advocated that individual airports should be relinquished from centralised state control and run as commercial enterprises for the first time. As in the US 20 years previously, British civic competitiveness encouraged local authorities to 'outdo' neighbouring air facilities in terms of the scale and scope of their buildings and infrastructure, and municipal airport design became highly competitive. However, in order to construct the required infrastructure, considerable building work was often required. The transformation of the redundant RAF Castle Donington airfield into the new civilian East Midlands Airport in central England in the early 1960s necessitated the removal of 630,000 cubic yards of earth, the infilling of thousands of tonnes of fly ash from the local power station to level the site, the construction of a new east–west runway, a 235,000-square-feet concrete aircraft apron complete with five stands, a 722-feet-long terminal building, an air traffic control tower, 1.5 miles of internal roads, and, arguably on the grounds of convenience and public utility rather than an appreciation of their future revenue-earning potential, a car park with space for 850 vehicles. At the same time, other nations were embarking on far more challenging airport development projects that variously involved land reclamation, coastal, estuarine and fluvial realignment, the removal and resettlement of local communities, and sculpting local terrain to smooth gradients and remove proximate obstructions.

The introduction of bigger and higher-capacity commercial aircraft during the 1960s caused air fares to fall and passenger demand to increase, and necessitated the construction of larger terminals and airside areas. The first generation of jet aircraft also resulted in the development and widespread adoption of new technologies, including the air bridge, moving walkway and automated baggage reclaim carousel, while growing incidents of terrorist attacks against aircraft and airports in the 1960s and 1970s resulted in the introduction of more rigorous and technologically mediated security screening. However, these rapid technological advances, combined with growing levels of traffic and the need to finance capital-intensive development programmes, had meant the business of running airports had become increasingly complex.

In 1965, the British government passed the Airports Authority Act, which established the British Airports Authority (BAA) as a new government-owned independent commercial enterprise. In April 1966, BAA assumed responsibility for four of the 22 government-owned airports – London Heathrow, Gatwick, Stansted, and Prestwick Airport on the Ayrshire coast in Scotland. Edinburgh, Aberdeen and Glasgow Airports followed in the early 1970s. Under the terms of the Act, the UK Civil Aviation Authority (CAA) retained statutory powers to regulate airport charges consistent with the terms of the 1977 Bermuda II air service agreement with the US, which obliged the government to adopt a single-till approach to airport charges.

The inauguration of Boeing 747 'jumbo jet' services in 1970 demanded a transformation in the scale and scope of airport operations. Apron areas, taxiways and runways had to be expanded and reinforced to support the aircraft's increased physical size and weight. Terminal buildings had to be expanded to accommodate the increased numbers of passengers, bags and cargo the aircraft could transport. However, while new higher-capacity wide-bodied aircraft such as the Boeing 747 were lowering the price of air fares and stimulating increased passenger demand for flight, they were also posing an environmental and public relations challenge for airports.

Although concern about aircraft noise had been articulated by local communities living near busy aerodromes as early as the 1920s, the widespread introduction of jet aircraft in the 1960s and 1970s spread the issue of noise pollution and emissions over a wider area, and forced some airports, including London Heathrow and Idlewild (later JFK) in New York, to introduce operating restrictions and noise curfews to manage and mitigate, as far as possible, the acoustic impact of aircraft operations on local communities. In theoretical terms, the global space of air traffic flows was now imposing ever-greater burdens on immobile local people and places.

While concerns about the environmental impact of aviation continued to grow (see Chapters 18 and 25), moves towards privatisation and increased commercialisation began to gain traction in the UK in the early 1980s. As part of its wide-ranging public sector reforms, the UK government announced its intention in the Airports Policy White Paper of 1985 to privatise BAA. In December 1985, BAA plc was incorporated under the 1986 Airports Act. This resulted in the transfer of BAA's property, rights and liabilities to a new public limited company. In July 1987, 500 million shares in BAA plc were offered for sale and the company was listed on the London Stock Exchange with a capitalisation of £1,225,000,000 (ICAO, 2013). The new company bought Southampton Airport in 1990 and sold Prestwick Airport to PIK facilities in 1992. In 1996, the UK government sold its remaining 2.9 per cent stake in BAA plc but retained a golden share to prevent a full takeover by foreign investors. This golden share was redeemed in September 2003 in response to a European Court of Justice ruling.

In 2006, a consortium led by the Spanish construction group Ferrovial took over BAA plc, delisted it from the London Stock Exchange and changed its name to BAA Ltd. In August 2008, the UK Competition Commission ruled that BAA Ltd must sell off two of its three London airports and one of its Scottish ones. London Gatwick Airport was duly sold to Global Investment Partners (GIP) and other investors in 2009/10, Edinburgh Airport was sold to GIP in 2012, and London Stansted Airport was sold to Manchester Airports Group (MAG) in 2013. By 2012, investments by foreign institutions and sovereign wealth funds, which included investments by the Chinese, Singaporean and Qatari governments, had reduced Ferrovial's stake to just over a third, and the remaining airports at London Heathrow, Glasgow, Aberdeen and Southampton were operated under stand-alone brands.

At the same time as BAA was being privatised, large local authority-operated regional airports in the UK, including Manchester, Birmingham, East Midlands and London Luton, were also being corporatised. The 1986 Airports Act required municipal airports with a turnover in excess of £1 million to become public airport companies. By 1993, changes in government borrowing requirements meant that the future development of these facilities could only be funded through private sector finance (ICAO, 2013). Subsequently, many UK airports have now been privatised (Ison et al., 2011).

## Airport privatisation

The British government's privatisation of BAA in 1987 started a trend towards greater private sector involvement in airports (Gillen, 2011). Privatisation aims to reduce government debt and liabilities, attract new investment, secure international expertise in operational efficiencies, open up the market to greater competition and remove government restrictions (Graham, 2011). Airport privatisation is often thought of as transferring the whole airport from public to private operation and/or ownership, but private sector involvement at airports can take many forms, from least to full privatisation (see Table 3.2). The decision to privatise some or all of an airport's property, assets and operations is motivated by many factors, including the need to secure cash injections by selling certain assets, repaying debt, enhancing revenues, improving levels of efficiency and productivity, and/or raising additional capital for development and expansion projects.

*Table 3.2* Types of airport privatisation

| Type | Characteristics |
| --- | --- |
| Least privatisation (management arrangement) | Services such as cleaning, maintenance, parking and non-police security are contracted out to private firms but the main airport asset remains in public ownership. |
| Public–private partnerships (PPPs) or concession arrangement | A partnership between the public and private sectors that delivers a project or service that has traditionally been provided by the public sector. A government grants a private company the right to develop, build, maintain and/or operate a public asset (such as an airport terminal) for a contracted period of time. The asset is still owned by the government but the private party generally assumes the financial risk for it. PPPs are intended to increase the quality, efficiency and competitiveness of an airport and/or raise additional finance or overcome budget restrictions. Governments retain responsibility for safety, security and economic oversight. |
| Full privatisation | Involves the long-term lease or sale of an entire airport to a private operator. |

*Source*: Derived from LeighFisher (2010).

*Table 3.3* The changing nature of private airport investors in the UK, 1980s to 2010s

| Decade | Type | Example companies | Example airport |
|---|---|---|---|
| 1980s | Airport operating companies | BAA (privatised from 1987) | London Heathrow |
| 1990s | Transport providers | National Express, Stagecoach, First Group | East Midlands |
| 2000s | Infrastructure funds/ companies | Macquirie, Infratil, Global Infrastructure Partners, Ferrovial, Balfour Beatty | Exeter |
| 2010s | Banks, sovereign wealth funds, overseas pension funds | Ontario Teachers' Pension Plan, Future Fund Boards of Guardians | Bristol |

*Source*: Data based on an original survey by LeighFisher (2010) with author additions.

By 2016, over 40 per cent of European airports had at least some private shareholders (ACI Europe, 2016). Significantly, the type of private shareholder has changed over time, with sovereign wealth funds and pension funds taking over from the first generation of private owners, which were predominantly airport operating companies or transport providers (see Table 3.3 for a UK example, and more generally Graham and Morrell, 2016).

Over the past decade, overseas banks, sovereign wealth funds and pension plans have become active airport investors. The Canadian Ontario Teachers' Pension Plan (OTPP), for example, began investing in airports in 2002 and currently owns 100 per cent of Bristol Airport in the UK plus stakes in Birmingham (UK), London City, Brussels and Copenhagen Airports.

Although some countries, including India, Brazil and South Africa, have chosen to sell off some or all of their airport assets to the private sector (see ACI, 2017 for an overview), other nations have sought to retain public ownership of them. Thus, it is important to state that the move towards privatisation is not universal. In the US, for example, municipalities and the Federal Aviation Administration (FAA) retain ownership and control of most major commercial facilities. Hartsfield-Jackson Atlanta International Airport in Georgia, the busiest passenger airport in the US, for example, is owned by the City of Atlanta and operated by the Atlanta Department of Aviation. Worldwide, as of 2013, 70.8 per cent of airports were still in public ownership, with 15.4 per cent operated as a PPP and only 13.8 per cent in full private ownership, which equates to 66.7 per cent, 17.9 per cent and 15.4 per cent of global passengers, respectively (ACI, 2015). Consequently, despite the moves towards privatisation in certain markets, public ownership remains an important aspect of the airport industry.

## Airport profitability

Airports and other transport infrastructure are often considered to be attractive assets in which to invest, not least because ACI (2016) reported an industry net profit margin of 16 per cent, a global return on invested capital of 6.3 per cent and global industry year-on-year growth (2014–2015) of 8.2 per cent. However, it is important to realise that these figures hide significant variation. Although some airports are profitable, many smaller facilities still operate at a loss and have relied on continued public subsidy to remain operational (see Chapter 12). In 2014, ACI estimated that 69 per cent of airports worldwide operate at net loss. In Europe, 51 per cent of airports make a loss. The majority of these loss-making airports (81 per cent of the world total) are small facilities handling under 1 million passengers per annum, and so do not have the traffic or passenger volumes to generate sufficient levels of revenue. In Europe, 77 per cent of these smaller airports make a loss (ACI Europe, 2017).

One such example of a loss-making airport in the UK is Glasgow Prestwick Airport, a facility that was bought back into public ownership in late 2013 for a token price of £1 amid concerns that the facility could close. In the 2015–2016 financial year, Prestwick handled 624,000 passengers and 11,409 tonnes of cargo but reported a loss of £9.2 million, an increase on the £8.9 million reported the previous year, with some sources suggesting the bailout could reach £40 million by 2018 (BBC News, 2017).

Although it is presumed that larger airports are more likely to be profitable, ACI figures show that even some airports that handle over 25 million passengers a year still report a loss. However, analysis by CAPA (2015) suggests that geographic location as well as passenger throughput influences airport profitability, with airports in some countries in the Far East outperforming the financial performance of comparatively sized facilities in neighbouring countries. Thus, it would appear that both size and the regulatory environment in which an airport operates are key to profitability.

Losses, combined with increased pressures on public spending, have led to the desirability (and even the legality) of state interventions and subsidies to be questioned. In 2004, for example, the European Commission (EC) stated its intention to introduce tighter regulations for state aid for airports and airlines in an attempt to prevent overcapacity and market distortion. The intervention was controversial, with many criticising the policy and claiming it would damage the competitiveness of European aviation vis-à-vis the still heavily state-subsidised markets of the Middle East and other regions. New regulations in this area, still very contentious, were agreed by the EC in 2014 (EC, 2014).

One of the main issues would appear to be the ability of airports to recoup the cost of infrastructure provision. It is rare for airports to cover the cost of their operation from aeronautical charges alone, and so airport operators and owners have been forced to develop alternative revenue streams from non-aeronautical sources (see Chapter 12 for a discussion of the complementarities between the aeronautical and non-aeronautical areas). Of the total global industry revenue of US$142.5 billion, 55.5 per cent comes from aeronautical charges, 40.4 per cent from non-aeronautical sources and 4.1 per cent from non-operating revenues. The revenues from non-aeronautical activities (which include car parking, property development, airport retailing and consultancy) have become increasingly important in recent years, as the airport ownership model has become increasingly diverse and complicated. In 2014, non-aeronautical revenue accounted for 40.4 per cent of total airport revenues, with retail, car parking and property accounting for 28 per cent, 22 per cent and 15 per cent of this total, respectively (ACI, 2016). Although some critics and commentators claim airports have become giant shopping malls, retail is a vital revenue source for airports, and many airports would not be profitable or even viable if retail revenues were removed. In the year to 31 December 2016, Heathrow Airport Holdings reported that 'retail performed strongly' thanks to a rise in retail revenue of 7.6 per cent to £612 million (£569 million in 2015); £138 million came from tax and duty-free, £115 million from specialised airside shops and a further £114 million from car parking (Heathrow Airport Holdings Limited, 2016).

The progressive commercialisation of airports, both in Europe and around the world, has had far-reaching consequences for airlines, airports and consumers. Airports now increasingly have to compete for traffic in a competitive marketplace and appeal to both airlines and passengers. Competitive forces compel airports to offer a range of inducements (such as free or reduced price landing charges, marketing assistance or other forms of incentive) to get airlines to fly from their facility (see Chapter 14), while pressure from shareholders obliges airport operators to streamline their services and provide a high-value but cost-efficient service that not only enhances service quality, but also offers an attractive opportunity to potential investors while being resilient to changes in consumer demand, currency fluctuations and the dynamics of airline route development and withdrawal. Such market pressures are not discriminating, and exert an influence irrespective of whether an airport is publicly or privately owned.

## Conclusion

The global airport industry is highly dynamic, diverse and spatially uneven, and comprises complex internationally focused operations that exist within an increasingly competitive and market-oriented environment. The industry faces a range of challenges, including long-term commercial viability, growing environmental pressures, and ever-evolving and dynamic security concerns. In saying this, each airport is unique in terms of its geographical location, type of provision, traffic mix, infrastructure, size, ownership structure, and passenger and cargo volumes. The last century evolved from publicly owned transport interchanges into complex commercially oriented enterprises, often with considerable private sector financing and management involvement. However, the move towards greater airport privatisation is by no means universal, with many airports remaining under public ownership and control.

## References

ACI (Airports Council International) (2015). *Airports Economic Report*, 19th edition, Montreal, ACI.

ACI (Airports Council International) (2016). *Airport Economics Report and KPIs for Financial Year 2014*, 20th edition, Montreal, ACI.

ACI (Airports Council International) (2017). *Airport Ownership, Economic Regulation and Financial Performance*, Montreal, ACI.

ACI Europe (Airports Council International Europe) (2016). *The Ownership of Europe's Airports 2016*, Brussels, ACI Europe.

ACI Europe (Airports Council International Europe) (2017) *Fast facts*. Online. Available at: www.aci-europe.org (accessed 8 May 2017).

ATAG (Air Transport Action Group) (2016). *Aviation: Benefits Beyond Borders*, Geneva, ATAG.

BBC News (2017) *Losses increase at Glasgow Prestwick Airport*. Online. Available at: www.bbc.co.uk/news/uk-scotland-scotland-business-3879248 (accessed 8 May 2017).

Bonnefoy, P., de Neufville, R. and Hansman, J. (2008). Evolution and development of multi-airport systems: a worldwide perspective, *Journal of Transport Engineering*, 136(11), 1021–1029.

CAPA (Centre for Aviation) (2015) *Airport financial results 1H2015: primary airports, hubs, alliances, retail sustain profitability*. Online. Available at: https://centreforaviation.com/insights/analysis/airport-financial-results-1h2015--primary-airports-hubs-alliances-retail-sustain-profitability-240555 (accessed 8 May 2015).

CIA (Central Intelligence Agency) (2016a). *The world factbook field listing: airports*. Online. Available at: www.cia.gov/library/publications/the-world-factbook/fields/2053.html (accessed 16 November 2016).

CIA (Central Intelligence Agency) (2016b). *The world factbook field listing: airports with paved runways*. Online. Available at: www.cia.gov/library/publications/the-world-factbook/fields/2030.html (accessed 16 November 2016).

EC (European Commission) (2014). *Communication from the Commission: Guidelines on State Aid to Airports and Airlines*, Official Journal C99, 4 April.

Gillen, D. (2011). The evolution of airport ownership and governance, *Journal of Air Transport Management*, 17(1), 3–13.

Graham, A. (2011). The objectives and outcomes of airport privatisation, *Research in Transportation Business & Management*, 1(1), 3–14.

Graham, A. and Morrell, P. (2016). *Airport Finance and Investment in the Global Economy*, Abingdon, Routledge.

Heathrow Airport Holdings Limited (2016) *Annual Report and Financial Statement for the Year Ended 31 December 2016*, Hounslow, Heathrow Airport Holdings Limited.

ICAO (International Civil Aviation Organisation) (2013). *Case Study on commercialization, privatization and economic oversight of airports and air navigation services providers: United Kingdom*. Online. Available at: www.icao.int/sustainability/CaseStudies/UnitedKingdom.pdf (accessed 11 November 2016).

Ison, S., Francis, G., Humphreys, C. and Page, R. (2011). UK regional airport commercialisation and privatisation: 25 years on, *Journal of Transport Geography*, 19(6), 1341–1349.

LeighFisher (2010). *The Global Airport Industry: Searching for the 'New Normal'*, London, LeighFisher.

Sealy, K. (1976). *Airport Strategy and Planning*, Oxford, Oxford University Press.

# 4

# Air traffic management and air navigation service providers

*Marc Bourgois, Eduardo García and Peter Hullah*

## Introduction

Air transport is vital for Europe's competitiveness. The safe, orderly and expeditious flow of this air traffic is ensured by the provision of airport and air traffic management (ATM) infrastructure, and air navigation services (ANS), whose provision is a state obligation under the Chicago Convention (ICAO, 2006) and is performed in accordance with global standards.

An air navigation service provider (ANSP) must be able to adjust service provision dynamically to the heterogeneous performance requirements of their customers, the airspace users (both civil and military). While European airlines currently focus on questions relating to the cost-efficiency of ATM, safety is paramount, and capacity and environmental criteria are equally important to enhancing competitiveness.

At the turn of the century, it was apparent that the continuous increase in air transport demand in Europe, together with growth in Eastern Europe, the Middle East and Asia, would cause severe capacity and safety deficiencies in Europe's ATM system. Delays in European air traffic also increased sharply because every country had a national approach to route structures, fragmenting the airspace on national, rather than functional, boundaries (see Chapter 16 for a discussion on issues relating to airport capacity). The European Union's (EU) Single European Sky (SES) legislation was developed to overcome these problems (EC, 1999). Two SES packages were adopted, in 2004 and in 2009, to reduce fragmentation, to better define the responsibilities of regulators and operators, to enhance the performance of ANSs and to reduce the cost of these services.

This chapter focuses on the major legal, technical and transversal aspects of modern ATM. It begins with a discussion of the applicable regulatory, organisational and business frameworks. This is followed by a description of the new technical developments designed to equip ATM for the twenty-first century. The transversal aspects of network management, the environment and safety are then expounded. The final section provides a conclusion. The chapter focuses on the European situation, but also has relevance to other dense air traffic areas such as the US, and to areas experiencing rapid air traffic growth such as from the Middle East through to South East Asia and China.

# ATM frameworks

## Institutional and regulatory framework for ATM

The normative framework for air navigation service provision is set: globally by the Chicago Convention, and its annexes developed and agreed by ICAO and its member states; at a European level by relevant EU legislation; and nationally by individual states. Globally binding ICAO standards are an essential basis for ensuring global interoperability, but they are usually the lowest common denominator and require complementary regional and local rules so that specific operational requirements may be taken account of. Sensible exemptions at local or national levels must continue to be possible to ensure the highest level of safety and service quality at European airports and in European airspaces.

European ATM rule-making competencies are exercised by the EU and the individual states. The European Commission (EC) entrusted the European Aviation Safety Agency (EASA) with the drafting of aviation safety legislation and providing technical advice to the EC and the EU member states. Since its creation in 2002, the remit of EASA has gradually increased. The European Organisation for the Safety of Air Navigation (EUROCONTROL) is an intergovernmental organisation committed to developing safe and seamless ATM across Europe. It does not have rule-making powers, but provides support to its member states at their request.

States have sovereignty over their national airspace, and are therefore responsible for ensuring the provision of ANSs and implementing global and European regulation, including the supervision of its application by public or private ANS entities, within their territory. The designation of certified ANSPs, and the system for certifying them, for a particular airspace respects this sovereignty, and will continue to do so. However, cross-border operations must be optimised, and cooperation in rule-making between groups of states to support cross-border arrangements for service provision is encouraged.

Regulatory functions such as certification of organisations or systems, supervision, enforcement and target-setting should be executed by organisations that are independent of interest groups, stakeholders and the regulated entities themselves, as well as of the legislative and rule-making entities. Their decisions should be subject to an appeal process in the respective national legal system.

Cooperation and collaboration between national supervisory authorities (NSAs) at all levels will be vital for increased harmonisation in rule-making, contributing to the creation of a level playing field, and enhancing cost-efficiency. EASA is complementary to the NSAs and performs regulatory functions in the ATM domain. These cover rule-making, supervision and certification of multinational or non-European service providers, certification of safety critical systems, peer review of NSAs, and the development of acceptable means of compliance (AMC) and/or guidance material to support the application of ATM regulation.

The current ATM regulatory framework is mainly prescriptive and requires comprehensive regulatory guidelines prescribing detailed acceptance criteria for meeting regulatory requirements. A 'performance-based' approach focuses on desired, measurable outcomes rather than prescriptive processes, and can become an important tool for managing and enhancing performance despite the significant growth in air traffic expected. Performance indicators allow for an assessment of the observed situation, measuring trends, providing feedback and helping to identify the means of achieving the specified goals. In the last decade, ICAO has stressed the importance of implementing a performance-based approach at all levels (global, regional and national), and the 11th Air Navigation Conference in 2003 urged ICAO to develop a performance framework for air navigation systems and to ensure that the future global ATM system is performance-based. The EC and EASA have also shown their intention to further develop a European approach to a performance-based environment (EASA, 2014).

Legislation and rules ('hard law') are complemented by guidance material, AMCs, industry standards and specifications, and non-binding material ('soft law'), which support the implementation of rules, interoperability of systems, harmonisation of specifications, and deployment of new technology and operational procedures.

There is an increased need for new technical standards arising from the transition to performance-based regulation, global and regional interoperability of ATM systems, and SESAR[1] deployment. Standards can provide details of methods and evaluation criteria that are too complex to include within the regulations themselves and provide means of complying with the requirements. For example, technical standards are adopted by EASA as AMCs to illustrate means of establishing compliance with the EASA basic regulation and its implementing rules.

In 2016, the EC established the European Air Traffic Management Standards Coordination Group (EASCG)[2] to coordinate the ATM-related standardisation activities in Europe, essentially stemming from the European air traffic management master plan (ATM MP), in support of SES implementation. The main responsibility of the EASCG is to develop, monitor and maintain a rolling European ATM standardisation development plan based on the standardisation road map from the SESAR framework and inputs from the EASCG members (including the military). In 2017, the EC established a similar group, the European Unmanned Aircraft Systems (UAS) Standards Development Group, to streamline the numerous standards developing activities related to UAS currently performed in Europe.

The evolution of the regulatory and standardisation roles of the various global and European institutions is summarised in Table 4.1.

*Table 4.1* Evolution of the regulatory and standardisation roles in ATM

| Organisation | Current role | Future role |
| --- | --- | --- |
| ICAO | Global standards (binding), recommendations, Procedures for Air Navigation Services (PANS), guidance material (non-binding) | Unchanged |
| ISO | Global industry standards (not ATM-specific) | Unchanged |
| RTCA | Aeronautical industry standards in the United States (US) | Unchanged |
| EUROCAE | Aeronautical industry standards in Europe | Main standardisation body for ATM in Europe |
| CEN/CENELEC | European industry standards (including in support of SES interoperability rule) | European industry standards (not ATM-specific) |
| ETSI | European industry standards (including in support of SES interoperability rule) | European industry standards (not ATM-specific) |
| EASA/EAA | AMC and guidance material (GM) (in support of EASA regulations) | Principally unchanged; AMC and GM should as far as possible be based on industry standards |
| EUROCONTROL | EUROCONTROL specifications and guidelines | Unchanged |

*Note*: Acronyms not yet mentioned in this chapter are International Civil Aviation Organisation (ICAO), International Organisation for Standardisation (ISO), Radio Technical Commission for Aeronautics (RTCA) and European Aviation Agency (EAA).

## SES and Functional Airspace Blocks (FABs)

Each European state has developed different ways of organising the provision of ANSs, with each using a different ATM infrastructure. Rather than routes designed to optimise the operational requirements of airspace users across the continent, national approaches caused gross inefficiencies in the route structure. In the 1990s, EUROCONTROL's European Air Traffic Control Harmonisation and Integration Programme (EATCHIP) brought some progress towards efficiency in the system and laid the necessary groundwork for the SES, initiated by the EU in 1999 (EC, 1999). The SES was designed to bring an end to delays that would otherwise be exacerbated by constant growth in the volume of traffic and increased safety requirements.

The first SES package was published in March 2004, based on four regulations (EC, 2004a, 2004b, 2004c, 2004d): a framework – the basic layout of the SES; airspace organisation – FABs; interoperability – making different air traffic control (ATC) systems interoperable; and service provision – harmonised certification of ANSPs for service provision. A second package of legislation, SES II, was launched in 2008 (EC, 2008a). SES II concerned improving performance. It consisted of four pillars:

- *Regulating performance*: An independent performance review body (PRB) was established to oversee the performance of the system and set targets. It foresaw the designation of a European network manager.
- *Safety*: The competency of EASA was extended to cover aerodromes, air traffic management and air navigation services, so that safety regulation could be harmonised and applied uniformly.
- *Technology*: The SESAR project was launched to provide the technical solutions to enable SES objectives to be achieved.
- *Airport capacity*: An airport observatory was established to assist the EC in addressing airport capacity, which must remain aligned with ATM capacity to preserve the overall efficiency of the network, and quality challenges.

The FABs are defined (EC, 2004a) as:

> an airspace block based on operational requirements and established regardless of state boundaries, where the provision of air navigation services and related functions are performance-driven and optimised with a view to introducing, in each Functional Airspace Block, enhanced cooperation among air navigation service providers or, where appropriate, an integrated provider.

The SES II regulation required all EU members to be part of an FAB by the end of 2012. Nine FABs have been established, each including a selection of entire states (see Table 4.2 and Figure 4.1). FABs were created to: enhance safety – remove the risk of border interference and national inconsistencies in safety procedures by enabling aircraft to fly seamlessly across borders; and reduce costs and fuel consumption – save fuel and reduce delays by enabling aircraft to fly straighter lines at better altitudes. The latter will improve the service delivered to passengers, bring benefits to the environment, both in terms of reduced noise and emissions, and greatly reduce the cost of flying.

In July 2015, the EC launched infringement proceedings against some member states that it believed were slowing down the process of implementing FABs, costing some €5 billion annually (EC, 2015). Also in 2016, the PRB (2016) stated that:

Marc Bourgois et al.

> FABs as implemented . . . bring more fragmentation . . ., blur accountability . . ., generate additional costs . . . and sometimes act as obstacles . . ., all of which goes against performance and adds significant costs in additional millions of euros.

The establishment of FABs enabled coordination at all levels (state, NSA, ANSPs) to deploy a number of changes that address the obligation of achieving performance improvements. This has led to various successes, such as joint airspace design, joint development of technical systems, joint training centres and, perhaps the most valuable benefit, free route airspace (FRA) projects. In some cases, FABs, particularly the smaller ones, seem to have been superseded by industrial partnerships (IPs). ANSPs claim that the results achieved by IPs, such as the Borealis

*Table 4.2* FABs and participating states

| Name of the FAB | Participating states |
| --- | --- |
| BALTIC FAB | Poland, Lithuania |
| BLUE MED | Italy, Malta, Greece, Cyprus (Egypt, Tunisia, Albania, Jordan as observers) |
| Danish-Swedish FAB/NUAC | Denmark, Sweden |
| DANUBE | Bulgaria, Romania |
| FABCE (FAB Central Europe) | Austria, Bosnia and Herzegovina, Croatia, Czech Republic, Hungary, Slovak Republic, Slovenia |
| FABEC (FAB Europe Central) | Belgium, France, Germany, Luxembourg, the Netherlands, Switzerland |
| NEFAB (North European FAB) | Estonia, Finland, Latvia, Norway |
| SW FAB (South West FAB) | Spain, Portugal |
| UK-IRELAND FAB | United Kingdom, Ireland |

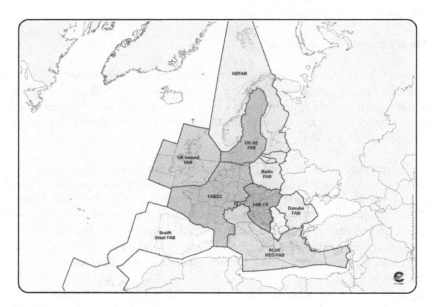

*Figure 4.1*   FABs and participating states

*Source*: With permission from EUROCONTROL.

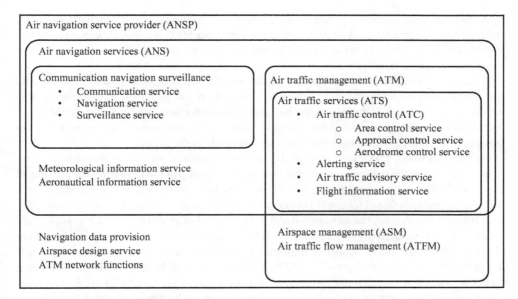

*Figure 4.2* Scope of ATM/ANS

*Source*: Authors.

and COOPANS[3] alliances, may become more important than FABs, at least in driving technological progress.

## New service provider business models

Figure 4.2 presents a breakdown of the different ATM and ANS functions as specified in the AMC/GM of Commission Implementing Regulation (EU) 2017/373 (EC, 2017b). It is important to note that ATM/ANS include more services than 'air traffic management' and 'air navigation services' together. In future, states could manage these functions through direct designation, regulation or certification, but the entities fulfilling them will, as today, include state-owned ANSPs, corporatised/privatised ANSPs, EU agencies and private companies. By 2035, it is likely that there will be a move towards liberalisation and consequent outsourcing (subcontracting) of certain ATM/ANS services, and subsequently competition. There could also be centrally provided services and functions (even if the provision of central services is likely to be a result of a competitive process).

A number of different infrastructure ownership options and models are currently in place. These not only vary between ANSPs, but also within ANSPs, depending on the type of infrastructure. A given element of infrastructure can be owned by: the ANSP or an alliance of ANSPs; the state or an alliance of states; one or more local or regional authorities; a private company or an IP or consortium; or a public–private partnership (PPP) between one or many authorities or states and one or many private companies.

As ATM moves towards a more service-based system over time, it will require a data network system such as system-wide information management (SWIM), and current 'local' ownership may no longer be appropriate. This could bring a shift towards joint ownership of infrastructure (through alliances, PPPs or IPs), in some cases leased from or managed by private entities or consortiums.

At present, data provision is fragmented, but it will have significantly evolved by 2035, bringing the potential for cross-border applications, and thus for new entrants to provide ANSs. SWIM will be in place, creating a more holistic system enabling significant changes for the provision of communication.

There are a number of drivers for change that need to be evaluated to determine the role that ANSPs have in delivering communications, navigation and surveillance (CNS) services in the future. There is likely to be a move towards outsourcing (subcontracting by ANSPs) and liberalisation of certain services. This discussion also links back to infrastructure ownership in terms of how ANSPs will manage their data service needs in the future.

As infrastructure, ANS functions and data provision dimensions evolve through to 2035, so will the models for delivering air traffic flow management (ATFM). SWIM will provide all players with information about the state of the network from six months before a flight through to the real-time situation. This could change the distribution of the network optimisation functions between the central, the subregional and the local level. The drivers for such change could come from users who, in developing optimal 4D trajectories for their flights, will enhance flight planning tools to include all available information, and from new entrants wanting to provide different solutions. This will provide ANSPs with opportunities both in terms of developing their own network management tools and, from the point of view of being an ATFM 'customer', the ability to obtain network management services in the most cost-effective way.

## New ATM technologies and concepts

The ICAO Global Air Navigation Plan (GANP) (ICAO, 2013a) provides a long-term vision to assist ICAO, states and industry in ensuring continuity and harmonisation among their various modernisation programmes (i.e. SESAR, the Next Generation Air Transportation System [NextGen], and Collaborative Action for Renovation of Air Transport Systems [CARATS]). Europe's modernisation programme is called SESAR and is driven from research and development to deployment by the European ATM MP (SESAR JU and EUROCONTROL, 2015). Continuous collaboration between European stakeholders and ICAO has given international visibility to the European perspective it describes. However, the baseline of ATM systems is still a complex patchwork, and the timely and successful implementation of changes will require flexibility so that it can be adapted to local conditions and operation-specific factors. This is particularly important because these conditions have enabled the establishment of a strong safety culture, and Europe can be proud of its safety record. While it is recognised that improvements in cost-effectiveness and quality of service are still expected, these changes will have to be introduced in an incremental manner to ensure they are not detrimental to safety, and in compliance with regulatory requirements (e.g. supported by safety cases approved by NSAs and/or EASA).

'Seamless operations' – functioning, from an airspace-user perspective, as if a single entity were managing the airspace – will be achieved through harmonised evolution of ATM architecture, supported by standards and specifications developed by industry for ATM stakeholders. ANSP involvement in SESAR and its successor SESAR2020 shows that they recognise the need to increase their collaboration on operational and technological issues. In addition, the SESAR development process supports the timely availability of necessary standards and guidance material facilitating the introduction of operational and functional ATM changes. A service-oriented approach, key to ensuring and facilitating interoperability between stakeholders, enables the facilitation of upgrades and provides increased agility for introducing innovative solutions into the ATM system.

A comprehensive implementation of performance-based navigation (PBN) is expected by 2030. In the EU, this is likely to be accompanied by a rationalisation plan for navigation infrastructure to control maintenance and replacement costs. The evolution of ground automation and communications integrated with appropriate aircraft systems, in particular through the exchange of intent data from air to ground, will provide the foundation for an ATC environment based much more on strategic management than on tactical control, relegating voice communication to non-routine, recovery and/or emergency cases.

## SESAR

The EU's SES policy initiated a major disruption in how Europe's ATM was organised and run, and it was obvious that the operations and technologies in use at the time would not cope with the increased capacity that SES, when fully realised, should bring. A major research effort was necessary, involving substantial investment. This technical research and development arm of the SES is the SESAR programme that is divided into three phases: definition, development and deployment. The definition phase ran from 2005 to 2008 and cost €60 million (€50 million from the EU, €10 million from industry) and led to the creation of the initial ATM MP.

The SESAR Joint Undertaking (SJU) was jointly founded by the EC and EUROCONTROL and established by EU regulation in 2007 (EC, 2007) to manage the development phase. The SJU is a PPP ensuring stakeholder buy-in and financing of its work. The undertaking's €2.1 billion budget from 2008 to 2016 was provided a third each by the EC, EUROCONTROL and the industrial partners. A second part of this phase, branded SESAR2020, runs to 2024 at a similarly financed cost of €1.6 billion.

The SESAR Deployment Manager (SDM), appointed in December 2014, is responsible for the deployment phase, beginning with the pilot common project (PCP) – 24 solutions to be deployed across Europe between 2015 and 2024 (EC, 2014). SESAR deployment will run to 2035 and will cost between €18 billion and €28 billion, approximately 90 per cent of which will come from the industry, the remainder funded by the EU.

The EC set the following high-level objectives for the SES, and thus for SESAR: a threefold increase in capacity; safety improved by a factor of 10; a 10 per cent reduction in environmental impact per flight; and at least a 50 per cent reduction in the cost of ATM service provision. These ATM goals are independent of the impact of improved aircraft technologies. Estimated benefits by 2030 due to SESAR are listed in Table 4.3.

The initial SESAR development phase consisted mainly of industrial research – bringing technologies that were already in the pipeline to a point where they could be deployed. SESAR2020 will have an emphasis on exploratory research (around 50 per cent of its budget) and very large-scale demonstrations. It will focus on four areas: airports, air traffic services, ATM network optimisation and aviation infrastructure. It will also take on board modern questions that were barely on the horizon during the SESAR definition phase: the safe integration of drones into the airspace, and cyber security.

*Table 4.3* Benefits of full SES/SESAR implementation by 2030

| | |
|---|---|
| 20 million | Flights handled per year |
| 10-minute | Reduction in average flight time |
| Within 1 minute | Punctuality (compared with planned arrival time) |
| €3 billion | Efficiency savings |
| €6 billion | Flight efficiency savings |
| 18 million | Tonnes of carbon dioxide ($CO_2$) saved per year |

*Source*: Adapted from Airline Leader (2015).

The SESAR operational concept is based on an airspace user's preferred 'business trajectory', defined with high precision in four dimensions without predefined routes. It is the job of air transport systems (ATSs) to enable this trajectory safely and cost-efficiently within infrastructure and environmental constraints. Airports will be fully integrated into the system, and interoperability between civil and military systems will be a key feature. The ATM system will be supported by a net-centric SWIM environment, including aircraft and ground facilities, to assist collaborative decision-making.

## Common support services

The deployment of the SWIM framework will enable a seamless exchange of information and will foster collaboration between aviation stakeholders, especially ANSPs, with the aim of providing more cost-efficient, safer and more sustainable ATM. The evolution towards an open ATM architecture and the virtualisation of technical rooms and control rooms will enable the introduction of common support services designed to improve operational performance and provide cost-effectiveness and flexible use of resources.

Common support services are defined in the ATM MP (SESAR JU and EUROCONTROL, 2015) as: "services that provide ATM capabilities in the same form to consumers that might have otherwise carried them out themselves, thus reducing fragmentation, enabling economies of scale, facilitating synergies and improving safety." The main aim of these common support services is to improve cost-effectiveness and resilience, and they should therefore only be introduced where they are seen as being beneficial and delivering customer value in meeting, or at least responding to, customer needs. Common support services could be provided at global, regional and local levels by one single organisation, or there could be several such providers (the decentralised approach). These services should be performance-based and technology-agnostic. Their definition and standardisation is essential for their successful implementation.

This service-oriented approach must be based on flexible, simple and transparent governance; in particular, it must address the issues of liability and continuity of service, both for individual ANSPs and for industrial partnerships. Such governance will play a supporting role in the rationalisation of infrastructure at a regional level and will probably also be a key trigger for the move towards virtualisation (e.g. the implementation of virtual centres).

## Remote tower services

In April 2016, LFV, the Swedish ANSP, put the world's first remote ATC tower into service – the remote control position is at Sundsvall, 150 kilometres south of the controlled airport at Örnsköldsvik. There are two parts to the set-up of a remote-control tower. At the airport, high-resolution cameras provide a 360° view, with a pan-tilt-zoom camera to replace the binoculars of traditional towers. These may be infrared-sensitive for viewing at night or under low-visibility weather conditions. At the remote-control centre, a conventional controller working position with its suite of decision support tools is complemented by a panoramic display system reproducing the out-of-the-window view via high-speed image transmission. Appropriate redundancy is engineered into this to cope with occasional outages.

In just 11 years since the first research project on the remote tower was awarded public funding,[4] this technology has rapidly matured to a level where several commercial products from companies such as Saab, Frequentis or Indra are competing. The fact that remote tower technology closely mimics current operations is one of the reasons it has been approved by ATC unions. Allowing controllers to work in more attractive locations has also played a role in creating the win-win required for successful technology adoption.

Remote tower operations have many benefits. Airport operations are lifelines to regional economies, and the remote tower concept offers the possibility of operating commercial flights at local airports where the construction or operation of a physical tower might not make economic sense given the low traffic volumes.

The solution at Sundsvall is the first of a series of gradually more complex operational scenarios. It is expected that the remote tower concept will move, through further validation exercises and demonstrations, from controlling low-density airports to higher density airports. Ultimately, two or more airports may be controlled from the same centre, bringing substantial financial benefits, essentially based on a more optimal use of controllers, although there are considerable challenges in situational awareness to be faced. Other operational scenarios have spun off from the original remote tower concept. Several service providers are looking at remote towers as a means of making tower control services resilient to, for example, fire or terrorist attacks – the remote tower would be a fallback system if the physical tower became unusable.

EASA now has a rule-making task that covers the technical requirements for remote tower operations and has published guidance on the implementation of the remote tower concept from an operational point of view, and air traffic controller licensing aspects (EASA, 2015a).

## Remotely piloted aircraft systems

The total number of remotely piloted aircraft systems (RPASs), a subclass of UASs,[5] already exceeds that of manned aircraft by a factor of 10. In the next five years, small 'toy' RPASs are likely to treble in number, whereas the (currently small) number of commercial RPASs, which will need to share controlled airspace, is expected to grow tenfold over the same period (FAA, 2017). RPASs can take many forms, sizes and employ different propulsion methods. Although there is no pilot on board, they are still aircraft and need to operate safely alongside other air traffic. For this, they have to carry on-board technology for sustaining reliable command and control communications, accurate navigation and cooperative surveillance. In particular, 'detect and avoid' technology needs to guarantee an equivalent performance to the classic 'see and avoid', combined with collision avoidance safety nets. Detect and avoid, whether air-based or ground-based, is a major research area.

RPASs are an indispensable tool for the military and for police forces, and their other potential commercial uses are numerous: inspecting infrastructure networks (pipelines or high-tension power lines); crop monitoring; firefighting; and delivery of urgent medication (Airbus, 2015). Most mainstream RPAS operations will take place in low-level, sometimes urban, airspace, although others will use the airspace generally reserved for commercial aviation. This integration poses several main challenges to ATC: widely varying aircraft performance; intermittent communication delays; differing contingency procedures; and the limited visibility of small RPAS, all have to be dealt with. Much work is currently being undertaken, by national agencies (e.g. NASA), private companies and partnerships between the two, to develop Unmanned Aircraft System traffic management (UTM) systems that allow operators, pilots, drones and flights to be identified, planned, managed and logged, ensuring the safety of other drones, manned aircraft and third parties.

There are many open regulatory issues such as: how to ensure vehicle or operator identification, vehicle airworthiness, pilot qualification, safety of people on the ground; adequate respect for privacy; and security. All these issues are being studied by regulators at national and international levels, in particular by the Joint Authorities for Rulemaking on Unmanned Systems (JARUS). Basic, shared regulatory principles are already emerging, for example, that regulation should be proportional and risk-based (EASA, 2015b). This leads to a large consensus on a scheme for regulation such as the one given in Table 4.4.

*Table 4.4* Schema of regulatory principles for RPAS

| Category | Weight | Airspace | Regulation | Regulator | Risk analysis |
|----------|--------|----------|-----------|-----------|---------------|
| 'Harmless' | < 250 g | Very low/non-urban | 'Toy' directive | EU | Avoid carelessness |
| 'Open' | < 25 kg | To be determined | Operational limitations | National + EU | Product safety |
| 'Specific' | Beyond 'open' | | Numerous existing | National | Operations-specific |
| 'Certified' | > 150 kg | Controlled airspace | To be determined | EASA | As per manned aviation |

*Source*: Authors.

## Satellite applications

The Global Navigation Satellite System (GNSS), which provides global coverage without the requirement for ground-based navigation aids, is the main enabler of the transition to satellite-based CNS/ATM, a major pillar of ATM modernisation and rationalisation. A GNSS has three elements: earth-orbiting satellites; ground stations to track and monitor them; and users who rely on them to compute their position and motion. There are four independent GNSSs in operation today:

- The American Global Positioning System (GPS), originally a military system, became fully operational in 1994 with 24 satellites. It now has 31 satellites.
- Russia's global naviation satellite system called Globalnaya Navigazionnaya Sputnikovaya Sistema (GLONASS) currently has 24 operational satellites.
- The European Galileo system, planned to be fully operational by 2020 with 30 satellites, will be completely interoperable with GPS and GLONASS.
- The Chinese BeiDou Navigation Satellite system currently operates with 15 satellites servicing the Asia-Pacific region. Plans include a full-scale global navigation system of 35 satellites by 2020+.

New dual-frequency multi-constellation GNSS receivers will support the more demanding system performance provided by this robust multi-constellation environment, enabling new applications and advanced operations.

Satellite-based (SBAS), ground-based (GBAS) and aircraft-based augmentation systems (ABAS), defined in the ICAO GNSS standard (ICAO, 2013b), guarantee the levels of accuracy, availability, continuity and integrity of GNSS as required for aviation applications. Whereas GBAS broadcasts corrections from a base station on the ground directly to users, SBAS ground stations send corrections to geostationary satellites, which then broadcast the signals back to SBAS-capable on-board receivers. ABAS uses measurement redundancy and/or integrates the information obtained from the other GNSS elements with information available on board an aircraft to provide integrity.

Despite extensive non-ATC use, satellite communication (SATCOM) is currently only used for a small proportion of en route ATM communications. In the future, it will be the main means of communication over oceanic regions and, in the long term, over continents. GNSS's ability to provide navigation guidance for all phases of flight, from en route to precision approach, enables the PBN concept.

Automatic dependent surveillance-broadcast (ADS-B) is a surveillance technology with which an aircraft determines its position via satellite navigation and periodically broadcasts it to simple ground receiver stations (ground-based ADS-B), enabling the aircraft to be tracked by other aircraft, by controllers and by public 'radar-tracking' applications. In the near future, 'space-based ADS-B' reports, collected and distributed by low earth orbit (LEO) satellites, will facilitate continuous global coverage, including polar and oceanic areas. The first such system is expected to be available in 2017.

The introduction of PBN is a high priority in ICAO's GANP 2013–2028 and ICAO assembly resolution A37-11 (ICAO, 2010) called for implementation of required navigational performance (RNP) approach procedures with vertical guidance (APV) using either SBAS or barometric vertical navigation (Baro-VNAV). Although GNSS is expected to become more robust through the use of multi-frequency and multi-constellation technologies, the GANP still considers a reversionary mode based on purely non-GNSS technologies – instrument landing system (ILS), distance measuring equipment, and a gradually reduced network of VHF omnidirectional ranges (VORs) – to be necessary.

## Free routes

Aircraft originally navigated a path over beacons on the ground between their origin and destination, the directness of routes being limited by the number of ground beacons. On-board computers made it possible to triangulate between beacons, and thus to navigate independently of their geographical location. Despite this, it is estimated that an aircraft in European airspace today flies 20 kilometres more than it would do following a direct route.

Replacing the fixed route network with direct or user-preferred routes (UPRs) is the next step in optimising flight efficiency.

In FRA, users may freely plan a route between defined entry and exit points, possibly routing via intermediate waypoints, without reference to the fixed route network (SKYbrary, 2017). If intermediate waypoints are used, the route is called user-preferred; otherwise, it is called direct. In FRA, flights remain subject to ATC. This is one of the most cost-efficient operational improvements proposed today since it requires almost no new technology: existing avionics can deal with FRA and updates to the ATC ground systems are minimal. To maximise the benefit of FRA, there is a need for airlines to update their flight planning systems.

Shorter distances under FRA save time and fuel, and thus reduce costs and emissions. Full implementation of the FRA in Europe would save 17 million kilometres, 45,000 tonnes of fuel (worth €37 million) and 150,000 tonnes of $CO_2$ per year (EUROCONTROL, 2017a). There are, however, challenges linked to the introduction of FRA. Conflicts may become harder to detect due to the fact that they are more spread out and cannot be located as predictably. The likelihood of conflicts happening close to sector boundaries also requires increased vigilance and coordination. With a more dynamic route pattern, control sectors, which are tightly linked to traffic flows, and thus to the current route network, will have to evolve, and perhaps their boundaries adapted. Implementation, which started in 2008, is progressing gradually, first with night-time operations, then expanding into sets of predefined direct routes covering specific flows. It is estimated that by the end of 2021, most of European airspace will enable FRA (see Figure 4.3).

There are no specific regulations governing the implementation of free and user-prefereed routes. The use of free routes is authorised and promoted in Annex 1 of the EC's Network Manager regulation (EC, 2011a). Work is now progressing to the next level through merging FRAs from several FABs or ANSPs. As shown in Figure 4.3, cross-border implementation has already been achieved in a number of FABs, between FABs or between groups of ANSPs across FABs. Several ANSPs from different FABs have been awarded EU funding to implement the next phase of its FRA programme (NATS, 2016a).

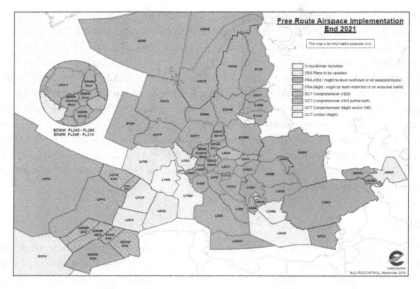

*Figure 4.3* Expected implementation of FRA in European airspace

*Source*: With permission from EUROCONTROL.

## Network issues

### *The Network Manager*

By the late 1980s, delays due to lack of ATC capacity became so damaging to the travelling public and to the economies of Europe that political intervention was unavoidable. A series of meetings of European air transport ministers (MATSE) took place, at the first of which it was agreed to create a centralised system of ATFM. EUROCONTROL took on the task of implementing this ATFM, and the central flow management unit (CFMU) was phased in from 1989, becoming fully operational and replacing earlier national and regional centres in 1996 (McInally, 2010). This task was extended in the second legislative package of the SES (SES II) and became known as 'network management'. The Network Manager was officially established in 2011 in the Network Manager Implementing Rule (NM IR) (EC, 2011a), and EUROCONTROL was officially nominated to this task for the period 2011–2019 (EC, 2011b).

Network management is a crucial component of the ATM performance scheme. The functions of the Network Manager are: developing route network design; management and operation of ATM functions, including ATFM; centralised frequency allocation; and coordinating the improvement of SSR code allocation. The NM IR lists the tasks to be performed by the Network Manager in relation to these functions.

Through a process of collaborative decision-making involving ATC units (currently 64 centres), airports, airlines flying through European airspace, and the miltary, the performance of the network is optimised (see Figure 4.4). This process relies on a hierarchy of shared traffic distribution plans, with the strategic time frame at the top, ahead of the winter or summer season, and the tactical planning of the day of operation at the bottom.

As in all air traffic tasks, there is a prominent concern for safety. In network management, safety translates primarily into protecting traffic control centres (or more specifically, sectors)

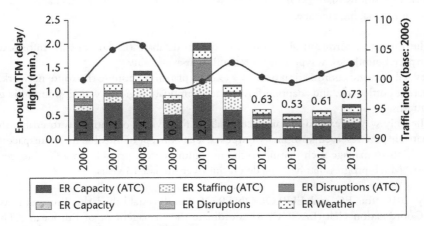

Figure 4.4   Evolution of ATFM delay, 2006 to 2015

*Source*: With permission from EUROCONTROL.

from over-deliveries. This means that the flows are managed centrally, such that the amount of traffic in a sector at any given time is not more than the number of planes the control team for that sector can handle simultaneously: the 'capacity' of the sector. A control centre supervisor can modulate the capacity by merging or splitting sectors, so that more or fewer controllers are available to handle the traffic demand. Note, however, that splitting a sector increases the inter-section coordination workload of the control team.

The coordination mechanisms available for the daily management of network traffic are also ideally suited to dealing with exceptional circumstances. Some events are exceptional but fore-seeable, such as major sports or political events generating additional traffic. Others are less fore-seeable, such as bad weather situations leading to reduced capacity at certain airports or large en route deviations due to wind or dangerous cloud or ice formations. Industrial actions of traffic control, airline or airport staff fall into this category. Other events are even more of a complete surprise, testing the network resilience to its utmost. A good example was the closure of large parts of European airspace following the volcanic eruptions in Iceland in 2010 that stranded up to 7 million passengers for eight days (Oxford Economics, 2010). In response to these more dramatic circumstances, the network management tasks were enlarged to cover crisis management.

Every day, operators of commercial flights in European airspace submit 35,000 mandatory flight plans, well in advance of departure. These are checked for consistency with the route structure, call-sign similarities (a known safety risk in radiotelephony communication between controllers and pilots) are deconflicted, and flights from airlines on the European blacklist are refused. Validated plans are distributed to the control centres along the planned routes, while corrections (in fewer than 9 per cent of submissions) and alternatives are suggested to airlines where appropriate.

It is possible that ATFM and capacity management measures could fail to prevent airport or airspace overload. As an ultimate measure to manage this overload, the Network Manager can delay departing flights by imposing 'first come, first served' departure slots that include a 15-minute window to allow controllers to build optimum sequences (e.g. due to wake vortex issues). In recent years, a better demand–capacity balance has been achieved by using collaborative processes, involving the different stakeholders, supported by a web-enabled Network Operations Plan (NOP). The Network Manager has various mechanisms and tools available for managing airspace:

- The European aeronautical information system database (EAD) contains information on airspace boundaries, waypoints, routes and their availability.
- Several strategic coordination processes exist to plan and optimise the route network, eliminating bottlenecks and adapting flow to accommodate regional variation in traffic growth patterns.
- The only way to extend the airspace available for civilian operations is to enable them to share airspace reserved for military purposes. The concept of 'flexible use of airspace' covers attempts to manage such sharing to the maximum extent possible on a flexible, real-time basis. Much progress has been made on this over the last 15 years.

In May 2010, the EC and EUROCONTROL jointly established the European Aviation Crisis Coordination Cell (EACCC) to coordinate the management of European ATM network responses to crisis situations. The EACCC establishes a consistent approach across Europe through close cooperation with corresponding structures in the states, including linking national contingency plans with others on a network level, proposing measures and taking initiatives, coordinating a response with mitigation actions and, in particular, acquiring and sharing information with the aviation community (decision-makers, airspace users and service providers) in a timely manner.

The EACCC consists of a representative of each of: the EU member state holding the Presidency of the European Council; the EC; EASA; EUROCONTROL; the Network Manager; the military; the ANSPs; airports; and airspace users.

## Environmental impact

The environmental impact of air transport is both a global and a local issue (see Chapters 17, 18 and 25). In terms of its effect on global warming, air transport contributes 3.5 per cent of global anthropogenic radiative forcing (IPCC, 1999). The aviation industry, through the Air Transport Action Group (ATAG), has agreed that emissions should stabilise by 2020 (carbon-neutral growth), and thereafter reduce to half of their 2005 values by 2050 (ATAG, 2012) (see Figure 4.5).

As discussed in Chapter 25 and shown in Figure 4.5, despite new technologies and operations, air transport emissions will increase in absolute terms (excluding alternative fuels and market-based measures) because the number of flights is increasing faster than technology can account for. Projections indicate sustained long-term growth, albeit at a low rate of 1.7 per cent compared with 4 per cent pre-2008, with 14 per cent more traffic in 2023 than in 2016 (STATFOR, 2017).

ATM's potential contribution to reducing climate impact is small. The introduction of reduced vertical separation minima (RVSM) in European airspace in January 2002 gave rise to a reduction of 1.6 to 2.3 per cent in fuel burn, and 0.7 to 1.0 per cent in emissions of nitrogen oxides ($NO_x$) (Jelinek et al., 2002). Current system optimisation means that fuel savings from direct routes or from more optimal climb and descent trajectories is limited to a few per cent, and the SES goal of a 10 per cent reduction in the environmental effect of an individual flight must be taken as a theoretical upper bound, only attainable if all flights flew perfect great-circle trajectories at optimal altitudes.

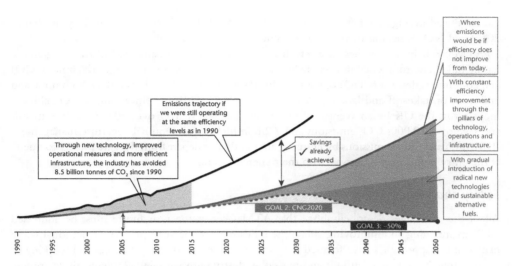

Where emissions would be if efficiency does not improve from today.

With constant efficiency improvement through the pillars of technology, operations and infrastructure.

With gradual introduction of radical new technologies and sustainable alternative fuels.

Emissions trajectory if we were still operating at the same efficiency levels as in 1990

Through new technology, improved operational measures and more efficient infrastructure, the industry has avoided 8.5 billion tonnes of $CO_2$ since 1990

Savings ✓ already achieved

GOAL 2: CNG2020

GOAL 3: –50%

*Figure 4.5*   A sustainable flightpath towards reducing emissions

*Source*: With permission from ATAG/IATA.

ATFM is a major contributor to fuel burn and $CO_2$ emission reduction by ensuring that an aircraft cannot take off until it can be certain to land without performing wasteful holding patterns. ADS-B implementation over oceanic areas could save about 440 kilotonnes (kt) of fuel annually by 2020 and 480 kt by 2025, giving carbon reductions of 1.4 million tonnes (Mt) and 1.5 Mt, respectively (Marais, 2016).

There has been much scientific debate about the impact of the condensation trails ('contrails') that an aircraft may create, and which may persist for long periods under specific atmospheric conditions, evolving into cirrus clouds. These can reduce warming during the day and reduce cooling at night. Similarly, aircraft climate impact may be subject to a 'multiplier effect' since emissions (e.g. $NO_x$, particulates and water vapour) from air transport take place directly in the upper atmosphere, where chemical processes are different and more harmful. Estimates for this radiative forcing factor have varied between 1 (no extra effect), through 1.9 (Sausen et al., 2005) and 2.7 (IPCC, 1999), but consensus seems to exist around 2.0 (DEFRA, 2007). In the future, ATM could help avoid contrail production and other climate impacts by optimising trajectories to avoid them (REACT4C, 2015). This will require detailed weather information, possibly transmitted via SWIM, and advanced computing techniques.

Aviation was integrated into the EU Emissions Trading Scheme (ETS) in 2010 (EC, 2008b). Initially, all aviation originating or terminating in the European Economic Area (EEA) was included in the scheme; however, from 2013, only intra-EEA traffic has been involved, while ICAO decides on a global market-based measure (GMBM). A GMBM scheme called the Carbon Offsetting and Reduction Scheme for International Aviation (CORSIA) was established by ICAO assembly resolution A39-3 (ICAO, 2016). It will be implemented in three phases from 2021 to 2029 (see Chapter 25 for details).

Environmental concerns at airports (see Chapters 18 and 25) stem from three effects of airport operations: fine particulates, $NO_x$ and noise. These all pose major health risks, from asthma to myocardial infarction, to the population living around an airport, as well as the psychosocial impacts caused by noise and poor air quality. These impacts are due not just to aircraft, but also to ground transport and airport infrastructure. Developments in engine and airframe technology have reduced average aircraft noise by around 20 decibels (dB) over the last 50 years (Huff, 2013) and $NO_x$ emissions by over 30 per cent (Chang et al., 2013).

ATM can help reduce these impacts through several measures, and the SESAR programme has included environmental impact analysis in many of its solutions. Continuous climb (CCO) and continuous descent (CDO) operations (EUROCONTROL, 2017b) reduce both noise and emissions on take-off and landing. According to NATS (2016b): "Increasing CDO achievement across the UK by an average of just 5 per cent will deliver over 30,000 quieter arrivals and save over 10,000t $CO_2$ emissions and £2m in fuel costs." Optimal departure management (DMAN) can reduce emissions by ensuring aircraft do not depart from the gate merely to queue at the entry points to the runway with their engines running.

## Safety challenges

All of the challenges described above that ATM faces in the near future must be addressed while maintaining and improving safety, the industry's number-one priority. Traditional safety management approaches have focused on understanding why things go wrong and working to prevent this. Now that aviation is an ultra-safe industry with very few accidents, there are few data to inform safety improvements. Such improvements are still possible, however, by focusing on what works well, determined using safety barrier measurements and practical methods. These approaches are complementary, and both can increase understanding of how to make aviation even safer. The CANSO global strategy for the future of safety in air traffic management (CANSO, 2014) is an example of a safety strategy that juxtaposes both approaches. It is built around four key themes.

### Safety intelligence

An organisation needs quantitative information to identify and assess various threats. Traditionally, incident data and other safety information on past events have given reasonable predictions about likely accidents and measures needed to avoid them. Today, however, predicting threats must also include talking to managers and front-line staff about the present and future to help detect weak signals. Safety intelligence for continuous improvement of safety performance involves three main steps:

1   *Get the data*: Implement an open reporting system to gather safety reports from across the business. Complement manual reporting with automatic safety data acquisition tools (e.g. about separation minima infringements).
2   *Understand the data*: Focus on the systemic factors that contributed to an incident. Performance measurements should not only explain the risk, but also help anticipate risks.
3   *Use the data*: Make use of the data that have been gathered to identify actions to be taken to control safety and to understand whether a change has been effective.

### People create safety

A positive and supportive safety culture and the provision of a working environment that reflects a just culture, promoted by the leaders of the business and understood by everyone, is essential. In such a culture, staff are not punished for actions, omissions or decisions they take that are commensurate with their experience and training, but gross negligence, willful violation and destructive acts are not tolerated. Leaders who demonstrate real commitment to safety generate a corresponding commitment and ultimately create a safety culture throughout the organisation.

## Tailored and proportionate

Safety is the aviation industry's number-one priority. However, there are economic and performance pressures on the industry, and it is important to understand the real risks to operations and focus on what really matters. It is therefore essential to ensure that new regulations are proportionate to the associated risks and are applied consistently.

## Challenging and learning

Managing the safety challenges of the future requires all the aviation stakeholders – ANSPs, airlines, airports, manufacturers and regulators – to work together as a community on risks they all share, and to learn from one another. Equating safety with regulator satisfaction can create a false sense of assurance since it may mean that organisations miss glaring safety issues that are outside the regulatory framework. Safety requires a culture of challenge that strives for the highest possible standards, challenging others on the pace and rigour of their risk mitigation actions.

## Information security

Information security is one of the major emerging challenges that the aviation industry is currently facing. Information security is explicitly considered, by different legislations, to be a binding requirement considering the need to protect both critical infrastructure in general and civil aviation systems and information in particular. Annex 17, 'Security – Safeguarding International Civil Aviation against Acts of Unlawful Interference', of the ICAO convention (ICAO, 2006) sets minimum standards for aviation security worldwide and creates a global legal and policy framework. The ICAO *Aviation Security Manual* (ICAO, 2002) provides guidance on minimum measures required for protecting critical information systems against unauthorised access and use.

In Europe, EU directives (EC, 2016, 2017a) specify such things as: the need to consider security in general, and information security in particular, for its potential effects on safety; a formal consideration of the information and cybersecurity domain within the security management system required for any ANSP; and the need for specific information security training for Air Traffic Safety Electronic Personnel (ATSEP).

EASA is planning to establish a European Centre for Cyber Security in Aviation (ECCSA), which will serve as a platform for sharing relevant cybersecurity information such as vulnerabilities, events and incidents with the aviation community. ECCSA aims to be a key enabler for the implementation of a resilient cyberspace for aviation.

## Conclusion

The organisation of ATM in Europe, and by analogy in other parts of the world with dense air traffic, such as the US and soon the axis from the Middle East through to South East Asia and China, has become dramatically more complex in the last 15 years.

The intricate interplay of the gradual privatisation of service provision, attempts at economic regulation in order to drive down costs and stimulate cross-border consolidation in what nevertheless remains a natural monopoly, and the need for faster implementation of technological modernisation has led to an ever-more complex framework of institutional and regulatory bodies. These numerous new bodies are starting to consolidate their roles and delimit their responsibilities with respect to one another. A more efficient network of national oversight authorities and EASA can be expected.

The performance scheme is controversial and strongly resisted by incumbent ANSPs and their staff associations. As a result, the EU is likely to reorient its legal initiatives but not give up on its intention to reduce fragmentation and ATM's inherent cost. Further unbundling of CNS services from ATSs, wider acceptance of cost-efficient common support services, increased use of virtualisation technologies – possibly initially by the smaller ANSPs who have less room for internal cost optimisation – will gradually lead ANSPs to refocus on their core business: assuring safe separation. Since this core business is rapidly becoming more complex because of the introduction of new air vehicle types with widely different performance characteristics, and of satellite technologies that allow for the implementation of far more flexible operational concepts, such a refocusing is greatly needed. Hopefully, it will be followed by tighter collaboration or integration, as many of these concepts require larger sectors of airspace for their optimal deployment.

## Notes

1  The Single European Sky ATM Research (SESAR) project will be discussed later in this chapter.
2  The EASCG is composed of the European Organisation for Civil Aviation Equipment (EUROCAE), EUROCONTROL, the EC Directorate-General for Mobility and Transport (DG MOVE), EASA, Single European Sky ATM Research Joint Undertaking (SESAR JU), and the European Standards Organisations (e.g. the European Committee for Standardisation [CEN], the European Committee for Electrotechnical Standardisation [CENELEC], and the European Telecommunications Standards Institute [ETSI]). The EASCG also counts on the support of organisations such as the AeroSpace and Defence Industries Association of Europe (ASD), the Civil Air Navigation Services Organisation (CANSO), the European Defence Agency (EDA) and the SESAR Deployment Manager (SDM).
3  Borealis is an international partnership between the ANSPs of Denmark (Naviair), Estonia (EANS), Finland (Finavia), Iceland (ISAVIA), Ireland (IAA), Latvia (LGS), Norway (Avinor), Sweden (LFV) and the UK (NATS). COOPANS is an international partnership between the ANSPs of Austria (Austro Control), Croatia (Croatia Control), Denmark (Naviair), Ireland (IAA) and Sweden (LFV), with Thales as the chosen industry supplier.
4  Advanced remote tower (ART) led by LFV and funded in 2005 by the sixth framework programme (FP6) of the EU's framework programme for research and technological development.
5  RPASs are generally seen as a first step towards fully automated aircraft. As other UASs will play a significant role only in the longer term, they are not considered further in this chapter.

## References

Airbus (2015). *Small RPAS Operations Near Regional Airports: Operational Description, Impacts, and Issues*, Dulles, VA, Airbus/ProSky Inc.

Airline Leader (2015). *Global ATM enters a new age – and the cost benefit potential is immense*. Online. Available at: www.airlineleader.com/categories/finance/global-atm-enters-a-new-age---and-the-cost-benefit-potential-is-immense-235716 (accessed 21 June 2017).

ATAG (Air Transport Action Group) (2012). *A sustainable flightpath towards reducing emissions: position paper presented by the global aviation industry, UNFCCC climate talks, Doha, November 2012*. Online. Available at: www.atag.org/component/downloads/downloads/203.html (accessed 21 June 2017).

CANSO (Civil Air Navigation Services Organisation) (2014). *Global Strategy for the Future of Safety in Air Traffic Management*, Amsterdam, CANSO.

Chang, C.T., Lee, C.M., Herbon, J.T. and Kramer, S.K. (2013). NASA environmentally responsible aviation project develops next-generation low-emissions combustor technologies (phase I), *Journal of Aeronautics & Aerospace Engineering*, 2(4), 1–10.

DEFRA (Department for Environment, Food and Rural Affairs) (2007). *Act on CO2 Calculator: Public Trial Version – Data, Methodology and Assumptions Paper*, London, DEFRA.

EASA (European Aviation Safety Agency) (2014). *A Harmonised European Approach to a Performance Based Environment (PBE)*, Cologne, EASA.

EASA (European Aviation Safety Agency) (2015a). *Notice of proposed amendment 2015–04: technical and operational requirements for remote tower operations*. Online. Available at: www.easa.europa.eu/system/files/dfu/NPA%202015-04.pdf (accessed 27 July 2017).

EASA (European Aviation Safety Agency) (2015b). *Technical Opinion: Introduction of a Regulatory Framework for the Operation of Unmanned Aircraft*, Cologne, EASA.

EC (European Commission) (1999). *Communication from the Commission to the Council and the European Parliament of 1 December 1999: The Creation of the Single European Sky*, COM(1999) 614 final, Brussels, EC.

EC (European Commission) (2004a). *Regulation (EC) No 549/2004 of the European Parliament and of the Council of 10 March 2004 Laying Down the Framework for the Creation of the Single European Sky*, Brussels, EC.

EC (European Commission) (2004b). *Regulation (EC) No 550/2004 of the European Parliament and of the Council of 10 March 2004 on the Provision of Air Navigation Services in the Single European Sky*, Brussels, EC.

EC (European Commission) (2004c). *Regulation (EC) No 551/2004 of the European Parliament and of the Council of 10 March 2004 on the Organisation and Use of the Airspace in the Single European Sky*, Brussels, EC.

EC (European Commission) (2004d). *Regulation (EC) No 552/2004 of the European Parliament and of the Council of 10 March 2004 on the Interoperability of the European Air Traffic Management Network*, Brussels, EC.

EC (European Commission) (2007). *Council Regulation (EC) No 219/2007 of 27 February 2007 on the Establishment of a Joint Undertaking to Develop the New Generation European Air Traffic Management System (SESAR)*, Bruseels, EC.

EC (European Commission) (2008a). *Communication from the Commission to the European Parliament, the Council, the European Economic and Social Committee and the Committee of the Regions of 25 June 2008: 'Single European Sky II: Towards More Sustainable and Better Performing Aviation'*, COM(2008) 389 final, Brussels, EC.

EC (European Commission) (2008b). *Directive 2008/101/EC of the European Parliament and of the Council of 19 November 2008 amending Directive 2003 87 EC so as to Include Aviation Activities in the Scheme for Greenhouse Gas Emission Allowance Trading Within the Community*, Official Journal L 8, 13/1/2009, Brussels, EC.

EC (European Commission) (2011a). *Commission Regulation (EU) No 677/2011 Laying Down Detailed Rules for the Implementation of Air Traffic Management (ATM) Network Functions*, Official Journal L 185/1 15/7/2011, Brussels, EC.

EC (European Commission) (2011b). *Commission Decision of 7.7.2011 on the Nomination of the Network Manager for the Air Traffic Management (ATM) Network Functions of the Single European Sky*, C(2011) 4130 final, Brussels, EC.

EC (European Commission) (2014). *Commission Implementing Regulation (EU) No 716/2014 of 27 June 2014 on the Establishment of the Pilot Common Project Supporting the Implementation of the European Air Traffic Management Master Plan*, Brussels, EC.

EC (European Commission) (2015). *European Commission – Fact Sheet: July Infringements Package: Key Decisions, July 2015*, MEMO/15/5356, Brussels, EC.

EC (European Commission) (2016). *Directive (EU) 2016/1148 of the European Parliament and of the Council of 6 July 2016 Concerning Measures for a High Common Level of Security of Network and Information Systems Across the Union*, Official Journal L 194, 19/7/2016, Brussels, EC.

EC (European Commission) (2017a). *Commission Implementing Regulation (EU) 2017/373 of 1 March 2017 Laying Down Common Requirements for Providers of Air Traffic Management/Air Navigation Services and Other Air Traffic Management Network Functions and their Oversight*, Official Journal L 62, 8/3/2017, Brussels, EC.

EC (European Commission) (2017b). *EC Decision 2017/001/R Common Requirements for Providers of Air Traffic Management/Air Navigation Services and Other Air Traffic Management Network Functions and their Oversight*, Brussels, EC.

EUROCONTROL (2017a). *Free route airspace*. Online. Available at: www.eurocontrol.int/articles/free-route-airspace (accessed 21 June 2017).

EUROCONTROL (2017b). *Continuous climb and descent operations*. Online. Available at: www.eurocontrol.int/articles/continuous-climb-and-descent-operations (accessed 21 June 2017).

FAA (Federal Aviation Administration) (2017). *FAA Aerospace Forecast Fiscal Year 2017–2037*, Washington, DC, FAA.

Huff, D.L. (2013). NASA Glenn's contributions to aircraft engine noise research, *Journal of Aerospace Engineering*, 26(2), 218–250.

ICAO (International Civil Aviation Organisation) (2002). *ICAO Security Manual for Safeguarding Civil Aviation Against Acts of Unlawful Interference, Doc. 8973/6*, Montreal, ICAO.

ICAO (International Civil Aviation Organisation) (2006). *Convention on International Civil Aviation*, ICAO Doc. 7300/9, Montreal, ICAO.

ICAO (International Civil Aviation Organisation) (2010). *Assembly Resolution A37-11, Performance-Based Navigation Global Goals*, Montreal, ICAO.
ICAO (International Civil Aviation Organisation) (2013a). *ICAO 2013–2028 Global Air Navigation Plan*, Montreal, ICAO.
ICAO (International Civil Aviation Organisation) (2013b). *ICAO GNSS Manual*, ICAO Doc. 9849, Montreal, ICAO.
ICAO (International Civil Aviation Organisation) (2016). *ICAO Resolution A39-3: Consolidated Statement of Continuing ICAO Policies and Practices Related to Environmental Protection – Global Market-Based Measure (MBM) Scheme*, Montreal, ICAO.
IPCC (Intergovernmental Panel on Climate Change) (1999). Aviation and the global atmosphere. In: J.E. Penner, D.H. Lister, D.J. Griggs, D.J. Dokken and M. McFarland (eds). *Special Report of the IPCC*, Cambridge, Cambridge University Press.
Jelinek, F., Carlier, S., Smith, J. and Quesne, A. (2002). *The EUR RVSM Implementation Project Environmental Benefit Analysis*, EEC/ENV/2002/008, Brussels, EURONTROL Experimental Centre.
Marais, K. (2016). *Environmental benefits of space-based ADS-B*. Online. Available at: https://engineering.purdue.edu/VRSS/research/benefits-space-adsb (accessed 21 June 2017).
McInally, J. (2010). *EUROCONTROL History Book*, Brussels, EUROCONTROL.
NATS (2016a). *Borealis free route airspace programme part 2 to receive European funding*. Online. Available at: www.nats.aero/news/borealis-free-route-airspace-programme-part-2-to-receive-european-funding/ (accessed 21 June 2017).
NATS (2016b). *A Guide to Continuous Descent Operations: For Controllers and Pilots by Controllers and Pilots*, Whiteley, NATS (on behalf of Sustainable Aviation).
Oxford Economics (2010). *The Economic Impacts of Air Travel Restrictions Due to Volcanic Ash*, Oxford, Oxford Economics.
PRB (2016). *PRB White Paper – RP3 Performance Objectives*, Brussels, EC.
REACT4C (2015). *Final Report Summary: Reducing Emissions from Aviation by Changing Trajectories for the Benefit of Climate*, Brussels, EC.
Sausen, R., Isaksen, I., Grewe, V., Hauglustaine, D., Lee, D.S., Myhre G., et al. (2005). Aviation radiative forcing in 2000: an update on IPCC (1999), *Meteorologische Zeitschrift*, 14(4), 555–561.
SESAR JU and EUROCONTROL (2015). *European ATM Master Plan: The Roadmap for Delivering High Performing Aviation for Europe, Executive View, Edition 2015*, Brussels, SESAR JU and EUROCONTROL.
SKYbrary (2017). *Aviation safety wiki*. Online. Available at: www.skybrary.aero (accessed 22 June 2017).
STATFOR (2017). *EUROCONTROL Seven-Year Forecast February 2017: Flight Movements and Service Units 2017–2023*, Brussels, EC/EUROCONTROL.

# 5

# The commercial
# aerospace industry

*Fariba E. Alamdari, Jan Hogrefe and Wendy R. Sowers*

## Introduction

The commercial aerospace industry has, through a century of innovation, become one of the most technologically advanced manufacturing industries of our time. This chapter gives a concise overview of key innovations that led to the current global dimensions of commercial aerospace. It also paints a picture of the current industry's structure, assesses its economic importance, and provides an outlook into the future. First, the chapter describes some of the major development milestones for products and manufacturing processes. A key example is the development of jet aircraft, which allowed faster and farther travel at lower cost. Another major step is the use of composite materials in modern jetliners. These allow efficiency improvements but also alter production technology and improve the passenger experience in the final product.

The chapter's main part assesses key characteristics of today's industry. It looks at the main manufacturers' output and how the industry has undergone significant consolidation over the decades. Regarding the industry's main product, commercial jetliners, this chapter discusses the size of the global fleet and its geographical distribution. The global jet fleet of about 23,000 aircraft is geographically diversified, but North American and Asian airlines represent the largest shares. Middle East airlines have large fleets relative to the size of their home markets, highlighting their importance for global connecting traffic via major hubs. Trends in aircraft development are discussed against the backdrop of demand (see Chapters 1 and 19) and strategy considerations (see Chapters 8 and 9). This is a key insight as new aircraft are generally developed with a potential market in mind. Contrary to consumer products, aircraft capabilities are often the key to a successful business model of an airline. This holds true for global super connectors as well as for many low cost carriers (LCCs). In the discussion about today's commercial aerospace industry, supplier relations are also highlighted, as are freighter aircraft.

Given the size and reach of the commercial aerospace industry, the chapter contains brief discussions of the economic importance of the industry and of a key future challenge crucial to the success of the industry – environmental sustainability (see Chapters 17 and 25). Finally, the chapter concludes with an outlook for the near and far future of the industry. While much of the next decade is determined by existing aircraft products and large manufacturer backlogs, new aircraft and new destinations will certainly emerge from an industry with a proven track record of innovation. Advanced propulsion technologies and space travel are just two of the many possibilities that lie ahead for the commercial aerospace industry.

## A century of innovation in the commercial aerospace industry

Commercial aviation has come a long way since mankind first took to the skies. In about a century's time, the commercial aerospace industry has grown into a force of globalisation that has changed the way people perceive and travel the world. Aircraft today are almost ubiquitous in the skies above large cities. Yet in the early twentieth century, no one could foresee the role commercial aviation would play in today's modern society.[1] Before commercial aerospace could take off, flying was either an adventurous endeavour following the Wright brothers' first successes, or part of military operations when aircraft became part of warfare during the First World War. After the war, commercial aviation also prospered in the form of air cargo services (see Chapter 2). For example, it was in 1919 that William Boeing's fledgling company operated its first commercial aircraft, the B-1, to deliver mail between Seattle in the United States (US) and Canada (Boeing, 2016a). This business grew considerably in the following years, yet scheduled passenger flights would take many more years to become established. While bigger and more reliable aircraft allowed passenger operations to develop throughout the 1930s, it was not until the arrival of the Douglas DC-3 that passenger flights would turn a profit outside of the business of carrying mail (Boeing, 2016a). However, the technology did not yet allow for air travel to become a means of mass transport, and thus flying remained a luxury experience. A prominent example is the Boeing 314 Clipper that flew international trips for the world's affluent class.

The Second World War put an abrupt end to intercontinental leisure travel, yet it also led to an acceleration of aerospace innovations that ultimately enabled commercial aviation's development. The key breakthrough was the development of the jet engine in combination with the swept-wing design that still marks the appearance of jetliners today. The De Havilland Comet, first introduced into commercial service by the British Overseas Airways Corporation, was the first jet airliner when it made its debut in passenger operations in 1952. However, structural weaknesses limited its commercial success. Then, for a couple of years, the Tupolev Tu-104 was the only jet airliner in service, but it was the Boeing 707 that took aviation to new heights and – according to Boeing (2016a) – helped air travel exceed travel by rail and sea for the first time after its introduction in 1957.

The next big leap came in 1970 with the Boeing 747, then the world's largest civilian aircraft, which made air travel available to large groups of passengers. Its twin-aisle design was unique at the time and allowed for significant increases in seating capacity, thus bringing down per-seat cost. The appearance of the Boeing 747 ushered in not only the age of mass air travel, but also a period of incremental innovation in commercial aerospace. Revolutionary aircraft capable of supersonic travel, such as the Tupolev Tu-144 and the Concorde, remained technologically advanced niche products. The 1970s also saw Airbus entering the stage of commercial aircraft manufacturing, significantly increasing competition, and hence spurring further innovation. The next key change was the introduction of twin jets, which allowed for further improvements in fuel efficiency. The Boeing 777-200LR also capped a development of rapidly increasing range for airlines. The example of the so-called kangaroo route makes this clear. While passengers travelling on a Qantas Super Constellation in the 1950s had to endure a trip over several days with at least a half-dozen refuelling stops, some modern jetliners can now fly London to Sydney direct in just under 20 hours. This design took the industry into the twenty-first century and remains the backbone of aircraft manufacturing today. On the manufacturing side, processes also improved. For instance, computer-aided design and engineering became widespread in parallel with computer use penetration in manufacturing.

While the basic design of commercial jetliners has not changed much in decades, one key innovation is hidden under the skin of the aircraft. Modern airliners such as the Boeing 787 Dreamliner and the Airbus 350 are largely made of composite materials. The corresponding weight reduction allows for a 20 per cent increase in fuel efficiency compared to predecessor variants. It also allows for a better passenger experience via increased cabin pressure and humidity levels. As a result, today's traveller will enjoy an experience of comfort that could not be more different from the thrill the first pioneers of aviation were seeking when they took to the skies. The aerospace industry has made reaching almost any place on earth a matter of days – and made it available to as many people as never before. Within about 100 years, and through many significant innovations, it has made the world a smaller place.

## The commercial aerospace industry today

Today's commercial civil aerospace industry is dominated by two large aircraft manufacturers, Boeing and Airbus. Between them, they accounted for over 80 per cent of aircraft deliveries in 2015. Embraer and Bombardier, which build smaller aircraft, make up another roughly 10 per cent of deliveries. Figure 5.1 shows the manufacturers' deliveries, including both jets and turbo props, over time since 1960. Several observations immediately stand out. One is the emergence of Airbus as a manufacturing powerhouse. While for its first decade in existence the company had a miniscule share of the global market, that quickly changed, and Airbus now delivers almost as many aircraft annually as rival Boeing. The second story that emerges from Figure 5.1 is one of consolidation. The top four clearly dominate the number of deliveries. While the number of companies delivering aircraft has fluctuated but not fallen much – it was at 8 in 1960, 12 in 1990, and 9 in 2016, respectively – the companies outside the main four are now mostly small by comparison. For the US aerospace industry, Spreen (2016) provides an overview of decades of consolidation in both the military and commercial space.

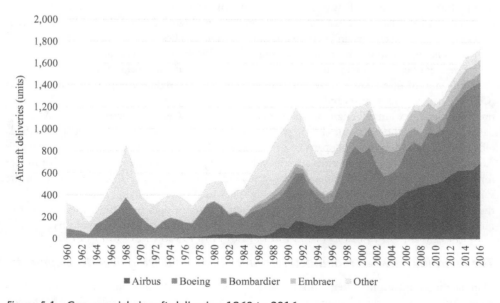

*Figure 5.1*  Commercial aircraft deliveries, 1960 to 2016

*Source*: Data from Teal Group Corporation (2016).

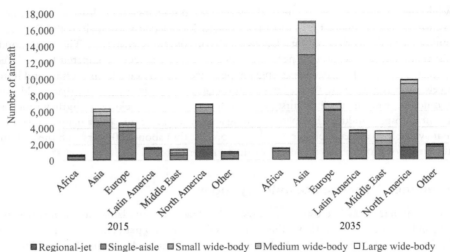

■Regional-jet  ■Single-aisle  ■Small wide-body  ▨Medium wide-body  □Large wide-body

*Figure 5.2*  Regional fleet composition by aircraft type, 2015 and 2035

*Source*: Data from Boeing (2016c).

The history of aircraft deliveries built a current fleet of commercial aircraft that is well diversified around the globe. Figure 5.2 shows the 2015 jet fleet distribution by aircraft type and airline domicile region. In 2015, there were more than 22,500 aircraft in service, with about 700 airlines globally (Boeing, 2016b). While North America and Europe make up 51.2 per cent of the global jet fleet, other regions are gaining in importance (see Figure 5.2), and the North American and European share is expected to decrease to 39.2 per cent by 2035. Economic development in emerging markets (see Chapters 7 and 19) is a key factor, as is the establishment of long-haul connecting hubs in the Middle East (see Chapters 1 and 3). The latter gives this region a larger share of aircraft capacity than mere economic size would justify. Figure 5.2 also shows that single-aisle aircraft dominate the current and expected future world fleet. These versatile intra-regional aircraft have become the backbone of airline operations in domestic markets around the world. Twin-aisle aircraft remain the key to connecting continents and allow airline networks to span the globe.

While output of aircraft is a key measure driven by the original equipment manufacturers (OEMs), it is also closely related to and crucially enabled by the supplier industry. The most prominent parts are aircraft engines, where companies such as General Electric, Pratt & Whitney, Safran, and Rolls Royce work closely with aircraft OEMs to develop and produce new fuel-efficient engines. Moreover, big parts of aircraft fuselages are produced by suppliers such as Spirit AeroSystems, and seats and interiors are generally crucial pieces from the supply chain that matter for on-time deliveries. In addition, there is a myriad of small and specialised companies in the supply chain that often build crucial and highly specialised parts. Soshkin (2016) describes how these suppliers historically were able to capture better margins than the OEMs themselves. But increased price competition is being felt along the supply chain in the modern industry.

## The interplay between manufacturers and airlines is driving fleet developments

Manufacturers and airlines often work together in determining the next step of aircraft development. Aviation is a dynamic industry that continuously adapts to a multitude of market forces. Moreover, the commercial aerospace industry is eager to identify trends in customer demand that will ultimately determine the success of new innovations in the marketplace. Some of the key market forces that can impact aircraft fleet dynamics are economic in nature, such as economic growth and development trends and fuel prices, while others are more aviation industry-specific, such as environmental regulations, infrastructure, market liberalisation, aircraft capabilities, airline business models and strategies evolution, and competing modes of transport. Aircraft development does not happen in isolation, and it is crucial to briefly look at some of the main drivers of aircraft demand when analysing the modern commercial aerospace industry.

## Fleet evolution

The global fleet composition has changed over the last two decades, with continued evolution expected as new technologies are introduced into the market and regulatory, infrastructure, and airline business models evolve. Airlines make fleet decisions based on the aircraft's versatility, asking questions such as does the aircraft have the efficiency and cost profile to open new routes, does it have the ability to go longer distances, and will it provide the right amount of seats at the right seat mile economics for the airline's network and markets. As airlines continue to focus on versatility, there has been a move from larger twin-aisle aircraft types to smaller twin-aisle ones. For instance, in 1995, the majority of twin-aisle aircraft were of either the small or large size categories. Today, and most likely in the near future, airlines are gravitating towards smaller and medium-size twin-aisle aircraft (see Figure 5.3) as more capable aircraft have entered the market in the medium-size segment. As an example, the Boeing 787 fleet represents approximately 5 per cent of the global twin-aisle in-service fleet. Despite this fact, 20 per cent of new routes since 2011 have been launched with Boeing 787s and over 100 new non-stop markets have been announced or started.

As emerging markets (see Chapter 7) and the airline business models (see Chapter 8) continue to diversify, single-aisle aircraft have dominated and are expected to gain market share (see Figures 5.2 and 5.3). As the LCC business model continues to grow, more point-to-point flying is occurring. Two decades ago, LCCs provided less than 10 per cent of all short-haul

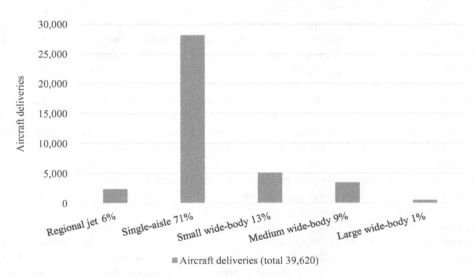

*Figure 5.3* Aircraft fleet evolution, 2015 to 2035

*Source*: Data from Boeing (2016c).

flights (less than 3,000 miles), the majority of which were flown on the US carrier Southwest. Today, LCCs fly almost 30 per cent of short-haul flights. There are regions of the world such as Europe, South East Asia, and North America where this trend is more common. As the rest of Asia-Pacific, Latin America, and the Middle East continue rapid growth, more point-to-point flying in these regions is expected, and again it has been the availability of ultra-efficient aircraft such as the Airbus 320 and Boeing 737 families that were crucial ingredients for these business models to succeed. As the industry has become less regulated and more competitive (see Chapters 6 and 7), airlines are focusing on improving service levels (see Chapter 22). Non-stop flights and increased frequencies provide better service from the passenger perspective by reducing travel times and providing more choices. This development is expected to boost the share of single-aisle aircraft in the global fleet even more. As shown in Figure 5.3, single-aisle aircraft are expected to make up over 70 per cent of the deliveries through 2035. Regionally, most growth is expected in Asia, where a dynamic economy is raising living standards and the need to connect a vast number of cities at short and medium distances. In fact, it is expected that by 2035, the Asian fleet will easily outsize the North American one for the number-one spot globally.

Fleet trends tend to be a mirror image of traffic growth trends around the world. Keeping supply and demand in balance, aircraft manufacturers are seeing greater diversity in their customer base. According to Boeing (2016c), airlines in Europe and North America carried 64 per cent of global passenger traffic in 1995. By 2015, that share had fallen to 48 per cent and is projected to continue declining to 37 per cent by 2035 as Asia-Pacific and the Middle East become more prominent regions for global passenger traffic. Varying regional and business model characteristics also drive different fleet requirements. Middle East airlines will still favour twin-aisle aircraft and premium passenger services to take advantage of the area's centrality and prominence in business travel. European and North American airlines respond to growing competition from LCCs by replacing older, fuel-inefficient aircraft with larger, more economical single-aisle models. In Asia, rising demand across the board will require a mix of single- and twin-aisle aircraft.

Growth of new travel demand is not the only source of demand for aircraft manufacturers. Replacing the existing aircraft is an important source of aircraft demand as well. Many factors can drive the need for replacement. Age is a primary one, but others include relative aircraft economics, maintenance requirements, and the overall market environment. In the early years of the twenty-first century, high fuel costs have played a larger role in influencing decisions to remove aircraft from service. Over 40 per cent of today's fleet is expected to be replaced over the next two decades (see Figure 5.4).

Finally, airlines also partake in international goods trade – be it with passenger airlines with extra cargo in the belly of their aircraft next to passengers' luggage or with dedicated freighter aircraft (see Chapter 2). Today, there are almost 1,800 main deck freighters in the global market. While a smaller portion of the overall aircraft market, air cargo is an important part of the global transport infrastructure. Air cargo accounts for less than 1 per cent of world trade tonnage, yet 35 per cent of world trade value is carried by air. Passenger aircraft and dedicated freighters both carry air cargo. Lower-hold cargo capacity on passenger flights has been expanding as airlines deploy new jetliners with excellent cargo capability. However, dedicated freight services offer shippers a combination of reliability, predictability, and control over timing and routing that is often superior to that of passenger operators. As a result, there is continued demand for the speed and reliability benefits that air freight offers. Industries that require transport of time-sensitive and high-value commodities such as perishables, consumer electronics, high-fashion apparel, pharmaceuticals, industrial machinery, and automobile components recognise the value of air freight, and this value will continue to play a significant role in their shipping decisions.

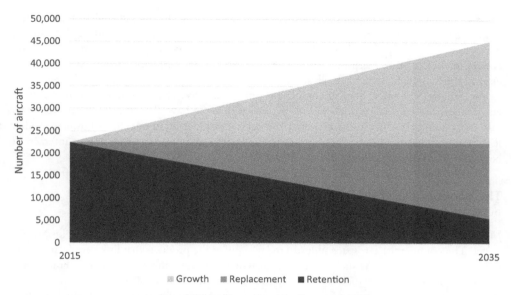

*Figure 5.4* Aircraft retention, replacement and growth, 2015 to 2035

*Source*: Data from Boeing (2016c).

The restructuring of logistics chains to serve the rapidly growing e-commerce industry also requires the unique capabilities that air cargo provides and offers a new area of growth. Direct involvement of companies such as Amazon in air freight activities serves as a good example of the importance e-commerce will have going forward (*Seattle Times*, 2016). As a result, freighters are expected to continue carrying more than half of global air cargo to satisfy the demanding requirements of air cargo markets.

## Regulatory and infrastructure developments

Liberalisation of aviation services stimulates competition in the airline industry, grows traffic, and historically has given passengers more choices and contributed to lower ticket prices in real terms, which in turn has bolstered demand for air travel and commercial jets (Cristea et al., 2015; Pearce and Smyth, 2007; Winston and Yan, 2015). While the aviation industry remains heavily regulated in many parts of the world, the pace of liberalisation has been steady (see Chapters 6 and 7).

Strong air travel demand growth requires infrastructure investments. Airport authorities around the world are investing in large capital projects, including new or improved runways, terminal expansions, and entirely new airports. These investments can significantly increase airport capacity, but are substantial, and development times typically extend more than a decade from initial planning to completion of construction. Initiatives to modernise air traffic management provide crucial enhancements to both system capacity and efficiency (see Chapter 4). Many national and regional airspace management agencies are engaged in programmes to overhaul airspace systems. For example, the US is implementing the NextGen programme to help airports run more smoothly and reduce flying and aircraft taxi times. This type of programme is implemented gradually, and the improvements in airport efficiency will be realised over time. Airline strategies (see Chapters 8 and 9) also play a key role in managing infrastructure and air space challenges. For example, many airlines have replaced smaller aircraft such as regional jets with larger single-aisle aircraft, helping to ease demand for take-off and landing slots during peak periods. Creating secondary hubs and expanding service to secondary airports can also ease congestion at the busiest airports. Airline alliances have proven effective in allowing airlines to expand route systems without duplicating services.

Overall, the current state of the industry is one of an active symbiosis between manufacturers, airlines, and other operators. Trends in market demand have shaped the industry for years into its present form. With the aircraft as the central product in an operator's business model, it is expected that the future evolution of the industry will continue to be one of interaction between aircraft manufacturers and their customers.

## The economic and environmental impact of the commercial aerospace industry

Modern societies and economies are unthinkable without the global connectivity provided by air travel. The commercial aerospace industry today supplies the products that link people and businesses across continents. As such, it enables growth and development along many dimensions. The value of the aerospace industry to economies around the world will also make it imperative that the industry be a champion for environmental sustainability research and implementation.

According to a recent report by ATAG (2016), 3.57 billion passengers were carried by the world's airlines in 2015, flying a total of 6.2 trillion kilometres on almost 35 million commercial flights. There are more than 17,000 unique city pairs connected by air travel services today. This global reach delivers vast benefits to economies worldwide. It is estimated that around 63 million jobs are supported by the aviation industry – jobs ultimately enabled by the supply of aircraft by the commercial aerospace industry. About 1.1 million people globally are directly employed in civil aerospace occupations. They are at the origin of a system that powers airlines and airports, enables indirect jobs at the latter, and ultimately facilitates the success of entire related industries such as travel and tourism. Overall, ATAG (2016) sees this system supporting 3.5 per cent of global gross domestic product (GDP).

Being connected to the world via aviation also enables a country to foster economic growth and increase development. Aviation allows access to large global markets at higher frequencies and reduced travel times compared to other modes of transport. Air travel is essential in the modern business world. It enables companies to find the optimal spot in a global value chain. Research by Arvis and Shepherd (2013) has shown a positive link between air connectivity and supply chain trade. Importantly, most value chains linked by aviation are producing high-value products. As such, a good aviation system can help economies in moving up the value chain. Shepherd et al. (2016) also highlight the value air cargo brings to an economy.

Connectivity is also crucial for attracting foreign direct investment (FDI), which is key for economic growth since FDI is an important technology transfer mechanism. Using data from the World Economic Forum's *Global Competitiveness Report*, it can be shown that there is a strong relationship between the quality of the air infrastructure and the availability of the latest technology (Schwab, 2015). However, it is more than technology that often comes into a country by air. Bel and Fageda (2008) show that quality jobs in headquarter functions often flourish in places connected to the world by aviation. Bloningen and Cristea (2015) highlight the overall benefits of air service for urban economic growth.

Finally, aviation can make a country's economy function more efficiently by connecting regions other than the capital to the centre of economic activity. Rural flower producers, for instance, now have the opportunity to fly their product both to domestic markets and out into the world. Lower-cost airlines also play a role in improving efficiency in labour markets by delinking the place of work and residence within a country, thus allowing for increased efficiency in allocating labour market resources across the country. In sum, aviation increases participation in an economy, and it can often do so at lower cost than rail or roads, in particular in challenging terrain.

Bringing these benefits to countries across the globe also means a large responsibility for a sustainable approach from an environmental perspective. Air travel today even ousts driving in terms of energy efficiency per mile travelled (Sivak, 2015). Furthermore, aircraft have become significantly more fuel-efficient and substantially quieter over time. Over time, modern aircraft achieved about an 80 per cent reduction in $CO_2$ emissions per seat kilometre and more than a 75 per cent reduction in perceived noise levels compared to the first jetliners, respectively (ATAG, 2016). The products of the commercial aerospace industry are able to spread the benefits of air connectivity and foster economic growth and developments worldwide. While they have a large financial impact, they are leaving behind a smaller environmental footprint. For both economic and environmental reasons, airline customers demand ever-increasing fuel efficiency. In a framework anchored at the UN (2014), the aviation industry has committed to ambitious carbon dioxide emissions targets to achieve carbon-neutral aviation growth beyond 2020 and halve net carbon emissions by 2050 (compared to 2005). The aviation industry is addressing environmental challenges with a three-pronged strategy of designing more efficient and safer aircraft, improving operational procedures, and developing sustainable biofuels that produce better than 50 per cent lower life cycle carbon dioxide emissions than conventional fuels (see also Chapter 25). In addition, a carbon-offseting scheme will help generate significant reductions in $CO_2$ emissions.

## What will the future of commercial aerospace look like?

With the last 100 years as guidance, the future of commercial aerospace will undoubtedly be one of further innovation. At first, this will mostly be incremental innovation, pursued by an enlarged set of industry actors regarding aircraft performance and production technology. But it will soon also encompass innovation leading to more intelligent machines and processes enabled by computing power and network systems to act in an ever-more integrated way. Furthermore, more disruptive changes are likely. The shape of aircraft could change and propulsion technology could be revolutionised. Entirely new destinations will be put on an expanded travel map, including space. The latter has also attracted new private entrants into the industry such as SpaceX, Blue Origin, and Virgin Galactic. Dubbs and Paat-Dahlstrom (2011) give an overview of this industry segment. At the outset of aviation, more than 100 years ago, it was hard to imagine the aviation industry of today. Likewise, there is only a rough idea of where the industry's drive for innovation will take it in the next century.

In an industry marked by long product cycles spanning several decades, the story of the immediate future is largely written already. Major manufacturers today have vast backlogs of aircraft to be delivered, and new aircraft programmes and updates are in various planning, testing, and production stages. At the end of the third quarter of 2016, Boeing and Airbus alone had a backlog of over 12,000 unfilled orders for commercial aircraft (Airbus, 2016; Boeing, 2016c). Working through these orders and delivering on new programme development will largely dominate the next decade in commercial aerospace. Looking further to 2035, Boeing predicts the global fleet of aircraft with more than 30 seats to more than double to 45,240 aircraft (Boeing, 2016c). This implies over 39,000 new deliveries. Most of these aircraft will look familiar and be built by familiar manufacturers such as Boeing and Airbus. Yet emerging competitors such as Embraer, Bombardier, Mitsubishi, the United Aircraft Corporation (UAC), and China's Commercial Aircraft Corporation (COMAC) will also take a share of the market as they improve their products and manufacturing processes. Although not specified in detail, some of these emerging manufacturers even have plans to build twin-aisle aircraft. For the near future, these companies will try to become bigger players in a market defined by the big manufacturers of today. Given the scale, knowledge, and capital requirements, it is unlikely that they will quickly disrupt the industry even if successful in capturing more market share.

A familiar appearance does not mean a lack of innovation, however. Many changes will be hidden under the skin of aircraft. One example is the spread of new manufacturing techniques making parts and components using additive manufacturing. This 3D printing is already present in today's aerospace industry. In 2016, the US Federal Aviation Authority (FAA) approved for the first time a 3D printed component for a commercial jet engine build by GE Aviation to be retrofitted to Boeing 777 jet engines (Fell, 2016). For Boeing's next generation of large twin-aisle aircraft, the Boeing 777X, the manufacturer will employ a tool that currently holds the world record for the largest solid 3D printed item (Guinness World Records, 2016). Additive manufacturing is also a key opportunity for the production of spares and enables new designs for lighter and stronger parts. Given the importance of weight reduction in commercial aerospace and the cost associated with maintenance of large aircraft, the future will only see 3D printing become a larger and more important part of manufacturing in the aerospace industry. With increased capabilities and higher computing power, advanced manufacturing robotics will play a larger role in aerospace as well. These machines allow much of the repetitive work to be completed more efficiently and safely.

Another important change not immediately visible on the outside of an aircraft is the more and more sophisticated connectivity of both the passengers and the aircraft itself. Passengers will be able to enjoy universal gate-to-gate Internet access and largely use their own devices for in-flight entertainment rather than expensive and heavy traditional in-flight entertainment systems. More importantly, the e-enabled aircraft itself will collect a host of data from sensors that can be used in predictive modelling applications to improve maintenance, safety, and fuel performance, manage maintenance records to increase asset value, and lower operating costs. According to Boeing (2016d), the annual aircraft data generated will increase 140-fold from 6.9 terabytes in 2010 to 1 petabyte by 2030. The use of data will extend to all of the airline's operations, and affect manufacturers and the supply chain via the use of optimised inventory management and parts procurement. The aircraft of the near future will be a smart and connected one, allowing airlines to more effectively run their passenger and cargo operations. The trend of more encompassing connectivity will transcend aircraft development steps and be a part of any new product introduced by the industry for the foreseeable future.

Looking beyond current backlogs, product developments, and already emerging trends, there is almost infinite room for imagination of what the world of aviation will look like in 50 to 100 years' time. Some basic research into fascinating technologies is already under way. Technology for hypersonic aircraft, able to shuttle passengers from New York to London in just about half an hour, is already being tested, even if still many years from commercial viability. So-called scramjet engines without moving parts will be able to accelerate planes to more than five times the speed of sound both on earth and in space. Other alternative propulsion technologies will also likely take hold and include electric and hybrid technologies. Aircraft might eventually have different shapes that better fit these new engine technologies. These changes will be long term, as the airport infrastructure will have to adjust with them. Aircraft might eventually also penetrate the area of personal vehicles and replace cars with personal electric rotorcraft. All of these trends are certainly possible, and if there is enough market demand it will only be a matter of time until they become a reality. Others might emerge that are currently beyond imagination. The fascination of flight will not subside, and will continue to power the imagination of generations of inventors and engineers.

## Conclusion

The commercial aerospace industry has come a long way since its inception roughly 100 years ago. This century has been marked by great innovation and developments few could have foreseen when people first took to the skies. The industry grew along with the aircraft capabilities. Just as flights now routinely cross oceans and routes span continents, so do supply chains and customer bases. The commercial aerospace industry of today is a truly global one. It is also an industry active in the pursuit of reducing its environmental footprint. While Boeing and Airbus are the largest manufacturers, emerging manufacturers are growing in the market for smaller aircraft. As with all manufacturers, supply chain companies will be challenged to succeed in an ever-changing environment marked by new technologies and market entrants. The industry today produces, operates, and maintains a fleet of aircraft in the tens of thousands with an ever-larger geographical reach. The future will only see the world's fleet of aircraft grow. Most of that growth over the next two decades will see aircraft that mostly look familiar to the current observer, yet they will be built using modern technologies and advanced materials such as carbon fibres. They will be connected aircraft, gathering data used to improve operations.

Many questions await the industry in the years to come. What kind of aircraft will the market demand in the future, and in what kind of overall mobility concept will those be embedded? What will be the environmental impact, and can the industry maintain its record of efficiency improvements and establish a successful carbon-offseting scheme? Who will build the aircraft of the future, and how will supply chains be structured?

The future will likely see many more innovations shaping the industry. New propulsion technologies are likely to power aircraft of the future, and they might connect destinations in significantly less time. Given its first century of innovation, the next 100 years are quite likely to once again open horizons and make the impossible possible.

## Note

1 This chapter provides but a snapshot of the many developments that took the commercial aviation industry to where it is today. For a more complete overview of both historical developments and current industry structure, see, for example, Eriksson and Steenhuis (2016) or Wensveen (2015).

## References

Airbus (2016). *Orders and deliveries*. Online. Available at: www.airbus.com/company/market/orders-deliveries/ (accessed 28 October 2016).

Arvis, J.F. and Shepherd, B. (2013). Global connectivity and export performance, *World Bank Economic Premise*, 111, 1–4.

ATAG (2016). *Aviation: Benefits Beyond Borders*, Geneva, ATAG.

Bel, G. and Fageda, X. (2008). Getting there fast: globalisation, intercontinental flights and location of headquarters, *Journal of Economic Geography*, 8, 471–495.

Bloningen, B. and Cristea, A. (2015). Air service and urban growth: evidence from a quasi-natural policy experiment, *Journal of Urban Economics*, 86, 128–146.

Boeing (2016a). *A century in the sky*. Online. Available at: www.theatlantic.com/sponsored/boeing-2015/a-century-in-the-sky/652/ (accessed 28 October 2016).

Boeing (2016b). *Orders and deliveries*. Online. Available at: www.boeing.com/commercial/#/orders-deliveries (accessed 28 October 2016).

Boeing (2016c). *Current Market Outlook 2016–2035*, Seattle, WA, Boeing.

Boeing (2016d). *Services Market Outlook 2016–2035*, Seattle, WA, Boeing.

Cristea, A.D, Hillberry, R. and Mattoo, A. (2015). Open skies over the Middle East, *The World Economy*, 38(11), 1650–1681.

Dubbs, C. and Paat-Dahlstrom, E. (2011). *Realizing Tomorrow: The Path to Private Space Flight*, Lincoln, NE: University of Nebraska Press.

Eriksson, S. and Steenhuis, H.-J. (eds) (2016). *The Global Commercial Aviation Industry*, New York, Routledge Studies in the Modern World Economy.

Fell, J. (2016). *3D printing in the aviation industry*. Online. Available at: https://eandt.theiet.org/content/articles/2016/10/3d-printing-in-the-aviation-industry/ (accessed 28 October 2016).

Guinness World Records (2016). *Largest solid 3D printed item*. Online. Available at: www.guinness worldrecords.com/world-records/432579-largest-solid-3d-printed-object (accessed 28 October 2016).

Pearce, B. and Smyth, M. (2007). *Airline Liberalisation – IATA Economics Briefing No. 7*, Geneva, IATA.

Schwab, K. (ed.) (2015). *The Global Competitiveness Report 2014–15*, Geneva, World Economic Forum.

*Seattle Times* (2016). *Amazon lines up fleet of Boeing jets to build its own air-cargo network*. Online. Available at: www.seattletimes.com/business/boeing-aerospace/amazon-to-lease-20-boeing-767s-for-its-own-air-cargo-network/ (accessed 1 November 2016).

Shepherd, B., Shingal, A. and Raj, A. (2016). *Value of Air Cargo: Air Transport and Global Value Chains*, Geneva, Report for IATA.

Sivak, M (2015). *Energy Intensities of Flying and Driving, Report No. UMTRI-2015-14*, Ann Arbor, MI, University of Michigan Transportation Research Institute.

Soshkin, M. (2016). The US aerospace industry: a manufacturing powerhouse, *Business Economics*, 51(3), 166–180.

Spreen, W.E. (2016). *Marketing in the International Aerospace Industry*, New York, Routledge.

Teal Group Corporation (2016). *Teal Group World Aircraft Production History* (subscription database).

UN (United Nations) (2014). *Transport Aviation Action Plan: Climate Summit 2014*, New York, UN.

Wensveen, J.G. (2015). *Air Transportation: A Management Perspective*, New York, Routledge.

Winston, C. and Yan, J. (2015). Open skies: estimating travelers' benefits from free trade in airline services, *American Economic Journal: Economic Policy*, 7(2), 370–414.

# 6

# Impacts of liberalisation in global mature markets

*David Gillen*

## Introduction

This chapter examines aviation markets in developed economies, including the United States (US), European Union (EU), Canada and Australasia that have gone through the deregulation process, and examines new industry strategies that have emerged in the face of evolving government policy in domestic and international aviation markets. While deregulation has taken place in developed and developing economies (see also Chapter 7), the focus here is on mature markets. Mature markets are generally associated with developed economies; economies that were the first to move to deregulation in their domestic aviation markets and also initiate more liberal international bilaterals. Such institutional innovation led to rapid traffic expansion as prices fell and costs decreased. However, once a market has a relatively small amount of migration (immigration), urbanisation has stabilised and the middle class is a relatively stable proportion of the population (the income distribution is not shifting significantly), and deregulation has worked through the economy to exploit most opportunities it provided, the markets will tend to grow at a steady pace, at a trend value reflecting population and economic growth (see Chapter 19). These are mature markets. Such markets are a challenge to any firm, but especially airlines, as they seek to grow their international presence while maintaining their domestic markets in the face of new and evolving business models (see Chapter 8).

The chapter traces the factors that led to deregulation and how deregulation in air transport may or may not be tied to other trade initiatives. It looks at the evolution of the industry, the growth of airline alliances, the introduction of joint ventures (JVs) and the recent development of metal neutral joint ventures (MNJVs). The consequences of this evolution for competition and the benefits of liberalised markets are considered. The chapter finishes with a discussion of where to next for these markets and the key forces at work. Both airports (see Chapter 3) and the air traffic control system (see Chapter 4) are important components of the aviation system and affect the benefits of introducing deregulation. However, this chapter does not discuss either of these industries as they are considered elsewhere in the book.

## Airline deregulation: factors affecting the process

Airline deregulation was first introduced in the US domestic market in 1978 following a somewhat lengthy debate as to its merits. In the US, airline services are a federal jurisdiction since air routes cross state borders. However, California and Texas were geographically large enough to have intra-state services. These services were not regulated by the federal regulators. Studies demonstrated that fares on the intra-state routes in California and Texas where there was competition were significantly lower than elsewhere in the US and that service quality was higher. This evidence together with disenchantment with the current system led, after a series of congressional hearings, to the move to deregulation. This outcome subsequently spread to other aviation markets, first to most other developed countries (Canada, Australia, New Zealand, various member countries of the EU) and then to a few developing economies. In developing economies, such liberalisation was gradual and selective; Brazil gradually introduced domestic deregulation beginning in 1992, India introduced deregulation in 1990 and China began deregulating in 2000, for example.

A distinguishing feature of the move to airline deregulation in the US was the speed of the process; almost overnight, the Civil Aeronautics Board, the federal regulatory body, removed restrictions on fares, market entry and numbers of flights. In every other country, developed or developing economies, the deregulation process was more gradual; there was an evolution to final deregulation. A single important difference between the US approach and that in other countries that may provide an explanation was the US was the only country that did not have a dominant national government-owned airline; it was an entirely private system. Therefore, there were no vested interests that wanted a slow process of liberalising aviation so the incumbents could entrench their positions in the domestic markets before being faced with increased competition. Elsewhere, some countries had a mix of public and private carriers (e.g. Canada, Australia) while others had public monopolies (e.g. New Zealand).

The regulations governing the airline industry differed considerably across countries. The US controlled almost everything from fares to route entry, networks and frequencies, while Australia had entry restrictions, informal price control and no control over networks, and the United Kingdom (UK) had price and entry controls and weak network controls. New Zealand had a public monopoly, and therefore did not have explicit price and route controls (see Forsyth, 1998). Canada had a near public monopoly but did have private airlines, albeit always placed at a disadvantage relative to the national carrier, and had rigid controls on entry, routes flown, conditions of service, complete control of air fares, regulation of exit, geographic regions that could be flown, and controls on the level of service an airline could provide.

International liberalisation was a more gradual affair, with the US again leading the way by establishing liberal, near open skies, agreements with smaller European countries. These agreements had a cascading effect that led to subsequent deals with neighbouring countries. For example, the US signed an open skies agreement with the Netherlands in 1992, and in 1996 Germany, the Czech Republic, Italy, Portugal, Malta and Poland all followed suit. Over the next two decades, those countries that had first adopted domestic deregulation took differing approaches to liberalising their international aviation markets. The US adopted an open skies model in 1991 that provided that all airlines of both countries to the bilateral agreement had unlimited market access, unlimited fifth freedom rights, break-of-gauge rights, free pricing and permitted code-sharing (see Button, 2009). In the 1978–1991 period, the US air bilaterals had more limiting conditions. As of 2016, the US had open skies bilateral agreements with 119 foreign partners and three multilateral open skies accords: the agreement with Multilateral

Agreement on the Liberalisation of International Air Transportation (MALIAT) (which included New Zealand, Singapore, Brunei, Chile, Samoa, Tonga and Mongolia), Canada and the EU.

The deregulation and international liberalisation in other developed economies generally followed that of the US, but at a slower pace, and not with nearly the degree of openness. It might be said that the US focused at the outset on the gains to consumers and the development of trade, while the others were more concerned with domestic producer protection, although some countries eventually followed the US model. The EU deregulated in three tranches since the creation of a single European sky from a web of interlinked air transport bilaterals and a host of national carriers was quite different than the case of the US in 1978; the US had a single regulator and one set of rules, while the EU had multiple regulators and multiple, often conflicting, rules. The first package occurred in 1987, and permitted partial capacity and fare liberalisation and sought to begin the process of dismantling existing bilaterals by granting increased access across EU member borders. The second package introduced in late 1990 expanded the freedoms of fare-setting and expanding capacity, allowing third and fourth freedoms between all airports and expanding fifth freedom traffic. The Third Package introduced in early 1993 removed the remaining constraints and provided for full access to international and domestic routes. The single EU market was established, and carriers were considered for third-party bilaterals to be union ownership and control, not national or home country. A significant outcome of creating the single European aviation market was the creation of opportunities for low cost carriers (LCCs) to enter and develop; by 2003, LCCs' share of available seat kilometres (ASKs) was 20.2 per cent (InterVISTAS, 2006).

Australia and New Zealand, which both deregulated domestic markets in the early 1990s, have evolved into one of the freest aviation markets in the world, with a single aviation market agreed to in 1996, where a single aviation market (SAM) carrier was able to operate without restriction trans-Tasman and in the domestic market of either country (effectively cabotage), but beyond rights were still governed by bilateral agreements. A SAM carrier was one that was at least 50 per cent owned and effectively controlled by either an Australian or New Zealander, with its head office and operational base in either country. Forsyth (1998) makes the point that the original emphasis of aviation reform in both countries was to increase competition. Therefore, the reforms undertaken in both Australia and New Zealand were designed to increase the practical possibility of domestic and international competition. Such reforms included removing barriers to entry, privatising Qantas in 1995, and taking a highly liberal approach to international air service agreements to allow access by foreign carriers.

Canada deregulated domestic markets gradually with some minor moves to liberalising fare restrictions in 1984. This evolution continued and formal domestic deregulation was enshrined in the National Transportation Act of 1987. The national airline Air Canada was privatised in 1988, and when it was sold it was provided with significant advantages over its private sector counterpart, Canadian Airlines International, which it subsequently took over in 2000. Canada signed an open skies agreement with the US in 1995 that allowed any airline from either country to join any two cities in either country (there were some temporary restrictions on US carrier access to Toronto, Montreal and Vancouver for two to three years). As a result of this agreement, the number of transborder (Canada–US) routes expanded enormously from 38 to 59. A new somewhat revised open skies agreement was signed in 2007 with new liberalised fifth and sixth freedoms. These freedoms have been used extensively by Air Canada to build its markets into the EU, Asia and South America. In international markets, Canada has been highly protectionist and has limited access to foreign carriers, in many cases to three times per week, and/or has placed restrictions on city designations and fares. The result has been a significant shift of Canadians flying out of US gateway airports.

David Gillen

## Airline market structures after deregulation

With most major developed and many developing economies deregulating their domestic aviation markets by the mid-1990s, there was a differing outcome with regard to the evolution
of the domestic airline market structure. Such outcomes were a result of a number of factors,
including the size of the market, the way deregulation was structured, the degree of liberalisation
of international air policy, the adoption of aircraft technologies, the power of airline alliances
in the domestic economy, access to airport capacity (see Chapter 16), the strength and enforcement of competition laws, and the entry of differing airline business models (see Chapter 8).

There seem to be distinct phases in the evolution of market structures post-domestic deregulation
that applied to all countries; differences were matters of degree rather than kind. The key outcomes
were the change in network strategy, the choice of airline business model and the numbers of firms
in the market. The numbers of firms increased due in part to natural market growth but also by the
increase in demand resulting from lower fares and the expansion of services as a result of deregulation.

Large markets such as the US and EU saw a significant amount of entry both because of the
opportunities for route development and because of the availability of capital. Smaller markets such
as New Zealand, Australia and Canada saw limited entry both because of the smallness of the market
but also because of limits on available capital and the restrictions on foreign ownership; Australia and
New Zealand overcame the access to capital problem by allowing rights of establishment (a foreign
owner can establish a domestic airline but is restricted to flying only domestic routes).

The amount of entry, the network strategy and the selection of business model are not independent. Gillen and Morrison (2005) argue that the choice of business model leads naturally
to a network strategy that is consistent with that model. Choosing to enter as an LCC (e.g.
JetBlue, WestJet, easyJet, Ryanair, Wizz), for example, will lead naturally to the choice of a
point-to-point network structure because this is the only network structure that is consistent
with the underlying drivers of low costs; a hub-and-spoke model is a high-service quality but
also high cost strategy. Thus, what was seen in each country was the incumbent legacy airlines
shifting to a hub-and-spoke network strategy; this was particularly evident in the US because it
was a large aviation market, it is a large country geographically, and most hubs were 360-degree
hubs, meaning they could be used to connect flights in all directions. In Europe, the incumbent national and former national carriers had established hubs as gateways for international
flights. Generally, as experienced in the US, the EU and elsewhere, with deregulation there are
opportunities and entry will occur. However, the effects of this shock generally will take time
to stabilise as there is a shake-out from the new entrants, perhaps with some consolidation and
the development of new strategies; Button (2001) illustrates the entry, volatility and survival
rates for various member countries in the EU following deregulation. Certainly, looking at the
medium- to longer-term outcomes in each country that has deregulated, there are more carriers, there are a variety of airline business models (see Chapter 8), fares on average have fallen,
particularly on routes where the number of effective competitors has increased, and the number
of routes and frequency of service has increased. Deregulation has led to increased connectivity
and increases in trade and economic growth (see Fu et al., 2010; Kincaid and Tretheway, 2013).

## Alliances and JVs

### Alliances and cross ownership

The next step in the evolution of airline markets as they matured was the growth of airline alliances (see also Chapters 1 and 9) and their subsequent evolution into JVs (see also Chapter 11).

Airlines had formed marketing arrangements for a number of years, and international carriers had interline agreements where passengers could connect at gateways (e.g. London, Paris, New York). However, domestic deregulation and international liberalisation provided both a need and an opportunity for airlines to establish some closer ties and agreements.

Deregulation in domestic markets provided airlines with an opportunity to exploit the significant economies of density that characterise the supply of airline service. There is a large body of literature that has shown airline cost functions do not exhibit economies of scale, but do have significant economies of density (Caves et al., 1984; Gillen et al., 1990) and economies of spatial scope (Basso and Jara-Diaz, 2005). The shift to hub-and-spoke networks allowed the airlines to capture the cost economies from density in domestic markets and the economies of scope in linked networks. As international markets liberalised the demand side, the value of more frequencies and destinations favoured large firms, but the restrictions on foreign ownership and having no direct access to beyond the gateway market (cabotage not allowed) led to the development of strategic alliances. Table 6.1 presents the foreign ownership restrictions for some selected countries.

The key economic features of the airline industry that supported alliance formation were the strategic complementarity of alliance partner products, the significant cost economies, the demand-side complementarity of linked flight segments, and the ability and incentive for alliance partners to internalise pricing externalities (Brueckner, 2001; Park et al., 2001). The other important factor that promoted strategic alliance formation was market power.

*Table 6.1* Foreign ownership restrictions on airlines for selected countries

| Country | Status of foreign ownership restrictions |
| --- | --- |
| Australia | 49% for international (25% single), 100% for domestic |
| Brazil | 20% of voting equity |
| Canada | 25% of voting equity (15% single) |
| Chile | Principal place of business only |
| China | 35% |
| Colombia | 40% |
| EU | 49% for international (25% single), 100% for domestic |
| India | 26% for Air India, 49% for privately owned domestic carriers, 74% for charter and cargo |
| Indonesia | Substantial ownership and effective control |
| Israel | 34% |
| Japan | 33.3% |
| Kenya | 49% for international (25% single), 100% for domestic |
| Korea | 50% |
| Malaysia | 45% for Malaysia Airlines (20% single), 30% other |
| Mauritius | 40% |
| New Zealand | 49% for international, 100% for domestic |
| Peru | 49% |
| Philippines | 40% |
| Singapore | None |
| Taiwan | 33.3% |
| Thailand | 30% |
| United States | 25% voting equity, {1/3} of board at maximum, cannot be chairman of board |

*Source*: World Economic Forum (2016).

David Gillen

Alliances can and do take a variety of forms, ranging from simple marketing relationships to co-investments; the former is a simple contract alliance, whereas the latter is a strategic alliance.[1] The simpler marketing and contract type of alliance generally has benefits for both passengers and carriers that exceed the costs of alliance formation. However, as the alliances move to become strategic where schedules are aligned, there is joint use of facilities and the partners become more integrated; for example, costs increase and the benefits of expanding markets may not be enough to justify the tighter alliance. Added benefits of higher revenues were available through reduced competition as a result of alliance partner cooperation rather than competition and the dominance of an alliance at a gateway hub (e.g. Star at Frankfurt, SkyTeam at Schiphol, Oneworld at London Heathrow).

Initially, there were four global alliances, and with various mergers and takeovers three global alliances exist today: Star, Oneworld and SkyTeam (see also Chapter 1). Star was the first alliance formed by SAS, Thai Airlines, United Airlines, Air Canada and Lufthansa in 1997; in 2016, it had 28 member airlines. Oneworld was formed in 1998 by founding airlines American Airlines, British Airways, Canadian Airlines International, Cathay Pacific and Qantas; there were 14 member airlines in 2016. SkyTeam was founded in 2000 by Aeromexico, Air France, Delta Airlines and Korean Airlines; Continental, Northwest and KLM joined in 2004; in 2016, it had 20 member airlines.[2] The relationship of the different member airlines within the alliance can be quite different. Where Lufthansa and United might have a strong widely based strategic relationship with co-investments, Singapore and Air New Zealand, both members of Star, may have only code-sharing and other marketing affiliation.

Tables 6.2 and 6.3 provide summary information for the three global alliances. Star is by far the largest in every dimension – geographic coverage, available capacity and market share. However, the return on sales (net profit/revenue) was highest for Oneworld at 8.2 per cent, with Star having 6.8 per cent and SkyTeam 3.9 per cent. There are a number of non-aligned carriers in the world, and these carriers accounted for 38 per cent of global revenue passenger kilometres (RPKs) in 2015. Notably, LCCs do not belong to alliances since it does not fit their business model. The Middle East carriers, Emirates and Etihad, also do not belong to any alliance. Emirates is a true global airline and has grown capacity to access most major gateway cities

Table 6.2 Financials of three global alliances

|  | Star | Oneworld | SkyTeam |
| --- | --- | --- | --- |
| Revenue (US$ billion) | 184 | 137 | 149 |
| Operating profit (US$ billion) | 14.6 | 12.5 | 14.7 |
| Net profit (US$ billion) | 12.6 | 11.3 | 5.8 |
| Market share (% RPK in 2015) | 24.2 | 18.5 | 20.8 |

Source: Airline Business (2016).

Table 6.3 Alliance networks weekly schedule operations

|  | Destinations | | Countries served | Frequencies (000s) | Capacity | |
| --- | --- | --- | --- | --- | --- | --- |
|  | Total | Duplicates |  |  | ASK (billions) | Share |
| Star | 1,203 | 462 | 192 | 135 | 41.0 | 23.3 |
| Oneworld | 966 | 275 | 161 | 94 | 29.3 | 16.7 |
| SkyTeam | 1,050 | 350 | 177 | 116 | 32.7 | 18.6 |

Source: Airline Business (2016).

in the world. It has formed a partnership, a mini-alliance with Qantas, while Qantas remains in the Oneworld alliance.

There are two evolutionary trends that have emerged from the initial alliance strategy. First, airlines are taking major ownership stakes in alliance member carriers; and second, the strategic alliance has become, for a subset of alliance members, MNJVs.

Table 6.4 provides a listing of the cross-ownerships between various airlines in different parts of the world. The motivation for these ownership stakes varies. In the case of Etihad, it provides them a means of influencing routings and obtaining some of the benefits of being in an alliance without having membership. In other cases, it is a means of obtaining passenger feed where the gateway may be dominated by another alliance (e.g. South African Airways hub at Johannesburg). In other cases, it is to access airports that have severe slot shortages or where slots are expensive (e.g. Delta's stake in Virgin Atlantic and Aeromexico to access London Heathrow and Mexico City, respectively). Delta is also able to obtain code-share agreements; after investing in Virgin Atlantic, it announced over 100 new code-share agreements.

## MNJVs

The second evolution from the initial alliance strategy was the development of MNJVs, which are considered as close as one can be to a full merger, without the merger. Members of the JV can share information on pricing, capacity, frequency, revenue management, marketing, sales

*Table 6.4* Cross-regional ownership

| Airline region | Owner | Airline | Amount (%) |
|---|---|---|---|
| Europe | Qatar Airways | IAG (UK) | 20 |
| | Korean Air | Czech Airlines (Czech Republic) | 44 |
| | HNA Group | Aigle Azur (France) | 48 |
| | Qatar Airways | Meridiana (Italy) | 49 |
| | Etihad Airways | Etihad Regional (Switzerland) | 33 |
| | Etihad Airways | Air Serbia (Serbia) | 49 |
| | Etihad Airways | Alitalia (Italy) | 49 |
| | Etihad Airways | Air Berlin (Germany) | 29 |
| | Azuk/HNA Group | TAP Portugal (Portugal) | 45 |
| | Delta Airways | Virgin Atlantic Airways (UK) | 49 |
| Asia-Pacific | Etihad Airways | Jet Airways (India) | 24 |
| | Etihad Airways | Virgin Australia (Australia) | 22 |
| | Austrian | Alliance Airlines (Australia) | 12 |
| | Delta | China Eastern Airlines (China) | 4 |
| Latin America | Delta | Grupo Aeromexico (Mexico) | 4 |
| | Delta | Gol (Brazil) | 9 |
| | Air France-KLM | Gol (Brazil) | 2 |
| | Qatar Airways | LATAM (Chile) | 10 |
| | HNA Group | Azul (Brazil) | 24 |
| | United Airlines | Azul (Brazil) | 5 |
| Africa | ASL Aviation Group | Safair (South Africa) | 100 |
| | KLM | Kenya Airways (Kenya) | 27 |
| | Etihad Airways | Air Seychelles (Seychelles) | 40 |
| | HNA Group | Comair (South Africa) | 6 |

*Source*: Airline Business (2016).

and route strategies, a government-sanctioned cartel. There were a number of reasons these came to be. First, most if not all JVs required antitrust immunity by the competition authorities of each partner airline; the US had a condition that antitrust immunity would be granted only if there was an open skies agreement. The public benefit emanating from a JV depended on the incentives of partner airlines to create an integrated joint network. Only with an MNJV would the benefits be realised; better route choice, better scheduling and lower fares (at least for connecting passengers) (see Aviation Economics, 2011).[3] Second, JVs and MNJVs included only a handful of airlines within the alliance, generally the larger carriers and the older members. These ventures were appearing since all the low-hanging fruit, the easy alliance relationships had been developed, and as alliance membership increased there were conflicts among alliance members as internal differences emerged. Third, there had been significant consolidation in the domestic airline industry in the US and Europe, and there were opportunities to consolidate market power. EU carriers in particular faced significant competition from LCCs in the European market, whereas yields on long-haul international traffic were much larger. In the US, there are now three legacy airlines where there used to be several more; domestic air fares are rising as the oligopoly reduces capacity and reduces competition.

The first MNJV took place in 1993 between KLM and Northwest. Subsequent MNJVs (in the transatlantic market) took place in 2007, 2009 (Star) and 2010 (Oneworld). The two key players in these JVs were the US and EU, and granting an MNJV required that an open skies agreement with the US was in place. The US was not willing to grant antitrust immunity to allow a consortium of airlines to act as a legal cartel unless there was unfettered access to all other airlines that wanted to serve the market.

MNJVs dominated traffic flowing across the Atlantic, with 73 per cent of traffic carried in 2011 in one of three MNJVs: Star (Lufthansa, United, Air Canada), Oneworld (BA, Iberia, American), and SkyTeam (Delta, Air France-KLM, Alitalia). In 2016, the three MNJVs controlled 80.8 per cent of transatlantic capacity. The Atlantic market has pioneered the MNJV because the US Department of Transportation (DOT), which has authority to grant antitrust immunity (not the US Department of Justice), and the EU competition authorities have taken a positive view of MNJVs. The claimed precondition to signing off on an MNJV is that an open skies agreement between the two jurisdictions must be in place. While this may be true between the US and EU, it is certainly not the case elsewhere, for example with Canada, where Air Canada is an active member of a number of MNJVs. Canada does not have a full open skies agreement with the EU, although it does with the US, and it has market dominance in the majority of significant transborder routes, with an MNJV in place between United and Air Canada on these transborder routes.

The three global alliances have also established or tried to establish MNJVs in the north and south Pacific markets. In the north Pacific, Japan's competition authorities, who take a conservative and protectionist position on international bilaterals and have no open skies agreements, had to sign off on antitrust immunity for Star and Oneworld. In the south Pacific market, antitrust immunity has been sought by Delta-Virgin Australia (in which Etihad has a 22 per cent stake), Qantas-American and Air New Zealand-United. In 2011, All Nippon Airways and Lufthansa sought antitrust immunity despite no open skies agreement between Japan and the EU or Germany (see Mifsud, 2011).

There have been several significant outcomes as a result of the growth in these MNJVs. First, as Mifsud (2011) notes, the gap between the major and minor players within an alliance is growing. The major players, generally the larger or founding member airlines, who are members of the MNJV are required as a condition of receiving antitrust immunity to cooperate and act as if they were a single firm and compete even against their alliance partners. The smaller and more recent alliance partners are able to obtain benefits from being a member of an alliance, which may be upstream or downstream in the aviation supply chain (e.g. common maintenance contracts) and not necessarily directly from passenger feed. Therefore, the smaller partners not included in an MNJV benefit on the cost side, whereas the MNJV members benefit from the demand/revenue side. These benefits are derived from greater market power and reduced competition.

A second outcome has been higher fares; fares are higher in open skies markets with antitrust immunity than in open skies markets with no antitrust immunity. The claim was the public benefits exceeded the detriments. The public benefits were increased competition in the beyond and before markets, more one-stop travel, joint frequent flyer benefits, seamless connectivity for passengers and luggage, and schedule coordination. The claim, at least of the US DOT, was these benefits could only be realised through an MNJV where no individual airline had an incentive to act in its own best interests rather than in the interest of the airline group within the JV. These benefits came at a cost of higher fares, particularly for non-connecting passengers and non-alliance passengers. Fare increases were possible because of increased market power at hub airports and increasing rivals' costs. This results in stealing market share from non-aligned competitors. Under the MNJV, there was an ability to fix prices and capacity in previously competitive markets.

A third outcome is a longer-term and more general one. When there are rents in markets, increased supply in the form of new firms or more output from incumbent firms occurs. New technologies play an important role in augmenting this supply; a good example is the development of fracking that had a dramatic impact on increasing the supply of oil in world markets. So too are forms of technological change seen in the Atlantic and Pacific aviation markets with LCC long-haul entry and airlines-within-airlines growing the number of routes (e.g. Eurowings [Lufthansa], Rouge [Air Canada] and Scoot [Singapore Airlines]). LCCs such as WestJet, WOW Air and Norwegian are increasing their presence in the transatlantic market along with leisure airlines (e.g. TUI Group and Thomas Cook) and the low cost operators of the legacy carriers. In Pacific markets, AirAsia X, Scoot (Singapore Airlines) and Jetstar (long-haul division) were active in developing long-haul routes. The Asian market was ripe for such new services, with a large growing middle class and the subsequent increased demand for leisure travel. These carriers are serving some existing routes (the leisure carriers) but the LCCs are opening new routes. For instance, CAPA (2016a) reports in 2016 there were 45 new routes linking 26 European airports and 27 North American airports. In only a few cases, these were new airports that are being linked. In all cases, they are growing the aggregate market and increasing their albeit modest market share. An important technological contributor to the LCC long-haul growth has been the Boeing 787 and Airbus 330/350 variants (see also Chapter 5). These have allowed the non-aligned carriers or non-JV carriers (e.g. Turkish, Virgin Atlantic, LCCs) to open new routes that are point-to-point and do not rely on connecting traffic (with the exception of Turkish).

There were in 2016 several LCCs operating long-haul routes between Asia and Europe, and Europe and North America: Eurowings, Norwegian, Jetstar Airways, Air Canada Rouge, Lion Air, Azul, Cebu Pacific, WestJet, Scoot, Jin Air and AirAsia X all operate routes in excess of 7,000 kilometres (see CAPA, 2016b). Some of these carriers are airlines-within-airlines (Rouge, Eurowings, Scoot), but regardless all long-haul LCCs operate point-to-point routes. The airlines-within-airlines in domestic markets are designed as a fighting brand against LCCs (see Homsombat et al., 2014) (see also Chapter 8). They also replace the primary carrier on some routes in order to increase returns since the LCCs have lower costs.[4] In international markets, they operate to secondary markets and take some feed traffic from other alliances and non-aligned carriers. However, LCCs not aligned with a legacy carrier enter major markets and compete with all other carriers.

David Gillen

## Alliances versus global network carriers

While the development of alliances was the strategy followed by the legacy carriers of North America, Europe and to some degree North and South Asia, there was a group of carriers who chose to develop global networks.[5] The comparative advantage of these carriers was based on geographic location and the access to long-haul international passengers, particularly through sixth freedom rights.[6] The primary impact of the Middle East carriers (Emirates, Qatar and Etihad) has been to flow North American and European traffic over their hubs to South and East Asia and Australasia. This has had an impact on transatlantic RPKs for the major North American carriers and their JV partners. The Middle East carriers' penetration of secondary European cities, their access to major airports in North America and code-share agreements they have with some US carriers (e.g. Jet Blue) means they take a significant amount of traffic away from Star and SkyTeam alliances, so traffic does not flow over or through European hubs.

Emirates was founded in 1985, Qatar in 2003 and Etihad in 1993. These carriers together with Turkish Airlines have focused upon developing global networks; Turkish is a member of Star Alliance, but it appears to follow a strategy of developing a network that has a primary hub at Istanbul Ataturk Airport. This hub is fed by spoking into Europe, Africa and to some extent North America. In other words, for the most part, Turkish does not feed Star Alliance partners, nor do Star Alliance partners feed Turkish to any great extent, and in fact Turkish is in direct competition, notably with Lufthansa, and many of its Star Alliance partners. Turkish served more destinations (in 2016) than any other airline in the world.[7] However, terrorist events in Turkey, coupled with a failed coup attempt and a significant shift in the political regime, has resulted in a dramatic downturn in Turkish Airlines' fortunes.

The formation of alliances was a response, in part, to more restrictive bilaterals and constraints on foreign ownership. In domestic markets, alliance partners, generally smaller regional airlines, provided feed for trunk routes and internationally alliance partners provided access to beyond the gateway markets. The Middle East carriers could see the alliances that were dominated by large European and US carriers offered very little to them and their mission of increasing connectivity of the Middle East to other global destinations. Their domestic markets were also small, and therefore feed traffic for behind the gateway markets was also small.

Alliances work well when connecting long-haul with long-haul traffic. In the case of Emirates, it flies exclusively long haul and hubs through a single airport, Dubai, so there is no real value in alliances.[8] Qatar joined Oneworld in 2013; it did not have the size or market access in either the EU or US. Joining an alliance provided some demand-side benefits for it but also for the major partners in Oneworld. Having Qatar as a member means IAG (BA and Iberia) have access to high growth markets in Asia, Africa and the Middle East, markets that Qatar serves and where SkyTeam and Star have a larger presence than Oneworld. Etihad has, after remaining isolated in its own global growth strategy, decided on strategic partnerships and equity investments (see Table 6.4). These investments go across airline business models (LCCs and legacy carriers) and across alliances. It has also actively pursued code-share arrangements, in excess of 40, primarily with SkyTeam member airlines, including Air France-KLM.

The mature markets continue to rely on alliance membership, and particularly MNJVs, to maintain their market positions and to consolidate access to and market power in major developing markets such as India and China. Alliances have evolved so there are major and minor partners, and these minor partners will form within alliance code-share agreements among themselves. The global network carriers, Middle East carriers, and independent carriers such as Virgin Atlantic that originally shunned alliance membership have evolved and formed at minimum code-sharing agreements. LCCs have, for the majority of cases, shunned alliance-type relationships since they do not fit the LCC business model nor their point-to-point network structure (see also Chapter 8). However, as long-haul LCCs develop, there may be opportunities for developing feed, and thus alliance (code-share) relationships.

Alliances have been very good at delivering benefits in the form of higher revenues but they have been relatively poor at delivering cost synergies. The revenue benefits arise from both some increases in market power but also in developing feed traffic relationships and growing the market; internalising the externality of double marginalisation, for example. Cost gains result mostly from realising economies of density. The other area where cost gains have been made are co-locating alliance members at a single terminal at a multi-terminal airport (e.g. London Heathrow, Los Angeles) or adjacent in a single terminal. Common information technology platforms and shared lounge facilities, as well as pooled check-in facilities and shared ground handling, have also brought cost savings while at the same time improving customer service. In 2013, 55 per cent of capacity (seats flown) were under alliances, but much less of revenue passenger miles (RPMs) (see CAPA, 2013).

## Airline consolidation: coming full circle with fewer numbers and less competition?

After a country deregulates its domestic aviation market, there is generally new airlines and entry into a number of markets. Entry is most always as an LCC or smaller regional carrier. In no case has a new airline been in the form of a full service network carrier (FSNC) with a complex array of markets, hubs and service offerings. This has been the pattern in the US, Canada, the EU, Australia and New Zealand, as well as in developing countries such as China, India, Brazil, Russia, Chile, Mexico and various countries in South East Asia. Generally, the numbers of carriers have increased but the number of carriers in a market has stayed relatively flat (see Swan, 2005).

In the US market over the last several years, there has been significant consolidation. Whereas in the early 2000s there were several FSNCs, by 2016 there were three (American, Delta, United), but the presence of Southwest, Jet Blue, Alaska (merging with Virgin America in 2016) and Spirit has provided for more competition. Wittman (2013) describes what he terms capacity discipline emerging after 2010; the four largest carriers were clearly restricting the number of seats in markets. The result has been an increase in fares (on average about 20 per cent), increase in load factors, increasing profits and, for the FSNCs, nearly 100 per cent of flights to and from hubs.

Huschelrath and Muller (2011), investigating the US market, found different patterns of market entry, particularly by the network carriers. From 1996 to 2009, there was considerable entry by both network carriers and LCCs. However, the network carriers' market entry fell significantly after 2003, while LCC entry has increased, and they are entering more long-haul domestic markets.

The European single aviation market is quite different than the US market. Distances are much shorter and population density is higher; the US has an average density of 35 people per square kilometre and a total population of 318 million, while the EU has a density of 112 per square kilometre with a total population of 510 million, and 743 million in all of Europe; the US is 9.2 million square kilometres, while the EU is 3.7 million square kilometres.

The population size and density in the EU has resulted in an airline industry with 237 airlines (or airline groups), whereas in North America there are 172. There are significant differences in the distribution of the seat capacity; the top five airlines in North America control 72 per cent of seats, while in Europe they have 43 per cent, and in Asia-Pacific only 33 per cent (see CAPA, 2016c). Measuring the share of seats to calculate a Herfindahl-Hirschman Index (HHI),

*Table 6.5* HHI by region based on share of seats

| Region | HHI |
| --- | --- |
| North America | 1,215 |
| Middle East | 889 |
| Latin America | 742 |
| Europe | 487 |
| Africa | 400 |
| Asia-Pacific | 341 |

*Source*: Based on OAG seat data for 30 May 2016 to 5 June 2016.

the relative concentration of the markets can be compared.[9] Table 6.5 shows that consolidation in the US and the presence of an effective duopoly in Canada results in North America having the highest level of concentration. Europe, on the other hand, has an HHI that is 40 per cent the value of North America at 487.

In other respects, North America and the EU are quite similar; like the US, there are three major (FSNC) airline groups: Lufthansa, IAG and Air France-KLM. In the US, Southwest, an LCC, is a major airline, while in the EU LCCs Ryanair and easyJet are both major airlines.

## Conclusion

The evolution of the industry has been driven fundamentally by changing airline industry economic regulations and burgeoning global trade as a result of trade liberalisation under the World Trade Organisation (WTO). Domestic airline deregulation led to greater competition, which in turn led to fundamental changes to airline management practices and to the development of new business models. Competition pressured the airlines to be more cost-competitive, to reorganise their networks, and to respond to demand-side pressures for geographic reach and route frequency.

The opportunities within the industry led to the growth of LCCs, initially in the US, as others copied and refined the Southwest Airlines model. The LCC model was an effective entrant since entry costs were low and it was a sustainable model since it did not require large investments in hubs. The LCC business model expanded into other jurisdictions and, as in the US, morphed into different variants (Mason and Morrison, 2008).

The emergence of a global airline industry was both a facilitator and facilitated by the growth in global trade. Liberalisation of trade under the WTO allowed globalisation to change the way supply chains were organised. This was facilitated by improvements in transportation (containerisation and large vessels), advances in communications (Internet and computerisation), highly skilled, adaptable and low cost labour, and facilitating government policies. EU carriers were the first to develop truly international networks. US carriers had such a large domestic market, their international activity was until recently a relatively small proportion of their total business. The international business was principally oriented to the EU and to pockets in South East Asia. This has changed as a result of the growth of LCCs in domestic markets, which has placed downward pressure on yields and the increasing opportunities in international markets that were being further liberalised to entry. The growth in globalisation in trade also stimulated demand.

The growth in international airline activity brought carriers face-to-face with the restrictions of market access beyond gateway airports and the limitations on foreign ownership. The outcome was the development of international airline alliances, which certainly had the outcome of extending networks but also of reducing effective competition. Three alliances emerged: Star, SkyTeam and Oneworld. Alliances moved from being coordinated marketing arrangements to integrated pricing and capacity agreements. These eventually led to (MN)JVs, which dominated the transatlantic markets, and soon after the trans-Pacific ones. These MNJVs were claimed to be net welfare increasing, but there is mixed evidence. These arrangements are as close to a merger as is possible without an actual merger. Connecting passengers gain on balance, but OD passengers face higher fares. The benefits from the JVs are also available through a looser alliance. The stumbling block is the alliance participants need to optimise over the alliance rather than for themselves within the alliance. An MNJV achieves this alliance optimisation.

The increased concentration in domestic markets of countries with mature airline industries, including the US, the EU, Australia and Canada, for example, has provided the incentives to develop new business models to take advantage of the higher fares the higher concentration has brought about. In domestic markets, the ultra-LCC has emerged (Spirit [US], Allegiant [US], Frontier [US], Enerjet [Canada], Fly Too [Canada], Flydubai [United Arab Emirates], Wizz Air [Hungary]), and the LCCs are now also flying long haul. Norwegian and Eurowings are flying between the EU and US, Wowair flies between Iceland and the US, WestJet flies between Canada and the EU, AirAsia X joins countries in South East Asia, and JetStar joins Australia with various countries in South East Asia. The success of these long-haul LCCs will depend on keeping down traditional factor costs, such as labour and fuel. The development of fuel-efficient aircraft, linking to domestic networks and achieving density economies in large city pair markets are the necessary ingredients to sustain long-haul LCCs.

The airline industry in 2017 has just emerged from the most profitable few years in its history. However, it faces uncertain times. Threats to the balance and pattern of global trade, a slowdown or even reversal in globalisation, terrorism, and a general decrease in economic growth are all threats to the industry. Yet what it has also seen is the extensive migration to developed economies that has taken place over the last several decades has created a natural demand for route development. As an example, there has been an 84 per cent increase in unique city pairs served since 1995; in 2016, IATA reported that 18,429 city pairs were served (IATA, 2016). The upcoming generations are also eschewing assets in favour of greater mobility and freedom. This generation has a 23 per cent greater propensity to travel than older generations (Machado, 2014). With mature aviation markets, it can be seen that there is a continued increase in the number of markets served, rather than in the size of markets.

## Notes

1 All alliances require the approval of the competition authorities of the two carriers forming the alliance relationship. In most cases, strategic alliances receive antitrust immunity.
2 Interestingly, the airlines have different alliance relationships on the cargo side.
3 The argument is that airlines with connecting traffic need to be incentivised to internalise the externality of ignoring how prices on one segment affect demand on a connecting segment (known as double marginalisation). Only under an MNJV is this likely to happen. The evidence is connecting fares decline but origin-destination (OD) fares increase.
4 As an example, Air Canada had Rouge take over all transborder routes except high-yield business routes.
5 LCCs do not join alliances since they operate point-to-point networks. They do, however, occasionally have code-share agreements with other carriers, in particular those carriers that do not belong to one of the three global alliances, or in cases where the domestic market is dominated by one alliance (e.g. Canada) and carriers from other alliances cannot access beyond markets easily. The dominant domestic alliance tends to have excessive interline fees for non-own alliance carriers.
6 An exception here is Virgin Atlantic, which is based in the UK and competes with global alliance carriers, especially British Airways. Virgin began in 1983 prior to the formation of the EU, the EU single aviation

market and European deregulation. This was a period prior to the development of global alliances. Virgin developed in a regime of fairly strict bilateral agreements and benefited from the high yields on these regulated markets.

7  In fact, one could argue that Turkish competes with Lufthansa to carry traffic from Europe to the Middle East, Asia and Africa.

8  Emirates did sign a five-year code-share partnership with Qantas, which allowed Emirates access to a large number of markets and increased Qantas's access to a larger number of European destinations through Dubai.

9  The HHI is a measure of market concentration, and is calculated by squaring the percentage market share of each firm in a defined market and summing these numbers; the index varies between 0 and 10,000, and a value of 10,000 would indicate a pure monopoly (100 squared).

# References

Airline Business (2016). Special report: alliances, *Airline Business*, September.

Aviation Economics (2011). North Atlantic: the metal neutral market, *Aviation Strategy*, 161, March.

Basso, L.J. and Jara-Diaz, S.R. (2005). Calculation of economies of spatial scope from transport cost functions with aggregate output with an application to the airline industry, *Journal of Transport Economics and Policy*, 39(1), 25–52.

Brueckner, J. (2001). The economics of international codesharing: an analysis of airline alliances, *International Journal of Industrial Organization*, 19(10), 1475–1498.

Button, K. (2001). Deregulation and liberalization of European air transport markets, *Innovation: The European Journal of Social Science Research*, 14(3), 255–275.

Button, K. (2009). The impact of the US-EU open skies agreement on airline market structures and airline networks, *Journal of Air Transport Management*, 15, 59–71.

CAPA (2013). *Airline alliances: what future? Global, multilateral and bilateral partnerships are evolving.* Online. Available at: http://centreforaviation.com/analysis/airline-alliances---what-future-global-multilateral-and-bilateral-partnerships-are-all-evolving-144593 (accessed 26 May 2017).

CAPA (2016a). Europe to North America in 2025: a gradual evolution, *Airline Leader*, 35 (July–August), 34–41.

CAPA (2016b). Long haul LCCS in ascendance: Scoot prepares to fly to Europe in 2017, the world's longest LCC route, *CAPA*, 9 July.

CAPA (2016c). European airline consolidation and profitability. Part 1: top 5 airline groups have only 43% share, *CAPA*, 8 April.

Caves, D., Laurits, R.C. and Tretheway, M.W. (1984). Economies of density versus economies of scale: why trunk and local service airline costs differ, *The RAND Journal of Economics*, 15(4), 471–489.

Forsyth, P. (1998). The gains from the liberalisation of air transport: a review of reform, *Journal of Transport Economics and Policy*, 31(1), 73–92.

Fu, X., Oum, T. and Zhang, A. (2010). Air transport liberalization and its impacts on airline competition and air passenger traffic, *Transportation Journal*, 49(4), 24–41.

Gillen, D. and Morrison, W. (2005). Regulation, competition and network evolution in aviation, *Journal of Air Transport Management*, 11, 161–174.

Gillen, D., Oum, T. and Tretheway, M. (1990). Airline cost structure and policy implications: a multi-product approach for Canadian airlines, *Journal of Transport Economics and Policy*, 24(1), 9–34.

Homsombat, W., Lei, Z. and Fu, X. (2014). Competitive effects of airlines within airlines strategy: pricing and route entry, *Transportation Research Part E: Logistics and Transportation Review*, 63, 1–16.

Huschelrath, K. and Muller, K. (2011). *Patterns and Effects of Entry in U.S. Airline Markets*, Discussion Paper No. 11–059, Mannheim, Centre for European Economic Research.

IATA (2016). *Economic performance of the industry-end year 2016 report.* Online. Available at: www.iata.org/.../economics/IATA-Economic-Performance-of-the-Industry-end (accessed 26 May 2017).

InterVISTAS (2006). *The economic impact of air service liberalization.* Online. Available at: www.intervistas.com/?insight=the-economic-impact-of-air-service-liberalization-final-report) (accessed 26 May 2017).

Kincaid, I. and Tretheway, M. (2013). Economic impact of aviation liberalization. In: P. Forsyth, D. Gillen, K. Huschelrath and H. Niemeier (eds). *Liberalisation in Aviation, Competition, Cooperation and Public Policy*, Aldershot, Ashgate.

Machado, A. (2014). How millennials are changing travel, *The Atlantic*, 18 June.

Mason, K.J. and Morrison, W.G. (2008). Towards a means of consistently comparing airline business models with an application to the 'low-cost' airline sector, *Research in Transportation Economics*, 24, 75–84.

Mifsud, P. (2011). Metal neutrality and the nation-bound airline industry, *Air and Space Law*, 36(2), 117–130.

Park, J.-H., Zhang, A. and Zhang, Y. (2001). Analytical models of international alliances in the airline industry, *Transportation Research Part B: Methodological*, 35(9), 865–886.

Swan, W. (2005). *Consolidation in the Airline Industry*, Mimeo, Sauder School of Business, University of British Columbia.

Wittman, M. (2013). *New Horizons in U.S. Airline Capacity Management: From Rationalization to Capacity Discipline*, Cambridge, MA, MIT International Center for Air Transportation.

World Economic Forum (2016). *A new regulatory model for foreign investment in airlines*. Online. Available at: www.weforum.org/whitepapers/a-new-regulatory-model-for-foreign-investment-in-airlines/ (accessed 26 May 2017).

# 7

# Liberalisation developments in key selected emerging markets

*Eric T. Njoya and David Warnock-Smith*

## Introduction

While there is no specific definition of what constitutes an emerging market, the majority of countries classified as emerging economies appear to fall into the World Bank's upper middle income and lower middle income categories (Tuncer, 2012). Thus, an emerging market can be defined as a market that is characterised by rapid economic growth, low to medium per capita income and increased participation in world trade. Thanks to strong economic and demographic developments, emerging markets are increasingly playing significant roles in the global aviation industry, with yearly revenue passenger kilometre (RPK) growth rates in the short to medium term expected to surpass that of more economically developed regions (Airbus, 2016) (see also Chapter 19). According to Airbus (2016), the aviation sector of emerging markets has grown rapidly over the past few decades, with RPK expected to grow at 5.8 per cent annually between 2015 and 2034 in emerging and developing economies, as compared to 3.5 per cent in advanced economies. The growth observed in recent years can also be explained by the gradual removal of restrictions on trade in air transport services in emerging economies.

Historically, the airline industries of emerging economies have been highly regulated, with high entry costs and protectionism of flag carriers. Most countries had a single flag carrier, which was nationalised and faced virtually no competition on the routes they operated. However, since the beginning of the 1990s, there has been a paradigm shift towards a market-oriented system that emphasised the liberalisation of air transport services and the role of the private sector as the engine for growth. Although these changes have happened to different degrees in emerging markets, in general they have resulted in the emergence of a variety of new market participants, which in turn has had a positive impact on levels of competition.

This chapter examines the degree of air transport liberalisation in emerging economies and its effect on the state and intensity of competition (see Chapter 6 for mature economies). Using the Air Liberalisation Index (ALI) developed by the World Trade Organisation (WTO) (WTO ASAP Database, 2016), it provides a brief overview of the bilateral and multilateral policies used by emerging markets to expand their air services (the ALI is also considered in Chapter 19). The ALI is a synthetic measure of the level of liberalisation of the air transport policy of a given signatory. Its value ranges between 0, for very restrictive ASAs, and 50, for very open ones. Indicators used to assess the degree of competition include the average number of effective competitors in the market, the type of airlines in the market, airline market shares at the route level, and barriers to entry. Furthermore, trends in market structure and the extent of competition in city pair markets are measured using the Herfindahl-Hirschman Index (HHI) (also mentioned in Chapter 6). The HHI is a measure of market concentration that is computed by squaring the market share of each firm competing in the market and then summing the resulting numbers. The HHI takes on values closer to 0 when there are many firms with small market shares and 10,000 when a monopoly exists. The scope of this chapter is limited to passenger scheduled air services.

The remainder of this chapter is organised into two sections. The first section reviews the literature on air transport liberalisation and competition in emerging economies, and their role in facilitating this growth. The second section presents four case studies in which air policy and the structure of the airline industry are analysed in detail. The chapter concludes with a summary that emphasises the need for further liberalisation and competition policies to safeguard consumer interests.

## The record so far

The world's two biggest commercial aircraft manufacturers, Airbus and Boeing, have collectively pinned much of their aircraft demand hopes on emerging markets over the last 5 to 10 years (see Chapter 5). Recent history suggests that higher than average gross domestic product (GDP) growth has quickly driven up living standards and has generated a much higher propensity to travel from a typically low base (see Chapter 19), which in turn generates significant aircraft orders both by airlines based in emerging economies and by airlines based elsewhere wishing to profit from such market growth. Boeing, for instance, sees a strong relationship between the predicted 4.1 per cent average GDP growth in Asia, the predicted 6.1 per cent growth rate in air traffic within Asia, and the expected 15,130 new aircraft orders by 2035 (Boeing, 2016). Similarly, Airbus contends that there is a strong relationship between growth in private consumption and propensity to travel, with emerging economies predicted to represent 43 per cent of all private consumption by 2034, up from the current 31 per cent (Airbus, 2016).

Perhaps the most interesting contribution of emerging economies to both the global economy and global air transport markets has been their role in the dispersion of wealth, and therefore the spread of air transport demand (see Chapter 19). Twenty years ago, 70 per cent of the world's population represented less than 10 per cent of global wealth, whereas now it is nearer 20 per cent (Airbus, 2016). In 1995, 64 per cent of world passenger traffic was transported by carriers based in North America and Europe, while in 2015 this figure had dropped to 48 per cent (Boeing, 2016). Rather strikingly, by 2035, these figures are expected to change to 30 per cent in terms of wealth distribution and a mere 37 per cent of air traffic concentrated in North America and Europe, with China, the Middle East and the rest of Asia being the primary drivers for growth over the next 20 years.

There have been a number of consultancy and academic studies looking into the relationship between emerging economies and air transport markets, with the role of liberalisation and competition in facilitating this growth being a major focus. Back in 2001, Goldstein (2001) found that there was a relationship between levels of market openness and the upgrading of air transport infrastructure in the Sub-Saharan Africa region, with the main finding being that continued policy restraints had restricted market access and investment in comparison to similar regions such as Central America. Cline et al. (1998) carried out a study of air transport demand in emerging markets in 1998 using Kyrgyzstan as a case country. As part of the study, economic development measures were computed for 30 countries and fed into air traffic forecasts, which were found to be dependent on underlying trends in GDP and trade, especially when economies such as Kyrgyzstan moved from centrally planned to market-based economic structures.

Zhang and Chen (2003) found that limited air traffic rights in China during the 1990s stifled the supply of international air services and were motivated primarily by protection of what were non-competitive, home-based airlines, as well as the infrastructure constraints and limited human capital that were prevalent at the time. More recently, under a backdrop of stronger home-based carriers (which became known as the Big Three: China Southern, China Eastern and Air China), and a relaxation of travel restrictions for Chinese residents, many of whom enjoying higher levels of disposable income, China has looked to partially liberalise air transport markets, though with a clear focus on the Big Three carriers, who have been allowed to dominate many domestic and international trunk routes (Wang et al., 2016).

There has been recent evidence of mixed performance across some of the main emerging economies. Among the BRIC economies (Brazil, Russia, India and China), for example, only India, and to a lesser extent China, have consistently seen strong growth in air transport markets and underlying economic performance. Brazil and Russia have both suffered from recent setbacks. Political turmoil and economic sanctions, respectively, have started to hit economic performance in both countries, which in turn has had a knock-on effect on air traffic levels. Commodity price decreases have also had a marked effect on underlying economic conditions in Brazil and Russia, both of which are energy-dependent. IATA (2015) adds that airlines in Brazil pay some of the highest fuel charges in the world, an issue that is recently going through reform in India after its home carrier fuel costs became unsustainably high (up to 50 per cent of total operating costs in 2009, according to O'Connell et al., 2013). Domestic capacity and traffic both contracted in Brazil and Russia compared to January 2016 and 2015 levels, though in Russia airlines have responded much quicker with capacity cuts than their Brazilian counterparts (see Table 7.1).

While it appears the BRIC economies have not been immune from economic and air transport market setbacks, the overriding regulatory prognosis has been quite uniform, with those BRIC countries liberalising at a faster pace providing a platform for higher levels of competition between carriers in domestic and international markets, and the more protective, restrictive countries having to rely more on a smaller selection of home-based and foreign carriers to serve growing or retracting markets (e.g. Russia).

Due to this well-documented divergence of fortunes between the BRIC emerging markets, it is of paramount importance to broaden the geographical scope of emerging markets to include lesser-studied transition states that will help to paint a fuller picture of the degree of divergence or convergence in the development of their respective air transport markets. To cover as wide a geographical scope as possible, four emerging countries located in different world continents are selected for further analysis, namely Kenya, Indonesia, Mexico and Saudi Arabia. A review of economic, air policy and air transport market developments is provided in each case.

*Table 7.1* Domestic air transport markets in Brazil and Russia, January 2016 versus 2015

| Air transport market | Capacity change (seats) | Traffic change (passengers) |
| --- | --- | --- |
| Domestic Brazil | −2.6 | −4.1 |
| Domestic Russia | −5.2 | −2.0 |

*Source:* IATA (2016).

## Case examples

### Kenya

Kenya, like most African economies, has faced unprecedented economic growth over the past decades, confirming the country's status as an emerging market. Between 2000 and 2015, Kenya's GDP grew on average by 5.9 per cent annually, but it is expected to improve by 6.5 per cent over the next 15 years, making it one of the fastest-growing economies in Sub-Saharan Africa (World Bank, 2016). Located in East Africa, Kenya has a population estimated at 46 million in 2015 and an estimated GDP per capita of US$1,380 (World Bank, 2016). The country is the dominant economy in the East African Community (EAC) (accounting for 40 per cent of the region's GDP) and is ranked the ninth largest economy in Africa and the fourth largest in Sub-Saharan Africa (Kimenyi et al., 2016). Its comparative advantage lies in its strategic location in the region, serving five landlocked countries (Ethiopia, South Sudan, Uganda, Rwanda and Burundi), its market-based economy, and its middle class, which accounts for 44.9 per cent of its population, proportionally the largest in the East African region.

One sector that has experienced particularly strong growth in the past decade is the aviation industry. The Kenyan aviation industry is a vital catalyst for economic growth, acting as a facilitator for tourism and for the transport of high yielding exports and perishable goods such as floriculture and fish products. Oxford Economics (2011) points out that the sector contributes 1.1 per cent directly to the country's GDP and supports 46,000 jobs. Passenger traffic at the largest airport, Jomo Kenyatta International Airport (JKIA), grew at an average annual rate of 3 per cent between 2010 and 2015, boosting volumes to 6.4 million (see Table 7.2). This has been achieved despite a fall in tourism revenues after the 2014 terrorist attacks in Nairobi.

There have been a number of significant changes with regard to the regulatory context for air transport in Kenya in the past decades. Liberalisation policies have been introduced since the 1990s (World Bank, 2005), and the Kenya Civil Aviation Authority has been established as an autonomous body, in charge of administering policies set by the government. Although the average level of liberalisation in Kenya's air service agreements (ASAs) is very low at 8 out of 50 according to the WTO ASAP Database (2016), the country has demonstrated greater flexibility in the granting of third and fourth freedom traffic rights and relaxation of fifth freedom traffic, frequency and capacity (Njoya, 2016). Kenya has also actively participated in regional and sub-regional economic blocs for the development of more open markets (MoT, 2009). Domestic routes in Kenya are liberalised and operators are free to fly any route without a special licence. Kenya has also embraced multiple designation. It sets the ownership limit at 49 per cent for both domestic and international airlines, and the remaining 51 per cent can be owned by private individuals (MoT, 2009).

Liberalisation policies have been accompanied by partial privatisation of the former state-owned carrier (IFC, 2008). However, despite the positive progress in privatisation, government involvement in the air transport sector has not disappeared entirely. In fact, with the exception

Table 7.2 GDP and air passenger indicators for Kenya and JKIA, 2010 to 2015

| Kenya | | JKIA | |
|---|---|---|---|
| GDP growth (%) 2010–2015 cumulated | GDP (US$ mn) 2015 current | Passenger growth (%) 2010–2015 cumulated | Passenger volume (mn) 2015 |
| 35.7 | 63,398 | 18.2 | 6.4 |

Source: KAA (2016) and World Bank (2016).

of Ethiopia and Rwanda, government interference with the day-to-day operation of airlines is prevalent in Kenya like in many African countries. In addition, airport charges are very high, owing to lots of inefficiencies in airports, low traffic volumes and government intentions to use aviation as a way of generating additional revenues for non-aviation purposes (Chingosho, 2009; Schlumberger and Weisskopf, 2014).

The Kenyan aviation industry is a dynamic and competitive one, dominated by the flag carrier, Kenya Airways, which held a 46 per cent share of weekly capacity in 2014 on international routes. Foreign African airlines operating in Kenya include Ethiopian Airlines (7.1 per cent in 2014) and Precision Air (5.6 per cent). These airlines operate intra-African traffic and competition is very limited, owing to thin markets on most routes, which do not justify the operation of several airlines (Abate, 2016). The World Bank (2005) argues that fares are relatively lower in the EAC compared to West and Central Africa, which is attributable to higher traffic concentration (especially in the Nairobi hub) and the resulting economies of scale. In order to provide an assessment of fare levels in the EAC, Schlumberger and Weisskopf (2014) compared fares for selected dates for domestic and intra-EAC routes with routes in other regions that are currently operated by low cost carriers (LCCs). They found that on the routes where the LCC Fly540 is present in Kenya, Kenya Airways actually undercuts the LCC by a small margin on the chosen dates, thereby displaying some signs of fare convergence in the market. The authors argue that competition with the LCCs seems to have brought down fares to a similar level on some trunk routes, such as the Nairobi to Mombasa route.

With regard to domestic capacity share by airline, Kenya Airways retained a 53.1 per cent share in 2014 – whereas the next largest market shares, of Five Forty Aviation and SafariLink, were 19.8 per cent and 7.5 per cent, respectively. As a result of the country's move towards a deregulated domestic market, some key routes have seen competitor entry. LCCs have been the key driver in domestic and regional air transport developments in Kenya (Schlumberger and Weisskopf, 2014). In 2013, almost a fifth (23 per cent compared with 10 per cent in 2001) of domestic seats in Kenya were operated by LCCs, led by Fly540 and Kenya Airways subsidiary Jambo Jet (see Table 7.3). Approximately 9 per cent of total international seats available were with Kenyan LCCs (CAPA, 2013).

A market analysis in terms of seats supplied between Mombasa and Nairobi shows that although there has been little change in the average number of effective competitors between 2000 and 2015, the HHI decreased from 8,735 to 6,650. In fact, the number of competitors in this domestic route increased slightly from two full service carriers in 2000 to two LCCs (with market shares of 80 per cent and 18 per cent) and one full service carrier in 2015. Thus, although the market is still highly concentrated, LCCs have expanded since 2000, thereby adding competition into

Table 7.3 LCCs based in Kenya

| Airline | Base | Operating since | Number of routes in 2013 | |
|---------|------|-----------------|--------------------------|---|
| | | | Domestic | Regional |
| Jambojet[1] | Nairobi | 2014 | 7 | 0 |
| JetLink Express | Nairobi | 2006 | Ceased operations 2012 | |
| Fly540 | Nairobi | 2005 | 6 | 2 |
| AirKenya Express[2] | Nairobi | 1987 | 8 | 1 |

Source: Author's compilation based on airlines' annual reports and data from CAPA.

Notes:
1 Kenya Airways' low cost subsidiary.
2 Hybrid carrier operating domestic scheduled and charter services.

the market. Competition has also increased on short-haul intra-regional services with the expansion of Fastjet, the largest LCC in Africa's international market based in Dar-es-Salam, Tanzania. Fastjet launched Tanzania to Nairobi flights in January 2016, stepping up competition with Kenya Airways and its associate Precision Air, which also flies the same route (CAPA, 2016).

At the international route level, the capacity analysis shows that the number of competitors offering direct flights increased between, for example, Nairobi and London Heathrow, experiencing a transition from a monopoly in 2000 to a duopoly in 2015. However, it is important to note that international competition is more intense on trunk routes operated by more than two airlines such as Nairobi–Paris/Amsterdam and Nairobi–Dubai. On these long-haul, fast-growing markets, competition is typically driven by network carriers such as Emirates Airlines, Qatar Airways, Swiss International Air Lines and Air France-KLM.

## Mexico

Mexico's status as an emerging economy has been secured by decades of strong growth in population and GDP (see Table 7.4), and it is now classified by the World Bank as an upper-middle-income economy. A stronger jobs market, real wage increases and expansion of credit have combined to drive substantial growth in private consumption. Mexico is also a significant exporter of international tourism, with a healthy 26 per cent growth in the 2010 to 2014 period, serving 29.3 million international tourist arrivals in 2014 (Index Mundi, 2016). Healthy private consumption has also led to an increase in outbound visits from Mexico, growing by 4 million in the 2010 to 2014 period to a total of 18.3 million in 2014 (Index Mundi, 2016).

Growth in air traffic and related international tourist visits have both outstripped GDP growth in Mexico, demonstrating a positive propensity to travel and a healthy stimulation effect of the travel industry on the Mexican economy. Air traffic growth between 2010 and 2015 has been particularly impressive at some of the larger gateway airports, namely Mexico City, Cancun and Monterrey (59, 58 and 57 per cent, respectively), with some of the country's smaller airports and regions also benefitting from the greater domestic and international connectivity provided at these airports, particularly in the case of Mexico City and Monterrey, with around 73 per cent growth in the 2010 to 2015 period at airports such as Villahermosa, Leon and Tuxtla Gutierrez.

Mexico has traditionally taken a protectionist stance on commercial air transport policy, though there have been some exceptions to this based on the reciprocal interests of bilateral partners and home-based airlines. By far the most significant agreement is the Mexico–United States (US) bilateral, which accounts for the main share of international traffic to and from Mexico, and which has been subject to various rounds of ASA revisions. According to the WTO Air Service Agreements Projector (ASAP), the Mexico–US ASA has been partially liberalised, with some evidence of fifth freedom rights being granted and freedom in fare-setting. Adjustments made in 1991 to the Mexico-US ASA paved the way for significant Delta services into provincial regions of Mexico, for example, with 170 per cent traffic increases on the Atlanta–Guadalajara city pair after Delta initiated services in 1999 (InterVISTAS, 2006). Areas

*Table 7.4* GDP and air passenger indicators for Mexico, 2010 to 2015

| GDP growth (%) 2010–2015 cumulated | GDP ($US bn) 2015 current | Passenger growth (%) 2010–2015 top 50 airports cumulated | Passenger volume (mn) 2015 top 50 airports |
|---|---|---|---|
| 10.2 | 1,144 | 46.6 | 113.5 |

*Source*: Gobierno de Mexico Secretaria de Comunicaciones y Transporte (2016) and World Bank (2016).

of designation, capacity and ownership have remained more restricted, however, preventing the types of consolidation and capacity-focused competition seen in more liberal markets.

There has been a recent push, nevertheless, to further liberalise the Mexico–US ASA, with the two parties signing a more liberal agreement in late 2015 to remove some of the remaining restrictions on designation, capacity and ownership that would prevent a proposed joint venture between Aeromexico and Delta on routes between the US and Mexico from taking place (Lay Yeo, 2015). The latest ASA update is still awaiting Senate approval in Mexico, and both the US Department of Transportation (DOT) and Mexican Competition Commission (COFECE) are also investigating the proposed competitive effects of the Delta/Aeromexico joint venture, which could lead to the carriers being forced to remove duplicate routes and reduce their joint presence in Mexico City. The various policy updates have started to take effect on many city pair markets, with the Mexico City to Houston, Texas market improving its HHI competitiveness indicator from 5,900 to 4,400 between September 2000 and September 2016, primarily due to the permitted introduction of LCC services (namely Interjet, with a 12 per cent market share of seats) to compete with incumbents Aeromexico (29 per cent) and United Airlines (58 per cent).

The average level of liberalisation for Mexico's ASAs is quite low (14 out of 50), according to the WTO ASAP Database (2016), ranging from very restrictive (1 out of 50 on Mexico-Venezuela) to moderately liberal (29 out of 50 on Mexico–New Zealand). Domestically, privatisation and freedom of operation has been permitted since the late 1980s (OECD, 2014), though this has led to mixed results over the intervening period, with Mexicana and Aeromexico first being privatised at the end of the 1980s, but then being left unchecked, and then being forced to merge in 1993, leading to an almost 80 per cent market share on domestic and international flights. The long-overdue introduction of LCCs from 2005 had a positive effect on levels of traffic and competition. This, combined with a sell-off of Mexicana and Aeromexico once again to private investors, led to an aggressive competitive environment initially in the domestic market and then extending to international markets. Mexicana became a well-publicised casualty of this cut-throat environment, having to cease operations in 2010.[1] The popular Mexico City to Guadalajara domestic market, for example, saw the overall number of seats offered increase by around 19,000 between September 2000 and September 2016, with the HHI competitiveness indicator strengthening from 3,500 to 3,000 primarily through the increased presence of privately owned and well-funded LCCs Interjet (26 per cent market share), Volaris (23 per cent) and Ryanair-backed VivaAerobus (9 per cent) competing head-to-head with the sole incumbent Aeromexico (42 per cent) after Mexicana's departure.

The competitive situation as of 2015 was quite positive from the consumer's perspective, with no fewer than eight carriers and a good mix of business models sharing the domestic market, with Aeromexico and Aeromexico Connect having a combined share of 35 per cent and Interjet and Volaris battling it out for second place at 25 per cent and 24 per cent of the market, respectively. The other five carriers shared the remaining 16 per cent of the domestic market between them (anna.aero, 2016), contributing to positive traffic growth overall every month since mid-2011.

Internationally, US and foreign carriers have benefitted more from the various ASA revisions than Mexican carriers (e.g. Delta and later Southwest), though recent evidence suggests that this is starting to change as home-based carrier Aeromexico and the best-performing LCCs strengthen and solidify their financial and market positions. By May 2016, the Mexican carrier share in international markets has grown to 29.1 per cent, with Aeromexico (and AM Connect) taking 64 per cent of these passengers, followed by Volaris (22 per cent) and Interjet (11 per cent). An important prerequisite for airlines benefitting from additional traffic rights is strong market capitalisation and asset leverage to take advantage of new opportunities. After many years of missed opportunities captured instead by US and foreign carriers (such as American Airlines and

Delta), Aeromexico is now in the position to operate to new gateways in the US (e.g. Mexico City–Boston commencing on 1 June 2015) and to negotiate joint ventures and other alliance arrangements with interested foreign carrier investors (e.g. Delta).

## Indonesia

Indonesia has emerged as one of the world's most dynamic and biggest aviation growth markets. As an archipelago with much mountainous terrain, the country is highly dependent on maritime and air transport links to connect the over 17,000 islands, 5,000 of which are inhabited with an estimated population of 257.5 million in 2015 (World Bank, 2016). The combination of physical geography, reasonable levels of GDP growth, rapid urbanisation (53 per cent in 2014 versus 31 per cent in 1990), a large population and a rapidly expanding middle class are driving soaring demand for domestic air travel. According to the World Bank (2016) and the Indonesian Angkasa Pura (2015), over the past five years, GDP grew at an average annual rate of 5.6 per cent, while the growth rate of the 10 largest airports in terms of passenger traffic was 13 per cent annually, accumulating to 33.8 per cent and 67 per cent, respectively (see Table 7.5).

Most of this growth was experienced in the domestic market, with the number of domestic passengers reaching 84.4 million in 2015, up from 51.8 million in 2010. Although growth in the domestic market has slowed considerably over the last two years, owing in part to constraints at Indonesia's largest airports and government impositions on price controls, this remarkable growth in air traffic services across Indonesia is projected to continue over the near to medium term, with Indonesia likely to contribute 183 million additional passengers by 2034 (Airline Leader, 2016; IATA, 2014). Currently, the country is home to over 600 airports, of which 233 are state-owned and -operated. Indonesian airports are managed by two corporative authorities, namely PT Angkasa Pura 1 and 2. Soekarno-Hatta, Juanda, Ngurah Rai and Polonia are the four largest Indonesian airports (FME-CWM, 2012).

Liberal aviation policies are another key reason why the aviation sector has grown quickly in recent years. First, passed in 1958, the basic aviation law is laid down by the Indonesian parliament. The most recent regulation (Law No. 1 of 2009) regulates wider issues, including airports and scheduled/non-scheduled air passenger services (Saraswati and Hanaoka, 2013). The aviation law authorises the Ministry of Transport (MoT) to control, supervise and implement further regulations. The Indonesian airline industry has been gradually liberalised since 1991, with positive effects on the performance of the industry (OECD, 2014). A review of the bilateral air services agreements (BASAs) using the ALI developed by the WTO shows that post-1991 BASAs are less restrictive with respect to the main market access features as compared to those concluded prior to the liberalisation process, with the average level of liberalisation standing at 14 out of 50 (WTO ASAP Database, 2016). However, the country has in recent years reviewed its BASAs. For instance, a recent BASA between Indonesia and Japan concluded in 2010 provides for multiple designations and entry points: 75 weekly frequencies for designated

*Table 7.5* GDP and air passenger indicators for Indonesia, 2010 to 2015

| GDP growth (%) 2010–2015 cumulated | GDP (US$ mn) 2015 current | Passenger growth (%) 2010–2014 10 largest airports cumulated | Passenger volume (mn) 2014 10 largest airports |
|---|---|---|---|
| 33.8 | 861,934 | 67 | 130 |

*Source*: Angkasa Pura (2015) and World Bank (2016).

Japanese carries and 14 for Indonesian carriers, with no limits on code-sharing between the two countries, as well as on domestic services (CAPA, 2010).

Areas where significant changes in policy have taken place include the number of carriers that can be designated as the country's flag carriers and the basis for the negotiation of traffic rights and routes. For instance, restrictions on domestic routes and frequencies have been eliminated. The aviation law also provides opportunities for the private sector to participate in operating public airports through a public–private partnership (PPP) scheme (Balfour and Rukmasari, 2015). Added to liberalisation progress at the bilateral level has been the shift in the regulatory approach taken at the plurilateral level. Indonesia is a signatory state of the Indonesia-Malaysia-Thailand Growth Triangle (IMT-GT), the Brunei-Daressalam-Indonesia-Malaysia-Philippines East ASEAN Growth Area (BIMP/EAGA) and the Association of Southeast Asian Nations (ASEAN) Sectoral Integration Protocol for Air Travel, which are subregional cooperation associations established in 1993, 1994 and 2005, respectively. The European Union (EU) and Indonesia signed a horizontal agreement on 29 June 2011 removing nationality restrictions in BASAs between 19 EU member states and Indonesia.

Despite the trend towards liberalisation, there remain considerable restrictions on airline access, pricing and ownership. The eighth and ninth freedoms of the air are prohibited. The aviation law regulates domestic air fares by imposing a tariff ceiling above which domestic airlines are prohibited from selling economy tickets (Balfour and Rukmasari, 2015). The principal restriction on access to the domestic market for foreign airlines is the ownership and control requirement, which is limited to 49 per cent of total shares. It is also argued that the government has policies that promote and protect stated-owned Garuda rather than fostering the growth of the budget sector (Bentley, 2009). According to Tan (2009), the Indonesian government had in 2005 sealed off its four major cities (Denpasar, Surabaya, Medan and Jakarta) to prospective foreign LCCs in an effort to protect the national carrier Garuda. According to CAPA (2016), the ban is still in place. However, the government welcomes the carriers at secondary destinations, as can be seen in the following quote from Santoso Eddy Wibowo, Director of Air Transport at the Minstry of Transportation of Indonesia (CAPA, 2016):

> If we open for the LCCs, we are afraid that passengers will shift from our airlines to foreign airlines. If they shift, our airlines will collapse . . . . We are not reviewing our policies on foreign LCCs with regard to the four major cities [Denpasar, Surabaya, Medan or Jakarta]. We encourage operators to help open up the tourist markets [at the 23 other international airports in Indonesia].

In terms of market structure, the number of airlines operating in the Indonesian market has until recently been very limited. However, the gradual removal of restrictions has brought genuine competition in both domestic and international markets (Airline Leader, 2016). The number of airlines has grown from 7 in 1999 to 27 in 2004, but declined to 20 airlines in 2015. The four main groups, namely Garuda, Lion, Sriwijaya Air and AirAsia, account for over 90 per cent of Indonesia's domestic market. There are only two Indonesian airlines classified by Indonesia as being full service carriers, namely Garuda and Batik Air, and both airlines compete on almost all routes (Airline Leader, 2016). An analysis of the state of competition in selected city pair markets indicates that during the last 15 years, the number of competitors has slightly changed in both domestic and international markets, despite airline bankruptcies. On the domestic route Soekarno-Hatta International Airport to Juanda International Airport, the number of competitors slightly increased from five in 2000 to six in 2015. Although there has been little change in the number of effective competitors, the market was less concentrated (as measured by HHI) in 2015 as compared to 2000. Moreover, HHI decreased from 3,909 (highly concentrated) in 2000 to 2,003 (moderately concentrated) in 2015. In fact, this market was dominated in 2000 by the flag carrier Garuda, with 56 per cent market share, but by 2015, although Garuda still dominated the market, its share had dropped to 29 per cent and the remaining 71 per cent was controlled by five LCCs. Indonesia has LCC penetration rates of 50 per cent and there is still room for more growth (Airline Leader, 2016). Major LCCs include Lion Air, Garuda's budget subsidiary Citilink and Indonesia AirAsia. According to Airline Leader (2016), Lion Air, a privately held LCC that serves predominantly domestic routes, is by far the largest carrier in terms of passengers.

Indonesia's international market consisted of less than 10 million passengers in 2012 (Airline Leader, 2016). In fact, most Indonesian carriers have been slow to expand in international markets, preferring to content themselves with domestic expansion. The slow expansion in international markets can be explained by the failure of some Indonesian carriers to meet International Civil Aviation Organisation (ICAO) safety standards that led the EU to ban Indonesian carriers from its airspace in recent years, and to some extent kept Indonesian carriers from properly expanding outside the country. Although there are signs of improvement, aviation safety remains a central concern in Indonesia. As a result of the slow growth in international markets, the Indonesian international market is primarily exploited by Gulf carriers and the big airline groups of Asia. Singapore Airlines, the largest foreign airline in Indonesia, is a large and aggressive sixth freedom competitor in the Indonesia–Europe market (Airline Leader, 2016). As an example, the route between Singapore Changi and Soekarno-Hatta International helps illuminate some of the changes in the number of competitors in the international market. The number of competitors on this route decreased from 12 in 2000 to 7 in 2015, with Singapore Airlines controlling 32 per cent of the market share by 2015, followed by Garuda Airlines (21 per cent) and Citilink (18 per cent). This market can be regarded as moderately concentrated, with an HHI of 2,138 in 2000 and 2,030 in 2015. The realisation of open skies for the ASEAN market through full ratification of the ASEAN open skies agreements in April 2016 is expected to stimulate more competition in the region, and hence even higher growth. It should be noted that the ASEAN open skies concept is less ambitious than the EU single market, for instance with seventh freedom rights and cabotage being notable exclusions to the agreement.

Whereas there is no detailed policy on airline competition, the aviation law adopts two key principles in undertaking aviation businesses in Indonesia, namely anti-monopoly and transparency. A new competition legal framework was set up in 1999 (Law No. 5 of 1999), which also applies to aviation. Actions that are extensively regulated in the law are cartels, acquisitions, price-fixing, monopolistic practices, writing contracts and boycotts (Balfour and Rukmasari, 2015).

## Saudi Arabia

Saudi Arabia is considered to have many of the typical characteristics of an emerging economy. As the largest member of the Gulf Cooperation Council (GCC) and a member of G20, Saudi Arabia has been able to take full advantage of its vast hydrocarbon reserves, with average incomes increasing 28 per cent from 2010 to 2015. This, combined with its 2.4 per cent population growth rate (over the 2010–2015 period) and its 2030 economic diversification plan, aimed at moving the economy away from its heavy reliance on hydrocarbon reserves and public sector jobs, and towards entrepreneurial and private sector businesses in trade, tourism and sport (Kingdom of Saudi Arabia, 2016), makes Saudi Arabia a medium-term prospect for achieving industrialised economy status.

*Table 7.6* GDP and air traffic indicators for Saudi Arabia and GACA airports, 2010 to 2015

| Saudi Arabia | | GACA airports | | | |
|---|---|---|---|---|---|
| GDP growth (%) 2010–2015 cumulated | GDP ($US bn) 2015 current | Passenger growth (%) 2010–2015 | Passenger volume (mn) 2015 | Air cargo growth (%) 2010–2015 | Air cargo volume (mn tonnes) 2015 |
| 22.6 | 646 | 70.6 | 81.9 | 78.0 | 1.2 |

Source: GACA (2016) and World Bank (2016).

Note: GACA is the operator of five international, nine regional and 13 domestic airports in Saudi Arabia.

Despite the recent downturn in the Saudi economy due to weak oil revenues and increased fiscal deficits (estimated to be US$118 billion in 2016) (World Bank, 2016), cumulative GDP growth in the 2010–2015 period was still a healthy 22.6 per cent (see Table 7.6). Both air passenger and air cargo traffic growth has significantly surpassed that of GDP growth, which, according to the Saudi Arabian General Authority of Civil Aviation (GACA), grew by 70.6 per cent and 78.0 per cent for passengers and cargo, respectively, over the 2010–2015 period.

Saudi Arabia's air transport market is quite well balanced between: domestic (43 per cent) and international traffic (57 per cent) (GACA, 2015); business (34 per cent of inbound visits) and leisure traffic (66 per cent, including large seasonal traffic figures for Hajj and Umrah pilgrimages, accounting for 40 per cent of inbound visits) (MAS Tourism Statistics, 2011); and incoming (49 per cent foreign visitors) and outgoing traffic (51 per cent Saudi residents) (Oxford Economics, 2010).

The country's air transport sector has been subject to a moderately restrictive, protectionist approach to domestic and international air policy. The overall level of liberalness of Saudi Arabia's BASAs, according to the WTO ASAP Database (2016), is estimated to be only 7 out of 50, though there have been moves to create a more liberal approach within the GCC region and the wider Arab Civil Aviation Commission (ACAC) member area (GCC average of 15 out of 50). Until 2006, national carrier Saudi Arabian Airlines enjoyed single designation monopoly status on domestic routes and exclusive rights as the only designating Saudi-registered carrier to operate in international markets. The introduction of LCCs Nas Air (now called Flynas) and Sama, which was poorly funded by its private investors before going bust after only three years of operation, went only some way to creating additional domestic competition. Notorious fare caps on domestic markets, though popular with passengers, have also served to stifle open competition.

As a sign that the tides are turning, the Saudi GACA confirmed its intention in late 2011 to open up its domestic market to further home-based and foreign carriers without preconceived restrictions on access points, capacity and tariffs (CAPA, 2011). This marked a significant change in direction from the preceding policy approach, though to date further policy implementation work is required to stimulate additional suppliers and traffic, presuming the right economic conditions are present. Minor changes to the domestic fare cap (e.g. removing restrictions on base fare-setting and allowing some revenue management in the last 10 days before departure) have also been welcomed by the incumbent carriers (Rivers/Flightglobal, 2016).

An OAG analysis in January 2016 showed that the Jeddah–Riyadh city pair is by far the biggest market, and growing rapidly, with 125,000 weekly seats available in January 2016 compared to only 100,000 just a year earlier, though this sort of growth has not been matched on many of the smaller domestic city pairs. This is reflected by the two incumbents Saudia and Flynas going head-to-head on this, the only very high-demand, high-growth market, but competing less aggressively on other lower-growth, lower-volume domestic pairs (e.g. Jazan–Riyadh). It is interesting to note that despite government and GACA efforts to deregulate, the domestic market is still effectively a duopoly. Dammam-based SaudiGulf Airlines has been more than three years in the making and only recently obtained its AOC (Rivers/Flightglobal, 2016), and still has not been able to commence scheduled operations. A seat capacity analysis using data from OAG to compare the Riyadh–Dammam market in September 2000 and September 2016 also serves to further illustrate the situation on domestic secondary pairs, with the overall market shrinking from around 76,000 seats to only 60,000 seats by 2016. The HHI in this market has improved from 8,800 to 5,200 with the entry of Flynas services, though this has clearly not been enough to stimulate true competition.

Saudia Arabia's marginally more open approach to GCC and ACAC partner countries has led to some entry of mainly foreign-based carriers at the same time as continuing the flag carrier-based, dual designation approach to intercontinental markets. A seat capacity analysis using data from OAG for the Jeddah–Cairo market, for instance, shows an increase in market competitiveness over the 2000–2016 period, with the HHI being 5,000 in October 2000 and reducing to 3,900 by October 2016. Despite the continued market dominance of incumbent carriers Saudia Arabian Airlines and EgyptAir, the permitted market entry of a number of newly established carriers on the route such as Flynas (Saudi-based LCC) and Nile Air (Egypt-based full service carrier) has led to a significant shift in the competitive dynamics of this and other regional markets. The overall market size has also more than doubled over the period, from around 40,000 seats in October 2000 to almost 108,000 seats in October 2016.

## Conclusion

This chapter sought to examine the degree of air service liberalisation in emerging markets and its effects on levels of competition. Emerging markets have witnessed continuous GDP growth in recent decades driven by a growing middle class, rapidly urbanising populations, and reforms in trade and policy. The cases of Kenya, Mexico, Indonesia and Saudi Arabia have served to illustrate the continued pace of air transport liberalisation in emerging countries. While the studied countries are different from each other in terms of population, GDP per capita, commercial aviation industry development and the degree to which they have begun their transition to more open sky policies, their air transport markets have evolved in recent years from ones dominated by one or a few airlines to ones characterised by larger numbers of home-based and foreign airlines. Growing competition between market participants, particularly in domestic markets, but also in some international markets, have led to improvements in service quality (e.g. choice) and to some price reductions, with positive impacts on demand being observed. Unlike airlines where private sector involvement is more common, emerging market airports have largely remained in public hands. However, this is starting to change, with the private sector increasingly playing an active role in the commercialisation of airports.

The four case countries presented in this chapter add to the body of literature on air transport liberalisation and competition in emerging markets. The divergence of fortunes (in air transport markets and in the general economy), as recently witnessed across the BRIC countries, has not been observed across the countries of Kenya, Mexico, Indonesia or Saudia Arabia, though it is entirely possible that geopolitical and macroeconomic forces can affect any of these four case countries just as much as it has done Russia and Brazil of late. Building resilience through efficiency and commercially driven growth in air services, along with further multilateral efforts to commercialise and liberalise air transport policy, can assist each of the studied countries in being better prepared for the inevitable bumpy periods along their route towards market maturity.

Looking to the future, political and economic factors are likely to push regulators to further relax currently restrictive conditions. Further liberalisation of air transport is likely to contribute to competition and diversity in the aviation sectors studied in this chapter. This is important if the benefits of aviation and tourism are to be exploited. For effective competition to take place, it would be imperative to eliminate government interference in airline operations. Emerging markets will also need to focus on the implementation of sector-specific competition law as these economies look to shift their focus from prohibitive regulation to effective policing. Despite the growing competition between airlines and diverse forms of collaboration now taking place, most emerging countries still do not have sector-specific competition policies in place.

## Note

1  As an interesting aside to the impact of ASAs, designation limitations on the Mexico–US ASA meant that technically Mexicana's air operator certificate (AOC) has never ceased, being adopted by other airlines such as Volaris and Interjet wishing to operate internationally to the US until the point when a more liberal ASA could be signed between the two states.

## References

Abate, M. (2016). Economic effects of air transport market liberalisation in Africa, *Transportation Research Part A: Policy and Practice*, 92, 326–337.
Airbus (2016). *Global Market Forecast, Flying by Numbers: 2015–2034*, Blagnac, Airbus.
Airline Leader (2016). Indonesia: slower growth in the world's fifth largest domestic airline market, *Airline Leader*, 33 (March).
Angkasa Pura (2015). *Annual Report 2015*, Jakarta, Angkasa Pura.
anna.aero (2016). *Passengers up 10% in Mexico in first five months of 2016*. Online. Available at: www.anna.aero/2016/07/26/passengers-up-10-percent-in-mexico/ (accessed 2 February 2017).
Balfour, W. and Rukmasari, A. (2015). Indonesia air transport 2015. In: J. Balfour and M. Bisset (eds). *Getting the Deal Through*. Online. Available at: https://gettingthedealthrough.com (accessed 26 May 2017).
Bentley, D. (2009). *Low Cost Airports and Terminals (LCATs)*, Sydney, CAPA.
Boeing (2016). *Current Market Outlook 2016–2035*, Seattle, WA, Boeing.
CAPA (Centre for Aviation) (2010). Japan and Indonesia expand bilateral air services agreement, *CAPA*, 30 April.
CAPA (Centre for Aviation) (2011). Saudi Arabia to take the plunge and open the domestic market, *CAPA*, 30 December.
CAPA (Centre for Aviation) (2013). Low-cost airlines start to penetrate African international market, led by fastjet, *CAPA*, 22 October.
CAPA (Centre for Aviation) (2016). Fastjet 2016 outlook Part 1: Kenya expansion following breakthrough Tanzania-Kenya launch, *CAPA*, 21 January.
Chingosho, E. (2009). *African Airlines in the Era of Liberalisation*, 2nd edition, Nairobi, Dr Elijah Chingosho.
Cline, R.C., Ruhl, T.A., Gosling, G.D. and Gillen, D. (1998). Air transportation demand forecasts in emerging market economies: a case study of the Kyrgyz Republic in the former Soviet Union, *Journal of Air Transport Management*, 4(1), 11–23.
FME-CWM (Dutch Employers' Organisation and Trade Association for the Technological-Industrial Sector) (2012). *Indonesia Market Analysis Airport Sector*, Zoetermeer, FME-CWM.
GACA (General Authority of Civil Aviation) (2015). *Statistical Yearbook 2015*, Riyadh, GACA.
GACA (General Authority of Civil Aviation) (2016). *Statistical Yearbook 2016*, Riyadh, GACA.
Gobierno de Mexico Secretaria de Comunicaciones y Transporte (2016). *Statistics by airport*. Online. Available at: www.sct.gob.mx/transporte-y-medicina-preventiva/aeronautica-civil/5-estadisticas/55-estadistica-operacional-de-aeropuertos-statistics-by-airport/ (accessed 26 May 2017).
Goldstein, A. (2001). Infrastructure development and regulatory reform in Sub-Saharan Africa: the case of air transport, *The World Economy*, 24(2), 221–248.

IATA (International Air Transport Association) (2014). New IATA passenger forecast reveals fast-growing markets of the future, *IATA Press Release No. 57.* 57, 16 October.

IATA (International Air Transport Association) (2015). IATA air passenger forecast shows dip in long-term demand, *IATA Press Release No. 55*, 26 November.

IATA (International Air Transport Association) (2016). *Air passenger market analysis.* Online. Available at: www.iata.org/whatwedo/Documents/economics/passenger-analysis-dec-2016.pdf (accessed 26 May 2017).

IFC (International Finance Corporation) (2008). *Public-private partnership stories: Kenya – Kenya Airways privatisation.* Online. Available at: www.ifc.org/wps/wcm/connect/ (accessed 2 February 2017).

Index Mundi (2016). *Mexico: international tourism.* Online. Available at: www.indexmundi.com/facts/mexico/international-tourism (accessed 26 May 2017).

InterVISTAS (2006). *The Economic Impact of Air Service Liberalization*, Washington, DC, InterVISTAS.

KAA (Kenya Airport Authority) (2016). *Kenya Airport Authority.* Online. Available at: https://kaa.go.ke/ (accessed 26 May 2017).

Kimenyi, M.S., Mwega, F.M. and Ndung'u, N.S. (2016). *The African lions: Kenya country case study.* Online. Available at: www.brookings.edu/wp-content/uploads/2016/07/kenya-country-case.pdf (accessed 2 February 2017).

Kingdom of Saudi Arabia (2016). *Saudi Vision 2030*, Riyadh, Kingdom of Saudi Arabia.

Lay Yeo, G. (2015). *What will a Delta-Aeromexico joint venture offer?* Online. Available at: www.flightglobal.com/news/articles/analysis-what-will-a-delta-aeromexico-joint-venture-410819/ (accessed 2 February 2017).

MAS Tourism Statistics (2011). *Saudi tourism demand statistics.* Online. Available at: www.mas.gov.sa/en/QAS/Pages/statistical.aspx (accessed 2 February 2017).

MoT (Ministry of Transport) (2009). *Integrated National Transport Policy*, Nairobi, MoT Kenya.

Njoya, E.T. (2016). Africa's single aviation market: the progress so far, *Journal of Transport Geography*, 50, 4–11.

O'Connell, J.F., Krishnamurthy, P., Warnock-Smith, D., Lei, Z. and Miyoshi, C. (2013). An investigation into the core underlying problems of India's airlines, *Transport Policy*, 29, 160–169.

OECD (Organisation for Economic Co-operation and Development) (2014). *Airline competition.* Online. Available at: www.oecd.org/competition/airlinecompetition.htm (accessed 2 February 2017).

Oxford Economics (2010). *Economic Benefits from Air Transport in Saudi Arabia*, Oxford, Oxford Economics.

Oxford Economics (2011). *Economic Benefits from Air Transport in Kenya*, Oxford, Oxford Economics.

Rivers/Flightglobal (2016). Analysis: old players eye new Gulf boom, *Flightglobal*, 19 July.

Saraswati, B. and Hanaoka, S. (2013). Aviation policy in Indonesia and its relation to ASEAN single aviation market, *Journal of the Eastern Asia Society for Transportation Studies*, 10, 2161–2176.

Schlumberger, C.E. and Weisskopf, N. (2014). *Ready for Takeoff? The Potential for Low-Cost Carriers in Developing Countries*, Washington, DC, World Bank.

Tan, A.K.-J. (2009). Prospects for a single aviation market in Southeast Asia, *Annals of Air and Space Law*, 34, 253–283.

Tuncer, G. (2012). 'Movin' on up . . .': emerging markets' rising importance in the global economy, *Asset Management Viewpoint*, 16(3), 1–3.

Wang, J., Bonilla, D. and Banister, D. (2016). Air deregulation in China and its impact on airline competition 1994–2012, *Journal of Transport Geography*, 50, 12–23.

World Bank (2005). *East Africa Air Transport Survey*, Washington, DC, World Bank.

World Bank (2016). *World Bank data.* Online. Available at: http://data.worldbank.org/ (accessed 2 February 2017).

WTO ASAP Database (2016). *WTO ASAP Database.* Online. Available at: www.wto.org/asap/index.html (accessed 2 February 2017).

Zhang, A. and Chen, H. (2003). Evolution of China's air transport development and policy towards international liberalization, *Transportation Journal*, 42(3), 31–49.

# 8

# Evolving airline and airport business models

*Marina Efthymiou and Andreas Papatheodorou*

## Introduction

Unlike neoclassical theory, evolutionary economics considers competition as a dynamic process where the so-called unique steady state equilibrium does not exist. On the contrary, the economy is understood to be in a constant state of flux as multiple equilibria are reached temporarily, only to be subsequently disturbed by a combination of exogenous and endogenous factors in the macro- and microeconomic system (Papatheodorou, 2004). Over the last 70 years since the end of the Second World War, business dynamics in the air transport sector are notably characterised by this evolutionary process. First, creative destruction à la Schumpeter (1996) is apparent as advancements in engineering and technology result in new generations of aircraft and passenger service systems, which drastically reduce the economic value and functional use of their predecessors. Moreover, the evolving business models in the air transport sectors are structurally intertwined, with both exogenous and endogenous systemic changes. The former are largely related to the gradual development of international tourism since the early 1960s and the opening of the airline, and subsequently the airport market a few decades later; the latter concern competition dynamics within a liberal environment (see Chapters 6 and 7) and the emergence of business model differentiation and specialisation, followed by a gradual blurring to maximise market share.

In summary, the early years after the Second World War were dominated by flag carriers, quite often heavily subsidised, operating scheduled point-to-point services in a highly regulated business environment (at both national and international levels) out and into state-owned airports almost exclusively, depending on aeronautical revenue (see also Chapter 1). Subsequently, charter airlines entered the foreground in the 1960s to cover leisure needs on a seasonal basis. Thus, by the mid-1970s, the first wave of airline business model differentiation was complete. Since then, airline deregulation/liberalisation, first in the United States (US) in 1978, and then in Europe between 1988 and 1997 (which emerged because of growing public dissatisfaction over high air fares and low service quality), led to notable market entry and a second wave of airline specialisation where, in addition to the two previous models (gradually redefined as full service network carriers [FSNCs] operating scheduled services over a hub-and-spoke network, usually in the context of strategic alliances, and leisure airlines offering predominantly seasonal services to holiday destinations), three others were added. Low cost carriers (LCCs), or low fare airlines (LFAs), as they prefer to identify themselves from a customer-centric point of view, are the major success story of the post-liberalisation period, offering a basic, very competitively priced scheduled service usually out of regional airports on a point-to-point basis, while at the same time all-business-class carriers and regional airlines (which are not recognised by all analysts as a separate business model) also emerged in the market.

Soon after the opening up of the airline market, the public sector mentality characterising the large majority of airports until the early 1990s started receding (see also Chapter 3). Gradual commercialisation (emphasising non-aeronautical revenue) and steps towards privatisation redefined the airline–airport relationship and rendered competition dynamics meaningful in the sector. This led to the first wave of specialisation into hub airports servicing FSNCs; regional bases/satellite airports servicing LCCs but also leisure, all-business-class and regional airlines; and spokes/peripheral airports willing to serve all but usually ending up with few services predominantly from LCCs but also from leisure and regional airlines – only occasionally from FSNCs.

Finally, corporate rivalry in the last 10 years and the willingness to capture an increasing market share led to gradual business convergence à la Hotelling (1929) using differentiation and specialisation at other levels (see Chapter 9). Differences between FSNCs and LCCs have become gradually blurred as each of them has incorporated characteristics of the other in their business model, while the very existence of leisure carriers as a separate business model is questioned. All business-class carriers still exist, but often battered by recession and other factors, while regional carriers usually try to secure their financial viability as affiliates of FSNCs. In this environment of airline business model convergence, the main differentiator seems to be distance, for instance short-haul, where many carriers now offer a service closer to the LCC original concept, and long-haul, where the concept of frills is often still valid despite the entry of LCCs into this sector too.

Airport business model convergence seems to be taking place with a limited time lag, as hub airports become increasingly interested in serving LCCs. Thus, the main differentiation now occurs not at an airport, but at a terminal level, as different airport services are provided to different airline customers based on the latter's profile (see Chapter 10). Interestingly, this whole idea of convergence steps beyond the micro-level as airlines gradually develop themselves into travel supermarkets (due to their emphasis on ancillary revenue derived from sources very different to their core product), while airport terminals have become major shopping malls. In fact, the very emergence of the airport city and aerotropolis highlights the role of airports as concession managers and creates interesting (both synergistic but also antagonistic) dynamics with the neighbouring destinations. Within this context, there needs to be acknowledgement of the role of the triangular relationship among airlines, airports and destination authorities.

The remainder of this chapter discusses in detail the evolutionary journey outlined above. First, the chapter highlights the business environment before the opening up of the airline market. Then, it presents major developments in the post-liberalisation period, essentially focusing on business model specialisation. Subsequently, the chapter analyses the very issue of convergence at both airline and airport business models, and continues by elaborating on the role of airport cities and the triangular relationship. The final section summarises and concludes.

## Business models before the opening up of the airline market

In the aftermath of the Second World War and until the deregulation/liberalisation of the airline market between the late 1970s and mid-1990s in much of the Western world (see Chapter 6), traditional scheduled carriers dominated the business scene. These carriers offered a typical three-class service (i.e. first, business and economy class), where different fare levels were largely justified by service quality disparities in in-flight catering, seat pitch and ground handling services (Doganis, 2005, 2010). In many cases, these airlines operated as national flag carriers, acting as government agencies. Due to their ownership status and importance for connectivity and accessibility of remoter regions in a country, governmental support in the form of subsidies and/or tax exemption motives became the norm. Moreover, many routes were developed for political rather than commercial reasons; hence, the airline network configuration was heavily influenced by government decisions (Papatheodorou, 2002). Traditional carriers also became active in cargo services (see Chapter 2). The first cargo flight was in 1910 between Albany and New York. In fact, air cargo played a key role in international trade, aid and relief operations.

The development of international tourism in Europe and the chase of Florida sun by Americans residing in the northern US states led to the gradual rise of charter, non-scheduled airlines in the 1960s. These airlines focused on leisure passengers, offering services usually as part of package holidays sold by tour operators with whom charter airlines, mostly in Europe, often entered vertical business relationships (Papatheodorou, 2002). Leisure passengers were interested in direct, reliable flights with low fares, and hence charter airlines were not seeking to compete on high service quality with traditional carriers. Destinations in the European Mediterranean region became popular thanks to charter airlines. Due to their dependence on sunlust operations characterised by high seasonality, operating off-season was a challenge for charter airlines. To increase aircraft utilisation and avoid extremely low load factors during winter, their aircraft were usually leased to airlines serving areas facing reverse seasonality, for instance in the Caribbean and Australia. Later, the gradual development of the winter sports market enabled European charter airlines to also serve winter destinations such as those in the Alps (Doganis, 2005, 2010).

Because of heavy airline regulation prevailing in this period, traditional carriers were protected by barriers to market entry, and capacity- and fare-setting constraints. At an international level, protectionism took the form of restrictive bilateral agreements. In the beginning, charter airlines faced more traffic restrictions compared to scheduled carriers, but these were later relaxed (DLR, 2008). Nevertheless, non-scheduled carriers were not allowed to distribute their tickets individually (via their city ticket office and/or call centre) or via computer reservation systems (CRSs); moreover, they were not allowed to carry freight or mail either. Scheduled and charter carriers in Europe became equally treated only after the implementation of Council Regulation (EEC) No. 2408/92 (EU, 1992), which abolished all related traffic, capacity and pricing legal restrictions.

In fact, although the air transport sector was one of the first to be regulated, it was also one of the first to be deregulated (Dempsey and Goetz, 1992). Initial considerations on market failure led to regulation; however, the inflexible and over-regulated airline business environment often resulted in passenger dissatisfaction due to poor value for money (see Chapter 23), thus setting the fundamentals for a change in the civil aviation regime (Borenstein, 1992). The assumption behind deregulation was that new airlines entering the market would provide more variety of choice in flight services and lower fares (Smeth et al., 2007). Moreover, and as per the European Commission (EC, 1996a: 1), the aim of liberalisation was "the gradual creation of a truly single market based upon the freedom to provide services throughout the Community in accordance with a single set of rules." Unlike the US, where the market was almost instantly deregulated in 1978, the liberalisation process in Europe was stepwise and implemented in three packages (see also Chapter 6). The first, adopted in 1987, relaxed the restrictions of the bilateral framework and allowed several smaller airlines to enter some of the important intra-community routes. The second package, agreed in 1990, relaxed restrictions on fifth freedom services, eased restrictions on multiple designation of airlines on specific routes, and introduced the element of double disapproval for fares. The third package was introduced in 1993, but due to the economic recession at the time the pace only accelerated in 1995 and 1996 (EC, 1996a). The third package was based on three interrelated pillars: the first offered free market entry and exit in the European Common Aviation Area (ECAA) by including full cabotage rights from 1997 onwards; the second extended pricing freedom; and the third pillar established harmonised licencing and certificates for airworthiness procedures.

Finally, and during this first period under consideration (i.e. up to the opening up of the airline market), and leaving aside infrastructural projects, commercial developments in airports were rather limited (see Chapter 3). For the large majority, airports operated as government agencies based on a public sector mentality that saw no real role for commercialisation and non-aeronautical revenue (Graham, 2014). As many traditional airlines were also owned by their respective states at the time, an indirect vertical business relationship developed between airlines and airports. This meant, among others, that aeronautical charges were not necessarily set by market criteria, but chiefly determined by political decisions. As both traditional scheduled carriers and charter airlines operated a point-to-point network, airports were distinguished mainly in terms of size rather than in terms of differing business models and networks.

## Business models in the aftermath of liberalisation: the phase of specialisation

Traditional carriers continued to play a very significant role in the post-liberalisation period (see Chapter 9). While the early years of the market opening up were characterised by enthusiastic new market entry, consolidation eventually prevailed as many ventures proved financially unsustainable. For example, in 1978, there were 15 major airlines in the US, while in 1988 there were only eight, with a joint market share of 91.7 per cent, proving that the market had turned into a solid oligopoly (Smeth et al., 2007). Moreover, in the post-1978 business environment, traditional carriers in the US replaced their previous point-to-point network with a hub-and-spoke system, as major airlines established hub bases recording incoming and outgoing traffic from feeder routes to smaller airports (i.e. the spokes) (Smeth et al., 2007). This system allowed carriers to achieve higher load factors while keeping the connectivity at the same level (i.e. serving the same number of airports). Moreover, network economies allowed the introduction of new spokes at very low marginal costs. In this way, traditional carriers were transformed into network carriers offering a full service (as opposed to LCCs, discussed later), hence the abbreviation FSNCs. Some examples of FSNCs are British Airways, Lufthansa and Air France-KLM in Europe, and American Airlines, United Airlines and Delta Airlines in the US.

Hubbing proved a successful market entry deterrent in many cases, and the construction of fortress hubs in Europe restricted competition, particularly in the absence of alternative airports nearby (Dobruszkes, 2009). Dempsey and Goetz (1992) quote that in 1989, the US General Accounting Office found that fares in hub airports characterised by a monopoly, or at best a duopoly, were 27 per cent higher than the competitive benchmark. Moreover, Polk and Bilotkach (2013) argue that large hub airports have local monopoly features; hence, they need to be regulated to prevent abuse of their dominant position in the market. In addition, the future of the home carrier and its hub airport become structurally interdependent, characterised by asset-specific investments from both sides. Not surprisingly, airports may end up bearing a higher level of risk due to the inherently sunk nature of their infrastructure: while an airline can always redirect its services to another airport, the latter is spatially fixed. Hence, hub airports often require FSNCs to partly fund their infrastructure (e.g. in the context of joint ventures, as is the case of Munich Airport Terminal Two, where the local airport collaborated with

Lufthansa). In any case, it should be also acknowledged that hub airports do face competition from other hub airports for transfer passengers (see Chapter 10). This may lead to a war of hubs, especially in cases where sixth freedom carriers vertically associated with hub airports (e.g. both being state-owned) follow aggressive expansionary strategies. The Big Three carriers in the Middle East (Emirates, Etihad and Qatar Airways) and their hub airports are a notable example. Conversely, a highly congested hub airport can also affect the network strategy of FSNCs (Elhedhli and Hu, 2005), leading to de-hubbing (Redondi et al., 2012) and/or new traffic opportunities at less congested airports. This phenomenon is mitigated in the case of multi-hub airlines (e.g. Lufthansa Group's Frankfurt, Munich, Zurich and Vienna Airports), where traffic can be rerouted to another hub airport.

In addition to operating a hub-and-spoke network based on a high frequency of conveniently scheduled regular flights, FSNCs tend to follow complex revenue management practices based on price discrimination (see Chapter 11). In Europe, this is also related to the fact that further to market liberalisation, the large majority of FSNCs were eventually privatised, thus using sophisticated revenue management techniques to ensure profitability became of much greater importance. FSNCs also provide a wide range of pre-flight and on-board services, including different service classes. Moreover, and to capitalise on their extensive network, FSNCs put emphasis on building loyalty schemes, the well-known frequent flyer programmes (FFPs), which raise switching costs to other carriers (see Chapter 11). The value of FFPs was greatly enhanced in the 1990s by the establishment of strategic airline alliances, which streamline collaboration of carriers on fares, marketing and capacity, especially when granted antitrust immunity, and act as a second-best solution to cross-country mergers and acquisitions, which until today have proved difficult due to international regulatory constraints (Papatheodorou and Iatrou, 2008). Leick and Wensveen (2014) argue that the success of the first alliance between Northwest and KLM in the early 1990s led to the subsequent creation of the three major global alliances that exist today (Star Alliance, Oneworld and SkyTeam). These alliances are now truly global and aim at creating a seamless network for participating carriers around the world. For example, in September 2016, Star Alliance served 1,203 destinations in 192 countries; SkyTeam served 1,050 destinations in 177 countries; and Oneworld served 966 destinations in 161 countries (Flight Airline Business, 2016) (see also Chapter 6).

Throughout the period under consideration, air freight remained an important revenue source for many FSNCs for high-value commodities (e.g. high-tech products, capital equipment) and shock-sensitive goods (e.g. chemicals, gold) that need fast, reliable and secure transportation (see Chapter 2). Unlike the all-cargo carriers such as Cargolux that operate a dedicated fleet of freighter aircraft, and the integrators such as DHL that provide a comprehensive door-to-door service, most FSNCs that participate in the cargo market rely either on the belly cargo or the combination model. Belly cargo carriers are passenger airlines that carry cargo in the holds of their aircraft to generate additional revenue. Similarly, combination carriers (e.g. All Nippon Airways) operate combi-aircraft (i.e. multi-compartment aircraft designed with additional freight capacity and, in some cases, air freighters). They also have the flexibility to shift from belly capacity to freighter capacity depending on the cargo demand. Combination carriers serve a wide range of destinations since they usually operate on a hub-and-spoke network (Morrell, 2011). The competitive dynamics in cargo operations pushed carriers to sign commercial agreements usually on a route-by-route basis and form alliances (such as WOW and SkyTeam Cargo) to coordinate/streamline activities and network configuration (subject to regulatory approval) and reduce total and unit costs; in most cases, however, such alliances have not proved as successful as in the case of passenger traffic, predominantly due to complexities in joint supply chain management (Morrell, 2011).

While the transformation of traditional carriers into FSNCs is a case of mild business model evolution, the real market disruption in the post-liberalisation environment was brought by LCCs. Southwest was the very first LCC worldwide commencing operations in Texas back in 1971. The LCC model, however, became popular in Europe from the mid-1990s onwards and then spread to become a global phenomenon. LCCs offer a basic service without frills, charging lower prices than FSNCs. Some of them were new entrants (e.g. easyJet), some were the outcome of radical business transformation (e.g. Ryanair), while others were founded by FSNCs (e.g. Buzz). Leisure passengers are frequent users of LCCs without being at the same time loyal to a specific LCC. Furthermore, several previously off-track areas (from a tourism perspective) were popularised thanks to LCCs; Carcassonne in France served by Ryanair is a good example (Palaskas et al., 2006). In contrast to charter carriers, LCCs serve a variety of destinations with diverse profiles, ranging from city breaks in mainland Europe (e.g. Barcelona) to summer holiday islands (e.g. Rhodes).

To improve their value for money and effectively compete on price rather than service quality, LCCs aim to actively reduce the unit cost of their operations. Therefore, they use a single aircraft type with a single class, very dense seat configuration and offer all services apart from the flight itself (such as seat selection, airport check-in, checked baggage, in-flight catering and entertainment, as well as other on-board services) at an additional cost. Moreover, LCCs sell direct predominantly on the Internet without relying on global distribution systems (GDSs) and often outsource non-core activities to third parties. Thus, LCCs focus on low fares, no frills and depend heavily on ancillary revenue, relying on a revenue management model that does not only comprise the flight per se (as is the case with FSNCs), but other services too. Interestingly, though, in the first few years of their operation, LCCs did not provide cargo services as they believed that the complications arising from entering the logistics supply chain outweighed any potential benefits.

In essence, therefore, LCCs focus on short-haul, point-to-point flights bypassing hub airports to avoid high airport taxes, slot constraints and often unavoidable (due to congestion) terminal delays that extend their turnaround time and decrease the aircraft utilisation. For the converse reasons, they prefer to use satellite and/or secondary airports due to the short turnaround times, the availability of slots and the low risk of delays, but most importantly due to the low airport taxes/charges. Such airports, on the other hand, rely heavily on LCCs.

There are cases where the LCCs' cooperation with certain airports proved mutually beneficial, as in the example of Ryanair and Brussels Charleroi Airport (Barbot, 2006). To attract LCCs, satellite and/or secondary airports are willing to reduce airport taxes/charges or even offer subsidies, which in some cases are on the borderline of being characterised as illegal state aid (Barbot, 2006; Fichert and Klophaus, 2011; Nunez-Sanchez, 2015; Papatheodorou, 2003; Wittman, 2014). In retrospect, LCCs have positively affected passenger traffic at secondary airports (Barrett, 2004; Graham and Dennis, 2007). If many of these airports were not served by LCCs, their traffic would be quite low or they would be so-called hedgehog airports, relying only on charter flights and characterised by acute seasonality. Therefore, LCCs do benefit secondary airports and the wider regions, not necessarily on a per capita basis, but primarily due to the sheer scale of newly generated traffic (Choo and Oum, 2013; Lei and Papatheodorou, 2010; Papatheodorou and Lei, 2006).

By the early 2000s, the airline environment in the Western world had polarised around the two business models discussed above (i.e. the evolving FSNC and the nascent yet powerful LCC model). As a result of this gradual polarisation, charter airlines (now better known as leisure carriers) felt insurmountable pressure as, on the one hand, they could not deliver the service quality and convenience of FSNCs, while, on the other, they found it very difficult to effectively compete on price and seat-only, one-way ticket flexibility of the LCCs (Papatheodorou, 2002). Many US charter carriers collapsed (Doganis, 2010), while in Europe the large majority of those that survived either sought comfort in vertical integration with large tour operators such as Thomson and subsequently TUI, or transformed themselves usually into LCCs (Dobruszkes et al., 2016).

Two other airline business models are also worth discussing: premium or business-class-only airlines and regional airlines. Premium or business-class-only airlines may be regarded as the opposite of LCCs, focusing solely on business passengers. They fly only on long-haul routes to and from central airports like the FSNCs, although major satellite airports (such as London Luton) may also be chosen to avoid congestion. These airlines offer a similar service quality to the business class of FSNCs, but have a higher unit cost since they do not operate a hub-and-spoke network to take advantage of scale and network economies. Eos, MaxJet and Silverjet first appeared in 2007, offering point-to-point connection on the London–New York route, which is very popular among business passengers, and reached a traffic peak during that period (Claussen and O'Higgins, 2010). The 2,000 premium seats offered per day generated US$1.4 billion in 2007 to the airlines serving this route (O'Connell, 2007). The three premium carriers had a combined market share of 21 per cent (Avery, 2007, cited in Claussen and O'Higgins, 2010) on that route. Nonetheless, the initial success of these airlines proved short-lived as all of them eventually ceased operations. Financial problems in a period of unprecedented economic recession (which started in 2008), in conjunction with weak schedules, high fares, low utilisation and the growing market acceptance of private jets, were some of the reasons why these airlines did not survive. Regent Air and MGM Grand Air that operated a similar model in the 1980s went bankrupt for similar reasons (Kuchta, 2006, cited in Claussen and O'Higgins, 2010).

Nevertheless, the all-business-class model is still deemed viable by some investors at least (Claussen and O'Higgins, 2010). A recently established company operating this model is La Compagnie. This has daily services between New York/Newark and Paris Charles de Gaulle and London Luton operating with two Boeing 757–200 aircraft. The company focuses on upmarket entertainment, in-flight catering, customer service, on-ground operations and facilities, and exhibits an environmentally friendly behaviour. An FFP is also provided to further steer passenger choice. Another interesting element of La Compagnie is its cooperation with Icelandair in aircraft maintenance. Yet despite an average load factor above 77 per cent on the London–New York route, the airline suspended this operation in summer 2016, quoting the forthcoming Brexit as the main reason; at the same time, it increased the frequency on the Paris–New York route, where loads were already exceeding 80 per cent (La Compagnie, 2016). In general, airlines that follow this business model have the flexibility to amend their operations at short notice, since business passengers do not usually book their tickets very early in advance; moreover, the frequency as well as the schedule of their operations is such that changes can be rapidly implemented.

Regional airlines are part of the last (but not least) business model to consider. Interestingly, this model originally appeared when the market was still regulated in both the US and Europe. Nonetheless, the very focus of FSNCs on hub-and-spoke operations gave a new impetus to regional airlines. Using turbo-props or small regional jets, some of them specialised as providers of commuter or feeder services to FSNCs, often engaging in horizontal business relationships, if not integration, with them. Such agreements allowed regional airlines to use the name and livery of FSNCs, but also to further participate in regular flight plans and appear in GDSs (Smeth et al., 2007). Other regional airlines decided to offer stand-alone, point-to-point services on routes that could not be profitably served by FSNCs or LCCs whose fleet structure was unsuitable for certain smaller-scale operations. Among others, regional airlines specialised in state-subsidised routes known as Essential Air Services in the US and Public Service Obligations in Europe. For all these reasons, regional airlines may be perceived as being part of a separate model of growing importance; for example, while the European Regional Airlines Association (ERAA) had only five founding airline members in 1980, it had about 200 members, including 22 airports and 52 airlines, by 2017 (ERAA, 2017).

All five business models have played a significant role in reshaping the airline–business relationship. In fact, from a period where the scale of traffic was the main, if not the only, differentiator among airports, the post-liberalisation period gave rise to different airport models based on the type of airline operations sought. As discussed, FSNCs focused on the creation of major hubs while LCCs set their own alternative bases and empowered satellite, regional and peripheral airports. Airlines associated with the remaining three business models usually sought similar airports to LCCs. Irrespective, however, of their specialisation, the large majority of airports in the post-liberalisation period actively pursued commercialisation by increasingly focusing on the generation of non-aeronautical revenue (Koo et al., 2016) (see Chapter 12). The end of duty-free sales in intra-EU flights in 1999 had a negative effect on many airports (Lei and Papatheodorou, 2010), but many of them have since become more aggressive and effective in non-aeronautical facilities management, with notable outcomes (Graham, 2014).

In certain cases, commercialisation was accompanied by privatisation, bringing the previously dominating public sector mentality in airports to an end (see Chapter 3). In Europe, this process was initiated in Britain with the privatisation of BAA in 1987, but subsequently moved forwards across the continent. For example, Act 13/2010 modernised the management of Spanish airports by transforming AENA (acronym for Spanish Airports and Air Navigation) to Aena Aeropuertos, which became a public–private entity in 2015 (Nunez-Sanchez, 2015). In 2010, 74 per cent of the publicly owned European airports operated as corporatised entities, while another 20 per cent were private or public–private partnerships (PPPs) (ACI Europe, 2010). The phased liberalisation of ground handling services in the EU introduced in 1997 with Directive 96/67/EC and the continuous consultation on slot allocation (EC, 1996b) are also in line with this mindset change.

## Business models in maturing liberal markets: the phase of convergence

In his seminal 1929 paper, Harold Hotelling used a linear city model to show that producers may rationally use a minimum product differentiation strategy to capture as large a market share as possible (Hotelling, 1929). Such competition dynamics are also apparent in the air transport sector, as in the recent post-liberalisation years, business models in air transport have gradually converged.

When the world economy entered recession in 2001, it became apparent that, unlike FSNCs, LCCs had a robust business model that equipped them (if properly managed) to survive, irrespective of the business cycle stage. As FSNCs recorded major losses and faced severe financial problems, many of them engaged in active cost-reduction strategies involving flight and cabin crew; fleet planning and scheduling; as well as passenger ground (e.g. check-in) and on-board (e.g. in-flight catering) services. Consequently, the business models of FSNCs and LCCs are not as diverse as in the first post-liberalisation years, since increased competition led to a reconfiguration of their operations. FSNCs adopted some elements of the easily copied strategy of LCCs or created an LCC division within their group (see Chapter 9). Porter (1980) argues that the motives for airline group diversification are closely related to strategic market positioning and growth. For instance, the Emirates Group responded to the threat of Air Arabia by supporting flydubai in its establishment stage (Redpath et al., 2016). FSNCs adopted less complicated yield management, improved their aircraft utilisation, unbundled services (Leick and Wensveen, 2014) and put greater emphasis on ancillary revenue, just like LCCs do. For example, United Airlines generated almost US$6.2 billion in 2015 from selling ancillary services to its passengers (Sorensen, 2016).

In the meantime, LCCs also adopted FSNC practices, giving rise to the so-called hybrid LCC business model (see Chapter 9). A hybrid LCC may be a member of an alliance (e.g. Value Alliance consisting of eight LCCs; the now bankrupt Air Berlin being part of Oneworld) or use a mix of short- and long-haul aircraft types (e.g. Aer Lingus). In addition, the emphasis on single-class cabin configuration can be put aside with the selective introduction of a business class (e.g. Jazeera Airways). Hybrid airlines also offer a wide range of airport and on-board services to divert business passengers' demand away from FSNCs. In other words, the new business model added frills. easyJet and Ryanair have implemented allocated seating across their network, and AirAsia X offers lie-flat seats. Moreover, LCCs such as easyJet and Ryanair have decided to partner with GDSs in addition to selling direct. Furthermore, new developments have shown LCCs (such as Norwegian) offering an FFP. This is very important since the FFP is the third determinant for selecting an airline after price and schedule. For business passengers, the existence of a loyalty scheme is ranked even higher than competitive pricing (Borenstein, 1992). Some LCCs have also modestly engaged in cargo operations with Boeing 737 or Airbus 319/320 aircraft that have 0.5- to 1-tonne cargo capacity; they also sell space to forwarders, as is the case with AirAsia X (Morrell, 2011).

In addition, and although none of the major European LCCs (i.e. Ryanair, easyJet, Wizz Air and Norwegian) have signed a code-sharing agreement, this practice has been adopted by other LCCs such as Virgin Australia, which is a code-share partner with Etihad (i.e. a major FSNC), despite differences in service quality. Several LCCs have also started flying from or into primary airports. For instance, Ryanair flies from Athens International Airport and Barcelona El Prat, while Aer Lingus (now part of IAG) has kept its valuable slots at London Heathrow.

Some LCCs are also stepping beyond short- and medium-haul routes, aiming at long-haul ones by relying on wide-body aircraft. Wensveen and Leick (2009) claim that low cost long-haul (LCLH) flights have a different cost structure compared to short-haul routes due to the different set of operational and marketing aspects. Whyte and Lohmann (2015) argue that the actual flight management concerns (i.e. cruising speed and altitude, approaches, fuel burn and aircraft weight) are more critical for long-haul flights, and delays can prove an impediment to the LCLH concept. Still, some of these concerns may be overcome by an appropriate choice of aircraft and revenue management techniques. Moreover, operating an LCLH flight does not necessarily mean that a primary airport will be used. Frequency, network aspects such as the possible lack of feeder flights, target groups and in-flight services are aspects that the LHLC should take under consideration to succeed. In the past, People Express, Zoom Airlines and Laker Airways attempted to offer no-frills long-haul flights, but the venture ended up in failure (Shaw, 2007; Whyte and Lohmann, 2015). AirAsia X operated in 2009 for a short period on the route Kuala Lumpur to London and Paris (Daft and Albers, 2012). Other cases, however, prove the potential viability of the LCLH concept. Norwegian currently operates on the North Atlantic route connecting London Gatwick to several US cities; Ryanair operates a medium-haul four-hour flight from London Stansted to Ponta Delgada in the Azores; and AirAsia X serves the Kuala Lumpur–Sydney route. Still, no LCLH airline has entered the Australia–EU open skies market (Whyte and Lohmann, 2015). The ultra-long-haul routes (i.e. over 12 hours of flight) can be very tiring for passengers; therefore, a certain level of frills and service quality may be required. On these grounds, it may be argued that in this stage of airline business model convergence, distance remains the last resort of differentiation: while the difference between

FSNCs and LCCs in short-haul flights has been significantly blurred, the LCLH model is only nascent while the ultra-long-haul routes are until now served only by FSNCs.

At the same time, the airports responded to the changing airline environment by adapting their infrastructure to the new needs and often changing their ownership structure (Efthymiou et al., 2016). High sunk costs of infrastructure combined with low marginal costs of processing extra passengers forced airports to increase their passenger scale and diversify their travellers' profile by attracting both FSNCs and LCCs (Francis et al., 2003; Starkie, 2012). Farmaki and Papatheodorou (2015) claim that many airports previously dependent on leisure carriers now consider targeting LCCs to mitigate seasonality. Moreover, increased airline competition and the risk of airline bankruptcies may affect hub airports that are dependent on a single operator. When Malév Airlines went bankrupt, Budapest Airport lost almost a quarter of its scheduled flights, with negative implications for business travellers (Bilotkach et al., 2014). The gap of Malév was filled by Ryanair and Wizz Air, who offered a solid traffic solution to Budapest Airport. Hence, many airports want to decrease their dependence from specific airlines and seek to diversify their customers by serving both FSNCs and LCCs to secure their airside and landside investment (Koo et al., 2016). However, from a customer's point of view, the major challenge to consider is that the airport facilities used by FSNCs and LCCs are usually different in terms of service and cost.

Therefore, and following a strategy like brand proliferation (Scherer and Ross, 1990), some airports have invested in low cost terminals (LCTs) designated only for LCCs (see Chapter 10). The LCT building cost is much lower compared to the cost of a terminal designed for hub-and-spoke operations (Kazda and Caves, 2015). This is because LCTs are linear and rely on finger piers that are more economical to build, and bear lower baggage handling system costs. LCT operating costs are also 30 to 40 per cent lower (O'Connell, 2007). LCTs usually have electronic kiosks that speed up the check-in process and reduce the dwell time and space requirements, and since LCCs emphasise rapid turnarounds for their aircraft, space requirements are even more limited (de Neufville et al., 2013). Therefore, offering an LCT to an LCC is cheaper. In fact, this strategy has been followed by airports such as Milan Malpensa (where Terminal 1 is built for hub-and-spoke operations and Terminal 2 for LCCs) and Bordeaux. Conversely, the purpose-built Terminal 2 at Munich Airport to serve Lufthansa's hub-and-spoke operations freed up space in Terminal 1 for use by other airlines, including LCCs. Having the above in mind, it may be argued that from an era of airport specialisation in the early post-liberalisation years, there is a movement towards a period of airport model convergence where differentiation and specialisation is now achieved at a terminal level.

## Emerging trends in airline and airport business models: stepping beyond the core product

At present, the current trend in business model convergence at both airline and airport levels shows no signs of receding. On the contrary, stepping beyond the core product to exploit synergies and complementarities with other activities seems to have become a priority for most air transport market participants. Having realised the potential of ancillary revenue from flight-related activities (e.g. baggage check-in fees and in-flight catering sales), LCCs, but also increasingly FSNCs, have transformed themselves into proper travel supermarkets by selling on their website not only tickets for their flights, but also complementary travel services, such as accommodation, travel insurance and car rental, usually in collaboration with large online travel agents, such as Booking.com. In this way, airlines capitalise on the popularity of their website, as well as on their overall brand recognition and reputation, to boost revenue, and thus counter by the sheer scale of sales the negative impact of competition on profit margins.

Likewise, airports gradually step beyond their initial focus on non-aeronautical revenue (see Chapter 12) from typical terminal activities (e.g. duty-free shops) to become proper concession managers at a wider level. The rapid expansion of airport-centric commercial development is now leading to airports with a city-like environment. The terminal, which is the spatial and functional core of the airport, is now transformed into an urban central square, leading to the creation of an airport city. This may set the fundamentals for the subsequent creation of an aerotropolis consisting of "an airport city core and extensive outlying areas of aviation-oriented businesses and their associated residential developments" (Kasarda, 2008: 13). In other words, an aerotropolis is an airport-integrated urban economic region. Some examples of this evolving model are Incheon Airport, Dubai, Hong Kong International Airport and Kuala Lumpur. According to Kasarda (2008), an aerotropolis economically influences the surrounding area of the airport. The constant growth in passenger and cargo traffic and the need for non-aeronautical revenues, in combination with the commercial sector's pursuit of affordable accessible land and the high interest of landside businesses, act as catalysts for the emergence of airport cities (Ashfold et al., 2011).

An appealing terminal can improve the airport experience, which can be a determining factor for transfer passengers when choosing an airline and its hub. Airport cities are attractive locations for regional and international corporate headquarters, conference and exhibition centres, among others. Moreover, airport cities offer a variety of services. For instance, Frankfurt International Airport has an airport clinic serving more than 36,000 patients per year (Kasarda, 2014). Xia and Li (2006) identify six major characteristics of an airport city. The airport is undoubtedly the core, which subsequently exercises agglomeration forces (i.e. the airport city attracts industries, service providers and workers who may also become interested in residing in the airport vicinity). In addition, industries are spatially spread according to different intensities of utilisation. Travelling time to and from the airport is also an important characteristic since airport proximity affects business flows and the transit of goods. Finally, global accessibility related to the extensiveness of the air transport network and the technological pre-eminence are major characteristics of airport cities. Some fundamental growth factors of airport cities are land availability, improved surface transportation access and intermodality (Efthymiou and Papatheodorou, 2015), growing passenger demand, airport revenue needs, and the site-specific commercial real estate opportunities (Kasarda, 2014). It should be noted that many airport cities are based around hub airports and serve mainly FSNCs. Nevertheless, the existence of LCTs is noted in some airport cities, proving that the latter can accommodate different passengers and different airlines at the same time.

The main challenges faced by an airport city and an aerotropolis are land use and congruence with their wider environment. Few airport cities were planned, and many emerged in a largely organic and rather uncoordinated manner. Traffic congestion, availability of land, parking shortages, inefficient multimodal ground transit systems and safety concerns are only some of the issues that need to be resolved should an airport be designed as an airport city in advance. Furthermore, all the involved stakeholders, and especially the local community, should have a synergetic relationship, aiming at improving the position of the region and achieving the broader goal of sound international competitiveness (Ashfold et al., 2011). In fact, the traditional love–hate relationship between airlines and airports should now explicitly consider the role of local community and destination authorities in a proper triangular setting where risk-sharing is of essence to resolve conflict and generate a business outcome that is beneficial to all (see Chapter 18). This is because such a relationship may be bruised by the lethal quartet, involving so-called white elephants, where extensive airport investment in grandiose infrastructure to establish an airport city and an aerotropolis is never fully recovered, to the detriment of investors and the environment; the winner's curse, where airports and/or tourism destination authorities thirsty for improved accessibility and large inbound traffic flows end up outbidding their peers by offering FSNCs and LCCs too preferential terms to benefit sustainably in the longer term; freeriding and coordination failure as local tourism service suppliers may have second thoughts when asked to financially assist regional airports and/or local tourism destination authorities to attract LCCs; and the previously discussed spatial, market and temporal risk of airports and destination authorities as a result of strategic partnerships with a single airline operator, either an FSNC or an LCC (Papatheodorou, 2016).

## Conclusion

This chapter has discussed the evolution of airline and airport business models in the post-Second World War period. Starting from a period of heavy regulation, which seriously constrained competition dynamics, both sectors now operate in a relatively liberal environment, at least in many parts of the world. Further to a period of intense differentiation and specialisation in the aftermath of market liberalisation, airline and airport business models are now characterised by greater convergence as participants in both sectors aim at maximising their market exposure. Concepts such as the travel supermarket and aerotropolis have become part of the contemporary air transport business environment. Along with changes in the airline and airport business models, air navigation service providers (ANSPs) (see Chapter 4) are also gradually subjected to institutional changes and liberalisation, at least in Europe: in addition to government-owned ANSP authorities, related companies organised under private law have emerged in various ownership statuses, such as 100 per cent owned by government (e.g. DFS in Germany), PPPs (e.g. NATS in the UK) and 100 per cent private (e.g. ACR in Sweden). Interestingly, all these recent developments have resulted in complex relationships, which involve new stakeholders (e.g. destination authorities, tourism service providers, online travel agents), and hence raise not only the prospects of higher returns, but also new risks. For this reason, skilful and enlightened negotiators are needed to build trust on rational business terms and make such complex relationships evolve from a transactional to a relational and even possibly a transformational level.

## References

ACI Europe (Airports Council International Europe) (2010). *The Ownership of Europe's Airports*, Brussels, ACI Europe.
Ashfold, N.J., Mumayiz, S. and Wright, P.H. (2011). *Airport Engineering, Planning, Design, and Development of 21st Century Airports*, Hoboken, NJ, John Wiley & Sons.
Barbot, C. (2006). Low-cost airlines, secondary airports, and state aid: an economic assessment of the Ryanair–Charleroi Airport agreement, *Journal of Air Transport Management*, 12(4), 197–203.
Barrett, S. (2004). How do the demands for airport services differ between full service carriers and low-cost carriers? *Journal of Air Transport Management*, 10, 33–39.
Bilotkach, V., Mueller, J. and Nemeth, A. (2014). Estimating the consumer welfare effects of de-hubbing: the case of Malév Hungarian Airlines, *Transportation Research Part E: Logistics and Transportation Review*, 66, 51–65.
Borenstein, S. (1992). The evolution of U.S. airline competition, *Journal of Economic Perspectives*, 6(2), 45–73.
Choo, Y.Y. and Oum, T.H. (2013). Impacts of low cost carrier services on efficiency of the major U.S. airports, *Journal of Air Transport Management*, 33, 60–67.
Claussen, J. and O'Higgins, E. (2010). Competing on value: perspectives on business class aviation, *Journal of Air Transport Management*, 16, 202–208.
Daft, J. and Albers, S. (2012). A profitability analysis of low-cost long-haul flight operations, *Journal of Air Transport Management*, 19, 49–54.

de Neufville, R., Odoni, A.R., Belobaba, P. and Reynolds, T.G. (2013). *Airport Systems, Planning, Design and Management*, 2nd edition, New York, McGraw-Hill Education.

Dempsey, P.S. and Goetz, A. (1992). *Airline Deregulation and Laissez-Faire Mythology*. Westport, CT, Quorum Book.

DLR (German Aerospace Centre) (2008). *Topical Report: Airline Business Models*, Cologne, DLR.

Dobruszkes, F. (2009). New Europe, new low-cost air services, *Journal of Transport Geography*, 17, 423–432.

Dobruszkes, F., Mondou, V. and Aymen, G. (2016). Assessing the impacts of aviation deregulation on tourism: some methodological considerations derived from the Moroccan and Tunisian cases, *Journal of Transport Geography*, 50, 115–127.

Doganis, R. (2005). *The Airline Business*, 2nd edition, Abingdon, Routledge.

Doganis, R. (2010). *Flying Off Course: Airline Economics and Marketing*, 4th edition, Abingdon, Routledge.

EC (European Commission) (1996a). *Communication from the Commission to the Council and the European Parliament: Impact of the Third Package of Air Transport Liberalization Measures, COM (96) 514*, Brussels, EC.

EC (European Commission) (1996b). *Council Directive 96/67/EC of 15 October 1996 on Access to the Ground-Handling Market at Community Airports*, Brussels, EC.

Efthymiou, M. and Papatheodorou, A. (2015). Intermodal passenger transportation and destination competitiveness in Greece, *Anatolia: An International Journal of Tourism and Hospitality Research*, 26(3), 459–471.

Efthymiou, M., Arvanitis, P. and Papatheodorou, A. (2016) Institutional changes and dynamics in the European aviation sector: implications for tourism. In: N. Pappas and I. Bregoli (eds). *Global Dynamics in Travel, Tourism and Hospitality*, Hershey, PA, IGI Global.

Elhedhli, S. and Hu, F.X. (2005). Hub-and-spoke network design with congestion, *Computers & Operations Research*, 32(6), 1615–1632.

ERAA (European Regional Airlines Association) (2017). *Overview*. Online. Available at: www.eraa.org/about/overview (accessed 27 May 2017).

EU (European Union) (1992). *Council Regulation (EEC) No 2408/92 of 23 July 1992 on Access for Community Air Carriers to Intra-Community Air Routes*, Brussels, EU.

Farmaki, A. and Papatheodorou, A. (2015) Stakeholder perceptions of the role of low-cost carriers in insular tourism destinations: the case of Cyprus, *Tourism Planning and Development*, 12(4), 412–432.

Fichert, F. and Klophaus, R. (2011). Incentive schemes on airport charges: theoretical analysis and empirical evidence from German airports, *Research in Transportation Business & Management*, 1, 71–79.

Flight Airline Business (2016). Alliances, codeshares and beyond, *Flight Airline Business*, September, 39.

Francis, G., Fidato, A. and Humphreys, I. (2003). Airport–airline interaction: the impact of low-cost carriers on two European airports, *Journal of Air Transport Management*, 9, 267–273.

Graham, A. (2014). *Managing Airports: An International Perspective*, 4th edition, Abingdon, Routledge.

Graham, A. and Dennis, D. (2007). Airport traffic and financial performance: a UK & Ireland case study, *Journal of Transport Geography*, 15(3), 161–171.

Hotelling, H. (1929) Stability in competition, *Economic Journal*, 39, 41–57.

Kasarda, J.D. (2008). *Airport Cities: The Evolution*, London, Insight Media.

Kasarda, J.D. (2014). *Gateway airports: commercial magnets and critical business infrastructure*. Online. Available at: www.aerotropolis.com/files/MHFIGI-Gateway-Airports-Updated.pdf (accessed 12 September 2016).

Kazda, A. and Caves, R.E. (2015). *Airport Design and Operation*, 3rd edition, Amsterdam, Pergamon.

Koo, T., Halpern, N., Papatheodorou, A., Graham, A. and Arvanitis, P. (2016) Air transport liberalisation and airport dependency: developing a composite index, *Journal of Transport Geography*, 50, 83–93.

La Compagnie (2016). *Brexit: La Compagnie suspends its London–New York route. Second daily flight to be introduced from Paris–New York*. Online. Available at: www.lacompagnie.com/sites/default/files/press-release/la_compagnie_suspends_london-ny_uk.pdf (accessed 12 September 2016).

Lei, Z. and Papatheodorou, A. (2010). Measuring the effect of low-cost carriers on regional airports' commercial revenue, *Research in Transportation Economics*, 26(1), 37–43.

Leick, R. and Wensveen, J. (2014). The airline business. In: D. Prokop (ed.). *The Business of Transportation*, California, Praeger.

Morrell, S.P. (2011). *Moving Boxes by Air: The Economics of International Air Cargo*, Abingdon, Routledge.

Nunez-Sanchez, R. (2015). Regional public support to airlines and airports: an unsolved puzzle, *Transportation Research Part E: Logistics and Transportation Review*, 76, 93–107.

O'Connell, J.F. (2007). *The Strategic Response of Full Service Airlines to the Low Cost Carrier Threat and the Perception of Passengers to Each Type of Carrier*, PhD Thesis, Bedford, Cranfield University.

Palaskas, T., Papatheodorou, A. and Tsampra, M. (2006). *Cultural Heritage as a Growth Factor in the Greek Economy* (in Greek), Athens, Academy of Athens.

Papatheodorou, A. (2002). Civil aviation regimes and leisure tourism in Europe, *Journal of Air Transport Management*, 8(6), 381–388.

Papatheodorou, A. (2003). Do we need airport regulation? *Utilities Journal*, 6(10), 35–37.

Papatheodorou, A. (2004) Exploring the evolution of tourism resorts, *Annals of Tourism Research*, 31(1), 219–237.

Papatheodorou, A. (2016). *The airline–airport–tourism destination authority relationship: an eternal business triangle? Presented at GAD, Lisbon, December 2016.* Online. Available at: www.icbi-events.com/blog/GAD-Blog/post/id/7864_The-Airline--Airport--Tourism-Destination-Authority-Relationship-An-Eternal-Business-Triangle (accessed 16 March 2017).

Papatheodorou, A. and Iatrou, K. (2008). Leisure travel: implications for airline alliances, *International Review of Aerospace Engineering*, 1(4), 332–342.

Papatheodorou, A. and Lei, Z. (2006). Leisure travel in Europe and airline business models: a study of regional airports in Great Britain, *Journal of Air Transport Management*, 12(1), 47–52.

Polk, A. and Bilotkach, V. (2013). The assessment of market power of hub airports, *Transport Policy*, 29, 29–37.

Porter, K. (1980). How competitive forces shape strategy, *Harvard Business Review*, March–April, 137–145.

Redondi, R., Malighetti, P. and Paleari, S. (2012). De-hubbing of airports and their recovery patterns, *Journal of Air Transport Management*, 18(1), 1–4.

Redpath, N., O'Connell, J.F. and Warnock-Smith, D. (2016). The strategic impact of airline group diversification: the cases of Emirates and Lufthansa, *Journal of Air Transport Management*, 1–18.

Scherer, F.M. and Ross, D. (1990). *Industrial Market Structure and Economic Performance*, 3rd edition, Boston, MA, Houghton Mifflin.

Schumpeter, J.A. (1996). *Capitalism, Socialism and Democracy*, London, Routledge.

Shaw, R. (2007) Laker Airways Skytrain: the world's first LCC, *Airliners*, July/August, 42–46.

Smeth, J.N., Allvine, F.C., Uslay, C. and Dixit, A. (2007). *Deregulation and Competition, Lessons from the Airline Industry*, 1st edition, Singapore, Sage.

Sorensen, J. (2016). *2015 Top 10 Ancillary Revenue Rankings*, Shorewood, WI, IdeaWorksCompany.

Starkie, D. (2012). European airports and airlines: evolving relationships and the regulatory implications, *Journal of Air Transport Management*, 21, 40–49.

Wensveen, J. and Leick, R. (2009). The long-haul low cost carrier: a unique business model, *Journal of Air Transport Management*, 15(3), 127–133.

Whyte, R. and Lohmann, G. (2015). Low-cost long-haul carriers: a hypothetical analysis of a 'kangaroo route', *Case Studies on Transport Policy*, 3(2), 159–165.

Wittman, M.D. (2014). Public funding of airport incentives in the United States: the efficacy of the small community air service development grant program, *Transport Policy*, 35, 220–228.

Xia, Z.Y. and Li, P. (2006). *Study on Airport Economy*, Beijing, China Economic Publishing House Press.

# Part II
# Application of management disciplines to airlines and airports

# 9

# Airline business strategy

*Gui Lohmann and Bojana Spasojevic*

## Introduction

Airlines are notorious for providing lower returns on investment when compared with other corporations. As a result, airline executives implement business strategies aiming to obtain higher than normal financial returns. With the liberalisation process that airlines have enjoyed around the world (see Chapters 6 and 7), some carriers have been quite creative in fostering new approaches in terms of their business models, product differentiation and cost reduction (see Chapter 8). In addition, because of the international multiple-business-related nature of airline operations (which includes aircraft manufacturers and maintenance, distribution channels and airport logistics), these characteristics make airline strategic management a very complex exercise. A number of approaches have been used to explain strategic issues related to airlines. One of them is Shaw's (2011) application of Porter's classic Five Forces model to the airline industry, a framework for analysing competitive forces, for instance rivalry, substitution, new entry, power of customers and power of suppliers. Scholars have also focused their attention on analysing airline strategic decisions relating to several managerial issues, with a particular emphasis on mergers and alliances (Gudmundsson and Lechner, 2011; Iatrou and Oretti, 2016).

This chapter is structured into four main sections. The first one provides some generic strategies. The second section focuses on airline differentiation strategies and niche products, mainly charter and leisure carriers. The third section tackles growth strategies, examining the four distinct strategies proposed by Ansoff's Matrix: market penetration, product development, market development and diversification. The fourth section considers different strategic growth methods, including organic growth, mergers and acquisitions, industry cooperation and franchising. In order to illustrate these concepts, examples from airlines around the world are discussed. The chapter concludes by extracting from this discussion lessons that can guide future trends in the airline industry.

## Generic strategies

The deregulation of air transport in different parts of the world has resulted in airlines becoming more susceptible to the pressures of competition (see Chapters 6 and 7). Before deregulation, the industry was predominantly characterised by a wide network of destinations where passengers flew in comfort and luxury. Airlines operating in that environment projected a brand associated with status, perks and, as a consequence, an expensive product affordable only to a few. This business model is traditionally called the full service network carrier (FSNC). In contrast, in most countries, the deregulation process resulted in the flourishing of airlines, operating with diverse business models (see Chapter 8). The most common airline business model following deregulation is the low cost carrier (LCC). LCCs try to focus on providing an efficient and punctual service while eliminating unnecessary costs and perks, offering only the basic elements required for a safe flight. As a result, LCCs are associated with low air fares. With the airline industry maturing in the deregulated environment, new airlines are entering the market, based on a variety of business models that fall between the traditional FSNC and the emerging LCC models. These new airlines are usually called hybrid airlines (Corbo, 2017). This section defines in more detail the various airline business models, providing examples from well-known airlines (see also Chapter 8).

Prior to the first airline deregulation process that took place in the United States (US) during the late 1970s, most airlines operated as FSNCs and were usually government-owned enterprises. Governments viewed these airlines as vehicles for advancing their national interest, flying either domestically or internationally. They were also called national or flag carriers. Examples include Air France, Air New Zealand and British Airways, which operated under some form of legislative protection as part of their respective national governments. With the wave of privatisation in many countries around the world during the 1980s, in large part due to financial pressures on governments to focus on core activities, many governments sold their stakes in their airlines, with British Airways being among the first to be privatised in 1986. Air New Zealand was privatised a few years later, in 1989. The 1990s were characterised by the emergence of a new competitive threat in the form of LCCs, while the 2000s saw airlines operating in an environment with record high fuel prices, increasingly stringent security measures, an overcapacity of airline seats, and intense competition in almost every domestic and international market.

One of the key characteristics of the FSNC model is the hub-and-spoke network (see Chapter 15), with routes concentrated on one or more major hubs that connect the rest of the network using radiating spoke services. A number of FSNCs have taken this approach to a global scale by joining strategic alliances offering code-share and interline ticket agreements to connect hundreds of destinations in dozens of countries. Hence, global marketing and distribution alliances such as Star Alliance, Oneworld and SkyTeam were formed.

Because of the superior product offered by FSNCs, these airlines predominantly target the corporate and government sectors, as well as individuals who are frequent flyers and are prepared to pay a premium fare for air travel. These airlines offer loyalty schemes such as frequent flyer programmes (FFPs) to enable their frequent passengers to collect and redeem points for free flights and other products and services. FFPs often offer partnerships such as with other airlines, banks, mobile phone companies and retailers who buy frequent flyer points and use them to reward customers for their loyalty (see also Chapter 13).

LCCs started with Southwest Airlines in the US in the late 1970s, then proliferated into Europe in the 1990s and to most countries in the world in the 2000s. LCCs have become well established, particularly in domestic markets and also in the medium-haul international markets, notably in Europe, Asia and Australasia. Establishing long-haul LCCs has proven to be a very difficult exercise, considering the challenges of providing sufficient comfort required by passengers flying more than nine hours and of working out the complex logistics approach required to set up such operations (Whyte and Lohmann, 2015a). While there are some features common to all airlines deploying the LCC model, the sector is not homogenous, with carriers modifying the model according to their location and market. LCCs generally opt for a single-class service with a narrow seat pitch, basic terminal facilities, without the use of air bridges if possible, and fast turnaround times in order to increase the utilisation of their fleet. A number of LCCs have unbundled the air travel product to its bare basics, making passengers pay for any extra product or service. Examples include requiring passengers to pay for selecting pre-assigned seats, in-flight meals, entertainment and checked hold baggage.

In order to resist the LCCs' attempts to penetrate the FSNC market, a number of FSNCs have tried to establish their own LCC subsidiary. However, several attempts to establish low cost carrier-within-a-carrier (CWC) strategies have resulted in unprofitable businesses because of the inability of FSNCs to foster a truly LCC organisational culture within their established subsidiaries (Whyte and Lohmann, 2015b). Successful examples include Jetstar and Scoot, established, respectively, by Qantas and Singapore Airlines, while cases of failed attempts include British Airways' Go Fly and United Airlines' Ted.

As airlines continue to mature in a competitive and deregulated environment, not only have traditional FSNCs departed from their established models, but LCCs have also developed variations in terms of picking and choosing attributes from both FSNCs and LCCs (Klophaus et al., 2012). The challenges of defining these new business models as either FSNCs or LCCs has led to the establishment of hybrid airlines (Whyte and Lohmann, 2016). Jetstar, for example, takes advantage of its parent airline Qantas to blend low cost traits with FSNC product differentiation, including operating from major airports, seeking route expansion beyond short-haul operations, and using travel agents and other commissionable sources as a distribution channel (Whyte and Lohmann, 2015b). Customer relationship management (CRM), including the introduction of FFPs, has been implemented to win repeat business. The United Kingdom (UK) based LCC easyJet, for example, now offers optional extras such as speedy boarding and the use of airport lounges, while the New York-based JetBlue has broadened its route portfolio and introduced new products to attract higher-yielding passengers. Its premium intercontinental product Mint offers lie-flat beds, thereby arguably having more in common with a traditional FSNC product than an LCC product. At the same time, FSNCs have started charging for certain perks that in the past were free, such as checked bags and complimentary hot meals.

With FSNCs and LCCs becoming increasingly indistinguishable, separating their differences is less obvious, making a re-evaluation of how both models are classified timely (Bell and Lindenau, 2009; Lieberman and Asaba, 2006). Homogenisation of the business model has been taking place through two principal methods. In the first, imitation takes place where firms mirror each other's strategies to avoid falling behind. In the second, market convergence, the previously blatant differences between FSNCs and LCCs (e.g. relating to pricing, product offering, fleet and network design) are blurred, moving to the mainstream middle and offering products and services that are a lot more similar. Within the two mainstream business models, there is a myriad of airlines utilising the best of each model, differentiating themselves through labour costs, fleet structuring or even creating a subsidiary to realise profitable gains.

In order to better represent this new reality, academics such as Daft and Albers (2013) and Lohmann and Koo (2013) proposed a spectrum where airlines can be classified in terms of their business models in a simple one-dimensional proposition. Using data from airlines based in the US from 2008 and 2009, Lohmann and Koo (2013) mapped out the airline business spectrum of nine US airlines (AirTran, Alaska, American, Continental, Delta, Hawaiian, JetBlue, SkyWest and Southwest). The results of this study, based on six different indices (see Table 9.1) show that carriers such as AirTran and Southwest were placed closer to the LCC model, whereas firms

*Table 9.1* Averaged benchmarked values for the six indices, 2008 to 2009

|  | AirTran | Southwest | JetBlue | SkyWest | Hawaiian | Alaska | Continental | American | Delta | SD |
|---|---|---|---|---|---|---|---|---|---|---|
| Revenue | 0.19 | 0.32 | 0.26 | 0.46 | 0.50 | 0.61 | 0.66 | 0.67 | 0.83 | 0.21 |
| Connectivity | 0.27 | 0.47 | 0.47 | 0.56 | 0.61 | 0.48 | 0.53 | 0.66 | 0.72 | 0.13 |
| Convenience | 0.70 | 0.58 | 0.83 | 0.27 | 0.35 | 0.40 | 0.61 | 0.61 | 0.41 | 0.18 |
| Comfort | 0.31 | 0.56 | 0.40 | 0.65 | 0.21 | 0.71 | 0.57 | 0.56 | 0.54 | 0.16 |
| Aircraft | 0.37 | 0.23 | 0.24 | 0.59 | 0.60 | 0.41 | 0.51 | 0.79 | 0.73 | 0.20 |
| Labour | 0.14 | 0.36 | 0.38 | 0.17 | 0.54 | 0.55 | 0.79 | 0.83 | 0.71 | 0.25 |
| SD | 0.20 | 0.14 | 0.22 | 0.19 | 0.16 | 0.12 | 0.10 | 0.11 | 0.15 | |
| Average | 0.33 | 0.42 | 0.43 | 0.45 | 0.47 | 0.53 | 0.63 | 0.65 | 0.66 | |

*Source*: Lohmann and Koo (2013).

such as American and Delta were shown to be closer to the FSNC model. While these results only confirm the overall perception of these airlines' business models, the ability to spot airlines in the middle of the spectrum, or the so-called hybrid airlines, is of value, notably visualising the position of JetBlue, SkyWest, Hawaiian and Alaska along the spectrum. Also valuable is the opportunity to dissect how all airlines perform in terms of each of the indices used. A subsequent similar study updated these results by examining the managerial and operational indices of US carriers in the years 2011 to 2013, focusing on the results of post-US carriers' mergers and the global financial crisis (GFC) (Jean and Lohmann, 2016). Evidence from this more recent study suggests that US carriers that went through a merger process came out with a stronger position towards FSNCs. With the exception of SkyWest, the remaining four airlines (American, United, Delta and Southwest) all increased their revenue index towards the FSNC end of the spectrum. Three airlines (American, United and Southwest) increased their average index in terms of connectivity (impacted by factors such as average daily departures per airport, total number of destinations served and average sector miles), with market growth occurring from merger expansion. As FSNCs are primarily identified in this study through their revenue and connectivity indices, Southwest, post-merger with AirTran, respectively, had a 22 and 23 per cent increase towards the FSNC end of the spectrum. Prior to the merger, Southwest operated a single fleet type, but with the merger moved to a multiple fleet type. This caused a shift in their corporate strategy where Southwest increased its position along the continuum by 4 per cent. This pattern suggests that post-merger, there is a tendency to shift towards the FSNC model, with an increase in their overall operations and corporate size.

## Airline differentiation strategy and niche products: charter and leisure carriers

Among the various airline business models, one that has operated in a much less regulated environment is that of charter, non-scheduled services (see also Chapter 8). Buck and Lei (2004: 73) define charter airlines as predominantly serving:

> leisure routes [. . .], carrying clients for tour operators [with a particular focus on the . . .] seasonal, locational and event-specific nature of leisure tourism [, enabling . . .] charter air services and travel companies to achieve economies of density [. . . to . . .] reduce passenger unit costs.

While charter airlines operate all over the world, Europe, in particular, has provided a perfect regulatory and socio-economic environment for this type of differentiation strategy. Charter flights are particularly well suited to flying the short international routes that service the seasonal market of European sunseekers, most notably the wealthier markets such as the British and German travellers (Lobbenberg, 1995). In both countries, very large tour operators have established their own charter airlines, with successful operations from companies such as First Choice and Thomson in the UK that belong to the German TUI Group, and are expected to operate under the single TUI name by 2018. Perry (1994) has mapped out a number of mainstream and niche airline operators flying for tour operators, including: (1) very large mainstream charter airlines, some of which fly to dozens of destinations worldwide; (2) small in-house airlines operating a handful of aircraft; (3) non-aligned or less-aligned airlines that serve high-quality niche markets for smaller tour operators requiring an out-house carrier; (4) wholly owned charter subsidiaries of FSNCs; (5) specialist niche operators focusing on small aircraft targeting less popular and non-mainstream destinations; and (6) seat-only level brokers and specialists booking predominantly foreign carriers, particularly during the peak season.

The air inclusive tour industry's success in using charter flights is attributed to the ability of operators to control the distribution channels, either through physical stores (still predominant in the UK, even in the current age of electronic distribution channels) or online reservation systems. This provides them with buying power, used against smaller accommodation providers based in less-developed countries in Europe or overseas and a deregulated air transport environment fostering the flourishing of a myriad of different types of airline business models (Evans, 2001a). In a number of countries, charter flights have also been offered in isolation from other tourism products, in effect competing with LCCs in the budget leisure travel segment.

Charter airlines have a number of different operational strategies in comparison to traditional carriers. One example is that while LCCs ground their aircraft during off-season periods, holiday charters opt to outsource their fleet through wet lease arrangements (i.e. when an airline leases an aircraft to another airline or business broker also offering complete crew, maintenance and insurance). De Wit and Zuidberg (2016) report that LCCs such as Ryanair ground at least 20 per cent of their aircraft during their winter season.

## Growth strategies

After liberalisation and deregulation of air transport markets in different parts of the world, airlines started to develop different strategies for market growth and increased profit. Some of these strategies are more commonly used by FSNCs, while others are mostly deployed by LCCs. This section discusses different strategic directions adopted by airlines, providing examples from FSNCs, LCCs and hybrid carriers (for airports, see Chapter 10).

Strategic planning is often used to set priorities, strengthen operations and ensure that companies work towards establishing goals. The strategic direction of airline companies can be successfully measured by using the Ansoff Matrix. Igor Ansoff, a Russian/American mathematician, applied his work to the world of business in order to help managers consider the growth of their business, either through existing or new products and markets (Martinet, 2010). The Ansoff Matrix is based on four distinct strategies: market penetration, product development, market development and diversification (see Figure 9.1). All of these strategies are used in the airline industry.

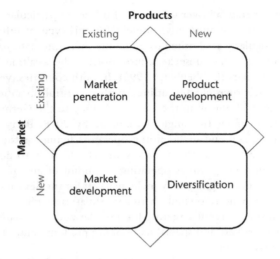

*Figure 9.1*  The Ansoff Matrix

*Source*: Drawn by the authors based on Ansoff (1957).

## Market penetration

Market penetration is a strategy used by companies to increase their market share. It is usually used by an airline company to grow its market share by focusing on its existing markets and product range. When there is an opportunity for further growth in a particular market, market penetration is found as an appropriate strategic direction (Dale, 2016). Some of the strategies used to increase market share include more aggressive pricing policies, an increase in supply, or the introduction of new products and services.

A global trend among FSNCs fostering market penetration includes the establishment of LCCs, through a CWC strategy. The CWC strategy, also called dual-brand strategy, was taken by Qantas with its subsidiary Jetstar. In this particular case, the positive results have inspired other companies to implement the same strategy. According to Whyte and Lohmann (2015b), the Jetstar model is a very basic proposition whereby the airline focuses on a low-fare market position, which is achieved through direct sales, self-service, user-pay offerings, a simplified fleet structure, and a lean and accountable business culture. This planned approach emphasises a long-term, highly systematic and deterministic process of strategic planning, aiming to achieve the best fit between the organisation and its environment. This strategy was implemented in an incremental way, with Jetstar emerging from being a purely domestic carrier into an international one. In the international market, the airline started by operating first to New Zealand, targeting the trans-Tasman market, before purchasing wide-bodied aircraft to serve Asia and Hawaii. Jetstar also benefits from a well-established strong parent owner that has the engineering, technical, planning, financial and marketing capabilities to support its subsidiary airline.

Despite the success enjoyed by the Qantas Group, many attempts to develop a successful CWC strategy have failed, as the demise of Continental Lite, Delta Express, Shuttle by United, Song, Ted, Tango, Go Fly (Go), bmibaby, Freedom Air, and many others has shown. However, CWCs have succeeded in the Asia-Pacific region, which hosts some of the best initiatives of CWCs (Pearson and Merkert, 2014). These include Singapore Airlines' subsidiary Scoot, Malaysian Airlines' subsidiary Firefly, Korean Air's subsidiary JinAir and All Nippon Airways' subsidiary Peach.

## Market development

The market development strategy involves offering existing products to new segments, new users and new geographies (Johnson et al., 2008). By following this strategic direction, airline companies enter new markets using its existing products. Because the success of the market development strategy is highly dependent on market research and planning, airline analysts play an important role in developing this strategy. There are numerous industry examples of successful market development strategies being employed by airline companies, including Emirates and Singapore Airlines (Lohmann et al., 2009), but also other Middle East carriers such as Qatar Airways.

By developing Dubai as an international and intercontinental hub, Emirates established an alternative to the traditional European airline hubs such as London Heathrow Airport, Amsterdam Schiphol and Frankfurt Airport. In the past, many European airlines have used these airports as gateways from smaller airports serving long-haul destinations. For example, instead of flying Budapest–Amsterdam–Singapore–Sydney, today passengers can choose a more convenient route with only one stop in Dubai. In 2016, Emirates operated over 150 direct routes across six continents from its hub at Dubai Airport. Additionally, Emirates owns the largest Airbus 380 fleet in the world, with 71 of these mega aircraft serving 36 destinations (The National, 2015). Because of Emirates' strategic air route planning, Dubai is heavily promoted as a destination, and thanks to the developed air route network is a logical stopover destination for many long-haul travellers.

One of Emirates' competitors, Qatar Airways, is applying a similar strategic direction by opening new international routes. As recently as 2011, Qatar Airways launched 15 new routes, and another nine in 2012, many of which were not served by either Emirates or Etihad (Mayasandra, 2011), their direct competitors in the Middle East. Currently, Qatar Airways operates to more than 150 destinations, and with 14 new routes starting in 2016, and another seven to commence operations in 2017 (Qatar Airways, 2016). Furthermore, a new-build airport in Doha, which is specially designed to accommodate Airbus 380 aircraft, suggests that Qatar Airways is working towards becoming the dominant airline in the Middle East (O'Connell, 2011).

Another interesting example of market development is Singapore Airlines' project called Capital Express. As of September 2016, for the first time in Australia and New Zealand's history, their national capital cities will be served by non-stop flights. In fact, this route is the first international route originating at Canberra Airport for more than a decade. The new route, Singapore–Canberra–Wellington, will complement Singapore Airlines' existing network in Australia that so far includes Adelaide, Brisbane, Melbourne, Perth and Sydney, with additional flights to Cairns and Darwin served by its subsidiary SilkAir (Canberra Airport, 2016). Singapore Airlines has used a wise strategy of developing a unique route such as Capital Express to enter a new market. As it is currently the only international flight serving Canberra, it has opened an unexploited market. Also, breaking the long-haul Singapore–Wellington flight into two parts allows more flexibility in terms of aircraft choice and route profitability.

## Product development

The product development strategy is implemented when the company brings a new or modified product or service to the existing market (see also Chapter 13). Product development can be the consequence of changed passenger preferences or a convenient way to attract new passengers and compete. This strategic direction is one of the best ways to compete with others, especially through innovation. Interestingly, some airline product development innovations can become a service standard. One of those examples is on-board Wi-Fi, which was a dream only a decade ago. Today, a number of airlines offer free Wi-Fi on board, including Emirates, JetBlue, Norwegian, Turkish Airlines, Air China, Philippine Airlines, Hong Kong Airlines and Nok Air. The convenience of having the Internet connection during the whole flight might help to attract a certain group of passengers, such as business travellers who might be willing to pay extra for this service (some airlines are offering it for free). Even though this product has not yet reached its full potential, it is expected that in the future, on-board Wi-Fi will be a component of regular service.

Other airlines are competing to attract different passenger segments, such as families with young children. Offering family-friendly services has proven to be a win-win strategy. Not only do these passengers have higher satisfaction rates, but so do passengers travelling without children. For example, a *Sydney Morning Herald* poll identified crying babies as the top irritant on planes (Small and Harris, 2014). As a response to this issue, a new, free service called Air Sky Nanny was introduced by Gulf Air (2016). This family-friendly product was later also offered by Etihad Airways on their long-haul flights, as well as their partner company, Air Serbia, on their first long-haul flight between Belgrade and New York.

As one of the world's leading airline companies, Emirates has one of its strategies to be the first airline to introduce new products (Nataraja and Al-Aali, 2011) – something that has distinguished it from other airlines. For example, Emirates was the first commercial airline in the world to offer an in-flight spa and free shower facility to first-class passengers on their Dubai to Sydney and Dubai to Auckland flights operated on the Airbus 380. As a Middle East market leader, Emirates is constantly challenged to expand its market and develop new products before its competitors (McKechnie et al., 2008).

## Diversification

Diversification as a strategic direction can be defined as an organisation's expansion out of its current products and markets into new areas (Yashodha, 2012). It is important to mention that a diversification strategic move can be related or unrelated to its current offerings. Related diversification is represented by the entry into a new market with a new product, which is related to the core business activity, while unrelated diversification represents the entry into a new market with a new product that is unrelated to the core business (Dale, 2016).

The most common airline-related diversification strategies involve cargo, maintenance, repair and overhaul, catering, information technologies and leisure management (Redpath et al., in press). The main aim of this strategic direction is to support passenger operations and improve the quality of existing services. A successful industry example of extended related diversification can be found in the case of easyJet, a British budget airline company and the second largest LCC in Europe, according to the number of passengers carried. Established in 1995, it was the first company established within the easyGroup. Since 1995, easyGroup has expanded their business by opening new 'easy brand' companies, mainly in the area of travel, leisure, accommodation and hospitality (Rae, 2001). Today, more than 60 different brands are part of easyGroup.

The Virgin Group is a noteworthy example of unrelated diversification. The Virgin Group has more than 200 companies that range from Virgin Bridal Stores to Virgin Airlines. Virgin is recognised as a famous brand, with travel, entertainment and lifestyle as its core business areas (Vincent, 2010). Unrelated diversification involves taking high risks and requires new operational systems and structures to be applied as a part of the strategy.

## Different strategic methods

After deciding on its strategic direction, the airline will identify and adopt an appropriate strategic method. Most business studies identify the following strategic methods (Dale, 2016): organic growth, inorganic growth through mergers and acquisitions, strategic alliances and franchising. This section discusses each of these strategic methods and its implications for the airline industry (for airports, see Chapter 10).

### Organic growth

Organic growth as a strategic method involves expanding the organisation's market or products by using its own resources. In comparison to inorganic growth, where growth is achieved through mergers and acquisitions, organic growth has its own advantages and disadvantages. Some of the main advantages are full control over the expansion plan, an increase of market share and improvement of customers' retention (Dale, 2016). On the other hand, in comparison with other strategic methods, organic growth can be a slower process with a risk as competitors can apply external/inorganic growth strategies with faster results. Companies focused on the organic growth method have a great potential to accelerate sustainable innovations, but this requires well-organised top-level strategic leadership (Ronald, 2005).

The literature has identified a number of examples of organic growth strategies in the airline industry. A classical often cited case is Southwest Airlines, which for over 30 years has been profitable by growing its business by meticulously expanding its network to selected destinations, while at the same time developing a very specific organisational culture (Boyer et al., 2002; Gittell, 2003; Ronald, 2005). Nevertheless, Southwest Airlines merged with AirTran in late 2014, outlining two major benefits of this acquisition: (1) access to Atlanta (the largest airport in the US in terms of passenger numbers); and (2) instant access to international markets in Latin America and the Caribbean operated by AirTran (CAPA, 2015).

Another successful organic growth example is Emirates. Based in Dubai, Emirates is the fastest-growing Middle East carrier and one of the most profitable airline companies in the world (Nataraja and Al-Aali, 2011). Emirates has experienced a constant growth rate in terms of air fleet, number of operated destinations and flight frequency without reporting a loss since its establishment in 1985. These results have positioned Emirates as a world-leading airline company. Figure 9.2 illustrates Emirates' growth over its main competitors, Etihad and Qatar Airways. Emirates had an exponential growth of available seat kilometres (ASKs) of 99 per cent between 2010 and 2016 (CAPA, 2016) and a 636 per cent growth in its fleet between 2000 and 2015 (Schonland, 2015). Furthermore, in the financial year 2015–2016, Emirates operated to 151 destinations from Dubai and carried 51.9 million passengers (The Emirates Group, 2016). Since Emirates is not part of any formal airline alliance, nor has it pursued any mergers or acquisitions, the company's success is based on an organic growth strategy.

Even though Emirates is still the leading Middle East and world airline company, some business analysts predict that it has reached limits of organic growth (Galani, 2011) and that it is time to consider another growth strategy. The fast growth of its competitor Qatar Airways provides credence to the advantages of change management and the implementation of new strategies that follow the driver of competition (Dale, 2016). In 2011, Qatar Airways overtook Emirates in the number of destinations served and has grown more than twice as fast (23 per cent) as Emirates (CAPA, 2016).

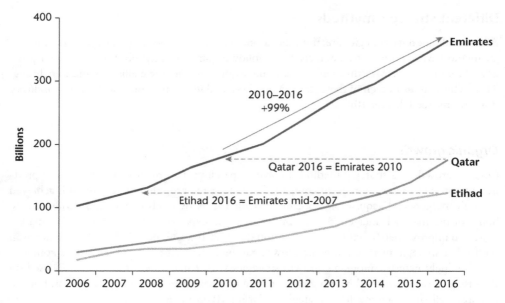

*Figure 9.2*   Middle East carriers' annual ASKs, 2006 to 2016

*Source*: Used with permission from CAPA (2016).

## Mergers and acquisitions

Mergers and acquisitions are common inorganic strategic growth methods. Even though these two strategic directions have the same ultimate goal of effective and quick growing market share, they comprise very different processes. A merger is a strategic decision of two or more companies to combine their resources and to become one organisation, while acquisition occurs when one company purchases the assets of another (Dale, 2016). The main potential issue of this strategic decision is a failure of the successful integration of the combined companies. This issue can be overcome through a well-structured operation management plan that can bring together different business philosophies.

In today's highly competitive and turbulent aviation market, mergers and acquisitions are often considered as an effective way of surviving financial crises (Merkert and Morrell, 2012) or achieving a fast recovery. Some of the key reasons for airlines to seek out a merger or acquisition are: stagnation or slower growth; a limitation on growth outside the home market; getting access to slots at key airports; or network expansion (Merkert and Morrell, 2012). The US market provides a clear example of successful mergers and acquisitions where a number of airlines were saved from financial loss by taking over another airline. The study conducted by Jean and Lohmann (2016) analysed the results of eight US companies between 2011 and 2013, after the GFC and after several mergers. Their results show that post-2009, the merged airlines' position moved closer to the FSCN end of the business model spectrum. The revenue index (a measure of an airline business that comprises a number of benchmarks) (see Jean and Lohmann, 2016 for more details) of all merged airlines (i.e. AirTran, Southwest, Continental, American, Delta) increased, except for SkyWest. Individual airlines (i.e. Alaska, Hawaiian and JetBlue) that did not merge during the post-GFC period moved towards the LCC end of the spectrum.

Meanwhile, in the European aviation market, the merger between KLM and Air France is considered as one of the most important market changes. According to European Union

(EU) law, a proposed merger between two or more airlines must be notified to the European Commission (EC) (Németh and Niemeier, 2012). Since 1995, when the first relevant merger case occurred (Swissair/Sabena), the point of origin-destination (OD) approach was used by the EC to assess the airlines' market position (Németh and Niemeier, 2012). According to this approach, every combination of a point of origin and destination is considered to be a disjoint market from the customer's standpoint. During the analysis, the EC looks not only at the direct flights between two airports, but also all other different transport possibilities in that market. In the case of the KLM and Air France merger (2004), a network competition analysis was used for the first time, instead of the traditional OD approach. The uniqueness of this merger case where Air France and KLM belonged to different global alliances was expected to create a mega-merger containing four of the world's largest airlines (Air France, KLM, Delta and Northwest) (Brueckner and Pels, 2005). This case emphasises that the mergers and acquisitions strategy opens a door for new business cooperation such as global alliances.

## Strategic alliances

Industry cooperation as a strategic direction is evident in many industries. One of the most active sectors within this strategic direction is the airline industry (Evans, 2001b). Airline alliances as a form of industry cooperation can be defined as the sharing of resources between two or more airlines, with the aim of mutual benefit, efficiency and market growth (French, 1997). The development of strategic airline alliances is strongly connected with the globalisation of tourism (Page, 2005). Even though most alliances were formed after 1992 (Bennett, 1997), the early stages of alliance development go back to the 1970s (French, 1997). Some of the main features of strategic alliances developed by airlines include code-sharing, joint services, joint marketing, franchise agreements and frequent flyer benefits (French, 1997). If airline alliances are analysed from the hierarchical perspective, the main types would include bilateral form, code-sharing, joint activities, marketing alliances and open skies, with open skies as the most dynamic form of commitment (Wang et al., 2004).

As mentioned earlier, airline alliances influence not only the overall performance of partner companies, but also the tourism industry. Destinations such as Australia, which is a long-distance destination from most of its potential tourism markets (apart from New Zealand), are most likely to experience the impact of alliances. Different forms of transport partnerships on a destination level play a significant role in competitive positioning (Page, 2005). The research conducted by Morley (2003) emphasised the following positive effects of airline alliances on Australian tourism: a decrease in fares; a reduction in total travel time; easier connections; more efficient marketing for Australia as a tourism destination; and more convenient air service scheduling. The recent boom of Chinese tourists visiting the Gold Coast in Australia supports this view. The benefits of new financial alliances between HNA Aviation Group, which owns Hainan Air, and has a stake in Virgin Australia, are already visible through a 32 per cent increase in Chinese tourists on the Gold Coast between June 2015 and June 2016 (Doherty, 2016).

## Franchising

Franchising is a business model method where one company grants another company the right to use its branding through a licensing agreement. The second company then sells the first company's products or services according to the rules and guidelines established by the first company. Franchising is a common practice in many industries (Price, 1997) but it is less common in the airline industry. In the US in the mid-1980s and in Europe in the 1990s, franchising was used as a strategic response by the airline industry to the deregulation of air transport. The airline franchising model does not differ markedly from other sectors. From the European practice, one airline (the franchisor) sells to another airline (the franchisee) its brand (aircraft livery and interior, crew uniforms, customer service and flight designator code), together with other intellectual property and know-how (Denton and Dennis, 2000). As in other industries, there are certain benefits and risks for both franchisor and franchisee. The main benefits for the franchisee include purchasing a well-known brand (Denton and Dennis, 2000) and gaining access to the franchisor's sales system and all additional support and training (Pender, 1999). The main benefit for the franchisor is a cheap method for extending the brand presence with minimal financial risk (Denton and Dennis, 2000). Also, there are some disadvantages for both parties with the biggest risk that any negative or impermissible activities carried out by the franchisee will reflect badly on the franchisor's brand.

Airline franchising, like airline alliances, has substantial implications for tourism. Franchising is a successful way for FSNCs to compete with charter carriers on important tourism routes (Pender, 1999). For example, British Airways handed the majority of its Mediterranean tourist routes to its franchisees, allowing these other airlines to offer lower standards more suitable to the leisure market. Another important implication of airline franchising is present in the development of peripheral regions, which rely heavily on air transport services. Pagliari (2003) explored the case study of the Highlands and Islands of Scotland and the benefits that accrued for this region from the British Airways Express franchise agreement with BA CitiExpress and Loganair in 1994. The process of franchising these two companies by British Airways terminated the existing competition between those carriers and created a development-ready environment.

## Conclusion

Strategic business decisions affect a wide range of managerial and operational areas of any airline. As discussed in this chapter, airlines have used a number of different approaches to suit their business decisions in accordance with their markets, regulations and business models. The examples provided in this chapter illustrate that in recent decades, airlines are becoming more creative in adjusting their strategies. For example, it is no longer a straightforward exercise to identify airlines as purely belonging to one of the traditional business models such as FSNC or LCC. Many airlines are adopting aspects of both FSNC and LCC models in order to become more competitive, with the establishment of individual hybrid models along the FSNC–LCC spectrum.

In terms of alliances, mergers and acquisitions, airlines similarly do not follow a one-model-fits-all solution. While in the 1990s and early 2000s survival was associated with the airlines needing to belong to one of the major global strategic alliances, a number of the emerging players like the Gulf carriers grew independently or negotiated specific operational strategic agreements such as the one established between Qantas and Emirates. The kangaroo route enables these airlines to feed the route between Australia and Europe via Dubai, instead of Asia. Another example from Australia is the case of Virgin Australia, which has established partnerships involving, for example, code-sharing and reciprocal FFPs with several airlines in different parts of the globe (e.g. Delta, Etihad, Singapore Airlines and Air New Zealand) outside the structure of one of the main airline alliances (i.e. Star Alliance, Oneworld and SkyTeam). Also, while the airline sector is far from becoming a truly multinational business across the world, new forms of mergers and acquisitions are becoming more evident, as regulations become more flexible to enable airlines to compete for markets in different regions. Airlines in the EU can now operate without a number of regulatory constraints, while groups such as Latam (created through the merger between Lan Chile and Tam Airlines) form a powerful airline in South America. Also, the Virgin-branded airlines (Virgin America, Virgin Atlantic and Virgin Australia) stretch their presence in different countries. Southwest Airlines, which grew organically for many decades, has undertaken its first ever merger – with AirTran. It seems that the future ahead for airline business strategies is one of unpredictable opportunities, with airline strategic managers innovating even more in the decades ahead in the twenty-first century.

## References

Ansoff, H.I. (1957). Strategies for diversification, *Harvard Business Review*, 35(5), 113–124.

Bell, M. and Lindenau, T. (2009). Sleepless nights, *Airline Business*, 25, 70–72.

Bennett, M.M. (1997). Strategic alliances in the world airline industry, *Progress in Tourism and Hospitality Research*, 3(3), 213–223.

Boyer, K.K., Hallowell, R. and Roth, A.V. (2002). E-services: operating strategy – a case study and a method for analyzing operational benefits, *Journal of Operations Management*, 20(2), 175–188.

Brueckner, J.K. and Pels, E. (2005). European airline mergers, alliance consolidation, and consumer welfare, *Journal of Air Transport Management*, 11(1), 27–41.

Buck, S. and Lei, Z. (2004). Charter airlines: have they a future? *Tourism and Hospitality Research*, 5(1), 72–78.

Canberra Airport (2016). *Singapore Airlines to make history with new 'Capital Express'*. Online. Available at: www.canberraairport.com.au/2016/01/singapore-airlines (accessed 29 September 2016).

CAPA (Centre for Aviation) (2015). *Southwest Airlines closes the chapter on AirTran. What's next for the middle aged LCC?* Online. Available at: http://centreforaviation.com/analysis/southwest-airlines-closes-the-chapter-on-airtran-whats-next-for-the-middle-aged-lcc-205437 (accessed 30 September 2016).

CAPA (Centre for Aviation) (2016). *Gulf 3 airline growth: Emirates steady, Qatar Airways accelerates & Etihad Airways slows*. Online. Available at: http://centreforaviation.com/analysis/gulf-3-airline-growth-emirates-steady-qatar-airways-accelerates--etihad-airways-slows-275457 (accessed 30 September 2016).

Corbo, L. (2017). In search of business model configurations that work: lessons from the hybridization of Air Berlin and JetBlue, *Journal of Air Transport Management*, 64, 139–150.

Daft, J. and Albers, S. (2013). A conceptual framework for measuring airline business model convergence, *Journal of Air Transport Management*, 28, 47–54.

Dale, C. (2016). Business planning and strategy. In: P. Robinson, P. Fallon, H. Cameron and J.C. Crotts (eds). *Operations Management in the Travel Industry*, Wallingford, CABI.

De Wit, J.G. and Zuidberg, J. (2016). Route churn: an analysis of low-cost carrier route continuity in Europe, *Journal of Transport Geography*, 50, 57–67.

Denton, N. and Dennis, N. (2000). Airline franchising in Europe: benefits and disbenefits to airlines and consumers, *Journal of Air Transport Management*, 6(4), 179–190.

Doherty, D. (2016). *Boom in Chinese tourism on Gold Coast sparks Virgin airline alliance*. Online. Available at: www.goldcoastbulletin.com.au/news/sun-community/boom-in-chinese-tourism-on-gold-coast-sparks-virgin-airline-alliance/news-story/931dd6c58ef8894a0a7db87d5180c6f5 (accessed 13 October 2016).

Evans, N. (2001a). The UK air inclusive tour industry: a reassessment of the competitive positioning of the 'independent' sector, *International Journal of Tourism Research*, 3(6), 477–491.

Evans, N. (2001b). Collaborative strategy: an analysis of the changing world of international airline alliances, *Tourism Management*, 22(3), 229–243.

French, T. (1997). Global trends in airline alliances, *Tourism and Travel Analyst*, 4, 81–100.

Galani, U. (2011). *Emirates reaches limits of organic growth strategy*. Online. Available at: www.reuters.com/article/uk-breakingviews-emirates-idUSLNE83H02F20120418 (accessed 29 September 2016).

Gittell, J.H. (2003). *The Southwest Airlines Way: Using the Power of Relationships to Achieve High Performance*, New York, McGraw-Hill.

Gudmundsson, S.V. and Lechner, C. (2011). Multilateral airline alliances: the fallacy of the alliances to merger proposition. In: J.F. O'Connell and G. Williams (eds). *Air Transport in the 21st Century: Key Strategic Developments*, Aldershot, Ashgate.

Gulf Air (2016). *Sky Nanny*. Online. Available at: www.gulfair.com/on-board/sky-nanny (accessed 29 September 2016).

Iatrou, K. and Oretti, M. (2016). *Airline Choices for the Future: From Alliances to Mergers*, Abingdon, Routledge.

Jean, D.A. and Lohmann, G. (2016). Revisiting the airline business model spectrum: the influence of post global financial crisis and airline mergers in the US (2011–2013), *Research in Transportation Business & Management*, 21, 76–83.

Johnson, G., Scholes, K. and Whittington, R. (2008). *Exploring Corporate Strategy: Text and Cases*, Essex, Pearson Education.

Klophaus, R., Conrady, R. and Fichert, F. (2012). Low cost carriers going hybrid: evidence from Europe, *Journal of Air Transport Management*, 23, 54–58.

Lieberman, M. and Asaba, S. (2006). Why do firms imitate each other? *The Academy of Management Review*, 31, 366–385.

Lobbenberg, A. (1995). Strategic responses of charter airlines to single market integration, *Journal of Air Transport Management*, 2(2), 67–80.

Lohmann, G. and Koo, T.R. (2013). The airline business model spectrum, *Journal of Air Transport Management*, 31, 7–9.

Lohmann, G., Albers, S., Koch, B. and Pavlovich, K. (2009). From hub to tourist destination: an explorative study of Singapore and Dubai's aviation-based transformation, *Journal of Air Transport Management*, 15, 205–211.

Martinet, A.C. (2010). Strategic planning, strategic management, strategic foresight: the seminal work of H. Igor Ansoff, *Technological Forecasting and Social Change*, 77(9), 1485–1487.

Mayasandra, V. (2011). *Qatar Airways expands via niche markets, opening 24 new routes in 2 years time*. Online. Available at: www.airlinetrends.com/2011/12/11/qatar-airways-niche-markets/ (accessed 29 September 2016).

McKechnie, D.S., Grant, J. and Katsioloudes, M. (2008). Positions and positioning: strategy simply stated, *Business Strategy Series*, 9(5), 224–230.

Merkert, R. and Morrell, P.S. (2012). Mergers and acquisitions in aviation: management and economic perspectives on the size of airlines, *Transportation Research Part E: Logistics and Transportation Review*, 48(4), 853–862.

Morley, C.L. (2003). Impacts of international airline alliances on tourism, *Tourism Economics*, 9(1), 31–51.

Nataraja, S. and Al-Aali, A. (2011). The exceptional performance strategies of Emirates Airlines, *Competitiveness Review: An International Business Journal*, 21(5), 471–486.

Németh, A. and Niemeier, H.M. (2012). Airline mergers in Europe: an overview on the market definition of the EU commission, *Journal of Air Transport Management*, 22, 45–52.

O'Connell, J.F. (2011). The rise of the Arabian Gulf carriers: an insight into the business model of Emirates Airline, *Journal of Air Transport Management*, 17(6), 339–346.

Page, S. (2005). *Transport and Tourism*, Essex, Pearson Education.

Pagliari, R. (2003). The impact of airline franchising on air service provision in the Highlands and Islands of Scotland, *Journal of Transport Geography*, 11(2), 117–129.

Pearson, J. and Merkert, R. (2014). Airlines-within-airlines: a business model moving East, *Journal of Air Transport Management*, 38, 21–26.

Pender, L. (1999). European aviation: the emergence of franchised airline operations, *Tourism Management*, 20(5), 565–574.

Perry, A. (1994). The changing face of flying to the sun, *Journal of Air Transport Management*, 1(4), 251–254.

Price, S. (1997). *The Franchise Paradox*, London, Cassell.

Qatar Airways (2016). *Discover our destinations around the world*. Online. Available at: www.qatarairways.com/global/en/destinations.page (accessed 29 September 2016).

Rae, D. (2001). EasyJet: a case of entrepreneurial management? *Strategic Change*, 10(6), 325–336.

Redpath, N., O'Connell, J.F. and Warnock-Smith, D. (2017). The strategic impact of airline group diversification: the cases of Emirates and Lufthansa, *Journal of Air Transport Management*, 64, 121–138.

Ronald, S.J. (2005). Driving sustainable growth and innovation: pathways to high performance leadership, *Handbook of Business Strategy*, 6(1), 197–202.

Schonland, A. (2015). *Emirates: 30 years of remarkable growth*. Online. Available at: www.ondair.net/emirates-30-years-of-remarkable-growth/ (accessed 30 September 2016).

Shaw, S. (2011). *Airline Marketing and Management*, Aldershot, Ashgate.

Small, J. and Harris, C. (2014). Crying babies on planes: aeromobility and parenting, *Annals of Tourism Research*, 48, 27–41.

The Emirates Group (2016). *Annual report 2015/2016*. Online. Available at: http://content.emirates.com/downloads/ek/pdfs/report/annual_report_2016.pdf (accessed 30 September 2016).

The National (2015). *Emirates announces three new A380 superjumbo routes for 2016*. Online. Available at: www.thenational.ae/business/aviation/emirates-announces-three-new-a380-superjumbo-routes-for-2016 (accessed 29 September 2016).

Vincent, J. (2010). *Unrelated diversification: a look at the Virgin Group*. Online. Available at: https://vinjyr.wordpress.com/2010/02/08/unrelated-diversification-a-look-at-the-virgin-group/ (accessed 17 October 2016).

Wang, Z.H., Evans, M. and Turner, L. (2004). Effects of strategic airline alliances on air transport market competition: an empirical analysis, *Tourism Economics*, 10(1), 23–43.

Whyte, R. and Lohmann, G. (2015a). Low-cost long-haul carriers: a hypothetical analysis of a 'kangaroo route', *Case Studies on Transport Policy*, 3(2), 159–165.

Whyte, R. and Lohmann, G. (2015b). The carrier-within-a-carrier strategy: an analysis of Jetstar, *Journal of Air Transport Management*, 42, 141–148.

Whyte, R. and Lohmann, G. (2016). Airline business models. In: L. Budd and S. Ison (eds). *Air Transport Management: An International Perspective*, Abingdon, Routledge.

Yashodha, Y. (2012). AirAsia Berhad: strategic analysis of a leading low cost carrier in the Asian region, *Elixir International Journal of Management Arts*, 51, 11164–11171.

# 10

# Airport business strategy

*Nigel Halpern*

## Introduction

Business strategy refers to the ways a business goes about achieving its objectives within an industry or industry segment (Carpenter and Sanders, 2009). It considers the changing competitive landscape in which a company operates, and is very much associated with finding ways to gain a competitive advantage. This is interesting from an airport perspective because the traditional view has been that airports act as natural monopolies, and are therefore exposed to minimal competition. That view is, however, challenged by a growing belief that airports increasingly compete, and in an environment of sustained uncertainty. The formulation and implementation of effective strategies is therefore of growing importance.

This chapter examines literature and key issues associated with airport business strategy (for airlines, see Chapter 9). It is concentrated largely on the formulation rather than implementation of strategy – that is, the competitive landscape within which airports operate and their strategic decisions. This is where the focus of literature on the subject is. Implementation is more related to decisions regarding how airport resources will be aligned and mobilised towards strategic objectives. This is scarcely covered by the literature, possibly because it is specific to individual airports and therefore has less generic appeal compared to issues relating to strategy formulation. The chapter consists of four main sections. The first section considers the competitive landscape. The next two sections focus on strategic decisions within the context of generic and growth strategy frameworks. The final section provides a conclusion.

## Competitive landscape

### Airport industry environment

Increased deregulation and liberalisation of air transport markets (see Chapters 6 and 7) has resulted in a restructuring of the airline industry with the emergence and growth of new airline business models (see Chapter 8) such as low cost carriers (LCCs) and increased consolidation among legacy carriers (e.g. see Forsyth et al., 2013). LCCs have offered opportunities for airports to compete and have brought much-needed traffic to many underutilised secondary and regional airports, as well as to some longer-established airports (CAPA, 2008). However, they tend to be footloose in terms of their willingness to change routes or move to alternative airports, which results in a greater volatility of traffic (Thelle et al., 2012). The gains can be significant at affected airports, but so too can the losses, which is of concern if the airport is dependent on just one or a few airline customers (e.g. see Halpern and Graham, 2017; Halpern et al., 2016).

Airline consolidation through the development of alliances, joint ventures, mergers or acquisitions (see Chapter 9) creates threats and opportunities for airports because links with alliances and other airline groupings may bring access to larger markets and allow airports to serve a wider choice of destinations (Bilotkach et al., 2013). However, it may also result in the realignment of airline schedules and capacity, or even the dropping of a hub entirely, to streamline services and avoid duplication (McCormick, 2015). Hub airports are, of course, also vulnerable to the possible failure of their hub carrier (e.g. see Linkweiler, 2013).

To keep up with changes in their business environment, many airports have adopted a more businesslike management philosophy, are operated as commercial enterprises rather than public infrastructure, and have loosened their ties with government (see Chapter 3). This is especially the case in Europe, where 40 per cent of airports in 2016 were under full or part private ownership. The figure was just 20 per cent in 2010. Of the airports that remain under full public ownership, almost 80 per cent are corporatised, meaning that they are operated largely as commercial companies, and at arm's length from their public owner (ACI Europe, 2016). Commercialisation and privatisation provides greater incentives for airports to compete for air services, passengers and cargo, but also to develop non-aeronautical and non-aviation activities. It also allows for the creation of multi-airport and international companies.

In the case of privatisation, the key drivers appear to be associated with a need for improved efficiency and greater investment. However, evidence of whether there are actual benefits to be gained is inconclusive (Graham, 2011). Another issue is related to the concern that larger airports may abuse their market power and not always act in the best interests of airport users, for instance by raising charges, underinvesting in facilities, and reducing the quality of service for airlines, passengers and other users. This has resulted in economic regulation being introduced with privatisation at some airports and has a major impact on their freedom to make decisions (e.g. on pricing) (see Chapter 12). There is also the question on whether non-aeronautical revenues should be included as part of any economic regulation (e.g. see Gillen and Mantin, 2014; Kratzsch and Sieg, 2011). This has implications for an airport's ability to develop competitive advantages on the non-aeronautical side of their business.

Carney and Mew (2003) investigate the strategic management perspective of airport governance reform and warn that while public owners often want to see reforms that bring a commercial and strategic orientation to their airport(s), they often create regulatory and governance structures that inhibit such an approach. This may be due to their reluctance to provide full autonomy to their airport(s) but also due to their desire to direct any gains from reform towards particular stakeholder interests.

All airports, whether privatised or not, operate in a strict regulatory environment that affects their decisions on diverse areas such as planning, security, safety, persons with reduced mobility, consumer protection, access to ground handling, slot access, funding and state aid. The airport regulatory and political environment therefore has a potential impact on the extent to which airports can control and influence decisions about the products and services that they offer, and therefore their ability to develop strategies to gain a competitive advantage. In addition, the location of an airport is a primary source of competitive advantage and is fixed. This also affects the ability of an airport to compete. Airport products and services are discussed in more detail in Halpern and Graham (2013), while the extent to which airports can control different elements of their products and services to gain competitive advantages is discussed in more detail in Graham (2010).

The global financial situation has also had a significant impact on airports in recent years, and has created a period of sustained uncertainty, for instance resulting from slower traffic growth rates (especially in mature markets but also in emerging markets), increased volatility of traffic, and a reduced availability of funding and investment for both publicly and privately owned airports. LeighFisher (2012) assess how these factors affect airport strategic planning, primarily from the perspective of the United States (US) where airports are still almost entirely owned by government entities. The headline for airport operators is: "You're increasingly on your own – a new operating environment requires new strategies to remain ahead of the game" (LeighFisher, 2012: 1), and the report states that in response to the new environment, airport strategies need to emphasise self-sufficiency, flexibility and agility as airports complete their transformation from cost-recovery organisations to actively managed, independent commercial enterprises.

Similarly, Sentence (2013) considers how airport strategic decisions are affected by the 'new normal' – a term that is now commonly used when referring to conditions following the financial crisis of 2007–2008. From an airport strategic management perspective, Sentence (2013) recommends cautious capacity expansion, the spread of risk among suppliers and business partners, including more flexible contract agreements to deal with volatility and potential shocks, such as to a major airline customer, and diversification of revenue across a range of geographies and market sectors.

## Competitive environment

Despite the changes taking place in the airport industry environment, there is still much debate about the extent to which airports compete. Copenhagen Economics published a report on Airport Competition in Europe in 2012, which has been a source of much debate in recent years. The report claims that changes such as the commercialisation and in some cases privatisation of airports, in addition to increased liberalisation of air transport markets and more experienced and demanding travellers, have encouraged a more competitive airport sector in Europe (see Thelle et al., 2012). This is refuted by the International Air Transport Association (IATA), which claims that airports continue to enjoy market power over airlines and their customers, and that this leads to excessively high prices and service standards that are lower than they should be (see Wiltshire, 2013). ACI Europe, who commissioned the report on Airport Competition in Europe by Thelle et al. (2012), then published a response to IATA's claims in Wiltshire (2013) with its own response (see ACI Europe, 2014). The claims and counterclaims highlight the extent to which airlines and airports disagree, for instance, on the methodologies and assumptions regarding assessments of potential airport market power.

Bush and Starkie (2014) draw on the report by Copenhagen Economics, and while they recognise that some positions of dominance remain, they add that significant market power of airports can no longer be assumed, and they suggest that airports are now subject to competitive constraints from several sources. This is reflected to a large extent by the extensive body of literature on airport competition, especially in more liberal markets such as Europe (e.g. see Forsyth et al., 2010a).

An analysis of the competitive environment is important for airports in order to understand the relative strengths and weaknesses of their position in the industry. The analysis provides a basis from which they can then go on to formulate strategies that enable them to gain competitive advantages. The Five Forces model developed by Porter (1980, 2008) provides a framework from which the competitive environment of an organisation can be analysed, and it has been used when assessing competitive forces affecting the airport industry (e.g. see Graham, 2010). The framework suggests that competition in an industry depends on five forces: industry rivalry, the threat of new entrants, the threat of substitutes, the bargaining power of buyers and the bargaining power of suppliers. The competitive environment will vary according to the circumstances of individual airports (Bush and Starkie, 2014). However, a review of literature reveals some general assumptions.

Competitive rivalry between airports is likely to be higher when airports are in close proximity to other airports (Lieshout, 2012) and when catchment areas overlap, especially if they can be continually expanded or contracted, depending on the nature of air services and surface links on offer at neighbouring airports (Lian and Rønnevik, 2011). In comparison, airports that are located in a remote region without any other airports nearby, and with limited opportunities for developing air services, are likely to have few direct competitors.

Competition is likely to be higher at airports with a greater concentration of point-to-point services provided by more price-sensitive low cost and charter carriers. The bargaining power of airlines may be quite high at such airports because of there being alternative airports to choose from, especially if the airport in question is underutilised (Lin et al., 2013), but also because of the flexibility of their point-to-point business model. The concept of route churn (the discontinuity or air routes) has become of interest to researchers in recent years, partly due to the operational flexibility exercised by LCCs at airports (e.g. see De Wit and Zuidberg, 2016). Thelle et al. (2012) report an annual churn rate of 15 to 20 per cent among point-to-point carriers at airports in Europe from 2002 to 2011, and this is predominantly due to LCCs (Wiltshire, 2013).

Encouraging LCCs to base aircraft at an airport (i.e. use their aircraft flexibly across their networks during the day but fly their aircraft and crew back to a base at the end of each day) results in a greater commitment to the airport because aircraft will be parked at the airport overnight, crew is likely to live locally, and the base airport is likely to be used by the LCC for routine aircraft maintenance. In response to the liberalisation of air transport markets in Europe, LCCs have been keen to develop bases throughout the region (see CAPA, 2013), often at secondary or regional airports that are seeking to compete with other airports to be a base for LCCs. According to airline websites in May 2017, Europe's three largest LCCs, Ryanair, easyJet and Norwegian, had 86, 28 and 21 bases, respectively. Norwegian is one of few LCCs to be opening bases outside of Europe with its US bases at Fort Lauderdale, John F. Kennedy International, Providence (T.F. Green Airport) and Stewart International. However, LCC bases are still vulnerable to the operational flexibilities of LCCs; for instance, Ryanair closed its base at Oslo Rygge Airport from October 2016 after the Norwegian government introduced a new air travel tax of 80 Norwegian kroner on departing passengers. The loss of Ryanair's based aircraft resulted in a significant reduction in traffic at Rygge and meant that the airport was no longer commercially viable, and closed to civil operations from November 2016.

The growth of many secondary and regional airports, largely because of growth from LCCs (e.g. see Halpern et al., 2016), means that passengers and other airport users now have a greater choice of airports. For instance, almost two-thirds of Europeans can reach two or more airports within a drive time of two hours. In addition, there is a large amount of route overlap at airports because over 50 per cent of the destinations served at the largest airport are also served by one or more airports around it (Thelle et al., 2012). On the cargo side, Tretheway and Andriulaitis (2010) suggest that the growing power and influence of freight forwarders has shifted the relative bargaining power from airlines to freight forwarders, and unlike airlines that have traditionally routed cargo according to the needs of their passenger operations, forwarders are not tied to existing passenger gateways or hubs, and are therefore more open to alternatives that better serve their customers. This has provided greater opportunities for airports to compete for cargo traffic.

Airports serving a distinct catchment area with a wide network of services may have few direct competitors unless they are competing as a hub with the opportunity for flight connections and transfer services for passengers (Grosche and Klophaus, 2015) and/or cargo (Wong et al., 2016). This is because connecting traffic can easily shift from one airport to another to take advantage of a cheaper, faster or more convenient connection (Tretheway and Kincaid, 2010). Hub airports may find themselves competing with hubs in their own world region but also with hubs in other world regions (Redondi and Gudmundsson, 2016). The choice for passengers and cargo can be quite high when transferring through a hub. Thelle et al. (2012) find that 62 per cent of transfer passengers at European hub airports have one or more realistic alternatives to transfer through. The bargaining power of hub carriers, however, may be low on the basis that they operate networked services and are less able to switch to an alternative airport, for instance, compared to more footloose low cost and charter carriers (Graham, 2010). The potential market power of hub airports has been a source of much debate in academic literature (e.g. see Bilotkach and Mueller, 2012; Polk and Bilokach, 2013) (see also Chapter 12).

Maertens (2012) investigates market power at Europe's 50 largest airports. The findings reveal relatively high market power for the largest airports such as Paris Charles de Gaulle, Frankfurt, Rome Fiumicino, Munich and Amsterdam Schiphol. Market power for some major hubs such as London Heathrow and Madrid Barajas is much lower than for similar-sized airports due to the presence of greater competition. Tourist airports such as Ibiza, Alicante, Malaga, Faro, Gran Canaria and Palma de Mallorca appear to have high market power, which can be explained by their remote or island location and the fact that they are owned as part of an airport group. However, market power is likely to be lower than the model suggests since the respective holiday regions that they serve are to a certain extent interchangeable from the incoming tourist's perspective. Most remaining airports in the study were found to have relatively low levels of market power from both the passenger and airline perspective.

Competition does not only come from other airports. It may also come from substitutes, including alternative modes of transport such as high-speed rail (Albalate et al., 2015; Jiang and Zhang, 2016) or alternative options to travel such as video conferencing (Denstadli et al., 2013). In addition, airports are increasingly focused on commercial sources of revenue (Graham, 2009) (see also Chapter 12), and airports that have developed non-aeronautical and non-aviation facilities and services, online and offline, and within and beyond the airport boundary, are likely to experience competition from a broad range of sources such as offsite car parks, downtown tax-free shopping, Internet retailers, hotels, conference facilities, consultancy companies, providers of real estate, and investment and infrastructure management companies (e.g. see Freathy, 2004), although the buying power of suppliers may be relatively low in the case of non-aeronautical activities at airports due to the attractiveness of the captive and often affluent passenger market (Graham, 2010).

The buying power of suppliers of operational services at airports is complicated because the provision of some services such as air traffic control (see Chapter 4) and security (see Chapter 21) may be determined by government policy, while others such as ground handling may be governed by strict rules or regulations. In addition, some airports may decide to offer the services themselves, as may be the case with ground handling. The degree of power will therefore vary significantly by airport, and is complicated further by the fact that in some cases, suppliers will charge the airline directly for their services (Graham, 2010).

The threat of new entrants is generally low in the airport industry. This is largely due to the huge levels of investment needed for new infrastructure, but also the long and complex planning and regulatory process associated with new airport developments (Graham, 2010) (see also Chapter 16). In addition, there are challenges associated with finding new sites (e.g. see Helsey and Codd, 2014). However, there are several former military or general aviation sites that have provided opportunities for new developments such as Berlin Brandenburg. There is also a rapid development of airport infrastructure in some emerging markets, such as in Dubai, Turkey and China, where new or expanded infrastructure is developed with relative ease compared to in more mature markets that have slower and more complex planning and regulatory processes (e.g. see Mazzanti, 2015).

## Generic strategy framework

Having assessed competitive forces and their underlying causes, airport managers can devise strategies that take into account the resources and capabilities of the company (by undertaking an internal analysis), strengths and weaknesses in relation to competitors, and opportunities and threats arising from the business environment within which they operate. When discussing strategic options for airports (or for airlines, such as in Chapter 9), literature tends to use Porter's (1979) generic strategies model that describes three options a company can use to gain a competitive advantage: cost leadership (having the lowest cost of production of a product or service), differentiation (creating differentiated products or services for different segments) and focus (focusing on a narrowly defined segment of the market – a so-called niche segment).

As mentioned previously, deregulation and liberalisation of air transport markets has resulted in the emergence and growth of LCCs. Twenty-six per cent of scheduled seat capacity worldwide was provided by LCCs in 2015 (CAPA, 2015). LCCs often have different requirements at airports compared to traditional legacy carriers (Barrett, 2004; Warnock-Smith and Potter, 2005). In some cases, this has resulted in the development of low cost airports (de Neufville, 2008) (see Chapter 8). Several secondary airports in metropolitan multi-airport systems in Europe have taken this approach, such as Brussels South Charleroi, Frankfurt Hahn, Girona, London Stansted, Stockholm Skavsta and Torp Sandefjord. Examples of low cost airports are scarce outside of Europe (although a number of airports, especially in Asia, have low cost terminals). An exception includes Ibaraki Tokyo. Several regional airports in Europe have also become low cost airports, such as Liverpool John Lennon. Branson is a rare example in the US, where, despite having a strong LCC market, there is little evidence of low cost airports or terminals – possibly due to the extensive public ownership of airports in the US and the way in which they are funded, but also due to cultural expectations, for instance regarding comfort at airports. Dedicated low cost airports or low cost terminals are also rare in the Middle East, Africa and Central/Latin America, possibly for similar reasons as in the US, but also due to a smaller market share of LCCs in those regions (CAPA, 2015).

Despite the presence of low cost airports in Europe, it can be questioned as to whether they are pursuing a true cost leadership strategy or not. Graham (2010) suggests that there is little evidence of cost leadership because of the high operating costs and investment needs of airports, but also their fixed location and apparent lack of economies of scale beyond a certain size means that it is difficult for them to achieve cost savings. In addition, she suggests that the relationship between costs and prices is weak at some airports, especially where public sector owners subsidise airport operations to achieve a broader objective, such as to stimulate regional economic development, or at airports operated as part of a group where uniform prices across the group do not reflect the costs of individual airports.

Instead, literature tends to advocate strategies based on differentiation, especially given the increased competition and sustained uncertainties highlighted in the previous section of this chapter (e.g. see Feldman, 2009, 2013; Graham, 2010; Herrmann and Hazel, 2012a, 2012b; Jimenez et al., 2014). Differentiation strategies aim to develop products or services that are perceived as being different or unique from those of their competitors. Differences may be real (e.g. through differences in design) or perceived (e.g. through the use of advertising). For instance, an airport may differentiate from its competitors through being in closer proximity to a particular area, offering enhanced service features, having a superior brand image, being more innovative, using more advanced technology, and offering more advanced operational capabilities (Halpern and Graham, 2013). Many multi-terminal airports have separate terminals for cargo or different types of passenger or airline (e.g. short-haul versus long-haul, domestic versus international, or by airline alliance). Some airports have competing terminals, such as at John F. Kennedy International, where most of the terminals are operated by different airlines or consortiums of airlines that use them. Airports may also offer dedicated products and services for different types of passenger (e.g. fast track for first- and business-class passengers) or airline (e.g. dedicated low cost terminals for LCCs) (Halpern and Graham, 2013).

According to Njoya and Niemeier (2011), dedicated low cost terminals contain elements of both cost leadership strategy and product differentiation. They represent an opportunity for airports to gain a competitive advantage and offer benefits in terms of potential traffic growth and economic contribution to the airport and its surrounding regions. However, they also present risks given the volatile nature of LCCs and the lack of flexibility associated with the terminal. The same view is shared by de Neufville (2008) in the context of low cost airports. The risk may be mitigated, or at least shared, if airlines are actively involved in the investment. However, this can of course have a negative effect on future opportunities for diversity or flexibility for either partner. Despite the concerns, several airports operate or are developing low cost terminals, such as Terminal billi at Bordeaux, mp² at Marseille Provence, Piers H and M at Amsterdam Schiphol, Terminal 4 at Melbourne and Terminal 3 at Narita International. However, some airports, such as with klia2 at Kuala Lumpur International, have selected a hybrid approach due to the risks associated with low cost terminals. Singapore Changi even decided to demolish the so-called Budget Terminal that it opened in 2006 and closed in 2012, and has built a larger hybrid terminal in its place.

Some airports specialise in serving one or a few specific markets, such as a particular type of airline (e.g. charter, low cost or cargo) or services to a particular geographic area. They may be too small or have limited infrastructure to target the whole market, and therefore pursue strategies of focus (sometimes referred to as niche strategies). Focus strategies can either be focused on cost (which is arguably more relevant than cost leadership strategies for airports targeting LCCs) or on differentiation (which is relevant to airports that provide specialist facilities such as for cargo at Liege) (Halpern and Graham, 2013).

London City is an interesting example of an airport that has a focus strategy based on differentiation. The airport primarily serves intra-European business travel markets. The airport, located close to London's Canary Wharf, offers what it calls a speed of transit proposition that enables the vast majority of passengers to pass through the airport in around 20 minutes on departure, and around 15 minutes on arrival (London City Airport, 2016). There are, of course, risks associated with having such a focused strategy. It may deter opportunities for other types of traffic such as LCCs (e.g. see Gooding, 2006), any major economic decline or reduced level of business activity in key markets is likely to affect traffic levels, and there is always a risk that the airport may struggle to deliver on its fundamental value proposition regarding the speed of transit.

Graham (2010) recognises that, in reality, there are many airports that fit into what Porter's model would define as being lost in the middle. This includes airports that have too high costs to lead on cost, too standardised a product to differentiate and too broad an appeal to focus. This is very much related to the less competitive environment that many airports still operate in.

Badanik et al. (2010) provide a slightly different perspective that recognises key differences in strategic approach according to airport size. They look at strategies of specialisation that are focused on developing the aeronautical activities of an airport and strategies of diversification that are focused on developing non-aeronautical and non-aviation activities. In terms of specialisation, they suggest that smaller/medium-sized airports may have more attention on low cost terminals, accessibility, communication, terminal capacity, commercial priorities and runway capacity, while larger airports may have more attention on improving infrastructure efficiency and intermodality. In terms of diversification, smaller airports may be more interested in services for passengers and commercial activities, while larger airports may be more interested in consultancy services, investments in other economic sectors or investments in other airports. Diversification is a type of growth strategy that will be considered in the following section of this chapter.

## Growth strategy framework

In addition to generic strategy models, literature tends to refer to growth strategies that are based largely on Ansoff's Growth Matrix (for airlines, see Chapter 9) – a strategic planning tool that provides a framework to help devise strategies for future growth depending on whether companies target growth in new or existing markets, and with new or existing products (Ansoff, 1987). The matrix distinguishes between four main strategies: market penetration (sometimes called concentrated growth), market development, product development and diversification. The latter may be classified according to concentric diversification, vertical integration or horizontal integration. Some airports are focused more on survival than growth, and will therefore need to consider retrenchment strategies such as turnaround, divestiture or liquidation (see Table 10.1).

There are also airports in less competitive markets that may simply aim to be better at what they do without seeking growth (this is sometimes referred to as harvesting). Many airports, including those that are targeting growth, tend to have harvesting-related strategies too. For instance, one of the strategic priorities for Sydney Airport is to improve the customer experience. The objective focuses on "listening to customers and improving the experience at every stage of the journey through superior customer service, operational efficiency and technological innovation" (Sydney Airport, 2016: 63). The airport has strategic priorities focused on growth, for instance in passenger numbers and aircraft movements through concentrated growth on

*Table 10.1* Strategies for accomplishing long-term objectives

| Strategy | Description |
| --- | --- |
| Concentrated growth | Direct resources towards capturing a larger market share |
| Market development | Market existing services to customers in new markets |
| Product development | Develop new products for current markets |
| Concentric diversification | Pursue opportunities that are synergistic with core aeronautical services |
| Vertical integration | Seek increased control of user support functions or suppliers |
| Horizontal integration | Combine with other organisations in the same industry |
| Joint venture or alliance | Seek benefits of collaboration without transferring ownership or control |
| Turnaround or retrenchment | Focus on cost reduction or asset reduction to regain financial strength |
| Divestiture or liquidation | Sale or closure of an airport, or part of an airport |

*Source*: Adapted from ACRP (2009).

existing services, but also market development by reaching out to new markets in Asia. The airport is also pursuing diversification by growing its property business. A balanced mix of growth strategies is recommended for airports as it helps to avoid over-reliance on one type of strategy (Halpern and Graham, 2013).

Graham (2010) describes a similar range of growth strategies to those that are listed in Table 10.1. However, she presents them according to how they can be achieved. This includes three main approaches: internal or organic growth (which applies to market penetration, market development, product development and diversification), integration (which may be vertical or horizontal), and retrenchment and divestiture (which includes turnaround and liquidation).

## Internal or organic growth strategies

Market penetration is a safer option for airports because it involves focusing on the growth of existing markets with existing products. It is therefore not likely to require much investment or carry much risk. However, it may be difficult for airports to capture gains in market share without implementing price reductions, promotional campaigns or product refinements – all of which may have a negative effect on the profitability of the airport (Halpern and Graham, 2013). Market penetration is particularly relevant for airports pursuing a focus strategy because much of their growth will come from existing products in existing markets. Internal approaches can be used for market penetration to increase use of the airport by existing customers, maintain or increase market share of existing products, or to dominate growth markets. For instance, many airports have introduced loyalty schemes for passengers that offer free or exclusive offers on retail, catering, car hire and parking, fast track services, lounge access, and exclusive competitions. An example of this is at Singapore Changi, where the seventh edition of its 'Be a Changi Millionaire' retail promotion was launched in 2016 with a grand prize of S$1 million (US$738,400). To participate in the draw, airport visitors and passengers needed to spend a minimum of S$50 (US$37), with increased chances of winning as more was spent. Airports also use growth incentives and marketing support (see Chapter 14) to encourage market penetration through the growth of existing air services (e.g. by increasing capacity or frequency) (Halpern and Graham, 2015).

Another strategy for achieving market penetration would be to restructure a mature market by driving out competitors and securing market dominance. Growth strategies based on market dominance have traditionally been less common in the airport industry, although they have become more common as air transport markets mature in some areas, such as in North America and Europe. There are four main types of competitive position: market leader, challenger, follower and nicher.

Halpern and Graham (2013) consider airport growth strategies based on market dominance. They suggest that market leaders occupy a dominant position in their main markets and seek to expand the market or their share of it, defend their position, or maintain the status quo (e.g. Dallas/Fort Worth International is the primary international airport serving the Dallas/Fort Worth area in the state of Texas). Challengers attack market leaders or other competitors to gain market share (e.g. Dallas Love Field was Dallas' main airport until Dallas/Fort Worth International opened; however, it has worked hard to regain market share in recent years). Followers are not in a dominant position, and instead of pursuing strategies to gain market share, they are more likely to play it safe and take any overflow from the market leader (e.g. Ontario has traditionally, and rather reluctantly, served the overflow from Los Angeles International). Nichers, as described in Porter's generic strategy framework, specialise in serving one of a few specific markets. Penetration is likely to be achieved as a result of the nichers' expertise and carefully targeted product and service offering for specific markets (e.g. Branson as a niche airport for LCCs).

Market development is where airports focus on marketing existing services to customers in new markets, for instance by targeting different customer segments or by reaching out to new geographical areas with existing services (e.g. by encouraging better surface access, an airport may be able to expand its catchment area). The strategy is not likely to require the development of new competencies because the new market is not expected to be too dissimilar to the markets that are already served (because the product offering is essentially the same). However, the strategy is likely to require something new and unique in order to gain leverage in the new market, for instance improved roads, rail or bus services or a high-speed rail connection being examples in the case of better surface access. The strategy also assumes that an increase in customers will improve the financial performance of the airport, for instance due to benefits arising from economies of scale. Toronto Pearson aims to grow its market, but also capture market share from other airports, and one of the steps needed to achieve this has been identified as the development of the airport "as a ground mobility hub – an interconnection point for air, rail, road and public transit. By making our airport even more accessible to the surrounding region" (Greater Toronto Airports Authority, 2011: 9).

Product development is where airports focus on marketing new products to customers in existing markets. This means that although markets will be familiar to the airport, the product may not, unless it is simply a modification of an existing product. The strategy may therefore require the development of new competencies to ensure that new or modified products appeal to existing markets. Product development will be important for airports pursuing differentiation strategies because they will need to develop and maintain differences from their competitors (Halpern and Graham, 2013). Internal approaches to product development could include encouraging long-haul services at an airport previously only offering short-haul, or by introducing an online option for booking car parking at an airport that previously only offered it offline. A problem for airports here is that it may be easy for competitors to imitate product development. A major challenge will therefore be to continually develop innovations and sources of competitive advantage that cannot be easily imitated. This means that there will be a need to continually invest in research and development of new products, which can be costly and does not always guarantee success.

Concentric diversification is where airports focus on new products in new markets. This is generally considered to be a high-risk strategy because it involves moving into markets that the airport has little or no experience in, and with products that the airport has little or no experience with. Airports pursuing diversification should therefore conduct a thorough and honest appraisal of the risks and be clear about what they expect to achieve (Halpern and Graham, 2013). A common approach is when airports diversify their revenue sources in order to exploit opportunities for non-aeronautical or non-aviation revenue and reduce their dependency on aeronautical revenue. Growth through diversification means that the airport no longer just competes as a facilitator of air transport activity, but also as a multipoint, and possibly multi-modal, service provider (Bracaglia et al., 2014; Jarach, 2001). This is closely related to the airport city concept (see Chapter 8), where, in addition to core aeronautical infrastructure and services, airports develop significant non-aeronautical facilities, services and revenue streams, as well as extending their commercial reach and economic impact beyond the airport boundary in non-aviation-related areas (Kasarda, 2013). Munich is one such airport that currently aims to expand its non-aviation business. The strategy states that "A wide array of products, services and events have helped increase the appeal of Munich Airport. Now we are driving development ahead to become an Airport City and are expanding the campus in close collaboration with surrounding municipalities" (Munich Airport, 2016).

Concentric diversification is also important for the aeronautical side of the airport business because an over-reliance on one or a few airline customers can leave the airport exposed to risk from airline failure or a reduction or withdrawal of air services (Koo et al., 2016). This was the case at Brussels, which lost most of its air services when the main airline customer Sabena went bankrupt in 2001. The airport still serves Brussels Airlines (formed after taking over part of Sabena's assets). However, the airport has diversified its customer base to include a wider range of traditional scheduled carriers and LCCs, along with a number of airlines offering charter and cargo services.

## Integration strategies

Internal or organic growth has been the traditional approach used by airports. This is largely because of limited options under public sector ownership but also because of the strict regulatory environment. The increased commercialisation, and in some cases privatisation of airports (see Chapter 3), has enabled other approaches for growth to be used, partly because it has made it possible for airports to buy other airports and pursue other forms of strategic growth (Graham, 2010). This leads on to other forms of diversification that are associated with horizontal or vertical integration.

Horizontal integration (sometimes referred to as related integration) is when organisations combine with other organisations in the same industry. There will therefore be some kind of a relationship or potential synergy between the organisations. There are two broad types of arrangements: mergers or acquisitions that create multi-airport groups (airports that are under common ownership), and strategic alliances (e.g. partnerships or joint ventures) between separately owned airports. Mergers or acquisitions effectively create a centralised governance structure for airports that belong to the group or system, while alliances allow partners to coordinate their strategies while staying independent (Forsyth et al., 2010b).

Forsyth et al. (2010b) describe seven main types of multi-airport group: government majority-owned national or regional airport corporations; companies that have been formed as a result of the sale of a group of airports by the government; major airports that own regional subsidiaries; corporations with a diverse portfolio of airports; airports that hold strategic (though minority) interests in other major airports; specialist investors such as infrastructure funds; and facility owners and operators, such as companies that own terminals in a range of airports.

Multiple-airport groups have a number of potential benefits, such as higher returns and increased shareholder value, reduced risk by spreading it over a wider geographical area, sharing of knowledge, expertise and resources, opportunities for bulk buying and joint purchasing, cost savings associated with centralising business functions, opportunities for joint staff training and procurement, cost advantages through combined marketing, greater resources for research and innovation, and the potential to develop a common brand (Graham, 2010). For multi-airport groups in a similar geographical area, there may be additional benefits associated with common approaches to contracting, quantity discounts on charging, agreements on the use of gates and other facilities, and investment and traffic coordination (Graham, 2013).

Another potential benefit for the operator is to reduce airport competition and gain market dominance (Forsyth et al., 2011). This is not so much of an issue for multi-airport groups consisting of airports that are geographical distant. However, if the different airports are in close proximity (or the same geographical region), and could therefore act as a substitute, the reduced competition and potential for market power may become a concern for competition authorities. This has been the case with the company formerly known as BAA, which was formed by the privatisation of the British Airports Authority to take responsibility for seven state-owned airports in the United Kingdom, including London Heathrow, London Gatwick and London Stansted. BAA later expanded into international operations (e.g. with a stake in Budapest International and retail and management contracts at airports in the US). The company has since changed ownership, and was required to sell off London Gatwick, London Stansted and Edinburgh due to competition concerns, and sold all of its airports other than Heathrow over the following years. The company was renamed Heathrow Airport Holdings in 2012 to reflect its main business.

Strategic alliances between separately owned airports are arguably of less concern to competition authorities and regulators. A number of them were established during the 1990s to 2000s, such as the Galaxy International Cargo Alliance in 1999 (established initially by Washington Dulles International and Chateauroux-Doels to cooperate in joint marketing), Aviation Handling Services in 2000 (established initially by a number of German airports to provide common standards for ground handling services), the Pantares Alliance in 2000 (established by Fraport and Schiphol to cooperate on terminal and retail management, handling of aircraft and cargo, facility management, information technology and international joint ventures) and the Hublink Alliance between Schiphol and Aéroports de Paris (now called Paris Aéroport) in 2008 (to enhance the functioning of the dual hub system of the respective hub carriers KLM and Air France that merged in 2004). However, such alliances seem to have offered few benefits (Forsyth et al., 2011; Graham, 2013; Tretheway, 2001).

More recently, there has been a growing interest in sister agreements between airports, normally formalised through a memorandum of understanding that agrees to work jointly on initiatives such as the development of new routes, sharing of information and best practice, and staff liaison (e.g. see Stone, 2011). For example, by the end of 2016, Chicago O'Hare had agreements to cooperate on a wide range of areas, including airport management, customer service, construction, planning, operations, information technology and sustainable development with nine different airports worldwide (Abu Dhabi International, Beijing Capital International, Belgrade Nikola Tesla, Birmingham, Hong Kong International, Incheon International, Istanbul Airports, Mariscal Sucre International and Shanghai).

Sister agreements seem to offer some benefits, such as in route development between the two airports. However, it could be argued that route development objectives can be achieved through more general cooperation and without the need for a memorandum of understanding between the airports. As with the previously mentioned alliances, sister agreements seem to have offered few benefits.

Vertical integration is when an organisation seeks to take greater control of parts of its supply chain. This may be forwards by taking greater control over distributors, or backwards by taking greater control over suppliers (Graham, 2010). It could be argued that airports have always used backward vertical integration because many have traditionally provided various parts of the supply chain themselves, such as ground handling, air traffic control, car parking or duty-free. However, this has primarily been due to historic rather than strategic reasons (Graham, 2010). Decisions to target growth through vertical integration are less common. However, there are some interesting examples. For instance, Travel Norwich Airport is an independent travel agent specialising in holidays and flights from Norwich International. It was established in 1987 as a department within the airport, and is a wholly owned subsidiary of Norwich Airport Limited. It is a form of forward integration because it provides a distribution channel for increasing awareness and the purchase of airport products and services.

An interesting issue is related to vertical integration between airlines (downstream) and airports (upstream) (see also Chapter 12). There is rationale for cooperation given that when choosing between two airports, passengers will typically consider the combined airport and airline offer rather than the airport alone (Barbot, 2009). However, formal integration can be problematic from a regulatory point of view due to the potentially dominant position of the airport and its airline. This was the case with the LAPA (acronym for the airline Líneas Aéreas Privadas Argentinas that ceased operations in April 2003) acquisition by the Argentine airport operator AA2000, which was blocked by the National Commission for Competition in 2002. Alliances between airports and airlines are, however, commonplace in the US because airport terminals are often rented or built and operated by airlines or other enterprises. Each airline with sufficient traffic then tries to operate its own terminal or at least its own gates (Albers et al., 2005). In addition, some domestic terminals in Australia are leased to Qantas. This practice is less common in Europe, although British Airways partially financed Birmingham's second terminal – Eurohub – and Lufthansa participated in the development of the second terminal at Munich (see Albers et al., 2005).

From an airline perspective, the alliance allows them to influence the planning and operations of the terminal so that it meets their needs and preferences, and allows them to optimise operations and transfer connection quality, as well as terminal quality. From an airport perspective, it reduces financial risk by sharing investment costs and reduces uncertainties because it signals a long-term traffic agreement and a commitment to coordinate strategic decisions for the mutual benefit of each partner (Albers et al., 2005). There are, however, potential problems associated with reduced flexibility in contractual arrangements for both partners, and there will also be a reduction in decision rights. A possible over-reliance on the partner airline adds risk for the airport, and may subsequently increase the market power of the airline. The airport may also experience difficulties attracting airlines and business to older parts of the airport, and their relationship with the alliance partner may deter other airline customers, and weaken the airport's ability to diversify (Albers et al., 2005). There may also be concerns from other airlines that the charges they pay to use the airport will then subsidise the alliance partners' preferential treatment.

## Retrenchment strategies

Retrenchment strategies are used when an organisation seeks to restructure or discontinue parts or all of its business activities, for instance in order to improve its financial situation. At the simplest level, this may be achieved through turnaround strategies that involve withdrawing or retreating from an earlier decision. For example, Singapore Changi's decision to close its Budget Terminal to be replaced by a hybrid terminal was taken for a number of reasons. The growth from LCCs was stronger than expected, meaning that the terminal soon reached capacity. In addition, the terminal was primarily built for point-to-point services, even though Singapore is more of a hub than an origin or destination, and the terminal offered poor opportunities for connections. There were also limited options for expansion at the existing location.

Retrenchment can also be achieved through divestment strategies that seek to downsize the scope of the organisation's business activities, for instance by selling or liquidating one or more business activities in order to improve the organisation's financial situation. After being privatised in 1987, BAA made the most of its freedom and diversified its business with other airports and non-aviation interests. Parts of the business, such as property investment, hotels and fashion outlet centres, were sold off to reduce the company's debt after it was taken over by a consortium led by Ferrovial in 2006 (Graham, 2010).

The most drastic retrenchment strategy to be taken is liquidation, where the company's operations are brought to an end. This is fairly uncommon for airports. However, the current business environment has resulted in a number of recent casualties in Europe. For instance, Blackpool, which closed in 2014 after a new buyer for the airport could not be found (but reopened with very limited services in 2015), Lubeck, which closed in 2016 after the airport's relatively new owner declared bankruptcy, and Oslo Rygge, which, as mentioned already in this chapter, closed in 2016 as a result of Ryanair abandoning its base operations at the airport due to the introduction of a new passenger tax by the Norwegian government.

Airports that are dependent on one or a few carriers for most of their traffic are particularly vulnerable to downsizing or base abandonments from their main airline customer(s) (Koo et al., 2016). Hub airports that have experienced the failure of their hub carrier, such as Zurich, Brussels and Budapest, have been fairly successful at recapturing the traffic lost (e.g. see Linkweiler, 2013). However, this is not the case for smaller secondary or regional airports serving one or a few LCCs, where downsizing and base adandonments have intensified in recent years, and are more difficult to recover from (Malighetti et. al., 2016). Pressure on public finances may mean that there is also a reluctance for local or national governments to (re)invest in civil operations at airports that have failed under private control, meaning that there are few options available to such airports other than to close.

## Conclusion

This chapter has considered literature and key issues related to the formulation of airport business strategy, with a focus on the competitive landscape within which airports operate and form their strategic decisions. The chapter identifies some key drivers for change in the airport business environment, such as the restructuring of the airline industry, the commercialisation and in some cases privatisation of airports, and a period of sustained uncertainty resulting from the global financial situation. These drivers continue to encourage a more competitive airport industry.

While it seems that there are still many airports that operate in a less competitive environment, market power can no longer be assumed. Many of the products and services offered by airports are exposed to competitive forces, and airports should be devising effective strategies that enable them to gain competitive advantages. However, it should also be noted that there are many regulatory and governance structures that control or influence airport decision-making, and subsequently limit the strategic options available to many airports.

One issue that is not covered so much in literature is the role of stakeholders and stakeholder engagement in airport strategy. This includes internal stakeholders, such as employees, and external stakeholders, such as local communities, government, interest groups and business partners. Given the wider impacts of airports (e.g. on the environment and on social and regional economic development) and the influence and potentially conflicting expectations of their stakeholders, it would appear to be an important but challenging issue for airport strategic management.

In terms of airport strategies, literature tends to advocate strategies based on differentiation and growth through diversification. Differentiation allows airports to develop value propositions that are viewed as being different or unique from their competitors, while diversification allows them to expand their range of products and services, and spread risk across a range of markets and geographic locations. Increased commercialisation and privatisation of airports has offered greater opportunities for diversification in non-aeronautical and non-aviation activities. It has also encouraged diversification through a greater use of integration strategies such as mergers and alliances. However, more research is needed because there is currently little quantifiable evidence of the effectiveness of such strategies.

Whether they are publicly or privately owned, there is a growing need for airports to be more financially self-sufficient. Airports that fail to find a competitive advantage, especially mid-sized hubs and smaller secondary and regional airports that operate in competitive markets, and are over-reliant on one or a few customers for much of their business, may be in a particularly vulnerable situation and face a real threat of liquidation, which, from a strategic management perspective, is the endgame decision for an airport operator.

## References

ACI Europe (Airports Council International Europe) (2014). *ACI Europe Analysis Paper: Competition in the European Aviation Sector*, Brussels, ACI Europe.

ACI Europe (Airports Council International Europe) (2016). *The Ownership of Europe's Airports*, Brussels, ACI Europe.

ACRP (Airport Cooperative Research Program) (2009). *Strategic Planning in the Airport Industry*, Washington, DC, Transportation Research Board of the National Academies.

Albalate, D., Bel., G. and Fagenda, X. (2015). Competition and cooperation between high-speed rail and air transportation services in Europe, *Journal of Transport Geography*, 42, 166–174.

Albers, S., Koch, B. and Ruff, C. (2005). Strategic alliances between airlines and airports: theoretical assessment and practical evidence, *Journal of Air Transport Management*, 11(2), 49–58.

Ansoff, I. (1987). *Corporate Strategy*, London, Penguin.

Badanik, B., Laplace, I., Lenoir, N., Malavolti, E., Tomova, A. and Kazda, A. (2010). Future strategies for airports. In: *Proceedings of the 27th International Congress of the Aeronautical Sciences (ICAS)*, Stockholm, ICAS.

Barbot, C. (2009). Airport and airlines competition: incentives for vertical collusion, *Transportation Research Part B: Methodological*, 43(10), 952–965.

Barrett, S.D. (2004). How do the demands for airport services differ between full-service carriers and low-cost carriers? *Journal of Air Transport Management*, 10(1), 33–39.

Bilotkach, V. and Mueller, J. (2012). Supply side substitutability and potential market power of airports: case of Amsterdam Schiphol, *Utilities Policy*, 23, 5–12.

Bilotkach, V., Fageda, X. and Fillol, R.F. (2013). Airline consolidation and traffic distribution between primary and secondary hubs, *Regional Science and Urban Economics*, 43(6), 951–963.

Bracaglia, V.D., Alfonso, T. and Nastasi, A. (2014). Competition between multiproduct airports, *Economics of Transportation*, 3(4), 270–281.

Bush, H. and Starkie, D. (2014). Competitive drivers towards improved airport/airline relationships, *Journal of Air Transport Management*, 41, 45–49.

CAPA (Centre for Aviation) (2008). *Low Cost Airport Terminals Report*, Sydney, CAPA.

CAPA (Centre for Aviation) (2013). *The Airline Base Concept: European LCCs Love to Base Aircraft and Crew Abroad, Unlike Others*, Sydney, CAPA.

CAPA (Centre for Aviation) (2015). *Low Cost Airports and Terminals (LCATs)*, Sydney, CAPA.

Carney, M. and Mew, K. (2003). Airport governance reform: a strategic management perspective, *Journal of Air Transport Management*, 9, 221–232.

Carpenter, M.A. and Sanders, Wm.G. (2009). *Strategic Management – A Dynamic Perspective: Concepts and Cases*, 2nd edition, Upper Saddle River, NJ, Pearson Education International.

de Neufville, R. (2008). Low-cost airports for low-cost airlines: flexible design to manage the risks, *Transportation Planning and Technology*, 31(1), 35–68.

De Wit, J.G. and Zuidberg, J. (2016). Route churn: an analysis of low-cost carrier route continuity in Europe, *Journal of Transport Geography*, 50, 57–67.

Denstadli, J.M., Grupsrud, M., Hjorthol, R. and Julsrud, T.E. (2013). Videoconferencing and business air travel: do new technologies produce new interaction patterns? *Transportation Research Part C: Emerging Technologies*, 29, 1–13.

Feldman, D. (2009). *Diversify, Differentiate, Innovate: Airport Strategies for Success in a New World*, Geneva, Examblia Consulting.

Feldman, D. (2013). *Time for a re-think?* Online. Available at: www.airport-world.com/features/marketing-communications/2416-time-for-a-re-think.html (accessed 12 June 2017).

Forsyth, P., Gillen, D., Muller, J. and Niemeier, H.-M. (eds) (2010a). *Airport Competition: The European Experience*, Abingdon, Routledge.

Forsyth, P., Niemeier, H.-M. and Wolf, H. (2010b). Airport alliances and multi-airport companies: implications for airport competition. In: P. Forsyth, D. Gillen, J. Muller and H.-M. Niemeier (eds). *Airport Competition: The European Experience*, Abingdon, Routledge.

Forsyth, P., Niemeier, H.-M. and Wolf, H. (2011). Airport alliances and mergers: structural change in the airport industry? *Journal of Air Transport Management*, 17(1), 49–56.

Forsyth, P., Gillen, D., Hüschelrath, K., Niemeier, H.-M. and Wolf, H. (eds) (2013). *Liberalisation in Aviation: Competition, Cooperation and Public Policy*, Abingdon, Routledge.

Freathy, P. (2004). The commercialisation of European airports: successful strategies in a decade of turbulence, *Journal of Air Transport Management*, 10, 191–197.

Gillen, D. and Mantin, B. (2014). The importance of concession revenues in the privatisation of airports, *Transportation Research Part E: Logistics and Transportation Review*, 68, 164–177.

Gooding, R.E. (2006). Surviving the low-cost carrier challenge: London City Airport's business model, *Journal of Airport Management*, 1(1), 6–8.

Graham, A. (2009). How important are commercial revenues to today's airports? *Journal of Air Transport Management*, 15(3), 106–111.

Graham, A. (2010). Airport strategies to gain competitive advantage. In: P. Forsyth, D. Gillen, J. Muller and H.-M. Niemeier (eds). *Airport Competition: The European Experience*, Abingdon, Routledge.

Graham, A. (2011). The objectives and outcomes of airport privatisation, *Research in Transportation Business & Management*, 1(1), 3–14.

Graham, A. (2013). *Managing Airports: An International Perspective*, 4th edition, Abingdon, Routledge.

Greater Toronto Airports Authority. (2011). *Toronto Pearson Strategic Plan 2011–2015*, Toronto, Greater Toronto Airports Authority.

Grosche, T. and Klophaus, R. (2015). Hubs at risk: exposure of Europe's largest hubs to competition on transfer city pairs, *Transport Policy*, 43, 55–60.

Halpern, N. and Graham, A. (2013). *Airport Marketing*, Abingdon, Routledge.

Halpern, N. and Graham, A. (2015). Airport route development: a survey of current practice, *Tourism Management*, 46, 213–221.

Halpern, N. and Graham, A. (2017). Performance and prospects of smaller UK regional airports, *Journal of Airport Management*, 11(2), 180–201.

Halpern, N., Graham, A. and Dennis, N. (2016). Low cost carriers and the changing fortunes of airports in the UK, *Research in Transportation Business & Management*, 21, 33–43.

Helsey, M. and Codd, F. (2014). *Aviation: Proposals for an Airport in the Thames Estuary, 1945–2014*, Standard note SN/BT/4920, London, UK Parliament.

Herrmann, N. and Hazel, B. (2012a). *Different strokes*. Online. Available at: www.airport-world.com/features/economics/2044-different-strokes.html (accessed 12 June 2017).

Herrmann, N. and Hazel, B. (2012b). *The Future of Airports: Part 2 – Eight Ways Airports Can Differentiate Themselves from Competitors*, Zurich, Oliver Wyman.

Jarach, D. (2001). The evolution of airport management practices: towards a multi-point, multi-service, marketing-driven firm, *Journal of Air Transport Management*, 7(2), 119–125.

Jiang, C. and Zhang, A. (2016). Airline network choice and market coverage under high-speed rail competition, *Transportation Research Part A: Policy and Practice*, 92, 248–260.

Jimenez, E., Claro, J. and Pinho de Sousa, J. (2014). The airport business in a competitive environment, *Procedia: Social and Behavioural Sciences*, 111, 947–954.

Kasarda, J.D. (2013). Airport cities: the evolution, *Airport World*, April–May, 24–27.

Koo, T., Halpern, N., Papatheodorou, A., Graham, A. and Arvanitis, P. (2016). Air transport liberalisation and airport dependency: developing a composite index, *Journal of Transport Geography*, 50, 83–93.

Kratzsch, U. and Sieg, G. (2011). Non-aviation revenues and their implications for airport regulation, *Transportation Research Part E: Logistics and Transportation Review*, 47, 755–763.

LeighFisher (2012). Airport strategic planning: time to take a fresh look, *Focus: Airport Strategic Planning*, December, 1–4.

Lian, J.I. and Rønnevik, J. (2011). Airport competition: regional airports losing ground to main airports, *Journal of Transport Geography*, 19(1), 85–92.

Lieshout, R. (2012). Measuring the size of an airport's catchment area, *Journal of Transport Geography*, 25, 27–34.

Nigel Halpern

Lin, E., Mak, B. and Wong, K. (2013). The business relationships between LCCs and airports in Southeast Asia: influences of power imbalance and mutual dependence, *Transportation Research Part A: Policy and Practice*, 50, 33–46.

Linkweiler, H. (2013). What airports can do in the event of the failure of their main airline, *Journal of Airport Management*, 7(2), 129–135.

London City Airport. (2016). *Strategic Report 2015*, London, London City Airport Ltd.

Maertens, S. (2012). Estimating the market power of airports in their catchment areas: a Europe-wide approach, *Journal of Transport Geography*, 22, 10–18.

Malighetti, P., Paleari, S. and Redondi, R. (2016). Base abandonments by low-cost carriers, *Journal of Air Transport Management*, 55, 234–244.

Mazzanti, J. (2015). *Blog: shifting strategies at Chinese airports*. Online. Available at: www.airport-world.com/news/general-news/5087-blog-shifting-strategies-at-chinese-airports.html (accessed 12 June 2017).

McCormick, M.J. (2015). Airline consolidation and hub abandonment: the impact on regional economies, *Transportation Research Board (TRB) 94th Annual Meeting Compendium of Papers*, paper number 15-2409, 17 pages.

Munich Airport. (2016). *Corporate Strategy 2025*, Munich, Munich Airport.

Njoya, E.T. and Niemeier, H.-M. (2011). Do dedicated low-cost passenger terminals create competitive advantages for airports? *Research in Transportation Business & Management*, 1(1), 55–61.

Polk, A. and Bilotkach, V. (2013). The assessment of market power of hub airports, *Transport Policy*, 29, 29–37.

Porter, M.E. (1979). How competitive forces shape strategy, *Harvard Business Review*, 57(2), 137–145.

Porter, M.E. (1980). *Competitive Strategy: Techniques for Analyzing Industries and Competitors*, New York, Free Press.

Porter, M.E. (2008). The five competitive forces that shape strategy, *Harvard Business Review*, January, 86–104.

Redondi, R. and Gudmundsson, S.V. (2016). Congestion spill effects of Heathrow and Frankfurt airports on connection traffic in European and Gulf hub airports, *Transportation Research Part A: Policy and Practice*, 92, 287–297.

Sentence, A. (2013). What is the 'new normal' for aviation? In: *Airlines and Airports Today Are Looking at an Uncertain Future*, London, PwC.

Stone, R. (2011). *Sister act*. Online. Available at: www.airport-world.com/features/economics/1055-sister-act.html (accessed 12 June 2017).

Sydney Airport. (2016). *Annual Report 2015*, Sydney, Sydney Airport.

Thelle, M.H., Pedersen, T.T. and Harhoff, F. (2012). *Airport Competition in Europe*, Copenhagen, Copenhagen Economics.

Tretheway, M.W. (2001). Alliances and partnerships among airports. In: *4th Hamburg Aviation Conference*, Hamburg.

Tretheway, M.W. and Andriulaitis, R.J. (2010). Airport competition for freight. In: P. Forsyth, D. Gillen, J. Muller and H.-M. Niemeier (eds). *Airport Competition: The European Experience*, Abingdon, Routledge.

Tretheway, M.W. and Kincaid, I. (2010). Competition between airports: occurrence and strategy. In: P. Forsyth, D. Gillen, J. Muller and H.-M. Niemeier (eds). *Airport Competition: The European Experience*, Abingdon, Routledge.

Warnock-Smith, D. and Potter, A. (2005). An exploratory study into airport choice factors for European low-cost airlines, *Journal of Air Transport Management*, 11(6), 388–392.

Wiltshire, J. (2013). *IATA Briefing No. 11: Airport Competition*, Montreal, IATA.

Wong, J.-T., Chung, Y.-S. and Hsu, P.-Y. (2016). Cargo market competition among Asia Pacific's major airports, *Journal of Air Transport Management*, 56(Part B), 91–98.

170

# 11

# Airline economics and finance

*Anming Zhang and Yahua Zhang*

## Introduction

This chapter surveys topics in the field of airline economics. The debates in these areas are explored from an economic perspective to help build an understanding of contemporary economic issues and challenges facing the airline industry, and to provide airline management with an economic way of thinking in dealing with these issues (for airports, see Chapter 12). This chapter also aims to encourage air transport researchers to consider some under-researched areas.

The first two sections of this chapter centre on key issues and debates relating to cost and demand analysis. The core financial issues that an airline faces will then be discussed, followed by a review of the analysis of airline profitability and its determinants. The last section contains concluding remarks, including a brief discussion about some under-researched areas where definitive answers to some interesting issues are still lacking.

## Airline costs and production

As with other industries, airlines use various inputs such as labour, capital, fuel and materials to produce air transport services. The fuel cost is the largest cost component for most airlines. Koopmans and Lieshout (2016) show that depending on the type of airline, fuel costs accounted for around 20 to 50 per cent of the total costs in 2014. For example, the fuel cost was 46 per cent of the total cost for Ryanair, while it was only 21 per cent for Lufthansa. A flight sector comprises ascent and decent phases as well as the cruise phase. During the cruise, the fuel cost is proportional to the route distance. Also, fuel costs differ substantially from one country to another, due mainly to the differences in taxes and transport costs. International airlines pay fuel prices at airports they serve, and thus the average price paid by a carrier is roughly a weighted average of fuel prices of the destinations it serves. Although the fuel price is largely out of an airline's control, some airlines are keen to use more fuel-efficient aircraft to save costs by purchasing (or leasing) new aircraft. Other airlines choose to replace the seats, television monitors and even the beverage carts with newer and lighter versions (FAA, 2011). However, these measures may not be sufficient for airlines to retain profitability when the oil price is at a high level. Therefore, fuel hedging has also been used to reduce the airline's exposure to unexpected changes in fuel prices, which will be discussed later in this chapter.

Then there is an airline's capital input that consists of two categories: capital input in aircraft, and ground property and equipment. Since the same lease rates are applied to all airlines, the differences in aircraft capital costs across airlines largely reflect the differences in their fleet composition. Finally, the purchased materials (and services) are a catch-all expense category as it includes all the inputs other than labour, fuel and capital inputs.[1]

Some studies have supported the existence of cost economies of aircraft size, meaning that larger aircraft are more cost-efficient (Bitzan and Chi, 2006; Ryerson and Hansen, 2013; Zuidberg, 2014). An airline's maintenance cost is closely related to the airline's average aircraft age as the costly heavy checks are delayed for a few years for new aircraft, while older aircraft incur more frequent and expensive heavy checks (Vasigh et al., 2013). However, Zuidberg (2014) found that airlines using newer aircraft have higher average operating costs per aircraft movement, which suggests that ownership costs due to depreciation and leasing costs of new aircraft outweigh the increasing maintenance costs of old aircraft. A similar view that there is no obvious effect of aircraft age on airline costs is expressed in Berrittella et al. (2009) and Swan and Adler (2006). It is also believed that airlines with diverse aircraft fleets need to maintain a certain level of spare part inventory for every type of aircraft, which could be costly. Brüggen and Klose (2010) and Gitto and Minervini (2007) confirmed the positive effect of fleet commonality on the operating margin of an airline, indicating that airlines with a uniform fleet could be more cost-efficient.

Based on engineering technology, the airline cost per seat declines with the size of aircraft (up to some threshold). Furthermore, the cost per passenger falls as the per cent of seats sold on a flight (the so-called load factor) rises, since much of a flight's cost is fixed regardless of the number of passengers flown. Do these relationships imply economies of scale in airline operations (see also Chapter 12 for a discussion of possible economies of scale for airports)? White (1979) surveyed all major studies covering airline costs and concluded that economies of scale are negligible or non-existent at the overall firm level. Why, then, did the wave of airline mergers and alliances occur after airline deregulation in the United States (US) and Canada, and airline liberalisation in Europe and elsewhere? One possible reason is that a simple manufacturing industry concept of scale economies is inadequate for modelling the relationship between inputs and outputs in this network-oriented service industry.[2] Caves et al. (1984) distinguish between the economies of traffic density and the economies of scale (firm size). Under the latter, output is expanded by adding points to the network, whereas under the former, output expands by increasing service within a given network (set of points served). While Caves et al. (1984) applied the density concept to US airlines, Gillen et al. (1986) studied Canadian airlines, and developed it further by distinguishing between different types of airline traffic (scheduled, charter, freight).

These studies conclude that roughly constant returns to firm size exist for rather broad ranges of airline traffic. That is, adding or dropping cities from an airline's network does not raise or lower unit cost. In contrast, sizeable economies of traffic density seem to exist up to fairly large volumes of traffic. That is, having larger aircraft or more passengers per aircraft on a given route will result in a lower per passenger cost.[3] Intuitively, this makes sense. Adding a city to a network involves a set of fixed operation costs such as airline counters, station managers, mechanics, ticket offices, and advertising (Tretheway and Oum, 1992). Every time a new city is added, another set of these costs must be incurred. On the other hand, once a set of cities are being served, additional traffic does not require any increases in the fixed operating costs. For instance, advertising need not be increased. Thus, the fixed operation costs can be spread out over more traffic, allowing the unit costs to fall. Lakew (2014) examined the cost structure of the integrated air cargo carriers FedEx and UPS, and concluded that the integrated industry exhibits increasing returns to traffic density and constant returns to scale.

An important measurement of firm performance is productivity, which can be divided into the productivity of a given input (e.g. labour), which is so-called partial productivity, and total factor productivity (TFP). For example, Oum and Yu (2001) report that the overall labour productivity of North American airlines has been increasing during the 1990s. This is probably due to: (i) as labour input prices increase, airlines substitute capital for labour via automation; (ii) an increase in outsourcing of various services to third-party providers and/or alliance partner airlines; and (iii) an improvement in labour-saving technology. With respect to materials productivity, each carrier's performance was affected by the corporate policies towards outsourcing of various services. The carriers with the most outsourcing would likely have lower productivity related to the materials inputs because payments associated with outsourced services were all lumped together in the materials input costs.

TFP, on the other hand, is essentially a weighted average of all the partial factor productivity measures, and therefore gives a more comprehensive picture of airline productivity. The TFP regression results in Oum and Yu (2001) suggest the following factors affecting the airline's productivity (in addition to managerial control). First, average stage length (i.e. the distance of a flight segment) has strong and statistically significant positive effects on the observed TFP level: an airline with 10 per cent longer average stage length is expected to have 1.63 per cent higher TFP. Essentially, this is related to another fundamental aspect of airline costs, namely the average cost per kilometre flown declines as the number of kilometres flown increases. Significant amounts of fuel are expended simply in getting a plane up to cruising altitude. In addition, there are various flight preparation costs that are largely independent of the distance. Second, an airline's output size influences TFP levels significantly: a firm with 10 per cent higher output size is expected to have 0.44 per cent higher observed TFP. Third, the state of the economy affects productivity: an economic upturn gives an opportunity for the airline industry to improve TFP levels.

A recent study by Choi (2017) contends that US airlines have constantly sought new ways to improve their competitiveness (including merger and acquisition) after experiencing the 9/11 terror attacks, global financial crisis (GFC) and soaring oil prices over the last 15 years. For the period 2006 to 2015, the US network legacy carriers have exhibited the highest efficiency, and low cost carriers (LCCs) the lowest. It has also been found that the fluctuations in technical change, rather than in efficiency change, had a greater impact on the fluctuation of productivity (measured using the Malmquist index) for US domestic airlines.

## Airline demand and revenues

### Drivers of demand

For airlines, understanding demand is important for their strategic and operational decisions. For example, when an airline is preparing to transfer its services from a set of city pair routes to a hub-and-spoke network, it is crucial for the carrier to have a good knowledge of the demand in major cities when selecting the hub airport(s) and designing its networks. Demand for air service (see Chapter 19) depends on a set of factors that influence a passenger's decision as to whether to travel by air and how much they will do so in a given time period. First off, the demand is highly responsive to price. De Vany (1974) and Oum et al. (1986) estimate the price elasticity of demand at about −1.2, indicating that a 1 per cent increase in fare would, other things being held constant, induce a 1.2 per cent drop in demand.

The demand is also influenced by income, which is usually proxied by gross domestic product (GDP) per capita. Studies have shown that the demand elasticity with respect to income is around 2: for instance, if the economy grows by 5 per cent, then the air travel demand would grow by 10 per cent; similarly, if the economy contracts by 2 per cent, the demand would fall by 4 per cent. This pro-cyclical behaviour has an important implication for airlines' decisions on route entry and exit, and on aircraft orders, purchases and leases (airline leasing and financing will be discussed later in this chapter).

In addition to price and income, air travel demand is affected by availability of other modes of transport. For instance, the emergence of high-speed rail (HSR) services has been a serious threat to China's airline industry. It could, as shown by Zhang et al. (2018), reduce the domestic city pair air passenger flows by 17 per cent. Here, the modal choice is based on the so-called full price, which is the sum of ticket price and time cost. Behrens and Pels (2012) and Gonzalez-Savignat (2004) find empirically that total journey time is the main determinant of travellers' modal choices. Total journey time is the sum of access time, travel time, and expected schedule delay. For a given origin-destination (OD) pair, while air mode has a shorter travel time than HSR, it has longer access time, which includes the time of accessing to, and egressing from, the transport terminals (airport, train station), the time spent at the terminals, and the take-off/landing time. The schedule delay refers to the difference between a passenger's preferred and actual travel time, which is determined largely by the flight/train frequency (Douglas and Miller, 1974). A more frequent service reduces expected schedule delays, and hence is a more convenient service, increasing demand.[4]

Demand for air travel is also related to distance. The longer the travel distance involved, the fewer trips will be made. This is sometimes referred to as the gravity of law of travel demand: demand falls with the square of the distance between origin and destination, similar to the gravity law in physics. Much of the airline literature on OD bilateral air traffic flows employs a gravity model (see Chapter 19). However, unlike the gravity models in the international trade literature, where the distance variable is consistently statistically significant, distance does not seem to be a good proxy for bilateral cost after airline deregulation (or liberalisation), especially in the markets where LCCs are present (see Zhang et al., 2018 for a recent survey of the literature). That distance plays a smaller role for air transport may be because, first, over very short distances (say, less than 300 to 400 km) few air trips are made, owing to an increased cost/time ratio relative to alternative modes such as high-speed rail or automobiles. Second, very long distance eliminates alternative transport modes (such as HSR and cars), which tends to increase air travel.

Safety and security are top priorities in air transport since both are important determinants for air travel demand. Air travel drops whenever there is a major air disaster, and so there has long been a substantial emphasis on safety in aviation, for instance policies and procedures to minimise the risks of failures in the design and operation of commercial airlines and airports. Security is concerned with deliberate sabotage or other acts to cause harm to air operations and the travelling public (see Chapter 21). Since 11 September 2001, security has become the highest priority of the global aviation industry and many governments.

Other factors that influence demand for air travel include timing of services (peak versus off-peak hours of the day, day of the week, season of the year), demographics, and technological advancements (Tretheway and Oum, 1992). For instance, new communication methods such as Skype may factor into a traveller's decision to fly (i.e. if they can see family members or conduct meetings over this medium, they need not fly as often). In addition, consumers prefer an itinerary with less stops to an itinerary with more stops; for example, based on this observation, Bilotkach (2005) examines the competition between two airline alliances.

## Airport as an attribute in passenger demand

Airports affect passenger demand for air travel in two dimensions: price and service quality. First, passengers pay ticket prices, which will be affected by airline costs. One of the costs is the fee that airlines pay to airports, including landing/take-off, aircraft parking, terminal building charges, and air traffic control (see Chapter 12). This amounts to between 2 and 28 per cent of overall airline costs (Koopmans and Lieshout, 2016).[5] At many airports, passengers also need to pay fees that are imposed directly on them, for instance airport security charge and airport improvement fee (Czerny and Zhang, 2015; Lin and Zhang, 2016).

Second, a passenger is also interested in the non-monetary cost of the non-air flying parts of their journey. Here, airports (departure, transfer, and arrival) affect the demand through airport-related service quality perceived by passengers, including: (i) airport location, which affects the travel distance between a passenger's home and the departure airport or their final destination and the arrival airport; (ii) airport facility attributes, for example passenger terminal design and various directional signs that affect how easy it is for a passenger to access, get around and exit the airport; (iii) ground accessibility, for example availability of airport trains, car parking and parking fees, airport shuttle service; (iv) congestion delays at runways, the gates, and terminals; and (v) airport concession or commercial services – an attractive concession/commercial offer helps to stimulate passenger demand and also mitigate some of the negative impacts caused by airport delays (e.g. Czerny et al., 2016; D'Alfonso et al., 2013; Kidokoro et al., 2016).

## Revenue management

As mentioned previously in this chapter, per passenger costs fall as a flight's load factor rises. However, airlines may choose not to fly with 100 per cent of their seats sold in advance on every flight, which is the case when they engage in revenue management. Specifically, revenue management (also called yield management) is the process of understanding, anticipating, and reacting to consumer behaviour in order to maximise airline revenue. Airlines monitor, through the use of specialised software, how quickly their seats are being reserved, and offer discounts when it appears that seats will otherwise be vacant. This builds on the observation that there are passenger types with distinct sensitivities to price and time. To illustrate, consider two passenger types, namely business travellers and leisure travellers. Oum et al. (1986) report that the price elasticity for business travellers is −0.7 to −1.0, whereas for leisure travellers it is −1.5 to −1.8 (that the business demand is significantly less price-elastic than the leisure demand is, for instance, confirmed in a study by Lazarev, 2013; see also Chapter 19). Further, Morrison (1987), Morrison and Winston (1989), Pels et al. (2003), and Zhang (2012), among others, show empirically that business passengers have a greater value of time than leisure passengers.[6]

Given these features, a carrier can improve its revenue by engaging in price discrimination: offering discounted fares only to leisure passengers.[7] The trick is how to separate the two passenger groups from each other. Here, revenue management designs a list of fences to prevent passengers of a higher fare class (e.g. business passengers) from buying discounted fares (e.g. Smith et al., 1992). For example, Lazarev (2013) finds that leisure passengers start searching for a ticket at least six weeks prior to flight departure, while business passengers typically search in the last week. Thus, an airline can use advanced-purchase rebates to price-discriminate between the business and leisure passengers, and charge business passengers a high fare relative to leisure passengers (e.g. Hazledine, 2006; Stavins, 2001). The strategy is implemented as follows: For each fare class, airline planners estimate the demand and assign a fare. They then maximise revenue by allocating seats for each fare class subject to the capacities of the aircraft assigned to the flights. In particular, by offering early booking with discount-fare seats, an airline is able to gain revenue from seats that may otherwise fly empty. The number of such discount-fare seats is optimally determined to balance against the expected revenue gain from full-fare passengers. Littlewood (1972) proposed a seat inventory control rule, known as 'Littlewood's rule', that discount-fare bookings should be accepted as long as their revenue value exceeds the expected revenue of future full-fare bookings.

After Littlewood's contribution, significant progress has been made on the subject of seat inventory allocation – especially on the optimal protection level since the late 1980s. Most studies in the literature were concerned with operational decisions of a seat allocation problem that is intrinsically internal to airlines, although most markets (routes) are served by two or more airlines (see Bitran and Caldentey, 2003; Elmaghraby and Keskinocak, 2003; McGill and van Ryzin, 1999 for useful literature surveys). A small but growing literature has been developing that introduces competition into the seat allocation problem. For example, Li et al. (2008) introduce differential costs into the airline strategic rivalry model (previous studies have either abstracted away costs, or assumed that costs are symmetric among competing firms). This is necessary because cost asymmetry plays a critical role in the determination of airlines' seat allocation and pricing strategies. Using a game theoretical approach to competing airlines' seat allocation problem, Li et al. (2008) derive necessary conditions that assure the existence of a pure strategy 'Nash equilibrium'. They further examine both the competition and cooperation equilibria, as the issue of cooperation has become increasingly relevant in the era of strategic alliances among carriers with different cost structures. The authors demonstrate that the rivalry over seat allocation between carriers may lead to a classic 'prisoners' dilemma', a finding that helps shed light on what optimal decision-making regarding seat allocation would be in a repetitive environment.

## Airline finance

The core financial issues that an airline faces include: (i) aircraft investment; (ii) the carrier's capital structure; (iii) its decision to buy or lease aircraft; and (iv) its use of fuel hedging strategy to mitigate the risk associated with oil price fluctuations. These issues will be discussed below.[8]

### Aircraft investment

A major strategic decision of an airline is its investment in fleets. In general, the designed life of a jumbo jet is 30 years. In practice however, its useful life is mostly less than the designed life due to various factors such as safety and maintenance, and so airlines often set 20 to 25 years as the depreciation period for the airframe and engines. Meanwhile, because the economic life of the airframe is influenced by a variety of factors, especially during the last two decades, when a great number of new aircraft types have entered into service, and fuel price has been at a high level and fluctuated dramatically, most airlines have been forced to retire old aircraft ahead of their useful life, and airlines now appear to prefer the use of the economic life as the investment period in their evaluation of aircraft acquisition. Most of the used aircraft were sold to developing countries, and that is why the average age of aircraft fleets in Africa and Latin America tends to be higher (Bjelicic, 2012).

Airlines operate in a dynamic environment with a great number of uncertainties, and with airline revenues and costs being influenced heavily by overall economic activities. How to evaluate aircraft acquisition programmes in such a circumstance thus becomes crucial for airlines. Gibson and Morrell (2005) surveyed the investment criteria such as net present value (NPV), used by airlines, and reported data on actual discount rates used at airlines. They found that airlines prefer the NPV method to the ARR (accounting rate of return) method. The reason is that while cash-based NPV techniques take the time value of money into consideration, ARR does not. They concluded, nevertheless, that finance departments of airlines do not necessarily capitalise on all useful methods available.

The base for such a static NPV method is the traditional discount cash flow (DCF) approach, which has an implicit assumption that the investment will, once undertaken, be operated until the end of its useful life set at the very beginning. Under the predetermined scenario, cash flows are based on factors such as the estimation of future revenues, costs, and follow-up investments, regardless of the changing circumstances in the future and likely managerial responses to some realised uncertainty outcomes. The DCF methodology thus implies a rigid managerial strategy that may not reflect real business decision-making of most firms, particularly those operating in a multiple-risks environment such as airlines.

To survive in the dynamic environment, airline business strategy is likely to be more flexible than one implied by the static NPV approach. Hu and Zhang (2015) demonstrate that aircraft acquisition by airlines may contain a portfolio of real options (flexible strategies) embedded in the investment's life cycle, and that if airlines rely solely on the static NPV method, they are likely to underestimate the true investment value. Two real options are investigated: (i) the shutdown–restart option (a carrier shuts down a plane if revenues are less than costs, but restarts it if revenues are more than costs); and (ii) the option to defer aircraft delivery. The authors quantify the values of these options in a case study of a major US airline. The basic idea demonstrated in Hu and Zhang (2015) could help explain observed capital expenditures of airlines, and serve as a rule of thumb in evaluating their capital budgeting decisions.

## Airline capital structure

There are several instruments to finance an airline's capital expenditures (such as aircraft acquisition), leading to the important decision on capital structure. Raising equity is an important source of financing, especially for setting up a new airline (Bjelicic, 2012). To increase capital, many new airlines, particularly the LCCs in Asia such as Tiger Airways and Spring Airlines, use an initial public offering (IPO) to finance the purchase of new aircraft. Bank borrowing is another significant source for aircraft financing. Bjelicic (2012) notes that the market for aircraft financing is a global market, and airlines do not rely just on the banks in their own countries or regions. American banks played a leading role in global aircraft financing in the 1960s and 1970s, followed by Japanese banks in the 1980s. European banks were the main loan providers for aircraft acquisitions in the 1990s. However, since the 2008 GFC, banks around the world became more cautious in aircraft financing and tended to set more restrictive loan terms for airlines (Bjelicic, 2012).

Bjelicic (2012) also discussed other sources of financing for airlines, including issuing corporate bonds, operating leases, export credit, and manufacturer and pre-delivery payment financings. The author pointed out that for many years, access to capital was not a big issue for most airlines. However, this climate has changed since the GFC. Capital access is likely to be a barrier to market entry for some new airlines and financing airlines will be a challenging task in the future.

There is an extant literature investigating the question of whether airlines invest in aircraft capacity efficiently or not. For instance, Wojahn (2012) examines causes for the well-documented phenomenon of capacity overinvestment in the airline industry based on a data set covering all publicly listed airlines. He finds that the data support multiple causes: agency problems (e.g. myopia and empire building) and the shift towards low cost and Asian carriers, coupled with remnants of capital in legacy airlines, as well as economies of scale, are all associated with overinvestment. An important feature that is not investigated in his paper is the airline oligopoly rivalry, examined, for instance, by Brander and Lewis (1986) and Oum et al. (2000a). That is, with the limited liability effect of modern corporations, investment with debt financing serves as a so-called 'top dog strategy' in output rivalry, which leads to overinvestment in capacity.[9]

## Decision to buy or lease aircraft

Another important financial decision is the decision to buy or lease aircraft. Operating lease and direct purchase with bank finance are two commonly used methods of financing the aircraft acquisition. Should an airline purchase and own the aircraft? If purchased, should the airline pay 100 per cent cash or borrow some funds for the purchase? These decisions depend on the market conditions and the airline's circumstances (Accession Capital Corp, 2003). There is no one method that is superior to another. Interest rates, discount rates, lease rates, and aircraft resale values are relevant variables, and should be taken into account when making the lease or purchase decision. Today, around 40 per cent of the worldwide fleet is owned by leasing companies. So the leasing industry is large and is getting larger,[10] and leasing is crucial to accommodate the future growth of the airline industry. Main advantages of leasing include a decrease in capital investment requirement, and an increase in fleet plan flexibility. There is a strand of literature on aircraft investment concerning the choice between ownership and lease (e.g. Allonen, 2013; Bourjade et al., 2017; Gibson and Morrell, 2004; Gritta et al., 1994; Littlejohns and McGairl, 1998; Oum et al., 2000b, 2000c). For example, Bourjade et al. (2017) find, using public data on 73 airlines operating worldwide over the period 1996 to 2011, that there is a concave effect of leasing on an airline's profit margin, and the impact is stronger for an LCC than for a legacy carrier.

## Use of fuel hedging strategy

Oil price has been making front-page news in the last decade. In 2004, the price of a barrel of crude oil was only about US$30 before commencing an upward trajectory. The price reached its peak, US$147, in October 2008, and fell sharply due to the GFC, and then remained in the range of US$90–120 for several years. However, the price fell precipitously from about US$110 in 2014 to US$27 in early 2016, but rebounded to US$54 by the end of 2016. Large swings in oil price have a major impact on global economic activities, and air transport is one of the most affected sectors. Fuel hedging has been frequently used to reduce airline exposure to unexpected changes in fuel price, as it has been difficult for airlines to pass the rise in fuel cost on to consumers since airline deregulation.

Nevertheless, the benefit of fuel hedging appears controversial. Carter et al. (2006) and Sturm (2009) reported a positive impact of fuel hedging on the airlines' firm value. The hedging premium and increase in firm value may come from the fact that hedging can offset the underinvestment problem faced by airlines when fuel price rises. Treanor et al. (2014) found a positive hedging premium, although there has been a decline in premium in recent years when the fuel price was high. However, it appears that investors tend to value firms with significant and stable hedging programmes rather than rewarding airlines that hedge more when exposure is higher. Jin and Jorion (2004) claim that hedging does not necessarily affect a firm's market value. Lim and Hong (2014) even found that hedging has a negative but insignificant impact on operating costs, which means that the actual benefit of fuel hedging could be negligible. Although airlines could reduce fuel prices, though marginally, through their hedging programmes, they remained susceptible to fuel cost swings, as did the non-fuel hedging firms. Lim and Hong (2014) pointed out that merely engaging in fuel hedging is not sufficient to achieve cost reduction. Rather, effectively and skillfully applying fuel hedging to lower fuel expenses is more important.

In fact, even successful hedging imposes costs and other disadvantages on hedging companies (Berghöfer and Lucey, 2014). In 2008, many airlines suffered losses due to their hedging strategy, including the formerly successful fuel hedger Southwest Airlines (Tokic, 2012). There is also induced cost associated with fuel hedging. Rao (1999) estimates that the cost of hedging amounts to 1 per cent of an airline's fuel bill. In addition, given that airlines typically make hedging decisions based on the information from oil or fuel suppliers and middle men directly, there is also potential counterparty risk, which could pose a threat to the benefit of hedging activity, especially when an airline cannot reduce this risk by adjusting contracting terms (Berghöfer and Lucey, 2014; Mercatus, 2012). Turner and Lim (2015) show that airlines hedging with futures would create the most effective hedge by using heating oil futures contracts with a three-month maturity. The hedge effectiveness decreases beyond the three-month veil.

## Airline profitability and determinants

Over the last three decades, the airline industry has experienced severe volatility in earnings, with airlines recording periods of large profits that are then followed by periods of substantial losses (see Chapter 1). Numerous airlines have entered bankruptcy or liquidated. As discussed above, financing decisions affect an airline's value and profit. In addition, airline profitability is determined primarily by: (i) cost competitiveness; and (ii) airlines' market power. A firm's price-setting ability or market power is closely linked to non-price competition and is affected by the trend of airline deregulation and consolidation.

### *Factors determining airline cost competitiveness*

The first factor is average stage length. Carriers serving routes with longer stage length are expected to have lower direct operating cost per unit of output. As mentioned earlier, the decline of unit costs with increasing stage length is considered to be an important characteristic of airline economics. This is because airport charges and station costs, and costs associated with ground manoeuvring, ground handling, and take-off and landing activities become relatively smaller per passenger kilometre as stage length increases. Also, longer stage length leads to higher aircraft and crew utilisation. However, Zuidberg (2014) and Chua et al. (2005) found no economies of stage length. Brüggen and Klose (2010) also failed to establish a relationship between route length and an airline's operating performance. A negative relationship between stage length and operating profit margin was reported in Mantin and Wang (2012).

Next, there is average load factor. A high load factor indicates better utilisation of aircraft and crew. Aircraft have very high initial costs, and a large proportion of crew, aircraft, and flight costs are fixed. Therefore, unit costs should decline as the load factor increases. Almost all the relevant literature has confirmed the existence of economies of load factor, such as Chua et al. (2005) and Hansen et al. (2001). Mantin and Wang (2012) and Tsikriktsis (2007) confirm that there is a positive impact of the airline's load factor on its operating margin.

Observed differences in unit costs are also due at least partly to the differences in input prices. Zuidberg (2014) notes that on average, fuel and labour costs account for about 50 per cent of an airline's total costs. Studies have shown that the higher the fuel/labour price, the higher the total costs of the airline (Hansen et al., 2001) or the higher direct operating costs per departure (Ryerson and Hansen, 2013).

Theoretically, efficiency should explain cost differences between airlines that cannot be attributed to the variations in input prices, operating characteristics, or any other cost variables. Li et al. (2015) have conducted a survey of the studies on various measures of airline efficiency, including operating efficiency (Barbot et al., 2008; Mallikarjun, 2015), energy efficiency or fuel efficiency (Cui and Li, 2015a; Miyoshi and Merkert, 2010), and safety efficiency (Cui and Li, 2015b).

## Non-price competition

The demand that is discussed earlier in this chapter is the market, or industry, demand. The demand that is faced by each carrier is the firm-specific demand, which also incorporates the degree of price/output competition between airlines. In general, the firm-specific demand is more elastic than the market demand, especially after airline deregulation and liberalisation.[11] In addition, airlines compete with each other through various non-pricing competition strategies to retain passengers, and thus a certain degree of market power.

Frequent flyer programmes (FFPs) are an example of non-price competition. The FFP that was first introduced by American Airlines was a loyalty programme with an aim to maintain loyalty among those who travel frequently by rewarding them with free upgrades, free tickets, additional baggage allowances, and business lounge access (Martin et al., 2011). These days, the FFP also includes other partners such as banks, hotels, and supermarkets. Seelhorst and Liu (2015) found that FFP membership played a strong role in airline choice, especially for passengers with elite membership. Availability of FFPs tends to stimulate air travel, especially for business travel where the employers pay the bill while the travellers reap the (personal) benefits. However, in developing countries such as China, FFPs have been largely a failure for the major airlines in terms of increasing customer loyalty (H. Jiang and Y. Zhang, 2016). It has been found that Chinese travellers were not significantly influenced by airline brands when making a travel decision (H. Jiang and Y. Zhang, 2016; Zhang, 2012).

Numerous studies have shown that the quality of pre-flight, in-flight, and post-flight services had a significant effect on customer satisfaction, which, as a mediating variable, had a positive effect on customer loyalty (Anderson and Jacobsen, 2000; Calisir et al., 2016; H. Jiang and Y. Zhang, 2016; Namukasa, 2013). Airlines that provide better services than their competitors are able to build a solid foundation for customer loyalty (Curry and Gao, 2012). However, these factors might be less important in the decision of whether or not to fly, but more important in the choice of airline. Although the vast majority of literature suggests a direct, positive relationship between customer satisfaction and customer loyalty (Hussain et al., 2015; Wang, 2014), a key finding in Dolnicar et al. (2011) is that an attempt to improve customers' satisfaction has not proven to have a large impact on loyalty. Chen (2012) notes that past empirical evidence has shown the existence of difference in the strength of the relationship between customer satisfaction and loyalty. H. Jiang and Y. Zhang (2016) show that although customer satisfaction is significantly and positively associated with customer loyalty for leisure travellers, satisfactory service did not result in higher customer loyalty among business travellers in China's aviation market.

## Airline mergers and alliances

It has been well documented in the airline literature that: (i) intensified competition after deregulation has substantially lessened airline market power and reduced airline profits; and (ii) strong competition in the airline industry has increased with the emergence of LCCs and further eroded the profit margin of full service airlines. A major strategic action taken by airlines in the deregulated market environment involves the proliferation of mergers and alliances, both international and domestic (see Chapters 6 and 9). Internationally, the three major global alliance groups – namely Star Alliance, Oneworld, and SkyTeam – made up over 60 per cent of the world market in recent years. In 2016, Star Alliance and SkyTeam had roughly the same market share in the world market measured by passenger count (around 700 million), while Oneworld just slightly lagged behind and carried about 600 million passengers.

Within each alliance, joint venture (JV) partnerships have been popular. Oneworld includes a JV group including British Airways, Iberia, and Vueling. Star Alliance has a Lufthansa JV group including Lufthansa, Swiss, Austrian, and Brussels Airlines. In the SkyTeam group, Delta has equity interests in the Air France-KLM-Alitalia group (Alitalia filed for bankruptcy in May 2017). It also owns a 49 per cent stake in Virgin Atlantic. These JVs command about 75 per cent of the market share in the transatlantic market as of 2016 (Bhaskara, 2016). The same trend has appeared in the US domestic market since the late 1990s, with the mega-mergers of Delta and Northwest, United and Continental, and American and US Airways. While major mergers have occurred in Europe (e.g. Air France and KLM), European airlines seem to rely more on their global partners in both the international and European domestic markets.[12]

There are many reasons for why airlines merge and form strategic alliances, including expansion of seamless service networks, traffic feeding between partners, cost-efficiency (based mainly on economies of traffic density), quality improvement, various marketing advantages (e.g. FFPs), and the advantage of market power and cooperative pricing. At the international level, the most important motivators appear to be the regulatory restrictions on access to foreign markets and the foreign ownership limitations in most countries.[13] Many of these alliances have aimed primarily at the network-related benefits of increased traffic feed into established gateways, access to new markets by tapping a partner's unutilised route rights or airport slots, or greater profits from current markets via joint management of capacity. Other than the revenue and cost advantages described previously, alliance carriers may also attempt to gain market power to charge higher prices. In 1992, the US government began granting immunity from antitrust investigation to selective alliances. Generally, this privilege has been tied to a country's willingness to sign an open skies agreement with the US.[14] As such, antitrust immunity allows the alliance carriers to practise cooperative pricing without being subject to US antitrust law. These carriers could, as a result, have a major competitive advantage over their competitors.

## Market liberalisation and competitiveness

It is important to point out that market deregulation (or liberalisation) and a viable airline industry are not necessarily in conflict with each other. In the longer run, deregulation should improve firm efficiency and cost competitiveness. To illustrate this point, consider the airline industry in China. In fact, the long history of the centrally planned economic system had fettered the productivity and competitiveness of the Chinese airline industry. Only in recent years has the industry been given some freedom to operate and to reform itself. The operational freedom, combined with the airline competition unleashed by the policy relaxation, has markedly improved the industry's productivity and competitiveness, leading to the industry's dramatic growth (e.g. Zhang, 1998; Zhang and Chen, 2003; Zhang and Zhang, 2016). Furthermore, with the intensifying international competition, it may also be in the carriers' interest to have a freer and more liberal market domestically. The airlines, once requiring the government's protection, now need greater freedoms to grow and compete effectively at a global level. This is especially so when airlines face challenges from other modes of transport, such as HSR. These are actually reflected in the current situation, where

Chinese airlines demand a greater number of both domestic services and international traffic rights so as to optimise their networks (C. Jiang and A. Zhang, 2016).

More generally, Clougherty and Zhang (2009) test, empirically, the hypothesis that a high degree of domestic competition improves the airlines' competitiveness in international markets. Using comprehensive data covering the international airline markets between nineteen nations over the 1987 to 1992 period, they find that domestic rivalry – measured both in structural and behavioural terms – positively impacts the international market shares of airlines. Accordingly, airlines that experience substantial domestic rivalry tend to perform better in export markets.

## Conclusion

Air transport is an important component of a modern economy and an essential input to tourism and many trading sectors. An efficient air transport system benefits the economy and improves consumer welfare. Key topics in the field of airline economics have been explored in this chapter, including such areas as airline costs and production, airline demand and revenue management, airline financial issues, and airline profitability. A survey of relevant literature on these topics from an economic perspective will help enhance understanding of core economic issues and challenges facing the airline industry, and provide the airline management with an economic way of thinking in dealing with these issues.

This chapter also encourages air transport researchers to consider some under-researched areas where definitive answers to some interesting issues are still lacking. For example, fuel cost has replaced labour cost as the largest cost component for many airlines. However, studies on the effective ways of reducing fuel cost risks, including fuel hedging and the adoption of new technologies, remain relatively sparse. It is understood that worldwide airlines have in general been running on thin profit margins and have seen large fluctuations in profits. Airline finance issues, such as aircraft acquisition and financing, have also not drawn sufficient attention from air transport researchers.

Furthermore, airline deregulation has sparked considerable competition, bidding away airline market power. Establishing a strong brand identify could be a non-price competition strategy used by airlines to differentiate their products and retain a certain degree of market power. However, many airlines, especially those in developing countries, have failed to achieve this, which might be one of the causes of failures and demises of some airlines. Finally, airlines are under threat from other modes of transport, especially HSR in Asia and Europe. HSR has driven the changes of, among others, marketing strategy and network designing for airlines. The modal competition (and cooperation) and its welfare consequences are an area worth further examining in the future.

## Notes

1 It includes travel agency commissions, airport charges, building and office rents, advertising cost, parts and materials for aircraft and vehicle maintenance, passenger meals and other in-flight supplies, fees for consultants, fees related to computer reservation systems, all outsourced services costs, including third-party baggage and ground handling costs, travel expenses, and stationery and other office supplies.
2 Alternative to this cost-side rationale is demand-side explanations. There are several aspects of demand that favour larger carriers (see the section in this chapter on airline profitability and determinants).
3 The traffic density effect is confirmed by, for example, Brueckner and Spiller (1994). Brueckner and Pels (2005) and Brueckner and Spiller (1991) have explored the implications of the density effect for competition and mergers in airline networks.

4  For theoretical analyses of air-HSR modal competition incorporating both price and total journey time, see, for example, Xia and Zhang (2016) and Yang and Zhang (2012).

5  Note that the demand for airport service is different from the demand for airline service. Here, each airport is an upstream firm that provides input service to downstream airlines, which in turn produce output for final consumers (air passengers). Conditional on the airport charge, airlines operating from the airport compete among one another in the output market. From this equilibrium output, we can obtain the derived demand for airport service, which is a function of airport charge. This demand is the same as the direct demand for airport service only when the airlines are perfectly competitive (Basso and Zhang, 2008a, 2008b). For the implications of imperfectly competitive airlines for airport demand and pricing, see a recent survey of studies by Zhang and Czerny (2012).

6  According to the US Department of Transportation's guidelines of 1997, business passengers' travel time should be valued at 100 per cent of the wage, while leisure passengers' travel time at 70 per cent (US DOT, 1997). In general, the value of time depends on both the traveller's income and the nature of the trip. Indeed, von Wartburg and Waters (2004) have a detailed discussion on the relationship between the value of travel time savings (VTTS) and income. Their comprehensive literature survey indicates that the income elasticity of VTTS is positive. For instance, Mackie et al. (2001) report that this income elasticity is in the range of 0.72 to 0.82. Furthermore, positive estimates of VTTS for air travel time have been incorporated in many studies (e.g. Carlton et al., 1980; De Vany, 1974). In addition, the value of time depends on the nature of the trip the person is taking, with VTTS being higher for business trips than leisure trips.

7  Airlines are a frequently used example for markets where price discrimination is prevalent (e.g. Borenstein, 1985; Cowan, 2007; Czerny and Zhang, 2014; Dana, 1999a, 1999b; Gillen and Mantin, 2009).

8  Useful general references on airline finance include Morrell (2013) and Vasigh et al. (2015).

9  In practice, airlines do seem to exercise the managerial options (discussed in Hu and Zhang, 2015) by adjusting their flight schedules and overall capacity with the changes of business environment. Taken together, Hu and Zhang's (2015) results, while seemingly being in the opposite direction of explaining the observed overinvestment anomaly, suggest that the anomaly may be more pronounced than was thought previously. That is, the results may in effect provide some support to the hypothesis that airlines overestimate values of the shutdown–restart option and other options.

10 Gibson and Morrell (2004) indicated that 25 per cent of airlines' aircraft was leased (around the early 2000s), of which about 80 per cent are operating leases (see also Gritta et al., 1994).

11 Earlier studies include Brander and Zhang (1990, 1993) and Oum et al. (1993). For a recent literature survey, see Zhang et al. (2011).

12 For Canadian experience, see Oum and Zhang (2001).

13 Unlike many other industries, air transport is regulated internationally: in particular, virtually all commercial aspects of international air transport are governed by bilateral air services agreements. Negotiated by relevant national governments, these agreements usually specify services (passenger, cargo) and routes to be operated between the two countries, and designate the airlines with the right to fly on each route and their capacities. They generally exclude third-country airlines and prohibit cabotage. Consequently, airlines are constrained from directly serving domestic markets in a foreign country. The foreign ownership limitations in most countries further prohibit airlines from acquiring and owning foreign airlines. See, for instance, Findlay (2003) and Findlay and Nikomborirak (2002).

14 For example, in 1992, the KLM–Northwest alliance was the first to receive immunity, and this privilege followed the Netherlands being the first country to sign an open skies agreement with the US. Relatedly, an important policy question is not whether airlines should be allowed to cooperate, but rather how they should be allowed to do it – that is, whether antitrust immunity should be granted or whether carve-out should be imposed for airline alliance partners (e.g. Bilotkach, 2005; Bilotkach and Hüschelrath, 2013; Brueckner and Proost, 2010). See Zhang and Czerny (2012) for a recent literature survey.

# References

Accession Capital Corp (2003). *Commercial aircraft: lease, finance or purchase?* Online. Available at: www.connvaluation.com/caseStudies/Lease_Borrow_Purchase.pdf (accessed 1 December 2016).

Allonen, M. (2013). *Operating Lease or Purchase Analysis – Case: An Acquisition of Airbus A330-300 for Finnair*, Master's Thesis, School of Business, Aalto University, Finland.

Anderson, H. and Jacobsen, P.N. (2000). Creating loyalty: its strategic importance in your customer strategy. In: S.A. Brown (ed.). *Customer Relationship Management*, Ontario, John Wiley.

Barbot, C., Costa, A. and Sochirca, E. (2008). Airlines performance in the new market context: a comparative productivity and efficiency analysis, *Journal of Air Transport Management*, 14(5), 270–274.

Basso, L. and Zhang, A. (2008a). On the relationship between airport pricing models, *Transportation Research Part B: Methodological*, 42, 725–735.

Basso, L. and Zhang, A. (2008b). Sequential peak-load pricing: the case of airports and airlines, *Canadian Journal of Economics*, 41(3), 1087–1119.

Behrens, C. and Pels, E. (2012). Intermodal competition in the London-Paris passenger market: high-speed rail and air transport, *Journal of Urban Economics*, 71(3), 278–288.

Berghöfer, B. and Lucey, B. (2014). Fuel hedging, operational hedging and risk exposure: evidence from the global airline industry, *International Review of Financial Analysis*, 34, 124–139.

Berrittella, M., La Franca, L. and Zito, P. (2009). An analytic hierarchy process for ranking operating costs of low cost and full service airlines, *Journal of Air Transport Management*, 15, 249–255.

Bhaskara, V. (2016). *The transatlantic market in summer 2016*. Online. Available at: https://airwaysmag.com/industry/the-transatlantic-market-in-summer-2016 (accessed 1 December 2016).

Bilotkach, V. (2005). Price competition between international airline alliances, *Journal of Transport Economics and Policy*, 39(2), 167–189.

Bilotkach, V. and Hüschelrath, K. (2013). Airline alliances, antitrust immunity and market foreclosure, *The Review of Economics and Statistics*, 95(4), 1368–1385.

Bitran, G. and Caldentey, R. (2003). An overview of pricing models for revenue management, *Manufacturing & Service Operations Management*, 5, 203–229.

Bitzan, J.D. and Chi, J. (2006). Higher airfares to small and medium sized communities: costly service or market power? *Journal of Transport Economics and Policy*, 40(3), 473–501.

Bjelicic, B. (2012). Financing airlines in the wake of the airline markets crisis, *Journal of Air Transport Management*, 21, 10–16.

Borenstein, S. (1985). Price discrimination in free-entry markets, *Rand Journal of Economics*, 16, 380–397.

Bourjade, S., Huc, R. and Muller-Vibes, C. (2017). Leasing and profitability: empirical evidence from the airline industry, *Transportation Research Part A: Policy and Practice*, 97, 30–46.

Brander, J.A. and Lewis, T.R. (1986). Oligopoly and financial structure: the limited liability effect, *American Economic Review*, 76(5), 956–970.

Brander, J.A. and Zhang, A. (1990). Market conduct in the airline industry, *Rand Journal of Economics*, 21, 567–583.

Brander, J.A. and Zhang, A. (1993). Dynamic behaviour in the airline industry, *International Journal of Industrial Organization*, 11, 407–435.

Brueckner, J.K. and Pels, E. (2005). European airline mergers, alliance consolidation, and consumer welfare, *Journal of Air Transport Management*, 11, 27–41.

Brueckner, J.K. and Proost, S. (2010). Carve-outs under airline antitrust immunity, *International Journal of Industrial Organization*, 28(6), 657–668.

Brueckner, J.K. and Spiller, P.T. (1991). Competition and mergers in airline networks, *International Journal of Industrial Organization*, 9, 323–342.

Brueckner, J.K. and Spiller, P.T. (1994). Economies of traffic density in the deregulated airline industry, *Journal of Law and Economics*, 37, 379–415.

Brüggen, A. and Klose, L. (2010). How fleet commonality influences low-cost airline operating performance: empirical evidence, *Journal of Air Transport Management*, 16, 299–303.

Calisir, N., Basak, E. and Calisir, F. (2016). Key drivers of passenger loyalty: a case of Frankfurt-Istanbul flights, *Journal of Air Transport Management*, 53, 211–217.

Carlton, D.W., Landes, W.M. and Posner, R.A. (1980). Benefits and costs of airline mergers: a case study, *Bell Journal of Economics*, 11, 65–83.

Carter, D.A., Rogers, D.A. and Simkins, B.J. (2006). Does hedging affect firm value? Evidence from the U.S. airline industry, *Financial Management*, 35(1), 53–86.

Caves, D.W., Christensen, L.R. and Tretheway, M.W. (1984). Economies of density versus economies of scale: why trunk and local service airline costs differ, *Rand Journal of Economics*, 15, 471–489.

Chen, S.C. (2012). The customer satisfaction-loyalty relation in an interactive e-service setting: the mediators, *Journal of Retailing and Consumer Services*, 19(2), 202–210.

Choi, K. (2017). Multi-period efficiency and productivity changes in US domestic airlines, *Journal of Air Transport Management*, 59, 18–25.

Chua, C., Kew, H. and Yong, J. (2005). Airline code-share alliances and costs: imposing concavity on translog cost function estimation, *Review of Industrial Organization*, 26, 461–487.

Clougherty, J. and Zhang, A. (2009). Domestic rivalry and export performance: theory and evidence from international airline markets, *Canadian Journal of Economics*, 42, 440–468.

Cowan, S. (2007). The welfare effects of third-degree price discrimination with nonlinear demand functions, *Rand Journal of Economics*, 32(2), 419–428.

Cui, Q. and Li, Y. (2015a). Evaluating energy efficiency for airlines: an application of VFB-DEA, *Journal of Air Transport Management*, 44/45, 34–41.

Cui, Q. and Li, Y. (2015b). The change trend and influencing factors of civil aviation safety efficiency: the case of Chinese airline companies, *Safety Science*, 75, 56–63.

Curry, N. and Gao, Y. (2012). Low-cost airlines: a new customer relationship? An analysis of service quality, service satisfaction and customer loyalty in a low-cost setting, *Services Marketing Quarterly*, 33(2), 104–118.

Czerny, A.I. and Zhang, A. (2014). Airport congestion pricing when airlines price discriminate, *Transportation Research Part B: Methodological*, 65, 77–89.

Czerny, A.I. and Zhang, A. (2015). How to mix per-flight and per-passenger based airport charges, *Transportation Research Part A: Policy and Practice*, 71(1), 77–95.

Czerny, A.I., Shi, Z. and Zhang, A. (2016). Can market power be controlled by regulation of core prices alone? An empirical analysis of airport demand and car rental price, *Transportation Research Part A: Policy and Practice*, 91, 260–272.

D'Alfonso, T., Jiang, C. and Wan, Y. (2013). Airport pricing, concession revenues and passenger types, *Journal of Transport Economics and Policy*, 47(1), 71–89.

Dana, J.D. (1999a). Using yield management to shift demand when the peak time is unknown, *Rand Journal of Economics*, 30, 456–474.

Dana, J.D. (1999b). Equilibrium price dispersion under demand uncertainty: the roles of costly capacity and market structure, *Rand Journal of Economics*, 30, 632–660.

De Vany, A. (1974). The revealed value of time in air travel, *Review of Economics and Statistics*, 56, 77–82.

Dolnicar, S., Grabler, K., Grun, B. and Kulnig, A. (2011). Key drivers of airline loyalty, *Tourism Management*, 32(5), 1020–1026.

Douglas, D.W. and Miller, J.C. (1974). Quality competition industry equilibrium, and efficiency in the price constrained airline market, *American Economic Review*, September, 657–669.

Elmaghraby, W. and Keskinocak, P. (2003). Dynamic pricing in the presence of inventory considerations: research overview, current practices, and future directions, *Management Science*, 49, 1287–1309.

FAA (Federal Aviation Administration) (2011). *The Economic Impact of Civil Aviation on the US Economy*. Washington, DC, FAA.

Findlay, C. (2003). Plurilateral agreements on trade in air transport services: the US model, *Journal of Air Transport Management*, 9, 211–220.

Findlay, C. and Nikomborirak, D. (2002). Liberalization of air transport services. In: W. Martin and M. Pangestu (eds). *Options for Global Trade Reform: A View from the Asia Pacific*, Cambridge, Cambridge University Press.

Gibson, W.E. and Morrell, P.S. (2004). Theory and practice in aircraft financial evaluation, *Journal of Air Transport Management*, 10, 427–433.

Gibson, W.E. and Morrell, P.S. (2005). *Aircraft Financial Evaluation: Evidence from the Field*, paper presented at the Air Transport Research Society (ATRS) World Conference, Rio de Janeiro, ATRS.

Gillen, D.W. and Mantin, B. (2009). Price volatility in airline markets, *Transportation Research Part E: Logistics and Transportation Review*, 45, 693–709.

Gillen, D.W., Oum, T.H. and Tretheway, M.W. (1986). *Airline Cost and Performance*, Vancouver, Centre for Transportation Studies, University of British Columbia.

Gitto, L. and Minervini, F. (2007). The performance of European full service airlines after liberalization: an econometric analysis, *Rivista di Politica Economica*, 97, 105–122.

Gonzalez-Savignat, M. (2004). Competition in air transport: the case of the high speed train, *Journal of Transport Economics and Policy*, 38(1), 77–108.

Gritta, R.D., Lippman, E. and Chow, G. (1994). The impact of the capitalization of leases on airline financial analysis: an issue revisited, *Logistics and Transportation Review*, 30(2), 189–202.

Hansen, M., Gillen, D. and Djafarian-Tehrani, R. (2001). Aviation infrastructure performance and airline cost: a statistical cost estimation approach, *Transportation Research Part E: Logistics and Transportation Review*, 37, 1–23.

Hazledine, T. (2006). Price discrimination in Cournot-Nash oligopoly, *Economics Letters*, 93, 413–420.

Hu, Q. and Zhang, A. (2015). Real option analysis of aircraft acquisition: a case study, *Journal of Air Transport Management*, 46, 19–29.

Hussain, R., Nasser, A.A. and Hussain, Y.K. (2015). Service quality and customer satisfaction of a UAE-based airline: an empirical investigation, *Journal of Air Transport Management*, 42, 167–175.

Jiang, C. and Zhang, A. (2016). Airline network choice and market coverage under high-speed rail competition, *Transportation Research Part A: Policy and Practice*, 92, 248–260.

Jiang, H. and Zhang, Y. (2016). An investigation of service quality, customer satisfaction and loyalty in China's airline market, *Journal of Air Transport Management*, 57, 80–88.

Jin, Y. and Jorion, P. (2004). Firm value and hedging: evidence from US oil and gas producers, *Journal of Finance*, 61(2), 893–917.

Kidokoro, Y., Lin, M.H. and Zhang, A. (2016). A general equilibrium analysis of airport pricing, capacity and regulation, *Journal of Urban Economics*, 96, 142–155.

Koopmans, C. and Lieshout, R. (2016). Airline cost changes: to what extent are they passed through to the passenger? *Journal of Air Transport Management*, 53, 1–11.

Lakew, P.A. (2014). Economies of traffic density and scale in the integrated air cargo industry: the cost structures of FedEx Express and UPS Airlines, *Journal of Air Transport Management*, 35, 29–38.

Lazarev, J. (2013). *The Welfare Effects of Intertemporal Price Discrimination: An Empirical Analysis of Airline Pricing in U.S. Monopoly Markets*, Mimeo, Graduate School of Business, Stanford University.

Li, M.Z.F., Zhang, A. and Zhang, Y. (2008). Airline seat allocation competition, *International Transactions in Operational Research*, 15, 439–459.

Li, Y., Wang, Y. and Cui, Q. (2015). Evaluating airline efficiency: an application of virtual frontier network SBM, *Transportation Research Part E: Logistics and Transportation Review*, 81, 1–17.

Lim, S.H. and Hong, Y. (2014). Fuel hedging and airline operating costs, *Journal of Air Transport Management*, 36, 33–40.

Lin, M.H. and Zhang, A. (2016). Hub congestion pricing: discriminatory passenger charges, *Economics of Transportation*, 5, 37–48.

Littlejohns, A. and McGairl, S. (eds) (1998). *Aircraft Financing*, 3rd edition, London, Euromoney Publications.

Littlewood, K. (1972). Forecasting and control of passenger bookings. In *AGIFORS Symposium Proceedings*, 12, 95–117.

Mackie, P.J., Wardman, M., Fowkes, A.S., Whelan, G., Nellthorp, J. and Bates, J. (2001). *Values of Travel Time Savings in the UK: A Report on the Evidence*, ITS Working Paper No. 567, Leeds, Institute of Transport Studies (ITS), University of Leeds.

Mallikarjun, S. (2015). Efficiency of US airlines: a strategic operating model, *Journal of Air Transport Management*, 43, 46–56.

Mantin, B. and Wang, J.-H.E. (2012). Determinants of profitability and recovery from system-wide shocks: the case of the airline industry, *Journal of Airline and Airport Management*, 2(1), 1–33.

Martin, J.C., Roman, C. and Espino, R. (2011). Evaluating frequent flyer programs from the air passengers' perspective, *Journal of Air Transport Management*, 17, 364–368.

McGill, J.I. and van Ryzin, G.J. (1999). Revenue management: research overview and prospects, *Transportation Science*, 33, 233–256.

Mercatus (2012). *The State of Airline Fuel Hedging and Risk Management in 2012*, Houston, TX, Mercatus Energy Advisors.

Miyoshi, C. and Merkert, R. (2010). Changes in carbon efficiency, unit cost of firms over time and the impacts of the fuel price: an empirical analysis of major European airlines. In *Proceedings of the 14th Air Transport Research Society (ATRS) World Conference*, Porto, ATRS.

Morrell, P.S. (2013). *Airline Finance*, 4th edition, Abingdon, Routledge.

Morrison, S.A. (1987). The equity and efficiency of runway pricing, *Journal of Public Economics*, 34, 45–60.

Morrison, S.A. and Winston, C. (1989). Enhancing the performance of the deregulated air transportation system, *Brookings Papers on Economic Activity: Microeconomics*, 61–112.

Namukasa, J. (2013). The influence of airline service quality on passenger satisfaction and loyalty, *The TQM Journal*, 25(5), 520–532.

Oum, T.H. and Yu, C. (2001). *Final Report: Assessment of Recent Performance of Canadian Carriers*, a report submitted to Canada Transportation Review Panel.

Oum, T.H. and Zhang, A. (2001). Global strategic alliances and the impacts on the Canadian airline industry, *Journal of Air Transport Management*, 7, 287–301.

Oum, T.H., Gillen, D.W. and Noble, S.E. (1986). Demands for fare classes and pricing and airline markets, *Logistics and Transportation Review*, 22, 195–222.

Oum, T.H., Zhang, A. and Zhang, Y. (1993). Inter-firm rivalry and firm-specific price elasticity in airline markets, *Journal of Transport Economics and Policy*, 27(2), 171–192.

Oum, T.H., Zhang, A. and Zhang, Y. (2000a). Socially optimal capacity and capital structure in oligopoly: the case of the airline industry, *Journal of Transport Economics and Policy*, 34, 55–68.

Oum, T.H., Zhang, A. and Zhang, Y. (2000b). Optimal demand for operating lease of aircraft, *Transportation Research Part B: Methodological*, 34, 17–29.

Oum, T.H., Zhang, A. and Zhang, Y. (2000c). Efficiency and social value of the aircraft leasing industry, *International Journal of Transport Economics*, 27, 131–145.

Pels, E., Nijkamp, P. and Rietveld, P. (2003). Inefficiencies and scale economies of European airport operations, *Transportation Research Part E: Logistics and Transportation Review*, 39, 341–361.

Rao, V.K. (1999). Fuel price risk management using futures, *Journal of Air Transport Management*, 5(1), 39–44.

Ryerson, M.S. and Hansen, M. (2013). Capturing the impact of fuel price on jet aircraft operating costs with Leontief technology and econometric models, *Transportation Research Part C: Emerging Technologies*, 33, 282–296.

Seelhorst, M. and Liu, Y. (2015). Latent air travel preferences: understanding the role of frequent flyer programs on itinerary choice, *Transportation Research Part A: Policy and Practice*, 80, 49–61.

Smith, B., Leimkuhler, J. and Darrow, R. (1992). Yield management at American Airlines, *Interfaces*, 22, 8–31.

Stavins, J. (2001). Price discrimination in the airline market: the effect of market concentration, *Review of Economics and Statistics*, 83, 200–202.

Sturm, R.R. (2009). Can selective hedging add value to airlines? The case of crude oil futures, *International Review of Applied Financial Issues and Economics*, 1, 130–146.

Swan, W. and Adler, N. (2006). Aircraft trip cost parameters: a function of stage length and seat capacity, *Transportation Research Part E: Logistics and Transportation Review*, 42, 105–115.

Tokic, D. (2012). When hedging fails: what every CEO should know about speculation, *The Journal of Management Development*, 31(8), 801–807.

Treanor, S., Rogers, D.A., Carter, D.A. and Simkins, B.J. (2014). Exposure, hedging, and value: new evidence from the U.S. airline industry, *International Review of Financial Analysis*, 34, 200–211.

Tretheway, M.W. and Oum, T.H. (1992). *Airline Economics: Foundations for Strategy and Policy*, Vancouver, Centre for Transportation Studies, University of British Columbia.

Tsikriktsis, N. (2007). The effect of operational performance and focus on profitability: a longitudinal study of the U.S. airline industry, *Manufacturing and Services Operations Management*, 9(4), 506–517.

Turner, S.P. and Lim, S.H. (2015). Hedging jet fuel price risk: the case of U.S. passenger airlines, *Journal of Air Transport Management*, 44/45, 54–64.

US DOT (US Department of Transportation) (1997). *The Value of Saving Travel Time: Departmental Guidance for Conducting Economic Evaluations*, Washington, DC, US DOT.

Vasigh, B., Fleming, K. and Tacker, T. (2013). *Introduction to Air Transport Economics: From Theory to Applications*, 2nd edition, Aldershot, Ashgate.

Vasigh, B., Fleming, K. and Humphreys, B. (2015). *Foundations of Airline Finance: Methodology and Practice*, 2nd edition, Abingdon, Routledge.

von Wartburg, M. and Waters II, W.G. (2004). Congestion externalities and the value of travel time savings. In: A. Zhang, A.E. Boardman, D. Gillen and W.G. Waters II (eds). *Towards Estimating the Social and Environmental Costs of Transportation in Canada*, Research Report prepared for Transport Canada.

Wang, S.W. (2014). Do global airline alliances influence the passenger's purchase decision? *Journal of Air Transport Management*, 37, 53–59.

White, L.J. (1979). Economies of scale and the question of 'natural monopoly' in the airline industry, *Journal of Air Law and Commerce*, 44, 545–573.

Wojahn, O.W. (2012). Why does the airline industry over-invest? *Journal of Air Transport Management*, 19, 1–8.

Xia, W. and Zhang, A. (2016). High-speed rail and air transport competition and cooperation: a vertical differentiation approach, *Transportation Research Part B: Methodological*, 94, 456–481.

Yang, H. and Zhang, A. (2012). Effects of high-speed rail and air transport competition on prices, profits and welfare, *Transportation Research Part B: Methodological*, 46(10), 1322–1333.

Zhang, A. (1998). Industrial reform and air transport development in China, *Journal of Air Transport Management*, 4, 155–164.

Zhang, A. and Chen, H. (2003). Evolution of China's air transport development and policy towards international liberalization, *Transportation Journal*, 42, 31–49.

Zhang, A. and Czerny, A.I. (2012). Airports and airlines economics and policy: an interpretive review of recent research, *Economics of Transportation*, 1, 15–34.

Zhang, A., Zhang, Y. and Clougherty, J.A. (2011). Competition and regulation in air transport. In: A. de Palma, R. Lindsey, E. Quinet and R. Vickerman (eds). *A Handbook of Transport Economics*, Northampton, MA, Edward Elgar.

Zhang, Y. (2012). Are Chinese passengers willing to pay more for better air services? *Journal of Air Transport Management*, 25, 5–7.

Zhang, Y. and Zhang, A. (2016). Determinants of air passenger flows in China and gravity model: deregulation, LCC and high-speed rail, *Journal of Transport Economics and Policy*, 50(3), 287–303.

Zhang, Y., Lin, F. and Zhang, A. (2018). Gravity models in air transport research: a survey and an application. In: B.A. Blonigen and W.W. Wilson (eds). *Handbook of International Trade and Transportation*, Cheltenham, Edward Elgar.

Zuidberg, J. (2014). Identifying airline cost economies: an econometric analysis of the factors affecting aircraft operating costs, *Journal of Air Transport Management*, 40, 86–95.

# 12

# Airport economics and finance

*Anne Graham*

## Introduction

In the early years of air transport development, the volume and range of research related to airport economics and finance was very limited, particularly in comparison to the airline industry (which is covered in Chapter 11). However, in the last two decades or so, there has been a very significant increase in this activity, which has resulted in a much better appreciation of important knowledge and the critical debates that exist in this area. Nevertheless, gaps still remain, with incomplete or contradictory understanding in some areas, particularly as the airport industry adapts to meet the rapidly changing demands of the air transport environment. Therefore, it is the aim of this chapter to provide a comprehensive assessment of current issues and challenges in airport economics and finance. Since the purpose is to provide the most up-to-date picture, only research since 2004 is referenced, with the assumption that any seminal studies that were undertaken before this date have been incorporated in this later research. Key avenues for future research are identified.

This chapter is divided into six key parts. The first section considers pricing and explores the airport–airline relationship. This leads on to consideration of economic regulation and aeronautical revenues. Attention is then given to non-aeronautical or commercial revenues, which is an increasingly important aspect of the airport business. An assessment of arguably the most popular area of research, namely efficiency and economic performance, then follows before conclusions are drawn.

## Airport pricing and the airport–airline relationship

Airport pricing has been a major area of debate and theoretical research. Much of the early research was associated with discussing the efficiency of pricing practices and their potential ability to cope with congestion problems, as air transport grew and airports became much more crowded. Basso and Zhang (2008) and Zhang and Czerny (2012) argued that this research could be grouped into two different approaches. First, there is the traditional approach, which assumes that demand for an airport is the function of the airport's own decision, based on the full price, which includes the airport charge and the congestion costs. With this, the airline market is not formally modelled and demand is simply assumed to exist, with airport charges and airline delay costs being fully passed on to passengers. Examples of this research include investigating the effects of regulation and the presense of concessions (or non-aeronautical) revenues (Czerny, 2006; Lu and Pagliari, 2004; Oum et al., 2004).

The alternative thinking, which is much more popular now, is the vertical structure approach, where airports are considered to constitute the upstream market, which sells an essential input for the airline output. It is the equilibrium of this airline downstream market, typically with the airlines possessing market power rather than being atomistic, that determines the airport's demand. Therefore, the demand for airport services is considered as a derived demand, and the nature of the equilibrium determines how the airport charges and airlines costs are passed on to consumers. Much of this original research is related to optimum pricing, market power effects and to whether airlines internalise their self-imposed congestion (Basso, 2008; Brueckner, 2005; Pels and Verhoef, 2004; Zhang and Zhang, 2006). However, since the evidence for self-internalisation was mixed, more recent attention has been given to gaining a greater understanding of passenger types and time valuations (Czerny and Zhang, 2011; Morrison and Winston, 2007). Overall, the arguments show that congestion pricing is difficult to implement, although an alternative may be slot solutions, such as slot auctions or slot trading (Basso and Zhang, 2010; Verhoef, 2010), but this is beyond the scope of this chapter, and is considered in Chapter 16.

It has been argued (D'Alfonso and Nastasi, 2014) that the adoption of this vertical structure approach raises certain issues related to airport–airline interaction that need to be considered, including viewing airports as two-sided (or multi-sided) platforms. The concept of a two-sided business, which is a relatively new phenomenon, has been applied to areas such as credit cards or newspapers, where the businesses provide platforms for two distinct customers who both gain from being networked through the platform. It can be reasoned that airports serve both passengers and airlines, and so the positive interdependence between these two markets means that airport operators will be incentivised to compete for airline traffic and passengers, as these will influence both their aeronautical and non-aeronautical revenue. If passengers stay away, this will affect the airlines that might have to leave the airport. If airlines reduce or withdraw their services, this will reduce passenger numbers, and consequently non-aeronautical sales.

While the application of this concept to airports has been accepted by some (Gillen and Mantin, 2014; Ivaldi et al., 2015; Thelle et al., 2012), others have rejected it (Fröhlich, 2010), although acknowledging that the effects of the airport, airline and passenger vertical relationship, and the role of non-aeronautical revenues, have similar effects. The main reason for this rejection is that the passenger's decision to buy an airline ticket already reflects their willingness to pay airport charges, and so this is not affected by what the airport does in the non-aeronautical area, which is the assumption with the two-sided platform. This issue has been of particular concern to the United Kingdom (UK) economic regulator, the Civil Aviation Authority (CAA), when it recently assessed the market power of the London airports. The airports' basic argument was that since airports are a two-sided business and non-aeronautical revenues are important, they have an incentive to increase passenger numbers to generate these, which reduces the incentives to raise airport charges to airlines, which in turn reduces the extent to which the airport may exploit any market power (Charles River Associates, 2013; Gatwick Airport Ltd, 2010). However, the CAA argued that the pricing of non-aeronautical services does not affect the overall demand of either passengers or airlines, and so instead adopted the conventional approach based on derived demand in a vertical relationship with complementary services (CAA, 2013).

Clearly, this is an area that would benefit from further research. Moreover, while the concept of the two-sided business is comparatively new, the ideas link to complementary issues concerning the two main types of revenues, which have been explored by others (Czerny, 2013; D'Alfonso et al., 2013; Morrison, 2009a; Zhang and Zhang, 2010). However, this has been largely theoretical, and further insight could be gained from more empirical studies, particularly in relation to whether non-aeronautical services can influence passenger volume.

## Economic regulation

Another issue, also concerned with the airport–airline relationship and airport complementarities, which has received considerable research attention over the years, is economic regulation. As discussed in Chapter 3, up until the 1980s, virtually all airports were owned and operated directly by state-owned entities. However, over the last three decades, airport privatisation has become a popular trend, and with this many governments have felt the need to introduce formal economic regulation, with the aim of preventing the abuse of market power and correcting market failure. The nature of such regulation has varied considerably, generating considerable debate concerning its effectiveness, and hence the accompanying research literature has blossomed.

Two of the main types of regulation are rate of return (ROR)/cost plus regulation or price-cap/incentive regulation (ACI, 2013). ROR/cost plus regulation basically permits an airport operator to earn enough revenue to cover its costs and make a profit and/or reasonable rate of return on the asset base. By contrast, price-cap regulation, which is the most widely used type of incentive regulation, aims to provide incentives to reduce costs and increase productivity while simultaneously controlling price increases. While the exact type of incentive regulation varies, it is by far the more popular of these two methods.

One key issue regarding economic regulation relates to the choice of till or cost allocation method. This links back to the complementarities between the aeronautical and non-aeronautical areas. There are two basic alternatives (but with hybrids existing), namely the single-till approach, when all airport activities are included, and the dual-till approach, when just the aeronautical aspects of the operation are taken into account. With the single-till concept, growth in non-aeronautical revenue can be used to offset increases in aeronautical charges. By contrast, the dual-till concept treats the aeronautical and non-aeronautical areas as separate financial entities, and focuses on the monopoly aeronautical airport services. It has been argued (Yarrow and Starkie, 2013) that if a vertical airport–airline relationship approach is accepted, then the use of the single-till approach is irrational, but this point has been refuted by others (Charles River Associates, 2013).

The UK has a single-till, but Starkie (2008a) argued in favour of the dual-till for congested airports, stating that this would have positive effects on the allocation of scarce slot capacity and on investment decisions. More generally, others (Czerny, 2006; Lu and Pagliari, 2004; Yang and Zhang, 2011; Zhang and Czerny, 2012) agreed that a dual-till approach is desirable when aeronautical capacity is fully utilised or already over-utilised, while the single-till approach is preferable where excess capacity exists. However, practice varies, with 44 per cent of world airports having a single-till, 26 per cent a dual-till and 30 per cent a hybrid-till (ACI, 2017).

It is important to note that in the United States (US), there is a different regulatory situation, where US airports negotiate legally binding contracts with airlines and finance large investment projects with revenue bonds (Faulhaber et al., 2010). Fuhr and Beckers (2009) argued that this results in comparative efficient investments and a check on cost-inefficiency. Moreover, rather than having a single- or dual-till, US airports have a different cost allocation process, with either a residual or compensatory approach (or a hybrid approach). The residual methodology guarantees that the airlines will pay the net costs of running the airport after taking into account the commercial and other non-airline sources of revenue. Therefore, this is a somewhat extreme version of the single-till, where virtually all risks of running the airport are transferred to the airlines and other aeronautical users. By contrast with the compensatory system, the risks of running the airport are primarily left to the airport operator, with the airlines just paying agreed charges based on recovery of the costs related to the facilities and services that they have used. Compensatory airports have been found to be most financially efficient, while residual airports delivered higher levels of commercial performance (Richardson et al., 2014), although research in this area is relatively scarce.

As more and more airports have been subject to some type of economic regulation, this has enabled more comparative research to be undertaken, and it remains a topic of hot debate from many different perspectives (ACI, 2013; Biggar, 2012; Charlton, 2009; Forsyth et al., 2004; Marques and Brochado, 2008; Niemeier, 2009; Oxera, 2013). However, a number of areas remain relatively under-researched, including the role of pre-financing, which is a particular issue, for example for the London airports (CAA, 2015; Humphreys, 2015). This is largely because there is no guarantee that the airlines paying the charges will actually be the airlines that will benefit from the new infrastructure, and there may be no certainty that the airport charges will be efficiently spent to provide new facilities. The counterarguments used by airports is that pre-financing in certain circumstances can provide a useful, cheaper source for funding investment in addition to loans and equity, which can also be used as security for raising extra finance, and that it avoids large increases in charges when the new infrastructure comes on stream.

Another key uncertainty relates to the measurement of market power. While this has been frequently discussed in theory, there has been very limited developed application using empirical evidence – two notable exceptions being Bilotkach and Mueller (2012), who considered the market power of Amsterdam, and Polk and Bilotkach (2013), who assessed the market power of hub airports. Moreover, there is no consensus of view concerning an appropriate detailed methodology for measuring this, which led Maertens (2012) to develop a common approach that he used on a wide range of European airports. Even in countries where more detailed market power analysis has been undertaken, such as in the UK, considerable areas of disagreement remain.

Economic regulation of airports can have an effect on both airport efficiency and financial performance, through its impact on prices, cost and profits and its incentives or disincentives to invest. One of the first comparative assessments of this with a sample of global airports was undertaken by Oum et al. (2004), who concluded that dual-till price-cap regulation improves economic efficiency for large, busy airports compared to the single-till approach. Adler and Liebert (2014) looked at the efficiency of European and Australian airports and observed that dual-till price-cap appeared to be the most appropriate form in weakly competitive markets, whereas for relatively competitive markets, regulation appeared to be unnecessary to encourage cost-efficiency. Meanwhile, Bel and Fageda (2010) analysed airport charges at European airports and found no statistical difference between the regulation mechanism and the level of airport charges. Later research by these authors found that large airports, with substantial market power, tend to be subject to highly prescriptive regulation, and airports that have nearby competing airports tend to be subject to less prescriptive regulation (Bel and Fageda, 2013). Bilotkach et al. (2012) concluded that single-till regulation and more light-handed regulation both tended to produce lower charges. Arguably in the most comprehensive worldwide assessment of incentive regulation, Adler et al. (2015) suggested that this regulation type does encourage productive efficiency and is superior to cost plus in efficiency terms. Overall, the comparative research of the last few years has been a welcome addition to the earlier research, which tended to focus on particular country experience, as in the UK and Australia. However, the findings are somewhat incomplete and inconsistent. One reason is the methodological and data difficulties associated with assessing economic performance, which is discussed later.

Both ROR and price-cap regulation are generally defined as heavy-handed regulation because of the intrusive nature of the information-gathering process and the rigidity in the regulation requirements. An alternative is a more light-handed approach, often called reserve regulation or price monitoring, which has been adopted, for example, in Australia. The general principle is that the market power abuse of the airport is constrained by the threat of regulation, rather than actual regulation. Hence, this threat is used to provide an effective safeguard against anticompetitive practices and discipline the airport's behaviour. In recent years, primarily because of the increasingly competitive environment, the arguments for a more light-handed approach, or even total deregulation relying on competition law, has been given increased attention, particularly from an airport viewpoint (ACI Europe, 2014; Thelle et al., 2012). This approach has been supported by, among others, Arblaster (2014), Littlechild (2012a, 2012b) and Niemeier (2009). Bush and Starkie (2014) argued that more attention needs to be paid to the risks of economic regulation hampering the growth of competition and the development of commercial relationships between airports and airlines. Moreover, Yang and Fu (2015) modelled price-cap and light-handed approaches, and found that the light-handed approach may lead to higher welfare. However, the airlines collectively are understandably more cautious and have expressed different views (IATA, 2013). Nevertheless, with airport competitive pressures seemingly set to continue, this is not a development that is going away.

## Aeronautical revenues

One very notable consequence of the more competitive airport environment, and the changing airport–airline relationship, has been more negotiation of airports charges and the offering of incentives, which has resulted in the published standard charges becoming less relevant. This may be as the result of of the airport operator entering into a long-term contract with the airlines, perhaps because of light-handed regulation, or as a marketing initiative to encourage traffic development (see Chapter 14). Indeed, in Europe, in 2014, 84 per cent of airports offered some form of charges discount, either via formal incentive schemes or commercial contracts (ACI Europe, 2015). While information about negotiated charges can be limited because of commercial sensitivities, some research, at least in the case of European airports, has recently been undertaken (Fichert and Klophaus, 2011; Jones et al., 2013; Malina et al., 2012), but there is a significant gap of knowledge related to the exact impact of these on traffic development.

More generally, while there is now a rich collection of research related to the factors that enhance airport performance and efficiency, the empirical research (other than related to economic regulation) into what drives aeronautical revenues is much more scarce. In the US, it was observed that unit aeronautical revenues (aeronautical revenue per flight) declined with the amount of traffic and were lower at airports facing competition from neighbouring airports, but increased with airline concentration (Van Dender, 2007). Choo (2014) also found that large hub airports had higher aeronautical charges than other airports. Meanwhile, in Europe, Bel and Fageda (2010) concluded that the charges were higher at larger airports and lower when there are competing nearby airports. In addition, they found a negative relationship with airline concentration, suggesting that in this case the airlines had stronger countervailing market power. Bilotkach et al. (2012) also observed a positive relationship with traffic and hubs, but no nearby airport effect. Clearly, these contradictions need further investigation. The higher charges at large airports are particularly interesting given the possibility of economies of scale (discussed later), and suggests that there are indeed other important drivers that need consideration here.

There is certainly little empirical research related to the impact on airlines and passengers of changes in airport charges. If the total charge were to be passed through to passengers, the effect could be assessed with passenger fare/price elasticities. This is a complex, well-researched area in its own right, which is beyond the scope of this chapter, although in general terms these elasticities are in the region of $-1.2$ to $-1.5$ at the route or market level, and $-0.8$ at a national level (InterVISTAS, 2007) (see Chapter 19). Subsequently, it is often argued that as airport charges represent a fairly low share of total airlines costs or the passenger fare (typically around 14 per cent, including navigation charges) (IATA, 2013), the overall impact must be fairly small and inelastic. Even if some degree of airport substitution is taken into account, as with a recent analysis of the London Stansted case (assuming that airport charges make up 10 per cent of the fare), the produced estimates of final inelastic airport charges' elasticities were in the region of $-0.2$ and $-0.6$ (CAA, 2013).

However, in practice, consideration should be given to the airport and airline market, and the extent to which the airlines can pass on the charges in a competitive situation, or whether they choose to absorb at least some of the charges, with a supply-side response to adjust capacity by making changes to routes and schedules. Research in this area is scarce, but SEO Economic Research (2014) argued in a congested situation, such as with the London airports, on balance, airlines are unlikely to increase air fares, and instead any charge increase will lead to a fall in airline scarcity rents and margins. However, views about this vary (RBB Economics, 2013; SLG Economics, 2012). Burghouwt and de Wit (2015) argued that even with no pass-through of charges, the detrimental impact on the airlines' network because of supply-side responses may have a negative impact on passenger numbers. Thus, Starkie (2013) and Starkie and Yarrow (2013) contended that if the charges are passed through (resulting in lower load factors) or not, airlines will see their profit margins reduced, but because any supply response will involve lumpy rather than gradual reductions in airline capacity, this will potentially have considerable impacts on the passengers. They concluded that even if price-inelastic demand exists, a small increase in aeronautical charges can lead to a significant reduction in passengers. This suggests that it is not sufficient to focus just on the narrow view of price elasticity, but more empirical research to confirm this is clearly necessary.

## Non-aeronautical revenues

Non-aeronautical or commercial revenues have already been briefly discussed in relation to the complementarities of airport revenues. As a topic in its own right, traditionally this has been an area that has received less research, partly because of the commercially sensitive nature and poor quality of much of the data, but also because other economic areas, such as pricing, regulation and efficiency, have tended to be of broader interest to more stakeholders, such as governments and regulators, for policymaking decisions. However, the growing importance of these commercial revenues in recent years has meant that increasing attention has now been paid to them, particularly by applying other disciplines, such as marketing, service quality and behavioural/motivational theory, to gain more insights and understanding.

Some of the research has investigated the key factors driving these revenues. A key finding is that unit commercial revenues (usually commercial revenues per passenger) increase with traffic levels. Intuitively, this is as expected because generally larger airports will be able to provide a greater range of commercial facilities and services, and typically will have a higher proportion of international passengers, with a longer dwell time, and so will spend more on commercial facilities, especially on duty- and tax-free goods. Recent attention has also been given to comparing the impact of low cost carrier (LCC) and full service carrier passengers. Graham and Dennis

(2007) contended that LCC passengers are not necessarily budget spenders on commercial facilities, but while Gillen and Lall (2004) found that LCC passengers favourably contributed to non-aeronautical revenues, Castillo-Manzano (2010) observed the opposite. Lei et al. (2010) also observed lower non-aeronautical spend for LCC passengers.

Other passenger characteristics are influential. For example, Fuerst et al. (2011) found a negative influence of business travellers on unit commercial revenues, and likewise Castillo-Manzano (2010) observed a positive effect with passengers on vacation. This can be explained by business travellers having less desire to make purchases and a shorter dwell time. Castillo-Manzano (2010) also observed that age and frequency of flying had a significant impact, whereas gender did not, but by contrast Geuens et al. (2004) found that gender had an influence, but not travel frequency or purpose. At a more detailed level, Perng et al. (2010) found that male passengers were more likely to be attracted to brand name products, while passengers under 26 were more likely to shop in souvenir shops and cafes. These latter two studies are part of a growing research set considering passenger motivations, preferences and behaviours, with more recent research including Chung (2015), Chung et al. (2013) and Lin and Chen (2013). Lin and Chen (2013) concluded, among others, that impulse buying is important for airport shopping. Freathy and O'Connell (2012) allocated passengers with varying behaviour into different segments and discussed how this could be used in developing the airport's commercial revenues.

Two other intuitive factors that have proved important to commercial revenue generation are location/space and time. For example, Hsu and Chao (2005) created a space allocation model and showed that more revenue can be generated by placing certain facilities in more accessible positions. As regards time, Lin and Chen (2013) found that time pressures negatively influenced commercial spend, while Torres et al. (2005) confirmed that the more time spent in the airport, the greater consumption by passengers. Geuens et al. (2004) and Castillo-Manzana (2010) also found a positive influence of dwell time on passenger spending. Furthermore, in modelling airport congestion pricing, D'Alfonso et al. (2013) assumed that as congestion increases, dwell time increases, and so the money spent on commercial activities increases. Hence, they assumed there is a positive externality of congestion on commercial activities, and concluded that the airport could have an incentive to reduce its congestion charging to increase the passenger dwell and encourage spending. However, with empirical research, Fuerst et al. (2011) investigated whether there was a possible link between passengers on delayed flights (using the percentage of delayed flights) and commercial revenues, but found no significant relationship. In the US, Appold and Kasarda (2006) found that commercial sales per passenger actually decreased with passenger traffic, which they suggested showed that congestion actually discouraged sales.

Overall, the whole area of dwell time, congestion and commercial revenues is in need of more research. For example, there is little evidence as to whether congestion actually increases dwell time, as passengers may merely spend longer in queues related to the essential processes at the airport, such as check-in, security and border control. Moreover, these processes have changed dramatically in recent years, on the one hand because of technology and self-service developments, which may have a positive impact on dwell time, but on the other because of more stringent security measures, which may have a negative effect. It is not clear whether the impact of these developments overall is positive or negative, or in fact neutral, as passengers adjust their time at airports to take these into account.

More generally, one of the shortcomings with much of the non-aeronautical or commercial research is that it tends to involve single airport or country studies, often based on small sample sizes, which makes it difficult to generalise the results. A few notable exceptions include Fuerst et al. (2011), which included 19 countries in Europe, and LeighFisher (2011), which, although focusing in detail on US terminal commercial facilities, also researched the airports of Amsterdam, Copenhagen and Seoul. Moreover, the last few years have been a challenging time for airports as many have reached a mature stage in exploiting many of the commercial opportunities that exist, and as a result growing revenues has become that much more difficult, particularly with the increase in off-airport competition, especially from the Internet. In addition, the last decade has seen the global economic recession and much more stringent security controls, which have had an impact on passengers' ability, motivation and confidence to spend. While the impacts of this have been debated by some (Graham, 2009; Martel, 2009; Sevcik 2014), more detailed analysis needs to be undertaken to gain insight into future commercial revenue generation at this more mature stage in the evolution of the airport business.

## Efficiency and economic performance

Looking now at overall economic and financial performance, industry figures generally show that the airport industry achieves relatively high profit margins, for example in 2014 a 26 per cent operating margin (Airline Business, 2015) and 16 per cent net margin (ACI, 2016). This measure of profitability, though, fails to measure the effectiveness of using capital to generate profits, as the comparative return on invested capital (ROIC) in this year was just 6 per cent. If the ROIC exceeds the weighted average cost of capital (WACC), then this can be seen as a true economic profit. The evidence suggests that airports are in fact barely covering their WACC or falling slightly short of this (IATA, 2013; Tretheway and Markhvida, 2013).

However, profit alone cannot provide a robust and thorough indication of true economic performance, and for this reason the most popular area of airport economics empirical research has been concerned with efficiency and economic performance. Much of this has focused on one country, particularly in Europe or the US, but as the data sets have improved, whole region research has been undertaken, with examples including Europe (Marques and Barros, 2010), Asia-Pacific (Lam et al., 2009), North America (Zhao et al., 2014), South America (Perelman and Serebrisky, 2012) and Africa (Barros, 2011). Some research has considered a mixture of airports from different regions, such as Europe and Australia (Adler and Liebert, 2014), the US and Europe (Vasigh and Gorjidooz, 2006) and the UK, US and Latin America (Vasigh et al., 2014), while a growing area of research, particularly using the global database of the Air Transport Research Society (ATRS), have included airports from all regions of the world. Some of this research chose to investigate regional differences, with mixed findings. Vasigh and Gorjidooz (2006) found that US airports outperformed European airports, but by contrast Oum et al. (2006) observed that, compared to North American airports, operating in Asia and Europe had a negative impact on efficiency, while operating in Australia and New Zealand had a positive impact. Perelman and Serebrisky (2012) observed that Latin American airports were more efficient than European airports but were less efficient than Asian and North American airports. Industry reports (ACI, 2016) have shown much higher unit costs for the European region.

One of the key issues with airport costs is whether economies of scale exist, that is whether there are reductions in unit costs as the output increases. Early rare research in the 1970s of UK airports indicated that this was the case for airports handling around 3 million passengers until these scale economies were exhausted. By contrast, Bottasso and Conti (2012) estimated that long-run average costs decreased for UK airports handling up to 5 million passengers, were constant for 5 to 14 million passengers, and then started to increase. Meanwhile, Martin and Voltes-Dorta found that cost economies were not exhausted at any level of traffic for their sample airports in both their research of Spanish (Martin and Voltes-Dorta, 2011) and worldwide airports (Martin and Voltes-Dorta, 2010). Research here, and also in the related area of returns to scale, which investigates the relationship between input and output quantities, has blossomed in recent years. Many country studies have found increasing returns to scale (IRS), for instance Wanke (2012) in Brazil, Yoshida (2004) in Japan and Tsekeris (2011) in Greece. For the UK case, Assaf (2010) identified small UK airports operating under IRS, with the larger UK ones being mainly scale-efficient or operating under decreasing returns to scale (DRS).

From a cost viewpoint, a key reason for why there may be economies of scale, which is a long-term concept, is because airports tend to have a relatively high share of fixed costs that are associated with the provision of infrastructure (such as the runway and terminal) and certain services (such as safety, security and energy), which will be incurred relatively independent of the traffic levels. Likewise, it can be hypothesised that diseconomies of scale may well exist because of a number of disadvantageous factors for larger airports, such as the need to efficiently coordinate or duplicate services and facilities, particularly when multiple terminals are involved, the scarcity of cheap land and labour (due to higher unionisation and local shortages), greater costs associated with mitigating the environmental impacts, and difficulties associated with ensuring that there is adequate surface access to/from the airport (Kamp et al., 2007).

When just operating costs or inputs are being considered, and if there are economies when traffic increases, this can instead be seen as economies of capacity utilisation or density. For the North American case, both Lin et al. (2013) and McCarthy (2014) found evidence of such short-run economies, with McCarthy calculating a 0.27 per cent cost elasticity related to departure demand (i.e. a 10 per cent increase in departures will push costs up by 2.7 per cent). For the UK, a broad figure in the region of 0.3 to 0.5 for operating cost elasticities related to passenger demand has been estimated (Steer Davies Gleave, 2012). Similarly, in forecasts of operating costs for Dublin Airport, various different operating cost elasticities have been applied, ranging from 0.1 for energy costs to 0.3 for security staff costs and 0.7 for retail staff costs (Steer Davies Gleave, 2014). Interestingly, for the UK case, there was some additional evidence of greater cost elasticity responsiveness if the traffic is declining, but this is in conflict with more detailed and broader research of 194 worldwide airports between 2007 and 2009, which showed that overall operating costs actually grew more proportionally, suggesting that the airports had major problems with cost flexibility and control (Martin et al., 2013; Voltes-Dorta and Pagliari, 2012). In part at least, this was presumably due to a high fixed proportion of costs and a stepwise, rather than gradual, nature.

Relating possible cost economies to profit levels, it is interesting that while healthy profit margins tend to be generated at larger airports, the evidence shows that generally smaller airports experience a less favourable financial situation. Indeed, in Europe, the European Commission's (EC) view is that airports under 1 million passengers find it hard to cover all of their operating costs, let alone their capital costs. At a size of 3 to 5 million, they should be able to cover all their costs to a large extent, whereas beyond 5 million they should be profitable (EC, 2014). However, this idea has been challenged, for instance by Starkie (2008b), who argued that, for example in the UK, there is evidence that in certain market conditions, even small airports can make reasonable profits.

Other possible traffic characteristics affecting economic performance include the airport's role. Oum and Yu (2004) observed that a hub role lowered performance of an airport, whereas Assaf (2011), Barros and Dieke (2008), Fung et al. (2008), Lin and Hong (2006) and Perelman and Serebrisky (2012) observed that hub airports had better performance. Other significant relationships identified from analysis of the ATRS global database include a negative link with international traffic and positive link with cargo traffic and capacity-constrained airports (Oum and Yu, 2004).

A popular area of research has investigated the impact of ownership, governance and economic regulation. However, again, the findings are mixed and somewhat inconclusive. Vogel (2006) found that partially and fully privatised European airports operated more efficiently than public ones, and both Chi-Lok and Zhang (2009) and Fung et al. (2008) agreed that airports that had been publicly listed in China were more efficient than non-listed ones. Curi et al. (2010) and Scotti et al. (2012) found public airports in Italy to be more efficient, which contradicts the findings of Barros and Dieke (2008). Globally, Marques et al. (2015) observed that privatisation had a positive effect on efficiency. Oum et al. (2006) concluded that airports with government majority ownership were significantly less efficient than airports with a private majority ownership, and Oum et al. (2008) observed that there was a high probability that airports owned/operated by a majority private firm achieved higher efficiency than those owned/operated by a mixed enterprise with government majority ownership. However, others, including Lin and Hong (2006), Vasigh and Gorjidooz (2006) and Barros (2009), found no significant connection with performance and ownership. In the US, where no significant privatisation has taken place, Craig et al. (2012) instead analysed two types of public ownership, namely airport authorities and city-owned, and found that the airport authority airports were more efficient, which was consistent with the findings of Kutlu and McCarthy (2016) and Zhao et al. (2014), although in the latter case this effect was small.

Vasigh et al. (2014) also looked at ownership structures in the US, as well as in the UK and several Latin American countries, but the results were rather ambivalent, which led to a suggestion that the performance would be better evaluated in terms of market structure and competition. Indeed, others have recently argued that the impact of ownership cannot be separated from the impact of economic regulation or competition. This led Assaf and Gillen (2012) to conclude from a global empirical study that the best performers were fully private airports with price monitoring. Similarly, Adler and Liebert (2014) analysed European and Australian airports in this manner and concluded that in non-competitive conditions, public airports operated less cost-efficiently than fully private airports, but under potential regional or hub competition, economic regulation inhibited airports of any ownership from operating and pricing efficiently.

Other related research has also attempted to assess the influence of management strategy, for example by considering the degree of outsourcing or commercial activity diversification. Tovar and Rendeiro (2009) found that both these factors had a positive impact on the efficiency of Spanish airports, whereas Abrate and Erbetta (2010), when studying Italian airports, noted similar observations about outsourcing but were inconclusive about commercial diversification. Other global research has found that developing commercial activities had a positive impact (Oum and Yu, 2004) and that a high level of outsourcing reduces cost flexibility (Martin et al., 2013). This contradictory and limited evidence again suggests that this is another area to explore.

Some other potential influential factors seem relatively under-researched. One area relates to undesirable outputs, such as delays and aircraft noise, as ignoring these may mean that efficiency comparisons may be biased against the airports that have strictly controlled these. Pathomsiri et al. (2008) considered aircraft delays and Yu et al. (2008) looked at noise. Another important factor is service quality because of the trade-off with cost levels and the influence on commercial revenue generation (Merkert and Assaf, 2015). Here, there are major data problems, because although information may exist on an airport or country basis, there are no comprehensive and reliable data sets available in the public domain to enable international comparisons to be made.

Finally, some consideration must be given to the methodological issues. Traditionally, performance was just analysed with partial or one-dimensional measures or performance ratios/indicators, but, while having many useful applications, these cannot show how efficiently airports combine all their inputs to produce a combination of outputs. As a result, in the last two decades or so, there has been considerable interest in using economic techniques to produce a single multidimensional performance or efficiency measure. Generally, three key methods have been used, namely total factor productivity (TFP), which is an average index number approach;

the most popular data envelopment analysis (DEA) method, which relates a weighted input index to a weighted output index using a linear programming technique; and a production or cost function (historically estimated by using regression analysis, but more commonly now with an efficient frontier by using the stochastic frontier method). Considerable progress over the years has been made with these methods to make them more effective tools, but no one overarching optimal method has emerged, leaving open to debate their relative reliability and robustness. Interestingly, Lin et al. (2013) used all three methods in their analysis of 62 North American airports, and while they produced similar rankings in the top 15 and bottom ranked airports, considerable differences existed for airports in the middle range.

However, the choice of appropriate methods is not the only challenge in researching airport efficiency and research (ACI, 2012; Adler et al., 2013; Bezerra and Gomes, 2016; Graham, 2005; Hazel et al., 2011; Liebert and Niemeier, 2013; Merkert et al., 2012). Major impediments remain related to other comparability issues (e.g. degree of outsourcing, use of different accounting policies, different investment cycles) and data limitations, especially inconsistent or incomplete data sets. The measurement of capital costs or the capital input is a particular problem. For multi-airport studies, given the heterogeneous nature of the airport market, there is the challenge of selecting the most appropriate comparators (Vogel and Graham, 2013). As a result, there has been considerable debate as to what is the best way forward with this research (Adler et al., 2009; Morrison, 2009b). In a more recent assessment, Liebert and Niemeier (2013) argued that while data availability remains a methodological difficulty for airport performance research, the heterogeneous nature of airports is now more effectively taken into account with such research. Nevertheless, significant challenges within the area of airport efficiency and performance research still remain.

## Conclusion

This chapter has considered current knowledge and critical debate related to airport pricing and the airport–airline relationship, aeronautical and non-aeronautical revenues, and efficiency and performance measurement. With a chapter this length, it is impossible to give justice to all the important issues, and so a few key topic areas have not been given the attention they deserve. This particularly relates to airport investment, valuation and sources of finance, and so for these areas it is recommended that Graham and Morrell (2016) and Jorge-Calderon (2014) are consulted.

Overall, knowledge of airport economics and finance is considerably greater than it was 10 or 20 years ago. However, for some areas, there is still a lack of empirical evidence to support theories that have been developed, and there is a shortage of studies, as with much air transport research, concerning less developed areas such as Africa and South America. Moreover, much of the research is focused on individual airports or countries, often with small samples, and while these can provide significant insight into the specific case in question, it is difficult to generalise many of the interesting findings that have been made. This is often the result of data limitations and comparability issues, which is generally more of a problem in the airport than airline industry, and although improvements have been made, further inroads are needed.

Key themes identified in this chapter relate to whether airports should be considered as two-sided businesses, or rather whether a vertical relationship exists with airports, airlines and passengers, and complementary between the aeronautical and non-aeronautical aspects. This links with economic regulation, where significant debate still exists as to what is the most effective regulatory model, if any, especially in light of more competitive pressures within the industry. Within the aeronautical area, there remain unanswered questions relating to the actual impact of different levels of charges, and passenger and airline responses to these. Gaps still exist in the knowledge of commercial revenues, particularly concerning the relationship of changing dwell time on revenue generation and the drivers of the more mature and challenging commercial environment that faces airport operators today. The final theme, efficiency and performance, has been explored extensively, particularly regarding areas related to scale economies and ownership/governance, but no overriding conclusions can really be drawn.

# References

Abrate, G. and Erbetta, F. (2010). Efficiency and patterns of service mix in airport companies: an input distance function approach, *Transportation Research Part E: Logistics and Transportation Review*, 46(5), 693–708.

ACI (Airports Council International) (2012). *Guide to Airport Performance Measures*, Montreal, ACI.

ACI (Airports Council International) (2013). *ACI Guide to Airport Economic Regulation*, Montreal, ACI.

ACI (Airports Council International) (2016). *Airport Economics Survey*, Montreal, ACI.

ACI (Airports Council International) (2017). *Airport Ownership, Economic Regulation and Financial Performance*, Montreal, ACI.

ACI Europe (Airports Council International Europe) (2014). *Competition in the European Aviation Sector*, Brussels, ACI Europe.

ACI Europe (Airports Council International Europe) (2015). *Airport Charges Survey 2014*, Brussels, ACI Europe.

Adler, N. and Liebert, V. (2014). Joint impact of competition, ownership form and economic regulation on airport performance and pricing, *Transportation Research Part A: Policy and Practice*, 64, 92–109.

Adler, N., Oum, T. and Yu, C. (2009). A response to 'Understanding the complexities and challenges of airport performance benchmarking'. *Journal of Airport Management*, 3(2), 159–163.

Adler, N., Liebert, V. and Yazhemsky, E. (2013). Benchmarking airports from a managerial perspective, *Omega*, 41(2), 442–458.

Adler, N., Forsyth, P., Mueller, J. and Niemeier, H.-M. (2015). An economic assessment of airport incentive regulation, *Transport Policy*, 41, 5–15.

Airline Business (2015). Airport group financials, *Airline Business*, November, 40–41.

Appold, S. and Kasarda, J. (2006). The appropriate scale of US airport retail activities, *Journal of Air Transport Management*, 12(6), 277–287.

Arblaster, M. (2014). The design of light-handed regulation of airports: lessons from experience in Australia and New Zealand, *Journal of Air Transport Management*, 38, 27–35.

Assaf, A. (2010). Bootstrapped scale efficiency measures of UK airports, *Journal of Air Transport Management*, 16(1), 42–44.

Assaf, A. (2011). Accounting for technological differences in modelling the performance of airports: a Bayesian approach, *Applied Economics*, 43(18), 2267–2275.

Assaf, A. and Gillen, D. (2012). Measuring the joint impact of governance form and economic regulation on airport efficiency, *European Journal of Operational Research*, 220(1), 187–198.

Barros, C. (2009). The measurement of efficiency of UK airports, using a stochastic latent class frontier model, *Transport Reviews*, 29(4), 479–498.

Barros, C. (2011). Cost efficiency of African airports using a finite mixture model, *Transport Policy*, 18(6), 807–813.

Barros, C. and Dieke, P. (2008). Measuring the economic efficiency of airports: a Simar–Wilson methodology analysis, *Transportation Research Part E: Logistics and Transportation Review*, 44, 1039–1051.

Basso, L. (2008). Airport deregulation: effects on pricing and capacity, *International Journal of Industrial Organization*, 26, 1015–1031.

Basso, L. and Zhang, A. (2008). On the relationship between airport pricing models, *Transportation Research Part B: Methodological*, 42(9), 725–735.

Basso, L. and Zhang, A. (2010). Pricing vs. slot policies when airport profits matter, *Transportation Research Part B: Methodological*, 44, 381–391.

Bel, G. and Fageda, X. (2010). Privatization, regulation, and airport pricing: an empirical analysis for Europe, *Journal of Regulatory Economics*, 37, 142–161.

Bel, G. and Fageda, X. (2013). Market power, competition and post-privatization regulation: evidence from changes in regulation of European airports, *Journal of Economic Policy Reform*, 16(2), 123–141.

Bezerra, G. and Gomes, C. (2016). Performance measurement in airport settings: a systematic literature review, *Benchmarking: An International Journal*, 23(4), 1027–1050.

Biggar, D. (2012). Why regulate airports? A re-examination of the rationale for airport regulation, *Journal of Transport Economics and Policy*, 46, 367–380.

Bilotkach, V. and Mueller, J. (2012). Supply side substitutability and potential market power of airports: case of Amsterdam Schiphol, *Utilities Policy*, 23, 5–12.

Bilotkach, V., Clougherty, J., Mueller, J. and Zhang, A. (2012). Regulation, privatization and airport charges: panel data evidence from European airports, *Economics of Transportation*, 42(1), 73–94.

Bottasso, A. and Conti, M. (2012). The cost structure of the UK airport industry, *Journal of Transport Economics and Policy*, 46(3), 313–332.

Brueckner, J. (2005). Internalization of airport congestion: a network analysis, *International Journal of Industrial Organization*, 23(7–8), 599–614.

Burghouwt, G. and de Wit, W. (2015). *Scarcity Rents and Airport Charges*, Report for the Airports Commission, Amsterdam, SEO Economic Research.

Bush, H. and Starkie, D. (2014). Competitive drivers towards improved airport/airline relationships, *Journal of Air Transport Management*, 41, 45–49.

CAA (Civil Aviation Authority) (2013). *Market Power Determination for Passenger Airlines in Relation to Stansted Airport: Statement of Reasons*, CAP 1135, London, CAA.

CAA (Civil Aviation Authority) (2015). *Economic Regulation at New Runway Capacity*, CAP 1279, London, CAA.

Castillo-Manzano, J. (2010). Determinants of commercial revenues at airports: lessons learned from Spanish regional airports, *Tourism Management*, 31(6), 788–796.

Charles River Associates (2013). *Two-Sides Market Analysis in the Context of the CAA's Airport Market Power Assessments*, Report to the CAA, London, Charles River Associates.

Charlton, A. (2009). Airport regulation: does a mature industry have mature regulation? *Journal of Air Transport Management*, 15(3), 116–120.

Chi-Lok, A. and Zhang, A. (2009). Effects of competition and policy changes on Chinese airport productivity: an empirical investigation, *Journal of Air Transport Management*, 15(4), 166–174.

Choo, Y. (2014). Factors affecting aeronautical charges at major US airports, *Transportation Research Part A: Policy and Practice*, 62, 54–62.

Chung, Y.-S. (2015). Hedonic and utilitarian shopping values in airport shopping behaviour, *Journal of Air Transport Management*, 49, 28–34.

Chung, Y.-S., Wu, C.-L. and Chiang, W.-E. (2013). Air passengers' shopping motivation and information seeking behaviour, *Journal of Air Transport Management*, 27, 25–28.

Craig, S., Airola, J. and Tipu, M. (2012). General purpose of special district governance? Technical efficiency vs. rent dissipation in airport finances, *Public Finance Revenues*, 40, 712–735.

Curi, C., Gitto, S. and Mancuso, P. (2010). The Italian airport industry in transition: a performance analysis, *Journal of Air Transport Management*, 16, 218–221.

Czerny, A. (2006). Price-cap regulation of airports: single-till versus dual-till, *Journal of Regulatory Economics*, 30(1), 85–97.

Czerny, A. (2013). Public versus private airport behavior when concession revenues exist, *Economics of Transportation*, 2, 38–46.

Czerny, A. and Zhang, A. (2011). Airport congestion pricing and passenger types, *Transportation Research Part B: Methodological*, 45, 595–604.

D'Alfonso, T. and Nastasi, A. (2014). Airport–airline interaction: some food for thought, *Transport Reviews*, 34(6), 730–748.

D'Alfonso, T., Jiang, C. and Wan, Y. (2013). Airport pricing, concession revenues and passenger types, *Journal of Transport Economics and Policy*, 47, 71–89.

EC (European Commission) (2014). *Communication from the Commission: Guidelines on State Aid to Airports and Airlines*, Official Journal C99, 4 April.

Faulhaber J., Schulthess, J., Eastmond, A., Lewis, S. and Block, R. (2010). *Airport/Airline Agreements: Practices and Characteristics*, ACRP Report 36, Washington, DC, Transportation Research Board.

Fichert, F. and Klophaus, R. (2011). Incentive schemes on airport charges: theoretical analysis and empirical evidence from German airports, *Research in Transportation Business & Management*, 1(1), 71–79.

Anne Graham

Forsyth, P., Gillen, D., Knorr, A., Mayer, O., Niemeier, H. and Starkie D. (eds) (2004). *The Economic Regulation of Airports*, Farnham, Ashgate.

Freathy, P. and O'Connell, F. (2012). Spending time, spending money: passenger segmentation in an international airport, *The International Review of Retail, Distribution and Consumer Research*, 22(4), 397–416.

Fröhlich, K. (2010). *Airports as Two-Sided Markets? A Critical Contribution*, Bremen, Bremen University of Applied Sciences.

Fuerst, F., Gross, S. and Klose, U. (2011). The sky is the limit? The determinants and constraints of European airports commercial revenues, *Journal of Air Transport Management*, 17(5), 278–283.

Fung, M., Wan, K., Hui, Y. and Law, J. (2008). Productivity changes in Chinese airports 1995–2004, *Transportation Research Part E: Logistics and Transportation Review*, 44, 521–542.

Fuhr, J. and Beckers, T. (2009). Contract design, financing arrangements and public ownership: an assessment of the US airport governance model, *Transport Reviews*, 29(4), 459–478.

Gatwick Airport Ltd (2010). *Two-Sided Platforms and Airports*, discussion paper, Gatwick Airport, GAL.

Geuens, M., Vantomme, D. and Brengman, M. (2004). Developing a typology of airport shoppers, *Tourism Management*, 25(5), 615–622.

Gillen, D. and Lall, A. (2004). Competitive advantage of low-cost carriers: some implications for airports, *Journal of Air Transport Management*, 10(1), 41–50.

Gillen, D. and Mantin, B. (2014). The importance of concession revenues in the privatization of airports, *Transportation Research Part E: Logistics and Transportation Review*, 68, 164–177.

Graham, A. (2005) Airport benchmarking: a review of the current situation, *Benchmarking: An International Journal*, 12, 99–111.

Graham, A. (2009). How important are commercial revenues to today's airports? *Journal of Air Transport Management*, 15, 106–111.

Graham, A. and Dennis, N. (2007). Airport traffic and financial performance: a UK and Ireland case study, *Journal of Transport Geography*, 15(3), 161–171.

Graham, A. and Morrell, P. (2016). *Airport Finance and Investment in the Global Economy*, London, Routledge.

Hazel, R., Blais, J., Browne, T. and Benzon, D. (2011). *Resource Guide to Airport Performance Indicators*, ACRP Report 19A, Washington, DC, Transportation Research Board.

Hsu, C. and Chao, C. (2005). Space allocation for commercial activities at international passenger terminals, *Transportation Research Part E: Logistics and Transportation Review*, 41(1), 29–51.

Humphreys, B. (2015). Davies Commission exposes pre-funding dilemma, *Aviation Strategy*, July/August, 4–9.

IATA (International Air Transport Association) (2013). *Profitability and the Air Transport Value Chain*, IATA Economics Briefing No. 10, Geneva, IATA.

InterVISTAS (2007). *Estimating Air Travel Demand Elasticities*, Vancouver, InterVISTAS.

Ivaldi, M., Sokullu, S. and Toru, T. (2015). *Airport Prices in a Two-Sided Market Setting: Major US Airports*, CEPR Discussion Paper No. DP10658, London, CEPR.

Jones, O., Budd, L. and Pitfield, D. (2013). Aeronautical charging policy incentive schemes for airlines at European airports, *Journal of Air Transport Management*, 33, 43–59.

Jorge-Calderon, D. (2014). *Aviation Investment*, Farnham, Ashgate.

Kamp, V., Niemeier H.-M. and Mueller, J. (2007). What can be learned from benchmarking studies? Examining the apparent poor performance of German airports, *Journal of Airport Management*, 1(3), 294–308.

Kutlu, L. and McCarthy, P. (2016). US airport ownership, efficiency, and heterogeneity, *Transportation Research Part E: Logistics and Transportation Review*, 89, 117–132.

Lam, S., Low, J. and Tang, L. (2009). Operational efficiencies across Asia Pacific airports, *Transportation Research Part E: Logistics and Transportation Review*, 45(4), 654–665.

Lei, Z., Papatheodorou, A. and Szivas, E. (2010). The effect of low-cost carriers on regional airports' revenue: evidence from the UK. In: P. Forsyth, D. Gillen, J. Muller and H.-M. Niemeier (eds). *Airport Competition: The European Experience*, Aldershot, Ashgate.

LeighFisher (2011). *Resource Manual for Airport In-Terminal Concessions*, ACRP Report 54, Washington, DC, Transportation Research Board.

Liebert, V. and Niemeier, H.-M. (2013). A survey of empirical research on the productivity and efficiency measurement of airports, *Journal of Transport Economics and Policy*, 47(2), 157–189.

Lin, L. and Hong, C. (2006). Operational performance evaluation of international major airports: an application of data envelopment analysis, *Journal of Air Transport Management*, 12, 342–351.

Lin, Y. and Chen, C. (2013). Passengers' shopping motivations and commercial activities at airports: the moderating effects of time pressure and impulse buying tendency, *Tourism Management*, 36, 426–434.

Lin, Z., Choo, Y. and Oum, T. (2013). Efficiency benchmarking of North American airports: comparative results of productivity index, data envelopment analysis and stochastic frontier analysis, *Journal of the Transportation Research Forum*, 52(1), 47–68.

Littlechild, S. (2012a). German airport regulation: framework agreements, civil law and the EU Directive, *Journal of Air Transport Management*, 21, 63–75.

Littlechild, S. (2012b). Australian airport regulation: exploring the frontier, *Journal of Air Transport Management*, 21, 50–62.

Lu, C. and Pagliari, R. (2004). Evaluating the potential impact of alternative airport pricing approaches on social welfare, *Transportation Research Part E: Logistics and Transportation Review*, 40(1), 1–17.

Maertens, S. (2012). Estimating the market power of airports in their catchment areas: a Europe-wide approach, *Journal of Transport Geography*, 22, 10–18.

Malina, R., Albers, S. and Kroll, N. (2012). Airport incentive programmes: a European perspective, *Transport Reviews*, 32(4), 435–453.

Marques, R. and Barros, C. (2010). Performance of European airports: regulation, ownership and managerial efficiency, *Applied Economics Letters*, 18(1), 29–37.

Marques, R. and Brochado, A. (2008). Airport regulation in Europe: is there need for a European observatory? *Transport Policy*, 15(3), 163–172.

Marques, R., Simões, P. and Carvalho, P. (2015). The influence of the operational environment on efficiency of international airports, *Journal of Advanced Transportation*, 49(4), 511–522.

Martel, F. (2009). External factors and their impact on non-aeronautical revenue, *Journal of Airport Management*, 3(4), 337–344.

Martin, J.C and Voltes-Dorta, A. (2010). International airports: economies of scale and marginal costs, *Journal of the Transportation Research Forum*, 47(1), 5–22.

Martin, J.C and Voltes-Dorta, A. (2011). Scale economies in marginal costs in Spanish airports, *Transportation Research Part E: Logistics and Transportation Review*, 47(2), 238–248.

Martin, J., Rodríguez-Déniz, H. and Voltes-Dorta, A. (2013). Determinants of airport cost flexibility in a context of economic recession, *Transportation Research Part E: Logistics and Transportation Review*, 57, 70–84.

McCarthy, P. (2014). US airport costs and production technology: a translog cost function analysis, *Journal of Transport Economics and Policy*, 48(3), 427–447.

Merkert, R. and Assaf, A. (2015). Using DEA models to jointly estimate service quality perception and profitability: evidence from international airports, *Transportation Research Part A: Policy and Practice*, 75, 42–50.

Merkert, R., Odeck, J., Brathen, S. and Pagliari, R. (2012). A review of different benchmarking methods in the context of regional airports, *Transport Reviews*, 32(3), 379–395.

Morrison, S. and Winston, C. (2007). Another look at airport congestion pricing, *American Economic Review*, 97, 1970–1977.

Morrison, W. (2009a). Real estate, factory outlets and bricks: a note on non-aeronautical activities at commercial airports, *Journal of Air Transport Management*, 15(3), 112–115.

Morrison, W. (2009b). Understanding the complexities and challenges of airport performance benchmarking, *Journal of Airport Management*, 3(2), 145–158.

Niemeier, H.-M. (2009). *Regulation of Large Airports: Status Quo and Options for Reform*, International Transport Forum – Airport Regulation Investment and Development of Aviation, Paris, ITF.

Oum, T. and Yu, C. (2004). Measuring airports' operating efficiency: a summary of the 2003 ATRS global airport benchmarking report, *Transportation Research Part E: Logistics and Transportation Review*, 40(6), 515–532.

Oum, T., Zhang, A. and Zhang, Y. (2004). Alternative forms of economic regulation and their efficiency implications for airports, *Journal of Transport Economics and Policy*, 38(2), 217–246.

Oum, T., Adler, N. and Yu, C. (2006). Privatisation, corporatisation, ownership forms and their effects on the performance of the world's major airports, *Journal of Air Transport Management*, 12(3), 109–121.

Oum, T., Yan, J. and Yu, C. (2008). Ownership forms matter for airport efficiency: a stochastic frontier investigation of worldwide airports, *Journal of Urban Economics*, 64(2), 422–435.

Oxera (2013). *Regulatory Regimes at Airports: An International Comparison*, Report for Gatwick Airport Limited, Oxford, Oxera.

Anne Graham

Pathomsiri, S., Haghani, A., Dresner, M. and Windle, R. (2008). Impact of undesirable outputs on the productivity of US airports, *Transportation Research Part E: Logistics and Transportation Review*, 44(2), 235–259.

Pels, E. and Verhoef, E. (2004). The economics of airport congestion pricing, *Journal of Urban Economics*, 55(2), 257–277.

Perelman, S. and Serebrisky, T. (2012). Measuring the technical efficiency of airports in Latin America, *Utilities Policy*, 22, 1–7.

Perng, S.W., Chow, C.C. and Liao, W.C. (2010). Analysis of shopping preference and satisfaction with airport retailing products, *Journal of Air Transport Management*, 16(5), 279–283.

Polk, A. and Bilotkach, V. (2013). The assessment of market power of hub airports, *Transport Policy*, 29, 29–37.

RBB Economics (2013). *Why Increases in Airport Charges Adversely Affect Airline Passengers: A Response to Compass Lexecon*, London, RBB Economics.

Richardson, C., Budd, L. and Pitfield, D. (2014). The impact of airline lease agreements on the financial performance of US hub airports, *Journal of Air Transport Management*, 40, 1–15.

Scotti, D., Malighetti, P., Martini, G. and Volta, N. (2012). The impact of airport competition on technical efficiency: a stochastic frontier analysis applied to Italian airport, *Journal of Air Transport Management*, 22, 9–15.

SEO Economic Research (2014). *Impacts of Expanding Airport Capacity on Competition and Connectivity*, Paris, OECD/ITF.

Sevcik, T. (2014). The end of retail, the future of retail, *Journal of Airport Management*, 8(4), 308–311.

SLG Economics (2012). *Q6 Review of the Distribution of Economic Rent between Airport, Airlines and Passengers and Cargo Users at Heathrow and Gatwick*, London, SLG Economics.

Starkie, D. (2008a). A critique of the single-till. In: D. Starkie (ed.). *Aviation Markets*, Ashgate, Aldershot.

Starkie, D. (2008b). *The Airport Industry in a Competitive Environment: A United Kingdom Perspective*, Discussion Paper No. 2005-15, Paris, ITF.

Starkie, D. (2013). Why a small increase in airport charges might lead to a large passenger loss, *Airneth*, 31 October.

Starkie, D. and Yarrow, G. (2013). *Why Airports Can Face Price-Elastic Demands: Margins, Lumpiness and Leveraged Passenger Losses*, Paris, ITF.

Steer Davies Gleave (2012). *Review of Operating Expenditure and Investment*, London, Steer Davies Gleave.

Steer Davies Gleave (2014). *Dublin Airport Operating Expenditure Efficiency Study*, London, Steer Davies Gleave.

Thelle, M.H., Pedersen, T.T. and Harhoff, F. (2012). *Airport Competition in Europe*, Copenhagen, Copenhagen Economics.

Torres, E., Domínguez, J.S., Valdes, L. and Aza, R. (2005). Passenger waiting time in an airport and expenditure carried out in the commercial area, *Journal of Air Transport Management*, 11(6), 363–367.

Tovar, B. and Rendeiro, R. (2009). Are outsourcing and non-aeronautical revenues important drivers in the efficiency of Spanish airports? *Journal of Air Transport Management*, 15(5), 217–220.

Tretheway, M. and Markhvida, K. (2013). *Airports in the Aviation Value Chain*, Discussion Paper No. 2013-15, Paris, ITF.

Tsekeris, T. (2011). Greek airports: efficiency measurement and analysis of determinants, *Journal of Air Transport Management*, 12(4), 182–190.

Van Dender, K. (2007). Determinants of fares and operating revenues at US airports, *Journal of Urban Economics*, 62(2), 317–336.

Vasigh, B. and Gorjidooz, J. (2006). Productivity analysis of public and private airports: a causal investigation, *Journal of Air Transportation*, 11(3), 144–163.

Vasigh, B., Erfani, G. and Sherman, B. (2014). Airport performance and ownership structure: evidence from the United Kingdom, United States, and Latin America, *Journal of Aviation Technology Engineering*, 4, 40–49.

Verhoef, E. (2010). Congestion pricing, slot sales and slot trading in aviation, *Transportation Research Part B: Methodological*, 44, 320–329.

Vogel, H.-A. (2006). Impact of privatization on the financial and economic performance of European airports, *The Aeronautical Journal*, April, 197–213.

Vogel, H.-A. and Graham, A. (2013). Devising airport groupings for financial benchmarking, *Journal of Air Transport Management*, 30, 32–38.

Voltes-Dorta, A. and Pagliari, R. (2012). The impact of recession on airports' cost efficiency, *Transport Policy*, 24, 211–222.

Wanke, P. (2012). Efficiency of Brazil's airports: evidences from bootstrapped DEA and FDH estimates, *Journal of Air Transport Management*, 23, 47–53.

Yang, H. and Fu, X. (2015). A comparison of price-cap and light-handed airport regulation with demand uncertainty, *Transportation Research Part B: Methodological*, 73, 122–132.

Yang, H. and Zhang, A. (2011). Price-cap regulation of congested airports, *Journal of Regulatory Economics*, 39(3), 293–312.

Yarrow, G. and Stakie, D. (2013). *Review of the CAA's Stansted market power assessment*. Online. Available at: www.caa.co.uk/WorkArea/DownloadAsset.aspx?id=4294972561 (accessed 1 February 2017).

Yoshida, Y. (2004). Endogenous-weight TFP measurement: methodology and its application to Japanese-airport benchmarking, *Transportation Research Part E: Logistics and Transportation Review*, 40(2), 151–182.

Yu, M., Hsu, S., Chang, C. and Lee, H. (2008). Productivity growth of Taiwan's major domestic airports in the presence of aircraft noise, *Transportation Research Part E: Logistics and Transportation Review*, 44(3), 543–554.

Zhang, A. and Czerny, A. (2012). Airports and airlines economics and policy: an interpretive review of recent research, *Economics of Transportation*, 1(1), 15–34.

Zhang, A. and Zhang, Y. (2006) Airport capacity and congestion when carriers have market power, *Journal of Urban Economics*, 60, 229–247.

Zhang, A. and Zhang, Y. (2010). Airport capacity and congestion pricing with both aeronautical and commercial operations, *Transportation Research Part B: Methodological*, 44, 404–413.

Zhao, Q., Choo, Y. and Oum, T. (2014). The effect of governance forms on North American airport efficiency: a comparative analysis of airport authority vs. government branch, *Journal of the Transportation Research Forum*, 53(2), 93–110.

# 13

# Airline marketing

*Blaise P. Waguespack*

## Introduction

With the evolution of the airline marketplace and the variety of business models and technological influences within society, the role of airline marketing has rapidly expanded beyond a traditional focus of travel promotions that lead to a booking, to in-flight services offered, and then to a post-flight questionnaire that completed the marketing process. The role of airline marketing has now expanded to include a more expansive view of the travel planning process. From inspiration and research on possible travel locations and activities, through the travel experience to the post travel sharing, airlines are becoming involved in various roles, e-commerce sites and digital communications in order to influence the buying process (Hanke, 2016a). As this expansion has occurred over the past few years, airlines continue to examine the process utilised in the past, along with external influences, especially digital technological developments, that may provide airlines the means to influence the process and market the service options developed through the business strategy the airline pursues. While the focus has no doubt increased the span of marketing-related tasks that airlines must engage in, still the airline involved must maintain a focus on its underlying product and service offerings. This chapter will utilise a classic four P's approach – product, place, promotion and price – while reviewing some of the possible legal and regulatory concerns that impact on how airline marketing is addressed today. The focus of this chapter is on airlines – refer to Chapter 14 for a discussion on airport marketing.

## Product

Airlines are presented in numerous textbooks as a prime example of a service product (Grewal and Levy, 2017; Peter and Donnelly, 2015; Solomon et al., 2016) that represents an intangible product, requiring a mix of service personnel and automation, in conjunction with tangible assets, the aircraft and airport, to deliver to the customer. Despite being intangible, one aspect of the airline product that is often stressed when communicating service benefits, and might be considered as offering tangible features, are the seats.

An article entitled 'Seat Wars' by Karp (2007) presented many of the first modern generation of reclining and fully flat seats introduced by airlines around the world in the mid-2000s. While

United States (US) airlines were slow in their deployment of such seats due to the economic difficulties in the mid-2000s, including bankruptcy proceedings for the three remaining legacy carriers, since the mid-2000s many of the major global carriers have engaged in an ongoing escalation of the high-end premium cabin seat (Arnoult, 2007; Majcher, 2011).

While the launch of The Residence by Etihad (Reals, 2016) may have temporarily brought forth the highest standard in the marketplace, airlines continue to focus on developing the right premium cabin for the airline. Airlines must determine what is the right product for the premium passenger mix of the airline. Strategy and markets served to drive the debate as to whether to stay with a true first-class cabin and then a business cabin or eliminate the first-class cabin completely for a better premium cabin experience, merging the first and business class into one premium product offering (Nicas, 2012; Taylor, 2014; *The Economist*, 2016).

While the rightsizing of the cabin has been a major concern (Thomas, 2008), the issue of layout, passenger comfort and aisle access, without having to climb over another passenger, are major concerns now driving decisions (Michaels, 2012; Morrison, 2016a). Airlines debate a factor such as the pattern of the seat layout, from herringbone (broken v-shaped, like the cloth) to yin-yang (offset, checkers board pattern) to v-shaped staggered that the carrier may use in the premium cabin to best serve the needs of their passengers (McCartney, 2012). In the summer of 2016, both United Airlines and Delta Airlines announced new premium cabin products to their fleet, stressing the issues of aisle access, privacy and, in Delta's case, the addition of a new suite to the airline's long-haul product (Baskas, 2016). With a growing threat of the Middle East carriers promoting their airlines as the most luxurious in the world, the US legacy carriers are taking these actions as the carriers respond to what will likely be a continuing seat war among the world's international carriers.

While much research tends to focus on the premium cabin, because of the costs and features involved in serving the highest spending passengers, other cabin issues are continuing to arise. Among the seating decisions that will continue to drive airline marketing is the inclusion of premium economy cabins. As cash-strapped business travellers are no longer willing to purchase a true first-class product, and many corporate travel policies limit business-class flying to the highest of C-level executives (CEO and others with chief in their positon title, or senior vice presidents), airlines had to adjust. Across the world, airlines developed the premium economy cabin to meet the needs of fliers willing to pay more for extra features beyond basic economy and stay within corporate travel policies (Boynton, 2012; Kwoh and Korn, 2013). With many airlines eliminating a true first class, as United is doing with the Polaris rollout, and moving to one premium cabin, which many travellers may not be able to afford or corporations will not pay for, deploying a premium economy cabin is occurring across more airlines (Dunn, 2016; Michaels, 2014). Among the airlines to finally end their holdouts are Singapore Airlines and Lufthansa Airlines, which both in 2015 announced the deployment of premium economy cabins, and have evolved to true four-class cabins within their respective long-haul fleets (Chong, 2015; Russel, 2014).

While not as pronounced as the differences in the premium cabin with fully lie-flat seats and often the largest in-flight entertainment (IFE) installations, there is currently no set standard of a premium economy cabin or seat. For many of the US airlines, premium economy on domestic routes may at most mean some additional legroom and some additional services (e.g. free baggage, seat assignment, or food and beverage options) that would have to be paid extra for if flying on an economy fare. Only recently have US airlines begun to offer an international premium economy experience, matching the amenities provided by global carriers. American Airlines now offers a premium economy section with wider seats and additional amenities on board Boeing 787-900 aircraft that are flying intercontinental from hubs to South

America, with expansion planned across American Airlines' global routes, but leaving the domestic Main Cabin Extra product unchanged (Left, 2016). To other carriers introducing a premium economy product, especially in a long-haul situation, this is more of a true differential, with wider seats, fuller recline and a clear upgrade in cabin amenities (Muther, 2016).

Another major seating trend is in the economy section, with the addition of slimline seats and increasing the densification of the economy cabin (Reals, 2016). The new seats, bringing new firms to the marketplace, allow airlines to increase capacity without adding new aircraft (Broderick, 2015). Whether the airline is retrofitting current aircraft or is adding new capacity to the fleet, the addition of the slimline seats allows more product to sell, while adding benefits to the airline as such seats are noted for being thinner, lighter weight and manufactured with stronger materials, thereby providing maintenance savings (Caliendo, 2017; Morrison, 2016a; Thisdell, 2016). With the slimline seats, airlines are adding seats to the economy cabin while still claiming no change to the seat pitch, and more storage space under the seat due to the design of the seats. Airlines such as Frontier have added 12 seats to the Airbus 319s and 320s in the airline's current fleet, increasing the capacity of the aircraft to 150 seats for the 319s and 180 seats for the 320s. Additionally, Frontier is purchasing new Airbus 321 aircraft with a capacity of 230 with the new slimline seats (Sumer, 2015a, 2015b). Ryanair has announced that as part of the airline's ongoing 'Always Getting Better' plan, it will introduce new slimline seats as current aircraft are updated (Rokou, 2016). As Ryanair begins to receive the Boeing 737 MAX 200, the aircraft will be configured with seating for 197 passengers, with Ryanair stating that the new layout, adding eight seats to the planes from the current Ryanair configuration, will generate about US$1 million to the bottom line per year (Norris and Flottau, 2014).

While the addition of amenities and the creation of a new product such as premium economy have not stirred much debate in regulatory regimes, the actions within the economy cabin are being discussed. For not only have the short-haul low cost carriers (LCCs) moved to the slimline seats, but some long-haul carriers have reconfigured their economy cabins and increased seat density. Some long-haul carriers have increased the number of seats per row, as United is now doing by moving to Boeing 777s, with 10-abreast seating in coach rows instead of nine, dropping the seat width from 18 inches to 17 (Duncan, 2017; McCartney, 2016a; Morrison, 2016b). This continued shrinking of the economy class has, in the US, led to an attempt to legislate by the Federal Aviation Administration (FAA) for a minimum seat size standard for airlines, but these efforts were unsuccessful in early 2016 (Kunkle, 2016). The amendment, offered by New York Senator Chares Shumer, would have required the FAA to: establish a moratorium on airlines further reducing the size of their seats, ensuring that an airline's current seat size is maintained as the floor; directed the FAA, in consultation with experts, to set a minimum standard seat size and pitch for commercial flights; and increased transparency by requiring airlines to post their seat dimensions on their websites, providing a commercial incentive for airlines to offer more comfortable seating arrangements (Congressional Documents and Publications, 2016).

This is not the only seating issue that has caused legislative review. In combination with the move to unbundling fares and creating matching low cost fare products, many airlines have also stopped assigning seats unless a passenger pays extra for the privilege. This has led to a situation where families may be assigned seats throughout the plane and creates a situation when boarding the aircraft of families negotiating seat swaps as the aircraft is trying to leave the gate (McCartney, 2016b). With reports occurring in the news, two congressmen proceeded to file the Families Flying Together Act of 2015, which would mandate the Secretary of the US Department of Transportation (DOT) to "establish a policy to ensure, to the extent practicable, that a family that purchases tickets for a flight with that air carrier is seated together during that flight" (US Government Publishing Office, 2016: 1). While the full bill did not become law within the 2016 FAA reauthorisation, there was still a directive for the US Transportation Secretary to look at establishing a policy directing airlines to allow children aged 13 or under to sit next to an accompanying family member who is older (Yamanouchi, 2016). Therefore, while not dictated by law, this issue may arise again through the DOT rule-making progress for airlines to address.

## Price

The discussion for this chapter began with a focus on seats, as, beyond the route to be flown, seats are the base product many consumers think of when purchasing a flight. Additionally, airlines in many of their advertisements still focus on the seat. However, as the discussion goes forward, so will the need to integrate processes across the airlines' operations and information technology systems to focus on the issue of price. As airlines develop new fare products, airline information systems must be updated to deliver the variety of products and services, with multiple price points involved, to the consumer. Across the tourism and hospitality industries, researchers are investigating how the technological advances from data analytics, social media and expanding distribution channels may impact pricing and revenue management systems (Wang et al., 2015).

An example of these expanding price points and products is the introduction of differentiated fare products in the coach section of the economy cabin by US airlines (Carey, 2016). While revenue management systems assured different price points occurred in the economy section, these price points were not advertised as unique products. Now, in response to consumer preferences for low fares and competition from the growing ultra LCCs, three of the US majors, American, Delta and United, are introducing what are known as 'basic economy' fares (Elliott, 2017). The new fare product comes with very few amenities, and the fares are often not eligible for upgrades or full frequent flier status on some carriers. Additionally, the fare product has baggage restrictions, with no bags allowed in the overhead bin, and someone purchasing a ticket may find themselves squeezed into the middle seat on many flights (Carey, 2017). While launched in the US, speculation is already occurring that this fare product will spread quickly to European legacy carriers (Duncan, 2017).

As many fliers know, the idea of buying a complete bundled product, with all associated services, has disappeared from many airline product lines. While a few international carriers may still offer a fully bundled first-class product, beyond those few airlines, some form of product unbundling has occurred, and as consumers compare products, often what services are or are not part of the base service can greatly influence the final price paid. These additional services are ancillary revenue to the firm. IdeaWorksCompany, one of the leading research firms in the area of ancillary products, developed a definition of ancillary revenue now broadly accepted by the airline industry: "Revenue beyond the sale of tickets that is generated by direct sales to passengers, or indirectly as a part of the travel experience" (IdeaWorksCompany, 2017). Providing context to this definition, IdeaWorksCompany categorises ancillary revenue into five categories:

1   *À la carte features*. These represent the items on the ancillary revenue menu and consist of the amenities consumers can add to their air travel experience. The list continues to grow, and the following are typical activities: (1) onboard sales of food and beverages; (2) checking of baggage and excess baggage; (3) assigned seats or better seats within the same cabin; (4) call centre support for reservations; (5) fees charged for purchases made with credit cards; (6) priority check-in and screening; (7) early boarding benefits; (8) onboard entertainment systems; and (9) wireless Internet access.

2   *Commission-based products.* Ancillary revenue activities also include the commissions earned by airlines on the sale of hotel accommodation, car rentals and travel insurance. The commission-based category primarily involves the airline's website, but it can include the sale of duty-free and consumer products on board aircraft.

3   *Frequent flier programmes (FFPs).* The frequent flier category largely consists of the sale of miles or points to programme partners such as hotel chains and car rental companies, co-branded credit cards, online malls, retailers and communication services. Sales of miles or points made directly to programme members also qualify.

4   *Advertising sold by the airline.* This category, added in 2010, includes any advertising initiative linked to passenger travel. The following are typical activities: (1) revenue generated from the in-flight magazine; (2) advertising messages sold in or on aircraft, loading bridges, gate areas and airport lounges; and (3) fee-based placement of consumer products and samples.

5   *Fare or product bundle.* Airlines may allocate a portion of the price associated with an economy-class bundle or product bundle as ancillary revenue. This is determined by assigning a revenue value to the services included in the bundle, such as checked baggage, early boarding and extra legroom seating.

The scheme is not meant to be exhaustive, and not all airlines have completely adopted all the forms of ancillary revenue noted. In the US, Southwest Airlines is the last major airline that does not charge any baggage fees for the first two checked bags. While pressured by analysts who believe Southwest is surrendering a major revenue source, the airline continues to state that it will not start charging in the near future (Whiteman, 2016). The focus on ancillary revenue by airlines across all business strategies reflects the difficult operating conditions felt by many airlines across the globe since the mid-2000s and the airlines' efforts to find sources of revenue beyond ticket prices, which consumers want as low as possible. With airlines being encouraged to adopt a merchandising perspective (Ascend, 2016) for the ancillary products offered, combined with new technologies allowing the selling of ancillaries to be easier across distribution modes, airlines will continue to develop new ancillary offers.

With this development come five possible pricing strategies that may be adopted by an airline (see Table 13.1). Starting from the unbundled product, there exists a combination of building limited fare bundles and brand names for those bundled products. These branded bundles demonstrate to the consumer what the benefits of the branded product are over the strictly à la carte product.

The ability to create products across all five of the strategies and offer the products are very dependent upon the airlines' distribution channels and the information technology system supporting the strategy selected. The pricing strategies and airlines' efforts to generate ancillary revenue through the purchase process must be able to be coordinated with the airlines' revenue management practices to maximise the revenue that can be generated (Chatterjee and Jain, 2015). Combining these strategies with revenue management practices and increasing information system processing has some analysts wondering if airlines are soon to be able to offer dynamic pricing (Wittman and Belobaba, 2016) or what Boyd (2007) called scientific customer centric pricing. With the increasing use of customer relationship management (CRM) systems and data analytics, the increasing sophistication of revenue management programmes, and the information that may soon be available to airlines as IATA's New Distribution Capability becomes an accepted standard in the industry, will airlines be able to extend their pricing power to each individual customer? Examples exist from other industries (Boyd, 2007), with direct data channels and the ability to know where that customer is coming from, to offer individual prices. Will airlines, with the data available in the airline's customer data warehouse on who that customer is from the profile and external data gathered, be able to offer individual prices soon?

*Table 13.1* Types of airline pricing

| Types | Definition | Revenue management | Airline examples |
| --- | --- | --- | --- |
| À la carte (unbundled) | Consumers may add optional extras such as checked bags, assigned seats and pre-ordered meals to any fare. | Lower-priced fares sell out as demand increases, but optional extras remain available. | Wizz Air's optional services such as priority boarding, extra leg room and assigned seats. |
| Branded fares | Base fare provides minimal amenities and consumers may upgrade to higher-priced fares that offer more perks. | Each fare type is always available and has a fixed (predictable) price premium. | Wizz Air's Basic and Plus fares, and JetBlue's Blue, Blue Plus and Blue Flex fares. |
| Service bundles | Base fare provides minimal amenities and consumers may purchase packages that offer additional perks. | Bundles are always available and may have fixed-price premiums or are dynamically priced. | Jetstar's Starter Fare and its Plus (fixed premium) and Max (dynamic) bundles. |
| Fare families | Amenities are linked to existing fare categories, with higher fares providing more perks. | Lower dynamically priced fares sell out as demand increases, which limits the choices presented to consumers. | TAP Portugal's Discount, Basic, Classic and Plus fares. |
| Subscription | Club membership allows consumers to enjoy fare discounts or have access to a service feature. | Discount is applied to lowest available fares. Service features are usually provided without limitation. | United's subscriptions for bags and Economy Plus, and Volaris V-Club fare discount programme. |

*Source*: Sorenson (2015).

## Distribution

Figure 13.1 is a simplified diagram of how the area of distribution has changed over the last 50 years (see also Chapter 20). Starting in the 1960s, the first computer reservation systems (CRSs) were developed by the legacy airlines, and over time became free from airline control and are now known as global distribution systems (GDS) (Pilling, 2009). With the technological advancement that Channel 1 represents, airlines entered to the realm of electronic commerce that in its various modes and channels drives airline distribution today.

Channel 1, an indirect channel that shows the airline inventory or product distributed from the airline to the GDS to a travel agency to the customer, is still a very viable channel for many airlines. While numerous articles have existed in the aviation press over the last 20 years about how technological gains threaten to end this channel and provide the airlines with the means to pursue a strategy of disintermediation, or leaving this structure, the channel continues to provide major benefits to airlines, including the LCCs (Ferguson, 2015; McDonald, 2007a). While the percentage of tickets distributed through this channel has gone down over the last 20 years, reports from airline trade groups still place the costs of the channel close to US$7 billion in fees a year to the systems (O'Neill, 2017).

As successful as Channel 1 was, not all tickets were sold using this method and airlines still utilised direct channels. Channel 1A, as noted, represents those tickets sold by the airline directly

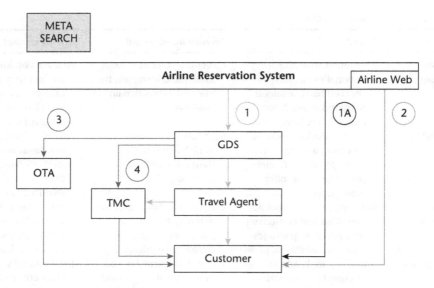

*Figure 13.1* Airline distribution channels

*Source*: Author.

through their call centre, the airline ticket counter and city ticket shops. Selling tickets at the airport is not as common as once occurred, but still ticket desks and airport travel agencies exist across the globe and are likely to continue in some areas of the world. While airline ticket shops have mostly disappeared from North America, the retail locations still exist in some localities across the globe to serve local ethnic groups or as a means of outreach in a traditional retail setting (McDonald, 2007b). Call centres still exist for customers wanting human contact through the booking process, but now some carriers charge fees when booking through the call centre as a means of paying for the channel. Additionally, the call centre allows the airline to utilise the opportunity to engage in upselling and gain additional ancillary revenue (Kahn, 2016).

The biggest factor to impact Channel 1 has been the spread of the Internet and the newer forms of digital commerce that have come about over the last 20 years. Along with the creation of e-tickets, airlines quickly realised the value of the web as a means of bypassing the GDS for sales to the public (Channel 2). The websites of many LCCs and ultra LCCs are the primary means of ticket distribution (Hanke, 2016a). It is also a crucial means for the airline to engage in merchandising activities associated with the air transport portion of the trip as airlines have unbundled services over the last decade in an effort to sell ancillary products. Besides the opportunity for selling ancillary services associated with the air travel portion of the trip, additional web content provides information and shopping for a wide variety of travel and tourism services beyond just air transport (Hanke, 2016b; Sobie, 2008a). Among the products and services consumers can book on airline websites are rental cars, hotels, trip insurance, amusement park tickets, cultural site tours and sporting event tickets.

Channel 3 in the diagram represents the other major channel structure that came about due to the Internet. Airlines were not the only firms who realised the ability of the web to provide customers with more information on choices and options when searching for travel information. With the growth of these firms over time, the term online travel agency (OTA) became a means of classifying a variety of firms that utilised web-based systems as their primary means of selling tickets to consumers. Created by a variety of firms, early OTAs had founders such as SABRE, a major GDS, beginning Travelocity (Schall, 2016). Some airlines, being afraid of Travelocity, launched Orbitz as a competing site. Microsoft, with expertise in the software industry, was a launch partner of Expedia, and other firms such as Priceline and regional firms such as C-trip in China became well-known web brands for travel shopping (Joyce, 2013). The OTA sites have a major advantage for many consumers as the OTA allows multiple airlines to be searched, unlike the stand-alone airline website, and the OTA offers a variety of means for searching for flights, price often being the main criterion for consumers to compare when shopping.

While the development of the OTA channel was occurring, the other major channel member, the travel agency, needed to evolve. Recognising the impact of the web and the digital world and not wanting to relinquish their position, the travel agency moved to become a travel management company (TMC), as shown in Channel 4 (McDonald, 2010). Offering a variety of travel services and functions, often aimed at the corporate travel manager, the TMC is customer-focused on serving business and corporate accounts looking to outsource the travel management process. Many travel agencies, utilising technologies from the marketplace, or the global distribution firms intent on keeping that business utilising the GDS, created their own TMC web portal and today are moving to direct connect arrangements with the airlines (Borgogna et al., 2017). The benefit of the TMC is that the firm will provide services to their corporate accounts, and often enforce corporate policies on travel expenses, freeing the firm from having an internal travel department to manage this expense.

As the channel structure has evolved due to technology, the ability of travellers to access these channels has also evolved with the creation of the meta search website. The meta search sites, perhaps the most well-known being Kayak and the United Kingdom (UK) based Skyscanner, aggregate flight information across the distribution structure to deliver to consumers the best fare to be found across the channels (Sobie, 2008b). The meta search sites offer many of the same search parameters as an OTA (e.g. by price, number of destinations and trip time); however, the person using the site is directed to the channel with the best results based on the parameters searched. While having the functionality of an OTA, the user does not purchase the flight at the actual site. While many consumers will use the site to find the lowest prices, controversy has arisen as many airlines complain that passengers buying tickets in this manner are not getting all the information needed for the purchase and the meta search sites drive traffic on the airline's information technology network with little benefit (Field, 2008; Painter, 2017).

The other major factor that is influencing the channel relationship is the ability to offer the ancillary products airlines now offer across the channels (McDonald, 2013). With airlines being concerned the GDS system has not kept pace with airline merchandising, IATA has led an effort to adopt new technological standards known as the New Distribution Capability (NDC) (Cowen, 2013). Working in partnership with the airlines, the goal was to create new standards in modern programming interfaces that would allow airlines, as the suppliers, to make available all the airlines' products, including ancillary offerings, to channel members (O'Neill, 2013). With NDC, the airlines hope to put in place standards that will allow the full range of products to be sold and consumers the opportunity to personalise the offering being shown, no matter what channel they are shopping on. NDC adoption is ongoing at many airlines, with IATA tracking airline activities as NDC standards are adopted by airlines (see IATA, 2017).

While the discussion has focused on channel structure, the method of delivery is undergoing rapid change. No doubt, the move to a smartphone or tablet app-based world is impacting travel distribution (Budd and Vorley, 2013). Mobile technology is introducing a new form of the direct channel that allows push messages to be sent to the recipient if so willing. The difficulty airlines may find is getting consumers to adopt the app. While travellers may be willing to download and use once a flight is purchased, this does not mean the app will become the preferred access for the consumer. While travellers are willing to use the app for the features of information updating and paperless boarding passes, this does not guarantee the irregular consumer will use the app for future booking purposes. Currently, beyond the basic ticketing purchase function, the most common feature on the apps for the top 25 airlines are à la carte features for selecting seat assignment and pre-pay baggage fees (Sorenson, 2017). Some reports put the number of apps for a consumer at 27 to 30 used on a regular basis, with travel-based apps hardly figuring in the hours used by consumers (O'Neil-Dunne, 2016). While the frequent flier may be more willing to adopt and use the app, driving business through the dedicated airline app by the non-frequent flier will be a challenge.

## Promotion and communications

Continuing the theme, technological innovations in digital media and social media have increased the means by which airlines can build awareness of the brand and attempt to shape passenger attitudes towards the airline and its product offerings. The tools of social media and digital communications in the form of blogs, media channels, social network sites and micro-blogging are now major concerns of airlines (Kahn, 2016). Airlines now must have digital media centres for monitoring the communications and conversations that are occurring in these channels. While airlines must become engaged in the social media world, the classic tools of promotions are still utilised by many airlines. This section examines the role of how a classic promotional tool, sponsorship, can be combined with the tools of social media to provide an overall promotion campaign to target audiences.

Sponsorship as a tool of the airline promotional mix has been known in the industry, but at times has had more of a community involvement and corporate social responsibility response (Dasburg, 1998). Airline management needed to be ready to respond to the request for services and assistance from the communities the airline served, and had long recognised the need to have a strategy to deal with these requests and get the stories to the public about the activities engaged. In the US, it is not uncommon in fact for the sponsorship links on the website to focus more on the charitable aspects of the firm and how the airline responds to a charitable request. An example of this would be the American Airlines Giving page (see American Airlines, 2017), which highlights the various non-profit and community-based organisations the airline and its employees participate with, along with links to how to engage the airline in a programme.

As the international airline industry has grown and firms strive to market across the globe, the active promotion of sponsorship activities has grown, especially across country borders. While local or domestic-related sponsorships are still common, catering to the events and demographics of an airline's home market, international and cross-border sponsorships are more common. For example, in the past, it was suggested that airlines should not become involved in dangerous sports such as auto racing (Shaw, 2004); however, airlines are now the major sponsor of Formula One Grand Prix races such as the Singapore Airlines Singapore Grand Prix, the Formula One Etihad Airways Abu Dhabi Grand Prix and the Formula One Gulf Air Bahrain Grand Prix. Across the globe, the growing Middle East airlines have especially become active in sponsoring soccer clubs in various leagues, most noticeably the English Premier League, the most watched soccer league globally (Total Sportek, 2017). In comments by Emirates founding CEO Sir Maurice Flanagan, the airline's investment in sponsorships is made clear. "Advertising never produces the same exposure for the money as the rights sponsorship, especially on TV," stated Sir Maurice, and that the rights deal struck between Emirates and Arsenal Football Club was the best deal the airline made as it began its sponsorship strategy (Halligan, 2015).

*Table 13.2* The five biggest spenders among the US airlines for sponsorships, 2015

| | Estimated total (US$ million) | Spending categories | | | | | |
| --- | --- | --- | --- | --- | --- | --- | --- |
| | | Sports | Arts | Entertainment | Cause | Festivals | Other |
| United | 35–40 | 45% | 24% | 18% | 8% | 4% | 1% |
| Delta | 25–30 | 58% | 15% | 4% | 17% | 6% | |
| American | 20–25 | 26% | 30% | 4% | 26% | 12% | 1% |
| Southwest | 10–15 | 57% | 3% | | 29% | 11% | |
| JetBlue | 5–10 | 60% | 3% | | 30% | 7% | |

*Source*: IEG (2016).

*Note*: Top sponsorship deals in 2015 for US airlines were:
United: Chicago Bears, PGA Tour, San Francisco 49ers, United Center – Chicago, US Olympic Committee.
Delta: Los Angeles Lakers, Madison Square Garden, New York Mets, New York Yankees.
American: AA Arena – Miami, AA Arena – Dallas, Dallas Cowboys, Los Angeles Clippers, Race for the Cure.
Southwest: Denver Nuggets, Phoenix Suns, Texas Rangers.
JetBlue: Boston Red Sox, Boston Bruins, New England Patriots, University of Southern California.

Examining the websites of the world's leading airlines, it is easy to see the role sponsorship has in the communication plans. Many of the leading global carriers have dedicated sponsorship pages across the sport and other cultural activities the airline is engaged in. The benefit of the sponsorship is recognised for brand exposure and building, while bringing to the airline a dedicated and known demographically profiled audience. With the ability to leverage the airline's website and social media platforms such as Facebook, Twitter and Instagram, airlines are well positioned to offer contests and sweepstakes, offering travel prizes to those who engage with the airlines on the social media platforms. With the data that may come from a sponsorship, targeted messages can be sent to find the right customer that may react positively to an offer from the airline (Yardley, 2016). Examining US airlines, Table 13.2 presents data from 2015 (IEG, 2016) that shows the amount spent by US airlines across the major categories and who the largest deals are with for the airlines. Table 13.2 clearly shows the commitment to sports sponsorships among the US airlines. Most of the top deals are clearly with teams that are either in an airline hub city or focused on key cities for the airline network and growth.

Besides the spending for the rights, for the sponsorship to be effective the firm must engage in leveraging and activation of the sponsorship. Leveraging encompasses all sponsorship marketing communication, while activation relates to those activities and messages for audiences to interact and become involved with the sponsor (Weeks et al., 2008). Table 13.3, adapted from O'Reilly and Horning (2013) presents some of the many ways a sponsorship can be leveraged across promotional and distribution networks today. The table demonstrates that depending upon the marketing strategy and tactics to be implemented, sponsorships can be utilised to do outreach in a variety of means, both traditional broadcast and person-to-person or across social networks.

While rates for spending beyond the rights acquired may vary by the activity selected, and include traditional media uses such as advertising and public relations, with a focus on the need to track dollars and show a marketing return, activation activities engaging in on-site hospitality, websites and social media utilisation are more often being engaged. As the range for leverage spending can be anywhere up to seven times the amount paid for rights (O'Reilly and Horning, 2013), the spending must be able to demonstrate its value. The additional aspect that the sponsorship and leveraged activities possess today is the ability to measure the responses and track data from the social media networks utilised (Rashidi et al., 2016). As concepts such as big data and data analytics of traveller behaviour (Kahn, 2016) have become

*Table 13.3* Sponsorship activation methods

| Type of sponsorship | Activation method |
|---|---|
| • Advertising – all forms<br>• Public relations/media coverage/Facebook Live<br>• Signage/banners/PA announcements<br>• Logo in arena, scoreboard or on uniforms<br>• In-store displays/point-of-sale promotions/samples<br>• Contests/sweepstakes/games<br>• Player sponsorships/meet-and-greets/product use<br>• On-site personnel for consumer interaction<br>• Social media influencer campaign | • Digital and social media/mobile media<br>• Online campaigns (websites, blogs, tweet-ups)<br>• On-site hospitality with geotags and Snapchat filters<br>• Events/client entertainment and VIP passes<br>• Off-site events with branded premiums and giveaways<br>• Direct marketing<br>• Cause-related tie-ins<br>• Internal marketing/employee programmes<br>• New products/services |

*Source*: Adapted from O'Reilly and Horning (2013).

topics of concern, sponsorships and the associated additional promotion and media tactics tools that can be leveraged can build data and relay to the airline aspects such as trip purpose, other transport modes utilised, and other sociocultural and demographic data. Some forms of social media are easier to track than others. Microblogs such as Twitter are perhaps the easiest to track as hashtags can be created that are often tied to events and locations. Social networks that utilise photographs, selfies and now live streaming videos taken by travellers may note the location and the purpose of the trip. Monitoring systems now allow firms to scan the background details to see the nature of the event and the demographics of the participants at the event (MacMillan and Dwoskin, 2014). Whereas in the past it may have been difficult to measure the associated value of sponsorships (Shaw, 2004), the social network and analytical systems today allow specific measurements to be determined.

## Conclusion

Airline marketing faces the challenge expressed by Brenneman (1998: 164) of meeting passenger expectations to "fly to places people wanted to go, when they wanted to go, in clean attractive airplanes; get them there on-time with their bags and serve food at mealtimes," while now providing a wide range of options and information to assist in determining the places where passengers want to go. Recently, a guest commentator on Tnooz.com noted, "an airline can only distinguish itself with regards to punctuality, luggage care, and safety by failing to provide them" (Walker, 2017). While separated by nearly 20 years, the comments reflect the base needs airlines still face as a service business. With the digital and mobile world of social media now surrounding airline operations, news of when that failure occurs spreads quickly, and even a casual observer of the industry can find daily examples occurring. As digital technology advances are now bringing about new communication possibilities that are affecting airline promotions and distribution, researchers are already starting to discuss how artificial intelligence may influence consumer decision information processing and decision-making. Airlines face the task of meeting the basic needs of passengers in a constantly changing technological and world marketplace. Research must focus on how customers are adopting the technologies and what are the barriers to implementing solutions that may help the airline serve customer needs while driving revenue and profitability for the airline.

# References

American Airlines (2017). *American Airlines: Giving.* Online. Available at: http://hub.aa.com/en/ju/home (accessed 19 November 2016).

Arnoult, S. (2007). Cabin fever, *Air Transport World*, 44 (April), 34–36.

Ascend (2016). Building customer memory: how airlines create a customer centric digital experience, *Ascend*, 4, 32–46.

Baskas, H. (2016). Suite seating at 35,000 feet, *USA Today*, 19 August, B5.

Borgogna, A., Agarwalla, A., Stroh, S. and Jakovljevic, I. (2017). Ticket to success, *Flight Airline Business*, 33 (March), 30–33.

Boyd, A.E. (2007). *The Future of Pricing: How Airline Ticket Pricing Has Inspired a Revolution*, New York, Palgrave MacMillan.

Boynton, C. (2012). The premium revolution, *Air Transport World*, 49 (March), 45–47.

Brenneman, G. (1998). Right away and all at once: how we saved Continental, *Harvard Business Review*, 76 (September/October), 162–179.

Broderick, S. (2015). Cabin upgrades will drive healthy retrofit market growth, *Aviation Daily*, 7 January, 4.

Budd, L. and Vorley, T. (2013). Airlines, apps, and business travel: a critical examination, *Research in Transportation Business & Management*, 9, 41–49.

Caliendo, H. (2017). *TexTtreme used to help lightweight aircraft seats.* Online. Available at: www.composites-world.com/news/textreme-used-to-help-lightweight-aircraft-seats (accessed 19 March 2017).

Carey, S. (2016). Airlines offer more coach choices, *Wall Street Journal*, 12 September, B3.

Carey, S. (2017). Low price, no fills: more airlines launch basic economy fares; American Airlines follow Delta in unveiling a cheaper economy-cabin product, *Wall Street Journal*, 18 January, A1.

Chatterjee, S. and Jain, Y. (2015). Steering airlines toward TRO, *Ascend*, 4, 55–57.

Chong, A. (2015). *SIA confident despite 'late-entry' into premium economy market.* Online. Available at: http://dashboard.flightglobal.com/app/#/articles/412627?context=newssearch (accessed 15 October 2016).

Congressional Documents and Publications (2016). *Schumer: airline amendment to allow more legroom & expand seat size defeated; Schumer vows to keep trying to return lost inches to travelers.* Online. Available at: www.schumer.senate.gov/newsroom/press-releases/schumer-airline-amendment-to-allow-more-leg-room-and-expand-seat-size-defeated-schumer-vows-to-keep-trying-to-return-lost-inches-to-travelers (accessed 17 September 2016).

Cowen, M. (2013). Hottest tickets in town, *Airline Business*, 29 (July), 36–38.

Dasburg, J.H. (1998). Northwest Airlines Aircares: a community support program combining community relations, marketing, promotion and public relations. In: G.F. Burler and M.R. Keller (eds). *Handbook of Airline Marketing*, New York, McGraw-Hill.

Duncan, C. (2017). Flying sinks to new low with 'basic economy', *Sunday Times*, 29 January, 2.

Dunn, G. (2016). Middle ground, *Airline Business*, 32 (May), 40–41.

Elliott, C. (2017). 'Basic economy' fares may lack basic amenities, *USA Today*, 9 January, B5.

Ferguson, M. (2015). Route to market, *Airline Business*, 31 (June), 42–43.

Field, D. (2008). Airlines battle with screen scrapers, *Airline Business*, 24 (October), 14.

Grewal, D. and Levy, M. (2017). *M: Marketing*, 5th edition, New York, McGraw-Hill.

Halligan, N. (2015). *Arsenal FC sponsorship was Emirates' best says founding CEO.* Online. Available at: www.arabianbusiness.com/arsenal-fc-sponsorship-deal-was-emirates-best-says-founding-ceo-579734.html#.V--_wPkrKM9 (accessed 10 December 2016).

Hanke, M. (2016a). *Airline E-Commerce*, New York, Routledge.

Hanke, M. (2016b) The race to cyberspace. *Airline Business*, 32 (March), 32–35.

IATA (International Air Transport Association) (2017). *Airline distribution.* Online. Available at: www.iata.org/whatwedo/airline-distribution/ndc/Pages/ndc-airlines.aspx (accessed 15 October 2016).

IdeaWorksCompany (2017). *Ancillary revenue defined.* Online. Available at: www.ideaworkscompany.com/ancillary-revenue-defined (accessed 15 October 2016).

IEG (2016). *Sponsor profiles: the five biggest spenders in the airline category.* Online. Available at: www.sponsorship.com/iegsr/2016/07/25/Sponsor-Profiles--The-Five-Biggest-Spenders-In-The.aspx (accessed 15 October 2016).

Joyce, S. (2013). *A brief history of travel technology: from its evolution to looking at the future.* Online. Available at: www.tnooz.com/article/a-brief-history-of-travel-technology-from-its-evolution-to-looking-at-the-future/ (accessed 16 October 2016).

Kahn, S. (2016). Trending forward: five crucial airline industry trends, *Ascend for Airlines*, 2, 20–22.

Karp, A. (2007). Seat wars, *Air Transport World*, 44 (April), 39–42.

Kunkle, F. (2016). *Senate kills measure that might have stopped sardine-seating on airlines*. Online. Available at: www.washingtonpost.com/news/tripping/wp/2016/04/08/senate-kills-measure-that-might-have-stopped-sardine-seating-on-airlines/ (accessed 8 October 2016).

Kwoh, L. and Korn, M. (2013). CEOs fly coach? Business travel turns frugal, *Wall Street Journal*, 13 February, B6.

Left, G. (2016). *An inside look at American Airlines brand new premium economy on the Boeing 787-9*. Online. Available at: http://viewfromthewing.boardingarea.com/2016/10/09/inside-look-american-airlines-brand-new-premium-economy-boeing-787-9/ (accessed 11 November 2016).

MacMillan, D. and Dwoskin, E. (2014). Smile! Marketing firms are mining your selfies, *Wall Street Journal*, 10 October, B1.

Majcher, K. (2011). Investing in interiors, *Aviation Week & Space Technology*, 173 (24 October), 94–96.

McCartney, S. (2012). The middle seat: the many ways to catch shut-eye in the sky, *Wall Street Journal*, 10 May, D3.

McCartney, S. (2016a). The middle seat: help airlines spend their windfall – a flier wish list, *Wall Street Journal*, 17 March, D1.

McCartney, S. (2016b). The middle seat: a fee too far? Paying to sit with family on a flight, *Wall Street Journal*, 26 May, D1.

McDonald, M. (2007a). A delicate balance, *Air Transport World*, 44 (May), 56–60.

McDonald, M. (2007b). Which channel works best? *Air Transport World*, 44 (August), 36–38.

McDonald, M. (2010). Direct to the customer, *Air Transport World*, 47 (April), 39–41.

McDonald, M. (2013). Distribution tail wind, *Air Transport World*, 50 (March), 53.

Michaels, D. (2012). Airlines escalate arms race in seating, *Wall Street Journal*, 8 March, B10.

Michaels, D. (2014). Why this plane seat is the most profitable, *Wall Street Journal*, 6 March, B1.

Morrison, M. (2016a). Room to improve, *Flight Daily News: Aircraft Interiors Expo*, 3 (7 April), 28–30.

Morrison, M. (2016b). Tight decisions, *Flight Daily News: Aircraft Interiors Expo*, 2 (6 April), 30.

Muther, C. (2016). How premium economy became the new hot seat: it's growing in popularity as airline seating space shrinks, *Boston Globe*, 24 April, M1.

Nicas, J. (2012). The long, slow death of a first class, *Wall Street Journal*, 20 July, B1.

Norris, G. and Flottau, J. (2014). Sweet spot, *Aviation Week & Space Technology*, 15 September, 20–21.

O'Neil-Dunne, T. (2016). *2017 predictions: a transformational year for airline distribution technology*. Online. Available at: www.tnooz.com/article/2017-prediction-airline-technology/ (accessed 14 January 2017).

O'Neill, S. (2013). *The real NDC: decoding the planned (r)evolution in airline distribution by IATA and airlines*. Online. Available at: www.tnooz.com/article/the-real-ndc-decoding-the-planned-revolution-in-airline-distribution-by-iata-and-airlines/ (accessed 14 January 2017).

O'Neill, S. (2017). *United signals it wants a better deal with reservation middlemen*. Online. Available at: https://skift.com/2017/01/20/united-signals-it-wants-a-better-deal-with-reservation-middlemen (accessed 28 January 2017).

O'Reilly, N. and Horning, D. (2013). Leveraging sponsorship: the activation ratio, *Sports Management Review*, 16, 424–437.

Painter, K. (2017). Up in the air: fractious time for airlines and online sites that sell tickets, *Star Tribune*, 28 January.

Peter, J.P. and Donnelly, J. (2015). *A Preface to Marketing Management*, 14th edition, New York, McGraw-Hill.

Pilling, M. (2009). Distribution confusion, *Airline Business*, 24 (May), 30–32.

Rashidi, T., Abbasi, A., Maghrebi, M., Hasan, S. and Waller, T. (2016). Exploring the capacity of social networks for modelling travel behaviour: opportunities and challenges, *Transportation Research Part C: Emerging Technologies*, 75, 197–211.

Reals, K. (2016). The big squeeze, *Aviation Week & Space Technology*, 178(7), 46.

Rokou, T. (2016). *Ryanair unveils 2016 (year 3) 'Always Getting Better' plan*. Online. Available at: www.traveldailynews.com/post/ryanair-unveils-2016-%28year-3%29-%E2%80%9Calways-getting-better%E2%80%9D-plan-71480 (accessed 14 October 2016).

Russel, E. (2014). *Lufthansa 'pleased' with initial premium economy demand*. Online. Available at: http://dashboard.flightglobal.com/app/#/articles/404591?context=relatedarticles (accessed 14 October 2017).

Schall, D. (2016). *The definitive oral history of online travel*. Online. Available at: https://skift.com/history-of-online-travel/ (accessed 14 October 2016).

Shaw, S. (2004). *Airline Marketing and Management*, 5th edition, Aldershot, Ashgate.

Sobie, B. (2008a). Weaving the web, *Airline Business*, 24 (March), 46–49.

Sobie, B. (2008b). Rise of the robots, *Airline Business*, 24 (March), 51.

Solomon, M., Marshall, G. and Stuart, E. (2016). *Marketing*, 8th edition, Boston, MA, Pearson.

Sorenson, J. (2015). *The airline manual for merchandising*. Online. Available at: www.ideaworkscompany. com/wp-content/uploads/2015/10/Manual-for-Merchandising.pdf (accessed 14 January 2017).

Sorenson, J. (2017). *Ancillary revenue goes mobile: the best methods used by the top 25 airlines*. Online. Available at: www.ideaworkscompany.com/wp-content/uploads/2017/03/Ancillary-Revenue-Goes-Mobile.pdf (accessed 24 February 2017).

Sumer, B. (2015a). Frontier Airlines plans to reduce dependence on A319s, *Aviation Daily*, 401(11), 11 June, 3.

Sumer, B. (2015b). *Frontier's new ultra low cost model is working*. Online. Available at: http://aviationweek. com/commercial-aviation/frontier-s-new-ultra-low-cost-model-working (accessed 14 January 2017).

Taylor, E. (2014). Class war, *Airline Business*, 30 (November), 42–44.

The Economist (2016). *Carriers are ditching first class cabins as business class becomes plusher*. Online. Available at: www.economist.com/blogs/gulliver/2016/06/changes-front-and-centre (accessed 14 October 2017).

Thisdell, D. (2016). Tony's Midus touch, *Flight Daily News: Aircraft Interiors Expo*, 3 (7 April), 1.

Thomas, G. (2008). You're FIRED! *Air Transport World*, 45 (November), 47, 50–52.

Total Sportek (2017). *25 world's most popular sports (ranked by 13 factors)*. Online. Available at: www.total-sportek.com/most-popular-sports/ (accessed 13 January 2017).

US Government Publishing Office (2016). *H.R.3334 – Families Flying Together Act of 2015*. Online. Available at: www.congress.gov/bill/114th-congress/house-bill/3334/text (accessed 28 March 2017).

Walker, M. (2017). *Dear airlines: online marketing works in other ways*. Online. Available at: www.tnooz.com/ article/airlines-online-marketing-works-other-ways/ (accessed 13 March 2017).

Wang, X., Yoonjoung, H., Schwartz, Z., Legoherel, P. and Specklin, F. (2015). Revenue management: progress, challenges, and research prospects, *Journal of Travel & Tourism Marketing*, 32, 797–811.

Weeks, C., Cornwell, T. and Drennan, J. (2008). Leveraging sponsorships on the Internet: activation, congruence and articulation, *Psychology & Marketing*, 25(5), 637–654.

Whiteman, L. (2016). *It's time for Southwest to make tough decisions on pricing and revenue*. Online. Available at: www.thestreet.com/story/13648190/1/it-s-time-for-southwest-to-make-tough-decisions-on-pricing-and-revenue.html (accessed 13 October 2016).

Wittman, M. and Belobaba, P. (2016). *Customized offers in airline revenue management*. Online. Available at: www.agifors.org/resources/Documents/Anna%20Valicek%20Papers/2016/Customized%20Offers%20 in%20Airline%20Revenue%20Management.pdf (accessed 13 October 2016).

Yamanouchi, K. (2016). Congress to airlines: keep families together – legislation doesn't actually impose seating rules, *The Atlanta Journal: Constitution*, 20 July, A11.

Yardley, S. (2016). *Game changer: the growing role of data in sponsorship*. Online. Available at: www.sponsorship. com/About-IEG/Sponsorship-Blogs/Guest/March-2016/Game-Changer--The-Growing-Role-Of-Data-In-Sponsors.aspx (accessed 12 March 2017).

# 14

# Airport marketing

*Nigel Halpern*

## Introduction

Airport marketing only really emerged as a field of interest to researchers during the 1990s. Even up until the 1980s, the general view was that airports were natural monopolies, and therefore not in a position to influence target markets through marketing (Halpern and Graham, 2013). Early research on airport marketing challenges the traditional view. For instance, Tretheway (1998) debates if airport marketing is an oxymoron. He concludes that it is not, and that as a result of changes taking place in their business environment, airports are increasingly exposed to competitive forces (see also Chapter 10) that can be exploited through marketing. Evidence of airport competition and the need for marketing is provided in later studies (e.g. Thelle et al., 2012; Tretheway and Kincaid, 2010).

By the late 1990s, it seemed that airports were allocating greater resources to marketing. For instance, Humphreys (1999) investigates the number of marketing staff employed at nine regional airports in the United Kingdom (UK) from 1991 to 1997. His study finds that the number grew at each airport. The ratio of marketing staff per passenger also grew at all but two of the nine airports. Additional examples are provided in later studies. For instance, Thelle et al. (2012) show that the number of full-time staff employed in marketing at Copenhagen Airport increased from two in 2000 to four in 2005 and eight in 2012. The same study also shows that expenditure on sales, marketing and administration at Zurich Airport increased from 17.6 million Swiss francs in 1999 to 39.1 million Swiss francs in 2011.

During the last few decades, there has been a growing interest in airport marketing as a field of academic study, and there are now various textbooks and book chapters that address general issues associated with airport marketing. For instance: Jarach (2005) examines the new management vision of airport marketing in his book *Airport Marketing: Strategies to Cope with the New Millennium Environment*; Halpern and Niskala (2008) consider the role of airport marketing on tourism development in the book *Aviation and Tourism: Implications for Leisure Travel*; Halpern (2010) looks at the marketing practices used by small regional airports in the book *Air Transport Provision in Remoter Regions*; Kramer et al. (2010) provide a *Marketing Guidebook for Small Airports* that helps airport managers to develop a marketing programme for their small general aviation or commercial service airport; Halpern and Graham (2013) apply marketing principles and practice to the airport industry in their book *Airport Marketing*; and each of the four editions of Graham's (2014) book *Managing Airports: An International Perspective*, which was first published in 2001, has included a chapter on the role of airport marketing.

There is also a growing body of literature on specific aspects of airport marketing that will be reviewed in this chapter (for airline marketing, see Chapter 13). Literature tends to focus on the marketing of airports to businesses (mainly to airlines) or to consumers (mainly to passengers). There is also some, albeit rather limited, literature on public sector marketing (which is directed at government) and social marketing (which is directed at communities and other stakeholders that have an interest in the activities of an airport).

This chapter consists of four main sections. The first section has provided an introduction. The second section considers the marketing of airports to businesses. The main focus is on aviation marketing to airlines and trade, and in particular the airport route development process. However, marketing to commercial business partners such as retailers is also considered. The third section considers the marketing of airports to consumers, and in particular the role of marketing communications and branding. The main focus of the third section is on the marketing of airports to passengers, but also to other airport users. The final section provides a conclusion.

## Marketing of airports to businesses

### Aviation marketing

The core purpose of an airport is to facilitate the landing and take-off of aircraft. Airlines are therefore the main customer of an airport, and aviation marketing, that is marketing directed at airlines, is crucial to the success of an airport and its surrounding communities (Griffin, 2012). It is important to note that aviation marketing may also be directed at trade partners such as tour operators or travel agents in the case of non-scheduled holiday charters, or freight forwarders or shippers in the case of cargo air services. In the case of general aviation, it may be directed at flying schools, clubs, specialist operators (e.g. of ambulance or offshore services), or personal aircraft owners that may base their aircraft at the airport.

The process through which airports market themselves to airlines has become known as airport route development (or air service development in some countries). Decisions regarding route development were traditionally considered to be an airline or government function, and the role of the airport was largely to respond to requests from airlines rather than proactively seeking their business (Halpern and Graham, 2013). However, this has been influenced by changes in the airport business environment, such as the increased liberalisation and deregulation of air transport markets (see Chapters 6 and 7), and the commercialisation and in some cases privatisation of airports (see Chapters 3 and 8). Airport route development has subsequently become a common activity among airports, and the tasks associated with it are of growing interest to researchers. For instance, route development is recognised by Spasojevic et al. (2017) as one of five areas of growing interest to researchers in the field of air transport and tourism.

Thelle et al. (2012: 81) define airport route development as the "marketing activities undertaken by airports with the aim of attracting new routes, for example through participation in route development conferences, offering incentive schemes, meetings with airlines, producing bespoke reports for airlines." However, it is not just for new routes. Martin (2009: v) states that route development "includes the attraction, initiation, expansion, retention, or any improvements of air service and can include changes in pricing, frequency, capacity, hub connectivity, or the number of non-stop destinations served." It is also a complex and dynamic process that

*Table 14.1* Main stages in the airport route development process

| Main stage | Associated tasks |
| --- | --- |
| Objectives | Develop objectives for route development; consider corporate values, vision and mission; consider wider objectives of the region. |
| Research | Define catchment area; assess internal and external business environment; identify unserved or underserved routes; analyse opportunities; produce forecasts for potential routes; target potential operators; assess financial viability. |
| Activities | Communicate opportunities; consider price incentives and marketing support; modify product/service offering if necessary; consider branding; seek opportunities for collaboration; lobby if necessary; consider management processes. |
| Implementation | Assess and allocate resources; determine processes and procedures for dealing with airlines; control and evaluate routes but also the route development process. |

*Source*: Adapted from Halpern and Graham (2016).

consists of four main stages (see Table 14.1). Complexity occurs as a result of airports being at various and multiple stages at any particular time, while dynamism is needed to constantly assess and adapt actions taken in response to changes taking place in the business environment. Griffin (2016) also recognises the complexities associated with airport route development. He identifies similar tasks to those listed in Table 14.1, but also states that route development ultimately involves negotiating a deal, and the formulation of a contract within the relevant legal framework. Considering the diversity of tasks, Griffin explains how a route development manager is expected to be skilled not only in marketing, but also in areas such as analysis, sales, politics, fundraising, accounting, negotiating and law.

In their survey of 124 airports worldwide, Halpern and Graham (2015) find that the majority of airports are actively involved in route development for a range of objectives. The most common objectives are to develop new routes (with new or existing airlines), grow existing routes and retain existing routes. Airports are less focused on influencing change to existing routes, which is arguably more of an airline function. The findings of their study show that route development practice is underpinned by intelligence-based and highly targeted and proactive approaches, especially to personal selling, and from a growing and dedicated team of personnel. Almost half of the airports surveyed have a route development team based at the airport itself, and a further 10 per cent have a route development team based within the head office of the airport authority. Route development activities at remaining airports, especially smaller airports, are typically carried out by the airport manager or their deputy, or by an employee in a different department.

In a subsequent study, but also based on the survey of 124 airports worldwide, Halpern and Graham (2016) find that the overall level of route development activity at an airport has a significant positive effect on performance in terms of the airport's ability to develop new routes, or grow, retain and influence change to existing routes compared to similar or competing airports. However, two factors associated with the airport business environment were also found to have a significant effect on performance; market growth has a positive effect, while airport constraints have a negative effect. This means that regardless of how much effort an airport puts into route development, there is no substitute for having a market that is growing or demonstrates potential for growth. In addition, airports that are constrained (e.g. by legal or regulatory conditions, infrastructure constraints, or limited operating conditions or capabilities) are inherently likely to be poor performers when it comes to route development.

Route development activities that are most used by airports are listed in Table 14.2. Airports often pursue multiple types of air service simultaneously (Halpern and Graham, 2015; Schano, 2008), and may therefore use different activities for different types of air service (e.g. see de Haan, 2012). However, the general principles are rather similar. For instance, Gardiner (2006) conducts a survey of 40 airports for his doctoral thesis on 'Airport choice factors for non-integrated cargo airlines'. The findings show that airports use personal approaches to cargo airlines most (used by 93 per cent of the airports). This was followed by work with freight forwarders (85 per cent), marketing support for joint advertising or promotional campaigns (82 per cent), flexibility on pricing (80 per cent), advertising brochures (80 per cent), cargo pages on their website (70 per cent), work with established shippers (68 per cent), print advertising in industry publications (63 per cent), work with the local business community (60 per cent), benchmarking with other airports (53 per cent) and sponsorship of cargo events (38 per cent). These approaches and the extent to which they are used are not too dissimilar to those listed in Table 14.2.

In measuring the effect that individual route development activities have on route development performance, Halpern and Graham (2016) find that collaboration (through the use of strategic marketing partnerships and collaborating with other airports), and the use of active and targeted forms of personal selling (including inviting target airlines to visit the airport and attending route development networking events), are the only activities that have a significant positive effect, while offering flexibility on pricing has a significant negative effect.

The need to collaborate emphasises that airport management must work with their stakeholders when developing route development strategies. Stakeholders here will typically include regional economic development agencies, destination management organisations, or tourism authorities, local businesses, Chambers of Commerce or other business associations. The importance of

*Table 14.2* Activities used in airport route development

| Activities | Average use |
| --- | --- |
| Attend route development networking events | 3.35 |
| Meet airlines in their offices and present to them | 3.25 |
| Use strategic marketing partnerships | 3.12 |
| Offer flexibility on pricing | 3.11 |
| Develop joint advertising or promotional campaigns | 3.07 |
| Target a specific airline with a bespoke report | 3.04 |
| Invite target airlines to visit the airport | 2.96 |
| Modify facilities or services to meet airline needs | 2.94 |
| Send marketing materials to airlines by email | 2.87 |
| Improve processes for providing assistance to airlines | 2.79 |
| Promote a recognised airport brand | 2.73 |
| Collaborate with other airports | 2.68 |
| Present itself on route development websites | 2.52 |
| Hire a consultant to conduct activities | 2.37 |
| Provide information on the airport website | 2.34 |
| Lobby for the removal of obstacles for further development | 2.33 |
| Send marketing materials to airlines by post/fax | 1.82 |
| Communicate with airlines via social media | 1.77 |

*Source*: Adapted from Halpern and Graham (2016) and based on their survey of 124 airports worldwide.

*Note*: Average use varies on a scale from 1 'not at all' to 5 'to a great extent'.

stakeholders such as tourism authorities in the case of tourism-related air services is highlighted by Wells (2016), who believes that their participation in the route development process can be a key factor for airlines when deciding whether to launch a new route.

Halpern and Graham (2016) highlight two key benefits from collaboration. First, it allows for the pooling of resources (e.g. in terms of gathering market intelligence or financial support for new or improved air services). This may be vital for smaller airports with more limited resources and expertise. Collaboration also encourages the development of an integrated approach that takes into account the wider regional objectives for route development, such as to attract inbound tourism or inward investment to the region, develop trade links for cargo, influence business activity and location decisions, or to encourage greater local use of the airport (e.g. in the case of general aviation). Airports, along with their stakeholders, can then develop active and targeted forms of personal selling (e.g. by inviting target airlines to visit the airport and attending route development networking events) in order to communicate potential opportunities. This is quite different to the passive approach that was typically used by airports in the past, when they simply responded to requests from airlines seeking to develop air services at their airport.

Airports may also need to gather support from government, local communities and other stakeholders that have an interest in the airport, and may affect or influence decisions, for instance relating to airport funding or investment, permission to expand or develop infrastructure and services at the airport, or goodwill towards the airport. This emphasises the importance of public sector and social marketing (e.g. see Appold and Kasarda, 2010; Kinsey, 2017).

Airport user charges have been known to play a key role in the decision of airlines to serve an airport, especially for low cost carriers (LCCs), because charges often contribute a greater proportion of their total operating costs than they do for other airline business models. However, increased competition means that they can influence the decisions of all airline business models, and discounts or incentive schemes have become something of an expectation from airlines when negotiating charges at airports that seek growth (see also Chapter 12). It was therefore surprising for Halpern and Graham (2016) to find that offering flexibility on pricing (e.g. with discounted user charges or other incentives) has a significant negative effect on route development performance. They suggest that it may be because airports that have poor performance due to inherent weak factors, such as a limited catchment area, feel that they have a greater need to offer flexibility in order to attract traffic that would not otherwise consider operating at the airport as a feasible option.

Halpern and Graham (2013) describe three main types of discount or incentive scheme used by airports: discounted user charges (which typically diminish over a set period of time and as the new route or change to a service or base becomes more established); risk-sharing arrangements (where the public and private sectors raise money to offer airlines a time-limited revenue guarantee to cover the costs associated with starting a new or changed route); and travel banks (where the public and private sectors guarantee booking a time-limited minimum number of seats with an airline during the start-up or change to the service). The first type fits into what Fichert and Klophaus (2011) classify as being within an established charging system, while the last two types are separate schemes introduced in addition to an established scheme. Some airports also offer marketing support (e.g. the payment of a one-off grant to be spent on advertising and promotion of a new route or other activities connected to route development).

The use of incentive schemes by airports has increased in recent years, and they are now commonplace at airports. For instance, a survey of 52 airports in the United States (US) finds that 65 per cent of airports offer incentive schemes or agreements for domestic air services and 48 per cent for international ones (Hargrove, 2010). More recently, Ryerson's (2016) survey of 70 US airports finds that 63 per cent have a published air service incentive programme for domestic or international air services. Similarly, Malina et al. (2012) find that 63 per cent of Europe's 200 largest airports offer incentives of some kind to airlines, whether through an official incentive scheme or through bilateral airport–airline or government–airline agreements. Other descriptive studies in this area include: Laurino and Beria (2014), who discuss incentive schemes used by three airports in Italy that are based on bilateral agreements rather than transparent incentive programmes; Jones et al. (2013) develop a taxonomy of incentive schemes based on an analysis of data for 46 European airports, and identify a significant magnitude and widespread use of such schemes; and Fichert and Klophaus (2011) classify incentive schemes and describe their potential advantages and disadvantages with examples from larger German and selected European airports. Other, more analytical studies investigate determinants for offering incentives from an airport perspective (Allroggen et al., 2013) and motivations for support from a regional public authority perspective (Núñez-Sánchez, 2015).

Key questions exist regarding the impact of such schemes and whether or not they are effective in meeting objectives for route development. For instance, Weatherill (2006) explains how many incentive programmes that are used at airports in North America do not accomplish their goals of securing long-term viable air services. Unfortunately, there has been little quantitative research that addresses these questions, possibly due to issues associated with accessing the necessary data from airports. One exception includes Barbot (2006), who finds that subsidies for secondary airports result in growth in demand, adding new users, and a switch of passengers from full service carriers to LCCs. More research is needed on the success of incentive schemes given that they are now widely and comprehensively used by airports, and this call is starting to be addressed. For instance, Ryerson (2016) finds that 26 of 44 US airports with air service incentive programmes that were able to recruit new routes spent a combined total of US$171.5 million between 2012 and the first quarter of 2015 to recruit them. Forty per cent of that expenditure was on routes that were not retained after the incentive period ended.

Most airports focus on developing air services that generate revenue, meaning that airport-specific incentives, with the exception of risk-sharing arrangements, may not always target routes that have a wider economic benefit to the region (Halpern and Graham, 2013). As a result, a number of European airports became involved in so-called Route Development Funds (RDFs) that are based on a partnership approach involving the public sector (e.g. regional administrations, development agencies and tourism authorities), airlines and airports. The aim is to encourage new air services that improve business connectivity and inbound tourism, thus focusing on regional economic development (see STRAIR, 2005 for more information).

RDFs have been credited with stimulating new routes with wider economic benefits to their regions (e.g. see Christodoulou et al., 2009; Scott Wilson, 2009). However, as with the incentive schemes mentioned earlier, their effectiveness is sometimes questioned because a number of routes end up being seasonal rather than year-round, or are discontinued after the funding period has expired (Pagliari, 2005). Recently introduced European guidelines on financing of airports and start-up aid to airlines departing from regional airports has now restricted the use of RDFs anyway (e.g. see EC, 2005, 2014). Similar issues elsewhere have also resulted in guidelines being produced (e.g. see FAA, 2010 for the US).

## Commercial sector marketing

Airports are increasingly focused on diversifying their business, and have a growing emphasis on the generation of non-aeronautical and non-aviation revenues (see Chapters 10 and 12). Forty-five per cent of total revenues at airports came from such activities in 2014 (ACI, 2015). There is therefore a growing need for airports to focus their efforts on marketing to commercial partners such as retailers, food and beverage service providers, car park management and car hire companies, advertisers, and companies interested in land use and real estate opportunities at airports.

Despite its importance, there is very little literature on the subject of airport commercial sector marketing. There is a chapter on 'Retail marketing within the airport environment' in Freathy and O'Connell (1998) – the first and perhaps only major book on airport retailing. However, it focuses on marketing to consumers rather than to businesses. Similarly, Bork (2007) considers why retail marketing is important and how it should be undertaken from a consumer perspective, while Topping (2010) investigates factors to consider when launching promotions and incentives for passengers in airport retailing. There are also a number of guidebooks published by the Airport Cooperative Research Program (ACRP) (e.g. Crider et al., 2011; LeighFisher, 2011; Oever et al., 2011). The ACRP guidebooks are very much focused on contracting aspects of commercial development rather than marketing. This is perhaps to be expected given that success in this area is to a large extent linked to the contractual relationships between airports and their tenants and/or concessionaires. However, evidence from airport operators such as Changi Airport Group's (CAG) approach to retail suggests that marketing also plays a role.

CAG provide brochures and information about their marketing activities to retail prospects on the corporate pages of their website (see CAG, 2017). This includes contact details, and information about the philosophy behind what they call the Changi Experience, the awards and accolades that they have accumulated, a newsroom that allows existing and potential partners to keep up to date on the latest happenings and projects, fun facts about the airport's retail offer, detailed information on terminal infrastructure and services, featured stories from tenants, and information on leasing opportunities and awarded leases.

In terms of marketing support, CAG offers tenants the opportunity to showcase brands via digital screens and king-size digital lightboxes throughout the airport, and digital 360-degree columns in strategic locations. CAG produces a printed shop and dine guide, and regularly organises events and promotional campaigns in collaboration with its retail partners to generate footfall and boost customer spending, for instance with seasonal marketing campaigns, Changi Millionaire, Changi First, and the You Shop, We Absorb GST absorption campaign. CAG also supports the efforts of its retail partners with engaging platforms for consumers, such as iShopchangi, iKiosks, the Changi Rewards loyalty programme, shopping concierges, and a strong social and digital media presence.

Operators such as CAG also rely on conferences and exhibitions that attract senior-level attendees and bring together airports, travel retail operators and brands. Such events offer opportunities for airports to exhibit, network and carry out personal selling initiatives with prospects in a similar way to networking events that are used by airports for route development purposes.

## Marketing of airports to consumers

Airlines have traditionally been viewed as the main customers of airports, while passengers have then been viewed as the main customers of airlines. However, as airports seek to reduce their reliance on aeronautical revenues, they increasingly view passengers and other users that may consume non-aeronautical products and services as their customers too. There is therefore much greater attention on the marketing of airports to consumers, and while airports are often viewed as being more conservative, and behind their airline counterparts in terms of marketing to consumers, there is growing evidence that the gap is beginning to narrow (McCullen, 2013). A good source of examples, albeit only for North American airports, is Airports Council

International's (ACI) Marketing and Communications Awards, which have been presented annually since 1990 (e.g. see ACI North America, 2016a). They recognise and honour airport marketing and communications efforts in 18 categories, including print communications, radio advertising, public relations campaigns, digital advertising, websites, social media campaigns and brand identity. In 2015, there were 350 entries from airports, demonstrating a hive of activity at airports. This section will focus on two main areas relating to the marketing of airports to consumers: marketing communications and branding.

## Marketing communications

Marketing communications is focused on the communication of meaningful messages that allow companies to create, develop and maintain relationships with existing or potential customers, and subsequently pursue their marketing objectives. Traditional forms include advertising (mass communications via display, print, radio or television), direct marketing (direct communications via post or telephone), personal selling (face-to-face communications), public relations (publicity, often via a third party such as the press) and sales promotions (short-term incentives such as via discounts or competitions).

Historically, airports relied largely on the standard method of advertising by pushing messages to customers (Nigam et al., 2011). In an attempt to manage the benefits and burdens of their operations, airports also conducted public relations activities, albeit with a rather cavalier attitude (Appold and Kasarda, 2010). Direct marketing, personal selling and sales promotion have been less extensively used by airports in the past. However, they are now widely used, as has been seen with the case of personal selling to airlines earlier in this chapter. Detailed information on each form, along with extensive examples from industry, and a discussion on their relative strengths and weaknesses, is provided by Halpern and Graham (2013).

With the exception of personal selling, traditional forms tend to communicate general messages to a mass audience. As in many other industries, airport consumer markets are increasingly fragmented (Halpern, 2016). In air transport, this is partly due to increased demand and the emergence of new segments such as LCCs and a wider range of airport users with distinct needs and wants, while existing markets are more experienced and demanding (partly as a result of increased trip frequency, but also from the availability of information via the Internet and other forms of digital media). In addition, potential customers generally have more alternatives available to them as a result of increased competition in the airport sector (see Chapter 10). Fragmentation reduces the effectiveness of mass media communications and erodes brand loyalty, meaning that airports need to develop strategies that foster closer relationships in more narrowly defined micro-markets. This has been further encouraged by the development of new technologies, and in particular digital forms of communication such as via the Internet, mobile and social media (Halpern, 2016). New technologies allow airports to engage and interact with individuals rather than simply push messages to a mass audience.

One of the greatest challenges with the changing communications landscape is that markets are increasingly crowded with messages and media as airports, but also companies in general seek to engage individuals via a broad media mix rather than communicating to a mass audience via a single or small selection of channels. Innovative approaches are therefore needed in order to break through the marketing clutter and be more effective at delivering the right messages to the right person via the right media at the right time. To help facilitate this, airports need to have a clearer understanding of the consumer and their willingness to engage across different media, and provide them with offers of true value rather than unwanted intrusion (Halpern, 2016).

In addition, users rarely distinguish between the different forms of media that are now used for marketing communications. Companies tend to integrate traditional and digital approaches, and many of the traditional media such as display, print, radio, television, post and telephone are now available digitally anyway. This means that airports need to focus less on the types of media that they use, and more on how they can develop creative and compelling messages, and initiatives that engage people (Halpern, 2016). The concept of engagement marketing that invites and encourages consumers to participate in the evolution of a brand has therefore grown in popularity in recent years.

Common engagement initiatives used by air transport companies can be classified as being mainly offline and experiential (e.g. mobile marketing, street marketing, marketing through amenities, events and micro-events, and thematic approaches) or mainly online and digital (e.g. digital and online advertising, email marketing, mobile technologies, social media, and crowd-sourcing) (Halpern, 2016). Airlines have been very active with engagement initiatives in recent years, and while airports have been much slower to adapt than their airline counterparts, they too are becoming more active.

For instance, many airports embrace thematic approaches to retail promotions. In 2015, Hong Kong International celebrated Christmas with festive promotions, including cash coupon redemptions for travellers meeting the minimum spend requirement and over 2,000 surprise gifts for travellers. The gifts were handed out by Santa Claus and the airport's own mascot. In addition, there were gift-themed exhibitions, music performances, displays that show how different countries around the world celebrate Christmas, and shopping and retail offers in collaboration with retailers. Details about offers were available by scanning quick release (QR) codes on the promotional materials, and the airport offered free delivery for certain purchases (DFNI, 2015).

Crowdsourcing is another interesting tool for engagement that is used by airports (Halpern, 2016). The aim of crowdsourcing is to solicit ideas and opinions from a large audience, and then to use that intelligence to make business decisions. It also aims to develop loyalty to the brand through a process that engages people and encourages them to associate with it. It should complement, rather than replace, more traditional feedback mechanisms. Copenhagen uses an online crowdsourcing platform called CPH Ideas, where users can suggest ideas for the airport of the future. Users can then vote on whether they like the idea or not, and the most popular suggestions are then considered for implementation (see CPH Ideas, 2017).

Initiatives do not need to focus solely on engagement. Traditional approaches such as advertising and public relations still play an important role, especially when targeted at certain markets. However, they increasingly coexist with experiential and digital approaches. For instance, Halpern (2016) mentions how Manchester Airport in the UK launched its Fly Manchester campaign in 2013 to promote Manchester Airport in the north-west of England as an alternative to London airports for long-haul flights to/from the UK. The airport used digital communications, including advertising via Google DoubleClick (which provides targeted Internet advertising services such as DoubleClick Ad Exchange), the airport's home page, and social media accounts such as Twitter and Facebook. However, traditional communications were also used, including strategically targeted advertising on the exterior of buses, 48 outdoor displays and the generation of publicity on local television.

One of the greatest influences on airport marketing communications is the evolution of traveller connectivity. According to SITA (2014), 95 per cent of air passengers use websites for some part of their travel arrangements. Ninety-seven per cent carry a laptop, tablet device or mobile phone when they travel. Eighteen per cent travel with all three. Approximately four in five passengers have a smartphone, and 76 per cent of smartphone users have travel-related mobile applications on their phone. The growing connectivity of air passengers offers additional opportunities for airports to engage with them, and across the entire travel chain via a wider range of touch points before, during and after their trip.

Airports are responding to such trends. Offering online services via airport websites has become widespread practice (Halpern and Regmi, 2013), and many airports are increasing their efforts here. For instance, Lynden Pindling International in the Bahamas concluded a US$410 million redevelopment of its terminals in 2013, with a more Bahamian sense of place and expanded amenities (e.g. for shopping and dining) (Burns, 2013). In order to reflect the transformation and promote the new amenities, the airport decided to improve its online presence and launched a US$14,000 redevelopment of its website in 2015 (ACI North America, 2016b). In addition, an increasing number of airports such as Singapore Changi now offer opportunities to shop online (e.g. for duty-free) and collect it at the airport on departure or arrival.

Airports are increasingly introducing dedicated and branded mobile applications. By 2014, 164 European airports that collectively serve 73 per cent of European passengers had mobile applications (ACI Europe, 2015). Studies suggest that larger airports have been using applications for mobile marketing, and especially for marketing communications and branding, but that the range of uses is rapidly expanding into other areas (e.g. see Florido-Benítez, 2016). This is supported by ACI Europe (2015), which finds that airport mobile applications have traditionally provided flight status and airport information on wayfinding, public transport links, and for passengers with reduced mobility. However, they are increasingly being used to advertise sales promotions, distribute non-aviation-related products and services (such as duty-free purchases or the pre-booking of airport car parking), and provide links to airport loyalty programmes and social media. There is also evidence to suggest that airport mobile marketing can have a positive impact on passenger experience and satisfaction at airports (e.g. see Florido-Benítez et al., 2016; Inversini, 2017).

Martin-Domingo and Martin (2016) investigate website and mobile innovations at 75 larger international airports, and while their study recognises a number of innovators such as Amsterdam Schiphol, Copenhagen, London Heathrow and London Stansted, they conclude that airports in general "are still at the very early stages of leveraging all the potential uses of websites and mobile devices" (Martin-Domingo and Martin, 2016: 110). Evidence from industry, however, suggests that airport innovations are gathering pace, especially as a result of new technologies such as QR codes, beacon technology and augmented reality (e.g. see Kressman, 2016; Thomas, 2015). For instance, QR code walls have been used by airports including Frankfurt, Gatwick and Delhi to enable passengers to do their shopping more easily; Nice Côte d'Azur introduced a beacon-enabled mobile application that sends retail information and promotions to passengers based on their location in the terminal – it also links to the airport loyalty programme, allowing passengers to collect points when they move through the airport; GVK Chhatrapati Shivaji International launched a mobile application that incorporates augmented reality with beacon technology in order to create an immersive physical and digital passenger experience; San Francisco integrated Apple's Voiceover technology with its mobile application in order to assist the visually impaired to navigate through the airport using their smartphone; and Dubai Airports introduced a smartwatch application that enables users to view flight information on their watch.

Growth in the use of social media during the last decade has been remarkable, and social media has provided additional opportunities for airports to engage with consumers. Stambaugh (2013) suggests that social media also allows airports to increase self-sufficiency by reducing expenditure on traditional approaches to marketing and communications. The number of airports that use social media has grown rapidly in recent years. Halpern (2012) investigates the use of social media by 1,559 commercial airports worldwide and finds that almost one-fifth used at least one type of social media; 13 per cent used Facebook, 12 per cent used Twitter, 7 per cent used LinkedIn and 4 per cent used YouTube. In a more recent study, ACI Europe (2015) estimates that of their 450 member airports, 292 were on Twitter (serving 87 per cent of European passengers), 289 were on Facebook (86 per cent), 141 were on YouTube (55 per cent), 77 were using Google+ (22 per cent), 38 used Instagram (35 per cent) and 12 used Pinterest (22 per cent). This is, of course, a dynamic area, and the situation at airports is likely to have changed dramatically since the aforementioned studies were carried out.

Passengers are typically the main focus for social media initiatives at airports, but they are also used by airports to connect, communicate, interact and share information with all publics. It allows airports to conduct marketing communications in a traditional sense (by communicating with customers) but also in a non-traditional sense (by allowing customers to interact with the airport and with each other) (Halpern, 2016). As with other digital forms of communication, marketing is not the only purpose, and this represents a general blurring of key business functions, such as marketing, sales and customer service. ACI Europe's (2011) classification of uses for social media at airports includes customer service, informal relationship building, crisis handling, corporate communications and commercial. Halpern (2012) adds research and development, because airports use social media and other digital and mobile technologies to survey customer satisfaction or opinions (e.g. about opportunities for new routes) and to collect intelligence (e.g. on passenger needs, preferences and behaviour). Social media is also used more generally to develop an airport's image and reputation through engaging directly and efficiently with its online community.

Launching social media campaigns is relatively cheap, quick and easy to do. For instance, Ottowa International launched a contest via Twitter in 2014 to name a new canine recruit to the airport security team (see ACI North America, 2015). The campaign cost just US$200 (for prizes). The first tweet resulted in over 10,000 impressions, with almost 600 engagements. Additional interest was generated from further tweets and Facebook engagement activities that resulted in 533 likes, 727 comments and 123 shares. During the time frame of the contest, the airport experienced 122 new page likes on Facebook, 87 new followers on Twitter, 432 clicked links compared to an average of 30 and a range of free publicity from local media.

The ease of social media means that many airports have rushed into using it for marketing purposes. However, the challenge for airports is to find out how to engage customers via social media rather than just using it as a broadcast channel (Nigam et al., 2011). For instance, Wattanacharoensil and Schuckert (2015) investigate how 10 major airports engage social media users on Facebook (for communications, promotions, product distribution, research and management relationship building). Their study identifies widespread use of Facebook by the airports, but suggests that there is a lack of a strategic approach and consistency to its use. This is supported to some extent by Malinowski (2016), who states that "a successful social media strategy is about more than posting a clever status or tweet alongside an artistically filtered photo. It is about cultivating an individual identity for a brand" (Malinowski, 2016: 245). It therefore takes a great deal of time and effort to develop and maintain an effective social media strategy, which Malinowski (2016) suggests should at least cover the platforms that are expected to be used, expectations regarding how often to post content, who will manage the social media and how much time they are expected to spend on it per day, and what the budget will be. In addition, Halpern (2016) emphasises the need to set clear and measurable objectives, and to understand how analytics will be used to assess and optimise performance.

Halpern (2016) also highlights a number of challenges associated with social media, including that the quality of content can vary, and it can be misused, abused and attract negative comments from users. There is a possibility that problems go viral and that heavy-handed responses or attempts to cover them up often make things worse. Airports therefore need to manage such communications in a calm, transparent and timely manner, which can actually turn any negative situations into a positive, and help to build trust and develop true brand advocates.

## Branding

As mentioned in Chapter 10, it is increasingly important for airports to differentiate themselves from their competitors, and in an attempt to stand out from the crowd, airports increasingly use branding. According to Bates (2012), early pioneers in terms of developing their own distinctive brand include Amsterdam Schiphol and BAA in Europe, Dubai Airports and Abu Dhabi Airports Company in the Middle East, Dallas/Fort Worth, Los Angeles International and Toronto Pearson in North America, Airports Company South Africa in Africa, and Singapore Changi, Hong Kong and Incheon in Asia-Pacific.

The concept of an airport brand is related to the airport product (Halpern and Graham, 2013). It is typically represented by a combination of features that give the airport an identity and differentiate it from rival airports. It can add tangible cues to what is essentially an intangible service, and a strong airport brand can promote preference and loyalty among target markets. Ultimately, the brand defines the airport and everything that it stands for. It therefore links closely to marketing communications because the brand should run through all marketing communications and behaviour from the airport and its partners.

The airport name is often considered to be an important part of branding. In their study of 1,562 commercial airports worldwide, Halpern and Regmi (2011) find that three-quarters of airports are named after a single place, with almost half of them including a reference to the scope of services available. Regional differences exist with other names. For instance, calling an airport after natural or man-made attractions – and primarily for touristic reasons – is most common in Europe, names associated with political leaders and/or revolutionaries is most popular in Latin America/the Caribbean, and royalty names are most common in the Middle East. The study also investigates the use of airport slogans. Only one-tenth of all airports used these. Slogans typically relate to the connectivity that the airport provides, location characteristics, the airport experience or opportunities that it provides, or some kind of play on words that is associated with famous people of the area or a local colloquial term.

According to Halpern and Graham (2013), there are additional ways that airports can develop their brand. For instance: a logo can be used to represent the company and everything that it stands for; branded merchandise and giveaways can be produced to reinforce image and identity; and distinctiveness can be created in the terminal by using a consistent style of signage or interior design, or a particular colour scheme. However, creating distinctiveness in the terminal can be problematic for airports because its effectiveness may be diluted by the existence of other brands (e.g. of retailers, airlines, alliance groups, and displays or spaces used by advertisers that contribute an important source of revenue to airports).

To a large extent, the demand for airports is derived. In general, people do not travel to an airport for the sole purpose of visiting it. Instead, airports are part of an overall tourism product (Martin-Cejas, 2006; Vujicic and Wickelgren, 2011). As a result, some airports link their brand to the destination that it serves by replicating key characteristics such as the scenery, history or culture (e.g. see Halpern, 2008), and can therefore act as a symbiotic attribute for a destination and its marketing messages (Warnaby, 2009). This may be achieved by using approaches that have already been mentioned, such as with the airport name or interior design, but also with airport architecture, staff uniforms, or by developing a local identity for the airport's commercial facilities with famous local brand outlets and the sale of local merchandise, handcrafted goods or gourmet products (Halpern and Graham, 2013). The latter can provide benefits in terms of increased retail expenditure and a more authentic and enjoyable airport retail experience. The importance of branding for the airport travel retail experience is discussed in more detail by Oswald (2015).

The discussion thus far has considered how to develop an airport brand. However, what airports really want to know is what are the key characteristics of a successful airport brand. Karamanos (2014) suggests that it should offer customers an experience that is valued, remain consistent and relevant to the customer experience, incorporate new technologies that allow customers to engage and interact with the brand, be underpinned by a good reputation, be meaningfully different, have a distinctive personality that reflects the key traits of the airport, have global appeal combined with local touches, and offer a memorable experience. He points out that some airports use different strategies when developing their brand for airline customers, including logos and slogans that are different from their corporate brand. This is generally considered poor practice by marketing experts, and may to some extent reflect the fact that airport marketing is still in an early stage. However, it also highlights the complexities associated with airports serving different customers with different needs.

If used successfully, Paternoster (2008) argues that branding can significantly improve customer satisfaction with the airport experience. However, there are significant challenges for airports. In particular, airports have a composite nature because they generally do not deliver all of the products and services on offer at the airport. Despite this, consumers rarely distinguish between the different service providers, and tend to hold the airport operator accountable for the level of service provided airport-wide. Airports therefore need to take a strategic and holistic approach to branding and to customer service in general in order to maximise customer satisfaction with the airport experience. This is particularly important given that there is often a direct relationship between customer satisfaction and airport net revenues (Paternoster, 2008).

In addition, it is important to note that a key element of branding is associated with the relationship that a company has with its customers, and how they perceive and feel about the brand and its performance. Brands are therefore very much in the heads of customers, and are effectively built by customers, not by companies. Strong brands rely on good customer feedback, and airports need to work hard to develop advocates, rather than adversaries, for their brand. This has become more important with the growth in digital and social media, where customers can engage and interact with brands and become involved in the co-creation of brands, including to co-create messages and ideas for improvements. It is therefore essential for airports to take a customer-centric approach to branding.

Airports appear to put a lot of time and effort into branding and into associated activities such as naming the airport (e.g. see Grey, 2015; Halpern and Regmi, 2011). The ultimate question is whether or not branding has a significant impact on the success of an airport, and if so, how. There is a distinct lack of scientific research that provides quantifiable answers to such questions. However, the opinion from industry seems to be that branding is a powerful and important tool, at least for larger hub airports. For instance, Bates (2012) conducts interviews with key personnel at Amsterdam Schiphol, Los Angeles International and Singapore Changi. According to Amsterdam Schiphol, an airport brand represents key values and is a guarantee for quality – it is the airport's promise to the travelling public that the product – the airport – will perform to a guest's expectations. Los Angeles International claims that it influences, educates and makes people aware of what the airport represents and offers – it differentiates the airport in what is becoming an increasingly competitive industry. Singapore Changi claims that a strong brand paves the way for an airport keen to market its services internationally. The latter is supported by an interview with a global brand consultancy in Bates (2010), where it is stated that a strong brand can transform an airport and elevate it to another level. For instance, successful branding has helped Fraport transform from being considered as an operator of a single, important destination (Frankfurt) to a global airport manager.

The changing airport business environment is mentioned in Chapter 10. As a result, many airports have experienced changes to the way in which they are owned and/or operated in recent years (see Chapter 3). There have also been many airports that have made more subtle yet significant changes, such as deciding to target new customers, seeking clearer differentiation between them and their competitors, trying to keep their brand current, developing changes to their products/services, or ultimately adjusting the strategic vision and mission of the company. When significant changes are made, airports may seek to refresh or rebrand in order to reflect the changes and convey them to existing and potential customers. The need to do this is reflected to some extent by Castro and Lohmann (2014) because their study shows how airport branding is linked to airport strategy, so if the strategic intentions change significantly, so too should the brand.

There are many examples of airports or airport groups that have refreshed or rebranded in recent years, such as London Gatwick (McMullen, 2014), Vantage Airport Group (Airport World, 2014), Toronto Pearson (Pulla, 2012) and Birmingham International (Allett, 2010). The examples highlight some key considerations to take into account when attempting to refresh or reinvent an airport brand. Perhaps the most important consideration is that it is not just about making visual changes (e.g. to the name, logo, design or colours). Although important and supportive of any branding efforts, these tend to be more superficial and short-term changes. The focus should be more on the formation of new and improved subjective and emotional relationships with customers that are developed over a longer period of time. There will also need to be a detailed understanding of how the airport has been viewed in the past, and how it wants to be viewed in the future. In addition to communicating any changes that are made (e.g. via the airport's marketing communications strategy), there will most likely need to be changes made to the organisational structure and processes used by the airport, and how it behaves. There will therefore need to be a significant level of support and commitment internally (e.g. by employees), but also externally (e.g. by customers and other stakeholders), and with both groups buying in to the changes that are made. Ultimately, there needs to be clear and compelling reasons for change, and not just change for change's sake.

## Conclusion

Airport marketing is often viewed as being a relatively new area of activity for both airports and researchers. However, as this chapter demonstrates, it is an area of great interest, and there is a growing body of research and debate on critical issues, especially relating to airport route development, marketing communications and branding.

Airports have clearly entered a new era in route development practice that is underpinned by intelligence-based and highly targeted and proactive approaches to personal selling. Two key areas of interest have emerged that are not yet sufficiently addressed by the literature. The first relates to the use of collaborations (e.g. between airports, airlines, and stakeholders such as tourism authorities or regional development agencies). The use of collaborations has become fairly widespread, and they have been found to have a significant positive effect on route development performance. However, little is known about the role of individual partners and how their level and nature of involvement may vary. In addition, little is known about the key criteria for success. The second relates to measuring the impact of airport discounts and incentives for

233

route development (e.g. on airport financial performance and regional development rather than just on traffic performance). Similar to collaborations, discounts and incentive schemes are now widely used by airports seeking growth, but there is a fair amount of uncertainty regarding what financial or regional development impacts they have.

As a result of a growing interest in developing the non-aeronautical side of their business, airports are increasingly focused on marketing to commercial partners or customers. Much of the research to date has been on contracting aspects of commercial development rather than marketing, so there is a large gap in literature on this aspect of airport marketing.

There is now a fairly good understanding of the different forms of marketing communications that are used by airports, and how they should seek to engage individuals rather than simply communicate to a mass audience. Future research could pay greater attention to how airports can better integrate the range of messages and media that they now use, and how to track and assess the effectiveness of their efforts. This is important because consumers' responses to brands may not always be associated with the level of engagement that is experienced. There is also a need to measure the effectiveness of airport branding and any efforts to refresh or reinvent an airport brand. Branding is widely used by airports, and a lot of time and effort goes into it. However, little is known about the quantifiable outcomes of branding.

Given the considerable benefits but also burdens that airports potentially have, and the subsequent influence that government and other stakeholders might have on airport decisions, it is surprising that little is known about approaches to airport public sector or social marketing. The benefits and burdens, and approaches to managing them, are covered extensively by literature on airport corporate and social responsibility (e.g. see Chapter 18). However, there is little research on this from an airport marketing perspective. This is important given that marketing is increasingly about engagement and the development of long-term relationships, which can subsequently be used as a powerful tool for managing government and stakeholder relations with an airport.

## References

ACI (Airports Council International) (2015). *2015 ACI Airport Economics Report*, Montreal, ACI World.
ACI Europe (Airports Council International Europe) (2011). *Airports 2.0: How European Airports Are Embracing Social Media*, Brussels, ACI Europe.
ACI Europe (Airports Council International Europe) (2015). *Digital Report 2014–2015*, Brussels, ACI Europe.
ACI North America (Airports Council International North America) (2015). *YOW social media campaign #NameOurDog: social media campaigns*. Online. Available at: http://aci-na.org/content/yow-social-media-campaign-nameourdog (accessed 15 November 2016).
ACI North America (Airports Council International North America) (2016a). *Peggy G. Hereford Award*. Online. Available at: www.aci-na.org/content/peggy-g-hereford-award (accessed 15 November 2016).
ACI North America (Airports Council International North America) (2016b). *A new NassauLPIA.com: websites*. Online. Available at: http://aci-na.org/content/new-nassaulpiacom (accessed 30 June 2017).
Airport World. (2014). Brand evolution, *Airport World*, 1 (April), 37.
Allett, T. (2010). Hello world, *Airports International*, November, 21–25.
Allroggen, F., Malina, R. and Lenz, A.-K. (2013). Which factors impact on the presence of incentives for route and traffic development? Econometric evidence from European airports, *Transportation Research Part E: Logistics and Transportation Review*, 60, 49–61.
Appold, S. and Kasarda, J. (2010). *Love thy neighbour*. Online. Available at: www.airport-world.com/features/marketing-communications/634-love-thy-neighbour.html (accessed 2 June 2017).
Barbot, C. (2006). Low-cost airlines, secondary airports and state aid: an economic assessment of the Ryanair-Charleroi Airport agreement, *Journal of Air Transport Management*, 12, 197–203.

Bates, J. (2010). *Brand conscious*. Online. Available at: www.airport-world.com/features/marketing-communications/31-brand-conscious.html (accessed 2 June 2017).

Bates, J. (2012). *All in a brand*. Online. Available at: www.airport-world.com/item/1864-all-in-a-brand (accessed 2 June 2017).

Bork, A. (2007). Developing a retail marketing strategy to promote both airport and retailers, *Journal of Airport Management*, 1(4), 348–356.

Burns, J. (2013). *Redevelopment of Bahamas Island Airport complete*. Online. Available at: www.airport-world.com/news/general-news/3199-final-stage-of-redevelopment-of-bahamas-island-airport-opened.html (accessed 30 June 2017).

CAG (Changi Airport Group) (2017). *Innovative strategies*. Online. Available at: www.changiairport.com/corporate/our-expertise/innovative-strategies.html?anchor=innovativeretailstrategy (accessed 15 June 2017).

Castro, R. and Lohmann, G. (2014). Airport branding: content analysis of vision statements, *Journal of Air Transport Management*, 10, 4–14.

Christodoulou, G., Smyth, A. and Dennis, N. (2009). The Route Development Fund (RDF): can we sustain air transport in the regions? In: *European Transport Conference Proceedings*, London, Association for European Transport.

CPH Ideas (2017). *CPH Ideas*. Online. Available at: https://expanding.cph.dk/cphideas/ (accessed 30 June 2017).

Crider, R., Preisler, M., Autin, E., Roth, S., Armstrong, R.W., Fulton, S., et al. (2011). *Guidebook for Developing and Leasing Airport Property*, ACRP Report 47, Washington, DC, Transportation Research Board.

de Haan, F. (2012). Airports developing air services for cargo versus passenger airlines, *Aerlines Magazine*, 52, 1–3.

DFNI (Duty Free News International) (2015). *Hong Kong International Airport reveals festive promotions*. Online. Available at: www.dfnionline.com/latest-news/retail/hong-kong-international-airport-reveals-festive-promotions-15-12-2015/ (accessed 30 June 2017).

EC (European Commission) (2005). *Community Guidelines on Financing of Airports and Start-Up Aid to Airlines Departing from Regional Airports (2005/C 312/01)*, Official Journal C312, 9 December, Brussels, EC.

EC (European Commission) (2014). *Communication from the Commission: Guidelines on State Aid to Airports and Airlines*, Official Journal C99, 4 April, Brussels, EC.

FAA (Federal Aviation Administration) (2010). *Air Carrier Incentive Program Guidebook: A Reference for Airport Sponsors*, Washington, DC, FAA.

Fichert, F. and Klophaus, R. (2011). Incentive schemes on airport charges: theoretical analysis and empirical evidence from German airports, *Journal of Air Transport Management*, 1(1), 71–79.

Florido-Benítez, L. (2016). The impact of mobile marketing in airports, *Journal of Airline and Airport Management*, 6(1), 1–18.

Florido-Benítez, L., Alcázar Martínez, B. and Gonzalez Robles, E.M. (2016). Analysis of the impact of mobile marketing on passenger experience and satisfaction at an airport, *International Journal of Innovation, Management and Technology*, 7(1), 8–15.

Freathy, P. and O'Connell, F. (1998). *European Airport Retailing: Growth Strategies for the New Millennium*, London, Macmillan Business.

Gardiner, J. (2006). *An International Study of the Airport Choice Factors of Non-Integrated Cargo Airlines*, PhD Thesis, Loughborough, Loughborough University.

Graham, A. (2014). *Managing Airports: An International Perspective*, 4th edition, Abingdon, Routledge.

Grey, E. (2015). What's in a name? A journey in airport rebranding, *Airport Technology Market & Customer Insight*, 29 June.

Griffin, T. (2012). *Route to success: airport route development marketing is crucial*. Online. Available at: www.airport-world.com/item/1923-route-to-success (accessed 2 June 2017).

Griffin, T. (2016). Are route development managers superheroes? *Routes News*, 1, 21–22.

Halpern, N. (2008). Lapland's airports: facilitating the development of international tourism in a peripheral region, *Scandinavian Journal of Hospitality and Tourism*, 8(1), 25–47.

Halpern, N. (2010). The marketing of small regional airports. In: G. Williams and S. Bråthen (eds). *Air Transport Provision in Remoter Regions*, Farnham, Ashgate.

Halpern, N. (2012). Use of social media by airports, *Journal of Airline and Airport Management*, 2(2), 67–85.

Halpern, N. (2016). Air transport marketing. In: S. Ison and L. Budd (eds). *Air Transport Management: An International Perspective*, Abingdon, Routledge.

Halpern, N. and Graham, A. (2013). *Airport Marketing*, Abingdon, Routledge.

Halpern, N. and Graham, A. (2015). Airport route development: a survey of current practice, *Tourism Management*, 46, 213–221.

Halpern, N. and Graham, A. (2016). Factors affecting airport route development activity and performance, *Journal of Air Transport Management*, 56, 69–78.

Halpern, N. and Niskala, J. (2008). Airport marketing and tourism in remote destinations: exploiting the potential in Europe's northern periphery. In: A. Graham, A. Papatheodorou and P. Forsyth (eds). *Aviation and Tourism: Implications for Leisure Travel*, Aldershot, Ashgate.

Halpern, N. and Regmi, U.K. (2011). What's in a name? Analysis of airport brand names and slogans, *Journal of Airport Management*, 6(1), 63–79.

Halpern, N. and Regmi, U.K. (2013). Content analysis of European airport websites, *Journal of Air Transport Management*, 26, 8–13.

Hargrove, M.R. (2010). *Airport incentive programs: legal and regulatory considerations in structuring programs and recent survey observations*. Presented at 2010 ACI North America Airport Economics and Finance Conference, Miami, 3–5 May.

Humphreys, I. (1999). Privatisation and commercialisation: changes in UK airport ownership patterns, *Journal of Transport Geography*, 7(2), 121–134.

Inversini, A. (2017). Managing passengers' experience through mobile moments, *Journal of Air Transport Management*, 62, 78–81.

Jarach, D. (2005). *Airport Marketing: Strategies to Cope with the New Millennium Environment*, Farnham, Ashgate.

Jones, O.C., Budd, L.C.S. and Pitfield, D.E. (2013). Aeronautical charging policy incentive schemes for airlines at European airports, *Journal of Air Transport Management*, 33, 43–59.

Karamanos, G. (2014). Adding value, *Airport World*, 1 (April), 20–22.

Kinsey, T. (2017). Strategically depositing into your 'goodwill bank': an important and necessary asset for airports, *Journal of Airport Management*, 11(2), 154–167.

Kramer, L., Fowler, P., Hazel, R., Ureksoy, M. and Harig, G. (2010). *Marketing Guidebook for Small Airports*, ACRP Report 28, Washington, DC, Transportation Research Board.

Kressman, J. (2016). *The airport beacon revolution: digital marketing news this week*. Online. Available at: https://skift.com/2016/08/19/the-airport-beacon-revolution-digital-marketing-news-this-week/ (accessed 30 June 2017).

Laurino, A. and Beria, P. (2014). Low-cost carriers and secondary airports: three experiences from Italy, *Journal of Destination Marketing & Management*, 3, 180–191.

LeighFisher (2011). *Resource Manual for Airport In-Terminal Concessions*, ACRP Report 54, Washington, DC, Transportation Research Board.

Malina, R., Albers, S. and Kroll, N. (2012). Airport incentive programmes: a European perspective, *Transport Reviews*, 32(4), 435–453.

Malinowski, H. (2016). The profession of being social: developing an effective and purposeful social media strategy for an airport, *Journal of Airport Management*, 10(3), 245–252.

Martin, S.C. (2009). *Passenger Air Service Development Techniques*, ACRP Report 18, Washington, DC, Transportation Research Board.

Martin-Cejas, R. (2006). Tourism service quality begins at the airport, *Tourism Management*, 27(5), 874–877.

Martin-Domingo, L. and Martin, J.C. (2016). Airport mobile internet an innovation, *Journal of Air Transport Management*, 55, 102–112.

McCullen, D. (2013). Airport marketing exchange: thinking differently, *Airport World*, 4 (September), 68–69.

McMullen, D. (2014). Airport marketing exchange: spotlight on Gatwick's rebrand, *Airport World*, 1 (April), 42–43.

Nigam, S., Cook, R. and Stark, C. (2011). Putting the joy back into the airport experience: can social networking platforms make a genuine contribution to increasing commercial revenues and engaging customers, *Journal of Airport Management*, 6(1), 7–11.

Núñez-Sánchez, R. (2015). Regional public support to airlines and airports: an unsolved puzzle, *Transportation Research Part E: Logistics and Transportation Review*, 76, 93–107.

Oever, K.V., Gittens, A., Warner-Dooley, S., Zaslov, A., Tremont, H., Snipes, T., et al. (2011). *Guidebook for Developing and Managing Airport Contracts*, ACRP Report 33, Washington, DC, Transportation Research Board.

Oswald, N. (2015). Maximising the brand, *Airport World*, 3 (July), 29–30.

Pagliari, R. (2005). Developments in the supply of direct international air services from airports in Scotland, *Journal of Air Transport Management*, 11(4), 249–257.

Paternoster, J. (2008). Excellent airport customer service meets successful branding strategy, *Journal of Airport Management*, 2(3), 218–226.

Pulla, S. (2012). *On cloud 10: Toronto Pearson's airport rebrand and American Express sponsorship*. Online. Available at: www.airport-world.com/features/marketing-communications/2178-on-cloud-10.html (accessed 2 June 2017).

Ryerson, M.S. (2016). Incentivize it and they will come? How some of the busiest U.S. airports are building air service with incentive programs, *Journal of American Planning Association*, 82(4), 303–315.

Schano, R. (2008). A balanced approach to airport marketing: the impact of low cost airlines on tourism in Salzburg, *Journal of Airport Management*, 3(1), 54–61.

Scott Wilson (2009). *Evaluation of the Scottish Air Route Development Fund*, Glasgow, Scott Wilson.

SITA (2014). *Passenger IT Trends Survey 2014*, Geneva, SITA.

Spasojevic, B., Lohmann, G. and Scott, N. (2017). Air transport and tourism: a systematic literature review (2000–2014), *Current Issues in Tourism*, in press.

Stambaugh, C. (2013). Social media and primary commercial service airports, *Transportation Research Record: Journal of the Transportation Research Board*, 2325, 76–86.

STRAIR (Strategic Development and Cooperation between Airport Regions) (2005). *Air Service Development for Regional Agencies: Strategy, Best Practice and Results*, Stockholm/Oslo, STRAIR.

Thelle, M.H., Pedersen, T.T. and Harhoff, F. (2012) *Airport Competition in Europe*, Copenhagen, Copenhagen Economics.

Thomas, D. (2015). *Future airports could become hi-tech pleasure domes*. Online. Available at: www.bbc.com/news/business-30830296 (accessed 30 June 2017).

Topping, P. (2010). Promotions and incentives in airport retailing, *Journal of Airport Management*, 4(3), 208–210.

Tretheway, M.W. (1998). Airport marketing: an oxymoron? In: G.F. Butler and M.R. Keller (eds). *Handbook of Airline Marketing*, New York, McGraw-Hill.

Tretheway, M. and Kincaid, I. (2010). Competition between airports: occurrence and strategy. In: P. Forsyth, D. Gillen, J. Müller and H.-M. Niemeier (eds). *Airport Competition: The European Experience*, Farnham, Ashgate.

Vujicic, S. and Wickelgren, M. (2011). Destination branding in relation to airports: the case of the City of Valencia, *European Journal of Transport and Infrastructure Research*, 11(3), 334–345.

Warnaby, G. (2009). Non-place marketing: transport hubs as gateways, flagships and symbols? *Journal of Place Management and Development*, 2(3), 211–219.

Wattanacharoensil, W. and Schuckert, M. (2015). How global airports engage social media users: a study of Facebook use and its role in stakeholder communication, *Journal of Travel and Tourism Marketing*, 32, 656–676.

Weatherill, J. (2006). North American airline incentives: best practices and emerging trends, *Journal of Airport Management*, 1(1), 25–37.

Wells, E. (2016). *Tourism authorities play an increasingly important role in the route development process*. Online. Available at: www.routesonline.com/news/29/breaking-news/267703/tourism-authorities-play-an-increasingly-important-role-in-route-development-process-/ (accessed 15 November 2016).

# 15

# Airline capacity planning and management

*Cheng-Lung Wu and Stephen J. Maher*

## Introduction

This chapter focuses on capacity planning and operational management for airlines (for airports, see Chapter 16). In general, the purpose of airline capacity planning is to respond to current and future travel demand of passengers (see Chapter 19). While the capacity of an airline is certain and can be planned, travel demand attracted to a particular airline is fairly uncertain. Travel demand typically depends on marketing, product offerings in the market, competition, and to some extent the market power (share) of an airline. Economies of density are identified in the literature for airlines running a hub-and-spoke network, while low cost carriers (LCCs) tend to run a point-to-point network on trunk routes and generate desired economies of scale (Button, 2002) (see Chapter 11 for a discussion of airline economies of density/scale). Since flights have various levels of demand, airlines respond to this capacity management issue by combining two techniques: the use of various fleets of different sizes, and the adjustment of service frequency on the route.

While airline capacity can be planned well ahead of operations, capacity management on the day of operation poses another challenge for airlines. Airline products (i.e. flight tickets) are offered according to a planned timetable that distributes the available capacity among routes, given certain capacity constraints. Unfortunately, daily operations are subject to stochastic disruptions from various sources, such as airport operating capacity (see Chapter 16), weather, air traffic control (see Chapter 4), aircraft availability and passenger processing. These disruptions cause varying levels of disturbance to airline operations. As such, an airline may need to reallocate capacity in its network to fulfil its transportation obligation to its customers. The management of daily capacity is called airline operations management, also known as disruption management in the industry.

Adjusting capacity allocation and flight frequency in a network gives rises to two challenging airline planning problems, namely schedule generation (SG) (also known as timetabling in the industry) and fleet assignment (FA). The issue of daily capacity management in airline operations then deals with the reallocation or withdrawal of capacity due to operational disturbances in disruption management. This chapter focuses on two main issues relating to airline capacity management: fleet assignment during schedule planning, and disruption management during operations.

## Routes and network structure with uncertain demand

### Uncertain demand and fleet capacity allocation

FA is critical in that it affects subsequent planning tasks in airline scheduling, including aircraft routing, crew pairing and crew rostering (Wu, 2010). FA also affects airline revenue management (RM) strategies. Hence, it has profound importance at an early stage of airline scheduling and capacity planning. For instance, route AC in Figure 15.1 has a forecast demand of 180, BC has 120, CD has 220 and CE has 80. The airline operating this network has three fleet types: Embraer 170 (80 seats), Airbus 320 (170 seats) and Airbus 330 (240 seats). It would be ideal to assign the Airbus 320 to route AC, Embraer 170 to route BC, Airbus 330 to CD and Embraer 170 to CE, based on the individual demand of sectors and the capacity of different fleet types. However, this assignment may not be entirely optimal from the RM perspective, unless routes AC and CD can be assigned the same fleet type (e.g. Airbus 330). By using the same fleet type, the airline can capture through revenues from A to D for services that are often priced higher due to the preferred shorter connection time at the hub airport C (Gopalan and Talluri, 1998; Sherali et al., 2006). This joint consideration of both a fleet assignment model (FAM) and RM can affect aircraft routing for this network.

### Routes and airline network development

Travel demand between origin-destination (OD) airport pairs drives the development of airline networks (Burghouwt, 2007). The development of an airline network then drives the selection of aircraft fleets (fleet purchase) and fleet assignment to flight sectors in a network (Clark, 2001). As with the example shown in Figure 15.1, if the demand between airport F and H is high enough to sustain a non-stop flight (FH), then such a sector will be added to the network. Otherwise, a one-stop flight from F to H via hub G will be provided (i.e. FG and GH). The flight GH can then be flown with a larger aircraft if this outbound flight collects enough OD and connecting traffic from other inbound flights into G, including the traffic from F and locally from G. While this hub-and-spoke network development concept is straightforward, a key question in airline schedule planning is whether a flight sector should be provided in the network (capacity allocation) and which fleet should be used to maximise profits. This gives rises to the SG and FA problems that are commonly seen in airline scheduling.

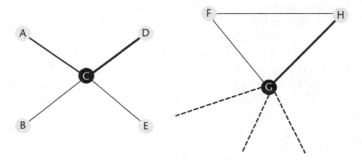

*Figure 15.1* An example airline network

*Source*: Authors.

## Fleet assignment models and profit maximization

### *Schedule generation and the integration with fleet assignment*

The fleet assignment problem has been studied by airlines since the late 1980s. With the improvement in computing resources and solution algorithms, airlines have reported significant benefits by developing in-house FAMs (Abara, 1989; Rushmeier and Kontogiorgis, 1997; Subramanian et al., 1994). Mancel and Mora-Camino (2006) and Sherali et al. (2006) provide good reviews on the early development of FAMs, both in industry and academia. The basic flight leg-based fleet assignment model (LFAM) is provided by Hane et al. (1995) as follows:

$$\text{Minimise} \sum_{i \in L} \sum_{f \in F} c_{f,i} x_{f,i} \text{ or } \text{Maximise} \sum_{i \in L} \sum_{f \in F} r_{f,i} x_{f,i} - \sum_{i \in L} \sum_{f \in F} c_{f,i} x_{f,i} \tag{1.0}$$

Subject to:

$$\sum_{f \in F} x_{f,i} = 1 \forall i \in L \tag{1.1}$$

$$y_{f,a,t^-} + \sum_{i \in I(f,a,t)} x_{f,i} - y_{f,a,t^+} - \sum_{i \in O(f,a,t)} x_{f,i} = 0 \,\forall f,a,t \tag{1.2}$$

$$\sum_{a \in A} y_{f,a,O^-} + \sum_{i \notin CL(f)} x_{f,i} \leq N_f \,\forall f \in F \tag{1.3}$$

$$x_{f,i} \in \{0,1\}, \forall f \in F, and \,\forall i \in L$$

$$y_{f,a,t} \geq 0, \forall f,a,t$$

The basic LFAM aims at minimising the total costs of FA, including passenger spill costs, spill recapture, passenger carrying costs and aircraft operating costs (aggregately modelled by the cost term, $C_{f,i}$ in (1.0)), given the assignment of fleet $f$ to flight leg $i$, $r_{f,i}$. An alternative objective function is to maximise expected profit contribution by incorporating the estimated expected revenues from fleet assignment $x_{f,i}$ (modelled by the revenue term, $r_{f,i}$ in (1.0)). Constraints (1.1) ensure that each flight is only covered by exactly one fleet type. This type of constraint arises in many planning and recovery problems, and is commonly termed the flight coverage constraint. Constraints (1.2) impose flow balance for the aircraft (fleet) across the planning horizon. Constraints (1.3) ensure that the size of each fleet is respected in the solution.

While airlines have long realised the importance of FA in schedule planning, the importance of SG has attracted less attention in the literature until recently. Gopalan and Talluri (1998) note the important role that SG may play and how the outcome of SG may affect fleet assignments and aircraft routings. Since airlines can change flight times in the timetable, research has found that the performance of FAM can be significantly improved if SG is incorporated or integrated with FAM. Belanger et al. (2006) and Rexing et al. (2000) use the concept of time windows to allow flexibility in setting flight departure times at the SG stage. Multiple copies of the original flight departure time are created to allow flexibility in choosing the optimal departure time in order to improve FAM results. Lohatepanont and Barnhart (2004) combine SG and FAM so the timetable is optimised according to the potential gains in FAM. More recently, Sherali et al. (2013) extend the process of integrating SG and FAM to further integrate with the aircraft routing model (ARM), while Pita et al. (2013) propose an integrated SG and FAM by explicitly considering the operational costing of aircraft and passenger delays under airport congestion scenarios.

## Moving from LFAM to origin-destination fleet assignment model (ODFAM)

As illustrated by Figure 15.1 earlier, FAM results can affect how flights are connected by different fleets in aircraft routing optimisation, and accordingly how airline tickets are offered in the market. Perhaps more importantly, the FAM affects how tickets are priced in RM systems of airlines. Earlier basic FAMs in the literature predominantly focused on LFAM that treated each flight leg independently without explicit consideration of the interdependencies of passenger spills due to FA and the implications on network revenues that an airline network can leverage (Barnhart et al., 2002). For an example of possible network effects on airline revenue management strategies and the comparison with LFAM, readers are referred to Barnhart et al. (2002).

An itinerary-based fleet assignment model (IFAM) is proposed by Barnhart et al. (2002) that incorporates a passenger mix model (PMM) in LFAM. PMM is developed to minimise passenger spill and carrying costs by capturing the network effects of passenger booking subject to flight capacity constraints and booking spills in the RM system. IFAM differs from the LFAM in that IFAM incorporates the PPM model by adding the PPM term in the objective function of LFAM:

$$\sum_{p \in P} \sum_{r \in P} (\widetilde{fare}_p - b_p^r \, \widetilde{fare}_r) t_p^r, \qquad (2)$$

where $\widetilde{fare}_p$ $(\widetilde{fare}_r)$ is the fare of itinerary $p$ $(r)$, $b_p^r$ represents the recapture rate of passenger spill from $p$ to $r$, and $t_p^r$ denotes the number of spilled passengers from itinerary $p$ to $r$. Further constraints are also added in the IFAM formulation to consider seat capacity allocation in the FAM part of the IFAM framework (Barnhart et al., 2002).

Recognising the fundamental importance of the interdependencies between flight sectors in FAM and RM, efforts have been focused on two areas: modelling passenger flows in the network and improving the revenue calculation (estimation) in FAM. Yan et al. (2007) combines SG and a passenger flow model (PFM) with FAM so to further exploit the potential gains of flight scheduling and FAM on passenger flows across an airline network. Jacobs et al. (2008) extend the basic LFAM and incorporate the network flow aspects of uncertain yield management in airline RM systems. This ODFAM formulation specifically incorporates RM systems that deal with passenger flows in the FAM framework to account for the probabilistic aspect of yield management in RM.

Dumas and Soumis (2008) develop a PFM that can be used to find an approximation of the expected passenger flows on an airline network given demand forecast data and an assumed booking process. Specifically, the PFM by Dumas and Soumis (2008) considers random distributions of itinerary demand, time distribution of itinerary bookings, and the estimation of passenger spill to a given itinerary. This PFM is then used in Dumas et al. (2009) to improve the outcome of FAM by focusing on the estimation of revenue loss that is commonly adopted in FAM to drive the passenger revenue component in the objective function of FAM. In the improved calculation, Dumas et al. (2009) are able to use the PFM to model spill and recapture between itineraries and account for leg interdependency of revenues.

Barnhart et al. (2009) focus on enhancing the revenue modelling part of LFAM by a different formulation called the subnetwork fleet assignment model (SFAM). The motivation of SFAM is the concern that assumptions made on the revenue estimation in the literature are too simplistic to reflect the complexity of RM systems commonly used by airlines, potentially leading to sub-optimal FAM results. The generic fleet assignment model (GFAM) proposed by Barnhart et al. (2009) is shown to be the generalised form of LFAM. Two factors are considered in formulating

SFAM: improving revenue modelling by partitioning a network into subnetworks, and reformulating GFAM into SFAM. The expected revenue function $r(x;h)$ in FAM is often provided in a linear form of fleet assignment $x$ under fare structure $h$ in the literature. The expected revenue is then approximated by $r(x;h) = \sum_{i \in L} \sum_{f \in F} r_{f,i} x_{f,i}$ in LFAM. The simplified and implicit assumption in the estimation of expected revenue lies in the allocation of the revenue share that a particular flight sector $i$ receives in a possible multi-sector itinerary booking.

IFAM improved LFAM by modelling the revenue function with an itinerary variable $p$ that replaces individual sector variable $i$ in the formulation, along with capacity side constraints and more detailed fare structures (Barnhart et al., 2002). SFAM uses the subnetwork concept and partitions an airline network into $k$ subnetworks to transform the revenue function to $r\left(x; \sum_{k=1}^{K} h^k\right) = \sum_{k=1}^{K} r\left(x; h^k\right)$ for a specific fare structure $h^k$ for subnetwork $k$. SFAM is then formulated by transforming the fleet assignment decision variable $x_{f,i}$ in (1) to a composite decision variable $\omega_j$ for fleet assignment configuration $j$. In essence, SFAM builds a stronger revenue estimation framework that is fully incorporated in the FAM formulation. This leads to better FAM results that are more consistent to RM strategies and passenger bookings observed in the industry.

## RM-driven fleet assignment

Given the sequential airline schedule planning paradigm, decisions made earlier in the scheduling process can have profound impacts on schedule execution and airline revenues. From the perspective of airline capacity management, and more specifically FA, decisions of fleeting can affect RM strategies (and revenues), aircraft routing, crewing and flight operations. Berge and Hopperstad (1993) question the suitability of FAM results on the day of operation given the long lead time (two to three months in advance) that FAM results are produced and the potential mismatch of FAM results and the continuing realisation of ticket booking levels up to the day of departure. A demand-driven dispatch ($D^3$) concept is then developed to take advantage of the updated ticket booking levels some time before the departure day, and accordingly adjusts FAM results to better suit realised demands. This type of RM-driven FAM tries to better match capacity allocation among flights via re-fleeting (re-FA) with updated booking demand forecasts during a booking period.

Although it appears ideal for RM to re-FA, the snowballing effects of re-FA due to the sequential schedule planning process cannot be ignored. Bish et al. (2004) then examine two key questions in RM-driven FAM, including timing (when re-FA by aircraft swapping should be carried out) and frequency (how often re-FA should be conducted). Arguably, with later timing and higher frequency, the re-FA can achieve better revenues because of superior demand forecasts and better matching between demand and capacity. However, late re-FA may greatly disturb aircraft routing and crew rosters, leading to higher schedule planning costs that are not always clear during the re-FA process. Regarding the inclusion of RM components in FAM, Wang and Meng (2008) is perhaps the most extensive with respect to RM modelling in FAM. A dynamic programming model that contains a continuous-time network yield management problem with $D^3$ is developed to integrate RM components when solving FAM. A small example implementing the integrated framework is provided by Wang and Meng (2008) to demonstrate this idea.

The idea of RM-driven FAM is further extended by Jiang and Barnhart (2009) and Warburg et al. (2008) with the concept of dynamic airline scheduling. Through flight retiming and re-FA, coupled with updated booking demand forecasts, dynamic scheduling aims to better match fleet capacity with stochastic travel demand that is gradually realised during the booking period. Flight retiming can generate new connection opportunities for offering new itineraries in the market, while re-FA can swap aircraft types among flights so to match new demand forecast with capacity while flight booking is in progress. In both papers, retiming and re-FA are reported to generate synergy when they are applied simultaneously, and result in significant profit gains for case study airlines. The dynamic airline schedule concept is further extended to include robustness from schedule generation (SG), in which the number of potentially connecting itineraries is maximised by using revenues as weighting factors (Jiang and Barnhart, 2013). This robustness is then embedded in the dynamic scheduling environment so the timetable can be more easily modified, reflecting changing demand in the booking period.

## Incorporating robustness in FAM and integrated capacity planning

Since FAM is solved early in the process of airline schedule planning, FAM results greatly affect subsequent scheduling tasks. Accordingly, researchers have focused on improving the robustness of FAM, and have recently extended this pursuit by integrating FAM with follow-up scheduling tasks. Early efforts of achieving robustness in FAM are through embedding schedule recovery options in FAM.

A simple recovery approach that has received academic and industry interest is aircraft swapping. A swap can be performed if two aircraft are planned to be on the ground at the same airport at the same time. If one aircraft is delayed, the other can be swapped to perform the alternate aircraft route. Ageeva (2000) presents a scheduling approach that aims to maximise aircraft swapping opportunities. Kang (2004) uses the concept of subnetwork to improve the robustness of the complete schedule. The subnetworks are given by a partitioning of the flights. In the scheduling process, each aircraft routing, crew pairing and passenger itinerary is constructed using flights of a single subnetwork. This idea tries to isolate the impact of disruptions. Ideally, a disruption will only affect a single subnetwork, and as a result only have an impact on a subset of aircraft, crew and passengers. Rosenberger et al. (2004) focus on creating short cycles in FAM, so when disruption occurs, short flight cycles (i.e. a pair of flights out and back to a hub) can be cancelled without affecting aircraft routing. The concept of station purity in FAM is developed by Smith and Johnson (2006), where the types of fleets that can be assigned to a single hub are limited by some criteria. By this, Smith and Johnson (2006) demonstrate that flow-on benefits from FAM make crew scheduling, maintenance scheduling (aircraft routing) and disruption recovery simpler, with reduced operational costs.

### Paradigm shift in airline scheduling

Airline scheduling is substantially driven by corporate resource utilisation and profit maximisation. Airline scheduling generally refers to the whole process of generating an airline schedule, including schedule generation, fleet assignment, aircraft routing, crew pairing and crew rostering. Due to the large-scale nature of real-world airline scheduling problems, airline scheduling has been approached by a divide-and-conquer philosophy. This strategy involves solving tasks sequentially, where the output of one task is used as the input to subsequent tasks (Bazargan, 2012; Wu, 2010; Wu and Maher, 2017).

The most notable drawback of this approach is that the solution quality (also the solution space) of a subsequent task heavily depends on the solution of the previous task. Often, the sequential approach lacks consideration of interdependence between tasks in airline scheduling. A characteristic of the sequential approach is the fixing of solutions for use as input to subsequent stages. This process typically results in suboptimal or even infeasible solutions across planning stages. As an example, Barnhart et al. (1998) state that the optimal FAM result in their case study did not always yield feasible aircraft maintenance routing solutions.

Additionally, the pursuit of corporate profit maximisation also pushes airlines to maximise asset utilisation, leaving little buffer for disruptions. As a result, airlines incur high operating costs due to disruption management actions, although the optimised schedule may have the potential to generate maximum profits with the least costs. The paradigm of airline scheduling, recognising the weakness of current scheduling practice, has gradually shifted to integrated schedule planning and robust scheduling.

The most intuitive form of integrated planning is the combination of two related planning problems, such as FAM and ARM (Barnhart et al., 1998), while the most complex involves optimisation problems that encompass the complete airline planning process, such as the one developed by Papadakos (2009). With a better understanding of solution algorithms and improved computing resources, the benefits of integrated planning can be realised.

The goal of integrated planning is to address the limitations of the sequential planning paradigm by considering multiple resources or tasks simultaneously. Further, the consideration of multiple resources provides the opportunity to impose extra planning conditions to improve operational performance.

## Integrating crew scheduling and aircraft routing

A very important direction of integrated planning is the simultaneous scheduling of crew and aircraft. Crew wages and fuel costs represent the two largest costs to an airline (see Chapter 11). As such, the improved planning solution given by combining the optimisation of crew and aircraft will have a significant impact on the profitability of an airline.

The combination of crew scheduling and aircraft routing is presented by Cordeau et al. (2001). In the airline planning context, a connection is defined as two flights that can potentially be operated by the same crew or aircraft consecutively. Specifically, given flight $i$ and flight $j$, the connection $(i, j)$ is valid if: (i) the destination of $i$ is the same as the origin of $j$; and (ii) the time between the arrival of $i$ and the departure of $j$ is greater than the minimum connection time at an airport, called the turn time for aircraft and sit time for crew.

The minimum sit time for crew is typically longer than the minimum turn time for aircraft. This leads to the definition of a short connection, which is a connection where the difference in the arrival of flight $i$ and the departure of flight $j$ is less than the minimum sit time but at least as long as the minimum turn time. Crew are permitted to use a short connection if an aircraft also uses the same connection. A key contribution of Cordeau et al. (2001) is the improved use of short connections in crew pairing, leading to lower planning and operational costs. The mathematical model integrating the crew pairing model (CPM) and ARM provided by Cordeau et al. (2001) is:

$$Minimise \sum_{f \in F} \sum_{\omega \in \Omega^f} c_\omega \theta_\omega + \sum_{k \in K} \sum_{\omega \in \Omega^k} c_\omega \zeta_\omega^r \tag{3.0}$$

Subject to:

$$\sum_{f \in F} \sum_{\omega \in \Omega^f} d_\omega^i \theta_\omega = 1 (i \in N), \tag{3.1}$$

$$\sum_{k \in K} \sum_{\omega \in \Omega^k} d_\omega^i \zeta_\omega = 1 (i \in N), \tag{3.2}$$

$$\sum_{k \in K} \sum_{\omega \in \Omega^k} b_{\omega}^{ij} \zeta_{\omega} - \sum_{f \in F} \sum_{\omega \in \Omega^f} b_{\omega}^{ij} \theta_{\omega} \le 0 \big( (i,j) \in C \big),$$

(3.3)

$$\sum_{\omega \in \Omega^f} \theta_{\omega} = 1 \big( f \in F \big),$$

(3.4)

$$\sum_{\omega \in \Omega^k} \zeta_{\omega} = 1 \big( k \in K \big),$$

(3.5)

$$\theta_{\omega} \in \{0,1\} \big( f \in F; \omega \in \Omega^f \big)$$

$$\zeta_{\omega} \in \{0,1\} \big( k \in K; \omega \in \Omega^k \big)$$

The objective (3.0) of this problem is to simultaneously minimise the cost of aircraft routing and crew pairing. The variables $\theta_{\omega}$ ($\zeta_{\omega}$) equal 1 to indicate the use of flight route (crew pairing) $\omega$. Constraints (3.1) and (3.2) ensure that all flights in the network are operated by exactly one crew and aircraft, respectively. These constraints are the flight coverage constraints. Constraints (3.3) enforce the condition that crew can only use a short connection if an aircraft is also using the same connection. Finally, constraints (3.4) and (3.5) ensure that each crew and aircraft are assigned to exactly one path through the network.

An important aspect that is presented in the above model is the use of variables to identify paths through a network. These paths are described as aircraft routings and crew pairings. Thus, a path is a sequence of flights that is performed by a single crew or aircraft over a predefined time period. Given that the total number of paths is exponential in the number of flights, it is not practical to completely enumerate all variables (i.e. paths). This difficulty is addressed by the use of the solution technique, column generation (Desaulniers et al., 2005).

Column generation is a solution technique used to solve linear programs by dynamically generating variables. Linear programs that are suitable for the application of column generation typically contain a large number of variables, most of which are expected to be zero in the optimal solution. The column generation solution algorithm initialises a restricted master problem (RMP), containing only a subset of all variables, and a sub-problem. The master problem solves to find an upper bound on the optimal solution and the sub-problem is tasked with identifying new variables that, when added to the master problem, will reduce the upper bound. When integer variables are present in the problem, the optimal solution is found using the related technique of branch-and-price.

Using problem (3) as an example, the RMP is given by (3.0)–(3.5), but formulated with only a subset of the variables $\theta_{\omega}$ and $\zeta_{\omega}$. This is achieved by replacing the sets $\Omega^f$ and $\Omega^k$ with $\bar{\Omega}^f$ and $\bar{\Omega}^k$, respectively, where the latter are subsets of the former. Given a solution to the RMP, the sub-problem, which is a resource-constrained shortest-path problem, is solved to identify variables from $\bar{\Omega}^f \backslash \Omega^f$ and $\bar{\Omega}^k \backslash \Omega^k$ to add to the RMP. The linear program is solved to optimality when no additional variables that could improve the solution to the RMP can be identified in the sub-problem. As mentioned above, branch-and-price would then be required to find the integer optimal solution.

## Integrating fleet assignment, aircraft routing and crew scheduling

Given the fundamental nature of the FAM within the airline planning process, the integration with other planning stages is expected to provide improved planning solutions. Haouari et al. (2009) integrate FAM with ARM so to provide higher quality solutions to the ARM by using a network flow-based approach. Since some constraints in FAM and ARM overlap (such as the constraints of aircraft flow balance and aircraft counts), many FAM elements can be replaced by ARM elements. Papadakos (2009) draws upon this idea and extends upon the work of Cordeau et al. (2001) and Mercier et al. (2005) to develop an integrated model that incorporates FAM, ARM and CPM:

$$\textit{Minimise} \sum_{f \in F} \sum_{r \in R^f} c_r^+ v_r + \sum_{f \in F} \sum_{p \in P^f} c_p \omega_p \tag{4.0}$$

*Subject to:*

$$\sum_{f \in F} \sum_{r \in R^f} e_{lr} v_r = 1, \forall l \in L \tag{4.1}$$

$$\sum_{p \in P^f} a_{lp} \omega_p - \sum_{r \in R^f} e_{lr} v_r = 0, \forall l \in L, \forall f \in F \tag{4.2}$$

$$\sum_{p \in P^f} s_p^{ij} \omega_p - \sum_{r \in R^f} s_r^{ij} v_r \leq 0, \forall (i,j) \in S^f, \forall f \in F \tag{4.3}$$

$$q_m - q_{m^-} + \sum_{r \in R^f} \left(e_{mr}^+ - e_{mr}^-\right) v_r = 0, \forall m \in M^f, \forall f \in F \tag{4.4}$$

$$\sum_{m \in M^f} q_m + \sum_{r \in R^f} \hat{e}_r v_r \leq n_f, \forall f \in F \tag{4.5}$$

$$v_r \in \{0,1\}, \forall r \in R^f, \forall f \in F$$

$$q_m \geq 0, \forall m \in M^f, \forall f \in F$$

$$\omega_p \in \{0,1\}, \forall p \in P^f, \forall f \in F$$

In this formulation, the objective is to minimise costs. Constraints (4.1) ensure that each sector is assigned to exactly one route of a single fleet. Constraints (4.2) assign leg $l$ to be included in one crew pairing for fleet $f$ if and only if $l$ is assigned to that fleet. Constraints (4.3) cover short crew connections if and only if the two consecutive flights are operated by the same aircraft. Constraints (4.4) describe the aircraft flow balance, which is essential in FAM and ARM. Constraints (4.5) limit the use of aircraft to the fleet size available. Salazar-Gonzalez (2014) operationalises the fully integrated model by Papadakos (2009) to solve the schedule planning problem of a regional Spanish carrier.

## Solving integrated planning problems

The above two problems present the integration of crew and aircraft. This integration is modelled by constraints (3.3) in the Cordeau et al. (2001) model, and constraints (4.2) and (4.3) in the Papadakos (2009) model. These constraint sets introduce a large number of additional constraints that are not present in the individual aircraft routing and crew pairing problems. The ability to handle this increase in problem size is an important challenge of integrated planning.

Relaxing the integration constraints allows the crew and aircraft problems to be solved independently. This idea is exploited by applying the solution technique of Benders' decomposition

(Benders, 1962). The crew and aircraft problems are solved independently using a master/slave solution algorithm. Using Cordeau et al. (2001) as an example, the aircraft problem is formulated with constraints (3.2) and (3.5) and the crew problem is formulated with constraints (3.1), (3.3) and (3.4). The solution to the aircraft problem is fixed and then provided to the crew problem as input, greatly simplifying the relationship between the resources that is defined by constraint (3.3). Using this fixed input, the solution to the crew problem generates additional constraints that are added to the aircraft problem. This may appear similar to the sequential solution approach, such as Dunbar et al. (2012) and Weide et al. (2010). However, the sequential approach is a heuristic while the Benders' decomposition algorithm finds the optimal solution to the integrated problem. The use of Benders' decomposition is demonstrated by Cordeau et al. (2001) and Papadakos (2009) to be an effective solution approach to improve the solving performance of the integrated problem.

## Airline capacity and disruption management

Disruptions to airline operations are commonplace. In 2015, 79.92 per cent of all arriving flights in the United States were on time, with the 10-year average on-time performance to December 2015 reported as 77.82 per cent (Bureau of Transportation Statistics, 2016). The on-time performance results demonstrate that schedule perturbations are an unavoidable part of airline operations. In response to the persistent nature of delays, airlines engage in the process of disruption management – a class of practices and decision-making processes designed to address the impact of schedule perturbations by managing airline capacity reallocation and sometimes performing re-optimisation.

Disruption management can be categorised into two classes – proactive and reactive disruption management. Proactive disruption management, commonly termed robust planning, is characterised by the development of airline planning solutions that are expected to be less susceptible to flight delays. A key example is the allocation of buffer times (increasing slack) between the arrival and departure of an aircraft (AhmadBeygi et al., 2008; Eggenberg, 2009; Wu, 2006). Proactive disruption management also includes embedding potential recovery possibilities into the planning solution. Examples of this technique include reducing the number of flights an aircraft performs away from a hub (short cycles) (Rosenberger et al., 2004) and providing aircraft swapping opportunities (Ageeva, 2000). Reactive disruption management, also termed airline recovery, is characterised by the repair of flight schedules, aircraft routings and crew pairings following a disruptive event (Clausen et al., 2010). In general, proactive disruption management aims to provide planning solutions that will reduce the potential impact of schedule disruptions, while reactive approaches respond to disruptions on the day of operations and provide tools and techniques to minimise the resulting impact.

### Proactive disruption management

The main aim of proactive disruption management is to efficiently allocate resources while minimising the expected impact of schedule perturbations. The areas of airline planning that have seen significant progress in the development of proactive disruption management approaches are aircraft routing and crew scheduling.

Many of the developments in proactive disruption management have arisen from the integration of aircraft and crew. The integration of aircraft and crew with a focus on restricted and short connections is presented by Cordeau et al. (2001) and Mercier et al. (2005). An extension of this work to include flight retiming is developed by Mercier and Soumis (2007). Additionally, proactive disruption management approaches that minimise a delay measure in an integrated aircraft and crew planning problem have been developed by Dunbar et al. (2012) and Weide et al. (2010). Alternatively, the concept of recoverable robustness is introduced for the tail assignment and maintenance planning problems by Froyland et al. (2014) and Maher et al. (2014).

In airline planning, there is a trade-off between the most efficient use of resources and the susceptibility of the planned solution to schedule disruptions. When planning solutions are found without considering the possibility of disruptions, the result is the most efficient use of resources with the lowest cost. However, such planning solutions are typically brittle and are highly susceptible to disruptions. In contrast, proactive disruption management approaches aim to identify alternative solutions that may appear to be suboptimal with respect to efficient resource usage and cost, but are expected to provide improved operational performance. The value of proactive disruption management techniques is realised only on the day of operations. The expectation is that the increase in planning costs due to using proactive disruption management planning techniques can be compensated by a decrease in operational costs.

## Proactive approaches to reduce flight delay propagation

The use of proactive disruption management to avoid flight delays is a major focus of research. There are two categories of flight delays: primary and secondary delays. Primary delays are those that are caused by disrupting events such as inclement weather, late passengers or unscheduled maintenance. Secondary delays are those that occur as the result of previously delayed flights, commonly caused by aircraft routing, crewing and passenger connections in the network.

The simplest approach to minimise the impact of flight delays involves the generation of aircraft routings and crew pairings that only use connections with a longer buffer time between consecutive flights. A more sophisticated approach applying this concept in an optimisation model is presented by Eggenberg (2009). The presented approach solves the maintenance routing problem to maximise the total slack or maximise the minimum slack between flight connections. It is noted that in an unconstrained problem, the maximum total slack may be infinite. However, the ARM by Eggenberg (2009) includes flight coverage constraints, and a constraint on the maximum number of aircraft ensures that the maximum total slack is finite. The approach developed by Eggenberg (2009) aims to better distribute connection slack across all flight connections. Flight retiming was employed by Lan et al. (2006) to reduce the prevalence of propagated delay in the solution to the aircraft routing problem. A more involved approach using estimates for the probability of propagated delay in the tail assignment problem is presented by Dovica (2014).

An example of propagated delay is presented in Figure 15.2. The horizontal axis represents time and the vertical axis is the location of an airport. The diagonal lines are flights and those of the same colour are operated by the same aircraft. In Figure 15.2, aircraft VH-435 experiences a primary delay when operating flight AR242 from BNE to MEL. This primary delay is greater than the buffer time planned for the next flight to be operated by VH-435, which is flight AR328 from MEL to SYD. As a result, some of the original primary delay on flight AR242 is propagated onto the subsequent flight for VH-435, flight AR328.

A proactive disruption management approach that considers the probability of delay propagation is presented by Dovica (2014). Using historical data, Dovica (2014) computes the

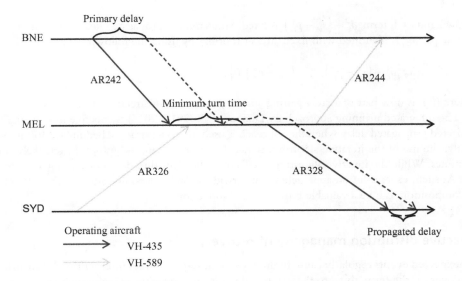

*Figure 15.2* **Example of propagated delay**

*Source*: Authors

probability of delay propagating between two consecutive flights. This computed probability is used to minimise the expected propagated delay. An interesting aspect of this work is that secondary flight delays are considered as a variable in the model, not as a historical data input. By considering flight delays as variables in the model, the actual delays that could be experienced are better represented. The resulting optimisation problem is then solved to minimise the probability of propagated delay. This approach attempts to more effectively use buffer times to address delays while ensuring a high utilisation of aircraft.

An integrated planning approach that explicitly minimises a propagated delay measure is presented by Dunbar et al. (2012). The amount of expected delay propagation for a given aircraft routing $\omega$ and crew pairing $\delta$ is computed using the following equations, respectively:

$$d_j^R = max\left\{d_i^R - \left(s_{ij}^R - p_{ij}^R\right), 0\right\} \forall (i, j) \in \omega, \tag{5}$$

$$d_j^P = max\left\{d_i^P - \left(s_{ij}^P - p_{ij}^P\right), 0\right\} \forall (i, j) \in \delta. \tag{6}$$

The optimisation problem presented by Dunbar et al. (2012) is an integrated aircraft routing and crew planning problem. The integration of aircraft and crew is achieved using an iterative algorithm. This algorithm treats each resource separately, but uses the solution for the alternate resource as input. Most importantly, the delay propagation with respect to crew is considered in the aircraft problem with the following modification to equation (5):

$$d_j^R = max\left\{d_i^R - \left(s_{ij}^R - p_{ij}^R\right), d_k^P - \left(s_{kj}^P - p_{kj}^P\right), 0\right\}, \tag{7}$$

where $(i, j)$ is part of an aircraft routing and $(k, j)$ is part of a crew pairing. For the aircraft routing problem, the crew pairings are fixed as given. As such, all crew pairing connections $(k, j)$ are known and each term $d_k^P - \left(s_{kj}^P - p_{kj}^P\right)$ is fixed. Similarly, the propagated delay for each flight in a crew pairing is identified with fixed aircraft routings by using the following equation:

$$d_j^P = max\left\{d_i^P - \left(s_{ij}^P - p_{ij}^P\right), d_k^R - \left(s_{kj}^R - p_{kj}^R\right), 0\right\}, \tag{8}$$

where $(i, j)$ is now part of a crew pairing and $(k, j)$ is part of an aircraft routing.

The integrated planning approach by Dunbar et al. (2012, 2014) is effective in reducing the expected propagated delay when the approach is used in robust airline scheduling. Most importantly, the use of the iterative algorithm is valuable in improving robustness in relatively small runtimes. While the iterative algorithm is effective, the algorithm does not guarantee optimality. As such, exact solution approaches that provide a similar decomposition, such as Benders' decomposition, can be a valuable future research direction.

## Reactive disruption management recovery

Unexpected events regularly cause flight delays that require direct intervention by an airline. Recovery is the term given to the reactive disruption management techniques employed by an airline on the day of operations to mitigate the impact of schedule perturbations. Airline recovery is a complex capacity management process that is commonly performed in a series of sequential stages that is analogous to that of the planning counterpart (Clausen et al., 2010). The stages of airline recovery typically consist of schedule, aircraft, crew and passenger recovery. Similar to the planning process, airline recovery solves each stage in order with the solutions to the preceding stage fixed and used as input for the following stage. The complexity of the airline recovery problem is similar to airline planning. However, while planning is performed over many months, a recovery solution is required within minutes or hours, depending on the scale of disruptions. Additionally, because disruptions can significantly affect the planned schedule, feedback is required in the airline recovery problem to repair any infeasibilities that result from using fixed inputs between the stages.

There are numerous actions that can be performed to mitigate the effects of schedule disruptions. The possible types of actions include, but are not limited to, delaying or cancelling flights (schedule recovery), changing the aircraft operating a flight (aircraft recovery), and changing the crew operating a flight (crew recovery). These actions aid the airline to manage capacity in operations by changing flight capacities (cancelling or changing aircraft types), and accordingly the crew that are required to operate the updated schedule.

### Aircraft recovery

In response to the complexity of airline recovery, early research was directed towards aircraft recovery. One of the first examples of aircraft recovery was presented by Teodorović and Guberinic (1984). A feature of the model presented by Teodorović and Guberinic (1984) is the use of only flight delays as a recovery policy. The limited use of recovery policies in early aircraft recovery problems was driven by the lack of computing resources to solve more complex problems in the required short runtimes. A prominent example of aircraft recovery problems with limited use of actions is the development of delay-only and cancellation-only models by Jarrah et al. (1993). A more comprehensive view of the aircraft recovery problem is presented by Thengvall et al. (2000), which incorporates aircraft swapping, flight delays and cancellations.

An interesting feature included in the model of Thengvall et al. (2000) is the objective of minimal deviation from the planned aircraft routings. This objective aids in forming solutions that are more human-friendly, and are expected to be more intuitive and easily implementable by operation controllers of airlines. Similar to the planning stages, advances in recovery problems have been made through the integration of related optimisation problems. Eggenberg et al. (2010) is a notable example, with the inclusion of maintenance routing constraints in the aircraft recovery problem.

An important feature of aircraft recovery problems is the structure design of the underlying network that is used to model airline schedule and resource connections. Three main network designs are the most prevalent – time–line, time–band and connection networks. The time–line network, used by Jarrah et al. (1993), Yan and Yang (1996) and Thengvall et al. (2000), provides an accurate description of the recovered schedule. However, this accurate description comes with a trade-off, typically resulting in very large problem formulations. The time–band network, as presented by Argüello (1997) and Eggenberg et al. (2010), attempts to address the large networks required to describe recovered schedules by aggregating activities into discrete time-bands. Finally, the connection network, which is also popular for airline planning problems, is used by Rosenberger et al. (2003) as an accurate and concise description of the recovered schedule and related activities.

## Integrated schedule and aircraft recovery model

The motivation for combining schedule and aircraft recovery is that flight delays and cancellation decisions rely on the availability of aircraft to operate the recovered schedule. Performing schedule and aircraft recovery separately requires a feedback process between the two problems to ensure that a feasible solution for both schedule and aircraft can be provided. Consider the aircraft recovery problem presented by Rosenberger et al. (2003):

$$\text{Minimise} \sum_{p \in Pr} \sum_{r \in R_{(p,f)}} c_r X_r + \sum_{f \in F} b_f K_f \tag{9.0}$$

*Subject to:*

$$\sum_{r \in R_{(p,f)}} X_r = 1 \forall p \in P, \tag{9.1}$$

$$\sum_{r \ni f} X_r + K_f = 1 \forall f \in F, \tag{9.2}$$

$$\sum_{r \in R_u} X_r \leq 1 \forall u \in U, \tag{9.3}$$

$$\sum_{r \in R_a} |H(r,a)| X_r \leq \alpha_a \forall a \in A, \tag{9.4}$$

$$X_r \in \{0,1\} \forall r \in R_{(p,f)}, p \in P,$$

$$K_f \in \{0,1\} \forall f \in F.$$

This model captures the main features of the aircraft recovery problem – flight delays and cancellations and the rerouting of aircraft. The objective of the aircraft recovery problem is to minimise the cost of flight delays and cancellations. The cost parameter $c_r$ in the objective function (9.0) is the unit cost of operating aircraft routing $p$, which includes the cost of delaying flights on that route. The parameter $b_f$ represents the cost of flight cancellations. This cost typically includes direct costs, such as lost revenues, and indirect costs, such as loss of passenger goodwill. Constraints (9.1) state that each aircraft can be assigned at most one routing. Constraints (9.2) state that each flight must be included in exactly one flight routing or is cancelled. An important feature of aircraft recovery is the management of available airport slots and capacity. These necessary restrictions are imposed by constraints (9.3) and (9.4).

There are many similarities between the aircraft routing planning and aircraft recovery problems. Specifically, the aircraft routing problem requires flight coverage constraints. Compare the aircraft routing and scheduling model presented by Desaulniers et al. (1997):

$$Minimise \sum_{k\in K}\sum_{p\in\Omega^k} c_p^k\theta_p^k, \tag{10.0}$$

Subject to:

$$\sum_{k\in K}\sum_{p\in\Omega^k} a_{ip}^k\theta_p^k = 1\forall i \in N, \tag{10.1}$$

$$\sum_{p\in\Omega^k} \left(d_{sp}^k - o_{sp}^k\right)\theta_p^k = 0\forall k \in K, \forall s \in S^k, \tag{10.2}$$

$$\sum_{p\in\Omega^k} \theta_p^k = n^k \forall k \in K, \tag{10.3}$$

$$\theta_p^k \geq 0\forall k \in K, \forall p \in \Omega^k,$$

$$\theta_p^k \text{ integer} \forall k \in K, \forall p \in \Omega^k.$$

The aircraft routing and scheduling model of Desaulniers et al. (1997) minimises the expected routing cost. In this model, $k$ represents the set of all aircraft types. As such, all aircraft of the same type are considered identical. In comparison to the aircraft recovery problem, only a single aircraft type is considered, but each aircraft is individually identified. Assuming that in the above model each individual aircraft is a unique type, then $n^k = 1\forall k \in K$. This makes the routing model of Desaulniers et al. (1997) and recovery problem of Rosenberger et al. (2003) in (9) directly comparable.

The main differences between the aircraft routing and recovery problem are given by the additional flexibility permitted in the latter. Namely, flight cancellations are permitted – modelled in constraint (9.1) – but are not permitted in the routing model, as indicated by constraint (10.1). Additionally, in recovery, flight delays are considered in the generation of recovery aircraft routes. There are also further restrictions that must be considered in the recovery problem. In particular, the recovery problem must manage the scarce resource of airport capacity (see Chapter 16).

## Crew recovery

Crew recovery is a very complex part of the airline recovery process. This is due to the large number of crew members and the complex working rules that must be satisfied. Early attempts developing crew recovery problems focused on the sequential recovery process, specifically using a modified flight schedule and aircraft routings as inputs. Examples of crew recovery with a fixed flight schedule include Medard and Sawhney (2007), Nissen and Haase (2006), Stojković et al. (1998) and Wei et al. (1997). Similar to the planning process, using fixed inputs from preceding stages results in suboptimal, or even infeasible, solutions. As such, it is important within the crew recovery problem to consider flight delays and cancellations. The use of flight cancellations is considered by Lettovsky et al. (2000) and the modelling of flight delays for crew recovery is presented by Stojković and Soumis (2001). A further development of the crew recovery problem to include both flight delays and cancellations is presented by Abdelghany et al. (2004). A novel aspect of the work by Abdelghany et al. (2004) is the use of a rolling time horizon in the solution algorithm. The rolling time horizon breaks the complete crew recovery problem into a number of smaller problems that are expected to be easier to solve.

## Integrated airline recovery

Similar to airline planning, there is a growing interest in the integration of airline recovery stages. The greatest impediment to the development of an integrated problem is the very restricted short time frames that are given to find an implementable solution in practice. However, many attempts have been made to develop partially and completely integrated airline recovery problems.

Many approaches developed for aircraft and crew recovery exhibit a partial integration with schedule recovery decisions. Examples of such partial integration are presented in the previous sections. Extending upon partially integrated approaches, there has been increasing interest in the integration of larger and more complex stages. In particular, the development of optimisation problems that integrate aircraft and crew recovery is a current research interest. Many integrated recovery problems extend models and solution algorithms developed for crew or aircraft recovery. For example, the model and solution methods presented by Abdelghany et al. (2004) are extended by Abdelghany et al. (2008) to include aircraft recovery decisions. In an integrated aircraft and crew recovery problem presented by Maher (2016), only a discrete set of delays at 15-minute intervals is considered due to the large number of possible delayed departure times for each flight. Discretisation of departure times is a common approximation approach employed in airline planning and recovery in order to improve the solving performance of the developed algorithm.

## Passenger recovery

Passenger recovery is a very complex part of the recovery process. During the airline planning stage, potential passenger itineraries are identified for revenue management based upon business decisions reflecting possible market demands in an airline network. Passenger itineraries, which are formed by flights from the original flight schedule, result in a different network structure for passenger flows compared to the network constructed for aircraft and crew. In the event of a disruption, the networks for passenger flow and aircraft movements are affected in different ways. For aircraft, a disruption changes the departure times of the affected flights. As such, the flights still exist (assuming no cancellations), but the set of feasible connections to subsequent flights may change. In regard to passengers, the change in the feasible connections for aircraft may cause some passenger itineraries to become ineligible.

Passenger recovery typically occurs as the final stage of the sequential recovery process. This timing is chosen in an effort to address the complexity of the optimisation problem. At the end of the sequential recovery process, all schedule, aircraft and crew recovery decisions have been made and fixed. As such, all eligible and ineligible itineraries of affected passengers are known so the passenger recovery problem is modelled as an assignment problem.

A very difficult optimisation problem results from the integration of passenger recovery with schedule, aircraft and crew recovery. An itinerary recovery problem is modelled and incorporated into the integrated airline recovery problem developed by Petersen et al. (2012). Alternatively, for those airlines that only provide point-to-point services, an itinerary recovery model may be overly complex. As such, the reallocation approach by Maher (2015) greatly simplifies the passenger recovery process.

The management of passengers, such as rebooking or providing alternative transport, in recovery systems is becoming more important from the airline perspective. Challenge ROADEF (2009) focused on optimisation techniques for an integrated aircraft and passenger recovery problem. The most successful contribution in the challenge was a heuristic approach developed by Bisaillon et al. (2011). Building on the success of this approach, Sinclair et al. (2014) refine the large neighbourhood search solution algorithm of Bisaillon et al. (2011) to achieve improved solving performance. While the solution algorithm of Sinclair et al. (2014) finds good solutions in short runtimes, it is possible that they are far from optimal. A post-processing step is introduced by Sinclair et al. (2016) to improve the final solution quality. This is achieved by applying column generation to a modified version of the original aircraft and passenger recovery problem. The results of Bisaillon et al. (2011), Sinclair et al. (2014) and Sinclair et al. (2016) demonstrate the difficulty of solving recovery problems and the value of heuristic approaches.

## Conclusion

Airline capacity management is a challenging topic that will receive ongoing attention in industry and academia. This chapter presents key concepts of airline capacity management focusing on the state-of-the-art airline fleet assignment model development and airline schedule recovery. There has been a long history of research into fleet assignment, with many of the developments flowing through to other critical schedule planning stages, such as crew scheduling and aircraft routing. A current focus of research for airline planning is the development of integrated planning approaches.

While the aim of airline schedule planning is to efficiently use available resources, achieving this goal is complicated as a result of uncertainties that emerge in daily operations. Proactive and reactive disruption management techniques have been developed to reduce the impact of schedule perturbation and minimise operating costs. Similar to the planning stages, there is much interest in the development of integrated approaches for disruption management. The knowledge gained in solving the capacity planning problems can be transferred to solving recovery problems that airlines face on a daily basis.

An important direction of future research is the handling of uncertainty in capacity planning using integrated models. In particular, airline fleet planning and purchase decision-making will receive more attention. As suggested by List et al. (2003) and Rosskopf et al. (2014), airlines still face the commercial risks of purchasing fleets based on uncertain long-term forecasts. Further, the growing pressure to reduce environmental impacts from operations (see Chapters 17 and 25) can drive different fleet purchasing behaviour of airlines, for example by purchasing fuel-efficient fleets.

The availability of airline planning data is important for continued research. Recently, Akartunali et al. (2013a, 2013b) proposed a framework aimed at developing benchmark research data. Freely available benchmark data will promote further research in airline planning and will provide a common base for the comparison of planning methods and algorithms. Ultimately, further research will achieve the necessary advances to improve the efficient deployment of airline resources and the effective management of capacity in daily operations.

## References

Abara, J. (1989). Applying integer linear programming to the fleet assignment problem, *Interfaces*, 19(4), 20–28.

Abdelghany, A., Ekollu, G., Narasimhan, R. and Abdelghany, K. (2004). A proactive crew recovery decision support tool for commercial airlines during irregular operations, *Annals of Operations Research*, 127(23), 309–331.

Abdelghany, K.F., Abdelghany, A.F. and Ekollu, G. (2008). An integrated decision support tool for airlines schedule recovery during irregular operations, *European Journal of Operational Research*, 185(2), 825–848.

Ageeva, Y. (2000). *Approaches to Incorporating Robustness into Airline Scheduling*, Cambridge, MA, Massachusetts Institute of Technology.

AhmadBeygi, S., Cohn, A. and Lapp, M. (2008). Decreasing airline delay propagation by re-allocating scheduled slack. In: *Proceedings: The Industry Studies Conference*, Pittsburgh, PA, Industry Studies Association.

Akartunali, K., Boland, N., Evans, I., Wallace, M. and Waterer, H. (2013a). Airline planning benchmark problems. Part I: characterising networks and demand using limited data, *Computers & Operations Research*, 40(3), 775–792.

Akartunali, K., Boland, N., Evans, I., Wallace, M. and Waterer, H. (2013b). Airline planning benchmark problems. Part II: passenger groups, utility and demand allocation, *Computers & Operations Research*, 40(3), 793–804.

Argüello, M.F. (1997). *Framework for Exact Solutions and Heuristics for Approximate Solutions to Airlines' Irregular Operations Control Aircraft Routing Problem*, Austin, TX, University of Texas.

Barnhart, C., Boland, N., Clarke, L.W., Johnson, E.L. Nemhauser, G.L. and Shenoi, R.G. (1998). Flight string models for aircraft fleeting and routing, *Transportation Science*, 32(3), 208–220.

Barnhart, C., Kniker, T. and Lohatepanont, M. (2002). Itinerary-based airline fleet assignment, *Transportation Science*, 36(2), 199–217.

Barnhart, C., Farahat, A. and Lohatepanont, M. (2009). Airline fleet assignment with enhanced revenue modeling, *Operations Research*, 57(1), 231–244.

Bazargan, M. (2012). *Airline Operations and Scheduling*, Aldershot, Ashgate.

Belanger, N., Desaulniers, G., Soumis, F., Desrosiers, J. and Lavigne, J. (2006). Weekly airline fleet assignment with homogeneity, *Transport Research Part B: Methodological*, 40(4), 306–318.

Benders, J.F. (1962). Partitioning procedures for solving mixed-variables programming problems, *Numerische Mathematik*, 4, 238–252.

Berge, M.E. and Hopperstad, C.A. (1993). Demand driven dispatch: a method for dynamic aircraft capacity assignment, models and algorithms, *Operations Research*, 41(1), 153–168.

Bisaillon, S., Cordeau, J.-F., Laporte, G. and Pasin, F. (2011). A large neighbourhood search heuristic for the aircraft and passenger recovery problem, *4OR*, 9(2), 139–157.

Bish, E.K., Suwandechochai, R. and Bish, D.R. (2004). Strategies for managing the flexible capacity in the airline industry, *Naval Research Logistics*, 51(5), 654–685.

Bureau of Transportation Statistics (2016). *Airline on-time statistics and delay causes*. Online. Available at: www.transtats.bts.gov/ot_delay/ot_delaycause1.asp (accessed 31 October 2016).

Burghouwt, G. (2007). *Airline Network Development in Europe and its Implications for Airport Planning*, Aldershot, Ashgate.

Button, K. (2002). Debunking some common myths about airport hubs, *Journal of Air Transport Management*, 8(3), 177–188.

Challenge ROADEF (2009). *Disruption management for commercial aviation*. Online. Available at: http://challenge.roadef.org/2009/en/ (accessed 31 October 2016).

Clark, P. (2001). *Buying the Big Jets*, Aldershot, Ashgate.
Clausen, J., Larsen, A., Larsen, J. and Rezanova, N.J. (2010). Disruption management in the airline industry: concepts, models and methods, *Computers & Operations Research*, 37(5), 809–821.
Cordeau, J.F., Stojkoviç, G., Soumis, F. and Desrosiers, J. (2001). Benders' decomposition for simultaneous aircraft routing and crew scheduling, *Transportation Science*, 35(4), 375–388.
Desaulniers, G., Desrosiers, J., Dumas, Y., Solomon, M.M. and Soumis, F. (1997). Daily aircraft routing and scheduling, *Management Science*, 43(6), 841–855.
Desaulniers, G., Desrosiers, J. and Solomon, M.M. (2005). *Column Generation*, Volume 5 of GERAD 25th Anniversary Series, New York, Springer.
Dovica, I. (2014). *Robust Tail Assignment*, Berlin, Technische Universität Berlin.
Dumas, J. and Soumis, F. (2008). Passenger flow model for airline networks, *Transportation Science*, 42(2), 197–207.
Dumas, J., Aithnard, F. and Soumis, F. (2009). Improving the objective function of the fleet assignment problem, *Transportation Research Part B: Methodological*, 43(4), 466–475.
Dunbar, M., Froyland, G. and Wu, C.L. (2012). Robust airline schedule planning: minimizing propagated delay in an integrated routing and crewing framework, *Transportation Science*, 46(2), 204–216.
Dunbar, M., Froyland, G. and Wu, C.L. (2014). An integrated scenario-based approach for robust aircraft routing, crew pairing and re-timing, *Computers & Operations Research*, 45, 68–86.
Eggenberg, N. (2009). *Combining Robustness and Recovery for Airline Schedules*, Lausanne, École Polytechnique Fédérale de Lausanne.
Eggenberg, N., Salani, M. and Bierlaire, M. (2010). Constraint-specific recovery network for solving airline recovery problem, *Computers & Operations Research*, 37, 1014–1026.
Froyland, G., Maher, S.J. and Wu, C.L. (2014). The recoverable robust tail assignment problem, *Transportation Science*, 48(3), 351–372.
Gopalan, R. and Talluri, K.T. (1998). Mathematical models in airline schedule planning: a survey, *Annals of Operations Research*, 76, 155–185.
Hane, C.A., Barnhart, C., Johnson, E.L., Marsten, R.E., Nemhauser, G.L. and Sigismondi, G. (1995). The fleet assignment problem: solving a large-scale integer program, *Mathematical Programming*, 70(2), 211–232.
Haouari, M., Aissaoui, N. and Mansour, F.Z. (2009). Network flow-based approaches for integrated aircraft fleeting and routing, *European Journal of Operational Research*, 193(2), 591–599.
Jacobs, T., Smith, B.C. and Johnson, E.L. (2008). Incorporating network flow effects into the airline fleet assignment process, *Transportation Science*, 42(4), 514–529.
Jarrah, A.I.Z., Yu, G., Krishnamurthy, N. and Rakshit, A. (1993). A decision support framework for airline flight cancellations and delays, *Transportation Science*, 27(3), 266–280.
Jiang, H. and Barnhart, C. (2009). Dynamic airline scheduling, *Transportation Science*, 43(3), 336–354.
Jiang, H. and Barnhart, C. (2013). Robust airline schedule design in a dynamic scheduling environment, *Computers & Operations Research*, 40, 831–840.
Kang, L. (2004). *Degradable Airline Scheduling: An Approach to Improve Operational Robustness and Differentiate Service Quality*, PhD Dissertation, Cambridge, MA, Massachusetts Institute of Technology.
Lan, S., Clarke, J.P. and Barnhart, C. (2006). Planning for robust airline operations: optimizing aircraft routings and flight departure times to minimize passenger disruptions, *Transportation Science*, 40(1), 15–28.
Lettovsky, L., Johnson, E.L. and Nemhauser, G.L. (2000). Airline crew recovery, *Transportation Science*, 34(4), 337–348.
List, G.F., Wood, B., Nozick, L.K., Turnquist, M.A., Jones, D.A., Kjeldgaard, E.A., et al. (2003). Robust optimization for fleet planning under uncertainty, *Transportation Research Part E: Logistics and Transportation Review*, 39(3), 209–227.
Lohatepanont, M. and Barnhart, C. (2004). Airline schedule planning: integrated models and algorithms for schedule design and fleet assignment, *Transportation Science*, 38(1), 19–32.
Maher, S.J. (2015). A novel passenger recovery approach for the integrated airline recovery problem, *Computers & Operations Research*, 57, 123–137.
Maher, S.J. (2016). Solving the integrated recovery problem using column-and-row generation, *Transportation Science*, 50(1), 216–239.
Maher, S.J., Desaulniers, G. and Soumis, F. (2014). Recoverable robust single day aircraft maintenance routing problem, *Computers & Operations Research*, 51, 130–145.

Mancel, C. and Mora-Camino, F. (2006). *Airline fleet assignment: a state of the art*. Presented at Air Transportation Research Society conference, Nagoya, May.

Medard, C.P. and Sawhney, N. (2007). Airline crew scheduling from planning to operations, *European Journal of Operational Research*, 183(3), 1013–1027.

Mercier, A. and Soumis, F.C. (2007). An integrated aircraft routing, crew scheduling and flight retiming model, *Computers & Operations Research*, 34(8), 2251–2265.

Mercier, A., Cordeau, J.-F. and Soumis, F. (2005). A computational study of Benders' decomposition for the integrated aircraft routing and crew scheduling problem, *Computers & Operations Research*, 32(6), 1451–1476.

Nissen, R. and Haase, K. (2006). Duty-period-based network model for crew rescheduling in European airlines, *Journal of Scheduling*, 9(3), 255–278.

Papadakos, N. (2009). Integrated airline scheduling, *Computers & Operations Research*, 36(1), 176–195.

Petersen, J.D., Sölveling, G., Clarke, J.P., Johnson, E.L. and Shebalov, S. (2012). An optimization approach to airline integrated recovery, *Transportation Science*, 46(4), 482–500.

Pita, J.P., Barnhart, C. and Antunes, A.P. (2013). Integrated flight scheduling and fleet assignment under airport congestion, *Transportation Science*, 47(4), 477–492.

Rexing, B., Barnhart, C., Kniker, T., Jarrah, A. and Krishnamurthy, N. (2000). Airline fleet assignment with time windows, *Transportation Science*, 34(1), 1–20.

Rosenberger, J.M., Johnson, E.L. and Nemhauser, G.L. (2003). Rerouting aircraft for airline recovery, *Transportation Science*, 37(4), 408–421.

Rosenberger, J., Johnson, E.L. and Nemhauser, G.L. (2004). A robust fleet assignment model with hub isolation and short cycles, *Transportation Science*, 38(3), 357–368.

Rosskopf, M., Lehner, S. and Gollnick, V. (2014). Economic-environmental trade-offs in long-term airline fleet planning, *Journal of Air Transport Management*, 34, 109–115.

Rushmeier, R.A. and Kontogiorgis, S.A. (1997). Advances in the optimization of airline fleet assignment, *Transportation Science*, 31(2), 159–169.

Salazar-Gonzalez, J. (2014). Approaches to solve the fleet-assignment, aircraft-routing, crew-pairing and crew-rostering problems of a regional carrier, *Omega*, 43, 71–82.

Sherali, H.D., Bish, E.K. and Zhu, X. (2006). Airline fleet assignment concepts, models and algorithms, *European Journal of Operational Research*, 172(1), 1–30.

Sherali, H.D., Bae, K. and Haouari, M. (2013). An integrated approach for airline flight selection and timing, fleet assignment and aircraft routing, *Transportation Science*, 47(4), 455–476.

Sinclair, K., Cordeau, J.-F. and Laporte, G. (2014). Improvements to a large neighborhood search heuristic for an integrated aircraft and passenger recovery problem, *European Journal of Operational Research*, 233(1), 234–245.

Sinclair, K., Cordeau, J.-F. and Laporte, G. (2016). A column generation post-optimization heuristic for the integrated aircraft and passenger recovery problem, *Computers & Operations Research*, 65, 42–52.

Smith, B. and Johnson, E.L. (2006). Robust airline fleet assignment: imposing station purity using station decomposition, *Transportation Science*, 40(4), 497–516.

Stojković, M. and Soumis, F. (2001). An optimization model for the simultaneous operational flight and pilot scheduling problem, *Management Science*, 47(9), 1290–1305.

Stojković, M., Soumis, F. and Desrosiers, J. (1998). The operational airline crew scheduling problem, *Transportation Science*, 32(3), 232–245.

Subramanian, R., Scheff, R.P., Quillinan, J.D., Wiper, D.S. and Marsten, R.E. (1994). Coldstart: fleet assignment at Delta Airlines, *Interfaces*, 24(1), 104–120.

Teodorović, D. and Guberinic, S. (1984). Optimal dispatching strategy on an airline network after a schedule perturbation, *European Journal of Operational Research*, 15(2), 178–182.

Thengvall, B.G., Bard, J.F. and Yu, G. (2000). Balancing user preferences for aircraft schedule recovery during irregular operations, *IIE Transactions*, 32(3), 181–193.

Wang, X. and Meng, Q. (2008). Continuous-time dynamic network yield management with demand driven dispatch in the airline industry, *Transportation Research Part E: Logistics and Transportation Review*, 44(6), 1052–1073.

Warburg, V., Hansen, T.G., Larsen, A., Norman, H. and Andersson, E. (2008). Dynamic airline scheduling: an analysis of the potentials of refleeting and retiming, *Journal of Air Transport Management*, 14(4), 163–167.

Wei, G., Yu, G. and Song, M. (1997). Optimization model and algorithm for crew management during airline irregular operations, *Journal of Combinatorial Optimization*, 1(3), 305–321.

Weide, O., Ryan, D. and Ehrgott, M. (2010). An iterative approach to robust and integrated aircraft routing and crew scheduling, *Computers & Operations Research*, 37(5), 833–844.

Wu, C.L. (2006). Improving airline network robustness and operational reliability by sequential optimization algorithms, *Journal of Network and Spatial Economics*, 6(3), 235–251.

Wu, C.L. (2010). *Airline Operations and Delay Management: Insights from Airline Economics, Networks and Strategic Schedule Planning*, Aldershot, Ashgate.

Wu, C.L. and Maher, S. (2017). Airline scheduling and disruption management. In: L. Budd and S. Ison (eds). *Air Transport Management: An International Perspective*, Abingdon, Routledge.

Yan, S. and Yang, D.H. (1996). A decision support framework for handling schedule perturbation, *Transportation Research Part B: Methodological*, 30(6), 405–419.

Yan, S., Tang, C. and Lee, M. (2007). A flight scheduling model for Taiwan airlines under market competitions, *Omega*, 35(1), 61–74.

# 16

# Airport capacity planning and management

*Dieter Wilken*

## Introduction

In their air traffic forecasts, the aircraft manufacturing industry (e.g. Airbus, 2014) has a strong message: air traffic in terms of revenue passenger kilometres (RPKs) will continue to grow and double in the next 15 years. However, EUROCONTROL has analysed the capacity development of European airports and compared future air traffic demand with airport capacity, with the result that by the year 2035, most likely 2 million flights out of a total of over 14 million flights will not be accommodated due to a capacity shortage at main airports (EUROCONTROL, 2013). In most instances, the capacity bottleneck is caused by the runway system, since people living around airports and exposed to aircraft noise and pollution (see Chapter 18) oppose the enlargement of runway capacity with the argument that further runways will intensify the noise problem.

In an environment of growing demand for air traffic services, on the one hand, and of strong resistance to capacity investments at airports, on the other, capacity planning and management will remain on the political and entrepreneurial agenda for a long time. To illustrate the problem, this chapter describes the capacity situation at airports, deals with the capacity-relevant components of airports, and provides some capacity estimates of major airport elements (for airlines, see Chapter 15). An administrative way of capacity management, that is handling traffic in capacity restrained conditions, is the widespread International Air Transport Association (IATA) type slot coordination, which has become an official regulatory instrument in Europe and some other parts of the world, but not in the United States (US). The main features and drawbacks of slot coordination will be described in this chapter in the context of efficient usage of slot capacity. Finally, the capacity management means of public authorities, airlines, airports and air navigation service providers (ANSPs) to cope with capacity constraints will be discussed.

## A global perspective of airport capacity constraints

Regardless of the mode, traffic is neither equally distributed over the network nor over the time of the day, week or year. Spatial and temporal concentrations are the rule in air traffic, as well as in road and rail traffic networks. It has been shown (Gelhausen et al., 2013) that the cumulative

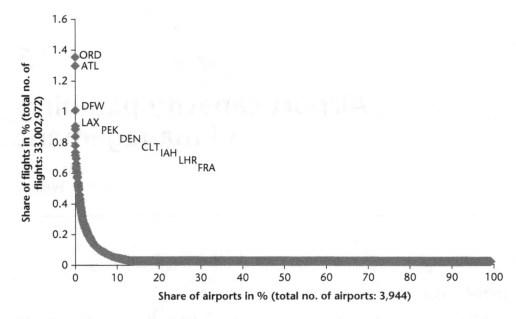

*Figure 16.1* Air traffic distribution in the global airport network, 2014

*Source*: OAG (2014), DLR.

distribution of air traffic in the global airport network is characterised by a high degree of concentration on a rather limited number of important airports, while, on the other hand, the great majority of airports handle relatively low traffic volumes well below capacity limits.

According to OAG (2014), air traffic reached a total volume of around 33 million flights in 2014 (corresponding to 66 million aircraft movements at airports) in a network of about 4,000 airports offering scheduled services. Figure 16.1 shows the distribution of airport traffic for the year 2014 (Berster et al., 2015). The number of flights (y-axis) and airports (x-axis) is shown as the share of total numbers of flights and airports. Each airport in the global network counts, therefore, for 0.0254 per cent of all airports. Dallas/Fort Worth (DFW) had, for example, a traffic volume of 333,000 flights, which corresponds to roughly 1 per cent of the total flight volume of 33 million flights worldwide.

The distribution of air traffic, as shown in Figure 16.1, demonstrates the concentration of traffic at a small number of high-volume airports and the great number of underutilised airports. Approximately 95 per cent of all airports (3,944) handle annual traffic volumes of below 3,300 flights, corresponding to 0.01 per cent of the total volume. The cumulative distribution, as shown in Figure 16.2, illustrates the concentration even more.

As can be seen, traffic share increases sharply over just a small share of all airports, 50 per cent of total traffic is handled by only 3 per cent of all airports and 90 per cent is handled by 24 per cent. In other words, the biggest 122 airports (3 per cent) handle half of the total traffic, that is 16.5 million flights, while the other 3,822 airports handle the same volume of traffic, on average each one handling 4,300 flights per year. Furthermore, the biggest 944 airports (24 per cent) handle almost 30 million flights, while the other 3,000 airports handle just 3 million (an average of 1,000 flights per year). The skewedness of the distribution function is typically described by the Gini coefficient,[1] which is in this case equal to 0.782.

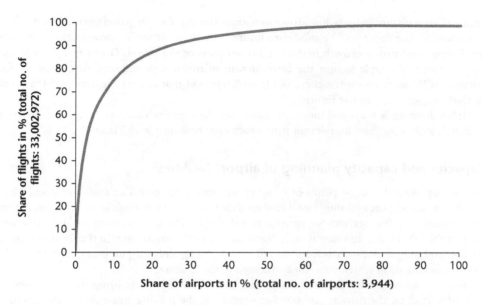

*Figure 16.2* Cumulative distribution of air traffic in the global airport network, 2014

*Source*: OAG (2014), DLR.

The global airport network therefore consists of a small number of airports with high traffic volumes, while the large number of airports handles traffic volumes of just a few flights a day. This latter group of airports is less likely to have the capacity problems that airports in the first group may have to deal with. Instead, their main concern is probably to attract more traffic to the airport in order to cover the cost of infrastructure and operations.

The interesting question is: Are these high-volume airports operating under unconstrained capacity conditions, such as the vast majority of small airports, or do they face more or less severe capacity problems, making it difficult for them and airlines to keep pace with the growing demand? A global constraints analysis (Gelhausen et al., 2013) has looked in detail into the capacity utilisation of airports with annual traffic volumes of more than 70,000 aircraft movements in 2008 by determining 5 per cent peak hour volumes and average daytime hourly volumes, and relating these to runway system capacities by establishing capacity utilisation indices (CUIs). A more recent analysis for 2014 (Berster et al., 2015) has identified 30 airports among over 170 airports with more than 70,000 aircraft movements with high utilisation rates and severe capacity constraints over longer periods of operating hours. More important, these airports are to a large extent identical to those with the highest traffic volumes. Among them are Beijing, Hong Kong, Shanghai, Istanbul, London Heathrow and Gatwick, Munich, Dubai, Atlanta, New York La Guardia, San Diego, Mexico City and Sao Paulo. A further 49 airports with high traffic volumes belong to a lower capacity utilisation class, indicating that they have peak hour congestion problems, among them Singapore, Delhi, Bangkok, Amsterdam, Frankfurt, Paris Charles de Gaulle, Chicago O'Hare, Detroit, New York JFK, San Francisco, Bogota and Sydney. There are therefore 79 airports belonging to the top-ranking airports worldwide that are both highly utilised and capacity-constrained during peak times or over many hours of the day.

In the past, airlines have deployed aircraft with higher seat capacity in order to try to overcome the bottleneck situation at major airports. That is one reason why air traffic in terms of aircraft movements has grown less than the number of passengers. Nevertheless, it is assumed that there will be moderate future growth of air traffic movements in the US and Europe and strong growth in Asia and other parts of the world. Given this growth and the resistance of people against the introduction of major new infrastructure projects, for instance in Western countries, there is a large likelihood that airport capacity problems will be further aggravated in the future.

Before looking at ways and means of improving the capacity situation at airports, the next section describes the capacity relevant parts of airports, both airside and landside.

## Capacity and capacity planning of airport facilities

Airports represent the access points of air transport users to the global air traffic network. They have become complex multifunctional entities if they are part of the public air transport system with scheduled airline services for passengers and goods. The large majority of airports, especially in the US, do not function as such, but serve primarily private users in the form of general aviation and special use, such as from aircraft owners for agricultural purposes or flight schools. These generally small airfields are not considered in this chapter.

Airports can be subdivided into airside and landside, with airside being the manoeuvring area for aircraft on the runway and taxiway system and the parking area either at the terminal or in reserved ramp areas. The controlled airspace surrounding airports is also regarded as being part of the airport's airside. The main components of the landside are the terminal buildings for passengers and cargo, parking areas and access roads for road vehicles, and public transportation facilities such as rail terminals. There are more airport facilities such as hangars, fuel farms, power plants and other support facilities, and non-aeronautical land use such as for hotels, office buildings and car rental locations, which are common components of each airport, however in many cases less critical with respect to capacity planning.

In an environment of air traffic growth, airport operators have an inherent interest in meeting demand by providing sufficient infrastructure capacity, today and in the future. The planning of facilities, including their capacity, has always been an important task for airport management, and also for public authorities, since airports are often regarded as part of the public transport infrastructure. While airport operators develop and decide on plans for the future layout of their airport, public authorities are responsible for providing regional or national air transport plans. These plans are of a strategic nature and are largely concerned with the functional division of airports in a country or region. Airport-specific plans, on the other hand, aim to provide detailed plans for airport facilities in the medium or long term. A classic example of long-term plans is the airport master plan.

According to the International Civil Aviation Organisation (ICAO), an airport master plan presents the planner's conception of the ultimate development of a specific airport (ICAO, 1987). The main working steps of master planning are: to produce an inventory of existing conditions; to forecast future traffic; to analyse capacities of airport facilities and compare with forecast demand, or the selection of a site if a new airport is required; to determine facility requirements; to develop several planned alternatives for comparative analysis; to select the most acceptable and appropriate master plan; to prepare the airport layout plan with a graphic presentation of facilities/functional units; and to schedule implementation of the plan with monetary estimates of investments, costs and sources of revenue.

While it is still general practice and often required by law to develop master plans, the drawbacks of these planning efforts have become more and more evident. The main critic comes from the fact that master plans rely just on one expectation of future traffic (de Neufville and

Odoni, 2003). While it typically needs several years to develop an airport master plan, the traffic forecast forming the basis for capacity estimates of airport facilities often turns out to be obsolete when the master plan is about to be adopted. Public authorities or interest groups opposing airport extensions often criticise traffic forecasts with the argument that recent factor developments have not been taken into account. Examples have been the weaker air transport demand development since the financial crisis in 2008–2009 or the tendency of airlines to deploy larger aircraft with higher seat capacities in recent years.

The basis for designing and dimensioning airport facilities is the future level and structure of air traffic. The traffic forecast (see Chapter 19) is therefore a central element of planning activities. It is generally understood that forecasts are estimates that should be based as far as possible on causal relationships, with input data, hypotheses and methods stated and described in a retrievable way for those who use them. In contrast to prophecies, forecasts yield 'if-then' results, meaning that only if specified framework conditions govern then the results may be used as forecast values in further planning studies. Nevertheless, the validity of these results is typically limited because of scarcity of data, lack of methodological quality, and uncertainty in the occurrence of influencing factors and premises.

In the past years, airports were often asked to alter their investment plans and long-term strategy in order to account for changing influences of planning factors such as the proliferation of low cost carriers (LCCs) and the increased prevalence of information technologies. Manchester Airport, for example, began to apply a dynamic strategic planning approach. The following steps were taken, and illustrate a difference to the working steps of master planning (Leucci, 2016): inventory of existing conditions; forecast range of future traffic for some scenarios describing traffic level and structure; determination of facility requirements suitable for several possible levels and types of traffic; selection of the most acceptable first-phase development, which enables subsequent and appropriate responses to possible future conditions; and development of plans that are flexible and agile enough to mitigate and correlate with future industry developments.

## Airside: airspace, runways, taxiways, aprons

Public authorities and semi-public or private companies providing air navigation services are responsible for safe and efficient movements of aircraft in the controlled airspace. The main functions of air traffic control are providing communication between air traffic controllers and pilots, ensuring surveillance of aircraft by providing positional information to air traffic controllers and the cockpit, and providing navigational services to pilots to fly on established air routes in structured airspace to the destination. Modern automation technologies (e.g. displays, computers and software), along with internationally agreed procedures and regulations, are used to guide aircraft if possible on direct routes from flight origin to destination by ensuring always sufficient separation between airspace users. For details of air traffic control (ATC) and air traffic management (ATM), see, for instance, FAA (1992), Horonjeff et al. (2010) and Nolan (1999) (see also Chapter 4).

The airspace surrounding airports, also called terminal area airspace or terminal control airspace (TCA), is of direct relevance to the capacity of airports, because aircraft approaching the airport or taking off from that airport have to follow specific procedures and separation rules in order to ensure safety for all airspace users. The longitudinal separation requirements thus determine the maximum number of aircraft that can be handled on a runway within a certain time span. A main reason for specifying separation minima is the fact that jet turbines of flying aircraft create wake vortices that endanger trailing aircraft when following too close to the leading aircraft. Since wake vortices depend on the power and size of the engines, the size of the wings, and thus the size and weight of the aircraft, each aircraft is assigned to one of three classes. The separation minima are specified for aircraft approaching an airport in units of distance (kilometres, nautical miles) and for aircraft departing from an airport both in units of time (minutes) and of distance units. The US Federal Aviation Administration (FAA) has issued such separation standards for US airspace, while ICAO has developed similar standards applicable to member states (ICAO, 2007).

As an example, according to ICAO, the maximum take-off mass (MTOM) determines the wake turbulence category for separation at a single-use runway. The categories are: heavy (all aircraft types of 136 tons or more); medium (aircraft types less than 136 tons but more than 7 tons); and light (aircraft types of 7 tons or less). The minimum separation between departing aircraft is one minute if aircraft are to fly on tracks diverging by at least 45 degrees immediately after take-off so that lateral separation is provided. For both arriving and departing aircraft that are not radar-separated, time-based wake turbulence separation minima for aircraft landing behind a heavy or medium aircraft are: two minutes for a medium aircraft behind a heavy aircraft, and three minutes for a light aircraft behind a heavy or medium aircraft. For departing aircraft not radar-separated, a minimum separation of two minutes is applied for a light or medium aircraft taking off behind a heavy aircraft, or a light aircraft taking off behind a medium aircraft.

In air traffic service (ATS) surveillance systems, especially arriving aircraft are radar controlled and distance-based wake turbulence separation minima are applied. For both the approach and departure phases of flight, the separation minima in Table 16.1 are specified.

Assuming a population of medium aircraft such as the Boeing 737 or Airbus 320 taking off, one following the other, with a minimum separation time of 60 seconds at a single-runway airport, there would be a theoretical runway capacity of 60 departures per hour. The corresponding capacity of aircraft in the final approach would be lower due to the greater wake turbulence separation. In practice, runway capacity is lower than the theoretical capacity, since aircraft are, for safety reasons, not typically spaced with exact minimum time intervals, but with additional buffer times to cope with uncertainties in aircraft spacing procedures.

Most of the airports that form part of the global network of scheduled air traffic are equipped with just one runway. However, due to the concentration of traffic at a small number of main airports, these airports often have more than one runway, frequently three runways or more. Very few airports have more than five runways in operation. These principal airports, such as London Heathrow, Hong Kong, Atlanta or Istanbul, suffer to a great extent from capacity constraints, mainly caused by lack of runway capacity. Since the runway system is crucial for the capability of the airport to handle current and future traffic, the maximum throughput of this airport component is of fundamental importance in airport planning. A large amount of research has been devoted to the subject of estimating runway capacity, especially in the US. The FAA has initiated and carried out many capacity-related studies, and issued Advisory Circulars on this subject. Recently, the FAA has published several reports in which runway capacities of the main US airports are presented as a result of benchmarking studies (e.g. see FAA, 2014).

*Table 16.1* Separation minima in ATS surveillance systems

| Preceding aircraft | Succeeding aircraft | Distance-based wake turbulence separation minima |
| --- | --- | --- |
| Heavy | Heavy | 7.4 km (4.0 NM) |
| Heavy | Medium | 9.3 km (5.0 NM) |
| Heavy | Light | 11.1 km (6.0 NM) |
| Medium | Light | 9.3 km (5.0 NM) |

Source: ICAO (2007).

Two prominent examples of textbooks describing methodological approaches to estimating runway capacity are de Neufville and Odoni (2003) and Horonjeff et al. (2010).

The term capacity usually refers to the capability of a facility to handle people, freight and vehicles. In a theoretical context, the capacity is identical to the maximum number of traffic units (i.e. vehicles) that can pass through the facility within a given time span, typically one hour, under specified conditions having regard to safety regulations, operating conditions, standards of expediency and comfort, and possibly other conditions (Wilken et al., 2011).

According to the concept of ultimate or maximum throughput capacity, the runway capacity is equal to the maximum number of flight movements – take-offs and landings – that the runway can accommodate, subject to regulations of ATC. The ultimate capacity does not take into account time delays that aircraft encounter when they are ready for take-off or landing in peak traffic conditions. As demand approaches ultimate capacity, delays to aircraft are likely to reach intolerably high levels. The phenomenon of sharply increasing delays in traffic situations approaching capacity without the possibility of reducing them by decreasing the demand can be observed in road and rail traffic alike.

To account for the delay problem, the concept of practical capacity has found wide application. Movement rates are determined in relation to average aircraft delay levels (FAA, 1969). In comparison to the level of service concept used in road traffic, a practical capacity was devised primarily for planning purposes, whereby a tolerable average delay per aircraft movement was the criterion for setting the capacity as a limit to the number of movements per hour for the runway system under day-to-day operating conditions. For many airports, the threshold value of tolerable delay was found to be in the order of four minutes, corresponding to the practical hourly capacity concept of the FAA. At an average delay of four minutes, single aircraft delays may exceed the average, however they are not likely to violate the punctuality criteria of 15-minute delay to a great extent. Only if delays exceed 15 minutes are the corresponding flights recorded as delayed flights in traffic statistics.

To answer the question of practical capacity, it is necessary to know that runway capacity is not a fixed value for all runways, but rather a function depending on a series of influencing factors. Since these factors vary from airport to airport, each runway has a specific capacity. The most relevant factors are (see also de Neufville and Odoni, 2003): number and geometric layout of the runways; separation requirements between aircraft imposed by ATC (as mentioned previously in this section); visibility, cloud ceiling and precipitation; wind direction and strength; mix of aircraft using the airport; mix of movements on each runway (arrivals only, departures only or mixed) and sequencing of movements; number, type and location of taxiway exits from the runway(s); state and performance of the ATC system (including the number and shape of standard instrument departures [SIDs] and standard arrival routes [STARs]); and noise-related and other administrative regulations regarding the usage of the runway(s) and surrounding airspace.

A specific concept of practical capacity is the declared capacity, the determination of which forms an integral part of the IATA slot coordination, which has become the legal form of airport capacity management in Europe and other parts of the world, but not in the US. Capacity values of slot-coordinated airports are documented as declared capacity and used by slot coordinators as stipulation for allocating slot requests of airlines at these airports. Details of the European Union (EU) slot regulation can be found in the Council-Regulation No 95/93 (EU, 2004) and are well documented in the IATA *Worldwide Slot Guidelines* (IATA, 2015).

The declared capacity specifies the number of aircraft movements that can be scheduled per unit of time (10 minutes, 30 minutes, one hour) at an airport, as estimated by the local airport stakeholders in the Coordination Committee. The declared capacity reflects the attempt to find a compromise between high-capacity and low-capacity conditions at an airport, which cannot

265

*Table 16.2* Declared capacities of selected airports by runway capacity class, 2016

| Airport | Declared capacity (aircraft movements per hour) |
|---|---|
| Single-runway airports | |
| London Gatwick | 50 |
| London Stansted | 36 |
| Dublin | 46 |
| Stuttgart | 42 |
| Geneva | 36 |
| Airports with two intersecting runways | |
| Hamburg | 48 |
| Warsaw | 42 |
| Perth | 38 |
| Lisbon | 40 |
| Airports with two close parallel runways | |
| Dubai | 65 |
| Manchester | 56 |
| Berlin Tegel | 52 |
| Nice | 50 |
| Düsseldorf* | 45 |
| Airports with two independent parallel runways | |
| Munich | 90 |
| London Heathrow | 89 |
| Helsinki | 80 |
| Oslo | 76 |
| Brussels | 74 |
| Palma de Mallorca | 66 |
| Taipei | 50 |

*Source*: National and airport-specific slot coordinator organisations.

*Note*: * Düsseldorf capacity is limited by administrative rules to a single-runway capacity.

be predicted a season in advance. Table 16.2 gives declared capacity values by runway capacity class for a selection of Level 3 airports for the year 2016, where runway capacities constrain the number of aircraft movements.

As can be seen in Table 16.2, declared capacities vary between airports depending largely on local conditions. In Europe, a single runway has a practical capacity under instrument flight rules (IFR) conditions of about 35 to 50 aircraft movements, if not factors as described previously in this section form more severe obstacles to higher movement rates. Two parallel runways, if being operated independently according to ICAO rules, have capacities of up to 90 aircraft movements.

In Europe, take-offs and landings are normally planned for IFR weather conditions. Visual flight rules (VFR) conditions typically govern in the US, although in poor weather conditions IFR flight rules will apply as well. Capacities are higher in VFR conditions, often by 10 to 20 per cent. The FAA has published a capacity analysis of 30 so-called core airports in the US (FAA, 2014), in which ATC reported and model-estimated profiles of practical capacity are given for three weather conditions – visual, marginal and instrument. San Diego Airport is the only single-runway airport among the high-volume core airports with a runway capacity of 48 movements per hour in IFR conditions and up to 57 in VFR conditions. Within the global airport constraint analysis mentioned above, mean practical runway capacities have been calculated on the basis of observed 5 per cent peak hour volumes of highly utilised airports, whereby the 5 per cent peak hour volume represents in most cases a value close to practical capacity (Gelhausen, 2012). By assuming a capacity utilisation index of 85 per cent – the value of London Heathrow, the highest value found – a mean runway capacity of around 40 aircraft movements has been estimated for operations under IFR conditions and 44 movements under VFR conditions. As can be seen, the actual values of San Diego Airport are even higher. All in all, good proxy value ranges of practical runway capacity seem to be 35 to 45 aircraft movements in typical European weather and operating conditions, and between 45 and 55 movements in good weather conditions in the US.

Taxiways and aprons form the infrastructural link between the runway system and passenger and cargo terminals, hangars, and other airport facilities. In fact, taxiways connect runways with terminals near aprons, while the latter serve primarily as aircraft stands close to terminals, so that passengers can directly board aircraft parked there, or as remote aircraft parking areas. Taxiways may be subdivided again into exit taxiways connecting runways with parallel taxiways, apron taxiways providing for aircraft circulation around or through apron areas, and taxilanes allowing aircraft to manoeuvre within larger aprons and accessing aircraft stands at terminals. Holding bays and bypass taxiways are often parts of taxiways allowing aircraft to wait for departure clearance near the runway in widened sections of the taxiway. At low traffic volume airports, runways are connected either directly with the apron by means of an exit taxiway or indirectly through a parallel taxiway, while high-volume airports need to have dual parallel taxiways in order to separate aircraft by direction – that is, aircraft after landing or before taking off.

As an example, Figure 16.3 shows the layout of Munich Airport, which has an independent parallel runway system with runways being 4,000 metres long, and two midfield terminals directly accessible from the landside. Each runway is accompanied by a series of high-speed exit taxiways that connect with dual taxiways for departing or landed aircraft. These taxiways are linked then with the apron areas in front of the two terminals and a third apron as a remote parking area for aircraft. At each of the four taxiway ends near the runways, holding bays are provided for aircraft waiting to enter the runway for take-off. The taxiway system at this airport is thus more complex than the runway system; the total length of taxiways measures about 30 kilometres, whereas the corresponding length of the runways is only 8 kilometres.

As shown in Table 16.2, the runway system at Munich Airport has a declared hourly capacity of 90 aircraft movements. The taxiway system and aprons have been planned in order to meet the capacity needs of the runway system. Due to the layout (i.e. the dual taxiways and high-speed exit taxiways), up to 90 aircraft per hour rolling from runways to aprons, and vice versa, can be handled without a risk of encountering delays, as long as exceptional short peak demand situations or capacity problems with ATM do not form additional obstacles.

As can be seen in Figure 16.3, the two runways are staggered by about 1,500 metres, meaning that the runway thresholds are offset, so that, independently of wind direction, an aircraft on approach always finds one runway for landing with short taxiways towards the terminal stands, and the other runway offers short taxiways for departures at the same time.

Finally, it should be mentioned that other airside facilities are needed to maintain the functioning of an airport; these are, in particular, the air traffic control tower and buildings and areas for servicing the aircraft between a landing and the successive take-off, or in the maintenance phase.

Dieter Wilken

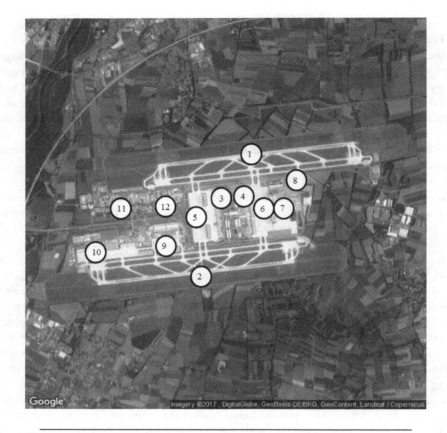

| | | |
|---|---|---|
| 1 RWY 08L – 26R | 5 Apron 1 | 9 Cargo area |
| 2 RWY 08R – 26L | 6 Apron 2 | 10 Aircraft maintenance |
| 3 Terminal 1 | 7 Apron 3 | 11 Central administration |
| 4 Terminal 2 | 8 General Aviation | 12 Visitors park |

*Figure 16.3* Layout of Munich Airport

*Source*: Google, Munich Airport (2012). Imagery ©2017, DigitalGlobe, GeoBasis-DE/BKG, GeoContent, Landsat/Copernicus.

## Landside: terminals, parking areas, road access, ground transportation facilities

Airside components of an airport such as runways, taxiways, ramps and aprons are essential elements without which the airport would not function. In contrast, the landside of airports typically includes facilities such as hotels and office and shopping areas in or near passenger buildings that, in a narrow sense, do not necessarily need to be there. However, such components often contribute to the attractiveness of the airport and to the revenue of the airport company (see Chapter 12). Essential landside facilities are the passenger and cargo buildings and road access and parking areas; in European countries, public transit and rail terminals for regional and intercity train services are regarded more and more as components of major airports that should be planned and incorporated from the beginning.

The main function of passenger terminals is to provide the interface between aircraft and passengers. While passengers find their way through the terminal, cargo has to be moved from the landside access, processed, sorted, consolidated and often stored in containers, until it is moved to the airside and finally loaded onto aircraft, and vice versa. Passenger terminals serve the needs of different types of passengers such as originating, terminating or transfer passengers, travelling either for business or leisure purposes. They also serve the needs of different airlines (i.e. full service network, charter, regional or LCCs) and of the airport operator. Terminals provide many services such as check-in counters, baggage processing devices, custom and security clearance, waiting areas in the landside as well as the airside part (i.e. gates), and transfer areas between these parts. In addition, passenger terminals are becoming partly shopping centres catering for visitors and passengers in the landside part and for passengers only in restricted areas after security. Passenger bridges allow access to the aircraft parked near the terminal; otherwise, bus gates are provided to bring passengers to the aircraft position away from the terminal. Finally, offices for airlines, government agencies, the airport operator and other airport users complete the spectrum of functions of terminals.

Passenger terminals have been developed with many different layouts, mostly following four basic configurations (see also de Neufville and Odoni, 2003): central buildings with finger piers (e.g. Frankfurt terminal one), central buildings with satellites (e.g. Tampa), central buildings with midfield concourses (e.g. Zurich) and linear buildings with one landside and one airside (e.g. Munich terminal one and two).

For the majority of airports with one runway and relatively small traffic volumes, linear buildings with road access on one side and gates on the airside is the standard configuration. Whatever the design solution, terminals should be developed so that their capacity conforms to the airside capacity (i.e. the runway capacity). In contrast to runways, terminals can be planned in more flexible ways regarding size, time of construction and passenger comfort. A basic requirement is therefore to adopt a dynamic strategic planning approach, as mentioned previously in this chapter, by taking account of the different interests of all stakeholders (i.e. airlines, passengers, forwarders, airport operators, government agencies and other users).

Whereas the runway capacity is measured in terms of aircraft movements per hour, passenger terminal capacity is related to the number of passengers handled in one hour. The hour selected is thereby a design peak hour that represents an hour with a relatively high traffic volume among all hours of the year (e.g. the 5 per cent peak hour, which reaches a traffic volume that is exceeded only in 5 per cent of all hours of the year). The design peak hour used, for instance, in the United Kingdom (UK) is the 30th busiest hour of the year, the volume of which is called the standard busy rate.

Assuming, for example, an airport has around 70,000 aircraft movements per year, such as Berlin-Schoenefeld in 2015, and with one runway in operation, a 5 per cent peak hour traffic volume of around 20 movements would be expected, corresponding to roughly 50 per cent of the capacity of that runway. Assuming further that the airport has an average passenger load per movement of 100 passengers (which corresponds to the European average), the terminal should have a capacity of handling at least 2,000 passengers per hour, and be built in such a way as to be able to expand if traffic grows in the future. According to design guidelines developed by the FAA (1988), the terminal building would need an area space of around 30,000 to 35,000 square metres with about 20 to 25 gates.

Obviously, such capacity, space and gate requirements are broad estimates. Final plans would be based on detailed analyses of the conditions and potential future developments of the airport under consideration. Such plans would include the concrete layout of the diverse terminal functions as there are terminal curb lengths for road access, passenger and visitor waiting areas, airline counters for ticketing, check-in and baggage handling, passenger security check areas, departure areas and lounges, corridors interrelating these functions, baggage claim facilities, office areas for airlines, customs and security, and airport management and other users such as car rentals, airside areas for aircraft handling, and – more and more – shopping areas and other passenger amenities. All these facilities would be designed in relation to a desired level of service, which may vary from country to country and even within a country depending on local requirements and constraints and expectations regarding the future demand development.

## Airport slot coordination

Administrative slot allocation at constrained airports has existed in some European countries for over 40 years and has been applied in EU member states as an official procedure since 1993, following the rules set forth in the European Council Regulation No. 95/93 (EU, 2004). The European rules are based on the IATA *Worldwide Slot Guidelines* (IATA, 2015), which form a procedural framework of slot coordination in many countries of the world, except in the US. In 2015, there were approximately 285 airports worldwide that were partly or fully slot-coordinated by means of the IATA coordination framework, of which 90 airports in the European Economic Area plus Switzerland were coordinated on the basis of the EU Regulation No. 95/93. Nearly 90 slot-coordinating institutions in 70 countries were responsible for carrying out the global slot allocation of flight schedules of around 250 airlines, including those of the US.

The basic principle of the EU/IATA slot coordination is not a market-based idea of getting access to scarce airport capacity, but an administrative right for an airline to use a slot (a given point in time for a take-off or landing in the next season) if the slot has been used in at least 80 per cent of all possible cases in the previous equivalent season (the 'use it or lose it' rule). This so-called grandfather right is the essential element of the slot coordination process and guarantees free market access to incumbent airlines, at least in the same way as in the previous season, whereas new entrants have only limited chances, depending on the scarcity of slots.

Around the grandfather right nucleus of EU/IATA slot coordination, a set of rules exist, and are applied in a biannual cycle following a predetermined schedule of coordination activities of stakeholders (i.e. coordinators, airlines, airports, ANSPs and governmental agencies) (see Figure 16.4).

Given the historical precedence of aircraft movements (in this context equal to slots), airlines have to apply for slots for the planning season, and these applications have to include the historic slots as well as new requests. Slot coordinators allocate these slot applications to the slots available, historic slots as requested and new slot applications, depending on free slots being available. If slots are still available after all historic slots have been allocated, 50 per cent of these slots are reserved for slot applications of new entrant airlines. At slot conferences, which take place twice annually, slot coordinators meet with about 1,000 airline and airport representatives in order to finalise schedule adjustments. Slots may be exchanged one by one within an airline and between airlines, provided the slot coordinator agrees and the slot swap has no effect on capacity. Slots that have been allocated can be returned to the slot coordinator some weeks after the slot conference so that they may be used by other airlines (i.e. new entrants). If these slots are not returned before the slot return deadline, airlines will lose the historic right to them. With the slot monitoring and the counting of grandfather slots, the new planning cycle for the following season restarts.

The IATA type slot coordination has received much criticism in the past, with the main argument being that scarce capacity is not optimally used since incumbent airlines do not pay for the airport access. Studies (e.g. see Steer Davies Gleave, 2011) have shown that the suboptimal

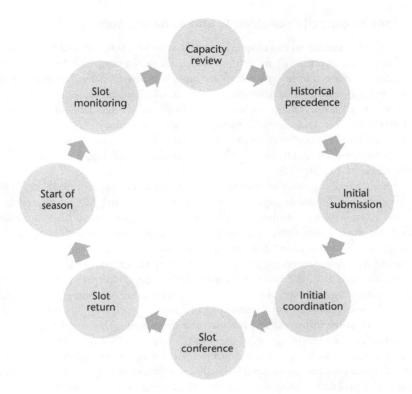

*Figure 16.4* Biannual slot coordination cycle

*Source*: Author.

use stems from the fact that a significant proportion of slots, although they have been allocated, have not been used, or, since passengers are no criterion in the coordination process, have been used by small aircraft, thus limiting passenger demand, which otherwise could have been satisfied within the constrained capacity. Analyses of flight data by the German Airport Coordinator, however, have shown that capacity utilisation at the three most important airports in Germany, Frankfurt, Munich and Düsseldorf, has been continuously high. In 2011, the capacity utilisation in terms of the ratio of slots used and declared capacity was 94 per cent at Frankfurt, 89 per cent at Munich and 80 per cent at Düsseldorf (Zang, 2015). These figures do not prove, however, that passenger markets have been served in the best way possible.

To optimise the utilisation, research studies have proposed to abandon the administrative IATA type slot coordination and introduce market-based instruments such as slot auctioning (e.g. see Technical University of Berlin, 2001). In addition, Steer Davies Gleave (2011) analysed and proposed a number of options, among them making the system of slot monitoring and enforcement more effective and introducing market mechanisms for the primary allocation of slots and/or for secondary allocation (secondary trading). The authors estimated that the net economic benefits from introducing secondary trading EU-wide were greater than the net economic benefits of all of the other options put together. Slot trading has occurred on quite a few occasions at London Heathrow Airport. For example, in early 2016, Oman Air bought a morning pair of take-off and landing slots for US$75 million. This shows the high monetary value of slots at congested hub airports.

## Implications of capacity constraints and enhancements

As has been described earlier in this chapter, air traffic is indeed concentrated at a relatively small number of important airports, the majority of which are facing capacity problems at present or in the near future. Air traffic is expected to continue to grow globally, however, with a pace that differs greatly between Asia, Australia and the Middle East, on the one hand, and Europe and North America, on the other (see Chapter 19). While in Asia the demand has only begun to grow during the last few decades, and is growing strongly, demand in North America is almost mature at a high level of propensity to fly, and demand development shows signs of saturation with a low growth tendency. Demand in Europe will still be growing, however, with decreasing growth rates (see Chapter 19).

These differing traffic growth expectations imply that future capacity problems will be less severe at major North American airports such as Atlanta, New York La Guardia and San Diego than at Asian airports such as Shanghai, Beijing, Hong Kong and others. Due to further traffic growth and the societal difficulties of developing new airport capacity in Europe, problems of overcoming constraints will most likely last into the future.

Solutions to the capacity problem will vary from airport to airport and from region to region. In some regions, such as in the London area, no enlargement of airport capacity has yet been achieved, in spite of many political propositions, whereas other regions, such as China or the Middle East, have experienced rapid extensions of runway systems or the construction of new airports. In many other instances, in particular in Europe, the delay of adding new facilities, especially runways, has been in the order of more than 20 years, a time span in which the traffic may have doubled. In such situations, airlines, airport operators and ANSPs have to look for means of optimising the throughput of facilities, applying perhaps congestion charges and improving ATM procedures. Airlines have already increased seat capacity of flights, primarily for economic reasons, at both unconstrained and constrained airports. It seems that all these measures have been exploited at London Heathrow, the airport with the highest capacity utilisation; the number of flights has not increased at Heathrow for years because the number of free slots has not increased and all available slots are held with incumbent airlines. The pressure to build a new runway, either at Heathrow or Gatwick, is strong and has been growing from year to year. In 2016, the British government has taken the formal decision in favour of developing a new runway at Heathrow Airport.

Among the options of how to deal with airport capacity scarcity, the alternative of adding new runways or a new airport is the solution with the highest capacity gain, however, typically, the one with the greatest problems of implementation. Another investment option is connecting the airport with regional and intercity train services, whereby regional trains would change the modal split of passengers originating or terminating their air journey at the airport, while intercity trains would enlarge the catchment area of the airport and reduce the demand for short-distance flights. While in Europe a great number of hub and other major airports are already complex rail and air nodes, intercity train services are offered only at a fraction of these airports.

Other options aim either at maximising throughput at the airport in terms of the number of flights, or at optimising throughput by pricing flights so that the revenue of airlines will rise accordingly, as is the case with intercontinental flights at London Heathrow, depending on the competitive situation of the market. Airports charge airlines with weight- and passenger-related landing fees per flight; since these fees have to be cost-related and adopted by government agencies in many countries, especially in Europe, airports often have no means to raise fees in relation to capacity scarcity (see also Chapter 12). The throughput-maximising options include: using more intensively off-peak times (incentive regulation and slot coordination measure); diverting traffic to less congested airports (slot coordination measure in airport systems); using aircraft with higher seat capacity (airline measure); or changing ATC rules (ANSP measure based on technological progress).

When airports are capacity-constrained in peak hours, requests to shift flights to off-peak hours may be handled through voluntary agreements between airlines, or through slot coordination at Level 3 airports. Diverting traffic to less congested airports is, in particular at hub airports, more a theoretical than a practical measure since many incoming and outgoing flights are interrelated in order to allow for transfer passengers to change flights. In airport systems, which are slot-coordinated, the coordinator has the means to shift flights from the principal airport to a secondary airport.

In order to satisfy growing demand without having to increase the number of flights accordingly, airlines have often deployed aircraft with higher seat capacity. This option has probably been the most effective operational measure. In the global network, the average aircraft size has increased from 114 seats per flight in 2006 to 132 seats in 2014 (see Figure 16.5). At the constrained airports mentioned earlier in this chapter, it has increased from 130 to 147 seats. While the global passenger demand has grown by 4.6 per cent per year on average during the time period, the number of flights offered has increased by just 1.6 per cent, primarily because of the growth in aircraft size and load factor.

Technological advancements in ATC (i.e. SESAR and NextGen) and air traffic flow management may lead to rule changes, which again may enhance the throughput of a runway system (see Chapter 4). Better communication, navigation and surveillance systems may allow an increase in the number of aircraft approaching an airport in the airspace surrounding airports. The current applied instrument landing system (ILS) calls for straight-line approaches of aircraft to the runway, with separation minima as indicated earlier in this chapter. Future navigational landing procedures will most likely be based on a satellite-based radio positioning and navigation system (e.g. using the US Global Positioning System [GPS]). GPS-based approaches allow aircraft to navigate around obstacles such as mountainous terrain and/or noise-sensitive urban areas, and to approach airports using more flexible jet precise navigation procedures, thus possibly permitting shorter separation distances between aircraft.

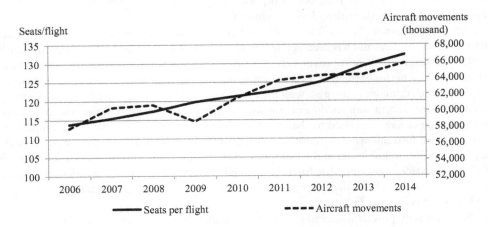

*Figure 16.5* Development of average aircraft size (seats per flight) and aircraft movements in the global airport network, 2006 to 2014

*Source*: OAG (2014), DLR.

All these organisational-type options can only slightly improve the utilisation of capacity-constrained airports. Since the development of new capacity-enhancing infrastructure is often doomed to failure on grounds of administrative obstacles and public resistance, efficient utilisation of the existing facilities gains in importance. The administrative non-market-based slot coordination is widely practised, but not a guarantee of the best usage of scarce capacity. Without market-based measures, it remains difficult to find out which airline would use the slots most efficiently. Secondary trading of slots will therefore improve the slot utilisation, and should be implemented.

## Conclusion

The global network of airports, which serve as nodes of scheduled air traffic, consists of around 4,000 airports, handling a traffic volume of about 66 million aircraft movements (take-offs and landings). Air traffic is very concentrated at a relatively small number of airports. In 2014, the largest 122 airports (3 per cent of all airports) handled half of the total traffic, that is, 33 million movements, while the other more than 3,800 airports handled the same volume, on average only 8,600 movements each.

A large proportion of the major airports with high traffic volumes struggle with capacity problems; around 30 of them have severe capacity constraints over longer periods of operating hours, and another 50 airports are constrained during daily peak hours. In an environment of growing demand for air traffic services, on the one hand, and of strong resistance of the public to capacity investments at airports, on the other, airport capacity problems are likely to continue. Capacity planning and management will therefore remain on the political and entrepreneurial agenda for a long time.

Given future air traffic growth, airport operators have an inherent interest to be in a position of meeting the demand by means of providing sufficient infrastructure capacity. Airport master plans have typically been developed in the past, following guidelines set up by ICAO. Airport master plans have relied on just one future development of air traffic that often turned out to be unrealistic. To account better for forecasting uncertainties, public authorities and airport planners are asked nowadays to adopt a more strategic airport planning approach, which does not aim at following one future path, but incorporates more flexibility by pursuing several handling options in relation to alternative developments of the air transport system.

Administrative slot allocation at constrained airports has existed in some European countries for over 40 years and has been applied by EU member states as an official procedure since 1993. In 2015, there were approximately 285 airports worldwide that were partly or fully slot-coordinated by means of the IATA coordination framework. This form of slot coordination has received much criticism in the past, with the main argument that scarce capacity is not optimally used since incumbent airlines do not pay for the airport access. To optimise the utilisation, research studies have proposed to abandon the administrative slot coordination and introduce market-based instruments such as slot auctioning. Because of industry and institutional unwillingness and political obstacles at the European level, however, slot coordination in Europe still follows the same regulation that has been applied since 1993. Political measures are needed more than anything else to improve the utilisation of airports, regarding both traffic organisation and capacity-enhancing investments.

Since capacity problems vary in type and size from airport to airport, solutions are airport-specific too. Capacity-enhancing investments such as new runways or new airports yield the highest gain in capacity, but are typically the type of action that experiences the highest level of public resistance, and thus long delays of realisation. Reflecting such difficulties, airport operators and ANSPs have been looking for means of optimising the throughput of facilities, applying, where politically possible, congestion charges and improving ATM procedures (see Chapter 4). Airlines have already increased seat capacity of flights, primarily for economic reasons, at both unconstrained and constrained airports. Price differencing strategies of airlines could be a means of deconcentrating traffic at congested airports. Since airport landing charges are regarded, at least in Europe, as fees that have to be non-discriminatory and cost-related, and adopted by public authorities, airports often have no means to vary fees in relation to capacity scarcity.

On the other side, technological advancements in air traffic flow management, such as satellite-based radio positioning and navigation systems, may lead to rule changes in ATC, with the objective to enhance the throughput of airport near airspace and runways. Nevertheless, all organisational measures can only improve the utilisation of constrained airports by small steps. Investment options are needed, together with incentive- and market-based regulation, such as secondary trading of slots, in order to keep the air traffic system functioning in the future.

## Note

1 The Gini coefficient is widely used in welfare economics for quantifying the relative concentration of income distribution of a population. Thereby, a Gini coefficient of 0 means an equal distribution (each person has the same [average] income), and a coefficient of 1 means the other extreme, that the whole income is concentrated on just one person.

## References

Airbus (2014). *Global Market Forecast, Flying on Demand 2014–2033*, Toulouse, Airbus.

Berster, P., Gelhausen, M. and Wilken, D. (2015). Constrained and underutilised airports: two sides of a coin. In: *Proceedings of the ATRS World Conference 2015*, Singapore, ATRS.

de Neufville, R. and Odoni, A. (2003). *Airport Systems, Planning, Design and Management*, New York, McGraw-Hill.

EU (European Union) (2004). *Council Regulation (EEC) No 95/93 of 18 January 1993 on Common Rules for the Allocation of Slots at Community Airports*, revised as per Regulation 793/2004 of 21 APR 2004, Brussels, EC.

EUROCONTROL (2013). *Challenges of Growth 2013*, Brussels, EUROCONTROL.

FAA (Federal Aviation Administration) (1969). *Airport Capacity Criteria Used in Long-Range Planning*, Advisory Circular AC 150/5060-3A, Washington, DC, FAA.

FAA (Federal Aviation Administration) (1988). *Planning and Design Guidelines for Airport Terminal Facilities*, Advisory Circular AC 150/5360-9, Washington, DC, FAA.

FAA (Federal Aviation Administration) (1992). *Air Traffic Control Handbook*, Order 7110.65G, Washington, DC, FAA.

FAA (Federal Aviation Administration) (2014). *Airport Capacity Profiles*, Washington, DC, FAA.

Gelhausen, M. (2012). *Model for Testing the Effects of Airport Capacity Constraints on Future Traffic Development at Airports Worldwide: The DLR Airport Capacity Constraints Model Suite*, DLR-Report, Cologne, German Aerospace Centre (DLR).

Gelhausen, M., Berster, P. and Wilken, D. (2013). Do airport capacity constraints have a serious impact on the future development of air traffic? *Journal of Air Transport Management*, 28, 3–13.

Horonjeff, R., McKelvey, F., Sproule, W. and Young, S. (2010). *Planning & Design of Airports*, New York, McGraw-Hill.

IATA (International Air Transport Association) (2015). *Worldwide Slot Guidelines*, Montreal, IATA.

ICAO (International Civil Aviation Organisation) (1987). *Airport Planning Manual, Part 1, Master Planning*, 2nd edition, Doc. 9184-AN/902, Montreal, ICAO.

ICAO (International Civil Aviation Organisation) (2007). *Procedures for Air Navigation Services: Air Traffic Management*, 15th edition, DOC 4444-ATM/501, Montreal, ICAO.

Leucci, G. (2016). Infrastructure development/investment (why airports invest), *Journal of Airport Management*, 10(3), 266–272.

Dieter Wilken

Munich Airport (2012). *Aerodrome Manual for Munich Airport*, Munich, Munich Airport.
Nolan, M. (1999). *Fundamentals of Air Traffic Control*, 3rd edition, Pacific Grove, CA, Brooks/Cole Wadsworth.
OAG (2014). *Official Airline Guide, Market Analysis 2014*, Dunstable, Reed Travel Group.
Steer Davies Gleave (2011). *Impact Assessment of Revisions to Regulation 95/93*, study prepared for the European Commission, London, Steer Davies Gleave.
Technical University of Berlin (2001). *Possibilities for the Better Use of Airport Slots in Germany and the EU*, Technical Report prepared by the Department of Infrastructure Economics, Berlin, Technical University of Berlin.
Wilken, D., Berster, P. and Gelhausen, M. (2011). New empirical evidence on airport capacity utilisation: relationship between hourly and annual air traffic volumes, *Research in Transportation Business & Management*, 1, 118–127.
Zang, V. (2015). *Slot management: airport coordination*. Presented at International University of Applied Sciences Bad Honnef, Bad Honnef, June.

# 17

# Airline sustainability and corporate social responsibility

*Robert Mayer*

## Introduction

Sustainability and corporate social responsibility (CSR) have developed over time from an environmental perspective into a broader and key management discipline for airlines, and focusing on these activities has become common in response to political and public pressure and expectations (for airports, see Chapter 18). For instance, British Airways published its first annual environmental report in 1991, which was later increased in scope to a social and environmental report (Becken and Lane, 2006). Similarly, SAS started its CSR activities by focusing on environmental aspects, and later extended it to include social responsibilities (Lynes and Andrachuk, 2008). In addition, it is increasingly recognised that the development of effective sustainability and CSR strategies can enable airlines to gain a competitive advantage in the market (Albers et al., 2009; Seo et al., 2015). Companies such as Southwest Airlines, for instance, have shown that social and commercial achievements are not conflicting targets (Beard and Hornik, 2011).

Addressing airline sustainability and CSR has become a global phenomenon, not only in practice, but also in academic research, where the airline sector has received significant attention, particularly in comparison to other sectors of the tourism industry (Coles et al., 2013). Studies in this field cover countries in many world regions, such as China (e.g. Wang et al., 2015), Scandinavia (e.g. Lynes and Andrachuk, 2008), New Zealand (e.g. Rigby et al., 2011) and the United States (US) (e.g. Sheldon and Park, 2011). Nevertheless, notwithstanding the global importance of sustainability and CSR in air transport, there are geographical, historical and cultural differences that affect attitudes towards airline sustainability (Goetz and Graham, 2004), and CSR actions will differ from country to country (Coombs and Holladay, 2012) and differ in comparison to other sectors (Godfrey et al., 2010).

This chapter defines sustainability and CSR from an airline perspective, and discusses the developments, communication strategies and reporting standards in airline sustainability and CSR. It takes a global approach, providing examples of developments in industry practice and latest research from around the world.

## Defining airline sustainability and CSR

### Defining airline sustainability

A commonly referred to definition of sustainability is from the World Commission on Environment and Development (WCED), which states that "sustainable development is the development that meets the needs of the present without compromising the ability of future generations to meet their own needs" (WCED, 1987: 43). Based on this definition, and applied to the transport sector, Black (1996: 151) defines sustainable transport as "satisfying current transport and mobility needs without compromising the ability of future generations to meet these needs," while Banister et al. (2000: 31) define sustainable transport systems as a system "which would imply a balance between economic development, broad access to transport facilities and a sufficiently high environmental quality." The definition by Banister et al. (2000) highlights common elements of sustainability definitions: economic, environmental and social sustainability, often referred to as the triple bottom line (Elkington, 2004). In practice, achieving all three simultaneously is challenging and might require some trade-offs (Upham, 2001).

Despite an abundance of definitions of sustainability, as well as its relevance in transport and particularly air transport, defining airline sustainability is difficult, often controversial and unbalanced. A key issue is the ambiguity that surrounds the word sustainability, which is interpreted differently by different stakeholders (Budd et al., 2013). Upham (2001) concludes, in this respect, that sustainability has no precise meaning, but is rather an aspiration to include environmental, social and economic concerns. Therefore, the link between airlines and sustainability cannot be easily assessed: there are questions of whether airlines can actually be sustainable (Budd et al., 2013), if transport contributes to problems, rather than to solutions (Peattie, 1995), or what role airlines should take in the sustainability debate (Copeland, 1992). Contrarily, others argue that environmental sustainability in air transport can be achieved, though at a cost (Forsyth, 2011).

Although the concept of sustainability includes the three elements of social, economic and environmental sustainability, their prominence in research and practice is unbalanced, with a stronger focus on environmental sustainability than economic and social sustainability (Walker and Cook, 2009). This also applies to airlines, with research predominantly looking at environmental aspects of sustainability, but also some focus on social elements (e.g. Graham and Guyer, 1999; Kuo et al., 2016), yet others try to combine at least two of the elements (e.g. Forsyth, 2011).

In this chapter, airline sustainable development is defined as actions that airlines undertake to reduced negative environmental impacts (environmental sustainability), enhance the social cohesion and access to transportation needs (social sustainability), while achieving long-term financial profitability (economic sustainability). Also, in this chapter, the focus mainly lies on the first two elements – this reflects the focus of current research and practice in airline sustainability.

### Defining airline CSR

As with the term sustainability, CSR lacks an accepted definition, but is seen as a broad concept (Coombs and Holladay, 2012; Van der Heijden et al., 2010). A definition commonly referred to in research (e.g. Coles et al., 2014; Cowper-Smith and de Grosbois, 2011; Sheldon and Park, 2011) is provided by the World Business Council for Sustainable Development (WBCSD, 1999: 3), which defines CSR as "the continuing commitment by business to contribute to economic development while improving the quality of life of the workforce and their families as well as of the community and society at large." In addition, the European Commission (EC, 2011: 6) defines CSR as "the responsibility of enterprises for their impacts on society." Further, the

EC states that "respect for applicable legislation, and for collective agreements between social partners, is a prerequisite for meeting that responsibility," and that "enterprises should have in place a process to integrate social, environmental, ethical, human rights and consumer concerns into their business operations and core strategies in close collaboration with their stakeholders."

From the definitions above, it becomes clear that CSR goes beyond a shareholder focus, but includes a wider perspective towards a stakeholder approach (e.g. including members of the community and employees), which is often at the centre of CSR discussions and definitions. Another characteristic that is often associated with CSR is that companies go beyond legal requirements and act voluntarily (or even philanthropically) to achieve societal benefits (Carroll, 1991; Coombs and Holladay, 2012).

Also, similarly to sustainability, CSR often refers to the triple bottom line concept of environmental, social and economic responsibilities (Moratis and Cochius, 2011; Van der Heijden et al., 2010). However, in practice, airlines' CSR activities are often dominated by environmental concerns rather than economic or social aspects. It needs to be borne in mind, though, that many environmental impacts affect social issues (Moratis and Cochius, 2011; Cowper-Smith and de Grosbois, 2011). The airline sector shows similar characteristics to heavy industries such as electric utilities, oil and gas refining, and energy trading, in contrast to other consumer service industries (e.g. banking, retail, insurance), with the latter focusing more on community involvement (Godfrey et al., 2010). One reason for why airlines particularly focus on the environmental aspects of CSR lies in their high dependency on fossil fuels (Sheldon and Park, 2011). Another reason is the financial benefits that accompany many environment-related actions (e.g. reduction in fuel consumption); these financial benefits are less tangible with regard to social commitments (Lynes and Andrachuk, 2008). Despite the dominant focus on environmental aspects of CSR, some studies have looked into the social dimension of CSR. For example, Rigby et al. (2011) discuss how Air New Zealand has incorporated indigenous cultures into their CSR strategy.

Following the WBCSD definition, airline CSR can be defined as the continuing commitment by airlines to contribute to economic development while improving the quality of life of the workforce and their families, as well as of the community and society at large. The definitions of airline sustainability and CSR illustrate that these two concepts are interlinked and overlapping. However, although both terms are often treated synonymously, Van Marrewijk (2003) suggests that they cover slightly different aspects, with CSR focusing on people and organisations, and their relationship with the community, while corporate sustainability (CS) focuses more on coherence and self-preservation of the organisation. Often, CSR is also seen as an element in achieving CS, particularly as CSR is characterised by a stakeholder orientation (Van Marrewijk, 2003; Zink, 2005). Zink (2005: 1049) highlights in this respect that: "sustainable success depends not only on the shareholder, but also on all (other) relevant stakeholders of an organization." Despite their subtle differences, but due to their close linkage, in this chapter, the concepts of airline CS and CSR will be addressed together.

## Developments in airline CS and CSR: environmental dimension

### Environmental impacts

The environmental dimension of airline CS and CSR takes a particular role in research and practice (Cowper-Smith and de Grosbois, 2011). Although the high dependency on fossil fuels is a major reason for this focus (Sheldon and Park, 2011), environmental impacts of airlines are not limited to emissions from the thermal combustion of fossil fuels. Daley (2010) identifies nine major impacts that air transport has on the environment: aircraft noise, air pollution, climate change, waste generation, water pollution, water consumption, ecological change, habitat degradation and land contamination.

While the latter three impacts can mainly be attributed to airports and only indirectly to airline and aircraft operations, the remaining impacts are mainly or at least partly directly caused by airlines (including airline maintenance and ground operations). Airlines' CS and CSR activities predominantly centre on the areas that are directly impacted on by airline operations, rather than those that are more aligned to the airport domain. The following themes with regard to airline environmental CSR activities can be identified (Cowper-Smith and de Grosbois, 2011): emissions (air pollution and gaseous emissions), noise, waste, energy, water and biodiversity.

Although airlines get involved in a range of different CS and CSR activities that are aimed at reducing their environmental impacts, applications and measurement of these activities vary significantly between airlines, which makes any comparisons between airlines difficult (Cowper-Smith and de Grosbois, 2011). Particularly with regards to the environmental dimension of CS and CSR, airlines are not purely (if at all) guided by a sense of altruism and social conscience, but by economic and financial benefits that accompany environmental initiatives through cost reductions (Lynes and Andrachuk, 2008).

Although regulations and laws around the environmental impacts of airlines have tightened, airlines have also seen increasing political and public pressure to reduce their environmental impacts (Gegg et al., 2014). A study by Gössling et al. (2009) finds that 57.6 per cent of air passengers believe that airlines should take responsibility for dealing with the environmental impacts of air transport. While regulatory and legal aspects, including the EU Emissions Trading Scheme (ETS) (see Chapter 25), are outside the scope of CS and CSR (in its strictest sense), particularly public pressure can be seen as an important driver for these more voluntary actions of companies. Voluntary and compulsory carbon markets are not completely independent of each other, though, as certain forms of voluntary carbon offsets sold by airlines can be exchanged in regulatory carbon markets (i.e. EU ETS) (Gössling et al., 2009). Notwithstanding that the EU ETS cannot be classified as a CSR activity (as it is not voluntary), Forsyth (2011) argues that it can improve the environmental sustainability of airlines.

## Atmospheric emissions

Within the environmental agenda of airline CS and CSR activities, atmospheric emissions and associated air pollution and global climate change take a key role (see Chapter 25). Many airlines focus on reducing their carbon dioxide ($CO_2$) emissions through different initiatives, such as fleet renewal programmes and weight-reduction measures (Cowper-Smith and de Grosbois, 2011). Although aircraft produce a range of greenhouse gas emissions, focus in research, government policy and practice is often on $CO_2$ (Budd and Suau-Sanchez, 2016; Dray, 2013; Gössling et al., 2009; Preston et al., 2012). Nevertheless, some airlines, such as American Airlines and Lufthansa, provide a broader view on greenhouse gases, including references to nitrogen oxides ($NO_x$), unburned hydrocarbons (UHC) and sulphur oxides ($SO_x$) in their CS and CSR reports (American Airlines, 2015; Lufthansa, 2016). Airlines are frequently criticised for their atmospheric emissions; therefore, it is not surprising that activities aimed at reducing emissions often feature highly on their CS and CSR agenda (Coles et al., 2013).

Technological improvements of aircraft, either by upgrading existing aircraft or purchasing newer, more fuel-efficient aircraft, are an important element of airline efforts to reduce their impacts on air quality and climate change. Besides the environmental benefits of newer aircraft, aircraft age can also be noticed by passengers, and therefore can generate marketing benefits (Mayer et al., 2015). Airlines such as easyJet, Virgin Atlantic and Flybe have been using their fleet and fleet renewal programmes to portray themselves as airlines that put significant effort and capital into reducing their emissions (Coles et al., 2013; Mayer et al., 2014). Improvements to existing aircraft often include retrofitting with winglets that reduce drag and improve fuel efficiency, and therefore lower emissions (Budd and Suau-Sanchez, 2016; Dray, 2013).

Many airlines offer carbon-offsetting schemes that enable their customers to voluntarily offset their flight-related $CO_2$ emissions. As of June 2016, IATA (2016) reports that over 35 airlines run these schemes. Offsetting can be achieved through investments in renewable energy, forestry projects (e.g. reforestation) or improvements in energy efficiencies (Gössling et al., 2007). Besides the different projects that airlines get involved in, a range of different methodologies for estimating emissions are also used by airlines (IATA, 2016). Carbon-offsetting schemes involve the passenger directly in the airline sustainability activities, and are thus sometimes referred to as consumer-involved sustainability programmes (Kim et al., 2014). Although uptakes by passengers are generally low, these schemes enable airlines to publicly show their intentions to reduce the environmental impacts of air travel (Albers et al., 2009; Mair, 2011). More recently, research in the area of carbon offsetting has focused around passenger behaviour, intentions, preferences and willingness to pay for voluntary schemes (e.g. Araghi et al., 2014; Chen, 2013; Lu and Shon, 2012; Mair, 2011). To improve the uptake of voluntary carbon-offsetting schemes, Chen (2013) recommends that airlines need to address emotive factors (e.g. contentment of doing something positive for the environment) in their communication strategy, and not only address rational aspects of offsetting. Despite the use of carbon offsetting as part of airline CS and CSR activities, the environmental benefits of carbon-offsetting schemes remain contested, with Gössling et al. (2007: 241) labelling them as an "ambiguous tool for sustainable tourism management." This is in contrast to many passengers who use carbon-offsetting schemes, as they perceive these voluntary schemes as a good tool to address climate change (Segerstedt and Grote, 2016).

As a way to reduce airline emissions, biofuels have received significant attention in research and practice, with many airlines having started to test these alternative fuels (e.g. Gegg et al., 2014; Mayer et al., 2014; Nair and Paulose, 2014). Sgouridis et al. (2011) calculate an emissions reduction potential of biofuels of between 6.6 and 17.0 per cent, dependent on the type of biofuel and when some form of carbon pricing is involved. Biofuels can be developed from a range of different sources; however, in air transport, the focus is on waste cooking oil (waste-to-liquid), animal fats and plants (e.g. algae, coconuts) to ensure the necessary fuel properties (e.g. chemical and flow characteristics) required in aviation (Gegg et al., 2014; Nair and Paulose, 2014; Rye et al., 2010). Besides the environmental benefits of biofuels (i.e. a reduction in pollution), they are also seen as particularly effective by passengers when it comes to airline efforts in reducing their environmental impact (Mayer et al., 2012). It can be noticed that biofuels play a significant role in airline CS and CSR activities and their communication strategies (Cowper-Smith and de Grosbois, 2011; Mayer et al., 2014).

## Noise

Historically, noise has been a major environmental impact of air transport, and has been seen as the most important environmental problem at airports (Copeland, 1992; Graham, 2014). Noise has featured in sustainability discussions for decades, but more recently the focus in research has shifted towards other environmental impacts. This is also noticeable with regard to environmental groups that see climate change as a bigger threat to the environment than noise (Bröer, 2013). Although aviation noise is predominantly, but not only, generated by airlines operating aircraft, research is mainly focused on airports (e.g. Martini et al., 2013; Postorino and Mantecchini, 2016; Sadr et al., 2014) or aspects related to the aircraft itself (e.g. Bernardo et al., 2016; Graham et al., 2014; Szodruch et al., 2011), rather than airlines. Relating to airline operations, Givoni and Rietveld (2010) examine noise exposure based on operating different aircraft. They conclude that larger aircraft on short-haul routes, with a high seat density and lower frequencies, can result in lower noise impacts. In practice, though, few airlines operate wide-body aircraft on short-haul routes, and noise is not a deciding factor when it comes to assigning wide-body aircraft to short-haul routes.

Noise features in many airline CS and CSR reports (e.g. British Airways, 2016a; Emirates, 2015), yet some airlines (e.g. Delta Air Lines, 2015; Garuda, 2014) hardly, if at all, cover the noise impact of airlines. Those airlines that mention actions addressing the noise impact of aircraft often refer to complying with noise standards and regulations rather than voluntary actions. As such, as these activities are not voluntary, they cannot be classified as CSR efforts (in its strictest sense). Mandatory noise restrictions are particularly in place in Europe, while in the US airlines have lobbied against different actions at different airports, which has resulted in a stronger focus on voluntary operating measures (Girvin, 2009).

## Waste

A common feature of many airline CS and CSR activities is the reduction of waste (Cowper-Smith and de Grosbois, 2011). The role of waste and waste management in airline environmental activities has been identified for decades, though has less prominence in comparison to noise and emissions activities (Copeland, 1992; Wheatcroft, 1991). From an airline perspective, waste management particularly addresses the large amounts created on board (e.g. catering), as well as waste generated as part of airline maintenance activities and office waste (Hooper and Greenall, 2005; Mak and Chan, 2007). For example, ANA recycles its plastic covers from cargo operations to produce plastic fuel and plastic bags (Mak and Chan, 2007). Similarly to activities that focus on a reduction in atmospheric emissions, voluntary waste management and reduction in waste generation is often driven by cost considerations (Lynes and Dredge, 2006). Although many airlines engage in waste management initiatives, implementation can be challenging. For example, SAS encountered opposition from unions when trying to make changes to their in-flight waste management (Lynes and Andrachuk, 2008). Despite its prominence in many airline CS and CSR activities (e.g. Japan Airlines, 2016; Southwest Airlines, 2016a; Turkish Airlines, 2016), waste management and reduction only marginally features in research on airlines' CS and CSR activities.

## Developments in airline CS and CSR: social dimension

### Airline social engagement

Although the focus of airline CSR and CS, and resulting from that any research that is conducted in this field, is often on environmental aspects, airlines and researchers also address the social dimension. Cowper-Smith and de Grosbois (2011) identify four themes related to the social (and economic) dimensions of airline CSR: employee well-being and engagement, diversity and social equity, community well-being, and economic prosperity. In this chapter, economic prosperity will be discussed under the economic dimension of CSR.

### Employee well-being and engagement

As defined by the WBCSD (1999), employees are a key component of CSR activities. As part of their CSR activities, many airlines introduce measures to improve employee health and well-being, focus on employee empowerment, and offer educational programmes to their staff (Cowper-Smith and de Grosbois, 2011). For example, Southwest Airlines is a company that, since the 1970s, has been guided by the strategy that if staff are happy, customer satisfaction and profits will follow. This strategy is based on meaningful interactions between management and employees, good relationships with unions, and the development of an ownership mentality among its employees. Southwest Airlines was also the first airline to introduce profit-sharing (Beard and Hornik, 2011). Another example of employee well-being and engagement is American Airlines, which has been working with Susan G. Komen, a breast cancer charity, to provide breast cancer education and awareness for its staff (Hoeffler and Keller, 2002).

## Diversity and equality

In the case of SAS, equality and diversity was one of the first elements of social responsibility that the airline included in its written CSR policies, and more recently the airline has expanded into external aspects (e.g. humanitarianism) of social responsibility (Lynes and Andrachuk, 2008). As part of their diversity and social equity agenda, some airlines address gender inequalities, such as trying to increase the number of female managers (Cowper-Smith and de Grosbois, 2011). Gender inequality is particularly prevalent on the flight deck, with only a small minority of flight crew being female. To increase the share of female pilots, it is therefore down to airlines (as well as other stakeholders) to promote career opportunities for women on the flight deck (McCarthy et al., 2015). Airlines need to address this under-representation as part of their CSR strategy.

Another element of equality and social equity within airline CSR activities is to focus on people with disabilities, both from an employment as well as a passenger perspective. It needs to be noted, though, that some of these activities fall outside the scope of CSR, as they are required by legislation, hence are not voluntary per se (Cowper-Smith and de Grosbois, 2011). Equality and diversity activities of airlines further include the lesbian, gay, bisexual and transgender (LGBT) communities, ethnic minorities (e.g. Native Americans), and war veterans (Southwest Airlines, 2016a; United Airlines, 2016a). For example, with regard to airline engagement with LGBT employees and communities, many airlines have undertaken a U-turn towards the end of the twentieth century. In the US, for decades, airlines had been discriminating against LGBT employees, especially after the discovery of HIV in the early 1980s, which led to HIV-positive flight attendants, many of whom were gay, losing their jobs. By the 1990s, attitudes had changed, and airlines developed a more inclusive approach. As an example, American Airlines changed its attitude towards LGBT employees and worked on overcoming its AIDS-phobic and homophobic reputation to become and market itself as a gay-friendly airline (Tiemeyer, 2013: 12). This example shows how airline attitudes towards certain issues can change significantly over time.

## Community well-being

Under community well-being, Cowper-Smith and de Grosbois (2011) record airline CSR activities that cover community projects, international projects and raising sustainable development issues. Local community involvement is, however, less well developed among airlines, as airlines often only have indirect relations with their local communities (e.g. unlike airports), and thus generate fewer direct benefits (Inoue and Lee, 2011). Local economic development is often focused on the home market of the airlines. In the case of United Airlines, the company has identified seven US hubs (Chicago, Denver, Houston, Los Angeles, New York/Newark, San Francisco and Washington, DC) where it concentrates its community involvement (United Airlines, 2016b).

The importance of CS and CSR in the airline sector has increased over time. However, the involvement of airlines in voluntary actions is not necessarily growing steadily. Airlines are less likely to participate in voluntary actions when they are under financial pressure (Forsyth, 2011), but for communities that are dependent on airline CSR activities, a long-term approach to CSR, rather than purely focusing on short-term activities, is necessary (Coles et al., 2011).

Community well-being activities of airlines are often linked to charitable partnerships. Charitable (sometimes referred to as philanthropic) activities are a key element of airline CSR approaches. Fenclova and Coles (2011) identify seven ways in which airlines support charities: online collections, on-board collections, staff donations, plane naming/design, other resource donations, percentage of product sales and monetary donations (e.g. share of company profits).

Charities often see airlines as good partners, due to their exposure to a large audience (e.g. through cabin announcements and in-flight magazines) (Fenclova and Coles, 2011). Directly targeting passengers (e.g. on the aircraft) can achieve immediate results for charities, without significant advertising, and is therefore seen as particularly cost-efficient (Kim et al., 2014; Pringle and Thompson, 1999). An example of the link between charities and airlines is the UNICEF Change for Good programme, in which passengers can donate loose change in any currency on board their flight. From 1987 to 2014, this programme has collected over US$120 million, with major airlines participating (UNICEF, 2014). From the passenger perspective, donating money during the flight might result in social approval and self-respect from fellow passengers, which can be a motivating factor to donate money (Hoeffler and Keller, 2002). Airlines that participated in the programme in 2014 were Aer Lingus, Alitalia, American Airlines, ANA, Asiana Airlines, Cathay Pacific, easyJet, Finnair, Hainan Airlines, JAL, Lan Peru and Qantas (UNICEF, 2014). Despite the prevalence of this high-profile charity partnership in the airline sector, so far there has been little research into the relationship between airlines and the Change for Good programme (Kim et al., 2014).

The number of participating airlines shows that involvement in this charity is independent of location, with airlines from many parts of the world being involved. Moreover, the airlines cover the spectrum of airline business models, from full service to low cost carriers (LCCs). Although the participation of LCCs in charitable partnerships seems to be counter-intuitive given their focus on costs, many LCCs support charities. These airlines are involved in charities such as cancer research and children's charities, as well as environmental charities (Fenclova and Coles, 2011). However, the UNICEF programme is not the only charity that partners with airlines. Until 2010, British Airways worked with UNICEF on the Change for Good programme, but in 2010 the airline switched charity partner and started a programme called Flying Start, where the airline collects money on behalf of the Comic Relief charity programme (Papworth, 2010). Another example is Singapore Airlines, which raised US$1.3 million for charity as part of auctioning seats for their first Airbus 380 flight (Heracleous and Wirtz, 2010).

## Developments in airline CS and CSR: economic dimension

### Socio-economic dimension

Although the economic aspect of CS and CSR often refers to financial profitability, Cowper-Smith and de Grosbois (2011) attach a social angle to this dimension by identifying three goals of airline economic CSR activities: procurement practices, job creation (including apprenticeships and internships) and local economic development. For example, LAN Colombia (part of LATAM) in 2015 introduced its Micro and Small Company programme (MyP) to support and promote smaller suppliers (LATAM, 2015). British Airways offers apprenticeships that include training, mentoring and development opportunities in a range of different areas, such as engineering, customer service and operations (British Airways, 2016a). With regard to local economic development, particularly LCCs in Europe have provided regional connectivity to (often remote) regions that enabled small and medium-sized businesses to enter new markets (Coles et al., 2011).

## CS/CSR and financial profitability

A more common focus of economic sustainability relates to financial profitability. Although financial performance is outside the scope of this chapter, the link between CS/CSR and financial performance has been discussed to some extent in research. Despite early opposition to CSR by many economists such as Levitt (1958) and Friedman (1970), with their strong views on firms' responsibility to generate profits for their shareholders, there is evidence that economic, environmental and social sustainability are not (completely) mutually exclusive. Nevertheless, in some cases, there might be a need for compromise between the different dimensions (Upham, 2001).

Several studies into the impact of CSR on financial performance in general (not only the airline sector) are inconclusive, with some suggesting positive, negative or no effects (Lee and Park, 2010). Recently, there has been some research into the impact of CSR on airline financial performance; however, there is no clear trend as to the impact of CSR on airline financial performance. Based on a sample of US airlines, Lee and Park (2010) identify a statistically significant positive relationship between airline CSR activities and their value performance (i.e. how financial markets value the company). This means that with increasing CSR activities, airline values increase. This trend has not only been noticed in the short term, but some longer-term effects can be noticed too. This long-term perspective might give airline managers additional motivation in addressing and incorporating CSR in their company's strategy. However, the same study finds that CSR activities have no statistically significant impact on accounting performance (i.e. return on assets, return on equity and return on sales). When breaking down CSR into different components, Inoue and Lee (2011) find no statistically significant positive impact of diversity-, employee- and product-related CSR activities on US airlines' short-term profitability, yet identify a negative impact of community-focused activities. A possible reason for this negative impact is the indirect relations that airlines have with local communities. With regard to long-term profitability, a statistically significant positive impact is identified for employee- and product-related CSR.

Although both LCCs and full service carriers are involved in CS and CSR activities, research on US airlines has shown differences with regard to the impact of CSR on airline financial performance. Full service carriers that focus on CSR (and service quality) can generate financial benefits as passengers are more likely to pay for the higher costs that airlines incur when taking environmentally and socially responsible actions. Contrarily, LCCs will see their cost basis increase as they adopt CSR practices for which passengers are less willing to pay for, which in return may result in LCCs losing their competitive advantage. As such, LCCs need to carefully evaluate the costs and benefits of certain CSR approaches (Seo et al., 2015). In practice, though, many LCCs get heavily involved in CS and CSR activities, for example easyJet and Flybe having extensively focused on environmental issues (Mayer et al., 2014) and Southwest Airlines on social aspects (Beard and Hornik, 2011).

Despite discussions of whether CS and CSR are compatible with financial profitability, Forsyth (2011) makes the case that, particularly in the long run, environmental sustainability and financial sustainability are achievable, while in the short run environmental actions of airlines will affect their profitability.

## Communication and reporting of CS and CSR

### *The role of communication and publicity*

The importance of communicating CSR activities has been identified early in the CSR and sustainability debate, as Parket and Eilbirt (1975: 6) point out: "Companies want these activities to be widely known and recognized." Airlines use advertising to position themselves as "good corporate citizens" (Shaw, 2011: 312). Therefore, communications can be an important reason for engaging in CS and CSR activities. In the case of the environmental dimension, companies like to associate themselves with green issues to generate a positive corporate image (Saha and Darnton, 2005). For example, for SAS, environmental reporting is a key vehicle to drive its environmental image (Lynes and Dredge, 2006). As such, there is a close connection between sustainability and marketing, with communication being a key component of any sustainability strategy. This includes external as well as internal communication. Related in this respect is the term corporate societal marketing (CSM), which is defined as "marketing initiatives that have at least one non-economic objective related to social welfare and use the resources of the company and/or one of its partners" (Drumwright and Murphy, 2001: 164). CSM is particularly applied by airlines when supporting charitable causes.

Saha and Darnton (2005) make the case that the volume of communications (i.e. how much companies communicate their commitments to the environment and social causes) is more important than the actual activities or how accurate claims are. This can also be witnessed in airline markets. A study by Mayer et al. (2015) shows that there is no statistically significant correlation between an airline's green image and their actual environmental performance (as measured by the average aircraft age, load factors and the atmosfair Airline Index, an environmental indicator produced by atmosfair, a German non-profit organisation – the atmosfair Airline Index ranks airlines by their carbon efficiency). There are many ways that airlines communicate CS and CSR activity, including CSR reports, their website, newspaper advertisements, online videos and press releases (Mayer et al., 2014). For example, Virgin Atlantic's publicity, communication and sustainability strategy has received some attention in literature. Kotler and Keller (2012: 672) refer to Virgin's CS and CSR activities by stressing the importance of these issues for Richard Branson, the founder of Virgin: "Clearly, Branson cares about Virgin's customers and the impact his companies have on people and the planet. That's why he recently made corporate responsibility and sustainable development (CR/SD) a key priority for every one of his companies." The airline uses public relations techniques to portray its green image as a company that cares for the environment. Other examples of airlines that have focused on environmental issues in their communication strategy in the past are easyJet and Flybe (Mayer et al., 2014).

Ecolabels have received some attention in airline CS and CSR communication. Gössling and Buckley (2016: 359) define ecolabels as "communication systems intended to influence consumer behaviour towards greater consideration of environmental concerns." Although following this definition the aim of these labels is to influence consumers, they also help airlines to be perceived as caring organisations. While in the wider tourism industry there are many different types of ecolabels (Gössling and Buckley, 2016), so far only two airlines seem to have introduced ecolabels, with little research covering this subject (Baumeister and Onkila, 2014). Flybe is often seen as a prime example of an airline that has introduced ecolabels in the airline sector. The airline claims to have been the first airline to do so (Mayer et al., 2014). Besides Flybe, Thomas Cook Airlines have also started to produce ecolabels for their aircraft (Thomas Cook, 2016). An external ecolabelling system used by the Canadian airline Air Transat (2015) is the previously mentioned atmosfair Airline Index. Araghi et al. (2014: 42) describe this index as a "recognized labelling system that ranks airlines according to their efficiency." Besides being used by some airlines, this index is also being referred to and used in academic research (e.g. Åkerman, 2011; Dobruszkes et al., 2014; Gössling and Buckley, 2016; Mayer et al., 2015).

As previously mentioned, many airlines associate themselves with charities, and while charities often see airlines as good partners (Fenclova and Coles, 2011), airlines also use this relationship to promote their social engagement. Airlines can either link their brand to an existing cause (e.g. airlines linking themselves to the UNICEF Change for Good programme), create a new programme or cause (e.g. Southwest Airlines Medical Transportation Grant programme) or use a combination of both (e.g. British Airway's Flying Start programme as part of the Comic Relief programme) (British Airways, 2016b; Hoeffler and Keller, 2002; Southwest Airlines, 2016b). Large fundraising campaigns, such as Comic Relief in the United Kingdom (UK), often receive significant media attention (Lim and Moufahim, 2015). This in return means that corporate supporters (in the case of Comic Relief, British Airways) receive media exposure by being associated with a particular cause or programme. For example, the boy band One Direction released a music video in aid of Comic Relief, which was partly filmed at Heathrow Airport, with British Airways' flight attendants appearing several times in the video (One Direction, 2013). Up until September 2016, the video had over 320 million views on YouTube.

CSR communication does not only focus on external stakeholders. It is important for companies to communicate their CS and CSR efforts to their employees as many of the activities are dependent on their support (Baldassarre and Campo, 2016). Employee well-being and engagement is an important part of CSR that relies on internal communication. For example, Southwest Airlines uses "aggressive internal communication" to strengthen employee ownership mentality (Beard and Hornik, 2011: 92). In the case of SAS, a strong internal culture and internal communication (top-down and bottom-up) has helped the company to develop environmental management practices (Lynes and Dredge, 2006). The examples of Southwest Airlines and SAS highlight the important role that internal communication plays in CSR. As important as communication is in CS and CSR, it is necessary that messages relating to CS and CSR are consistent, as any ambiguity can create more harm than benefits (Coombs and Holladay, 2012).

## Reporting standards and practices

The quantity and quality of CSR reporting of airlines has increased over time. CS and CSR activities are an important part of airlines' communication strategy. Although there is some criticism that there is no common approach to how airlines should report CS and CSR, different organisations have developed reporting standards. For example, two major reporting systems were developed by the Global Reporting Initiative (GRI) and by the International Organisation for Standardisation (ISO), with GRI being dominant worldwide for CSR and sustainability reports (Coombs and Holladay, 2012). In comparison to other guidelines, GRI offers sector-specific supplements on CSR reporting. Despite their prominence, GRI guidelines have also received criticism for being too simple and lacking an integrated view on sustainable development (Moneva et al., 2006). Standards such as GRI or ISO are voluntary, however some airlines follow these guidelines, particularly if they are part of a certification process (e.g. certain ISO certifications). Besides these guidelines, companies can also engage external organisations to validate their CSR reporting. A study by PwC in 2011 found that 37 per cent of airline CSR reports were independently verified (Heeres et al., 2011), giving these reports more credibility. An example in this respect are Flybe's ecolabels, which are validated by Deloitte & Touche (2007).

GRI produces a framework that is regularly referred to when addressing CSR reporting of airlines (e.g. Cowper-Smith and de Grosbois, 2011; Heeres et al., 2011; Rudari and Johnson, 2015). Besides giving an overview of the different topic areas, the GRI also provides an explanation on each area, as well as references to other sources, which should help airlines to develop their CSR reporting. Eccles et al. (2012) advocate the benefits of sector-specific standards, as these improve a company's ability to report on their environmental and social performance.

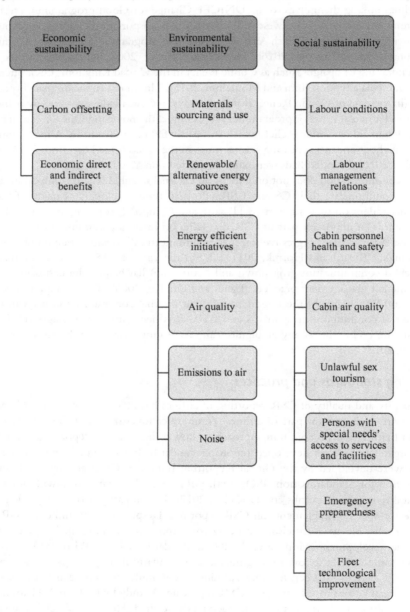

*Figure 17.1*   GRI Airline Framework

*Source*: GRI (2013).

Based on different stakeholder requirements, GRI (2013) has produced a list of topics that stakeholders in the airline sector deem relevant. Figure 17.1 illustrates the topics covered by the GRI framework. A study of 15 major US carriers found that seven produce sustainability reports based on GRI guidelines, and one produced a report that is not based on GRI (Rudari and Johnson, 2015). A similar adoption rate (60 per cent) was identified in a study by PwC on the use of GRI by airlines. The study finds that the airlines that apply GRI guidelines tend to have higher-quality sustainability reports (Heeres et al., 2011).

Similarly to GRI, ISO 26000 provides companies with guidelines on how to structure CSR reports and their content. ISO 26000 is a voluntary programme that does not specify any requirements and cannot be used for certification, unlike other ISO certification standards such as ISO 14001 (Environmental Management) or ISO 9001 (Quality Management) (Coombs and Holladay, 2012; ISO, 2014; Moratis and Cochius, 2011). ISO 26000 covers seven core subjects (ISO, 2014): organisational governance, human rights, labour practices, the environment, fair operating practices, consumer issues, and community involvement and development. Unlike GRI, ISO 26000 does not provide any sector-specific standards. Nevertheless, some airlines have started to prepare their CSR reports following ISO 26000 guidelines. For example, Japan Airlines has aligned its CSR reporting to follow ISO 26000 (Japan Airlines, 2016). Table 17.1 shows the seven ISO 26000 core subjects and how Japan Airlines pledges to address them.

GRI and ISO 26000 do not have to be used separately, but can also be combined. GRI and ISO therefore provide information on how these two guidelines can be used together (ISO and GRI, 2014). In the airline sector, for example, Asiana Airlines, in its 2015 sustainability report, uses GRI guidelines aligned with ISO 26000 to organise and present its CSR activities (Asiana Airlines, 2015). Besides the ISO 26000 guidelines, ISO also established the ISO14001 standard, which sets out the requirements for an environmental management system (ISO, 2015). Although narrower in scope (only environmental aspects, rather than the full triple-bottom-line approach), this standard offers an accredited certification process. In the airline sector, SAS (2016) followed this standard and had its business ISO 14001 certified in 2010.

Cowper-Smith and de Grosbois (2011) find that with regard to CSR reporting of airlines, many companies report activities under the branding of CSR while they are actually mandatory by law, and as such are not voluntary. While CSR reporting among airlines has increased over

Table 17.1 ISO 26000 core subjects of JAL Group

| ISO 26000 core subject | Japan Airlines pledge |
| --- | --- |
| Organisational governance | A system to promote corporate social responsibility (CSR). |
| Human rights | We respect all human rights in any and all situations. |
| Labour practices | We promote the creation of a comfortable workplace environment for every JAL Group staff, in accordance with the JAL Group Corporate Policy and JAL Philosophy. |
| The environment | JAL Group recognises that reducing impacts on the environment and conserving the environment are priority issues of management. |
| Fair operating practices | With our business partners. We promote fair and impartial procurement activities with an awareness of CSR. |
| Consumer issues | With our customers. We put ourselves in the customers' position and strive to maintain flight safety and enhance our services. |
| Community involvement and development | We conduct various activities with the participation of JAL Group staff to contribute to the betterment of society. |

Source: Japan Airlines (2016).

time (Heeres et al., 2011), there are airlines who do not report on CSR. Some managers in these airlines perceive CSR reporting as unnecessary (Kuo et al., 2016).

## Criticism and greenwash

The role of publicity in airline efforts to address environmental impacts is highlighted by Wheatcroft (1991: 124), who concludes: "The best that the air transport and tourism industries can do is gain as much publicity as possible for the genuine efforts to reduce environmental nuisances." Although many companies, including airlines, follow this recommendation, there is a question about what constitutes genuine efforts. Ambiguous claims related to the improvement of companies' environmental sustainability can lead to accusations of greenwash (a form of manipulation of a company's environmental image without actual advances in the company's environmental performance) (Benn and Bolton, 2011). Greenwash can then have the opposite effect to the initial intention and generate negative publicity if false claims are uncovered (Curtin, 2007). This fear of being accused of greenwash results in some companies not communicating their efforts, while other companies decide not to publish their achievements because they think it is not appropriate (Baldassarre and Campo, 2016). Fears of negative backlash from journalists also affect airline CSR reporting, with some airlines deciding not to communicate certain positive activities (Coles et al., 2013).

Frequently, airlines report their CSR activities, even when these measures are required by law, and are therefore not voluntary and would not classify as CSR (Cowper-Smith and de Grosbois, 2011). Although many airlines engage in CSR, Burns and Cowlishaw (2014) find that among UK airlines (with the exception of Virgin Atlantic), airlines often place the responsibility of climate change on the consumer, rather than themselves. Due to their ambiguous role in the sustainability debate, as to whether airlines can be sustainable at all, airlines are particularly vulnerable to criticism, and particularly to claims of greenwash. Despite this, to date, there has been little research on greenwash and other criticisms of airline CS and CSR activities.

Although many airlines refer to CSR activities and targets, few of them provide actual measures on how their CSR goals have been achieved. The measures that are given are often inconsistent between airlines, which makes comparisons very difficult (Cowper-Smith and de Grosbois, 2011). Coles et al. (2014) review the CSR communication of LCCs and conclude that CSR reporting often lacks detail and is selective with regard to the coverage and intended audience. For example, in the case of Flybe, they conclude that the airline CSR policy is rather a review of its past activities and not aspirational or providing future targets. A study by Eccles et al. (2012: 68–69), which includes seven airlines, finds that in many areas, the companies use 'Boilerplate Statements', which include "generic language about potential risks from future regulation and the inability to quantify financial impacts." Despite this criticism, Eccles et al. (2012) also identify areas such as fuel hedging where companies provide quantitative metrics rather than vague statements. Mayer et al. (2014) provide an overview and discussion of different types of criticisms and negative reactions to Virgin Atlantic, easyJet and Flybe's environmental marketing activities. These airlines, in their effort to become more sustainable or their effort to be perceived as doing something for the environment, have been accused of greenwash. This criticism is particularly driven by environmental groups, rather than consumers. An area that has particularly received criticism in research, is the use of carbon-offsetting schemes offered by airlines. In comparison to other environmental activities, the costs of carbon offsetting are not actually borne by the airlines, but directly by the passengers (Mair, 2011). Therefore, it can be argued that carbon offsetting is not a CS activity per se, as airlines only offer the vehicle for their customers to take measures that improve the environmental impacts of air travel.

Further, Gössling et al. (2007) argue that few schemes are based on a scientific and holistic approach, and there are no common standards for calculating emissions and how emissions offsets are communicated. Also, as there are no caps on emissions, offsetting schemes can be extended infinitely without major environmental benefits (Gössling et al., 2009). Due to the high likelihood of accusations of greenwash, Mayer et al. (2014) suggest that airlines need to be careful with regard to how they select the content of their CS and CSR communications, as well as preparing to counter any claims of greenwash that underpins their credibility as a sustainable and socially responsible organisation.

Criticism of airline CS and CSR activities extends beyond greenwash, though, and also includes the social dimension. As previously outlined, in the 1990s, US airlines changed their attitude towards LGBT employees. Yet by the late 1990s, United Airlines drew criticism from activists about its treatment of LGBT employees: "the activists particularly stressed United's hypocrisy in claiming to be a gay-friendly airline while also spending significant sums of money on legal actions designed to resist providing its employees with domestic partner benefits" (Tiemeyer, 2013: 203). An example of criticism to an airline's charity activities is Ryanair's sale of charity scratch cards. The airline suggests that proceeds are going to a children's charity. However, upon further investigation, an unsatisfied passenger claimed in a Facebook post (which has been shared nearly 20,000 times by October 2016), that only 0.3 per cent of the revenue generated was actually transferred to the named charity. In a statement, Ryanair rejected the claims as false. Regardless as to whether this claim is substantiated or not, several national newspapers (e.g. *The Independent, The Mirror, The Sun*) in the UK reported on this accusation (e.g. Blair, 2015; Cardy, 2015; Gillespie, 2016).

In many cases, market orientation is a key factor in airline CS and CSR activities. As earlier discussed, commercial and social interest are not necessary mutually exclusive, yet commercially profiting from these activities needs to be carefully managed, as passengers oppose when companies make money out of such initiatives (Mayer et al., 2014).

## Conclusion

CS and CSR have received significant attention in research and practice in the airline sector, particularly since the 1990s. While research on airline CS and CSR is often based on case studies (e.g. Lynes and Andrachuk, 2008; Lynes and Dredge, 2006; Mayer et al., 2014), more recently research in this field has also applied quantitative methods (e.g. Kuo et al., 2016; Lee et al., 2013). Environmental issues have been the core focus of airline CS and CSR, although airlines have also started to include social aspects, such as community involvement, employee engagement and charitable actions. Although the social dimension of CS and CSR is an emerging field, environmental elements still dominate, both in practice as well as in research. Very few researchers (e.g. Fenclova and Coles, 2011; Kim et al., 2014) have addressed the social dimensions, which highlights a gap in research.

Another research theme that has emerged is related to the content of airline CS and CSR (e.g. Burns and Cowlishaw, 2014; Coles et al., 2011; Cowper-Smith and de Grosbois, 2011). While this research gives valuable insight into the application of CS and CSR at a given time, it does not provide an understanding of how the content and the focus has developed over time. Coles et al. (2011) refer to the CSR activities of LCCs during the economic downturn in the UK in 2008/2009, yet it does not provide an insight into how economic hardship affects airline commitment to CS and CSR. A longitudinal study on the use of CS and CSR over time will have practical relevance to airlines, as well as their stakeholders, with regard to the role of external shocks on the commitment to CS and CSR.

Although airlines have seen a range of negative reactions over their CS and CSR activities, most notably relating to claims of greenwash, the research community so far has hardly addressed this issue. With consumers becoming more sceptical (Grant, 2008), the role and content of CS and CSR communication will become more scrutinised, and a better understanding is necessary for airlines to develop their future communication strategies. Related to this is the issue of CS and CSR reporting. Airlines have been criticised for their lack of standardisation and lack of tangible measures in their reporting. Although standards and guidelines have been developed (e.g. GRI and ISO), these standards hardly feature prominently in research. Future research should look into these guidelines with regard to their application in the airline sector. This research could help to address the criticism regarding the lack of comparability between airlines when it comes to CS and CSR reporting and measurements.

Airline CS and CSR is a highly topical area in research and practice. In comparison to many other industries and sectors, it has not had a full exposure in research, and some airlines still do not perceive CSR reporting as a necessity. With many gaps that need to be addressed, as well as still some opposition to CSR, future research can have a relevant practical impact for airlines and their stakeholders to improve the quality and quantity of CS and CSR commitment and actions.

# References

Air Transat (2015). *Air Transat still among the world's top 10 airlines when it comes to environmental performance.* Online. Available at http://news-releases.transat.com/Air-Transat-still-among-the-world-s-top-10-airlines-when-it-comes-to-environmental-performance (accessed 26 October 2016).

Åkerman, J. (2011). The role of high-speed rail in mitigating climate change: the Swedish case Europabanan from a life cycle perspective, *Transportation Research Part D: Transport and Environment*, 16(3), 208–217.

Albers, S., Bühne, J.-A. and Peters, H. (2009). Will EU-ETS instigate airline network reconfigurations? *Journal of Air Transport Management*, 15, 1–6.

American Airlines (2015). *2015 Corporate Responsibility Report*, Fort Worth, TX, American Airlines.

Araghi, Y., Kroesen, M., Molin, E. and Van Wee, B. (2014). Do social norms regarding carbon offsetting affect individual preferences toward this policy? Results from a stated choice experiment, *Transportation Research Part D: Transport and Environment*, 26, 42–46.

Asiana Airlines (2015). *Sustainability Report*, Seoul, Asiana Airlines.

Baldassarre, F. and Campo, R. (2016). Sustainability as a marketing tool: to be or to appear to be? *Business Horizons*, 59, 421–429.

Banister, D., Stead, D., Steen, P., Åkerman, J., Dreborg, K., Nijkamp, P. and Schleicher-Tappeser, R. (2000). *European Transport Policy and Sustainable Mobility*, London, E & FN Spon.

Baumeister, S. and Onkila, T. (2014). *Shaping the industry with a new standard: environmental labels in the aviation industry.* In: 18th Air Transport Research Society World Conference Proceedings, Bordeaux, Air Transport Research Society.

Beard, A. and Hornik, R. (2011). It's hard to be good, *Harvard Business Review*, November, 88–96.

Becken, S. and Lane, B. (2006). Air travel and the environment: an interview with Hugh Somerville, *Journal of Sustainable Tourism*, 14(2), 216–219.

Benn, S. and Bolton, D. (2011). *Key Concepts in Corporate Social Responsibility*, London, Sage.

Bernardo, J.E., Kirby, M.R. and Mavris, D. (2016). Probabilistic assessment of fleet-level noise impacts of projected technology improvements, *Journal of Air Transport Management*, 57, 26–42.

Black, W.R. (1996). Sustainable transportation: a US perspective, *Journal of Transport Geography*, 4(3), 151–159.

Blair, O. (2015). *Ryanair defend themselves over claims in-flight charity scratch cards are an 'utterly cynical' way to make money.* Online. Available at: www.independent.co.uk/travel/news-and-advice/ryanair-defend-themselves-over-claims-in-flight-charity-scratch-cards-are-an-utterly-cynical-way-to-a6729776.html (accessed 26 October 2016).

British Airways (2016a). *Corporate responsibility.* Online. Available at: www.britishairways.com/en-gb/information/about-ba/csr/corporate-responsibility (accessed 26 October 2016).

British Airways (2016b). *British Airways Flying Start*. Online. Available at: www.ba-flyingstart.com/ (accessed 26 October 2016).

Bröer, C. (2013). Sustainability and noise annoyance. In: L. Budd, S. Griggs and D. Howarth (eds). *Sustainable Aviation Futures*, Bingley, Emerald.

Budd, L., Griggs, S. and Howarth, D. (2013). Sustainable aviation futures: crisis, contested realities and prospects for change. In: L. Budd, S. Griggs and D. Howarth (eds). *Sustainable Aviation Futures*, Bingley, Emerald.

Budd, T. and Suau-Sanchez, P. (2016). Assessing the fuel burn and $CO_2$ impacts of the introduction of the next generation aircraft: a study of a major European low-cost carrier, *Research in Transportation Business & Management*, 21, 68–75.

Burns, P.M. and Cowlishaw, C. (2014). Climate change discourses: how UK airlines communicate their case to the public, *Journal of Sustainable Tourism*, 22(5), 740–767.

Cardy, P. (2015). *Ryanair plane unfair as charity lotto winner must pick €1m prize from 125 envelopes*. Online. Available at: www.mirror.co.uk/news/uk-news/ryanair-plane-unfair-charity-lotto-5920749 (accessed 26 October 2016).

Carroll, A.B. (1991). The pyramid of corporate social responsibility: toward the moral management of organizational stakeholders, *Business Horizons*, July–August, 39–48.

Chen, F.-Y. (2013). The intention and determining factors of airline passengers' participation in carbon offset schemes, *Journal of Air Transport Management*, 29, 17–22.

Coles, T., Fenclova, E. and Dinan, C. (2011). Responsibilities, recession and the tourism sector: perspectives on CSR among low-fares airlines during the economic downturn in the UK, *Current Issues in Tourism*, 14(6), 519–536.

Coles, T., Fenclova, E. and Dinan, C. (2013). Tourism and corporate social responsibility: a critical review and research agenda, *Tourism Management Perspectives*, 6, 122–141.

Coles, T., Fenclova, E. and Dinan, C. (2014). Corporate social responsibility reporting among European low-fares airlines: challenges for the examination and development of sustainable mobilities, *Journal of Sustainable Tourism*, 22(1), 69–88.

Coombs, W.T. and Holladay, S.J. (2012). *Managing Corporate Social Responsibility: A Communication Approach*, Chichester, Wiley-Blackwell.

Copeland, E. (1992). The role of airlines in the tourism and environment debate, *Tourism Management*, March, 112–114.

Cowper-Smith, A. and de Grosbois, D. (2011). The adoption of corporate social responsibility practices in the airlines industry, *Journal of Sustainable Tourism*, 19(1), 59–77.

Curtin, T. (2007). *Managing Green Issues*, 2nd edition, Basingstoke, Palgrave Macmillan.

Daley, B. (2010). *Air Transport and the Environment*, Farnham, Ashgate.

Deloitte & Touche (2007). *Assurance*. Online. Available at: https://es.flybe.com/pdf/deloitte_assurance.pdf (accessed 26 October 2016).

Delta Air Lines (2015). *Corporate Social Responsibility Report 2015*, Atlanta, GA, Delta Air Lines.

Dobruszkes, F., Dehon, C. and Givoni, M. (2014). Does European high-speed rail affect the current level of air services? An EU-wide analysis, *Transportation Research Part A: Policy and Practice*, 69, 461–475.

Dray, L. (2013). An analysis of the impact of aircraft lifecycles on aviation emissions mitigation policies, *Journal of Air Transport Management*, 28, 62–69.

Drumwright, M.E. and Murphy, P.E. (2001). Corporate societal marketing. In: P.N. Bloom and G. Gundlach (eds). *Handbook of Marketing and Society*, London, Sage.

EC (European Commission) (2011). *Communication from the Commission to the European Parliament, the Council, the European Economic and Social Committee and the Committee of the Regions: A Renewed EU Strategy 2011–14 for Corporate Social Responsibility*, Brussels, EC.

Eccles, R.G., Krzus, M., Rogers, J. and Serafeim, G. (2012). The need for sector-specific materiality and sustainability reporting standards, *Journal of Applied Corporate Finance*, 24(2), 65–71.

Elkington, J. (2004). Enter the triple bottom line. In: A. Henriques and J. Richardson (eds). *The Triple Bottom Line: Does It All Add Up?* London, Earthscan.

Emirates (2015). *The Emirates Group: Environmental Report 2014–2015*, Dubai, The Emirates Group.

Fenclova, E. and Coles, T. (2011). Charitable partnerships among travel and tourism businesses: perspectives from low-fares airlines, *International Journal of Tourism Research*, 13, 337–354.

Forsyth, P. (2011). Environmental and financial sustainability of air transport: are they incompatible? *Journal of Air Transport Management*, 17, 27–32.

Friedman, M. (1970). The social responsibility of business is to increase its profits, *The New York Times Magazine*, 13 September, 122–124.

Garuda (2014). *Garuda Indonesia green efforts*. Online. Available at: www.garuda-indonesia.com/id/en/csr/garuda-indonesia-green-efforts/index.page (accessed 26 October 2016).

Gegg, P., Budd, L. and Ison, S. (2014). The market development of aviation biofuel: driver and constraints, *Journal of Air Transport Management*, 39, 34–40.

Gillespie, T. (2016). *PIGS MIGHT FLY Ryanair slammed for 'Fly to Win' charity scratch card where odds of winning are 1.2BILLION/1 . . . and only small percentage of the profits go to good causes*. Online. Available at: www.thesun.co.uk/news/1982591/ryanair-slammed-for-fly-to-win-charity-scratch-card-where-odds-of-winning-are-1-2billion1-and-only-small-percentage-of-the-profits-go-to-good-causes/ (accessed 26 October 2016).

Girvin, R. (2009). Aircraft noise-abatement and mitigation strategies, *Journal of Air Transport Management*, 15, 14–22.

Givoni, M. and Rietveld, P. (2010). The environmental implications of airlines' choice of aircraft size, *Journal of Air Transport Management*, 16, 159–167.

Godfrey, P.C., Hatch, N.W. and Hansen, J.M. (2010). Toward a general theory of CSRs: the roles of beneficence, profitability, insurance, and industry heterogeneity, *Business & Society*, 49(2), 316–344.

Goetz, A.R. and Graham, B. (2004). Air transport globalization, liberalization and sustainability: post-2001 policy dynamics in the United States and Europe, *Journal of Transport Geography*, 12, 265–276.

Gössling, S. and Buckley, R. (2016). Carbon labels in tourism: persuasive communication? *Journal of Cleaner Production*, 111, 358–369.

Gössling, S., Broderick, J., Upham, P., Ceron, J.-P., Dubois, G., Peeters, P. and Strasdas, W. (2007). Voluntary carbon offsetting schemes for aviation: efficiency, credibility and sustainable tourism, *Journal of Sustainable Tourism*, 15(3), 223–248.

Gössling, S., Haglund, L., Kallgren, H. and Revahl, M. (2009). Swedish air travellers and voluntary carbon offsets: towards the co-creation of environmental value? *Current Issues in Tourism*, 12(1), 1–19.

Graham, A. (2014). *Managing Airports: An International Perspective*, 4th edition, Abingdon, Routledge.

Graham, B. and Guyer, C. (1999). Environmental sustainability, airport capacity and European air transport liberalization: irreconcilable goals? *Journal of Transport Geography*, 7, 165–180.

Graham, W.R., Hall, C.A. and Morales, M.V. (2014). The potential of future aircraft technology for noise and pollutant emissions reduction, *Transport Policy*, 34, 36–51.

Grant, J. (2008). Green marketing, *Strategic Direction*, 24(6), 25–27.

GRI (2013). *Air transportation: airlines*. Online. Available at: www.globalreporting.org/resourcelibrary/27-Airlines.pdf (accessed 26 October 2016).

Heeres, J.L., Kruijd, J., Montgomery, E. and Simmons, J.J. (2011). *Building Trust in the Air: Is Airline Corporate Sustainability Reporting Taking Off?* London, PwC.

Heracleous, L. and Wirtz, J. (2010). Singapore Airlines' balancing act, *Harvard Business Review*, July–August, 145–149.

Hoeffler, S. and Keller, K.L. (2002). Building brand equity through corporate societal marketing, *Journal of Public Policy & Marketing*, 21(1), 78–89.

Hooper, P.D. and Greenall, A. (2005). Exploring the potential for environmental performance benchmarking in the airline sector, *Benchmarking: An International Journal*, 12(2), 151–165.

IATA (International Air Transport Association) (2016). *Fact sheet: carbon offsetting*. Online. Available at: www.iata.org/pressroom/facts_figures/fact_sheets/Documents/fact-sheet-carbon-offsetting.pdf (accessed 26 October 2016).

Inoue, Y. and Lee, S. (2011). Effects of different dimensions of corporate social responsibility on corporate financial performance in tourism-related industries, *Tourism Management*, 32, 790–804.

ISO (International Organisation for Standardisation) (2014). *Discovering ISO 26000*, Geneva, ISO.

ISO (International Organisation for Standardisation) (2015). *ISO 14001: Key Benefits*, Geneva, ISO.

ISO (International Organisation for Standardisation) and GRI (Global Reporting Initiative) (2014). *GRI G4 Guidelines and ISO 26000:2010: How to Use the GRI G4 Guidelines and ISO 26000 in Conjunction*, Geneva/Amsterdam, ISO/GRI.

Japan Airlines (2016). *Actions for ISO26000 core subjects*. Online. Available at: www.jal.com/en/csr/iso/ (accessed 26 October 2016).

Kim, Y., Yun, S. and Lee, J. (2014). Can companies induce sustainable consumption? The impact of knowledge and social embeddedness on airline sustainability programs in the U.S., *Sustainability*, 6, 3338–3356.

Kotler, P. and Keller, K.L. (2012). *Marketing Management*, 14th edition, Harlow, Pearson Education.

Kuo, T.C, Okudan Kremer, G.E., Phuong, N.G. and Hsu, C.-W. (2016). Motivations and barriers for corporate social responsibility reporting: evidence from the airline industry, *Journal of Air Transport Management*, 57, 184–195.

LATAM (2015). *Sustainability Report 2015*, Santiago, LATAM Airlines Group.

Lee, S. and Park, S.-Y. (2010). Financial impacts of socially responsible airline companies, *Journal of Hospitality & Tourism Research*, 34(2), 185–203.

Lee, S., Seo, K. and Sharma, A. (2013). Corporate social responsibility and firm performance in the airline industry: the moderating role of oil prices, *Tourism Management*, 38, 20–30.

Levitt, T. (1958). The dangers of social responsibility, *Harvard Business Review*, September–October, 41–50.

Lim, M. and Moufahim, M. (2015). The spectacularization of suffering: an analysis of the use of celebrities in 'Comic Relief' UK's charity fundraising campaigns, *Journal of Marketing Management*, 31(5–6), 525–545.

Lu, J.-L. and Shon, Z.Y. (2012). Exploring airline passengers' willingness to pay for carbon offsets, *Transportation Research Part D: Transport and Environment*, 17, 124–128.

Lufthansa (2016). *Balance*, Frankfurt, Lufthansa.

Lynes, J.K. and Andrachuk, M. (2008). Motivations for social and environmental responsibility: a case study of Scandinavian Airlines, *Journal of International Management*, 14, 377–390.

Lynes, J.K. and Dredge, D. (2006). Going green: motivations for environmental commitment in the airline industry – a case study of Scandinavian Airlines, *Journal of Sustainable Tourism*, 14(2), 116–138.

Mair, J. (2011). Exploring air travellers' voluntary carbon-offsetting behaviour, *Journal of Sustainable Tourism*, 19(2), 215–230.

Mak, B.L.M. and Chan, W.W. (2007). A study of environmental reporting: international Japanese airlines, *Asia Pacific Journal of Tourism Research*, 12(4), 303–312.

Martini, G., Scotti, D. and Volta, N. (2013). Including local air pollution in airport efficiency assessment: a hyperbolic-stochastic approach, *Transportation Research Part D: Transport and Environment*, 24, 27–36.

Mayer, R., Ryley, T. and Gillingwater, D. (2012). Passenger perceptions of the green image associated with airlines, *Journal of Transport Geography*, 22, 179–186.

Mayer, R., Ryley, T. and Gillingwater, D. (2014). The role of green marketing: insights from three airline case studies, *Journal of Sustainable Mobility*, 1(2), 46–72.

Mayer, R., Ryley, T. and Gillingwater, D. (2015). Eco-positioning of airlines: perception versus actual performance, *Journal of Air Transport Management*, 44–45, 82–89.

McCarthy, F., Budd, L. and Ison, S. (2015). Gender on the flightdeck: experiences of women commercial airline pilots in the UK, *Journal of Air Transport Management*, 47, 32–38.

Moneva, J.M., Archel, P. and Correa, C. (2006). GRI and the camouflaging of corporate unsustainability, *Accounting Forum*, 30, 121–137.

Moratis, L. and Cochius, T. (2011). *ISO26000: The Business Guide to the New Standard on Social Responsibility*, Sheffield, Greenleaf.

Nair, S. and Paulose, H. (2014). Emergence of green business models: the case of algae biofuel for aviation, *Energy Policy*, 65, 175–184.

One Direction (2013). *One way or another (teenage kicks)*. Online. Available at: www.youtube.com/watch?v=36mCEZzzQ3o (accessed 26 December 2016).

Papworth, J. (2010). *How charity can use your unused foreign currency*. Online. Available at: www.theguardian.com/money/2010/sep/04/charity-unused-foreign-currency (accessed 26 October 2016).

Parket, I.R. and Eilbirt, H., (1975). Social responsibility: the underlying factors, *Business Horizons*, August, 5–10.

Peattie, K. (1995). *Environmental Marketing Management: Meeting the Green Challenge*, London, Financial Times Management.

Postorino, M.N. and Mantecchini, L. (2016). A systematic approach to assess the effectiveness of airport noise mitigation strategies, *Journal of Air Transport Management*, 50, 71–82.

Preston, H., Lee, D.S. and Hooper, P.D. (2012). The inclusion of the aviation sector within the European Union's Emissions Trading Scheme: what are the prospects for a more sustainable aviation industry? *Environmental Development*, 2, 48–56.

Pringle, H., and Thompson, M. (1999). *Brand Spirit*, Chichester, John Wiley & Sons.

Rigby, C., Mueller, J. and Baker, A. (2011). The integration of Maori indigenous culture into corporate social responsibility strategies at Air New Zealand, *Journal of Marketing Development and Competitiveness*, 5(6), 116–126.

Rudari, L. and Johnson, M.E. (2015). Sustainability reporting practices of Group III U.S. Air Carriers, *International Journal of Aviation, Aeronautics, and Aerospace*, 2(2), 1–19.

Rye, L., Blakey, S. and Wilson, C.W. (2010). Sustainability of supply or the planet: a review of potential drop-in alternative aviation fuels, *Energy & Environmental Science*, 3, 17–27.

Sadr, M.K., Nassiri, P., Hosseini, M., Monavari, M. and Gharagozlou, A. (2014). Assessment of land use compatibility and noise pollution at Imam Khomeini International Airport, *Journal of Air Transport Management*, 34, 49–56.

Saha, M. and Darnton, G. (2005). Green companies or green con-panies: are companies really green, or are they pretending to be? *Business and Society Review*, 110(2), 117–157.

SAS (2016). *Environmental Management System (ISO 14001)*. Online. Available at: www.sasgroup.net/en/environmental-management-system-iso-14001/ (accessed 26 October 2016).

Segerstedt, A. and Grote, U. (2016). Increasing adoption of voluntary carbon offsets among tourists, *Journal of Sustainable Tourism*, 24(11), 1541–1554.

Seo, K., Moon, J. and Lee, S. (2015). Synergy of corporate social responsibility and service quality for airlines: the moderating role of carrier type, *Journal of Air Transport Management*, 47, 126–134.

Sgouridis, S., Bonnefoy, P.A. and Hansman, R.J. (2011). Air transportation in a carbon constrained world: long-term dynamics of policies and strategies for mitigating the carbon footprint of commercial aviation, *Transportation Research Part A: Policy and Practice*, 45, 1077–1091.

Shaw, S. (2011). *Airline Marketing and Management*, 7th edition, Farnham, Ashgate.

Sheldon, P.J. and Park, S.-Y. (2011). An exploratory study of corporate social responsibility in the U.S. travel industry, *Journal of Travel Research*, 50(4), 392–407.

Southwest Airlines (2016a). *Southwest citizenship*. Online. Available at: www.southwest.com/html/southwest-difference/southwest-citizenship/index.html?clk=GFOOTER-ABOUT-DIFFERENCE-SOUTHWEST-CARES (accessed 26 October 2016).

Southwest Airlines (2016b). *Medical transportation*. Online. Available at: www.southwest.com/html/southwest-difference/community-involvement/charities/medical_transportation.html (accessed 26 October 2016).

Szodruch, J., Grimme, W., Blumrich, F. and Schmid, R. (2011). Next generation single-aisle aircraft: requirements and technological solutions, *Journal of Air Transport Management*, 17(1), 33–39.

Thomas Cook (2016). *Eco-label*. Online. Available at: http://cdn.thomascook.com/pdf/eco-label-16102012.pdf (accessed 26 October 2016).

Tiemeyer, P. (2013). *Plane Queer: Labor, Sexuality, and AIDS in the History of Male Flight Attendants*, London, University of California Press.

Turkish Airlines (2016). *Environmental and social responsibility report*. Online. Available at: http://investor.turkishairlines.com/documents/ThyInvestorRelations/download/icerikler/environmental_and_social_responsiblty.pdf (accessed 26 October 2016).

UNICEF (2014). *UNICEF's corporate partnerships*. Online. Available at: www.unicef.org/corporate_partners/index_good.html (accessed 26 October 2016).

United Airlines (2016a). *Diversity and inclusion initiatives*. Online. Available at: www.united.com/web/en-US/content/company/globalcitizenship/diversity-initiatives.aspx (accessed 26 October 2016).

United Airlines (2016b). *Community involvement*. Online. Available at: www.united.com/web/en-US/content/company/globalcitizenship/community.aspx (accessed 26 October 2016).

Upham, P. (2001). A comparison of sustainability theory with UK and European airports policy and practice, *Journal of Environmental Management*, 63, 237–248.

Van der Heijden, A., Driessen, P.P.J. and Cramer, J.M. (2010). Making sense of corporate social responsibility: exploring organizational processes and strategies, *Journal of Cleaner Production*, 18, 1787–1796.

Van Marrewijk, M. (2003). Concepts and definitions of CSR and corporate sustainability: between agency and communion, *Journal of Business Ethics*, 44, 95–105.

Walker, S. and Cook, M. (2009). The contested concept of sustainable aviation, *Sustainable Development*, 17(6), 378–390.

Wang, Q., Wu, C. and Sun, Y. (2015). Evaluating corporate social responsibility of airlines using entropy weight and grey relation analysis, *Journal of Air Transport Management*, 42, 55–62.

WBCSD (World Business Council for Sustainable Development) (1999). *Meeting Changing Expectations: Corporate Social Responsibility*, Geneva, WBCSD.

WCED (World Commission on Environment and Development) (1987). *Our Common Future*, Oxford, Oxford University Press.

Wheatcroft, S. (1991). Airlines, tourism and the environment, *Tourism Management*, June, 119–124.

Zink, K.J. (2005). Stakeholder orientation and corporate social responsibility as a precondition for sustainability, *Total Quality Management*, 16(8–9), 1041–1052.

# 18

# Airport sustainability and corporate social responsibility

*Christopher Paling and Callum Thomas*

## Introduction

Major changes have occurred to the global economy and society over the past half-century, driven to a significant extent by the growth and development of air transport (ATAG, 2016; Bråthen and Halpern, 2012). Airports provide accessibility for city regions to the rest of the world and support economic development (Airports Commission, 2013). They are the physical embodiment of the air transport sector, and as such are the focus for many of the socio-economic benefits the industry brings. However, their operations do give rise to adverse environmental impacts, the significance of which is increasing, and a trend that is unsustainable (Thomas and Hooper, 2013). The airport sector therefore faces similar challenges to other sectors of the economy in mitigating or compensating for these adverse environmental impacts in the context of limited global resources and tightening environmental constraints.

People travel by air to do business, for personal fulfilment (e.g. to go on holiday, to visit cultural and historical sites, or meet cultural and religious obligations), and to maintain social and family networks (see Chapter 1). Meanwhile, the global air freight industry provides high-speed transport of high-value and perishable goods over long distances (see Chapter 2). Global mobility supports regional competitiveness, and allows regions to source or supply goods, services and skills from and to the world. As a result, the economies of some locations are highly reliant upon air transport, particularly those that provide services to consumers in remote parts of the world. The development of the global economy and multicultural society has been driven by, and increasingly is driving, the growth of air transport, facilitated by growing affluence and a reduction in the cost of flying (see Chapter 19). For these benefits to be maintained, it is essential that airports and airlines take the necessary action to manage, mitigate and, if necessary, compensate for their environmental impacts. Failure to do so will act as a significant barrier in the pursuit of continued growth in response to demand.

The influence of environmental issues on the growth and development of air transport is a comparatively recent phenomenon. The advent of the jet engine in the late 1950s saw aircraft noise emerge as an issue for aviation, in particular airports. However, its impacts were restricted to a small number of large airports, almost exclusively in Europe, North America and Japan. It was not until 1969 that the International Civil Aviation Organisation (ICAO) convened a special conference that drafted a new international certification standard (ICAO, 2004) that limited permissible noise levels from aircraft, and established the Committee on Aircraft Noise (CAN).

The rising price of oil in the 1970s gave rise to efforts to cut energy use, but still environmental management at airports was in its infancy. Air quality in major cities in developed economies started to emerge as another phenomenon associated primarily with industrial pollution, and later the growth of private car use, but it was only in 1971 when the 1970 EC Directive 70/220/EEC came into force that local air quality started to emerge as a possible threat to the growth of airports. In 1988, the Intergovernmental Panel on Climate Change (IPCC) was established by the World Meteorological Organisation (WMO) and the United Nations Environment Programme (UNEP) in recognition of the problem of global warming. However, it was not until 1999, with the IPCC Report on Aviation and the Global Environment (IPCC, 1999) that the implications of aircraft emissions for climate change came into the political spotlight (see Chapter 25 for more on air transport and climate change). A decade later, the Airports Council International (ACI), the global industry body representing airports, established its carbon accreditation for airports in recognition of the fact that all sectors of the aviation industry needed to work together to prevent climate change (ACI, 2017a).

In 2003, EUROCONTROL published the results of a survey that demonstrated that in Europe, a wide variety of environmental issues were having a significant impact upon the growth and development of airports (EUROCONTROL, 2003). Such issues were acknowledged as increasing operating costs, limiting operational capacity and causing delays to planning applications. Thus, it became evident that engagement with the environmental agenda was a prerequisite to a successful airport business.

This chapter considers the concept of sustainability and corporate social responsibility (CSR) as it applies to airports (for airlines, see Chapter 17) from a largely United Kingdom (UK) or European perspective. It describes the variety of environmental issues arising from their operation, and in so doing it identifies that proactive and effective environmental management is key to enabling airport growth. Engagement with the environmental agenda is therefore as much a matter of commercial self-interest as one of sustainability and CSR.

## Sustainability and airports

As mentioned in Chapter 17, the term sustainability implies taking a holistic and long-term view to ensure something can continue in perpetuity. For a business, this implies a financial element; after all, no business can survive, or provide employment or other societal benefits, if it is not able to generate revenue. Indeed, historically, under the neoclassical model of the firm, financial issues were the sole consideration for all businesses (Tomer, 1999). Corporate activity would be defined only by the demands of the market, and by broad government regulations that ensured wider societal concerns were catered for. The 1956 Clean Air Act (DEFRA, 2015) is an example of this. More recently, however, many business leaders have become aware of the importance of foresight in developing robust business strategies that can maintain or grow revenue streams into the long term. This inherently implies consideration of externalities that can impact the performance of a company's business model, for instance economic, societal, legislative, technological, political or environmental issues, termed by Tomer (1999) as the socio-economic model of the firm. In terms of the environment, the critical issues are the finite supply of natural resources (in a consumption- and fossil fuel-driven economy), and the ability of the planet to absorb emissions and wastes from human activity (e.g. those causing climate change). The magnitude of these environmental business threats is evident from the fact that the majority of the planet's ecosystems are already in a state of decline (Secretariat of the Convention on Biological Diversity, 2010).

The definition of sustainability is contested, with no precise or single meaning (see Dresner, 2008 for a detailed account). There are different interpretations of the concept from those with different perspectives and viewpoints. It is understandable, therefore, that when it comes to a complex system such as the air transport sector (or even an airport), there is no commonly accepted definition, as discussed by Janić (2007) and Upham (2001). Very often, sustainability is represented as integrating three pillars – economic development, environmental protection and social progress – which are discussed later.

Environmental non-governmental organisations (NGOs) tend to approach the issue from the perspective of maintaining the stability of the earth's natural systems in relation to the rate of consumption of resources and production of pollution (e.g. Holmberg, 1998). They also acknowledge the issue of social equity, which, in the context of aviation, implies either that all human beings should have the same rights of global mobility, or that the adverse consequences of a small proportion of the world's population choosing to fly should not disproportionately affect those who do not. For instance, air transport is responsible for approximately 2 to 3 per cent of global anthropogenic climate change emissions (IPCC, 1999), but a far smaller proportion of people have access to air travel. Equally, at a local level, while the economic benefits of airports are spread across regions or entire countries (benefiting millions), the adverse costs (such as disturbance and the adverse health effects of aircraft noise, local air pollution, loss of green spaces and road traffic congestion) are borne by the residents of neighbouring communities.

This view proposes environmental or socially based growth limits that take little or no account of the resulting economic consequences. From this perspective, the current rate of growth of the air transport sector is unsustainable in the longer term because of its reliance upon a fossil fuel (a finite resource) and the fact that growth is outstripping technological and operational improvements in environmental performance, resulting in increasing fuel use and carbon emissions. Given forecast aircraft technologies and the likelihood that any step change in propulsion (e.g. hydrogen-powered aircraft) would be expensive and are decades away, one might question the role that air transport will play in a low-carbon world of the second half of the twenty-first century (an issue considered by Paling et al., 2014).

Governments seek to achieve a political balance between both the social and economic benefits of an activity, and the associated social and environmental costs, while still acknowledging limits to growth. *Mainstreaming Sustainable Development* (DEFRA, 2011) exemplifies this in the UK. It also acknowledges the imperative to deliver a strong, healthy and just society and a sustainable economy. Here, the emphasis is placed upon good governance (social and environmental responsibility) and decisions being based on sound science. The UK Department for Transport (2012) goes further, proposing a Sustainable Framework for Aviation that stresses the need for attaining a fair balance between airport benefits and adverse environmental and health impacts. Community involvement in the development of airport infrastructure, operations and environmental management plans is regarded as essential, and airport master plans (see Chapter 16) (explaining development, environmental impacts and mitigation measures) are required to underpin this dialogue. The use of the term 'fair balance' acknowledges that some adverse impacts cannot be avoided, and there is an implicit assumption that action may have to be taken to compensate those adversely affected, an issue returned to later.

Individual airports provide very different definitions of sustainability, but some consistent themes emerge. Industry, like government, frames the concept in terms of maximising the social and economic benefits that arise from the particular services offered by the organisation, while minimising the adverse social and environmental costs. London Heathrow Airport, for example, which arguably has one of the most advanced environmental management systems of any airport in the world, under the title Responsible Heathrow, talks about:

> Achieving our vision to give passengers the best airport service in the world relies on managing the airport responsibly. We're working hard to maximize the economic benefits that Heathrow brings, whilst carefully managing our environmental responsibilities and being a good neighbour to our local communities.
>
> *(Heathrow Airport Limited, 2017a)*

More recently, with the publication of *Heathrow 2.0: Our Plan for Sustainable Growth*, the company articulates a more challenging aspiration: "to expand to meet demand in a way that creates a positive impact upon our community, environment and economy" (Heathrow Airport Limited, 2017b).

Manchester Airport states that: "Our priority is to continually improve our performance and ensure that we maximise the social and economic benefits of our business, whilst minimising any harm to the environment and impact on our neighbours" (MAG, 2017a), and:

> By building enduring relationships with our local communities, we will seek to understand the issues that are important to them, how our operations affect them and how we can open up and improve the employment opportunities that we offer. We will use the skills and resources of airport partners to work together for mutual benefit.
>
> *(MAG, 2017b)*

ACI does not provide a specific definition of sustainable aviation, but does include the issue within the goals of its environment initiatives:

> The goals of ACI's environmental initiatives are to promote aviation and airport sustainable developments, limiting or reducing environmental impacts while supporting economic and social benefits – the key to community permission to operate and grow at both global and local levels.
>
> *(ACI, 2017b)*

All three organisations implicitly accept that for some environmental impacts, it will never be possible to completely mitigate the effects of airport operations and there will be residual adverse environmental impacts. Compensatory actions are therefore necessary, such as for the communities affected by noise (as noted by Rawson and Hooper, 2012), or through offset schemes for residual carbon emissions (as provided for in the ACI Airport Carbon Accreditation) (ACI, 2017a).

It is self-evident that industry perceptions of sustainability will be constrained by concerns about what is operationally feasible and commercially viable leading to a short- to medium-term focus, while still acknowledging longer-term challenges (such as the need to decarbonise energy use). Increasingly, however, airports are recognising that they face operational and growth constraints from a wide variety of environmental issues, and this has given rise to the concept of airport environmental capacity, discussed by Upham et al. (2003). When considering the operational capacity of an airport (see Chapter 16), the focus normally turns to the capacity of different elements of the airport infrastructure (such as the number of terminals, runways, apron stands and car parking spaces) or the operational management of the airport (such as the efficiency of security processes and aircraft manoeuvring). The concept of airport environmental capacity acknowledges the fact that even where sufficient infrastructure is provided, an airport's environmental impact may limit operating capacity. This is most easily illustrated by airports that must close at night due to aircraft noise issues, or by operational limits resulting from local air quality regulations.

For some environmental issues (such as energy and water use), sustainability and commercial agendas will often align. For other issues (such as investment in low-carbon energy generation), it can be more difficult to build a case for investment, despite the clear long-term business threat. A further commercial challenge arises from the fact that short-term investment in environmental management and mitigation may deliver long-term benefits, but benefits that do not conform to normal rates of return (e.g. investment in noise management and compensation). This is a common failing regarding environmental mitigation and investment, in that environmental impacts are rarely assigned any economic value, despite their clear value to society (Hawken, 2010).

Sustainability requires that the airport operator continually achieves an appropriate balance between commercial, environmental and operational objectives. When an airport wishes to secure external approvals for expansion, however, it is necessary to demonstrate not only good environmental stewardship, but also its wider contribution to regional development objectives, this being a matter of political sustainability; hence, the maxim of minimising the adverse impacts and maximising the social and economic benefits. Meeting the sustainability challenge is therefore a complex and difficult process, as evidenced by constraints to growth and protests against airport expansion that have emerged around the world (e.g. BBC, 2016). All too often, senior management only fully recognise the extent of the business risk and value of investment in the environment when it is too late, for example when planning permissions are delayed or refused, or when regulatory failure threatens penalties and clean-up costs. Proactive action has been shown to be cheaper than reactive responses to environmental issues, and early engagement with such issues gives greater control of the issue rather than being at the behest of others directing the response.

## CSR at airports

Like the term sustainability, and as mentioned in Chapter 17, the concept of CSR is also subject to a variety of definitions. The World Bank states that: "The World Bank manages its internal operations to safeguard the wellbeing of staff as well as the ecosystems, communities, and economies in which it works" (World Bank, 2017). The European Commission, meanwhile, states that: "Corporate social responsibility (CSR) refers to companies taking responsibility for their impact on society" (EC, 2017).

Both represent broad aspirations that can be interpreted by individual organisations in a variety of ways to meet their own needs. Dahlsrud (2008) reviewed (and helpfully reproduced) definitions of CSR used by 37 different organisations and found a degree of consistency in that they all refer to five dimensions – environmental, social, economic/financial, stakeholder and voluntariness (a willingness to go beyond regulatory requirement). Several of these elements are reflected in airport publications, reports and websites. London City Airport, for example, states that: "CSR is the continuing commitment by business to behave ethically and contribute to economic development while improving the quality of life of the workforce and their families as well as the local community and society at large" (London City Airport Limited, 2017).

The *Birmingham Airport Corporate Social Responsibility Report 2015–16* talks about: "striking a balance between the positive and negative impacts," and:

> to ensure that we grow sustainably, that our success is shared amongst all those who can benefit from it, and that where that success has an impact upon our neighbours we are prepared to act responsibly to manage that impact.
>
> *(Birmingham Airport Limited, 2017)*

The CSR commitments of the Manchester Airports Group (MAG) state that:

> Building and maintaining trust is paramount to business success and that this is achieved through a commitment to engage openly with our stakeholders and by acting with integrity. Our CSR objectives and strong corporate governance are designed to promote the long term interests of our business and colleagues.
>
> *(MAG, 2017a)*

The term 'colleagues' is used to refer to employees.

As this statement demonstrates, the motivation for CSR is to maintain business success while being accountable to stakeholders and the wider community. There is therefore a significant degree of overlap between the language used by airports to describe sustainability and CSR. Having said this, Steurer et al. (2005) maintain that there are distinct differences between the two, including that, in general, CSR is about meeting the demands of current stakeholders as opposed to sustainability, which extends to future stakeholders. In addition, the two issues have very different historical perspectives – CSR was initially focused upon issues such as human rights and working conditions, whereas corporate sustainability has developed out of an essentially environmental background.

Traditionally, businesses and corporations were viewed as having responsibility only to their shareholders; however, since the 1990s, there has been a shift away from this to a more stakeholder-based view (Hubbard, 2009). With an increase in stakeholder influence, there has been a move away from the traditional short-term profit maximisation view to one that seeks to simultaneously improve environmental and social performance (Darnall et al., 2010). Such changes do not necessarily represent a change in corporate philosophy. They may simply reflect increasing recognition of growing environmental pressures and changing social attitudes.

Several papers have also focused upon CSR in the airport sector. The Global Reporting Initiative (GRI) examined reports from airports around the world (GRI, 2009). It found that a growing number of airports are publishing data to demonstrate their economic performance alongside their environmental and social credentials. Skouloudis et al. (2012) carried out a content analysis of CSR reports from airports, commenting upon their comprehensiveness and quality. They note that while the publication of non-financial information by airports is increasing, it is still comparatively rare and restricted to certain parts of the world (almost exclusively Europe and North America). They also observed a tendency to focus upon direct social and economic benefits of their operations rather than the wider benefits that would accrue to the regions they serve.

The audience for airport CSR reporting ranges from shareholders, for whom financial return is paramount, service partners (e.g. airlines) that need to understand and support the airport's sustainability strategy, through to investors and insurance bodies. One of the most significant stakeholder groups are the residents of neighbouring communities and their elected representatives. Community opposition to the airport can severely constrain current operations and growth. This is particularly the case when the airport operator brings forward an application for infrastructure development or airspace change. In this situation, the airport must be able to demonstrate that it is taking appropriate action to minimise adverse environmental impacts and that it is taking action to compensate those adversely affected. In addition, it needs to make clear (and even take action to maximise) the social and economic benefits of its continued growth.

## Drivers for sustainability and CSR approaches at airports

Many organisations profess aspirations to be good corporate citizens, to move ahead of regulatory requirements and to be recognised as leaders in sustainability or CSR. The extent to which any company can deviate from its core activity to provide additional social benefit, over and above that which secures its own commercial development, can be limited by its Articles of Association, and this in turn is likely to be linked to the issue of ownership. Put simply, an airport operator that is wholly owned by private shareholders (especially international conglomerates) may focus upon profitability and shareholder return, and only invest in supporting regional social and economic development where this can be shown to directly facilitate business success. Indeed, the economist Milton Friedman (1967) is explicit in his claim that the priority of business must, and should only, be to generate revenue for shareholders. They lack the knowledge and expertise to adequately address externalities such as the environment – which he claimed should be dealt with by governments, via policy and regulation.

State-owned airports, on the other hand, or those whose shares are wholly or partly owned by public bodies (especially local government), are potentially more likely to incorporate regional development priorities into their commercial strategy. Route development provides a clear example of this. While some airports prioritise routes and slot allocation according to the social and economic benefits that would accrue to the city/region, others may seek to maximise direct and indirect income to the airport operator (through landing fees or passenger spend).

In the context of airport growth and development, there can therefore be a significant degree of overlap between CSR, sustainability and commercial development objectives. Such action can be seen as being of commercial self-interest. Meeting environmental regulations is an absolute minimum if airports are to avoid court actions and fines for non-compliance. If environmental issues (e.g. local air quality) present a constraint to business growth, then investment in quality environmental management is vital to avoid or unlock those constraints. Minimising energy and water use or waste production is a prerequisite to effective financial management. Finally, airports are major industrial complexes that cannot help but have a significant adverse impact upon the local environment and the lives of residents of surrounding communities. If community opposition is to be minimised, and if planning approvals for expansion are to be achieved, then it is critical that airports seek not simply to minimise their adverse impacts, but also to identify, promote and maximise the social and economic benefit arising from their continued development. Furthermore, by actively directing the benefits towards those adversely affected, airports can engender tolerance within their neighbouring communities.

## Airport environmental impacts

Airports are complex industrial and commercial sites. They include the activities of a wide variety of different organisations, including the airport operator, airlines, air traffic navigation service providers, ground handlers, catering and retail companies, engineering and maintenance organisations, hotels, and surface transport providers. The operations of these organisations are varied and give rise to a wide variety of environmental impacts.

Aircraft noise is regarded as the most significant local impact arising from the operation of airports, and is a common cause of operational restrictions and refusal of planning permissions

(Thomas et al., 2010). Noise can have adverse effects upon health and sleep (CAA, 2014; Hansell et al., 2013), the learning of children in schools (CAA, 2010), and cause disturbance to the daily lives of tens or even hundreds of thousands of people (Thomas et al., 2010). Improvements in aircraft noise technology and operations have been offset by traffic growth, changes to flight paths (exposing new people to overflight) and urban encroachment (Thomas et al., 2010). At the same time, growing affluence has made people more sensitive to noise (Thomas et al., 2010). In acknowledgement of the fact that aircraft will never be silent, and that airports have much broader impacts on their neighbours, many implement public engagement programmes and invest in local communities to compensate for disturbance in high-noise areas, as evidenced by London Heathrow Airport (Heathrow Airport Limited, 2017b). Effective management of aircraft noise and community relations is therefore a matter of both commercial self-interest as well as corporate responsibility.

Governments across the world are setting challenging carbon dioxide (referred to as $CO_2$ or carbon) reduction targets to avoid dangerous climate change, as exemplified in the UK by the Climate Change Act 2008 (HM Government, 2008). Aviation faces a particular challenge in contributing to these targets because forecasts suggest $CO_2$ emissions from airlines will grow (CCC, 2009). Airports, on the other hand, can deliver absolute reductions in $CO_2$ despite expansion, and should publicly demonstrate that they are doing so. Some large European airports are already included within the European Union's (EU) Emissions Trading Scheme (ETS) due to their energy use. In the future, governments may seek to impose carbon caps on airports, as exemplified by Stockholm Arlanda Airport in Sweden. Arlanda is subject to a $CO_2$ cap encompassing emissions associated with aircraft movements, surface transport vehicles, and heating and cooling of buildings (Wigstrand, 2010). The ACI Airport Carbon Accreditation provides a structured framework to guide airports to account for and manage their carbon emissions. In addition to the benefit of alleviating any capacity constraints, and financial benefits of reducing energy costs, effective carbon management helps airports adapt to an increasingly carbon-constrained world. Additionally, from a corporate responsibility perspective, all organisations need to contribute to efforts to prevent climate change.

Local air quality can restrict airport growth where regulations limit levels of pollution, as exemplified by Zurich Airport (2010), or where opposition arises from communities that fear the health implications of living close by. Poor air quality arises from the accumulation of pollutants such as nitrogen oxides, carbon monoxide, hydrocarbons, particulate matter, sulphur dioxide and ozone, all of which can have a detrimental impact on human health, increasing rates of mortality and morbidity (TRB, 2015). Aircraft operations, apron activities, energy generation, engine testing and fire training primarily affect air quality at the airport. In the immediate vicinity of the airport, road traffic emissions are the key contributor to reduced air quality. This road traffic will comprise airport-related and non-airport-related vehicles. The threat of local air quality constraints has resulted in airports investing efforts to promote public transport use, changes in apron vehicle fleets, encouragement of low-emission aircraft and improved air traffic management. At the time of writing, the issue is threatening proposals for a new runway at London Heathrow Airport (Airports Commission, 2017), and so can have major implications not simply for business growth, but also for the market value of a company.

Historically, economic growth (because of rising consumption levels) and population growth have been linked to increasing energy consumption in all sectors of the economy. Growing demand leads to increases in energy costs, but also incidences of power outages and grid network failures, with security of supply being most acute in countries undergoing rapid economic development. Climate change is significant also, not only because it will be necessary for airports to ensure their energy supplies come from renewable or low-carbon sources, but also, in some parts of the world, because the changing climate will lead to a significant increase in airport energy demand. Investment in energy efficiency and renewable energy generation by airports represents not just a move towards environmental sustainability, but is a way of maximising airport capacity, operational reliability and minimising operating costs, all clear business drivers.

Airports also consume large quantities of water to maintain essential services and provide appropriate levels of customer service. Water security will become increasingly challenging for some airports because the same factors that drive airport expansion (economic growth and increasing affluence) lead to increasing demand for water in all sectors of the economy. The Organisation for European Economic Co-operation and Development (OECD) *Environmental Outlook 2050* (OECD, 2012) suggests that global water demand will increase by 55 per cent during the period 2000 to 2050. Some airports will face a particular challenge where climate change leads to both an increased frequency of heatwaves (requiring more water for air conditioning and cooling) and droughts (reducing water availability). To remain commercially viable, airports need to secure low cost and adequate supplies. This in turn requires investment in water management programmes.

Surface and groundwater contamination arising from airport operations can damage watercourses, pollute soil, substrata and aquifers, threatening human health, as well as resulting in the death of plants and animals (Thomas and Hooper, 2013). Water pollution arises from aircraft handling, maintenance and washing activities, emergency services/fire training and de-icing activities. Management drivers include regulatory compliance, the avoidance of financial penalties and clean-up costs, as well as maintaining corporate reputation. In addition, the legacy of groundwater pollution can be a significant issue when airports are offered for sale because the clean-up costs can be high. Insurance companies and investors also examine such legacies.

Airport operations, aircraft and passenger handling activities all generate significant quantities of waste. London Heathrow Airport, for example, generates about 100,000 tonnes of waste per year (Heathrow Airport Limited, 2017c). A number of specific challenges apply to waste management in an airport environment, ranging from legal restrictions relating to international waste, the large number of organisations operating across the site, to security issues. At Manchester Airport, 85 per cent of the airport's waste comes from its service partners (MAG, 2010). Waste management practices that can reduce costs and generate income require the segregation of materials for reuse, to be sold on for recycling or used to generate energy (Mitie, 2014; WRAP, 2012).

Very often, airports close to major urban conurbations are located in areas of considerable value in terms of biodiversity, the green belt[1] or are highly prized for their recreational value by urban dwellers. The ability of an airport to extend its boundaries, or even build upon parts of its own land, can be restricted due to the ecological habitats threatened by the development. This problem has emerged at a number of airports in the UK (including Heathrow, Gatwick, Stansted and Manchester), where sites protected by national or international conventions have constrained infrastructure expansion. Given the commitments made starting with the Rio Earth Summit in 1992 (see Dresner, 2008 for a summary) to protect biodiversity, such constraints are very likely to become more pressing in the future. Investment in large-scale habitat management and compensation programmes designed to underpin airport development strategies are symptomatic of a growing focus upon the need for developments to be ecologically sensitive to secure approval. The UK CAA provides a useful web resource that links to biodiversity reports from different airports in the UK (CAA, 2017).

## Airport sustainability and CSR programmes

Every airport differs in terms of its physical setting, the weather, the sensitivity of surrounding countryside, the quality of supporting infrastructure (e.g. road, rail, electrical and water supplies) and its proximity to built-up areas. These factors, coupled with a need for further infrastructure provision, the level of air traffic operations and their timing (particularly day/night flights), will all determine how important different environmental issues will be in terms of airport operations, airport expansion and traffic growth. In addition to the environmental impacts of airport operations, airport operators can look to the GRI Sustainability Reporting Standards (GRI, 2017) for a checklist of topics to be included in sustainability or CSR programmes (Koç and Durmaz, 2015). These guidelines require the consideration of a broad range of issues, such as child labour, indigenous rights and anti-corruption, diversity, and equal opportunities.

An airport's environmental impacts arise principally from the activities of different service partners rather than the airport operator itself (e.g. the disturbance caused by aircraft noise arises from airline operations). For this reason, the environmental management system found at airports can be complex and requires the coordination of up to hundreds of companies. This has given rise to the concept of collaborative environmental management, an issue that has been the subject of particular attention in recent years in Europe (EUROCONTROL, 2013). In the long term, it is to the advantage of all airport service partners that they continually strive to improve their environmental performance. Only through such action will the airport be able to grow in response to demand and play the required role in supporting economic development within the region it serves.

The airport operator has a particularly important role in achieving a site-wide approach; in part, because for some impacts (e.g. water pollution) it has a legal requirement to do so, but also because this can be the most cost-effective or eco-efficient method. Moreover, as the over-arching landlord that links its comprising businesses, it has the ability to bring individual service partners together. For example, at London Heathrow Airport, the Heathrow Sustainability Partnership was created to help the airport's different tenants improve Heathrow's sustainability performance (Heathrow Airport Limited, 2017d). In addition, the airport operator can be essential to ensuring long-term airport growth. This involves achieving the sustainable balance between maximising operational capacity, maintaining safety, meeting customer service expectations, minimising operating costs and ensuring adequate environmental protection. This can require resolution of the sometimes conflicting priorities and interests of different services partners.

Therefore, a systematic approach is recommended. The most commonly adopted internationally recognised system for certifying environmental management systems is the International Organisation for Standardisation's ISO14001:2015 (ISO, 2015). The standard requires an airport to identify and control the environmental impacts associated with its activities and that of its service partners. Doing so facilitates continual performance improvements, promotes regulatory compliance, and can publicly demonstrate that the airport is meeting its environmental responsibilities, objectives and targets. Similar international standards exist for health and safety, energy management, and quality, which airports may choose to adopt.

A key part of any sustainability or CSR programme is engagement with neighbouring communities as they are key stakeholders for the organisation. Effective engagement, designed to facilitate airport operations and growth, involves the following activities: communication in an honest, open and transparent way, to identify the nature and extent of the airport's adverse impacts upon local residents' lives; implementation of a management programme that incorporates publicly stated targets for improvement that are meaningful to local people; effective action to mitigate impacts and compensate for those that cannot be avoided; and efforts to maximise social and economic benefits that arise from the airport's operation and growth, and to share these benefits with those areas worst affected.

Examples of such community investments include: providing financial support to local initiatives that improve quality of life (e.g. environmental improvement or investment in culture and arts); investing in local schools to improve educational achievement or providing opportunities for employment at the airport; and directing recruitment of employees to areas closest to the airport.

## Conclusion

It has become clear that the trend of tightening environmental pressures upon airports will continue in the future because of: the growth in air traffic and airport infrastructure; the spread of environmental regulations across the world; improved scientific knowledge leading to stricter environmental regulations; the application of more onerous environmental criteria to planning approvals for airport developments; hardening public attitudes to environmental degradation; increasing democratisation leading to more vocal and active opposition to airports and an expectation of being consulted on major developments; rising utility and waste management costs; increased requirements from banks and insurance providers; and the effects of the changing climate.

Airports, as commercial entities, face a particular threat from environmental issues for two principle reasons. The first is simply the size of their operations. Larger airports, in particular, can be the biggest industrial complexes in the regions they serve. The second arises from the fact that climate change emissions from aviation (see Chapter 25) will increase for the foreseeable future, at a time when governments and the United Nations (UN) are seeking to cut carbon emissions to prevent dangerous climate change (CCC, 2009; UN, 2016), and when other sectors are able to reduce their contribution to global emissions. Given that the growth of airports is directly linked to that of air traffic, and given that all airport activities produce greenhouse gases, including carbon, both airlines and airports are likely to remain in the political spotlight for the foreseeable future.

Business responses to the environmental threat can involve significant financial investment with no immediate or measurable return (e.g. investment in public transport infrastructure to improve local air quality or cut carbon). They can require the development of new business models such as the need to reduce reliance upon car park income. They can lead to new business risks such as the need for public engagement and far greater transparency than was previously the norm. As a result, airports should acknowledge environmental issues as a key business threat.

The problem is how to articulate such threats in a way that allows a business case to be developed. There is a requirement for further research into the development of environmental business risk assessment methodologies that consider: the direct and indirect implications of each environmental issue for the future growth and development of different parts of the airport business; the magnitude of those impacts and likely consequences; the timescales over which they are likely to impact the business; the certainty of the risk; and the options and costs of mitigation or compensation and the resulting business benefits.

Airport operators need to anticipate these changes, begin to plan for the long term, and implement a systematic approach to environmental business risk analysis, and subsequently environmental management systems. Alongside environmental management, airports should consider how they can maximise their economic benefit, such as through local employment, and support local communities and employee welfare in order to sustain growth.

## Note

1 In UK planning, the green belt is a ring of countryside around major urban conurbations where priority is given to nature conservation, agriculture, forestry and outdoor leisure.

## References

ACI (Airports Council International) (2017a). *Annual reports*. Online. Available at: www.airportcarbonac creditation.org/library/annual-reports.html (accessed 23 February 2017).
ACI (Airports Council International) (2017b). *Environment*. Online. Available at: www.aci.aero/About-ACI/Priorities/Environment (accessed 23 February 2017).
Airports Commission (2013). *Aviation connectivity and the economy*. Online. Available at: www.gov.uk/government/uploads/system/uploads/attachment_data/file/138162/aviation-connectivity-and-the-economy.pdf (accessed 23 February 2017).
Airports Commission (2017). *The Airports Commission report follow-up: carbon emissions, air quality and noise*. Online. Available at: www.publications.parliament.uk/pa/cm201617/cmselect/cmenvaud/840/84002.htm (accessed 24 February 2017).
ATAG (Air Transport Action Group) (2016). *Aviation: Benefits Beyond Borders*, Geneva, ATAG.
BBC (2016). *Heathrow expansion: protesters arrested on M4 spur road*. Online. Available at: www.bbc.co.uk/news/uk-england-london-38038313 (accessed 23 February 2017).
Birmingham Airport Limited (2017). *Birmingham Airport corporate responsibility report 2015–2016*. Online. Available at: www.birminghamairport.co.uk/media/3491/048255_bhx_corporate-responsibility-report-2016_pages.pdf (accessed 23 February 2017).
Bråthen, S. and Halpern, N. (2012). Air transport service provision and management strategies to improve the economic benefits for remote regions, *Research in Transportation Business & Management*, 4, 3–12.
CAA (Civil Aviation Authority) (2010). *Aircraft Noise and Children's Learning*, London, Environmental Research and Consultancy Department, CAA.
CAA (Civil Aviation Authority) (2014). *Aircraft Noise, Sleep Disturbance and Health Effects (CAP 1164)*, London, Environmental Research and Consultancy Department, CAA.
CAA (Civil Aviation Authority) (2017). *Aviation and biodiversity*. Online. Available at: www.caa.co.uk/Environment/Environmenta http://jncc.defra.gov.uk/page-1377l-information/Information-by-environmental-impact/Local-impact/Aviation-s-impact-on-biodiversity/ (accessed 23 February 2017).
CCC (Committee on Climate Change) (2009). *Aviation Report*, London, CCC.
Dahlsrud, A. (2008). How corporate social responsibility is defined: an analysis of 37 definitions, *Corporate Social Responsibility and Environmental Management*, 15, 1–13.
Darnall, N., Henriques, I. and Sadorsky, P. (2010). Adopting proactive environmental strategy: the influence of stakeholders and firm size, *Journal of Management Studies*, 47(6), 1072–1094.
DEFRA (Department for Environment, Food and Rural Affairs) (2011). *Mainstreaming Sustainable Development: The Government's Vision and What This Means in Practice*, London, DEFRA.
DEFRA (Department for Environment, Food and Rural Affairs) (2015). *Policy Paper 2010 to 2015 Government Policy: Environmental Quality*, London, DEFRA.
Department for Transport (2012). *Draft Aviation Policy Framework*, London, Department for Transport.
Dresner, S. (2008). *The Principles of Sustainability*, London, Earthscan.
EC (European Commission) (2017). *Corporate social responsibility (CSR)*. Online. Available at: http://ec.europa.eu/growth/industry/corporate-social-responsibility/ (accessed 23 February 2017).
EUROCONTROL (2013). *Specification for collaborative environmental management*. Online. Available at: www.eurocontrol.int/articles/collaborative-environmental-management-cem-specification (accessed 23 February 2017).
Friedman, M. (1967). The monetary theory and policy of Henry Simons, *Journal of Law and Economy*, 10, 1–13.
GRI (Global Reporting Initiative) (2009) *A Snapshot of Sustainability Reporting in the Airports Sector*, Amsterdam, GRI.
GRI (Global Reporting Initiative) (2017). *GRI's sustainability reporting standards*. Online. Available at: www.globalreporting.org/standards/ (accessed 23 February 2017).
Hansell, A.L., Blangiardo, M., Fortunato, L., Floud, S., de Hoogh, K., Fecht, D., et al. (2013). Aircraft noise and cardiovascular disease near Heathrow Airport in London: small area study, *BMJ* 2013, 347: f5432.

Hawken, P. (2010). *The Ecology of Commerce: A Declaration of Sustainability*, 2nd edition, New York, HarperCollins.

Heathrow Airport Limited (2017a) *Responsible Heathrow*. Online. Available at: www.heathrow.com/company/community-and-environment/responsible-heathrow (accessed 23 February 2017).

Heathrow Airport Limited (2017b). *Heathrow 2.0: Our plan for sustainable growth*. Online. Available at: https://your.heathrow.com/sustainability/ (accessed 3 March 2017).

Heathrow Airport Limited (2017c). *Waste and water*. Online. Available at: www.heathrow.com/company/community-and-environment/responsible-heathrow/reducing-environmental-impacts/waste-and-water (accessed 23 February 2017).

Heathrow Airport Limited (2017d). *Partnerships*. Online. Available at: www.heathrow.com/company/community-and-environment/responsible-heathrow/partnerships (accessed 23 February 2017).

HM Government (2008). *Climate Change Act 2008*, London, The Stationery Office.

Holmberg, J. (1998). Backcasting: a natural step in operationalizing sustainable development, *Greener Management International*, Autumn, 30.

Hubbard, G. (2009). Measuring organizational performance: beyond the triple bottom line, *Business Strategy and the Environment*, 18, 177–191.

ICAO (International Civil Aviation Organisation) (2004). *Noise certification workshop. Session 4: documentation. History of noise certification documentation*. Online. Available at: www.icao.int/Meetings/EnvironmentalWorkshops/Documents/NoiseCertificationWorkshop-2004/bip4_01.pdf (accessed 23 February 2017).

IPCC (Intergovernmental Panel on Climate Change) (1999) – J.E. Penner, D.H. Lister, D.J. Griggs, D.J. Dokken and M. McFarland (eds). *IPCC Special Report: Aviation and the Global Atmosphere*, Cambridge, Cambridge University Press.

ISO (International Organisation for Standardisation) (2015). *Environmental Management Systems: Requirements with Guidance for Use*, Geneva, ISO.

Janić, M. (2007). *The Sustainability of Air Transportation: A Quantitative Analysis and Assessment*, Farnham, Ashgate.

Koç, S. and Durmaz, V. (2015). Airport corporate sustainability: an analysis of indicators reported in the sustainability practices, *Procedia: Social and Behavioural Sciences*, 181, 158–170.

London City Airport Limited (2017). *CSR*. Online. Available at: www.londoncityairport.com/aboutand corporate/page/csr (accessed 23 February 2017).

MAG (Manchester Airports Group) (2010). *Waste management*. Online. Available at: www.magworld.co.uk/educationpack/waste_management.html (accessed 23 February 2017).

MAG (Manchester Airports Group) (2017a). *Sustainable development*. Online. Available at: www.magworld.co.uk/magweb.nsf/All+Content/sustainabledevelopment (accessed 23 February 2017).

MAG (Manchester Airports Group) (2017b). *Sustainable development plan*. Online. Available at: www.manchesterairport.co.uk/about-us/sustainable-development-plan/ (accessed 23 February 2017).

Mitie (2014). *Mitie and Birmingham Airport partnership recycles over 70 tonnes of food waste*. Online. Available at: www.mitie.com/news-centre/news/2014/mitie-and-birmingham-airport-partnership-recycles-over-70-tonnes-of-food-waste (accessed 23 February 2017).

OECD (Organisation for Economic Co-operation and Development) (2012). *The Organisation for Economic Co-operation and Development environmental outlook to 2050: the consequences of inaction*. Online. Available at: www.oecd.org/env/indicators-modelling-outlooks/49846090.pdf (accessed 23 February 2017).

Paling, C., Hooper, P.D. and Thomas, C. (2014). The sustainability of air transport. In: A. Goetz and L. Budd (eds). *The Geographies of Air Transport*, Farnham, Ashgate.

Rawson, R. and Hooper, P.D. (2012). The importance of stakeholder participation to sustainable airport master planning in the UK, *Environmental Development*, 2, 36–47.

Secretariat of the Convention on Biological Diversity (2010). *Global Biodiversity Outlook 3*, Montreal, Secretariat of the Convention on Biological Diversity.

Skouloudis, A., Evangelinos, K. and Moraitis, S. (2012). Accountability and stakeholder engagement in the airport industry: an assessment of airports' CSR reports, *Journal of Air Transport Management*, 18(1), 16–20.

Steurer, R., Langer, M.E., Konrad, A. and Martinuzzi, A. (2005). Corporations, stakeholders and sustainable development 1: a theoretical exploration of business-society relations, *Journal of Business Ethics*, 61, 263–281.

Thomas, C. and Hooper, P. (2013). Sustainable development and environmental capacity of airports. In: N.J. Ashford, H.P.M. Stanton, C.A. Moore, P. Coutu and J.R. Beasley (eds). *Airport Operations*, 3rd edition, New York, McGraw-Hill.

Thomas, C.S., Maughan, J.A., Hooper, P.D. and Hume, K.I. (2010). Aircraft noise and community impacts. In: R. Blockley and W. Shyy (eds). *Encyclopaedia of Aerospace Engineering: Volume 6 Environmental Impact, Manufacturing and Operations*, New Jersey, John Wiley & Sons.

Tomer, J.F. (1999). *The Human Firm: A Socio-Economic Analysis of Its Behaviour and Potential in a New Economic Age*, Routledge, London.

TRB (Transportation Research Board of the National Academies) (2015). *Understanding Airport Air Quality and Public Health Studies*, Washington, DC, TRB.

UN (United Nations) (2016). *Marrakech Climate Change Conference: November 2016*. Online. Available at: http://unfccc.int/meetings/marrakech_nov_2016/meeting/9567.php (accessed 23 February 2017).

Upham, P. (2001). A comparison of sustainability theory with UK and European airports policy and practice, *Journal of Environmental Management*, 63, 237–248.

Upham, P., Thomas, C., Gillingwater, D. and Raper, D. (2003). Environmental capacity and airport operations: current issues and future prospects, *Journal of Air Transport Management*, 9, 145–151.

Wigstrand, I. (2010). *The ATES Project: a sustainable solution for Stockholm-Arlanda Airport*. Online. Available at: http://intraweb.stockton.edu/eyos/energy_studies/content/docs/effstock09/Session_6_3_ATES_Applications/55.pdf (accessed 23 February 2017).

World Bank (2017). *Corporate responsibility*. Online. Available at: www.worldbank.org/en/about/what-we-do/crinfo (accessed 23 February 2017).

WRAP (Waste and Resources Action Programme) (2012). *Case study: Edinburgh Airport*. Online. Available at: www.wrap.org.uk/sites/files/wrap/ROTG_ENG_Case_Study_EdinAir_2P.pdf (accessed 23 February 2017).

Zurich Airport (2010). *Aircraft emission charges Zurich Airport*. Online. Available at: www.zurich-airport.com/the-company/noise-policy-and-the-environment/air-quality/ (accessed 23 February 2017).

# Part III
# Key selected themes

# Patterns and drivers of demand for air transport

*Xingwu Zheng and Anne Graham*

## Introduction

There is extensive coverage in both the academic and industry literature discussing the growth and patterns of air travel demand, and a number of the chapters in this book raise issues related to this (e.g. see Chapters 1, 2 and 5). However, there is a need to have a separate chapter here to consider the important features of air transport demand in depth as a detailed understanding of these is crucial for the successful management of the industry.

This chapter begins by considering the general growth patterns and characteristics of air transport demand. This leads onto an assessment of the drivers of demand and a discussion of elasticities, particularly in relation to income and price. The next section then examines how this understanding of drivers is incorporated into demand models and forecasts. Following on from this there is a detailed specific analysis of demand in emerging markets as these are predicted to experience very significant growth in the future. This is undertaken by selecting a mix of eight very different emerging markets. The final concluding section looks to the future, reflecting on the main findings of this chapter.

## Growth and patterns of air transport demand

Tables 19.1 and 19.2 summarise the general aggregate demand trends since 1990. There has been resilience and continual growth in air transport demand, albeit at a slower pace in more recent years, and a shift away from the historic dominant markets such as North America and Europe, to emerging markets in Asia and elsewhere. Revenue passenger kilometres (RPKs) have increased at a faster rate than passengers, indicating a growth in average length of haul, and load factors have risen, undoubtedly benefitting from more sophisticated yield management strategies and new airline business models such as low cost carriers (LCCs). In 2015, passenger traffic represented three-quarters of all revenue tonne kilometres (RTKs) and international traffic accounted for just over two-thirds of all traffic, having increased at a faster rate than domestic traffic, which was traditionally dominated by flights in the United States (US).

In terms of travel participation or the propensity to fly for different markets, IATA (2014) found that in 2013, the average air trips per passenger per year was 1.48 for those with high

Xingwu Zheng and Anne Graham

*Table 19.1* Global scheduled air transport demand, 1990 to 2015

|  | 1990 | 2000 | 2010 | 2015 | Average annual growth 1990–2015 |
|---|---|---|---|---|---|
| Passengers (million) | 1,165 | 1,672 | 2,698 | 3,533 | 4.5 |
| RPKs (million) | 1,894,020 | 3,037,530 | 4,910,282 | 6,601,465 | 5.1 |
| FTKs (million) | 58,830 | 118,080 | 186,230 | 197,549 | 5.0 |
| Total RTKs (million) | 235,240 | 403,960 | 643,670 | 817,030 | 5.1 |
| Domestic RTKs (million) | 104,460 | 130,870 | 196,275 | 250,368 | 3.6 |
| International RTKs (million) | 130,780 | 273,090 | 447,395 | 566,662 | 6.0 |
| Passenger load factor (%) | 68 | 71 | 78 | 80 | |

*Source*: ICAO (1992, 2001, 2011, 2016a).

*Table 19.2* Regional distribution of scheduled air transport demand (% RTKs), 1990 to 2015

|  | 1990 | 2000 | 2010 | 2015 |
|---|---|---|---|---|
| Europe | 32 | 28 | 25 | 26 |
| Africa | 2 | 2 | 3 | 2 |
| Middle East | 3 | 3 | 9 | 11 |
| Asia-Pacific | 20 | 27 | 29 | 33 |
| North America | 38 | 36 | 30 | 23 |
| Latin America and the Caribbean | 5 | 4 | 5 | 5 |
| Total | 100 | 100 | 100 | 100 |

*Source*: ICAO (1992, 2001, 2011, 2016a).

income, 0.29 for middle-income passengers, but only 0.04 for those with low income. For the same year, Airbus (2014) estimated that the equivalent figure for passengers originating in perspective geographic regions ranged from 1.59 in North America, 0.99 in Europe, 0.38 in the Middle East, 0.36 in Latin America and the Caribbean, 0.25 in the CIS, 0.24 in Asia-Pacific, and only 0.06 in Africa.

## Drivers of air transport demand

In order to understand the reasons for these patterns of air traffic, it is essential to appreciate the drivers of demand that have already been introduced in Chapter 11. These drivers are frequently the subject of much debate, and typically this involves distinguishing between those drivers outside and those inside the scope of airline control (Valdes, 2015). They have been classified in a number of different ways, with a useful distinction being between geo-economic and service-related categories, as identified by Jorge-Calderon (1997). He stated that the geo-economic categories could be subdivided between activity factors and locational factors. Activity factors typically cover the nature and level of trade and income, levels of personal disposable income, and often population size as well. As discussed below, these are very common variables used in demand models and forecasting. Activity factors may also include other economic, social and demographic influences, such as population and age distribution; historical, cultural and educational characteristics; and social factors such as length of paid holidays and attitudes to travel. The locational factors relate to where the air transport takes place, arguably the most common feature being the distance between origin and destinations, but this can also include the attraction of the destination for leisure or business tourism markets, proximity of competing airports, and the extent of surface transport competition.

Service-related variables are now seen as more important than in the past as the air transport environment has progressively become more competitive and deregulated. These cover both the quality of airline and airport services and the fare that is paid (see also Chapters 13 and 22). The quality aspects are typically related to frequency, schedules and timings; aircraft size and type; in-flight and airport service and amenities; frequent flyer programmes; and other factors, such as the airline/airport's image or safety/security reputation. Then there is the price influence, which often can be very important, but is increasingly very difficult to measure in a dynamic industry where there are multiple fares on offer. These will be linked to the price of fuel and exchange rates. The cost and convenience of alternative modes of transport may also play a role, as may the prices of complementary products such as hotels.

Numerous studies of air transport demand have chosen to consider some of these different drivers, with the specific choice of variables usually being determined by the market under consideration together with practical data availability issues. Traditionally, much of this research was related to the US because of its long history of aviation industry development (Wang and Song, 2010), but now a much broader coverage exists. For example, country studies have been undertaken for Australia (Hensher, 2002), Brazil (Marazzo et al., 2010), China (Hu et al., 2015), Greece (Tsekeris, 2009), India (Srinidhi and Manrai, 2014), Saudi Arabia (Abed et al., 2001), Sweden (Kopsch, 2012), and many more. The research of Valdes (2015) interestingly was one of the first to specialise in middle-income countries rather than including advanced economies. Other research concerning demand has focused on specific structural changes and public policies factors such as liberalisation (Ismaila et al., 2014; Oum et al., 2009; Piermartini and Rousova, 2008), carbon emission charging (Pagoni and Psaraki-Kalouptsidi, 2016), or high-speed train competition (Inoue et al., 2015; Ortúzar and Simonetti, 2008), to mention just a few. Meanwhile, Bieger et al. (2007) considered the effect of customer value, Graham (2006) assessed whether the relationship with key variables had fundamentally changed, and Wadud (2014) delved more deeply to try to understand the complex links between demand, air fare and fuel price.

Of particular significance in recent years has been the impact of 'shock' or crisis/disaster events. These are associated with terrorist attacks, war or internal conflict, climatic incidents, crime waves or health concerns. Such events have always been present, but now appear to be occurring more often and with greater severity, and so are creating a more volatile or uncertain market environment. Different approaches have been adopted here; for example, Njegovan (2006a) assessed all shocks over a certain time period to assess the impact on United Kingom (UK) air travel demand, while one of the most significant shocks of recent times, namely 9/11, has been separately analysed by, among others, Guzhva and Pagiavlas (2004) and Ito and Lee (2005a) for the US market, and Ito and Lee (2005b) for international air travel.

In looking at the drivers of demand, arguably it is equally important to assess the factors that also inhibit people from flying. However, these are more rarely considered, partly because data collection in this area is much more challenging. Graham and Metz (2017) found that such non-flyers and infrequent flyers make up a heterogeneous consumer group whose non-flying is influenced more by budget constraints and personal circumstances than specific aviation factors, such as concerns about air travel (e.g. safety, security), accessibility and the impact of the environment. More confirmation of these findings is needed.

## Demand elasticities

Shifting the focus back to the demand for flying, it was explained in Chapter 11 that the responsiveness of demand to these drivers can be measured by demand elasticities. These typically vary between different market segments by purpose; for example, business, holiday, visiting friends and relatives (VFR), trip length (e.g. short-haul, long-haul) and type of travel (e.g. domestic, international). The focus here is on income and price elasticities, as these are some of the most common ones discussed in the literature. Only elasticities for passenger demand are considered here as evidence of elasticities for freight demand is scarcer, with a rare exception being Chi and Baek (2012).

As regards income elasticities, Gallet and Doucouliagos (2014) undertook a meta-regression analysis to quantitatively survey the literature in this area. They found that for the majority of studies, the income elasticity value exceeded 1, suggesting that air travel was a luxury and an immature market, with only 12 of the 40 studies reporting mean income elasticity estimates of less than 1. Overall, they estimated an income elasticity of 1.186. Moreover, the research demonstrated that the elasticities were largely insensitive to different global regions, but were higher for international flights rather than domestic. Earlier, Gillen et al. (2002) looked at 21 studies and found a fairly similar median elasticity value of 1.39. Meanwhile, InterVISTAS (2007) and IATA (2008) discussed a review of 23 papers, and likewise observed that virtually all of these estimated income elasticities were above 1, generally between 1 and 2. They also estimated their own income elasticities for short-haul, medium-haul, long-haul and very long-haul markets, separately considering developed and developing economies, and again found values in this range (with the exception of very long-haul with values of 2 to 2.5). So the broad finding from the research in this area indicates that generally, air travel demand still increases at a higher rate than incomes.

It has been argued that when this ceases to be the case, air transport demand will be mature. Indeed, Graham (2000) suggested a theoretical five-stage model of maturity and saturation using income elasticities, with stage 4 (full maturity) when the elasticity value is 1, and stage 5 (saturation) when the elasticity value is 0. EUROCONTROL (2013) used a similar approach but had slightly different definitions. They assumed that if an increase in income produced a smaller increase in demand, then the market was becoming mature, whereas if an increase in income caused no increase in demand, then the market was totally mature. InterVISTAS (2007) found short- and medium-haul elasticities of 1.8 for developing economies but 1.3 to 1.4 for developed economies. These values will clearly differ by market, an example here being the UK, where overall a value of 1.3 was estimated, but this ranged from 1.0 for foreign business travel to 1.4 for UK leisure travel (Department for Transport, 2013). In looking to the future, assumptions were made to adjust downwards some of these values to take account of maturity.

Looking at price elasticities, Brons et al. (2002) undertook a meta-analysis of 37 studies and found a mean value of $-1.146$. At a more disaggregate level, Gillen et al. (2002) observed median price elasticity values of $-0.26$ for long-haul international business travel, $-0.99$ for long-haul international leisure, $-1.15$ for long-haul domestic business, $-1.12$ for long-haul domestic leisure, $-1.52$ for short- to medium-haul leisure, and $-0.73$ for short- to medium-haul business. InterVISTAS (2007), in their comparative study of 23 papers, also confirmed that, as expected, business travellers are less sensitive to fare changes than leisure travellers, and that fare elasticities on short-haul routes were generally higher than on long-haul routes. In part, they argued that this reflected the opportunity for intermodal substitution on short-haul routes. Some of the studies that they reviewed also supported the idea that the demand elasticity faced by individual airlines is higher than that faced by the whole market. With their own new analysis, the following price elasticities were estimated: $-1.4$ for the route level, $-0.8$ for the national level, and

−0.6 for the supranational level. Using the UK as a national example, this matches quite closely the more disaggregate estimates of the Department of Transport (2013), namely UK resident business −0.2, UK resident leisure −0.7, foreign business −0.2, foreign leisure −0.6, and domestic −0.5. Njegovan (2006b) also calculated a value of −0.7 for the UK market.

## Demand models and forecasts

Many of the demand drivers discussed above and the associated elasticity values have been key inputs for air transport demand and forecasting models. Typically, the aggregate demand will be linked to macroeconomic variables such as income, trade and fuel price, whereas route/country forecasts will try to consider more specific drivers such as air fares, competing transport modes and service-related variables, as well as more detailed economic data related to the origin and destination in question. Combining some of these drivers into a time-series econometric model is a popular and well-established means of forecasting future demand (ACRP, 2007). If both time-series and cross-sectional data can be mixed in a panel, this can often produce more robust findings, and so panel data studies have become more popular in recent years when the data has been available.

There are numerous academic examples of such econometric forecasts covering a diverse range of different countries and markets. For the industry, an example of an aggregate but relatively simple forecast is that of ICAO (2016b). The data set for this consisted of RPKs and FTKs, for both international and domestic operations, at city pair and carrier level from 1995 to 2012. The passenger forecasts were segmented into a total of 50 route groups (40 international and 10 domestic), and in order to obtain the flexibility of having different elasticity estimates based on income level and market maturity, these were assigned to six different tiers based on World Bank definitions of economies. For the freight forecasts, six regions rather than the 50 route groups were used. The final passenger model contained the variables' real gross domestic product (GDP) per capita and oil prices as a proxy for cost of air travel, together with dummy variables for shock events. The freight model was just based on GDP per capita.

Other industry forecasts cover more variables; for example, Airbus (2017) listed up to 15 for their forecasts, including GDP, private consumption, exports and imports, population, working age population, employment, crude oil price, as well as other drivers such as the evolution of airline business models, liberalisation and tourism development. An example of a more disaggregate forecast can be found in the UK (Department of Transport, 2013), which had 19 market sectors classified by residence, purpose and foreign origin and destination, and with explanatory variables related to GDP, consumption, imports and exports, fares, exchange rates, and dummies, when relevant.

As highlighted in Chapter 11, a special type of econometric model is the gravity model, which is in quite common use for explaining trade flows between countries. It has had some limited application in air transport, particularly in examining the impact of air transport policy and other determinants on bilateral air traffic flows. Examples include Bhadra and Kee (2008), Gillen and Hazledine (2015), Grosche et al. (2007) and Matsumoto (2007). A rare example of the application to the freight market can be found with the research of Alexander and Merkert (2017). However, in their review of such models, Zhang et al. (2018) were critical in that this research had not accounted for the advances in empirical estimation techniques developed in international economics, in particular with most studies failing to take account of multilateral resistance, which can be interpreted as the average trade costs with all trading countries.

Many of the modelling approaches discussed above can be applied on an aggregate or a disaggregated or route/airport level. However, in cases when the disaggregated market is being considered, there is often a need to understand individual passenger behaviour and the choices that passengers make in terms of choosing airlines, airports and surface access. An increasingly popular way of examining this is by looking at discrete choice models, when there are mutually exclusive alternatives to be considered, each with an associated utility or attractiveness. Such models work with the principle that the alternative with the highest utility is chosen. These can be calibrated with actual historic data (e.g. bookings), or revealed or stated preferences of passengers, typically through surveys. There are a number of different models that have been used, including binary logit and multinomial logit models, nested logit models and mixed logit models, with the evolution of new model structures allowing for an increasingly realistic representation of behaviour (Garrow, 2010).

Most of the early discrete choice research focused on the distribution of demand across one single dimension, such as specific airport choice with multi-airport systems. As discussed in Chapter 11, airports can affect passenger demand for air travel both in terms of the price and service quality offered. Examples include Pels et al. (2001) and Başar and Bhat (2004), who developed discrete choice models based on the multi-airport system in the San Francisco Bay Area. Another similar case is the research of Hess and Polak (2006), which looked at the combined choice of airport, airline and access mode in the Greater London area. Many of the initial discrete choice studies relied on revealed preference data, but increasingly stated preference data has become more popular, as it enables more data to be used and is more effective in identifying the significant effects of some of the crucial factors, particularly air fares (Hess et al., 2007). Another interesting and more recent development of this approach has been the use of more disaggregated itinerary choice models, which for each city pair can utilise data based on the characteristics of itinerary (e.g. price, departure/arrival times, connections, travel distance), the characteristics of passengers (e.g. income, age, gender) and the characteristics of the trip (e.g. business versus leisure, domestic versus international) (Abdelghany and Abdelghany, 2009; Coldren and Koppelman, 2005).

Rather than including a range of explanatory variables, there are also examples of time-series models of varying levels of sophistication, which use the basic assumption that demand is primarily a function of time. These can include different methods such as autoregressive moving averages (e.g. autoregressive integrated moving average [ARIMA] models), exponential smoothing techniques or Box Jenkins methods. They have been applied on a country basis, for example in the UK with Grubb and Mason (2001) and Coshall (2006), and in Portugal with Samagaio and Wolters (2010), as well as in a wider context, for instance with Dantas et al. (2017), who combined bootstrap aggregating with time-series analysis for 11 European countries, together with Australia, Brazil and the US.

In addition to these quantitative forecasting methods, some qualitative approaches have also been used, but not so commonly. Arguably the most formal of these is the Delphi method, which involves the recruitment of a number of experts and then uses an iterative process to reach consensual forecasts. A rare case of its use in the literature can be found with Mason and Alamdari (2007), who examined certain features of the European air transport market for the next 10 to 15 years by using 26 air transport experts. Moreover, faced with growing uncertainly within the world economy and air transport environment, there has been an increased use of different scenarios, often derived from more qualitative research, to inform quantitative models. For example, EUROCONTROL (2013) used four scenarios for their forecasts, namely global growth, regulated growth, happy localism and fragmenting world, while the Airports Commission in the UK, in considering the need for extra runway capacity in the London area, used five scenarios, defined as assessment of need, global growth, relative decline of Europe, low cost is king and global fragmentation (Airports Commission, 2015).

All these methods and some other less popular ones are explained in a number of practical guides produced by various industry stakeholders such as ACI (2011, 2016a), ACRP (2007), ICAO (2006) and OECD (2016). The overall message from these is that all the forecasts vary considerably in terms of scope, sophistication and data requirements, and hence there is no overarching best practice method. For assessing accuracy, ACRP (2007) provided tools for evaluating the forecasts, while ACI (2016a) emphasised the fact that the various air transport sectors have different time frames for long-term/strategic forecasts, namely: for airlines, it is three to five years; for airports and manufacturers, 20 to 25 years; and for civil aviation authorities. it is typically 30 to 40 years. OECD (2016) argued that the track record of airport demand forecasting appeared to be mixed, and suggested that the forecasts needed to be improved by: (a) using qualitative methods to analyse the key drivers of airport demand; (b) using expert guidance to help interpret the quantitative results (perhaps formalised through methods such as the Delphi technique); (c) quality-assuring the analysis and countering the risks of optimism bias; and (d) reflecting the risks and uncertainties that arise in even the best forecasts. Here, they argued that more use of scenario analysis, as mentioned above, could be effective.

## Air transport demand in emerging markets

### Definition of emerging markets

This section considers in detail emerging markets, as these are predicted to experience some of the most significant growth in the future. However, as discussed in Chapter 7, there is actually no universally agreed definition for such markets, although the term has been widely used since the 1980s, when Agtmael (1984) was involved in the development of the World Bank's International Finance Corporation (IFC) emerging markets database. At that time, Errunza (1983) argued that the emergence of capital markets in emerging markets was considered by some as one of the indicators of a developing country's ascendency into industrial development, while later on Hoskisson et al. (2000) stressed that emerging markets were often understood to mean emerging stock markets in international finance. Currently, according to the *Financial Times* (2017), emerging market is a term that investors use to describe a developing country in which investment would be expected to achieve higher returns but be accompanied by greater risk.

There are various global index providers, including the International Monetary Fund (IMF), Financial Times Stock Exchange (FTSE), MSCI, and Columbia University Emerging Market Global Players (EMGP), that try to define a commonly accepted list of emerging markets (see Table 19.3). However, these index providers fail to agree on precisely what constitutes an emerging market. As an example of the inconsistencies in the definitions, South Korea, a relatively developed market, is an emerging market in the MSCI's index, while the FTSE and S&P indexes exclude it. Both the IMF and the United Nations Conference on Trade and Development (UNCATD) also provide a country or economy classification, but do not provide precise details concerning emerging markets.

It is evident that there are a large number of diverse countries that potentially could be covered in an emerging markets analysis, but this would be too extensive for this chapter. Instead, Brazil, China, India, Mexico, the Philippines, Russia, South Africa and Turkey, which are consistently considered to be emerging markets by virtually all the global index providers in Table 19.3, will be the focus here. These specific emerging markets in air transport share some common characteristics, such as the relative fast growth of their economy, rapid development of air transport, the emergence of new airlines, and significant changes in their domestic and international air transport institutions.

Xingwu Zheng and Anne Graham

Table 19.3 Emerging markets by different sources

| Markets | BRICS+ Next Eleven¹ | FTSE | MSCI | S&P | EM bond index | Russell | Columbia University EMGP |
|---|---|---|---|---|---|---|---|
| Argentina | | | | | ✓ | | ✓ |
| Bangladesh | ✓ | ✓ | ✓ | ✓ | ✓ | | |
| Brazil | ✓ | ✓ | ✓ | ✓ | ✓ | ✓ | ✓ |
| Bulgaria | | | | | | | |
| Chile | | ✓ | ✓ | ✓ | ✓ | ✓ | ✓ |
| China | ✓ | ✓ | ✓ | ✓ | ✓ | ✓ | ✓ |
| Chinese Taipei | | ✓ | ✓ | ✓ | ✓ | ✓ | ✓ |
| Colombia | | ✓ | ✓ | ✓ | ✓ | ✓ | ✓ |
| Czech Republic | | ✓ | ✓ | ✓ | ✓ | ✓ | |
| Egypt | ✓ | ✓ | ✓ | ✓ | | | ✓ |
| Greece | | ✓ | ✓ | ✓ | | ✓ | |
| Hungary | | ✓ | ✓ | ✓ | ✓ | ✓ | ✓ |
| India | ✓ | ✓ | ✓ | ✓ | ✓ | ✓ | ✓ |
| Indonesia | ✓ | ✓ | ✓ | ✓ | | ✓ | |
| Iran | ✓ | | | | ✓ | | |
| Israel | | | | | ✓ | | ✓ |
| Malaysia | | ✓ | ✓ | ✓ | | ✓ | |
| Mauritius | | | | | ✓ | | ✓ |
| Mexico | ✓ | ✓ | ✓ | ✓ | ✓ | ✓ | ✓ |
| Nigeria | ✓ | | | | ✓ | | |
| Oman | | | | | ✓ | | |
| Pakistan | ✓ | ✓ | | | ✓ | | |
| Peru | | ✓ | ✓ | ✓ | ✓ | ✓ | |
| Philippines | ✓ | ✓ | ✓ | ✓ | ✓ | ✓ | ✓ |
| Poland | | ✓ | ✓ | ✓ | ✓ | ✓ | ✓ |
| Qatar | | | ✓ | | ✓ | | |
| Romania | | | | | ✓ | | |
| Russia | ✓ | ✓ | ✓ | ✓ | | ✓ | ✓ |
| Singapore | | | | | ✓ | | |
| Slovenia | | | | | | | ✓ |
| South Africa | ✓ | ✓ | ✓ | ✓ | ✓ | ✓ | ✓ |
| South Korea | ✓ | ✓ | | | ✓ | ✓ | ✓ |
| Thailand | | ✓ | ✓ | ✓ | ✓ | ✓ | ✓ |
| Turkey | ✓ | ✓ | ✓ | ✓ | ✓ | ✓ | ✓ |
| Ukraine | | | | | ✓ | | |
| United Arab Emirates | | ✓ | ✓ | | ✓ | ✓ | ✓ |
| Venezuela | | | | | ✓ | | |
| Vietnam | ✓ | | | | | | |

*Source:* FTSE (2015), MSCI (2016), S&P Dow Jones (2015), J.P. Morgan (2016), Russell (2016) and Columbia University (2016).

*Note:*
1 BRICS+ Next Eleven refers to the BRIC countries of Brazil, Russia, India and China, plus the Next Eleven countries: Bangladesh, Egypt, Indonesia, Iran, Mexico, Nigeria, Pakistan, the Philippines, Turkey, South Korea and Vietnam.

## Growth and patterns of demand

Generally, during 1990 to 2015, these eight emerging markets maintained a higher GDP growth than that of developed economies, especially China and India (see Table 19.4). In parallel with

Table 19.4 Economic and air transport performance of selected emerging markets

| Market | GDP growth (%) (1990–2015) | RTK growth (%) (1990–2015) | Number of airlines ranked in the top 100 by revenue (2015) | ALI (2006) |
|---|---|---|---|---|
| Brazil | 2.7 | 5.1 | 2 | 10.2 |
| China | 9.9 | 15.1 | 9 | 3.7 |
| India | 6.6 | 7.9 | 3 | 6.2 |
| Mexico | 2.6 | 5.9 | 2 | 7.4 |
| Philippines | 4.2 | 5.9 | 2 | 8.5 |
| Russia | 3.6 (2000–2015) | 10.1 (2000–2014) | 3 | 5.8 |
| South Africa | 2.5 | 4.5 | 1 | 8.7 |
| Turkey | 3.9 | 15.4 | 3 | 8.9 |

Source: Airline Business (2016), ICAO (1992, 2016a), IMF (2016) and WTO (2006).

GDP growth, air transport (RTKs) in the majority of these emerging markets also experienced a much higher growth than the world average of 5.1 per cent, with Turkey and China having the highest values. The number of airlines from these emerging markets ranked in the top 100 worldwide by revenue in Airline Business (2016) totalled 26 in 2015, more than a quarter of the top 100. Moreover, many of the strict restrictions on international air transport are now being gradually removed in these areas. The degree of liberalisation can be measured by the Air or ASA (air service agreement) Liberalisation Index (ALI), which values each individual air service agreement between 0 for the very restrictive ones and 50 for the very open ones. According to the WTO (2006), the weighted ALI in most of the selected emerging markets failed to reach the average world level of 8.96 in 2006, but since then the situation has changed. While complete comparative up-to-date figures are not readily available, China, for example, had an ALI in 2015 of above 10 points.[1]

Table 19.5 shows in more detail how generally the growth rates of RTKs in emerging markets have been higher than the world average. Overall, between 1990 and 2015, they were higher than 5 per cent in all the selected emerging markets except for South Africa. China and Turkey experienced double-digit growth in both domestic and international markets during

Table 19.5 Average annual growth rates (%) of selected emerging markets, 1990 to 2015

| Market | RTK growth | | | RPK growth | | | FTK growth | | |
|---|---|---|---|---|---|---|---|---|---|
| | Total | Dom. | Int. | Total | Dom. | Int. | Total | Dom. | Int. |
| Brazil | 5.1 | 6.7 | 3.1 | 6.1 | 7.3 | 3.8 | 1.3 | 1.1 | 1.5 |
| China | 15.1 | 14.9 | 15.3 | 14.8 | 14.7 | 15.0 | 14.2 | 13.1 | 14.8 |
| India | 7.9 | 9.6 | 6.6 | 8.9 | 9.7 | 8.1 | 4.1 | 7.8 | 3.0 |
| Mexico | 5.9 | 6.3 | 5.6 | 5.2 | 5.6 | 4.7 | 6.6 | 2.6 | 8.1 |
| Philippines | 5.9 | 8.4 | 5.4 | 6.7 | 8.4 | 6.2 | 1.8 | 2.4 | 1.7 |
| Russia | 10.1 | 8.8 | 11.5 | 10.0 | 9.3 | 10.9 | 10.7 | 4.1 | 12.6 |
| South Africa | 4.5 | 1.7 | 5.7 | 4.8 | 4.1 | 5.4 | 5.8 | 1.2 | 6.5 |
| Turkey | 15.4 | 14.5 | 15.6 | 14.9 | 13.9 | 15.2 | 14.4 | 4.7 | 14.7 |
| World | 5.1 | 3.6 | 6.0 | 5.1 | 3.7 | 6.3 | 5.0 | 3.1 | 5.3 |

Source: ICAO (1992, 2016a).

Note: As the Soviet Union was broken up in 1990, figures for Russia are from 2000 to 2015.

*Table 19.6* Domestic demand shares (%) of selected emerging markets, 1990 and 2015

| Market | 1990 | | | 2015 | | |
|---|---|---|---|---|---|---|
| | RTK | RPK | FTK | RTK | RPK | FTK |
| Brazil | 52.6 | 55.4 | 36.3 | 68.5 | 76.0 | 36.0 |
| China | 67.6 | 77.6 | 39.6 | 65.8 | 76.6 | 31.4 |
| India | 34.6 | 45.6 | 15.2 | 51.2 | 54.5 | 35.6 |
| Mexico | 47.6 | 50.0 | 51.4 | 52.3 | 55.5 | 15.8 |
| Philippines | 13.6 | 17.8 | 13.7 | 24.2 | 26.4 | 15.9 |
| Russia | 92.0 | 92.7 | 85.2 | 44.8 | 53.8 | 13.3 |
| South Africa | 41.7 | 46.9 | 20.5 | 21.3 | 39.2 | 6.8 |
| Turkey | 20.0 | 24.7 | 8.0 | 16.6 | 19.5 | 0.9 |
| World | 44.4 | 52.8 | 21.2 | 30.6 | 37.3 | 13.7 |

*Source*: ICAO (1992, 2016a).

that period. Brazil, India, Mexico and the Philippines experienced a higher growth rate in domestic RTKs than international, while China, Russia, South Africa and Turkey maintained much higher growth in international RTKs. However, in terms of RPK growth, most of the emerging markets had higher domestic versus international growth rates, except for China, South Africa and Turkey, while in terms of FTKs, only India and the Philippines achieved higher growth in domestic traffic.

This means that the domestic demand share in RTKs for half of the eight emerging markets increased during 1990 to 2015, but decreased for China, Russia, South Africa and Turkey. This share of RTKs in Brazil and China was over 65 per cent, while for South Africa it was under 25 per cent (see Table 19.6). In terms of passenger demand (RPKs), the emerging markets can be divided into two groups for 2015. One includes Brazil, China, India, Mexico and Russia, where the domestic demand share was over 50 per cent. Among them, the domestic share of Brazil and China was more than 75 per cent. The domestic demand share in the other group (the Philippines, South Africa and Turkey) was no more than 50 per cent, and in the Philippines and Turkey it failed to reach 30 per cent. Russia has been quite different from other emerging markets, as in 1990 the domestic demand dominated, whereas by 2015 the domestic demand share had dropped by half. As regards freight demand (FTKs), all of the eight emerging markets had considerably larger international demand by 2015. The domestic demand share of Russia decreased from 85 per cent in 1990 to 13 per cent in 2015, and in Mexico it dropped from 51 per cent to 16 per cent. The domestic demand for freight in Turkey was minimal in 2015.

## Drivers of demand

As discussed above, there are various drivers of demand that vary according to the market being considered. In this section, initially some findings from different studies are presented for some of the selected individual emerging markets, and then some original econometric analysis is undertaken to estimate the overall effect of key drivers for the chosen sample of emerging markets.

Table 19.7 presents the value of some demand elasticities for previous research. As with many other studies, income and fare elasticities tend to dominate. Other variables include population and foreign direct investment (FDI). A number of the findings match up with other general elasticity research, but some are somewhat inconsistent or not totally as expected. The income elasticities of Brazil, China and Turkey are mostly in line with what has been seen elsewhere,

Table 19.7 Examples of demand elasticities estimated for the selected emerging markets

| Market | Fare | GDP | Income per capita | Population | Inward FDI |
|---|---|---|---|---|---|
| Brazil | −0.245 (Marazzo et al., 2010) | 1978–1997: 1.453 (Alekseev and Seixas, 2002) 1996–2006: 1.661 (Marazzo et al., 2010) | | | |
| China | | 1995–2011: 1.317 (short run) 0.574 (long run) (Yao and Yang, 2012)** 2006–2012: 1.06 (long run) (Hu et al., 2015)** | | | |
| India | 1991–2010: −0.15* (Srinidhi and Manrai, 2014) 2005–2006: −0.157* (Srinidhi, 2010) | 0.125* (Srinidhi and Manrai, 2014) | 0.333* (Srinidhi, 2010; Srinidhi and Manrai, 2014) | 0.161 (Srinidhi, 2010) | 1.027* (Srinidhi and Manrai, 2014) |
| Philippines | | 0.2551 (Mehmood et al., 2015) | | | |
| South Africa | −0.863*** (Baikgaki and Daw, 2013) | 0.3293*** (Baikgaki and Daw, 2013) | | 6.5483*** (Baikgaki and Daw, 2013) | |
| Turkey | | 1.3*** (short run) 2.6*** (long run) (Demirsoy, 2012) | | 0.99*** (short run) 1.3*** (long run) (Demirsoy, 2012) | |

Notes: * international air transport; ** based on provincial GDP; *** domestic air transport. No values available for Mexico and Russia.

and suggest a relatively immature market. Specifically, for Brazil, Alekseev and Seixas (2002) estimated a GDP elasticity of 1.453 for 1978 to 1997, while Marazzo et al. (2010) calculated a fairly similar value of 1.661 between 1966 and 2006. However, in China, the long-term GDP elasticity estimated by Yao and Yang (2012) was much smaller than that calculated by Hu et al. (2015). According to Yao and Yang (2012), but not shown in the table, trade was another main driver of air passenger demand, with a 0.822 elasticity value. Yao and Yang (2012) also found that both GDP and trade were the main factors to stimulate the development of air cargo traffic in China. The elasticity coefficients were 1.12 and 0.67 in the long run, respectively. Unusually, GDP was not found to be the key driver in international air transport development in India (Srinidhi and Manrai, 2014), although income per capita played a more important role. Furthermore, inward FDI was a key influential factor.

Both economic development and population were the main factors to accelerate the growth of air passenger demand in Turkey (Demirsoy, 2012). Such a high GDP elasticity (1.3 in the short run and 2.6 in the long run) may help explain why Turkey achieved similar average traffic growth as in China, even though the average annual GDP growth rate from 1990 to 2015 in Turkey was much smaller than in China. However, usually the elasticity coefficients in the long run are smaller than those in the short run, but it seemed to be the reverse situation for Turkey, which was not explained. Meanwhile, the study of Baikgaki and Daw (2013) showed that population mainly drove the growth of domestic air traffic for passengers in South Africa, indeed more than income (although household consumption rather than GDP was actually used here). As with more general air transport research, fare has been shown to be a key factor to affect some of the emerging markets. Baikgaki and Daw (2013) observed that it played a comparatively important role in South Africa, with a price elasticity of −0.863 − close to the InterVISTAS (2007) national value of −0.8 − compared to around −0.1 to −0.3 in India and Brazil.

An econometric analysis has been undertaken using panel data for the eight emerging markets from 1992 to 2014 to identify the key influences on overall demand, particularly since the review of previous literature was somewhat inconclusive. RPKs and FTKs were used as the dependent variables for passenger and freight traffic. The economy was chosen as a major independent variable, but there were different measures that could have been used, such as GDP, GDP per capita or national income per capita. In relation to passenger traffic, population was also considered to be an important potential driver to include. However, as both GDP and population are aggregate variables, there is a strong relationship between them. To avoid this correlation between GDP and population, GDP per capita and national income per capita were therefore considered as the most appropriate independent variables for the economy in the analysis of RPKs. For FTKs, GDP was used.

As shown previously in Table 19.6, there are some emerging markets where domestic air traffic is less than half the total air traffic. International air services therefore provide the main source of air traffic in those markets. Thus, some variables concerning international relationships were needed. The value of trade in goods and in services were considered the appropriate explanatory variables for the passenger market. With air freight, FDI also plays an important role in current globalisation that has embodied the feature of production fragmentation. Thus, inward FDI and outward FDI were included as independent variables. As the FDI flows can be negative, the FDI stocks for both inward and outward were utilised. Unfortunately, due to unavailability of price data, the estimation could not identify the impact of price or fare on the air passenger traffic. In emerging markets, it is particularly hard to obtain the price information either in aggregate or at the route level.

The data sources were RPKs and FTKs (ICAO's Annual Reports of the Council); GDP, GDP per capita, population and GDP deflator (UN Statistic Division's National Accounts

Table 19.8 The estimation results for RPKs

|  | Model 1 | Model 2 |
|---|---|---|
|  | Lnrpk | Lnrpk |
| Lngdpp | 1.199*** |  |
|  | (10.25) |  |
| Lnnipc |  | 0.748*** |
|  |  | (6.92) |
| Lnpopl | 1.007*** | 0.700*** |
|  | (8.68) | (6.39) |
| Lntrag | 0.113* | 0.301*** |
|  | (1.68) | (4.37) |
| Lntras | −0.00526 | −0.00797** |
|  | (−1.53) | (−2.11) |
| Cons | −20.90*** | −16.15*** |
|  | (−9.57) | (−7.32) |

Notes: $t$ statistics in parentheses; * $p < 0.10$; ** $p < 0.05$; *** $p < 0.01$; gdpp = GDP per capita; nipc = national income per capita; popl = population; trag = trade in goods; tras = trade in services.

Main Aggregates Database); national income per capita (World Bank's World Development Indicators); trade (WTO trade database); and FDI inward and outward stocks (UNCTAD's database of World Investment Reports). All the nominal values in US$ were converted into real values in 2005 US$ with the GDP deflator.

Hausman's test confirmed that the panel data had to be estimated with fixed effects, but as there was heteroscedasticity across the panels and autocorrelation within panels, feasible generalised least square (FGLS) was used to solve these issues. Table 19.8 shows the estimation results for RPKs for the overall eight emerging markets. Model 1 has GDP per capita as a variable and Model 2 has national income per capita.

In line with previous research, economic growth and population growth are key explanatory factors. The coefficient/elasticity of GDP per capita is 1.199, while that of national income per capita is 0.748. In Model 1, the coefficient of population is 1.007, which is larger than that in Model 2. However, it needs noting that from 2003 through to 2014, the annual growth rate of population in China was only 0.5 per cent and in Russia it was negative, while in the same period of time the other emerging markets had a much higher growth rate in population, on average 1.3 per cent. Hence, population growth in China and Russia may not have been as important as in the other eight emerging markets. In addition, the impact of trade in goods is positive in both models, which indicates that this may have stimulated not only the international air passenger traffic, but also the domestic. However, unexpectedly, the coefficients of trade in services are negative, and in Model 1 are not significant. One possible explanation may be that there has been some travel substitution in relation to services. For example, after a year's operation of Disney World in Shanghai, the visitor numbers reached over 10 million. Before the opening of Shanghai Disney World, people in China had to go to Hong Kong, Tokyo, Paris, or even Los Angeles for a comparable trip. Further analysis is required with sub-sectorial data of trade in services to prove this assumption.

RPKs were disaggregated into domestic and international RPKs (see Table 19.9) and an estimation also carried out on domestic RPKs (DRPKs). With the exception of the coefficient of trade in goods in Model 3, which turned out to be insignificant, together with the coefficient

Table 19.9 The estimation results for DRPKs

| | Model 3 | Model 4 |
| --- | --- | --- |
| | Lndrpk | Lndrpk |
| Lngdpp | 1.375*** | |
| | (10.76) | |
| Lnnipc | | 0.983*** |
| | | (8.06) |
| Lnpopl | 1.347*** | 1.052*** |
| | (10.85) | (9.61) |
| Lntrag | 0.0622 | 0.348*** |
| | (0.77) | (3.87) |
| Lntras | −0.00852* | −0.0143** |
| | (−1.75) | (−2.30) |
| Cons | −28.18*** | −26.63*** |
| | (−13.15) | (−15.38) |

Notes: t statistics in parentheses; * $p < 0.10$; ** $p < 0.05$; *** $p < 0.01$; drpk = domestic revenue passenger kilometres.

of trade in services, which became significant, all others remain the same as with the aggregate estimation. However, it is evident that the coefficients of both the economic and population variables have become larger, suggesting that the economy and population are much more important to domestic air passenger traffic than the aggregate total market.

In the estimation of FTKs, two models were used, namely Model 5, which considered total traffic, and Model 6, which only considered domestic traffic (see Table 19.10). As expected, GDP is the key driver to air freight and was more critical to domestic air freight. Trade in goods does not affect domestic air freight, but it does the total, implying that the trade in goods could be a key driver of international air freight. The situation of trade in services is similar, but it appears to decrease the total air freight. Inward FDI seems to reduce domestic air freight but

Table 19.10 The estimation results for FTKs

| | Model 5 | Model 6 |
| --- | --- | --- |
| | Lnftk | Lndftk |
| Lnrgdp | 0.714*** | 1.385*** |
| | (6.28) | (6.63) |
| Lntrag | 0.343*** | 0.139 |
| | (3.44) | (0.88) |
| Lntras | −0.00931* | −0.000595 |
| | (−1.86) | (−0.06) |
| Lnfdii | −0.00612 | −0.152** |
| | (−0.14) | (−2.23) |
| Lnfdio | −0.0142 | 0.0572 |
| | (−0.41) | (1.10) |
| Cons | −7.658*** | −9.262*** |
| | (−4.07) | (−3.26) |

Notes: t statistics in parentheses; * $p < 0.10$; ** $p < 0.05$; *** $p < 0.01$; rgdpp = real GDP; fdii = FDI inward stock; fdio = FDI outward stock.

not the total air freight. As the coefficient of inward FDI for total air freight is very small and insignificant, it could be assumed that inward FDI may favour the development of international air cargo in these emerging markets. Indeed, inward FDI could reduce the domestic FTKs in two ways, namely by lowering the weight of freight carried by air or by shortening the distance for air freight transported. This is because inward FDI could accelerate the updating of the high-technology products such as computers, which could in turn reduce the weight of such high-technology goods that are more likely to be transported by air. Moreover, it could promote the optimisation of geographical distribution of industries or production, which might decrease the air transport distance of freight. More research in this area is again clearly needed.

## Conclusion

This chapter has discussed the main drivers of demand and associated elasticity values, and these will undoubtedly continue to play a key role in determining future demand levels. Whatever method is used to model past and future demand, there is general consensus (as discussed in other parts of this book as well) that overall air transport will continue to grow in the future, with average annual growth rates in the long term (i.e. to 2030–2040) in the range of 3.7 to 4.9 per cent for passengers and passenger kilometres, with slightly lower growth (2.3 to 4.2 per cent) in FTKs (ACI, 2016b; Airbus, 2017; Boeing, 2016; IATA, 2016; ICAO, 2016b). The fastest growth is continued to be predicted in the emerging/developing economies, and indeed Airbus (2017) has estimated an annual growth with these markets of 5.8 per cent, compared to 3.2 per cent for advanced economies, with trips per capita in India and China becoming 0.4 and 1.3, respectively, in 2036, compared to 0.1 and 0.4 in 2016. ACI (2016b) estimated that by 2040, 62 per cent of all passenger movements will be associated with emerging countries, compared to 44 per cent in 2015. This all assumes that supply can keep up with demand, which is a major challenge, and that growing environmental issues, such as those discussed in Chapters 17, 18 and 25, will not deter or prevent passengers from flying.

The specific case study of emerging countries has provided some confirmation of these general trends, but also raised some unanswered questions that need to be investigated. Historically, demand studies have focused on the traditional developed world markets, and so research gaps still exist for some of the less developed and emerging markets that need to be filled. As regards the more mature markets, there is now the question as to whether trends that have been well established in the past will hold equally true in the future, if and when maturity sets in, and to what extent current non-flyers in these markets will fly in the future. While there has been some limited consideration of these issues, it is nevertheless an area that is likely to become more important in future years. Moreover, the more uncertain world and aviation environment that exists suggests that greater use of scenario analysis, and more integration of quantitative and qualitative approaches, will be an appropriate way forward for the future to analyse and predict air transport demand.

## Note

1 Calculated by the author.

## References

Abdelghany, A. and Abdelghany, K. (2009). *Modeling Applications in the Airline Industry*, Farnham, Ashgate.

Abed, S.Y., Ba-Fail, A.O. and Jasimuddin, S.M. (2001). An econometric analysis of international air travel demand in Saudi Arabia, *Journal of Air Transport Management*, 7(3), 143–148.

ACI (Airports Council International) (2011). *ACI Airport Traffic Forecasting Manual: A Practical Guide Addressing Best Practices*, Montreal, ACI.

ACI (Airports Council International) (2016a). *ACI Guide to World Airport Traffic Forecasts*, Montreal, ACI.

ACI (Airports Council International) (2016b). *2016 world airport traffic forecasts infographics*. Online. Available at: www.aci.aero/Publications/ACI-Airport-Economics-and-Statistics/ACI-World-Airport-Traffic-Forecasts-20162040 (accessed 10 December 2016).

ACRP (Airport Cooperative Research Program) (2007). *Airport Aviation Activity Forecasting*, ACRP Synthesis 2, Washington, DC, Transportation Research Board.

Agtmael, A.W.V. (1984). *Emerging Securities Markets: Investment Banking Opportunities in the Developing World*, London, Euromoney Publications.

Airbus (2014). *Global Market Forecast 2014–2033*, Toulouse, Airbus.

Airbus (2017). *Global Market Forecast 2017–2036*, Toulouse, Airbus.

Airline Business (2016). World airline rankings traffic, *Airline Business*, July–August, 44–47.

Airports Commission (2015). *Final Report*, London, Airports Commission.

Alekseev, K.P.G. and Seixas, J.M. (2002). Forecasting the air transport demand for passengers with neural modelling. In: *Neural Networks, Proceedings of the VII Brazilian Symposium on Neural Networks*, Pernambuco.

Alexander, D.W. and Merkert, R. (2017). Challenges to domestic air freight in Australia: evaluating air traffic markets with gravity modelling, *Journal of Air Transport Management*, 61, 41–52.

Baikgaki, O.A. and Daw, O.D. (2013). The determinants of domestic air passenger demand in the Republic of South Africa, *Mediterranean Journal of Social Sciences*, 4(13), 389–396.

Başar, G. and Bhat, C. (2004). A parameterized consideration set model for airport choice: an application to the San Francisco Bay Area, *Transportation Research Part B: Methodological*, 38(10), 889–904.

Bhadra, D. and Kee, J. (2008). Structure and dynamics of the core US air travel markets: a basic empirical analysis of domestic passenger demand, *Journal of Air Transport Management*, 14(1), 27–39.

Bieger, T., Wittmer, A. and Laesser, C. (2007). What is driving the continued growth in demand for air travel? Customer value of air transport, *Journal of Air Transport Management*, 13(1), 31–36.

Boeing (2016). *Current Market Outlook 2016–2035*, Seattle, WA, Boeing.

Brons, M., Pels, E., Nijkamp, P. and Rietveld, P. (2002). Price elasticities of demand for passenger air travel: a meta-analysis, *Journal of Air Transport Management*, 8(3), 165–175.

Chi, J. and Baek, J. (2012). Price and income elasticities of demand for air transportation: empirical evidence from US airfreight industry, *Journal of Air Transport Management*, 20, 18–19.

Coldren, G.M. and Koppelman, F.S. (2005). Modeling the competition among air-travel itinerary shares: GEV model development, *Transportation Research Part A: Policy and Practice*, 39(4), 345–365.

Columbia University (2016). *Columbia University Emerging Market Global Players (EMGP)*. Online. Available at: http://ccsi.columbia.edu/publications/emgp/ (accessed 1 August 2016).

Coshall, J. (2006). Time series analyses of UK outbound travel by air, *Journal of Travel Research*, 44(3), 335–347.

Dantas, T.M., Oliveira, F.L.C. and Repolho, H.M.V. (2017). Air transportation demand forecast through Bagging Holt Winters methods, *Journal of Air Transport Management*, 59, 116–123.

Demirsoy, C. (2012). *Analysis of Stimulated Domestic Air Transport Demand in Turkey: What Are the Drivers?* Masters Research Thesis, Rotterdam, Erasmus University Rotterdam.

Department for Transport (2013). *UK Aviation Forecasts*, London, Department for Transport.

Errunza, V.R. (1983). Emerging markets: a new opportunity for improving global portfolio performance, *Financial Analysts Journal*, 39(5), 51–58.

EUROCONTROL (2013). *Challenges of Growth 2013 Summary Report*, Brussels, EUROCONTROL.

*Financial Times* (2017). *Definition of emerging markets*. Online. Available at: http://lexicon.ft.com/Term?term=emerging-markets (accessed 10 April 2017).

FTSE (Financial Times Stock Exchange) (2015). *FTSE annual country classification review*. Online. Available at: www.ftse.com/products/downloads/ftse-country-classification-update_latest.pdf (accessed August 2016).

Gallet, C.A. and Doucouliagos, H. (2014). The income elasticity of air travel: a meta-analysis, *Annals of Tourism Research*, 49, 141–155.

Garrow, L.A. (2010). *Discrete Choice Modelling and Air Travel Demand: Theory and Applications*, Farnham, Ashgate.

Gillen, D. and Hazledine, T. (2015). The economics and geography of regional airline services in six countries, *Journal of Transport Geography*, 46, 129–136.

Gillen, D.W., Morrison, W.G. and Stewart, C. (2002). *Air travel demand elasticities: concepts, issues and measurement*. Online. Available at: www.fin.gc.ca/consultresp/airtravel/airtravstdy_-eng.asp (accessed 30 September 2016).

Graham, A. (2000). Demand for leisure air travel and limits to growth, *Journal of Air Transport Management*, 6(2), 109–118.

Graham, A. (2006). Have the major forces driving leisure airline traffic changed? *Journal of Air Transport Management*, 12(1), 14–20.

Graham, A. and Metz, D. (2017). Limits to air travel growth: the case of infrequent flyers, *Journal of Air Transport Management*, 62, 109–120.

Grosche, T., Rothlauf, F. and Heinzl, A. (2007). Gravity models for airline passenger volume estimation, *Journal of Air Transport Management*, 13(4), 175–183.

Grubb, H. and Mason, A. (2001). Long lead-time forecasting of UK air passengers by Holt–Winters methods with damped trend, *International Journal of Forecasting*, 17(1), 71–82.

Guzhva, V.S. and Pagiavlas, N. (2004). US commercial airline performance after September 11, 2001: decomposing the effect of the terrorist attack from macroeconomic influences, *Journal of Air Transport Management*, 10(5), 327–332.

Hensher, D.A. (2002). Determining passenger potential for a regional airline hub at Canberra International Airport, *Journal of Air Transport Management*, 8(5), 301–311.

Hess, S. and Polak, J.W. (2006). Exploring the potential for cross-nesting structures in airport-choice analysis: a case-study of the Greater London area, *Transportation Research Part E: Logistics and Transportation Review*, 42(2), 63–81.

Hess, S., Adler, T. and Polak, J.W. (2007). Modelling airport and airline choice behaviour with the use of stated preference survey data, *Transportation Research Part E: Logistics and Transportation Review*, 43(3), 221–233.

Hoskisson, R.E., Eden, L., Lau, C.M. and Wright, M. (2000). Strategy in emerging economies, *Academy of Management Journal*, 43(3), 249–267.

Hu, Y., Xiao, J., Deng, Y., Xiao, Y. and Wang, S. (2015). Domestic air passenger traffic and economic growth in China: evidence from heterogeneous panel models, *Journal of Air Transport Management*, 42, 95–100.

IATA (International Air Transport Association) (2008). *Air Travel Demand*, Economics Briefing Paper No. 9, Geneva, IATA.

IATA (International Air Transport Association) (2014). *The shape of air travel markets over the next 20 years*. Online. Available at: www.iata.org/whatwedo/Documents/economics/20yearsForecast-GAD2014-Athens-Nov2014-BP.pdf (accessed 5 September 2015).

IATA (International Air Transport Association) (2016). *IATA forecast passenger demand to double over 20 years*. Online. Available at: www.iata.org/pressroom/pr/Pages/2016-10-18-02.aspx (accessed 1 April 2017).

ICAO (International Civil Aviation Organisation) (1992). *Civil Aviation Statistics of the World*, 17th edition, Montreal, ICAO.

ICAO (International Civil Aviation Organisation) (2001). *Annual Report of the Council 2000*, Montreal, ICAO.

ICAO (International Civil Aviation Organisation) (2006). *Manual on Air Traffic Forecasting*, 3rd edition, Montreal, ICAO.

ICAO (International Civil Aviation Organisation) (2011). *Annual Report of the Council 2010*, Montreal, ICAO.

ICAO (International Civil Aviation Organisation) (2016a). *Annual Report of the Council 2015*, Montreal, ICAO.

ICAO (International Civil Aviation Organisation) (2016b). *ICAO Long-Term Traffic Forecasts: Passenger and Cargo*, Montreal, ICAO.

IMF (International Monetary Fund) (2016). *World Economy Outlook April 2016*, Washington, DC, IMF.

Inoue, G., Ono, M., Uehara, K. and Isono, F. (2015). Stated-preference analysis to estimate the domestic transport demand following the future entry of LCCs and the inauguration of the Linear Chuo Shinkansen in Japan, *Journal of Air Transport Management*, 47, 199–217.

InterVISTAS (2007). *Estimating Air Travel Demand Elasticities: Final Report*, Vancouver, InterVISTAS.

Ismaila, D.A., Warnock-Smith, D. and Hubbard, N. (2014). The impact of air service agreement liberalisation: the case of Nigeria, *Journal of Air Transport Management*, 37, 69–75.

Ito, H. and Lee, D. (2005a). Assessing the impact of the September 11 terrorist attacks on US airline demand, *Journal of Economics and Business*, 57(1), 75–95.

Ito, H. and Lee, D. (2005b). Comparing the impact of the September 11th terrorist attacks on international airline demand, *International Journal of the Economics of Business*, 12(2), 225–249.

Jorge-Calderon, J.D. (1997). A demand model for scheduled airline services on international European routes, *Journal of Air Transport Management*, 3(1), 23–35.

J.P. Morgan (2016). *J.P. Morgan Emerging Markets Bond Index Monitor*, March.

Kopsch, F. (2012). A demand model for domestic air travel in Sweden, *Journal of Air Transport Management*, 20(1), 46–48.

Marazzo, M., Scherre, R. and Fernandes, E. (2010). Air transport demand and economic growth in Brazil: a time series analysis, *Transportation Research Part E: Logistics and Transportation Review*, 46(2), 261–269.

Mason, K.J. and Alamdari, F. (2007). EU network carriers, low cost carriers and consumer behaviour: a Delphi study of future trends, *Journal of Air Transport Management*, 13(5), 299–310.

Matsumoto, H. (2007). International air network structures and air traffic density of world cities, *Transportation Research Part E: Logistics and Transportation Review*, 43(3), 269–282.

Mehmood, B., Shahid, A. and Ilyas, S. (2015). Co-integration analysis of aviation demand and economic growth in Philippines, *International Journal of Economics and Empirical Research*, 3(6), 271–277.

MSCI (2016). *MSCI Emerging Markets Indexes*. Online. Available at: https://support.msci.com/documents/10199/a4d530c2-caac-44be-a4c3-5e9a693e73de (accessed August 2016).

Njegovan, N. (2006a). Are shocks to air passenger traffic permanent or transitory? Implications for long-term air passenger forecasts for the UK, *Journal of Transport Economics and Policy*, 40(2), 315–328.

Njegovan, N. (2006b). Elasticities of demand for leisure air travel: a system modelling approach, *Journal of Air Transport Management*, 12(1), 33–39.

OECD (Organisation for Economic Co-operation and Development) (2016). *Airport Demand Forecasting for Long-Term Planning*, ITF Round Tables, Paris, OECD.

Ortúzar, J.D. and Simonetti, C. (2008). Modelling the demand for medium distance air travel with the mixed data estimation method, *Journal of Air Transport Management*, 14(6), 297–303.

Oum, T.H., Fu, X. and Zhang A. (2009). *Air Transport Liberalisation and Its Impacts on Airline Competition and Air Passenger Traffic*, ITF 2009 Forum, Paris, OECD.

Pagoni, I. and Psaraki-Kalouptsidi, V. (2016). The impact of carbon emission fees on passenger demand and air fares: a game theoretic approach, *Journal of Air Transport Management*, 55, 41–51.

Pels, E., Nijkamp, P. and Rietveld, P. (2001). Airport and airline choice in a multiple airport region: an empirical analysis for the San Francisco Bay Area, *Regional Studies*, 35(1), 1–9.

Piermartini, R. and Rousova, L. (2008). *Liberalization of air transport services and passenger traffic*. Online. Available at: www.wto.org/english/res_e/reser_e/ersd200806_e.pdf (accessed 1 April 2017).

Russell (2016). *Russell Global Index Series*. Online. Available at: www.ftse.com/products/downloads/Russell-global-indexes.pdf?981 (accessed 1 August 2016).

S&P Dow Jones (2015). *S&P Dow Jones indices announces country classification consultation results*. Online. Available at: www.spindices.com/documents/index-news-and-announcements/20161215-spdji-country-classification-consultation-results.pdf. (accessed 1 August 2016).

Samagaio, A. and Wolters, M. (2010). Comparative analysis of government forecasts for the Lisbon Airport, *Journal of Air Transport Management*, 16(4), 213–217.

Srinidhi, S. (2010). Demand model for air passenger traffic on international sectors, *South Asian Journal of Management*, 17(3), 53–70.

Srinidhi, S. and Manrai, A. (2014). International air transport demand: drivers and forecasts in the Indian context, *Journal of Modelling in Management*, 9(3), 245–260.

Tsekeris, T. (2009). Dynamic analysis of air travel demand in competitive island markets, *Journal of Air Transport Management*, 15(6), 267–273.

Valdes, V. (2015). Determinants of air travel demand in middle income countries, *Journal of Air Transport Management*, 42, 75–84.

Wadud, Z. (2014). The asymmetric effects of income and fuel price on air transport demand, *Transportation Research Part A: Policy and Practice*, 65, 92–102.

Wang, M. and Song, H. (2010). Air travel demand studies: a review, *Journal of China Tourism Research*, 6(1), 29–49.

WTO (World Trade Organisation) (2006). *Quantitative air services agreements review (QUASAR)*. Online. Available at: www.wto.org/english/tratop_e/serv_e/transport_e/review2_e.htm (accessed 10 April 2017).

Yao, S. and Yang, X. (2012). Air transport and regional economic growth in China, *Asia-Pacific Journal of Accounting and Economics*, 19(3), 318–329.

Zhang, Y., Lin, F. and Zhang, A. (2018). Gravity models in air transport research: a survey and an application. In: B.A. Blonigen and W.W. Wilson (eds). *Handbook of International Trade and Transportation*, Cheltenham, Edward Elgar.

# 20

# The role of technology in airline management and operations

*Berendien Lubbe and Theunis Potgieter*

## Introduction

Airlines have a long history of technological innovation, with the commercial airline industry being one of the most technologically advanced industries in modern times. Technology drives aircraft design, airline planning and operations, distribution systems, e-commerce, and passenger processing. For instance, advances in aircraft design gave rise to the tremendous growth of the commercial airline industry, with the number of annual passengers increasing to well over 3 billion after 100 years of flight. On the operational side, the role of technology is the foundation for business intelligence and efficiency. The advent of digital information technologies has allowed airlines to streamline their operations by automating and effectively managing the vast amounts of information required by the industry. The Internet brought about structural shifts in the distribution of the airline product (see Chapter 13) and fundamentally changed the demands of consumers. The airline industry is characterised by its complexity, interdependencies and massive volumes of data requiring real-time solutions across the globe. Information and communication technologies (ICTs) provide the means for effective operational and commercial management, and airlines can no longer function or operate without technology. In meeting passenger demands, airlines try to distinguish themselves through their use of ICTs such as mobile technologies, social media, crew tablets and in-flight entertainment (see Chapter 13).

Airlines have been at the forefront of adopting new technologies, and this chapter begins with a brief historical overview of the most important developments. A discussion follows on the role of technology in supporting the various management and operational functions of an airline. One of the areas most affected by ICTs is the distribution of the airline product, particularly with the advent of the Internet, and this chapter then discusses airline distribution and e-commerce in some depth. The chapter ends with a look at some of the challenges and what the future may hold for airlines when it comes to ICTs.

## Brief overview of technological developments in the airline industry

Technological innovation in the airline industry has been seen in the aircraft itself, its impact on the environment and on airline management. Innovation began with the advent of the first sustained powered and controlled flight by the Wright brothers in 1903, which was followed by the pioneering era up to the First World War, where the focus was on attempts to establish stable machines. The period between the First and Second World Wars saw rapid advancement in aircraft technology, where aircraft evolved from wood and fabric low-powered biplanes to high-powered monoplanes made of aluminium. The 1930s saw the introduction of the jet engine, the development and production of which grew rapidly during the Second World War. Subsequent technological advances resulted in the arrival of long-range aircraft, with new large four-engine monoplanes coming into service after the war and revolutionary progress being made in flight speeds, distances and materials technology resulting in the growth of commercial aviation to where it is today (see Chapter 5).

From an environmental perspective (see Chapter 17), innovation in technology in the airline industry has led to a reduction in congestion and emissions, with today's aircraft being 80 per cent more efficient than the first jet aircraft (IATA, 2016a). Improved technology has also resulted in a marked reduction in the cost of fuel, with the new-generation jet aircraft being exponentially more efficient and with a 90 per cent reduction in noise footprint since the 1960s (Boeing, 2014). Great strides have also been made in technology related to sustainable alternative jet fuel.

One of the most important innovations in airline management and passenger interaction has been the way in which airlines sell their product to passengers (see also Chapter 13). While the sales processes of planning, publishing timetables and prices, booking, and flight handling have not fundamentally changed (Troester, 2016), the introduction of electronically supported processes saw the emergence of a new era. Before the move towards the automation of inventory through computer reservations systems (CRSs), airlines published fares and schedules in directories such as OAG, timetables and booklets. Booking an airline seat was a tedious three-step process by the travel agent (O'Connor, 1999) that incorporated: searching for suitable flights and fares; contacting the airline's reservations department to get flight details and an accurate fare quote to advise the client; after the client's approval, returning to the airline for the booking and reconfirmation of the details.

This manual system was costly and time-consuming for the travel agent, as well as for the airline, which had to maintain a large reservation of staff and pay commissions to travel agents. In 1946, American Airlines installed the first automated booking system, called the Electromechanical Reservisor. In 1953, American Airlines' CEO C.R. Smith sat next to an International Business Machines Corporation (IBM) sales representative and invited him to visit their Reservisor system and look for ways that IBM could improve it. American Airlines and IBM collaborated, and their idea of an automated airline system resulted in a 1959 venture known as the Semi-Automatic Business Research Environment, otherwise known as SABRE. The network was completed in 1964 and was the largest civil data processing system in the world (Ross, 2013). According to Buhalis (2004), SABRE proved to be much more than an inventory control system, with its technology providing the foundation for generating flight plans for aircraft, tracking spare parts, scheduling crews, and developing a range of decision-support systems for management.

Other airlines also created their own systems, with Delta Air Lines launching the Delta Automated Travel Account System (DATAS) in 1968 and United Airlines and Trans World Airlines following in 1971 with the Apollo reservation system and Programmed Airline Reservation System (PARS), respectively. In 1976, United Airlines began offering its Apollo to travel agents, and while it would not allow the agents to book tickets on United Airline's competitors, the convenience of having such a program proved indispensable. SABRE, PARS and DATAS were soon released to travel agents (Ross, 2013). Thus, from having a small regional focus, the systems moved towards a more global perspective, becoming the dominant instruments for handling flight reservations, and the term global distribution systems (GDSs) began to be used. The airlines began selling their shares in the GDSs in the mid-1990s, and these GDSs have mostly become publicly traded companies following a path of integration and consolidation.

Franke (2007: 24) asserts that:

> after years of operational improvement, the unique upturn phase of the 1990s drew the attention of airlines more to the revenue side. With the invention of network management as a central instrument to optimise profits, hubs achieved maximum connectivity, expanding service offerings to as many destinations and customer segments as possible.

The advent of the Internet in the mid-1990s gave airlines the opportunity of looking at new ways of distributing their product, and they had to invest heavily in their ICT systems in order to develop interfaces with consumers and the travel trade (Buhalis, 2004).

Airlines identified the Internet as a major opportunity to tackle distribution costs (the third most significant expense after labour and fuel), and by the end of the twentieth century nearly every scheduled airline had its own website. At the same time, a number of low cost carriers (LCCs) emerged in both Europe and the United States, concentrating on lowering input costs in many areas of their operations and making the industry re-engineer itself as it introduced a number of Internet- and ICT-enabled innovations (Buhalis, 2004), including: electronic/paperless tickets; transparent and clear pricing led by proactive and reactive yield management; single fare tickets with no restrictions on staying or Saturday night rules; commission capping and publication of net fares; financial incentives for self-booking online; auctions and online promotions; powerful customer relationship management (CRM) systems; and online and context-relevant advertising.

The Internet proved to be one of the most influential technologies that changed travellers' behaviour by moving the balance of power from suppliers to travellers. The new traveller has become more knowledgeable, seeking exceptional value for money and time, and is far less patient with delays or waiting. The Internet has allowed airlines to distribute their product not only directly via their websites, but also through a wide range of channels such as online travel agencies and metasearch engines.

The 1990s saw another milestone in the development of airline distribution systems with the introduction of electronic tickets. According to Hansman (2005), airline tickets are the ideal Internet product because a customer purchases a product online and goes to the point of delivery to receive the product. The proliferation of electronic tickets and online or kiosk check-in systems greatly improved cost-efficiency in passenger services. Since the early 2000s, self-service technologies (SSTs) have started to take centre stage on airlines' agendas. Most major airlines have invested in installing self-service technologies not only to bring down costs and improve services for the consumer, but also to distinguish themselves from competitors. Passengers use SSTs to reserve and pay for tickets online, check in over the Internet or mobile phones, pick up boarding passes at airport kiosks, and receive flight updates on mobile devices. According to Castillo-Manzano and López-Valpuesta (2013), the development of SSTs, specifically those for check-in through kiosks or over the Internet, reconciled the aims of both airlines and airports. In a global passenger survey conducted by the International Air Transport Association (IATA), it was found that travellers want more self-service options such as printing their own boarding baggage tags, automated boarding gate and security processing, tracking their own bags throughout their journey and direct notification of up-to-date information (IATA, 2016b). In the current decade, investment by airlines in ICTs is being prioritised in mobile and business intelligence, with a deeper integration of mobile services for passenger services, sales (including ancillary services) and crew to transform airline operations.

Airlines are global in nature and operate within a complex interdependent air transport system where demand and supply determine the way in which airlines and airports function. This system is further influenced by the geopolitical, environmental, economic and regulatory environments. To function within this complex system and environment, all airlines depend on ICTs for their strategic and operational management.

## Role of technology in airline management and operations

The complexity of the air transport system and environment makes information crucial to airlines, and the only way airlines can effectively manage the way in which information flows is through the use of ICTs. This section looks at how information management and decision support systems underpin the airline's core business processes and operations management. As depicted in Figure 20.1, the management of an airline can broadly be categorised into its commercial and operations functions.

The commercial function in an airline refers to all core airline activities that will affect the revenue generation ability of an airline. Key decisions on: aircraft economics; the network on which the aircraft will be deployed, the schedule the aircraft will operate, and the configuration of aircraft; and the optimisation of revenue from ticket sales, price levels, and how seats will be sold are some of the key questions asked in an airline on a day-to-day basis. These complex and interrelated questions require an airline to process large amounts of historic data to project and derive important business decisions that will affect the ultimate profitability of an airline.

Airline operations refer to all the activities related to the actual operation of a flight, such as crew, flight and maintenance planning, control systems, and in-flight entertainment, among

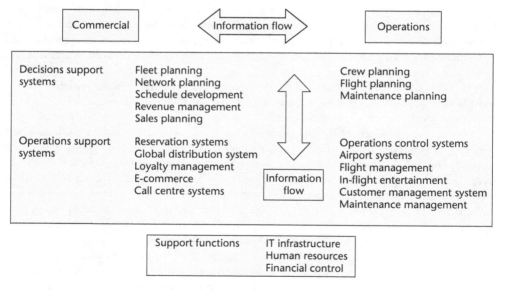

*Figure 20.1* Holistic view of the airline business

*Source*: Authors.

others. The primary objective of operating a safe, secure and on-time flight requires an airline to combine these activities to be able operate a successful flight. ICT systems are employed to support both the commercial and operational decisions through the analysis of information and the generation of recommendations and solutions.

The systems supporting both the commercial and operations functions of an airline can be categorised into decision support systems and operational support systems, which are further underpinned by the support functions of IT infrastructure, human resources and financial control. Airline systems are very specialised, and in many cases governed by a number of regulatory requirements and standards. These systems are all very integrated, with high dependencies on data transfer between them.

## Decision support systems

Decision support systems are sophisticated operations research models that use what-if analysis (Benckendorff et al., 2014) to determine the most optimal allocation of resources in the company. Numerous technology providers specialise in the development of complex operations research models that have the ability to process and derive business solutions that improve the bottom line of the company. Data flows across an airline requires systems to pass information from one system to another to enable a smooth travel process for passengers. Decision support systems in an airline are designed to improve the overall planning efficiency in both the commercial and operational functions, and are used on a daily basis to solve complex business problems. There are two types of decision support systems: commercial decision support systems and operational support systems.

## Commercial decision support systems

The primary focus of commercial decision support systems is to effectively manage processes and resources required for efficient operations, optimisation of resources and reduction of operating cost. The scope of these systems focuses on assisting an airline to plan its fleet of aircraft, where these aircraft will operate (i.e. its network), the schedule for the airline, how it will price each flight through revenue management, as well as how the flight will be sold.

In fleet planning, aircraft manufacturers provide aircraft performance data for all aircraft types; when selecting an aircraft to complete a flight, this performance and planning data includes fuel burn information, aircraft lease rates and maintenance rates. Taking into account the airport and meteorological information, fleet planning systems are able to compare the operating costs of different aircraft types across similar markers. This allows airlines to make key fleet planning decisions and tests different aircraft types for the selection of their fleet.

Network planning is essential because each airline has a unique network of where it operates, the demand within each airline network is different, and it has become a science to determine the most optimal network to operate. As more and more passenger demand data become available, network planning tools help to identify new markets, optimise the schedule, and more accurately model future demand based on historic trends, including time of day and day of the week demand. Network planning tools are available to determine the most optimal network plan an airline can operate and assign the appropriate fleet to maximise profitability.

Aircraft scheduling tools (see also Chapter 15) are used to match the type and number of aircraft and their utilisation with the network plan an airline operates. Scheduling systems take into account a number of rules developed to match the operational requirements with that of the scheduling planning system. As an example, certain airports have limitations in terms of the times they are open or the type of aircraft that can operate into the airport. A scheduling system also assists an airline in increasing its aircraft utilisation. Airlines in general attempt to maximise their aircraft utilisation to ensure improved profitability. These systems also manage the exchange of slot coordination messages according to IATA standards with the relevant airport authorities and manage the set-up of code-share flights. Once an optimised schedule has been developed, it is fed electronically to other planning and operational systems in an airline and published to external systems.

Technology plays a fundamental role in the revenue management function of an airline. Revenue management (see also Chapter 13) is the process in which various quantitative techniques and strategies are used to control the sale of (perishable) seats under uncertainty, such that an expected revenue/profit is maximised with scarce resources. An airline decides at what pricing levels it will be selling what percentage of its seats before departure, and decides, based on certain criteria, when to accept or reject group bookings. Historical data taking into account the spread of demand in days before departure, the market, special events, seasonality and when the departure will take place are some of the factors taken into account when deciding how to forecast the price per class level and revenue-manage a flight. Revenue management and pricing systems have become common practice in airlines and provide the data and inventory required for airline reservation systems to effectively operate. Revenue integrity applications optimise revenue while protecting the inventory from fictitious bookings. Bookings are analysed against set criteria to eliminate duplicate bookings, enforce payments based on booking class, and auto cancel bad bookings and release these seats back into the system for resale.

Sales planning is when airlines sell their inventory through a number of sales channels, and accordingly set their sales targets. The development of revenue budgets, and the setting of channel, sales territory and sales executive targets relies on data from the airlines' commercial systems, and requires revenue planning systems to process the volume of data to ensure the organisation is focused on achieving its revenue objectives.

## Operations decision support systems

The operation of an on-time flight requires an airline to plan for each service, and numerous systems are used for improved planning (see also Chapter 15).

The first of these systems is crew planning. Complex civil aviation rules stipulate the rules and regulations of how cockpit and cabin crew can legally operate a flight. The number of crew, their qualifications, limitations on their number of hours and rest between flights, as well as training, are all factors that need to be taken into account when selecting which crew to operate which flights. Large airlines employ thousands of crew across the globe, and crew planning systems are used to manage the rosters of crew to ensure that airlines can minimise the number of crew while ensuring they comply with the rules and regulations of operating a legal flight.

Flight planning is required because airlines operate flights that criss-cross the globe. This requires precision planning to enable airlines to operate safe and economical flights, for instance with electronic data for airports, aircraft performance, meteorological information, flight routing, fuel consumption, the aircraft maintenance condition, and alternative airports. This data and information must be processed by airlines to provide crew with optimal flight plans. Flight planning has become a science, as optimal flight planning takes into account all the factors for a flight and requires a complex simulation of the actual flight path, and can make a substantial difference to the bottom-line economics of an airline.

Aircraft maintenance is a major cost component for an airline, requiring meticulous maintenance planning. Unplanned maintenance events, an aircraft that goes out of service due to maintenance-related issues, or even just poor management of a spare part inventory can all play a major role in the reliability of an airline. Aircraft maintenance systems assist airlines in planning major and minor maintenance events for aircraft, taking into account the schedule an aircraft is required to fly. Such events are planned up to 24 months in advance, and with the maintenance planning system built around the commercial operations of an airline such maintenance events are well known and airlines are able to plan accordingly.

Commercial planning is enabled through technology and operational systems that require commercial planning information to plan operations. Whether this is for staffing levels and rosters at airports, the number of crew to employ, the number of spare parts to purchase, or how much fuel to procure are all decisions that require information from the commercial side of the business.

## Operational support systems

Operational support systems do not only support the actual flight operations, but also support a complex process of distributing the airline's inventory to its final customers. The process of selling seats and generating revenue is a key function enabled through technology.

### Commercial operational support systems

Airline reservations remain one of the most important commercial applications of information technology (IT) in an airline, and consist of four core functions: flight scheduling and availability; fare quotes and associated rules; passenger information; and ticketing (Benckendorff et al., 2014). Airline reservation systems (ARSs) manage the airline's bookings and help maximise booking opportunities by distributing airline and non-airline content to wide-reaching distribution channels. Various payment processes are offered and electronic tickets are generated upon payment. ARSs also offer ancillary services that can be purchased, such as preferred seating, upgrades and excess baggage. Airlines either operate an in-house ARS, which is connected to other systems, such as Internet booking engines (IBEs) and GDSs, or use a computer reservation system (CRS), which is hosted by a GDS or third-party vendor. IBEs (first developed in the 1990s) created the opportunity for airlines to increase direct sales via their own website, which is the most cost-effective distribution channel for airlines. Airline websites offer passengers flight schedules, availability, a range of fares to meet passenger needs, settlement and receipt of electronic tickets, as well as online check-in, seat selection, the sale of ancillary products and frequent flyer benefits. According to Harteveldt (2012), airlines have been increasingly successful in generating direct sales via their own airline websites and mobile applications, with LCCs generating most of their sales from their websites.

Before the advent of the Internet, GDSs traditionally distributed the majority of airline seats via travel agencies, providing a one-stop shop with value-added services such as car rental and accommodation. The cost of GDS representation and distribution increased considerably in the 1990s, and airlines have found it difficult to control. As a result, airlines have sought alternatives, and generally try to divert their indirect sales from GDSs onto their own direct reservations systems. Costs are not the only reason for airlines to try to divert their sales from GDSs as, according to Harteveldt (2012), there is also a lack of transparency of fare families (a group of fares that airlines use to market different travel options associated with an air fare, such as whether or not the ticket is refundable, changeable or mileage-accruable) and ancillary product merchandising in GDS-based distribution channels, with third-party intermediaries generally only providing limited airline content and only selling a part of an airline's ancillary product suite. In a study conducted by Accenture (2016), it was found that while airline executives believe digital technology has strengthened intermediaries such as online travel agents (OTAs) and metasearch engines such as Google Flights, these technologies are perceived as distancing carriers from their customers and commoditising the airline product. This has made airlines more intent on strengthening their own direct digital platforms.

A new development by IATA to overcome the interface problems related to data transmission between the various booking platforms (ARSs, GDSs and travel intermediaries) is the New Distribution Capability (NDC) project, which is an XML-based technology communication standard to help airlines offer a consistent customer experience, regardless of where and how their products and services are booked (see also Chapter 13). This includes the IBE operated by the airline itself, the GDSs and the OTAs. Troester (2016) says that new market participants, such as metasearch engines that previously could only slowly gain a foothold in the distribution landscape due to the limited interface flexibility, are already using this XML standard. Systems can directly receive and display listing data from the airline's reservation systems. Furthermore, it is also possible to transmit, display and reserve any product – with content-rich data such as images or movies – because of the XML format of the interface.

E-commerce is an extremely important concept in the airline industry, with its two key applications of electronic selling via the Internet and electronic ticketing, both of which dramatically transformed the way that airline services and products are marketed and distributed (Doganis, 2006). According to Harteveldt (2012), e-commerce has allowed airlines to become retailers, and as such require systems that can distribute their flights and merchandise their products[1] across all channels, and what airlines currently call distribution will be replaced by a focus on channel-based, value-creating commerce. Technology has enabled wider distribution and merchandising of airline products, and a greater understanding exists among travellers that paying extra for certain services is normal, with travel agencies also accepting and realising the benefits of offering ancillary services. The NDC of IATA is designed to deliver an enhanced airline merchandising experience to help airlines offer rich content and a consistent customer experience, allowing them to drive greater product differentiation. According to Sabre (2016b), some airlines are making significant investments in air merchandising platforms and are looking at NDC standards to enable this.

Related to the airline concept of e-commerce are loyalty programmes, more generally referred to as frequent flyer programmes (FFPs) (see also Chapters 1, 9 and 11). Since the mid-1980s, FFPs have been very popular among megacarriers, and a number of databases with customers' information have been created since that time. FFP databases became critical factors for CRM. Airlines set up loyalty programmes to attract and retain customers, with these programmes generally tracking flight activity and allocating points to customers in exchange for their loyalty. These points are then used towards payment of another flight, upgrades, ancillary services or shopping.

There is little doubt that consumer technology used by travellers has grown faster than the technology used by airlines, with mobile and social media (see also Chapter 13) fast becoming the preferred devices and platforms for passengers. "The world's airline passengers are online citizens, empowered through their extensive adoption of various consumer technology devices" (Harteveldt, 2012: 5). These devices include laptops, mobile smartphones and tablet devices, of which mobile is regarded as the most important due to its unprecedented growth. Passengers have shown a strong interest in using mobile devices to plan and book flights due to their portability and ease of use (Harteveldt, 2012). Mobiles and tablets are expanding the distribution of air travel sales, with mobile applications being increasingly used because they provide customers with a sense of control over their journey. Airlines are engaging more with their customer base via mobile technology across the entire travel experience, from the pre-travel phase of information seeking, booking, transfers and departures to the in-flight experience and arrival. Airlines attempt to create a seamless user experience, which includes using location-based services in mobile applications, selling ancillary products and services, sharing special offers on flights and hotels to encourage bookings, and notifying travellers about lounges and ground transportation.

Airlines were one of the early adopters of social media (Mistilis et al., 2004), using social media as promotional channels to improve customer service, raise brand awareness and drive customer loyalty. Social media has enabled airlines to interact with their geographically dispersed customers in new ways, such as via online brand communities (OBCs), which is defined by Dessart et al. (2015: 32) as "a grouping of individuals sharing a mutual interest in a brand, using electronic mediation to overcome real-life time and space limitations." Some airlines have integrated booking applications on their social media platforms, while others utilise these platforms for communicating with their customers, either one-directional, providing information, or bi-directional, where airlines respond to customer posts. These applications allow airlines to improve customer loyalty and brand awareness. Finally, a fairly old distribution channel, but still essential, are call centres used by airlines to book or change seats and offer customer services over the phone.

## Operations operational support systems

Operations control systems support on-time departures, which requires a multitude of different operational activities to be coordinated and tracked to ensure all these activities are running simultaneously, and that all time-critical tasks are completed in time. Sophisticated departure control systems are utilised in the operations control centres of airlines to ensure that alignment of activities takes place. For instance, tracking of aircraft, catering, baggage, fuel, crew, slots, airport passenger processing, maintenance, and ground equipment requires close alignment with information on passenger volumes, weight of aircraft, and weather conditions to determine whether a flight will be able to depart. Operations control centres in airlines are staffed by highly skilled staff utilising the latest in technology to process complex operations across the globe.

Airport systems provide support to airlines in their utilisation of departure control systems in the airport environment, for instance to ensure they are able to process passengers for check-in, generate passenger manifests, screen passengers for any security requirements, process baggage, and provide aircraft weight information. Airlines are focusing on improving the passenger experience in the airport environment and utilise their FFPs, for example, to install their passenger's frequent flyer card with a tracking chip to determine when they enter the airport environment and to allow fast-tracking through airport channels based on the status of the passenger.

Flight management systems are systems for automating many of the components of a flight, including the navigation, flight path, determining the positioning of an aircraft for tracking purposes, technical information on the airports, and runways the aircraft will be using. Flight management systems are an integral part of commercial airlines, with reliance on connectivity with the airline's operations control centre, air traffic navigation services and airports. Data retrieved from flight management systems are critical in improving flight performance in areas such as fuel usage improvement and maintenance control.

Maintenance management is essential because commercial aircraft have thousands of components that require to be tracked for usage, replacement and performance. Maintenance organisations plan major and minor maintenance intervals and must keep track of all the events required to ensure an aircraft is certified to operate. There is close alignment between the scheduling and the maintenance systems of an airline (see Chapter 15) to ensure that airlines' aircraft are operating the flights required for an on-time performance. Global megacarriers with hundreds of aircraft across the globe require advanced maintenance systems to ensure their aircraft remain serviceable at locations across the globe.

Providing in-flight entertainment has become a key component of the customer offering (see Chapter 13), especially on long-haul flights. In-seat personal televisions with hundreds of video and audio content channels have become a product differentiator for many airlines. The development of on-board wireless connectivity and the growth of personal devices used by passengers have created a platform for streaming of on-board content, as well as linking personalised customer information solutions to enhance the passenger's experience. Satellite connectivity has also created the opportunity for passengers to now use mobile devices for voice and Internet connectivity.

As more customer information becomes available, airlines are focusing on providing a more personalised passenger experience through on-board customer management systems. Customer data are now downloaded to tablets and provided to cabin crew. Cabin crew can access all logged preferences a customer could have, including what they would like to drink and how they want to be addressed. The capturing of any customer complaint can be done at the time of occurrence, and when the passenger travels again the cabin crew will have full knowledge of any experience the passenger may have had with the airline.

The flow of information and data is not a closed loop in an airline environment. In the same manner as operational systems require input from the commercial systems, there is a requirement that commercial systems be updated post-operational events. This information provides the opportunity for post-event optimisation of performance.

## Support functions

IT network connectivity and infrastructure is essential because airlines operate a number of complex systems that are integrated, operate across global locations and require 24/7 availability for a mobile workforce. All these requirements place high levels of reliance on the IT infrastructure to provide continuous connectivity, and where any break in continued service leads to passenger inconvenience, aircraft delays and lost revenue earning opportunities.

Airlines are required to invest in substantial infrastructure with data centres and network infrastructure to process the large amounts of data they require to operate all of their systems. Many of the systems required are procured from a range of different vendors, which further increases the potential risk of connectivity-related problems if an end-to-end service is not delivered.

Many of the systems driving an airline have seen major innovation in the last decade, with airport passenger innovation, e-commerce growth, social media, loyalty programme data development and increases in passenger volume driving the requirement for increased system capacity. Much of the infrastructure of the airline industry network was developed before the growth of new global megacarriers and customer-centric data systems, and requires continuous expansion and the development of future scalable solutions.

The airline industry has a range of employees performing duties across a wide geography, and in many instances a virtual or absent workforce that requires to be managed remotely. Traditional human resources (HR) systems are deployed, managing recruitment, enterprise resource planning, payroll, administration, performance management and the ability to drive statistical analysis across the company. HR systems in the airline environment (see also Chapter 24) require integration into the airline operational systems to ensure logging of activities, scheduling, training and tracking, and oversight of movement of staff.

Financial control systems cover a number of areas, such as revenue accounting, procurement and control, and reporting and analysis. The revenue accounting process is key for an airline to ensure there is no revenue leakage and to track all passenger sales revenue in real time. It is the process that accounts for a passenger ticket, and managing the sale and utilisation thereof. Revenue streams for LCCs and large global carriers that offer interline services between airlines have very different revenue accounting procedures. Global carriers such as British Airways and Emirates allow passengers to purchase a single ticket that permits passengers to connect between airlines. The revenue accounting process manages factors such as the proration of revenue across coupons and airlines, refunds, splitting of excess baggage charges, and management of services fees and taxes – requiring complex revenue control systems. These systems also track and ensure that airlines are able to collect all revenue due to them and highlight any weak internal controls that can be addressed.

Vendor selection, control, service delivery, tracking, invoicing and payment, and reporting are standard payment processes in procurement and control in an airline environment. Numerous standard industry systems provide airline procurement management and control. The global nature of the industry does, however, require the system's ability to comply with cross-country payments and local market requirements.

Reporting and analysis occurs through key performance metrics, which are an important element of managing the performance of an airline. Real-time performance measurement across the business is required to ensure the effective allocation of resources and focusing attention to areas that require improvement. Reporting is a key element of every IT system in an airline, and provides a single view and dashboard for performance across the organisation.

## Challenges in the ICT environment and future innovations

A number of challenges or obstacles have been identified that require airlines to invest in processes and tools that support operational efficiencies. These challenges range from increasing passenger volumes and constrained airspace (see also Chapter 4), which cause problems such as delays and cancellations, baggage processing inefficiencies, and customer service issues, which affect the passenger's journey.

Sabre (2016b) also identified limited access to real-time information, siloed systems, established organisational structure, as well as a lack of information sharing as the top obstacles to improving airlines' performance, and says that technology can bridge these gaps by automating workflows, enabling data sharing, and accelerating communication across the operation and its stakeholders – helping the airline evolve from a traditional airline into a so-called connected airline.

While engines and aircraft have become more digitally sophisticated, with greater connectivity being introduced into aircraft and airline management, the adoption of digital technology still faces certain barriers. First, there is an internal resistance in airlines to changing the organisational structure or functions. Second, integrating digital into the legacy systems is time-consuming and complex, and too many customer touchpoints need to communicate and connect. Third, there are concerns over data privacy and how data will be managed. Overcoming these barriers will allow streamlined workflows, enhanced productivity, greater protection against cyber threats, and an opportunity for differentiation in the distribution of the airline product and customer relationships (Accenture, 2016).

In terms of innovations, Franke (2007) asserted that the deployment of state-of-the-art technologies, such as those shown in Figure 20.2, help to raise efficiency, process stability and service quality in the airline industry.

Improving baggage movement and tracking, the customer airport experience and effective processing of passengers, improved standard technology for the distribution of airline content, and the introduction of biometric security measures are some of the initiatives that IATA is working with on behalf of the industry.

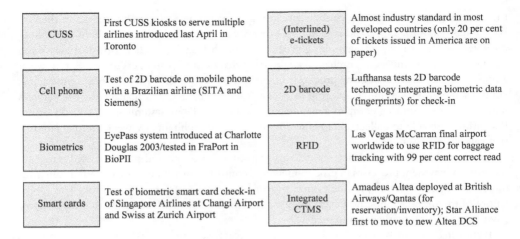

*Figure 20.2* Advanced technologies in terminal handling

*Source*: Based on Franke (2007).

According to SITA (2016), mobiles will continue to dominate the investment agenda of airlines for passenger services, while on the operational side investments include implementing electronic flight bags (EFBs)[2] and equipping staff and ground handlers with mobile technologies. Airlines are also increasingly recognising the potential of the Internet of Things (IoT)[3] in making air travel more efficient and improving the passenger experience. According to SITA (2016), airlines expect, over the next decade, to trial new technologies such as smart watches and smart glasses for staff, wearable-enabled services for passengers, a single biometric travel ticket for identity management, artificial intelligence, virtual reality services for passengers, and virtual reality services for staff.

Aviation Week (2016) suggests that the future of aircraft design lies in cleaner, quieter, faster, closer and cheaper ultra-efficient commercial aircraft. The world's airlines have committed to halt then reverse the growth in their carbon footprint to prevent their environmental impact constraining the future expansion of air travel (see also Chapters 17 and 25). Greater flight efficiency will align with the need for lower airport noise, reducing both fuel consumption and sound generation. So far, travel beyond supersonic speeds remains an ambition, and hypersonic aircraft will only come once the technology has matured (see also Chapter 5). The concept is closely linked to the increasing problem of congestion in urban areas, with aviation visionaries seeing aircraft as the means to escape the limitations of ground transport. These aircraft include so-called flying cars, personal air vehicles and taxis, with some experts foreseeing the feasibility of Uber-style on-demand aviation. The large aircraft manufacturers, namely Airbus and Boeing, have recognised that each new generation of aircraft cannot keep costing more than the last, and that by 2030 a great deal of advanced technology will have been developed to combat the problem of affordability.

## Conclusion

New technology, changing customer interaction with technology and behaviour, the increasing global nature of the industry, and passenger volumes require continuous investment to ensure survival in a competitive industry. Investment in technology remains a priority in an industry where profits are continuously under pressure. Technology has become more and more of a differentiator in cutting costs, improving productivity, enhancing customer service and increasing revenue-earning opportunities. Innovation within the industry is a tool for the industry to remain profitable, as well as for airlines to increase their competitiveness.

## Notes

1 Air merchandising refers to the bundling and unbundling of airline products and services. Within the industry, air merchandising can mean different things to different people. For some, it is the individual ancillary products on top of flight bookings; for others, it is the bundling of options to create fare packages suited to a particular type of traveller (Sabre, 2016a).

2 An EFB is a device that allows flight crews to perform a variety of functions that were traditionally accomplished by using paper references.

3 Everyday objects such as vehicles, watches, glasses and other consumables have network connectivity, allowing them to send and receive data, generally described as smart devices.

## References

Accenture (2016). *Digital readiness for customer experience in the airline industry*. Online. Available at: www.accenture.com/t00010101T000000__w__/gb-en/_acnmedia/PDF-36/Accenture-Digital-Readiness-Customer-Experience-Airline-Industry-Transcript.pdf (accessed 2 February 2017).

Aviation Week (2016). The future is . . . on the horizon for aerospace and defence, *Aviation Week: 100th Anniversary Issue*, 178(10), 90–93.

Benckendorff, P., Sheldon, P. and Fesenmaier, D. (2014). *Tourism Information Technology*, Wallingford, CABI.

Boeing. (2014). *Current Market Outlook 2014–2033*, Seattle, WA, Boeing.

Buhalis, D. (2004). eAirlines: strategic and tactical use of ICTs in the airline industry, *Information & Management*, 41(7), 805–825.

Castillo-Manzano, J. and López-Valpuesta, L. (2013). Check-in services and passenger behaviour: self service technologies in airport systems, *Computers in Human Behavior*, 29, 2431–2437.

Dessart, L., Veloutsou, C. and Morgan-Thomas, A. (2015). Consumer engagement in online brand communities: a social media perspective. *The Journal of Product and Brand Management*, 24(1), 28–42.

Doganis, R. (2006). *The Airline Business*, 2nd edition, London, Routledge.

Franke, M. (2007). Innovation: the winning formula to regain profitability in aviation? *Journal of Air Transport Management*, 13, 23–30.

Hansman, R.J. (2005). *The impact of information technologies on air transportation*. Presented at the 43rd AIAA Aerospace Sciences Meeting and Exhibit, Reno, AIAA.

Harteveldt, H. (2012). *The Future of Airline Distribution: A Look Ahead to 2017. A Special Report Commissioned by IATA*, Cambridge, MA, Atmosphere Research Group.

IATA (International Air Transport Association) (2016a). *Fact sheet: alternative fuels*. Online. Available at: www.iata.org/pressroom/facts_figures/Pages/index.aspx (accessed 2 February 2017).

IATA (International Air Transport Association) (2016b). *IATA Annual Review 2016*, Montreal, IATA.

Mistilis, N., Agnes, P. and Presbury, R. (2004). The strategic use of information and communication technology in marketing and distribution: a preliminary investigation of Sydney hotels, *Journal of Hospitality and Tourism Management*, 11(1), 42–55.

O'Connor, P. (1999). *Electronic Information Distribution in Tourism and Hospitality*, Wallingford, CABI.

Ross, G. (2013). *Airline reservation systems history 101*. Online. Available at: www.cbtravel.com/blog/2013/11/airline-reservation-systems-history-101/ (accessed 2 February 2017).

Sabre (2016a). *Whitepaper: Air Merchandising – Get Onboard*, Soutlake, TX, Sabre.

Sabre (2016b). *Whitepaper: The Connected Airline*, Southlake, TX, Sabre.

SITA (2016). *The Airline IT Trends Survey 2016*, Geneva, SITA.

Troester, J. (2016). *Airline sales yesterday, today and tomorrow*, unpublished lecture notes by J. Troester.

# 21

# Key aspects in aviation security

*William G. Morrison and Kathleen Rodenburg*

## Introduction

It is estimated that total global spending on airport security will reach or exceed US$45 billion by 2018 (Frost & Sullivan, 2012). Yet despite all of the resources devoted to deterrence, pre-emption and defence against attacks on aviation, the undisputable fact is that the threat of such attacks (which can be initiated and executed with relatively few resources) can never be completely eliminated. Consequently, aviation security necessarily defines an 'economic problem' in which scarce resources must be allocated to the prevention of attacks, while striving to preserve the rights, freedoms and quality of life that should be enjoyed and preserved for future generations. The economic nature of problems in aviation security underlies the importance of research and analysis that can help allocate resources as effectively and efficiently as possible.

However, research on aviation security is challenging for a number of reasons; accurate and complete data on the current state of aviation security is often unavailable, and as Jackson (2012) and Prentice (2008) point out, many of the economic costs and benefits pertaining to aviation security are both intangible and uncertain. In addition, the aviation security landscape is dynamic and constantly evolving, which creates a danger that research and analysis can become quickly irrelevant to current aviation security problems. The main reason for this is the strategic nature of the interaction between the defence agencies of nation states and the individuals or groups intent on attacking them. These interactions share similar features to the relationships of players found in simple cat-and-mouse games (Popescu, 2011). The government in this case represents the cat, while the mouse represents terrorists. Despite its efforts, the cat is unable to secure a definitive victory over the mouse, and although the mouse never defeats the cat, it inevitably avoids capture. It is a never-ending contest between players where the advantage is constantly shifting between cat and mouse (government and terrorist), which causes the aviation security landscape to continually shift as each player tries to re-establish its advantage. Benda (2015: 23) describes the evolution of this game as "a constant technology arms race between changing tactics and security capabilities."

The creation of new governing bodies (e.g. the Canadian Air Transport Security Authority [CATSA] in Canada and the Department of Homeland Security in the United States [US]), and the additional resources given to these bodies to improve security for its citizens in response to the 9/11 attacks, has little resemblance to the security efforts or practices prior to the attack (Hoffman, 2003). Consequently, the most applicable and pertinent research literature for this chapter is research conducted in the years following the 9/11 attacks.

This chapter reviews economic and related research on key aspects of aviation security. The chapter focuses on seven main areas: the extent to which aviation security is considered to be a private or public good, the cost–benefit approach to evaluating aviation security, efficient and risk-based approaches to aviation security, the human factor in aviation security, the role of new technology, layered screening and pre-emption in airport screening, and non-passenger screening and security. A conclusion briefly considers directions for future research.

## Aviation security: private or public good?

There is a general consensus in the post-9/11 literature that advocates the classification of airport security and safety as a public good (Coughlin et al., 2002; Frey et al., 2004b; Jackson, 2012; Prentice, 2008, 2015; Stewart and Mueller, 2008). This classification is predicated on economic theory. Aviation security passes the two conditions for a public good highlighted by Samuelson (1954): (1) non-rivalry, that is, the consumption of the good by one individual does not diminish the consumption of the same good by another individual; and (2) non-excludability, that is, once the good is provided, no one can be forced to pay for it. It is this second condition that leads to free-rider problems if the good is left for private provision.

In such cases, the public good will be underfunded by markets (which only equate private costs and benefits) so that governments (who equate social costs and benefits) must intervene to ensure its socially efficient provision. Furthermore, it is not difficult to see that airport safety measures have impacts on society beyond the immediate airport and airline community. Ito and Lee (2003) assess the impact of the 9/11 attacks on US airline demand and find that the demand for air travel decreased over 30 per cent immediately following the 9/11 attacks, with an ongoing reduction in demand of 7.4 per cent into 2003. This impact on air travel demand not only caused direct losses of revenues for airlines and airports; it also affected the entire travel industry (i.e. car rentals, hotels and tourism) (Ito and Lee, 2003). More importantly, the direct effects of the 9/11 attacks were to cause large-scale loss of life to civilians who were not air passengers or employed in the aviation sector, and destruction of ground targets beyond aircraft and airport infrastructure (Dillingham, 2001). Research published by the New York City Partnership and Chamber of Commerce (2001) estimated the total economic cost of the 9/11 attack (the sum of direct and indirect costs) to the city of New York to be US$83 billion. Aside from the tragic loss of lives, these costs included short- and medium-term loss of jobs, destruction of property, negative shocks to the financial, retail and tourism sectors, and rescue, clean-up and infrastructure repair costs (New York City Partnership and Chamber of Commerce, 2001). The 9/11 attacks made it very clear that air travellers are not the exclusive private beneficiaries of aviation security, and consequently ICAO (2004: 2) argues that:

> Governments have direct responsibility for aviation security and funding . . . as the security threat is against the state, the provision and cost of aviation security should be borne by the state from general revenues and not from taxes and user fees.

Coughlin et al. (2002) examine the economic issues relevant to airline and airport security in light of the (then) newly implemented security measures put in place following the 9/11 attacks. The article provides an overview of the network characteristics of civil aviation and highlights the strategic independence of airports in the provision of security. When one airport increases security, all other airports in its network benefit. They highlight the free-rider and public goods aspects of aviation security, in which unregulated private markets provide too little security from society's perspective. The article summarises key features of post-9/11 legislation using a production function approach and considers whether the federal role should be restricted to setting and monitoring standards, or whether the role should also include financing and implementation of security. While their analysis affirms a strong case for the government to be involved in funding aviation security, they catalogue the arguments both in support of and in opposition to government provision of aviation security.

Frey et al. (2004b) consider how to characterise the disutility experienced from a public bad, specifically the effects of terrorist attacks. They attempt to demonstrate how damage done by terrorism can be empirically measured. Following Enders and Sandler (1995), Sandler and Enders (2004) and Frey et al. (2004b), Frey et al. (2004a) apply a life satisfaction approach. That is, they assume people's assessment of their overall well-being can be determined by measures of reported well-being. In a survey, individuals are asked about their life satisfaction or happiness. This subjective well-being is then used as a proxy for utility. The ill effects of a terrorist attack then become the loss of well-being. They proceed by calculating the marginal disutility of the public bad and the marginal utility of income to provide a marginal rate of substitution between income and the public bad. Clearly, acts of terrorism lead to a considerable reduction in life satisfaction, and therefore individuals would need to receive a large compensatory increase in income to offset the inflicted harm caused by terrorism. The main conclusion of Frey et al. (2004b) is that the loss of well-being experienced as a result of terrorism could far exceed the purely monetary costs associated with such acts.

Rekiel (2012) investigates the impact of financing sources on aviation security; specifically, he compares the impact of the user pays principle versus government-funded, between the European Union (EU) and the Netherlands. He argues that ensuring security measures in the EU are consistent across member states is challenging given that in some states, costs are partly born by the government, and in other states the user pays principle applies. He reports that aviation security charges in the Netherlands increased by 43 per cent between 2003 and 2007, and that security charges and taxes form a considerable part of total revenues to the airports both in the Netherlands and other parts of the EU (27 per cent at Amsterdam Schiphol, 28 per cent at Brussels, 25 per cent at Zurich, and 24 per cent at Paris Charles de Gaulle, Frankfurt and Munich). Rekiel (2012) argues that there should be a reduction in user fees and an increase in the contribution from the government's general revenues because terrorism is targeted at the government and society indirectly through airlines. In particular, he argues that higher levels of government funding are associated with stricter security guidelines in excess of the minimum standard, and recommends increased transparency of security-related costs in order to harmonise the financing efforts of aviation security across EU member states.

Prentice (2015) highlights that although airport security is a public good as defined by economic theory, many countries do not treat it as such. While Mexico's aviation security is funded completely by the government, the US's security measure costs are shared between the public treasury and passengers, and at the extreme Canadian passengers foot the entire bill. Therefore, in Canada, passengers fund a service that provides benefits on a national level, far beyond the benefit received for their own protection (social benefits exceeding the private benefits). Prentice (2015) points out that in Canada, the government has essentially privatised the provision of the public good, and has consequently created a free-riding problem. However, in this case, the government has become the free-rider. He further identifies that this financing model (where users pay) is not a result of solid policy analysis, but is a result of reactionary measures taken given past and potential terrorist threats.

To date, the majority of research supports the notion of aviation security as a public good for which at least a significant portion of financing should come from general tax revenues rather than user-pay taxes on air travellers. However, as noted by Gillen and Morrison (2015a), the trend in practice seems to be in the opposite direction, with governments seeking to finance an increasing portion of aviation security costs from taxes on airlines and passengers. In 2014, the US federal government raised the September 11 security charge from US$2.50 per enplanement per passenger trip (with a maximum charge of US$5) to a flat fee of US$5.60 per passenger trip (irrespective of the number of enplanements). Moreover, this fee is scheduled to rise by 50 cents per year until 2019. In Canada, increases in the air travellers' security charge has resulted in security tax revenues exceeding the aviation security costs financed by the tax, so that between 2011 and 2014, the air travellers' security charge actually increased the government's general revenues (Gillen and Morrison, 2015a).

Estimates of price elasticity of demand for air travel (e.g. Brons et al., 2002; Gillen et al., 2007) (see also Chapters 11 and 19) show a range of demand sensitivity to price from relatively insensitive (inelastic) in business travel and international long-haul markets to relatively sensitive (elastic) in leisure travel and short-haul markets. Thus, instituting or increasing passenger security charges will have a distortionary and negative effect on air travel demand, with an associated decline in economic welfare through losses in consumer and producer surplus. Gillen and Morrison (2015b) estimate that in 2011, there were 690,000 fewer passengers flying to/from and within Canada as a result of the air transport security charge, resulting in a loss of C$227 million in forgone revenue to airlines and an economic welfare loss of C$2.2 billion (note that this estimated welfare loss does not include broader measures of economic impact on the economy). Therefore, it is unclear why many governments ignore the public good argument for financing aviation security from general revenues. Poole (2015) provides one explanation by arguing that if it is possible to successfully charge a toll for a roadway or a security tax to an air passenger, this is evidence that private benefits do exist and that private markets may indeed offer a better financing alternative to large bureaucratic government intervention. Button (2016) suggests a political economy explanation; that such decisions are made more out of political expediency, notions of equity and a perception that air passengers are able and willing to pay the full costs of aviation security.

## The cost–benefit analysis approach to evaluating aviation security

In general, cost–benefit analysis is used to measure the discounted present value of net benefits (benefits minus costs) flowing from some definable project or resource allocation. Such analysis can be used to either determine whether a given project defines a positive net benefit or to rank a number of competing projects. Applying cost–benefit analysis to aviation security is peculiar in at least one respect; aviation security measures do not create any benefit, but instead prevent losses from occurring.

Stewart and Mueller (2008) apply a cost–benefit approach to evaluating two specific security measures in the US: the programme to harden cockpit doors on aircraft and the US Federal Air Marshal Service. The former was implemented to make it harder for would-be hijackers to gain control of an aircraft and potentially use it to crash into targets on the ground. The latter was implemented to provide a means of resisting and preventing any in-flight attempt by individuals to hijack or damage an aircraft, or to harm passengers or crew. Their study reports the annual cost of hardening cockpit doors and the Air Marshal Service to be US$40 million and US$900 million, respectively. According to their cost–benefit analysis, the US programme to harden cockpit doors (with a cost per life saved of US$800,000) has created a strong net benefit to society; however, the Air Marshal Service (with a cost per life saved of US$180 million) far exceeds the upper bound of the value of a statistical life, which they conservatively estimate to be US$10 million for a life saved. In comparison, Viscusi (2000) states that overall, value of life estimates cluster in the range of US$3 million to US$9 million.

Given the number of strong assumptions needed to make these calculations, Stewart and Mueller (2008) recognise the need to conduct sensitivity analysis on their results. In particular, the cost per life saved depends crucially on assumptions made about the observed reduction in risk attributed to any given security measure. For each case, Stewart and Mueller (2008) calculate the cost per life saved as a function of the security measure's assigned risk reduction, which generates a break-even point. That is, the programme-specific risk reduction percentage can be calculated such that the cost per life saved just equals the upper bound on the value of a statistical life.

For the relationship between the reduction in risk of an attack and the cost per life saved for the hardening of cockpit doors programme, Stewart and Mueller (2008) find that any risk reduction attributable to this security measure equal to or greater than 1.33 per cent generates a cost per life saved equal to or less than US$10 million. That is, if the risk reduction associated with this security measure is very small, it is still generating net benefits to society. In contrast, even with air marshals present on 30 per cent of all flights, it is virtually impossible for this security measure to pass the cost–benefit test. Given Stewart and Mueller's assumptions, to reach a conclusion that the Air Marshal Service generates a net benefit to society would require an acceptance that the Air Marshal Service was the only source of reduction in total risk since 2001.

Using the same methodology, Stewart and Mueller (2015) investigate the net benefit of the US PreCheck or trusted traveller programme. Membership to this programme requires travellers to provide information in advance for background checks that result in expedited security screening for a five-year period. They find a reduction in risk associated with PreCheck of 0.5 per cent when PreCheck correctly identifies low-risk passengers, but there is an overall decrease in risk of 0.1 per cent when PreCheck passengers are selected at random, which leads them to conclude that the PreCheck programme generates a net benefit to society. In another cost–benefit analysis, Poole (2015) studies the US SPOT programme for behaviour detection and concludes that it does not pass a cost–benefit test. He highlights insufficient training received by the behaviour detection officers (BDOs), with four days of classroom training and only one day of on-the-job training. Poole (2015) also cites support for his argument from studies by the US Government Accountability Office (GAO) and the National Academy of Sciences, both of which find no evidence that the SPOT programme will be successful.

Prentice (2008) provides a qualitative investigation into the benefits (direct and indirect, and tangible and intangible) of transportation security, and asks how risk assessment affects social benefits of security in an effort to assess whether the cost of security is justified. He constructs an economic model where social benefit curves react to changes in risk levels and outlines the effects of transportation security measurements and their related welfare impact. Private and social benefits are broadly identified and classified as tangible (direct and indirect) and intangible (direct and indirect). Specifically, benefits are broken down into four main categories (sovereignty protection, terrorism protection, interdiction of illegal activities and personal security), and then further subdivided into tangible and intangible benefits. He suggests that transportation security measures provide a wide range of tangible and intangible benefits to society, businesses and individuals, and concludes that when all these benefits are taken into account, the benefits are more likely to outweigh the costs than if a more narrow economic definition of benefits is used; in this regard, Prentice (2008) and Frey et al. (2004b) come to a similar conclusion.

Jackson (2012) argues that all the costs paid by taxpayers for a particular security measure must be weighed against the level of security that the measure is expected to produce. However, he also recognises that there is much uncertainty in these estimates. Nevertheless, Jackson supports the use of cost–benefit analysis, using ranges of terrorist risk values to identify break-even points. The cost of security measures can be compared with risk levels over a range, to provide a measure of how good a security measure would have to be to reduce risk to a point of cost-effectiveness. The effectiveness value determines where the security measure would break even (i.e. where it would reduce enough risk that its cost would be worth paying). His approach helps provide a structured framework for addressing the cost-effectiveness of aviation security measures, without the need for a full cost–benefit analysis, thus avoiding the measurement issues related to the calculation of benefits of aviation security.

## Efficient and risk-based airport security

With global air passenger volumes predicted to at least double by 2030 to 2040 (see Chapter 19), there is real concern from governments and within the aviation industry that current (traditional) approaches to aviation security will come under increasing pressure and will eventually be unable to cope unless changes are made. Consequently, there is interest in understanding how current systems can become more efficient and how new technologies and approaches – such as risk-based security – can either taper with the existing system or replace it over time. The current (traditional) approach views each passenger as representing the same threat probability, and therefore demands that each passenger be subject to an equal and intense amount of security vetting at the airport. An alternative is to move to risk-based security systems.

Jackson and Frelinger (2012) argue that the first step in implementing more efficient security is properly assessing the risk. They outline three components in a framework for examining the risk to aviation from terrorism: threat (the probability of an attack being attempted), vulnerability (the probability of damage from an attempted attack) and consequences (the extent of damages from an attack). They examine and discuss historical risks and provide a historical account of attack incidence (incident data) and consequences. While acknowledging the limits to using historical data, Jackson and Frelinger (2012) explore ways to think rationally about possible future risks. They argue that the relevant questions are as follows:

1 How have terrorists attacked aviation targets in the past?
2 What might incremental improvements or deviations from these behaviours look like?
3 What problems have terrorists encountered in the past, and what changes could help them solve these problems?
4 What have the relevant adversaries said they want to do in the future?
5 How might new technologies and weapons influence terrorist choices?

Their main conclusion is that we must develop scenarios of hypothetical future attacks that are not just based on historical data, but take into consideration the potential for adaption and reaction by adversaries.

Jacobson et al. (2006) evaluate the cost effectiveness of explosive detection technologies (explosion detection systems [EDS] and explosion trace detection systems [ETD]) currently being used to screen passenger baggage. In their research, they consider both single-device (i.e. one system) versus two-device systems (i.e. EDS and ETD) using a cost–benefit analysis. First, they estimate expected annual direct costs of using EDS, ETD or a combination of them both for 100 per cent of checked baggage screening. In particular, they study the trade-offs between single- and two-device strategies. Second, they estimate the expected number of successful threats under different checked baggage screening scenarios using a risk-based screening strategy. Using the current security set-up, current costs and identical estimated probabilities of a successful threat, the authors conclude that the single device systems are less costly and have less numbers of expected successful threats than two-device systems. They observe that this result is due to how the second device affects the alarm or clear decision on the first device. That is, if the first device (a more advanced technology) identifies a potential threat, and the second device (a less advanced technology) clears the item, it is actually passing the inspection with less rigour. Previous work concerning cost–benefit analysis and the trade-offs concerning the use of EDS machines can be found in Virta et al. (2003) and Jacobson et al. (2005).

Wong and Brooks (2015) outline the key premises of risk-based aviation security as being that: the vast majority of airline passengers present a low risk; the more information that is known about passengers, the better the population can be segmented in terms of risk; and security can be increased by focusing on unknowns while expediting the known or trusted travellers. They also identify reasons for risk-based aviation security measures. First, it can lead to more efficient security by taking resources away from other menial tasks and putting them towards more risky areas. Second, it can reduce costs through more efficient processes, and finally, if done properly, it can improve passenger throughput, experience and safety. However, Wong and Brooks (2015) acknowledge that barriers to adoption of risk-based measures exist; in particular, the public perception that a risk-based approach implies removal or less security. There is also a concern that the increased scrutiny of passengers based on race identification, behaviour detection, passenger data and flight-based risk will lead to racial and/or other types of profiling. Finally, it may be difficult to coordinate bilateral or multilateral approvals of new risk-based systems being adopted around the world. Wong and Brooks (2015) argue that a risk-based model must be able to separate high-risk passengers and flights from low-risk trusted travellers, while maintaining a sufficient level of security.

Poole (2006, 2008) surveys post-9/11 aviation security measures in the US, Canada and Europe, focusing in particular on the need for a risk-based approach to aviation security. Poole is critical of aviation security in the US both pre- and post-9/11. In the years prior to 9/11, Poole (2008) catalogues a history of poor performance with respect to passenger and baggage screening, attributable to the Federal Aviation Administration (FAA) and airline-hired screening companies. In the post-9/11 period, Poole (2006) is most critical of the lack of a risk-based approach to aviation security. He argues that much of the references to risk-based systems in Canada, Europe and the US have been comprised of just words rather than tangible actions. In the US, he cites dissatisfaction from the GAO that the Department for Homeland Security still lacks a comprehensive and integrated strategy that would allow for a risk-based approach and the lack of a risk-management system (Poole, 2008). Poole (2008) argues that the lack of a risk-based approach has been a deliberate choice by the Transportation Security Administration (TSA) because the TSA believes that its registered traveller programme is not secure, and therefore current members should be subject to the same screening methods and procedures as regular passengers. These actions run counter to what Poole (2008) argues are the benefits of a truly risk-based system, and outlines an example of a three-tiered approach to screening air travellers and their baggage that entails separating low-risk (registered) travellers from high-risk individuals (about who either nothing is known or something negative is known) and ordinary (unregistered) passengers. Poole argues that the security of this system would be maintained by random checks on low-risk passengers and by the use of biometrics to verify identity, along with the potential use of behavioural screening. Citing a model developed at Carnegie Mellon University, Poole (2008) argues that the throughput efficiency gains could be extremely significant, not only for registered (low-risk) passengers, but for ordinary passengers as well (as screening lines for this group shorten).

A key aspect of Poole's argument lies in the efficiency gains that result from a reallocation of existing resources. In applying the risk-based approach to baggage screening, Poole argues that under reasonable assumptions, risk-based screening of all non-registered passengers, plus the screening of 10 per cent of registered passengers, could reduce the deployment of EDS machines by 50 per cent. Poole (2008) acknowledges that moving to a truly risk-based system requires a redesign of the physical airport screening space (i.e. screening of registered passengers will require more space to accommodate two tiers of screening).

Veisten et al. (2011) note that while costs are easy to quantify from market information, the impacts on attack probabilities and its potential consequences (i.e. benefits) are difficult to quantify. They suggest that the type of screening can influence the probability of the terror fatality risk. In their study, 421 potential passengers from Norway complete an Internet-based questionnaire. The subjects are first introduced to the concept of fatality risk (number of deaths) caused by accidents and acts of terrorism. They are then informed of the reduction in the expected terror fatality numbers given the additional time and costs associated with a new risk-based passenger screening method. Each individual is then introduced to six pairwise choices between travel alternatives, each with different levels of screening intensities. The screening intensity ranges from current uniform screening to risk-based screening where passengers are identified as high, medium or low risk using biometric identity cards. Those not identified as low risk would be required to undergo a full body scan. Each level of screening intensity is accompanied with the expected reduction in terror fatality numbers, time use and cost. Additionally, the authors gather income and other individual characteristics of the sample population. For the Norwegians who were surveyed, they found, with the existing levels of terrorist risks, protecting privacy is preferred to a new risk-based screening system, even if this system has the potential of preventing terrorist activities. Moreover, they found that this preference against intrusive screening is significantly stronger for persons who were not identified as a low-risk passenger.

Gillen and Morrison (2015a) outline five key elements that are required for a risk-based airport security system to operate effectively:

1  Trusted traveller programmes wherein passengers submit to a pre-screening process that assesses their risk level. Qualified individuals are then eligible for expedited screening procedures at the airport.
2  Random checks; lowest-risk passengers must still be subject to random selection for more intense screening at the airport.
3  Use of biometric identification technology to help ensure that individuals cannot steal or procure the identity of low-risk trusted travellers.
4  Real-time behavioural assessments wherein trained agents at an airport select passengers for more intense screening if their behaviour or answers to interview questions raise suspicions concerning their risk level.
5  Real-time intelligence and information; intelligence authorities with information on changes in a person's risk status convey that information in a timely manner to security personnel at the airport.

Incorporating these five elements into a comprehensive airport security system worldwide is complex and potentially costly, with the potential for many coordination and incentive problems among participants. Implementation will require collaboration, information sharing and mutual recognition of any passenger's risk assessment between participating nation states. Nevertheless, in 2014, the International Air Transport Association (IATA) and Airports Council International (ACI) launched Smart Security (IATA and ACI, 2015), a joint programme aimed at pilot testing integrated combinations of new risk-based methods and technologies with the goal of a coordinated broader implementation across airports. In a joint communication, IATA and ACI state that the following security system elements have been piloted or have been permanently installed in some airports: innovative use and integration of advanced and new security technology and passenger processing systems; use of biometrics and data for passenger differentiation; adaptable risk-based screening capabilities; dynamic lane screening; efficient resource allocation; security processes integrated seamlessly into the passenger journey from curb to boarding; and process efficiencies (IATA and ACI, 2015). However, there is no publicly available data or analysis from the pilot projects conducted to date.

## The human factor

Persico and Todd (2005) study two measures for improving airport security with emphasis on how human behaviour may impact the effectiveness of either. First, they examine whether the implementation of a Computer-Assisted Passenger Prescreening System (CAPPSII) introduces racial biases towards passengers by security screening officers (a system used to pre-emptively identify terrorists at the point of purchase of an airline ticket or in advance of boarding a plane). CAPPSII is a profiling technology that has been challenged in the past in lawsuits alleging unlawful discrimination. Second, they investigate whether better detection through higher-ability screeners and improvements to security training decrease crime. They use an extended version of a Knowles et al. (2001) theoretical model of police and criminal behaviour, which measures crime rates and hit rates (the latter represents the probability that a search of a member of a group is successful) to determine the presence of both racial bias and crime. In the model, they identify two types of passengers and they assume that screeners can distinguish between using CAPPSII but cannot distinguish passengers within the group (i.e. whether the passenger within the group is a criminal or not). A passenger's propensity to commit a crime is dependent on their expected utility from committing a crime, which includes the probability of a search and detection. In equilibrium, screeners must receive the same expected utility from searching either group. The paper shows that hit-rate tests for racial bias can be applied even when there are imperfections in monitoring. These tests can also serve to check whether CAPPSII introduces racial/ethnic bias in searching. Additionally, they find using the model that improved detection rates lead to reductions in crime.

Bolfing et al. (2008) investigate how both image-based factors and human factors contribute to threat detection performance at the baggage screening area. They observe three image-based factors identified by Schwaninger (2003) and Schwaninger et al. (2004): view difficulty (baggage contents are difficult to view), super position (items that are superimposed on top of another object) and bag complexity (the size and shape of bag is abnormal, making X-raying difficult). Additionally, they identify two human factors: training (number of hours spent in training using the X-ray tutor) and age of the screening officer. They conduct a trial consisting of 2,048 observations of 90 professional security X-ray screening officers and measure their accuracy in identifying objects that are prohibited during the screening process. During the trial, image-based factors are varied to determine what human factors contribute to successful identification of prohibited objects. They find that knowledge-based factors, such as knowing which objects are prohibited and what these objects actually look like on the X-ray screen, are critical in successful screening. Consequently, their results indicate that the number of hours spent using computer-based training greatly enhances the screener's knowledge in this area. The authors also acknowledge that vigilance, stress, heat and time pressure all impact human behaviour, and that these factors could consequently affect the ability to properly screen.

The BEMOSA project (Behavioural Modelling for Security in Airports) is a project co-funded by the EU (see http://bemosa.technion.ac.il/). The objective of the project is to develop a behavioural model that best describes how people make airport security decisions in and outside of crisis situations. Kirschenbaum et al. (2012) argue that human factors are a key determinant in the proper or improper identification and curtailment of security threats and that human behaviour has the potential to undermine risk management systems. To date, the BEMOSA group has conducted research at various airports across Europe to gather data and observe procedures on how human behaviour influences both the effectiveness and efficiency of current security measures. Three studies derived from the BEMOSA project are Kirschenbaum et al. (2012) and Kirschenbaum (2013, 2015).

Kirschenbaum et al. (2012) investigate how the type of information source (formal or informal) affects security employees' decisions to comply with security rules and directives. More specifically, they examine the conditions under which security staff are more apt to follow the rules and protocol when faced with a security threat. The study employs ethnographic observations, a full-scale field survey, detailed questionnaire, and detailed personal interviews with 514 security personnel. According to Kirschenbaum et al. (2012), the decision environment is characterised by: multiple sources of information concerning threats and alternative actions; information flowing through both formal and informal networks; the opportunity for employees to make a security decision that may comply or not comply with the rules (depending on the source of information); and a hierarchy of information sources such that one source of information may dominate another. The results indicate that security employees receive most updates from their supervisor/manager (71 per cent), by written orders (63 per cent), from friends (53 per cent) and from rumours (33 per cent). Moreover, the results show that information from informal sources leads towards less rule compliance than information from formal sources.

Kirschenbaum (2013, 2015) investigates how passenger behaviour – in particular passenger negotiations with security staff – influences the costs of security screening. He reports the results of an ethnographic study in which airport security operators were interviewed regarding the length of time it took to process a passenger when, for one reason or another, they needed to be stopped for questioning and examination. The interviews revealed that security personnel do not always follow the rules (may wave passengers through if they are focused on cost initiatives).

In addition, Kirschenbaum (2013) reports on a time-motion study in which the direct cost of manpower associated with security screening for different throughput times was calculated. The study used four general security-related behavioural categories for passengers who either: (1) pass through security without incident; (2) accept security's order to remove the prohibited item; (3) negotiate with the security officer to keep the item; or (4) refuse to give up the item to the security officer. Kirschenbaum provides evidence that the time to process each one of these behaviour types increases with movement from category 1 to category 4, and his results indicate that problematic passengers (who negotiate or argue) account for a significant portion of screening security costs. He argues that passenger behaviour has been a missing link when calculating the true costs of security, and that screening security could be more cost-efficient if passengers were sorted according to whether they are uninformed/forgetful or frequent flyers. This may also help streamline some of the processes. The study also highlights the importance of ensuring passengers are fully informed about screening security processes and requirements prior to arrival at the airport.

Kirschenbaum (2015) includes the reality of human behaviour within the current security model. In this new model, he strongly advocates that major investment for aviation security in the future should be placed on staffing, training and motivating employees.

Skorupski and Uchronski (2015) develop a model and a computer system that can evaluate the effectiveness of airport securities screeners' capabilities to identify prohibited items in baggage. In this model, they take into account the impact of human decision-making in the process. Additionally, they include many subjective factors, such as employees' experience, level of training and at-work attitudes. Experiments were conducted at Katowice-Pyrzowice Airport, enabling the evaluation of individuals and groups of employees working during the same shift. Their results suggest that comprehensive training sessions should occur every 12 months, with ongoing training sessions occurring every six months.

## Role of new technology

Security checks are performed on passengers, carry-on bags, luggage and cargo containers using various technologies in an effort to circumvent potential malicious attacks on the aviation infrastructure. The TSA (2013) identifies the following technologies currently in place at all airports: bottled liquid scanners (which differentiate liquid explosives from common benign liquids), EDSs that capture images of a single bag to determine if the bag contains a potential threat, ETDs where passengers' bags and hands are swabbed and the swab is placed in a scanner, and threat image projection (TIP), where an image of a gun or a weapon is projected on to the bag being scanned to check screening officers' ability to detect weapons or explosives. Full-body scanners have slowly replaced metal detection scanners – since 2007 in many countries. Full-body scanners detect objects on a person's body without the passenger having to physically remove their clothes. The advantage of the full-body scanner is that it can detect more than metal objects, and therefore, in addition to an enhanced detection system, no physical contact with the passenger by the security screeners is required. The TSA (2013) has identified the following pilot projects for future implementation: credential authorisation technology, biometric systems, and next-generation bottled liquid scanners.

Benda (2015) argues that the biggest challenge for technology is finding ways to dramatically improve throughput of passengers without compromising the level of security. As an example, Benda suggests that printable radio frequency identification (RFID) technology could enable the use of a risk-based approach in baggage screening to expedite screening and eliminate unnecessary and costly secondary screening of bags, stating that: "[RFID tag] readers could automatically assess each bag prior to entering the EDS, dynamically adjusting the EDS detection algorithms based on the risks presented by each bag's owner, potentially significantly lowering the number of bags that need secondary screening" (Benda, 2015: 48). Benda also argues that significant economies of scope could be realised if screening personnel are located remotely rather than at a single airport checkpoint location. Virtual interaction from a remote screening workforce would allow airport security authorities to allocate screening capacity efficiently across airports and terminals.

Academic literature related to technology adoption in aviation security tends to be focused on engineering and operations research approaches to modelling, simulating and testing the technical aspects and attributes of new technologies (e.g. Singh and Singh, 2002). There are relatively fewer articles covering economic aspects of technology adoption; however, one area identified above by the TSA in which there is a growing research interest is in biometrics – the science of recognising an individual based on a signal detection system that senses a raw biometric signal, processes the signal to extract important physical features, and compares these features against an existing database to validate or invalidate a claimed identity.

Jain et al. (2006) provide an overview of issues related to biometrics, focusing on examining applications where biometrics can enhance information security and establishing a number of

*Table 21.1* Comparison of various biometric technologies

| Biometric identifier | Factors | | | | | | |
|---|---|---|---|---|---|---|---|
| | Universality | Distinctiveness | Permanence | Collectible | Performance | Acceptability | Circumvention |
| Face | H | H | M | H | L | H | H |
| Fingerprint | M | H | H | M | H | M | M |
| Hand geometry | M | M | M | H | M | M | M |
| Iris | H | H | H | M | H | L | L |
| Keystroke | L | L | L | M | L | M | M |
| Signature | L | L | L | H | L | H | H |
| Voice | M | L | L | M | L | H | H |

*Source*: Jain et al. (2006).

*Notes*: Universality (do all people have it); distinctiveness (can people be distinguished based on an identifier); permanence (how permanent are identifiers); collectible (how well can the identifiers be collected and quantified); performance (speed and accuracy); acceptability (how willing are people to accept the technology); and circumvention (how foolproof is the technology).

challenges when using biometric technology in real-world settings. They also discuss potential solutions to address problems with current biometric technology for wide-scale application in areas such as airport security. Table 21.1 shows a ranking assessment by Jain et al. (2006) of seven key attributes of seven biometric technologies.

Jain et al. (2006) assign a discrete ranking to each biometric technology attribute: high (H), medium (M) and low (L). Table 21.1 indicates that iris scan technology, while rated highly in terms of universality, distinctiveness and performance, scores poorly in terms of acceptability and circumvention. In contrast, face recognition technology, while more acceptable and foolproof, does not rate highly on performance or permanence. They conclude that no single biometric system passes all three required factors for success: accuracy, available scale or size of database, and usability.

Similar to Jain et al. (2006), Acharya and Kasprzycki (2010) suggest that biometric technologies are vulnerable to physical attack (i.e. damage to hardware, the algorithms and templates are vulnerable to hacker attacks and data may be stolen or tampered with). Both Acharya and Kasprzycki (2010) and Jain et al. (2006) suggest that use of multimodal biometric technologies would at least partially address some of these issues.

Birney and Pidgeon (2012) study the relationship between biometric systems and the level of security and efficiency. They argue that biometric systems can simultaneously increase security while improving throughput efficiency and lowering costs. The key biometric system components identified by Birney and Pidgeon (2012) are: a sensor (e.g. fingerprint and/or iris scan), a feature extractor, and an enrollment database and a matching mechanism. They review field evidence from Ben Gurion International Airport, where a dual-sensor system (fingerprint plus iris) is employed, and report a decline in false positives and false negatives after implementation, along with improved accuracy in human matching techniques. They also report dramatic efficiency gains, whereby passenger time in passport control lines, which can take up to an hour, are reduced to 20 seconds using an automated inspection process. Birney and Pidgeon (2012) state that the most sophisticated biometric system could pay for itself in 10 years if accompanied by the reduction of one security agent at the lowest pay scale. Finally, they argue that from an ethics perspective, biometric systems do not impose any privacy issues over and above current (non-biometric) systems.

## Layered screening and pre-emption in airport security

Security can be viewed as a layering process; as new methods and technologies become available, new layers of security are added to enhance the level of security or to increase efficiency and lower costs of a given level of security. Each successful terrorist attack highlights weaknesses in the current aviation security system, and in response government agencies seek solutions to shore up the vulnerability. To this end, the TSA (2013) has identified 20 layers of defence against terrorist/malicious acts on aviation infrastructure. The approach as it pertains to layered screening is described as follows in the book *Understanding the Department of Homeland Security*:

> Each one of these layers alone is capable of stopping a terrorist attack. In combination their security value is multiplied, creating a much stronger, formidable system. A terrorist who has to overcome multiple security layers in order to carry out an attack is more likely to be pre-empted, deterred, or to fail during the attempt.
>
> *(Philpott, 2015: 80)*

LaTourrette (2012) examines the effectiveness of a layered security system, in which each layer provides some level of overlap and backup as a failsafe. LaTourrette argues that continued investment is characterised by diminishing returns in overall performance and that the degree of diminishing returns depends on the extent to which the layers in the system are complementary (meaning that one layer of security can affect a pre-existing layer of security's performance). Given that layers of security are not independent of one another, LaTourrette argues that there is a need to understand the dimensions and interrelations between security layers in the context of attack scenarios and pathways, security methods, passive versus active security, and human versus machine decision-making. Security elements can be characterised by identifying their important functional attributes and how these attributes interrelate across layers. As such, those interactions that enhance and those that downgrade system performance can be identified. Complementary capabilities and information transfer (information gained from one element is used for another) enhance performance, while lulling (shirking), offsetting or risky behaviour at checkpoints, interference between layers, and insider threats downgrade performance.

LaTourrette (2012) highlights that the interrelatedness of security layers can result in both positive and negative outcomes; a failure in one layer can cause an element in another layer to fail. In conclusion, LaTourrette argues that the more different each layer is from the prior layer, the greater the probability of preventing security risks. This type of security system would protect a broader range of potential threats. While some layering is beneficial, there is a need to recognise and account for a declining marginal benefit of additional security layers.

In a subsequent paper, Jackson and LaTourrette (2015) identify the challenge associated with determining the impact that the integration of several security measures together have in curtailing terrorist attacks. In their analysis, they consider the actions of the attackers to help determine areas of vulnerability in the current layered approach. They do this by evaluating the individual components, the combined performance, the completeness and the depth of protection of the layered security approach. They then identify four potential attack pathways – passenger entry, employee entry, baggage cargo and breach/covert entry – to determine where the layered security efforts are most effective. They find that the baggage and cargo and employee entry points are the most vulnerable targets with the least amount of layered security.

Chan et al. (2012) study whether targeted screening can improve security or improve costs, when it is based on an assessment of risk profile associated with the passenger. They construct a theoretical model of a trusted traveller programme (TTP) and assume the following:

1   There are two types of people: terrorists (representing a small percentage of the population) and citizens (the general public).
2   Some of these people will apply to the TTP programme (will volunteer for a background check) and some will not.
3   Some fraction of non-terrorist public will be incorrectly rejected.
4   Some fraction of terrorists will be incorrectly accepted.
5   The TTP will have special screening lines (less rigorous) while the balance of the people will go through public lines.
6   A reduction in the screening of trusted travellers results in security resources being freed, and these are redeployed to public screening lines.
7   These new resources provide more rigorous search in the non-trusted traveller line.
8   The shift in resources is cost-neutral.
9   In the TT line, there is still a chance of catching a terrorist.

By varying parameter values in the model, Chan et al. (2012) determine what percentage of the population should apply to the TTP (regardless of the number of terrorists) such that there would be improvement to security performance. The results of their analysis suggest that whether the TTP will improve or downgrade security depends on two factors: screening quality and the number of terrorists who successfully infiltrate the programme. The amount of any improvement will be dependent on the decisions of travellers and terrorists (i.e. the number who apply to the TTP). Their model demonstrates how (exogenous) decisions made by others can impact security performance, and it shows that even when the net benefits of the programme are dependent on the decisions of others, it is still possible to analyse consequences. They conclude that their model can be used to estimate the total number of explosive detection machines required per location, and to provide a complete picture of both staff and equipment needs.

Cavusoglu et al. (2013) develop a theoretical model to determine how the addition of passenger profiling impacts airport security operators when the profiler is vulnerable to the gaming of attackers. In their model, they identify two types of passenger screening: no profiling and profiling. In each type of screening, all passengers are sent through a security device, and those who raise an alarm are inspected, but in the profiling case, screening devices are configured differently for classified attackers versus normal passengers. Under the profiling set-up, it is assumed that the profiler is faced with the problem of attackers attempting to game the profiler by manipulating behaviour and attributes to represent normal passengers. The expected pay-off functions for both the TSA and the attackers are constructed, and the optimal detection rates that maximise TSA expected pay-offs are calculated. They conclude that a profiling set-up that achieves the optimal detection rate performs at least as well as the no profiling set-up on key performance measures (expected security costs, inspection rates of normal passengers and attacker detection ratios), even if gaming occurs.

## Non-passenger screening and security

This section draws heavily from Gillen and Morrison (2015a). While much of the public and media interest on matters of aviation security is focused on the safety and security of air passengers, the screening of non-passengers and air cargo is a less discussed but crucial element in aviation security. Air cargo includes passenger bags, mail and air freight in the hold of a passenger aircraft, and mail and freight transported in non-passenger (air freighter) aircraft. In the latter case, Gillen and Morrison (2015a) report that air freighters move 72 per cent of air freight from South East Asia to Europe and carry 80 per cent of trans-Pacific and 43 per cent of transatlantic air freight (see also Chapter 2). Screening of air freight has its own set of practical challenges; for example, it is difficult to screen air freight at short notice prior to take-off when cargo is loaded in containers or palletised. Also, the amount and range of screening equipment varies across airports, and some cargo is too large for X-ray equipment.

Peterson and Treat (2008) note that prior to 9/11, the International Civil Aviation Organisation (ICAO) set standards for shippers, freight forwarders and transportation firms to oversee and maintain the security of air cargo while in transit. Under the Chicago Convention, ICAO also recommended the use of risk management systems over physical inspection of cargo, acceptance of documents in an electronic format, and the use of pre-approved importers to increase the speed of customs processing. They highlight that by 2009, the IATA had only developed a list of best practices with respect to the protection of air cargo following a task force to establish a strategic plan on air cargo security (IATA, 2006, 2007).

Elias (2007) also notes that post-9/11, security in the US was primarily focused on passenger operations, and consequently, by 2007, an air cargo strategic plan had not been fully implemented. Elias (2007) argues that many improvements can and should be made, including industry-wide consolidation of known shipper programmes, increased cargo inspections, increased security at aircraft facilities, and increased oversight of aircraft operations.

The adequacy of security standards for air freight was brought into question in 2012 when terrorists in Yemen attempted to disguise bombs as printer toner cartridges as air freight bound for the US. ICAO standards require all air freight to be inspected and then held in secure areas prior to being shipped; this is also part of the Air Cargo Advance Screening Programme developed by the US Department of Homeland Security. While this programme relies on X-ray and screener inspection for air freight in belly hold, for larger air freight it relies on significant amounts of advance information concerning the items being shipped and all parties involved in shipping the freight. This is a risk-based approach such that more scrutiny is placed on cargo deemed to be of higher risk. However, compared to the TSA's 20 layers of security for air passengers, Jackson and LaTourrette (2015) calculate significantly fewer security layers at baggage, cargo and employee entry points in US airports, which they argue creates areas of vulnerability.

In Europe, the relative focus has been the risks to air freight arriving in EU member states from non-EU third countries. Macário et al. (2012) review the security of air cargo from third countries and highlight three areas of vulnerability: the capacity of member states to play their part in implementing a new regulatory framework; the dangers of over-regulation through different approaches across EU member states; and a policy bias towards air passenger security that affects the allocation of resources to secure air freight effectively. In particular, Macário et al. (2012) argue that more resources are required for implementation (e.g. the recruitment, selection and training of staff) relative to the administrative bureaucracy controlling consignments.

Nevertheless, by 2014, the EU had implemented a new Air Cargo or Mail Carrier Certificate (ACC3) programme. Under this programme, carriers bringing cargo from third countries must apply for ACC3 certification; meanwhile, independent validators for inspecting air freight have been trained and positioned in non-EU countries. In addition, an advanced screening programme similar to that employed in the US has been implemented, whereby firms can be registered to be an authorised economic operator to carry out security inspections.

Domingues et al. (2014) update their earlier analysis by re-examining the EU's legislative efforts to secure air freight from third countries, with a focus on the experience in Belgium. They conclude that the ACC3 framework is not satisfactory, in part due to a lack of an overarching strategy to serve the interests of all stakeholders. They argue that more emphasis should have been placed on collaboration between government and industry, and that there remains an urgent need to harmonise air freight security procedures.

# Conclusion

This chapter has reviewed economic and related research in key aspects of aviation security. More research is required to help address the challenges faced by current aviation security systems in a world where globalisation and terrorism coexist and co-evolve. In the coming years, growth of air passengers (see Chapters 1 and 19) and air cargo volumes, especially in Asia (see Chapter 2), will place new and increasing pressures on governments, airports and airlines to provide a sufficient level of security without major disruptions or costs to air transport networks and the economy. If terrorists are able to cripple transportation and inflict indirect damage to an economy through responses to terror threats (whether or not attacks occur), this becomes a victory for them.

The promise of new technologies and an evolution to risk-based approaches to security offer pathways to addressing these pressures, but such a transition is made that much harder without the support of academic research to assess current problems and provide guidance on the impact of potential solutions. The current lack of consistent and transparent data with which to conduct such research therefore represents a serious roadblock. Absent research and analysis, the political incentives surrounding new security methods and technologies will tend towards implementing new layers of security without removing or adapting existing layers. No politician or bureaucrat wants to risk blame for removing a security measure if that removal could be linked to a future successful attack. Notwithstanding the possible inefficiencies and detrimental effects arising from interactions between new security layers when there are no changes to current layers, this approach will cause security costs to continue to rise over time – a trend that surely is not sustainable. Governments and the institutions of aviation security must rectify this deficiency in data if they wish to reap the benefits of informed decision-making.

# References

Acharya, A. and Kasprzychi, T. (2010). *Biometrics and Government*, Library of Parliament Background Paper, Publication No. 06-30-E, Ottawa, Library of Parliament.

Benda, P. (2015). Commentary: harnessing advanced technology and process innovations to enhance aviation security, *Journal of Air Transport Management*, 48, 23–25.

Birney, Z. and Pidgeon, J. (2012). *Security in the Skies: Using Biometrics to Optimize Airport Security*, Pittsburgh, PA, University of Pittsburgh.

Bolfing, A., Halbherr, T. and Schwaninger, A. (2008). How image based factors and human factors contribute to threat detection performance in x-ray aviation security screening. In: A. Holzinger (ed.). *HCI and Usability for Education and Work*, Berlin, Springer Berlin Heidelberg.

Brons, M., Pels, E., Nijkamp, P. and Rietveld, P. (2002). Price elasticities of demand for passenger air travel: a meta-analysis, *Journal of Air Transport Management*, 8(3), 165–175.

Button, K. (2016). *The Economics and Political Economy of Transportation Security*, Cheltenham, Edward Elgar.

Cavusoglu, H., Kwark, Y., Mai, B. and Raghunathan, S. (2013). Passenger profiling and screening for aviation security in the presence of strategic attackers, *Decision Analysis*, 10(1), 63–81.

Chan, E.W., Jackson, B.A. and LaTourrette, T. (2012). The benefits of security depend on the trade-offs between intended and unintended consequences: the example of the trusted traveler program. In: B.A. Jackson, T. LaTourrette, E.W. Chan, R. Lundberg, A.R. Morral and D.R. Frelinger (eds). *Efficient Aviation Security: Strengthening the Analytic Foundation for Making Air Transport Security Decisions*, Santa Monica, CA, RAND Corporation.

Coughlin, C., Cohen J. and Khan, S. (2002). *Aviation Security and Terrorism: A Review of the Issues*, Working Paper 2002-009A, St. Louis, MO, Federal Reserve Bank of St. Louis.

Dillingham, G.L. (2001). *Aviation Security: Terrorist Acts Demonstrate Urgent Need to Improve Security at Nation's Airport*, testimony before the Committee on Commerce, Science, and Transportation, US Senate, GAO-01-1162T, Washington, DC, US GAO.

Domingues, S., Macário, R., Pauwels, T., Vande Voorde, E., Vanelslander, T. and Vieira, J. (2014). An assessment of regulation of air cargo security in Europe: a Belgian case study, *Journal of Air Transport Management*, 34(1), 131–139.

Elias, B. (2007). *Air Cargo Security*, CRS Report for Congress, Washington, DC, Congressional Research Service.

Enders, N. and Sandler, T. (1995). Terrorism: theory and application. In: K. Hartley and T. Sandler (eds). *Handbook of Defense Economics*, Amsterdam, Elsevier.

Frey, B.S., Luechinger, S. and Stutzer, A. (2004a). *Valuing Public Goods: The Life Satisfaction Approach*, CREMA Working Paper Series No. 2004-11, Basel, CREMA.

Frey, B.S., Luechinger, S. and Stutzer, A. (2004b). *Calculating Tragedy: Assessing the Costs of Terrorism*, CESifo Working Paper No. 1341, Category 1: Public Finance, Munich, CESifo.

Frost & Sullivan (2012). *Global Airport Security Market Assessment*, New York, Frost & Sullivan.

Gillen, D.W. and Morrison, W.G. (2015a). Aviation security: costing, pricing, finance and performance, *Journal of Air Transport Management*, 48, 1–12.

Gillen, D.W. and Morrison, W.G. (2015b). *Aviation Security: Design, Governance, Performance, Financing and Policy*, Technical Report, Ottawa, Public Safety Canada.

Gillen, D.W., Morrison, W.G. and Stewart, C. (2007). *Air Travel Demand Elasticities: Concepts, Issues and Measurement*, Ottowa, Government of Canada.

Hoffman, B. (2003). Al Qaeda, trends in terrorism, and future potentialities: an assessment, *Studies in Conflict & Terrorism*, 26(6), 429–442.

IATA (International Air Transport Association) (2006). *Simplifying Air Cargo: Cargo Security Strategy*, Montreal, IATA.

IATA (International Air Transport Association) (2007). *Cargo Services Conference Resolutions Manual*, Montreal, IATA.

IATA and ACI (International Air Transport Association and Airports Council International) (2015). *Smart security*. Online. Available at: www.iata.org/whatwedo/security/Documents/SMART%20SECURITY_ALL.pdf (accessed 5 February 2017).

ICAO (International Civil Aviation Organisation) (2004). *Aviation security issues, Assembly 35th session; Executive Committee, A35-WP/71*. Online. Available at: www.icao.int/Meetings/AMC/MA/Assembly%2035th%20Session/wp071r_en.pdf (accessed 5 February 2017).

Ito, H. and Lee, D. (2003). *Assessing the Impact of the September 11 Terrorist Attacks on US Airline Demand*, Working Paper, No. 2003-16, Providence, RI, Brown University.

Jackson, B.A. (2012). The costs of security can depend on what is being protected – and security can affect its value. In: B.A. Jackson, T. LaTourrette, E.W. Chan, R. Lundberg, A.R. Morral and D.R. Frelinger (eds). *Efficient Aviation Security: Strengthening the Analytic Foundation for Making Air Transport Security Decisions*, Santa Monica, CA, RAND Corporation.

Jackson, B.A. and Frelinger, D.R. (2012). The problem to be solved: aviation terrorism risk past, present and future. In: B.A. Jackson, T. LaTourrette, E.W. Chan, R. Lundberg, A.R. Morral and D.R. Frelinger (eds). *Efficient Aviation Security: Strengthening the Analytic Foundation for Making Air Transport Security Decisions*, Santa Monica, CA, RAND Corporation.

Jackson, B.A. and LaTourrette, T. (2015). Assessing the effectiveness of layered security for protecting the aviation system against adaptive adversaries, *Journal of Transport Management*, 48, 26–33.

Jacobson, S., McLay, L., Virta, J. and Kobza, J. (2005). Integer programming models for deployment of airport baggage screening security devices, *Optimization and Engineering*, 6(3), 339–359.

Jacobson, S., Karnani, T., Kobza, J. and Ritchie, L. (2006). A cost-benefit analysis of alternative device configurations for aviation-checked baggage security screening, *Risk Analysis*, 26(2), 297–310.

Jain, A., Ross, A. and Pankanti, S. (2006). Biometrics: a tool for information security, *IEEE Transactions on Information Forensics and Security*, 1(2), 125–143.

Kirschenbaum, A.A. (2013). The cost of airport security: the passenger dilemma, *Journal of Air Transport Management*, 30, 39–45.

Kirschenbaum, A.A. (2015). The social foundations of airport security, *Journal of Air Transport Management*, 48, 34–41.

Kirschenbaum, A.A., Mariani, M., Van Gulijk, C., Rapaport, C. and Lubasz, S. (2012). Airports at risk: the impact of information sources on security decisions, *Journal of Transport Security*, 5, 187–197.

Knowles, J., Persico, N. and Todd, P. (2001). Racial bias in motor vehicle searches: theory and evidence, *Journal of Political Economy*, 109(1), 203–229.

LaTourrette, T. (2012). The benefits of security depend on how different security measures work together. In: B.A. Jackson, T. LaTourrette, E.W. Chan, R. Lundberg, A.R. Morral and D.R. Frelinger (eds). *Efficient Aviation Security: Strengthening the Analytic Foundation for Making Air Transport Security Decisions*, Santa Monica, CA, RAND Corporation.

Macário, R., Vieira, J., Mano, P., van Renssen, S., Van de Voorde, E., Pauwels, T., Domingues, S., Dawkins, R. and Todd, J. (2012). *The Security of Air Cargo from Third Countries*, Brussels, European Parliament.

New York City Partnership and Chamber of Commerce (2001). *Economic Impact Analysis of the September 11th Attack on New York City*, New York, New York City Partnership and Chamber of Commerce.

Persico, N. and Todd, P.E. (2005). Passenger profiling, imperfect screening, and airport security, *The American Economic Review*, 95(2), 127–131.

Peterson, J. and Treat, A. (2008). The post 9/11 global framework for cargo security, *Journal of International Commerce & Economics*, March, 1.

Philpott, D. (2015). *Understanding the Department of Homeland Security*, London, Bernan Press.

Poole, R.W. Jr. (2006). *Airport Security: Time for a New Model*, Reason Foundation Policy Study 340, Los Angeles, CA, The Reason Foundation.

Poole, R.W. Jr. (2008). *Towards Risk-Based Aviation Security Policy*, Discussion Paper No. 2008-23, November, Paris, OECD/ITF.

Poole, R.W. Jr. (2015). Fresh thinking on aviation security, *Journal of Air Transport Management*, 48, 65–67.

Popescu, G. (2011). *Bordering and Ordering the Twenty-first Century: Understanding Borders. Political Science*, New York, Rowman & Littlefield.

Prentice, B.E. (2008). Tangible and intangible benefits of transportation security measures, *Journal of Transportation Security*, 1, 3–14.

Prentice, B.E. (2015). Canadian airport security: the privatization of a public good, *Journal of Air Transport Management*, 48, 52–59.

Rekiel, J. (2012). *EU and Dutch Perspective on Level Playing Field in Aviation Security*, Consultancy report for Ecorys, Netherlands and University of Amsterdam.

Samuelson, P.A. (1954). The pure theory of public expenditure, *Review of Economics and Statistics*, 36(4), 387–389.

Sandler, T. and Enders, W. (2004). An economic perspective on transnational terrorism, *European Journal of Political Economy*, 20(20), 301–316.

Schwaninger, A. (2003). *Object Recognition Test (ORT), Test Manual and User Guide*, Zurich, APSS.

Schwaninger, A., Hardmeier, D. and Hofer, F. (2004). Measuring visual abilities and visual knowledge of aviation security screeners. In: *Proceedings of the 38th Annual 2004 International Carnahan Conference on Security Technology*, IEEE.

Singh, S. and Singh, M. (2002). *Explosives Detection Systems (EDS) for Aviation Security: A Review*, Working Paper, Exeter, PANN Research, Department of Computer Science, University of Exeter.

Skorupski, J. and Uchronski, P. (2015). A fuzzy model for evaluating airport security screeners' work, *Journal of Air Transport Management*, 48, 42–51.

Stewart, M. and Mueller, J. (2008). A risk and cost-benefit assessment of United States aviation security measures, *Journal of Transportation Security*, 1(3), 143–159.

Stewart, M. and Mueller, J. (2015). Responsible policy analysis in aviation security with an evaluation of PreCheck, *Journal of Air Transport Management*, 48, 13–22.

TSA (Transportation Security Administration) (2013). *Official website of the Department of Homeland Security*. Online. Available at: www.tsa.gov (accessed 10 June 2017).

Veisten, K., Flügel, S. and Bjørnskau, T. (2011). Public's trade-off between a new risk-based airport screening and asserted terror risk impact: a stated choice survey from Norway, *Journal of Transportation Technologies*, 1, 11–20.

Virta, J., Jacobson, S. and Kobza, J. (2003). Analyzing the cost of screening selectee and non-selectee baggage, *Risk Analysis*, 23(5), 897–908.

Viscusi, W.K. (2000). The value of life in legal contexts: survey and critique, *American Law and Economics Review*, 2(1), 195–222.

Wong, S. and Brooks, N. (2015). Evolving risk-based security: a review of current issues and emerging trends impacting security screening in the aviation industry, *Journal of Air Transport Management*, 48, 60–64.

# 22

# Airline service quality and the consumer experience

*Dawna L. Rhoades*

## Introduction

As many airlines prepare to convince economy and low cost carrier (LCC) passengers that fixed-back seats are a better comfort option for flyers concerned about protecting their knees from the reclining seat in front of them, passengers in the front seats of the traditional full service carrier can expect to be offered a growing array of perks, from streaming video and music, often on their own devices, to gourmet, healthy meals prepared by renowned chefs. In between, airlines are exploring new classes of service that will offer passengers amenity and space options for a price (Reals, 2015). This differentiation in service is nothing new for airlines (see Chapter 9 for more discussion on airline differentiation). It is certainly familiar to any passenger in a deregulated air service market where market forces decide on price and service quality levels. As LCCs have gained market share across the globe, the idea of no-frills flying or paying for a growing list of amenities is an accepted trade-off for lower fares. Of course, the popular press has often highlighted carriers that have gone too far in their efforts to charge for additional services, as Spirit Airlines in the United States (US) and Ryanair in Europe can attest (LeBeau, 2016; Porter, 2014). Still, the International Air Transportation Association (IATA) has enshrined the idea of product differentiation and consumer choice into their New Distribution Capability (NDC) standard (IATA, 2016) (see also Chapters 13 and 20 for more details on NDC). Their argument is that airlines can best serve their customers by offering them a customised product that reflects their willingness to pay.

If there seems to be a complex array of service options available to airline customers, then it is not surprising that there is a wide and complex array of research on the topic of airline service quality, both popular press and academic. The purpose of this chapter is to explore the concept of service quality and the past two decades of research on the topic to help understand the relationship between the research and its findings, the future of airline service quality, and the approaches that management might take to address these issues.

## Defining the concept

Quality has been defined as excellence (Garvin, 1984) and value (Cronin and Taylor, 1992), but the most common definition is meeting or exceeding customer expectations (Parasuraman

362

et al., 1985). Theory posits that service quality leads to satisfaction, which leads to loyalty and repurchase (Fullerton, 2005; Rauyruen and Miller, 2007). Yet there remains some debate about the relationships in this chain because of the presence of mixed findings over the years (Szwarc, 2005; Szymanski and Henard, 2001). In part, the mixed findings are believed to be related to the multidimensional nature of the constructs and how they have been defined and viewed by different researchers (Oliver, 1999; Rauyruen and Miller, 2007). Still, there is general agreement that customers compare their expectations of service quality to their perceptions of the services received (Parasuraman et al., 1985, 1988). In fact, Parasuraman et al. (1988) gave rise to one of the most popular survey methods for evaluating service quality, SERVQUAL.

SERVQUAL examines expected and perceived service on five dimensions: tangibles, reliability, responsiveness, assurance and empathy. Expected service is believed to be shaped by such things as word-of-mouth communications, consumer needs and desires, and past experience. There is less agreement on the factors that affect consumer perception, but they include nationality and culture (Sultan and Simpson, 2000), reputation and branding (Ostrowski et al., 1993), and passenger segment (i.e. first, business, economy) (Makens and Marquardt, 1977). Cronin and Taylor (1992) even disagree regarding the inclusion of perception into the measurement of service quality, arguing that service quality is performance (SERVPERF).

Other approaches to analysing service quality have involved the use of secondary data on customer failures as represented by complaints or collected metrics on service features (e.g. response times, defective products, delays in shipping, arrival). Obviously, perception is not a factor in secondary research, except in that it may play a role in complaint behaviour, and researchers can only analyse data on the metrics collected. One advantage of secondary data research is that when the collected database is consistent across the years, researchers can evaluate longitudinal trends in customer service rather than reporting on snapshot, cross-sectional data.

## Prior research

This section will divide recent research into popular press reports and academic studies. The academic research is not an exhaustive list of the topic. It covers only research from the past 20 years, and does not include studies focused on frequent flyer programmes (FFPs), branding, airline financial performance, airline network issues, or service and alliance performance. This research is broken down into studies using either SERVQUAL or SERVPERF, other primary data methods, and secondary data studies. General findings, trends, strengths and weaknesses will be discussed.

### *Popular press*

Table 22.1 presents two of the most widely known popular press reports on airline quality: SkyTrax and JD Powers. While Conde Nast has occasionally released reports on airline quality, SkyTrax and JD Powers are annual reports and rankings/ratings that are frequently touted by airlines as proof of quality. These surveys usually include a large sample of frequent flyers, which means they do not capture the opinions of occasional flyers, although, as seen below, there are those who feel that firms should really only pay attention to their best customers. Due to the cross-sectional nature of these surveys, it is difficult to analyse overall trends or trends in specific categories. Further, these categories are subject to change from one year to the next. Finally, some of the popular press reports do not provide overall rankings, choosing instead to provide a winner per category or a top three per category.

Table 22.1 Popular press quality awards

|  | SkyTrax | JD Powers |
|---|---|---|
| Categories | Food and beverage<br>In-flight entertainment<br>Seat comfort<br>Staff service<br>Value for money | Overall satisfaction<br>Reservation experience<br>Check-in experience<br>Boarding experience<br>Aircraft experience<br>Staff experience<br>Service experience<br>Cost and fee experience |
| Rating system | 1 to 5 stars per each category with overall airline rating assigned | Power circle ratings calculated based on the range between the highest and lowest score in each category |
| Website | www.airlinequality.com | www.jdpower.com |

## SERVQUAL/SERVPERF

The largest category of studies reported here have used either SERVQUAL, SERVPERF, or both, as a means of studying airline service quality. Broadly, these studies have found the expected links between service quality and customer satisfaction, with some factors more strongly related, such as reliability and assurance (see Chou et al., 2011; Pakdil and Aydın, 2007). In addition, some studies have linked satisfaction to loyalty and behavioural intent (see Amiruddin, 2013; Huang, 2010; Park et al., 2004, 2005). A brief glance at the titles in Table 22.2 shows that many were conducted in international markets with airlines that could be expected to have a diverse cultural clientele. These provide some evidence of cultural differences in expectations (see Gilbert and Wong, 2002; Ladhari and Bressolles, 2011; Sultan and Simpson, 2000). Alqeed (2013) did examine business profitability, but only as a mediating variable between service quality and customer satisfaction.

The SERVQUAL/SERVPERF methodology is widely used, and there are a number of developed surveys for researchers to choose from for their study. Many have included factor analyses confirming the structure of the basic dimensions and items included. A close examination of the actual items under the five basic dimensions reveals that there are a number of variations in the features included across these studies, making an exact comparison of results difficult. Still, the overall conclusion is that service quality is positively related to customer satisfaction in the airline industry.

## Other primary studies

Studies in this section (see Table 22.3) examined primary data through surveys designed by the researchers/authors themselves or, in the case of Hossain et al. (2011), used latent semantic analysis (LSA) to examine customer comment documents as a means of evaluating factors in service quality (service expectations, caring/friendly staff and luggage handling were the main issues for passengers). As with the earlier studies examined, service quality is positively related to customer satisfaction and behavioural intentions (Adeola and Adebiyi, 2014; Khraim, 2013; Namukasa, 2013). Several articles looked at quality from a slightly different angle. Fageda et al. (2014) examined survey data from multiple airlines, and reported that the perceived quality of larger airlines was higher than their smaller counterparts and airlines in financial

*Table 22.2* Service quality studies using SERVQUAL/SERVPERF

| Study | Title |
|---|---|
| Abdullah et al. (2012) | A structural equation modelling approach to validate the dimensions of SERVPERF in the airline industry of Malaysia. |
| Alqeed (2013) | Service quality relationship with customer satisfaction and business profitability: a case study of Royal Jordanian. |
| Amiruddin (2013) | Price, service quality and customer loyalty: a case of Air Asia. |
| Ariffin et al. (2010) | Service quality and satisfaction for LCCs. |
| Aydin and Yildirim (2012) | The measurement of service quality with SERVQUAL for different domestic airline firms in Turkey. |
| Aydın and Pakdil (2008) | Fuzzy SERVQUAL analysis in airline services. |
| Baby (2014) | Passengers' expectation on service quality dimensions in domestic airline services. |
| Chou et al. (2011) | An evaluation of airline service quality using the fuzzy weighted SERVQUAL method. |
| Dias (2011) | *The Influence of Service Quality and Satisfaction in Consumer Behaviour Intention: An Empirical Study of a Charter Airline.* |
| Chikwendu et al. (2012) | Evaluation of service quality of a Nigerian airline using the SERVQUAL model. |
| Erdil and Yildiz (2011) | Measuring service quality and a comparative analysis in the passenger carriage of the airline industry. |
| Erdoğan et al. (2013) | A customer satisfaction model based on fuzzy TOPSIS and SERVQUAL methods. |
| Farid et al. (2014) | Offering a model to measure the impact of the SERVQUAL model to service quality on brand loyalty with an emphasis on the role of brand switching cost. |
| Gilbert and Wong (2002) | Passenger expectations and airline services: a Hong Kong based study. |
| Huang (2010) | The effect of airline service quality on passengers' behavioural intentions using SERVQUAL scores: a Taiwan case study. |
| Kalitesi and Araştırma (2012) | Service quality in the airline businesses: a research on THY. |
| Ladhari and Bressolles (2011) | Culture and personal values: how they influence perceived service quality. |
| Nagar (2013) | Perceived service quality with frill and no frill airlines: an explanatory research among Indian passengers. |
| Pakdil and Aydın (2007) | Expectations and perceptions in airline services: an analysis using weighted SERVQUAL scores. |
| Park et al. (2004) | The effect of airline service quality on passengers' behavioural intentions: a Korean case study. |
| Park et al. (2005) | Investigating the effect of airline service quality on airlines' image and passenger future behavioural intentions: findings from Australian international air passengers. |
| Prayag (2007) | Assessing international tourists' perception of service quality at Air Mauritius. |
| Saha and Theingi (2009) | Service quality, satisfaction, and behavioural intentions: a study of LCCs in Thailand. |
| Sultan and Simpson (2000) | International service variants: airline passenger expectations and perceptions of service quality. |

distress were perceived to have lower quality than stronger airlines. There were also differences in the perceived quality of airlines from different regions of the world. Curtis et al. (2012) found that satisfaction with overall airline quality, airline personnel in the gates, and aircraft cleanliness/appearance decreased the more passengers reported flying.

*Table 22.3* Other primary data service quality studies

| Study | Title |
|---|---|
| Adeola and Adebiyi (2014) | Service quality, perceived value and customer satisfaction as determinant of airline choice in Nigeria. |
| Atalik (2007) | Customer complaints about airline service: a preliminary study of Turkish frequent flyers. |
| Atilgan et al. (2008) | Measuring and mapping customers' perception and expectations for airlines: the SunExpress case with gaps model. |
| Balcombe et al. (2009) | Consumer willingness to pay for in-flight service and comfort levels: a choice experiment. |
| Curtis et al. (2012) | Satisfaction with airline service quality: familiarity breeds contempt. |
| Fageda et al. (2014) | Assessing airlines: quality as a competitive variable. |
| Hossain et al. (2011) | A consumer perspective of service quality in the airline industry. |
| Khraim (2013) | Airline image and service quality effects on travelling customers' behavioural intentions in Jordan. |
| Liou and Tzeng (2007) | A non-additive model for evaluating airline service quality. |
| Mostert et al. (2009) | The influence of service failure and service recovery on airline passengers' relationships with domestic airlines: an exploratory study. |
| Namukasa (2013) | The influence of airline service quality on passenger satisfaction and loyalty: the case of Uganda airline industry. |
| Tsaur et al. (2002) | The evaluation of airline service quality by fuzzy MCDM. |
| Urban (2013) | Perceived quality versus quality of processes: a meta concept of service quality measurement. |
| Zangmo et al. (2014) | The influence of passenger perceived service quality on passenger satisfaction and loyalty: case of Drukair Royal Bhutan Airlines. |

Overall, the general results of this group of studies supports the basic theories of the relationship between service quality, satisfaction, intent and loyalty, although they arrive at these conclusions from different methodologies. The different methodologies mean that direct comparison between studies is not possible, and some of the studies examined the questions from very different angles. Still, each provides a small piece of the complex puzzle.

## Secondary data studies

It should be noted at the outset that most of the research using secondary data involves US airlines because the US has made data on the industry publicly available since 1987 (via the so-called Air Travel Consumer Report of the US Department of Transportation [DOT]). As Table 22.4 shows, two groups of US researchers have used these data extensively. The Airline Quality Rating (AQR) report was first released in 1991. While it has changed extensively over the years, it continues to rank US airlines and release a public report annually (Bowen and Headley, 1991–2015). The second group of researchers has published studies since 1998 covering all the years that data are available. The most recent study looks at 25 years of airline quality (Waguespack and Rhoades, 2014). The focus of this group is less on yearly rankings and more on the overall trend in service quality, which corresponds closely to the economic cycle; specifically, the industry reports fewer service problems when traffic is down. This leads to the conclusion that high traffic levels create a burden on the existing aviation infrastructure, which results in more flight delays, denied boarding, cancellations, mishandled baggage and complaints. In a twist on the question of service quality, Nafchi et al. (2014) examined airline quality from the perspective of the websites to determine whether they delivered features that attracted customers.

*Table 22.4* Service quality studies using secondary data

| Study | Title |
| --- | --- |
| Bowen and Headley (1991–2015) | *Airline Quality Rating Report.* |
| Gursoy et al. (2005) | The US airlines relative positioning based on attributes of service quality. |
| Nafchi et al. (2014) | A new quality model to measure quality of airlines' websites. |
| Rhoades and Waguespack (1999) | Better safe than service: the relationship between service and safety quality in the US airline industry. |
| Rhoades and Waguespack (2000a) | Service quality in the US airline industry: variations in performance within and between firms. |
| Rhoades and Waguespack (2000b) | Judging a book by its cover: the relationship between service and safety quality in the US airline industry. |
| Rhoades and Waguespack (2004) | Service and safety quality in US airlines: pre- and post-September 11th. |
| Rhoades and Waguespack (2005) | Strategic imperatives and the pursuit of quality in the US airline industry. |
| Rhoades and Waguespack (2008) | Twenty years of service quality performance in the US airline industry. |
| Rhoades et al. (1998) | Service quality in the US airline industry: progress and problems. |
| Tiernan et al. (2008) | Airline alliance service quality performance: an analysis of US and EU member airlines. |
| Waguespack and Rhoades (2014) | Twenty-five years of measuring airline service quality or why is airline service quality only good when times are bad? |
| Waguespack et al. (2007) | An investigation into airline service quality performance between US legacy carriers and their EU competitors and partners. |
| Yayla-Kullu (2013) | A critical evaluation of US airlines' service quality performance: lower costs vs. satisfied customers. |

Clearly, one of the advantages of secondary data is the ability to look at trends across time. While there have been some changes over the years (elimination of smoking complaints, inclusion of cancellations), these have been relatively minor. Thus, the data reflect changes in the industry as well as changes in the carriers over the years of the study. As noted above, the data reveal an economic and traffic volume effect for the industry. They also show how some carriers have maintained, and even improved, in service quality while other airlines in financial trouble tend to show an increase in service-related quality problems. The major disadvantage of this type of research is that it does not specifically address customer satisfaction, intent to repurchase or repurchase behaviour. Even the complaint data are questionable in that they typically represent less than 2 per cent of the enplaned population, even in years that the popular press term bad for airline quality (Waguespack and Rhoades, 2014). Spirit Airlines posted the worst on-time arrival and complaint rate in the DOT's *Air Travel Consumer Report* at a time when it was witnessing growing passenger numbers and investment interest. Like Ryanair in Europe, Spirit's response was to note that it was in the business of delivering value at low prices, and customers expecting frills should shop elsewhere (DOT, 2016; LeBeau, 2016; Maxon, 2014).

## Discussion

A review of the last 20 years reveals that airline service has been the subject of extensive academic research and popular press focus. While the literature overall finds a positive relationship between service quality and customer satisfaction, as well as loyalty and intent to repurchase, several recent articles have pointed out a critical missing link, namely a link to airline financial performance. After all, if a reputation for excellent service quality resulted in a more profitable airline, then it would be expected that there would be a race to the top of the rankings among international carriers. Sadly, there is evidence to the contrary. A case in point is Virgin America, which ranked number one in the most recent AQR, but has failed to escape the label as an award-winning, money-losing carrier that is not succeeding with shareholders (Ali, 2016; Armstrong, 2012). In fact, a recent article in *The Economist* reported the results of a study by IATA, which found no proof that satisfied happy customers lead to commercially successful airlines (*The Economist*, 2015). As Mouawad (2016) has noted, the primary concern for airlines following the first decade of the twenty-first century with 9/11, SARS, the global financial crisis and erupting volcanoes is providing acceptable returns on investment and paying down debt accrued over the years of hardship. Consolidation in many markets and capacity discipline has allowed the industry to post successive years of profit, but service quality levels are not likely to rise for most passengers. If anything, airlines are likely to focus on efficiency. As Yayla-Kullu (2013) has reported, this does not necessarily mean that service quality will suffer, but the pursuit of lower cost-efficiency does not suggest that carriers will be raising service levels in an effort to improve customer satisfaction. Still, reliability is one of the SERVQUAL dimensions that is often noted as leading to customer satisfaction, and this does involve a high degree of efficiency. Customers who arrive on time with their bags tend to be happier than other customers. A nice meal or a good movie are not likely to help consumers forget a lost bag or a missed connection.

Service quality literature suggests that quality service leads to satisfaction, which leads to loyalty and returning customers. A firm with loyal customers is assumed to be a successful firm. Airline FFPs are called loyalty programmes for a reason; they are designed to create and ensure loyalty. Here, too, the evidence is not really supportive. Research cited in Bryan (2014a) by Aimia, a firm that runs a number of FFPs and other loyalty programmes, found that 73 per cent of consumers belonged to a supermarket loyalty programme, but only 12 per cent belonged to an airline FFP. Further, many did not use their FFP points for seats or any of the other items that many airlines offer. This has not stopped airline FFPs from evolving into profit centres for carriers who have spun them off to investors interested in the rich source of data they provide (Bryan, 2014a, 2014b). The idea of FFPs as short-term revenue generators is a far cry from the original American Airlines concept. In a special report on *The Price of Loyalty*, it is suggested that large carriers will likely focus on the cash-generating aspects of FFPs, while smaller carriers will try to use them as a customer relationship management (CRM) tool (IATA, 2012). Literature on customer satisfaction and loyalty would argue for the benefit of the latter approach, but when it comes to airlines the difference between theory and reality is often vast.

## Managerial implications

If there is no proof of a link between service quality and profitability, then it is unclear why this is an issue. It might be surprising to find that brand is considered to be a key factor in consumer choice, according to IATA (2015: 3), which states that: "Brand perception is everything" and cites on-time performance (75 per cent), aircraft quality and interior (66 per cent), and customer interaction (54 per cent) as the top three factors in branding. Of course, the survey then reports that the top three factors influencing ticket purchase are pricing (43 per cent), schedule and convenient flight time (21 per cent), and FFP (13 per cent). While there seems to be a disconnection between brand perception and the driving factor of price, this may be explained by an Australian survey that found that three-quarters of customers would not book with an unknown carrier because they were not aware of its brand reputation for safety and service. So, although brand loyalty does not stop customers from shopping for a better price, it does stop them from booking on a carrier whose brand they do not know (Leggatt, 2014). This would also indicate that an airline whose brand is not known for the former qualities would be advised to take action to change their image.

One further finding of the IATA survey is that customers want more proactive access to information and services – online check-in (with their bags), seat assignment in advance, flight status, baggage status and tracking, regulations updates, SMS service, and use of own devices for flight entertainment. Passengers are prepared, even willing, to print their own passes and luggage tags, check themselves in and deposit their luggage. In exchange, they want as much information as they can get on flights, connections, airports, rebooking and luggage location. If this is all mobile, then it is even better. This assumes that the information is accurate. A site that reports erroneously that baggage has not been loaded or is arriving at a different location is worse than not reporting at all.

IATA sold the NDC standard on the concept that the best way to serve passengers is to allow them to customise their experience, getting (and paying for) what they value most from the flight experience. While consumer critics opposed NDC, claiming that it was an effort by airlines to avoid publishing prices and to remove the price transparencies and comparison shopping that most consumers desire (Kelly, 2013), the theoretical argument over expectations and service quality would suggest that if passengers are allowed to design their own experience, then they are more likely to be satisfied with the service they get. The airline that makes this selection experience as painless as possible is likely to gain customers and loyalty.

## Conclusion

If the volume of research is an indication of the importance of a topic, then airline service quality is certainly important to academic researchers. It is also a complex, bedeviling construct to researchers, consumers and airlines. While a link between expectations and satisfaction is clear and there is research on the factors that lead customers to develop their expectations, the links become less clear when moving from satisfaction to loyalty to intent to repurchase, and seem to totally break down when it comes to firm profitability. As noted above, consumers appear to have a decision set of airlines whose brand they recognise as meeting basic standards for service and safety. Within this set, price and schedule become key factors in final choice. In other words, consumers are not rational decision-makers; they are satisficing (Simon, 1956). Airlines, on the other hand, seek to maximise revenue and profits. Airline service quality lies somewhere in the middle, subject to the winds of changing expectations, economic crisis and airline competition.

## References

Abdullah, K., Jan, M.T. and Manaf, N.H.A. (2012). A structural equation modelling approach to validate the dimensions of SERVPERF in airline industry of Malaysia, *International Journal of Engineering and Management Sciences*, 3(2), 134–141.

Adeola, M.M. and Adebiyi, S.O. (2014). Service quality, perceived value and customer satisfaction as determinant of airline choice in Nigeria, *International Letters of Social and Humanistic Sciences*, 20, 66–80.

Ali, H. (2016). *Virgin America Inc (VA) reports April 2016 performance*. Online. Available at: www.bidnessetc. com/68759-virgin-america-va-reports-april-2016-performance/ (accessed 11 May 2016).

Alqeed, M.A. (2013). Service quality relationship with customer satisfaction and business profitability: a case study of Royal Jordanian, *European Journal of Business and Management*, 5(1), 210–216.

Amiruddin, N.H. (2013). Price, service quality and customer loyalty: a case of Air Asia, *South East Asia Journal of Contemporary Business, Economics and Law*, 2(1), 34–40.

Ariffin, A.A.M., Salleh, L.H.M., Aziz, N. and Asbudin, A.A. (2010). Service quality and satisfaction for low cost carriers, *International Review of Business Research Papers*, 6(1), 47–56.

Armstrong, D. (2012). *Virgin America a hit, but losing money*. Online. Available at: www.sfgate.com/business/article/Virgin-America-a-hit-but-losing-money-3762763.php (accessed 11 May 2016).

Atalik, O. (2007). Customer complaints about airline service: a preliminary study of Turkish frequent flyers, *Management Research News*, 30(6), 409–419.

Atilgan, E., Akinci, S. and Aksoy, S. (2008). Measuring and mapping customers' perception and expectations for airlines: the SunExpress case with gaps model, *Journal of Global Strategic Management*, 3, 68–78.

Aydin, K. and Yildirim, S. (2012). The measurement of service quality with SERVQUAL for different domestic airline firms in Turkey, *Serbian Journal of Management*, 7(2), 219–230.

Aydın, O. and Pakdil, F. (2008). Fuzzy SERVQUAL analysis in airline services, *Organizacija*, 41(3), 108–115.

Baby, P. (2014). Passengers' expectation on service quality dimensions in domestic airline services, *Global Journal for Research Analysis*, 3(6), 1–3.

Balcombe, K., Fraser, I. and Harri, L. (2009). Consumer willingness to pay for in-flight service and comfort levels: a choice experiment, *Journal of Air Transport Management*, 15(5), 221–226.

Bowen, B.D. and Headley, D.E. (1991–2015). *Airline Quality Rating Report*, Prescott, FL/Wichita, KS, Embry-Riddle Aeronautical University/Wichita State University.

Bryan, V. (2014a). *Airlines are unlocking new value in their frequent flier programs*. Online. Available at: www.businessinsider.com/r-frequent-flyer-schemes-revamped-to-drive-profits-in-tough-times-for-airlines-2014-11 (accessed 11 May 2016).

Bryan, V. (2014b) *Frequent flyer schemes revamped to drive profits in tough times for airlines*. Online. Available at: www.reuters.com/article/airlines-frequentflyers-idUSL6N0P442420140811 (accessed 14 March 2017).

Chikwendu, E., Ejem, E. and Ezenwa, A. (2012). Evaluation of service quality of Nigerian airline using Servqual model, *Journal of Hospitality Management and Tourism*, 3(6), 117–125.

Chou, C., Liu, L., Huang, S., Yih, J. and Han, T. (2011). An evaluation of airline service quality using the fuzzy weighted SERVQUAL method, *Applied Soft Computing*, 11, 2117–2128.

Cronin, J.J. and Taylor, S.A. (1992). Measuring service quality: a reexamination and extension, *Journal of Marketing*, 56(3), 55–68.

Curtis, T., Rhoades, D.L. and Waguespack, B.P. (2012). Satisfaction with airline service quality: familiarity breeds contempt, *International Journal of Aviation Management*, 1(4), 242–257.

Dias, M.I.D.C. (2011). *The Influence of Service Quality and Satisfaction in Consumer Behavior Intention: An Empirical Study of a Charter Airline*, Master Thesis, Lisbon, Lisbon School of Economics & Management.

DOT (Department of Transportation) (2016). *Air Travel Consumer Report*. Online. Available at: www.transportation.gov/airconsumer/air-travel-consumer-report (accessed 10 May 2016).

Erdil, S. and Yildiz, O. (2011). Measuring service quality and comparative analysis in the passenger carriage of airline industry. *Procedia Social and Behavioral Science*, 24, 1232–1242.

Erdoğan, M., Bilişik, O.N., Kaya, I. and Baraçlı, H. (2013). A customer satisfaction model based on fuzzy TOPSIS and SERVQUAL methods, *Lecture Notes in Management Science*, 5, 74–83.

Fageda, X., Jiménez, J.L. and Suárez-Alemán, A. (2014). Assessing airlines: quality as a competitive variable, *International Journal of Transport Economics*, 41(3), 425–438.

Farid, F., Moghaddasi, S., Pakinasab, N. and Moghaddasi, S.O (2014). Offering a model to measure the impact of the servqual model to service quality on brand loyalty with emphasis on the role of brand switching cost, *Indian Journal of Fundamental and Applied Life Sciences*, 4(1), 2036–2043.

Fullerton, G. (2005). The impact of brand commitment on loyalty to retail service brands, *Canadian Journal of Administrative Sciences*, 22(2), 97–110.

Garvin, G. (1984). What does 'product quality' really mean? *Sloan Management Review*, 26(1), 25–43.

Gilbert, D. and Wong, R.K.C. (2002). Passenger expectations and airline services: a Hong Kong based study, *Tourism Management*, 24, 519–532.

Gursoy, D., Chen, M. and Kim, H.J. (2005). The US airlines relative positioning based on attributes of service quality, *Tourism Management*, 26, 57–67.

Hossain, M.M., Ouedraogo, N. and Rezania, D. (2011). A consumer perspective of service quality in the airline industry, *Tourism Management*, 26, 57–67.

Huang, K.Y. (2010). The effect of airline service quality on passengers' behavioral intentions using SERVQUAL scores: a Taiwan case study, *Journal of the Eastern Asia Society for Transportation Studies*, 8, 2330–2343.

IATA (International Air Transport Association) (2012). *Special report: the price of loyalty.* Online. Available at: http://airlines.iata.org/reports/special-report-the-price-of-loyalty (accessed 11 May 2016).

IATA (International Air Transport Association) (2015). *2015 IATA Global passenger survey.* Online. Available at: www.iata.org/whatwedo/passenger/gps/Documents/Highlights%202015-Global-Passenger-Survey-Final.pdf (accessed 11 May 2016).

IATA (International Air Transport Association) (2016). *New Distribution Capability.* Online. Available at: www.iata.org/whatwedo/airline-distribution/ndc/pages/default.aspx (accessed May 4, 2016).

Kalitesi, H.I.Z. and Araştırma, T.B. (2012). Service quality in airline businesses: a research on THY, *Kocaeli Üniversitesi Sosyal Bilimler Dergisi*, 24, 35–49.

Kelly, G. (2013). *BTC says opposition to IATAs New Distribution Capability mounting.* Online. Available at: www.travelpulse.com/news/features/btc-says-opposition-to-iatas.html (accessed 12 May 2016).

Khraim, H.S. (2013). Airline image and service quality effects on travelling customers' behavioural intentions in Jordan, *European Journal of Business and Management*, 5(22), 20–33.

Ladhari, P. and Bressolles, Z. (2011). Culture and personal values: how they influence perceived service quality, *Journal of Business Research*, 64(9), 951–957.

LeBeau, P. (2016). *Spirit Airlines triggered the most complaints.* Online. Available at: www.cnbc.com/2016/02/18/spirit-airlines-triggered-the-most-complaints.html (accessed 5 May 2016).

Leggatt, H. (2014). *Price ousts airline brand loyalty.* Online. Available at: www.bizreport.com/2014/03/price-ousts-airline-brand-loyalty.html (accessed 11 May 2016).

Liou, J.J.H. and Tzeng, G. (2007). A non-additive model for evaluating airline service quality, *Journal of Air Transport Management*, 13, 131–138.

Makens, J.C. and Marquardt, R.A. (1977). Consumer perceptions regarding first class and coach airline seating, *Journal of Travel Research*, 16, 19–22.

Maxon, T. (2014). *Spirit Airlines CEO Ben Baldanza responds to story about airline complaints.* Online. Available at: http://aviationblog.dallasnews.com/2014/04/spirit-airlines-ceo-ben-baldanza-responds-to-story-about-airline-complaints.html/ (accessed 12 May 2016).

Mostert, P.G., De Meyer, C.F. and van Rensburg, L.R.J. (2009). The influence of service failure and service recovery on airline passengers' relationships with domestic airlines: an exploratory study, *Southern African Business Review*, 13(2), 118–140.

Mouawad, J. (2016). *Airlines reap record profits, and passengers get peanuts.* Online. Available at: www.nytimes.com/2016/02/07/business/energy-environment/airlines-reap-record-profits-and-passengers-get-peanuts.html?_r=0 (accessed 11 May 2016).

Nafchi, M.Z., Gandomani, T.J. and Algunaid, A. (2014). A new quality model to measure quality of airlines' websites, *International Journal of Computer and Information Technology*, 3(5), 1160–1164.

Nagar, K. (2013). Perceived service quality with frill and no frill airlines: an explanatory research among Indian passengers, *Prestige International Journal of Management & IT- Sanchayan*, 2(1), 63–74.

Namukasa, J. (2013). The influence of airline service quality on passenger satisfaction and loyalty: the case of Uganda airline industry, *The TQM Journal*, 25(5), 520–532.

Oliver, R.I. (1999). Whence consumer loyalty, *Journal of Marketing*, 63, 33–44.

Ostrowski, P.I., O'Brien, T.V. and Gordon, G.L. (1993). Service quality and customer loyalty in the commercial airline industry, *Journal of Travel Research*, 32(2), 16–24.

Pakdil, F. and Aydın, O. (2007). Expectations and perceptions in airline services: an analysis using weighted SERVQUAL scores, *Journal of Air Transport Management*, 13, 229–237.

Parasuraman, A., Zeithaml, V.A. and Berry, L.L. (1985). A conceptual model of service quality for measuring customer perceptions of service quality, *Journal of Marketing*, 49(4), 41–50.

Parasuraman, A., Zeithaml, V.A. and Berry, L.L. (1988). SERVQUAL: a multiple-item scale for measuring customer perceptions of service quality, *Journal of Retailing*, 64(1), 12–40.

Park, J.W., Robertson, R. and Wu, C. (2004). The effect of airline service quality on passengers' behavioural intentions: a Korean case study, *Journal of Air Transport Management*, 10, 435–439.

Park, J.W., Robertson, R. and Wu, C. (2005). Investigating the effect of airline service quality on airline's image and passenger future behavioural intentions: findings from Australian international air passengers, *The Journal of Tourism Studies*, 16(1), 2–11.

Porter, L. (2014). *Ryanair: the truth about airline's customer services department.* Online. Available at: www.telegraph.co.uk/travel/news/ryanair/Ryanair-the-truth-about-the-airlines-customer-services-department/ (accessed 5 May 2016).

Prayag, G. (2007). Assessing international tourists' perception of service quality at Air Mauritius, *International Journal of Quality & Reliability Management*, 24(5), 492–514.

Rauyruen, P. and Miller, K.E. (2007). Relationship quality as a predictor of B2B customer loyalty, *Journal of Business Research*, 60, 21–31.

Reals, K. (2015). Take a seat: airlines differentiate their cabin products from premium to no-frill, *Aviation Week & Space Technology*, 23 November–6 December, 33.

Rhoades, D.L. and Waguespack, B. (1999). Better safe than service: the relationship between service and safety quality in the U.S. airline industry, *Managing Service Quality: An International Journal*, 9(6), 396–401.

Rhoades, D.L. and Waguespack, B. (2000a). Judging a book by its cover: the relationship between service and safety quality in the US airline industry, *Journal of Air Transport Management*, 6(2), 87–94.

Rhoades, D.L. and Waguespack, B. (2000b). Service quality in the U.S. airline industry: variations in performance within and between firms, *Journal of Air Transportation World Wide*, 5(1), 60–77.

Rhoades, D.L. and Waguespack, B. (2004). Service and safety quality in US airlines: pre- and post-September 11th, *Managing Service Quality: An International Journal*, 14(4), 307–316.

Rhoades, D.L. and Waguespack, B. (2005). Strategic imperatives and the pursuit of quality in the U.S. airline industry, *Managing Service Quality: An International Journal*, 15(4), 344–356.

Rhoades, D.L. and Waguespack, B. (2008). Twenty years of service quality performance in the US airline industry, *Managing Service Quality: An International Journal*, 18(1), 20–34.

Rhoades, D.L., Waguespack, B. and Treudt, E. (1998). Service quality in the US airline industry: progress and problems, *Managing Service Quality: An International Journal*, 8(5), 306–311.

Saha, G.C. and Theingi (2009). Service quality, satisfaction, and behavioral intentions: a study of low-cost airline carriers in Thailand, *Managing Service Quality: An International Journal*, 19(3), 350–372.

Simon, H.A. (1956). Rational choice and the structure of the environment, *Psychological Review*, 63(2), 129–138.

Sultan Jr., F. and Simpson, M.C. (2000). International service variants: airline passenger expectations and perceptions of service quality, *Journal of Services Marketing*, 14(3), 188–216.

Szwarc, P. (2005). *Researching Customer Satisfaction and Loyalty: How to Find Out What People Really Think*, London, The Market Research Society.

Szymanski, D.M. and Henard, D.H. (2001). Customer satisfaction: a meta-analysis of the empirical evidence, *Journal of the Academy of Marketing Science*, 29(1), 16–35.

*The Economist* (2015). *The price of being nice: treating flyers well is bad for airlines' business*. Online. Available at: www.economist.com/blogs/gulliver/2015/11/price-being-nice (accessed 11 May 2016).

Tiernan, S., Rhoades, D.L. and Waguespack, B. (2008). Airline alliance service quality performance: an analysis of US and EU member airlines, *Journal of Air Transport Management*, 14, 99–102.

Tsaur, S., Chang, T. and Yen, C. (2002). The evaluation of airline service quality by fuzzy MCDM, *Tourism Management*, 23(2), 107–115.

Urban, W. (2013). Perceived quality versus quality of processes: a meta concept of service quality measurement, *The Service Industries Journal*, 33(2), 200–217.

Waguespack, B. and Rhoades, D.L. (2014). Twenty-five years of measuring airline service quality or why is airline service quality only good when times are bad? *Research in Transportation Business & Management*, 10, 33–39.

Waguespack, B., Rhoades, D.L. and Tiernan, S. (2007). An investigation into airline service quality performance between US legacy carriers and their EU competitors and partners, *Journal of Air Transportation*, 12(2), 59–71.

Yayla-Kullu, H.M. (2013). A critical evaluation of US airlines' service quality performance: lower costs vs. satisfied customers, *Journal of Management and Strategy*, 4(5), 1–11.

Zangmo, M., Liampreecha, W. and Chemsripong, S. (2014). The influence of passenger perceived service quality on passenger satisfaction and loyalty: case of Drukair Royal Bhutan Airlines, *International Journal of Technical Research and Applications*, 2(8), 66–74.

# 23

# Consumer protection regimes and passenger complaints

*Paul Hooper*

## Introduction

"Airline service quality to many U.S. passengers may be the ultimate oxymoron based on stories, statistics and the perception that airlines help to foster" (Waguespack and Rhoades, 2014: 33). It is sentiments such as these that underlie pressures on governments to take strong action to protect passengers. But the proliferation of consumer protection laws presents problems for the global airline industry.

The International Air Transport Association's (IATA) view is that:

> There's a worrying trend in aviation policy these days – the spread of heavy consumer protection regimes around the world. While offering protection for consumers is a good thing, the purpose of many of these regulations appears to be to 'defend' passengers from airlines. This results in rules which reduce consumer protection and convenience – through higher fares, less choice, and more confusion.
>
> *(IATA, 2016)*

But if concerns about service quality are so high, it has not deterred people from flying – each year sees new records set for passenger demand. Also, the facts are that service levels have improved in core areas such as baggage handling (SITA, 2016). The International Civil Aviation Organisation (ICAO) also observed that complaints about on-time performance rose in the United States (US) despite reductions in delays. This led ICAO to conclude that:

> In light of this apparent contradiction, care should be taken not to attempt to pursue an elusive objective of absolute passenger satisfaction, which may well be unachievable. No matter how timely, cheap, comfortable, safe and secure the flight is, there will probably always remain irrational factors for passengers' dissatisfaction.
>
> *(ICAO, 2013: 9)*

Sound approaches to the development of public policy require a clear articulation of the problem to be solved, identification of policy options, and careful evaluation and implementation (Staroňová, 2010). Yet in the matter of passenger protection, a heavy weight is placed on mandating remedies for common types of complaints. Some airlines, though, are leaders in the marketing field and actively encourage complaints so that they have the opportunity to turn dissatisfaction into loyalty, and thereby benefit from repeat purchases and favourable word of mouth (WOM).

The US and the European Union (EU) are leaders in the field of passenger protection, and this chapter explains the key features of their regulatory regimes and relates some of their experiences. The chapter also examines the relationship between competition policy and consumer protection. The discussion traces the rise of consumerism as a social movement and its consequences for public policy and management. A legacy of consumerism activity in the 1970s is a well-developed body of research on consumer dissatisfaction, complaining behaviour and loyalty. This work provides insights into the apparent paradoxes noted above, and it highlights key findings relevant to policymakers and management alike. This field of research is promoted herein as a valuable resource, which can inform public policy debates and assist management in understanding how best to deal with dissatisfied passengers.

In addition to the introduction, this chapter consists of five sections. The first discusses the consumerism movement and its implications for regulation and management. The second section deals with regulating to protect passengers and it examines the scope of passenger protection and its treatment in the US and the EU. The third section is about understanding passenger complaints, including statistical evidence and published research into causes and consequences of passenger dissatisfaction. The fourth section then examines how best to deal with dissatisfied passengers – how to manage complaints and how to turn a dissatisfied passenger into a customer who has a long-term commitment to the brand. The final section presents conclusions and makes suggestions for further research.

## The consumerism movement and its implications for regulation and management

### Consumerism and regulation

Adam Smith, the eighteenth-century economist who advocated the laissez-faire market system, believed that profit was a powerful motivator leading producers to provide what consumers wanted. Competition was the force required to promote efficient production and to deliver the benefits of this in the form of low prices. But even in 1769, in his native Scotland, consumers felt the need to organise a cooperative society to improve their bargaining position. Arguably, this marked the birth of a 'consumerism' movement (Kaynak, 1985).

When the US enacted the Sherman Antitrust Act in 1890, it set out to prevent sellers restricting supply in order to charge high prices. Subsequently, competition laws were enacted in many countries, and they amount to "regulation of the marketplace to ensure private conduct does not depress free trade and competition" (Huffman, 2010: 7).

However, markets are messy even with well-intentioned competition laws. The risk of regulatory failure is ever-present, perhaps because of inadequacies in design and implementation. But there is another possibility – that powerful and well-organised interest groups influence the legislative agenda in order to protect their own interests (Boudreaux and DiLorenzo, 1993). The question arises whether it is necessary to mobilise countervailing forces to represent consumers more effectively.

Some of the earliest laws to protect consumers emerged in the US at the beginning of the twentieth century, and they mainly addressed product safety. The solutions were to mandate standards and to insist on disclosure in packaging. The provision of checks and balances against abuses of corporate power became a public policy issue again during the Great Depression of the 1930s. The focus was on food, drugs and banking, but other trends included the formation of consumer cooperatives, increased efforts to educate consumers, and the establishment of consumer divisions in government agencies (Cohen, 2010).

The prevailing economic, social and political conditions in the US in the 1960s and 1970s further strengthened the consumerism movement. Congress had conducted high-profile investigations into the safety of a variety of products and President John F. Kennedy championed the enactment of a Consumer Bill of Rights in 1962. This set out four basic consumer rights: the right to safety, the right to be informed, the right to exercise free choice and the right to be heard (Cohen, 2010).

Thus, consumerism as a social movement was now a reality (Kaynak, 1985), and it did not lack for influential leaders. Ralph Nader, for example, mounted a successful campaign in the mid-1960s against General Motors about dangerous design flaws in the Corvair model. Nader and fellow activists were demonstrating that the justice system could be relied upon to award compensation to parties injured by manufacturing defects. The consumerism movement gained strength through its popularity with an increasingly affluent middle class – and accompanying this trend were higher expectations about product quality.

In the realms of competition law, the best way to protect consumers is to prohibit anticompetitive, unfair and deceptive practices and exploitation of market power. However, governments now were enacting a variety of consumer protection laws designed to give consumers specific rights in their transactions with sellers, and notably to provide consumers with remedies (Agbonifoh and Edoreh, 1993; Crandall and Winston, 2003; Harris, 1978). Additionally, legislation and regulations dealing with deceptive advertising and product representations were strengthened.

The objectives of both competition laws and consumer laws are, in theory, the same – advancing the best interests of consumers. There is always the possibility that consumer protection laws are not necessary because competition law addresses the problem more effectively (Huffman, 2010). Nevertheless, consumerism is well established as a powerful, globalised social movement. In 1985, the United Nations (UN) adopted a set of Guidelines for Consumer Protection, including an expanded set of consumer rights. Another factor supporting the spread of consumer rights regimes in a wide spectrum of economies has been the formation of entities such as the International Consumer Protection Enforcement Network (ICPEN) – a global network of national consumer agencies that shares information, promotes best practices, and, among other activities, organises coordinated action on deceptive claims made on the Internet (Ramsay, 2006).

The consumerism movement in the US initially was the stimulus for similar policies and laws in the EU, but regulatory failures relating to health and safety during the 1990s led to public demands for stronger action. As a result, the EU became a global leader in areas such as product safety standard setting, product liability, the control of unfair contract terms, and access to justice, and a strong advocate of extending its consumer protection regimes to non-EU countries (Svetiev, 2013).

## Consumerism's impact on management

Regulatory responses to consumerism in the aviation sector will be explored below, but there are other consequences of the consumerism movement that should be introduced at this point. The first is that consumerism led researchers to investigate complaining behaviour. The legacy of this is that an extensive literature is available to guide the understanding of both policymakers and management about what causes a consumer to be dissatisfied, why they complain, and what they expect the seller to do.

At the same time, there were growing expectations that a business enterprise would:

> behave in a manner that is not detrimental to the overall interest of society, but that it should also help in finding solutions to societal and environmental problems such as environmental and cultural pollution, excessive materialism, inflation, unemployment and urban congestion.
>
> *(Agbonifoh and Edoreh, 1993: 43)*

It is a direct extension of this trend that many of today's airlines have corporate social responsibility policies (Kuo et al., 2016).

Consumers in the 1960s and 1970s also expected better standards in commodities such as motor vehicles, and their demands were being met by Japanese producers who had invested heavily in quality management. Many of their rivals in the US also embraced concepts such as total quality management (TQM) in order to improve their performance, but more generally the importance of satisfying the needs of consumers began to play a central role in thinking about business strategy. This was especially the case in highly competitive service industries, and the prescription for a sustainable strategy was to: (a) identify a target market; (b) decide what elements of service are valued most; (c) devise a way to produce the desired service elements in a profitable way; and (d) ensure that the service is delivered consistently. Southwest Airlines is often held up to be a good example about how such a business strategy works.

The satisfaction of customer demands continues to occupy a central role in modern strategic management, as exemplified by the management model promoted by the European Federation of Quality Management (EFQM) – a competitive strategy based upon the integration of efforts to develop, maintain and improve quality in the continuous pursuit to achieve excellence. According to this model: "Excellence, as optimal management, means the availability of a system for assuring the quality requisites of products and services. It includes customer satisfaction, process management and resource optimisation following a social responsibility approach" (Martin-Castilla and Rodriguez-Ruiz, 2008: 135).

The airline industry has been a pioneer in the design of loyalty programmes and in the development of customer relationship management (CRM) concepts (see also Chapter 22). CRM:

> enables companies to gather and access information about customer orders, complaints, preferences, and participation in sales and marketing campaigns. This information can then be used to better react to customer needs, automate some operations, and capture customer feedback to improve products and service.
>
> *(Chang and Cheng, 2007: 5)*

The highly competitive nature of the airline industry, the realisation that passenger satisfaction is much more important in generating repeat business, and the finding that it costs more to attract a new customer than to encourage repeat business are all factors underlying the relevance of CRM to even the low cost operators with their focus on pricing (Akamavi et al., 2015; Baker, 2013). Of course, there is a need to ensure that investments in quality generate an adequate return (Rust et al., 1995).

These modern management approaches rely on having a sound understanding about customers, and complaints take on significance far greater than meeting regulatory or societal expectations. Complainers transmit information vital to management, and proactive firms encourage dissatisfied consumers to communicate with them. Accordingly, the research on dissatisfaction, complaining behaviour and loyalty is highly relevant to today's management, and thus is a subject dealt with in more detail below.

## Regulating to protect passengers

### The scope of passenger protection

The aviation industry's uncompromising approach to safety earned it an excellent reputation, and though aviation safety is newsworthy, demands for consumer protection do not generally arise on this score. International treaties also provide for compensation of victims of aviation disasters. Notably, the Convention for the Unification of Certain Rules for International Carriage by Air (Montreal Convention) of 1999 (MC99) modernised and consolidated protection measures for passengers, including limits of liability for death or injury of passengers engaged in international air travel. At present, 119 countries plus the EU have ratified this treaty.

The MC99 also contains provisions concerning delays experienced by passengers, denied boarding, and damage or miscarriage of baggage. Currently, a passenger on a flight between countries that have ratified MC99 may claim up to 1,131 Special Drawing Rights (SDRs) for destruction, loss, damage or delay of baggage, which, at current rates published by the International Monetary Fund (IMF), amounts to about US$1,550. The corresponding level of compensation available to a passenger suffering a delay is 4,694 SDRs. The treaty specifies time limits for making claims, and it relieves an airline from an obligation to pay compensation if it can demonstrate it has taken all reasonable measures to avoid the damages or that it was impossible to take such measures.

IATA contends that, in ratifying MC99, a state agrees to its exclusive application. IATA therefore expressed its concerns that "Today, 55 jurisdictions have some form of aviation-specific passenger rights regime . . . The multitude of regimes today are not mutually recognised or coordinated . . . The potential for duplication in claims has profound cost implications for the industry" (IATA, 2013: 2). More countries have adopted specific aviation consumer protection regimes since this statement was made.

In an attempt to achieve operational convergence and compatibility in approaches, ICAO developed a set of Core Principles on Consumer Protection (ICAO, 2015). These principles describe general approaches without being prescriptive. For example, the principles say that consumers should be informed about their rights as well as about products available in the market. During travel, ICAO stresses the need to keep passengers informed, especially when services are disrupted. ICAO appeals to airlines, airport operators and all stakeholders, including government authorities, to plan in advance to ensure that passengers receive adequate attention and assistance during massive disruptions. In the post-flight stage, the ICAO Core Principles emphasise the need for efficient complaint handling procedures.

The scope of consumer protection in aviation can be gauged by examining the measures addressed by ICAO in its statement of polices and guidance on the economic regulation of international civil aviation (ICAO, 2008). It is further revealed in those measures adopted at the national or EU level. It can be seen that passenger protection extends to unfair pricing and unfair conditions of carriage, refunds and protection of consumers' payments, unfair and deceptive advertising (especially regarding so-called ancillary charges), and failure to inform the consumer about the identity of the actual carrier. Regulators do not tolerate discrimination, and many countries have special laws and regulations designed to assert the rights of persons with disabilities.

The US, as a pioneer in the field of aviation consumer protection, and the EU, in adopting regulations designed to promote a common aviation market, are worthy of special note. In the sections below, pertinent details will be presented about the approaches taken and about some issues that have arisen in recent years.

## The US

Specific application of consumer protection laws in aviation is the responsibility of the Department of Transportation's (DOT) Aviation Consumer Protection and Enforcement Office. According to the DOT:

> Consumer protection compliance and enforcement activities relate to areas such as unfair and deceptive practices and unfair competition by air carriers and travel agents, deceptive airline advertising (e.g. fare, on-time performance, schedule and code sharing), and violations of rules concerning denied boarding compensation, ticket refunds, baggage liability requirements, and charter flights.
>
> *(DOT, 2016a)*

The DOT also takes action to ensure that persons with disabilities "obtain non-discriminatory access to the air transportation system and that the public is not subjected by airlines to unlawful discrimination on the basis of race, religion, national origin or sex during the course of their air transportation" (DOT, 2016a).

The DOT offers a channel for passengers to register complaints, and this information is provided to the carriers as well as to the public in the form of statistical reports, which also contain factual information about denied boarding, on-time performance and flight cancellations. A summary record of complaints, expressed in terms of per million enplanements, is presented in Table 23.1. Despite the ease of registering a complaint, the rate of complaining has been low for a long period of time. One obvious fact is that the rate of complaints for the domestic airlines varies significantly from year to year. Another observation is that the rate of complaining is higher for foreign airlines.

The DOT enforces the laws and regulations by issuing warning letters, or by issuing consent orders, which may involve agreed penalties, or it can pursue litigation and seek civil penalties. Carriers are required to provide reports on a variety of matters, and actions are taken when they fail to meet their reporting obligations.

The DOT also provides information to passengers about how they can pursue legal redress through the courts. In the case of lost, damaged, delayed or pilfered luggage, the liability limits of MC99 apply to flights to and from the US. A higher level of compensation is possible for domestic flights, and the DOT reports the number of passenger reports of mishandled (domestic) luggage, including those not involving claims for compensation. In 2015, the rate varied from a high of 8.5 per thousand enplaned passengers to a low of 0.8. In 2005, the average across all the airlines was 6.0. In 2010, it was 3.5, and in 2015 it was 3.2.

*Table 23.1* Complaints (per million enplanements) received by the DOT, 2000 to 2015

|  | *2000* | *2005* | *2010* | *2011* | *2012* | *2013* | *2014* | *2015* |
|---|---|---|---|---|---|---|---|---|
| US airlines | 30.9 | 9.4 | 12.7 | 12.9 | 15.6 | 13.1 | 14.9 | 19.1 |
| Foreign airlines | 31.7 | 22.6 | 22.1 | 23.5 | 38.5 | 33.8 | 41.3 | 44.3 |
| All airlines | 31.0 | 10.5 | 13.6 | 13.9 | 17.8 | 15.2 | 17.7 | 21.9 |

*Source*: Bureau of Transportation Statistics (2016) and DOT (2016b).

The DOT recognised that there are net social benefits when airlines are able to overbook to avoid flying with empty seats when passengers do not present themselves on time for their flights (no-shows). Of course, this means that there will be occasions when some passengers have to be denied boarding, and the rule applying in such circumstances is that airlines must first seek volunteers before denying boarding to confirmed passengers. The DOT explains on its website that each airline is required to give all passengers who are bumped involuntarily a written statement about its policy and procedure and whether it will pay compensation, usually based on the price of the ticket and the length of delay. The carriers are required to report incidents of denied boarding, and this information is made public. Improved management procedures have made it possible to reduce the extent of denied boarding, and in 2015, for example, 7.6 people were involuntarily denied boarding out of every hundred thousand enplanements.

There are interesting lessons to be drawn from public policy debates in the US. Alfred Kahn, the former official who presided over the deregulation of the US domestic airline industry in 1978, acknowledged the frustration of consumers and "the flood of proposals for legislative enactment of 'travelers' bills of rights' engendered by clearly unsatisfactory air service to which they have been exposed in recent years" (Kahn, 2002: 39). However, he attributed the poor service levels to adverse weather conditions and inefficient pricing structure of infrastructure services, and he did not favour specific measures to protect passengers. Another former official added that:

> consumers consistently showed that they cared more about price than quality, the market gave them what they wanted, whereupon they became nostalgic for the service quality of the good old days (but wanted it at the new prices, of course).
>
> *(Levine, 2006: 22)*

Kahn noted demands for stricter regulations, including a passenger bill of rights, and Levine explained why, despite the pressures to do something, the government chose not to re-regulate.

A useful example to illustrate how such pressures manifested themselves and how policy-makers reacted is the so-called tarmac delay rule. Weather events in January 1999 resulted in extreme disruption to normal air services, and some passengers were held inside aircraft on the tarmac for up to 8.5 hours. The public outcry led to renewed demands for a passenger bill of rights. In the event, airlines agreed to make customer service commitments and to develop contingency plans with the cooperation of airports and other airlines so that they could improve the way they handled future emergencies. However, increasing congestion in the air navigation system continued to cause delays, especially in the north-east of the US. When severe weather was experienced in December 2006 and February 2007, considerable pressure was exerted on the DOT to take action. The result was a new rule issued in December 2009 that imposed strict requirements on the airlines and included penalties of US$27,500 for each passenger in the event that an airline did not begin deplaning within three hours of tarmac delay.

The rule continues to be a source of debate. Berg (2010), for example, argued that the likelihood that a flight will be cancelled increases after an aircraft is required to return to the gate. Berg also considered it more likely that an airline would take pre-emptive action and cancel a flight if it expected lengthy tarmac delays. When a flight is cancelled, passengers need to be rebooked and, with high load factors, overnight stays are more likely. The question arises whether passengers are better off avoiding lengthy tarmac delays versus having a higher risk of cancellation. However, Berg's criticism of the rule did not end there. He pointed out that there were only 903 delays of three hours or more out of more than 6 million flights in the US in 2009. He added that the DOT already had authority to investigate and penalise carriers for such delays.

The trend to unbundle the airline service and to apply ancillary charges for luggage, meals, priority boarding, seat allocation and other features, as well as the imposition of fuel levies, resulted in consumer complaints about deceptive advertising. In the early 1980s, the Federal Trade Commission (FTC) prohibited practices that had the capacity to mislead the ignorant, unthinking and credulous. As the FTC's policies developed, the test to prohibit deception required that an actionable injury had to be substantial, not reasonably avoidable by consumers, and not outweighed by countervailing benefits to consumers or competition (Pappalardo, 2012).

Policy debates continued about the relative importance of provision of information by the government, consumer education, and regulation of product/service characteristics. Regulators and policymakers also recognised the lessons researchers were deriving from the field of consumer choice behaviour involving contributions from both economics and psychology. It has been found that the quality of consumer decision-making does not necessarily improve simply by providing more information. "Indeed, it seems that when the cognitive load increases (e.g. because of complex pricing structure), individuals tend to use less of the available information" (van Boom, 2011: 361). Sellers have learned that the way a price is framed can make a significant difference to the way consumers respond. For example, higher discounts tend to have a disproportionate impact on propensity to buy. Accordingly, the protection of consumers from deception is understood to be a complex and difficult field (Pappalardo, 2012; van Boom, 2011), while some argue that deception poses a low risk because it generally is an unsustainable practice (Huffman, 2010).

Since January 2012, the DOT followed FTC policy in requiring that the first price presented to a consumer must be the full price, including all taxes, fees and all carrier surcharges. The DOT permits carriers to separately identify the elements of costs, including airport charges, government taxes and airline-imposed surcharges, in subsequent displays of the price. In further clarifications issued by the DOT, airlines were advised that it would be regarded as deceptive if the airline-imposed charges were incorrectly identified simply as additional fees. Moreover, claims of free flights, notably in association with redemption of benefits under frequent flyer programmes (FFPs), cannot be so regarded if the consumer must pay for additional charges.

## The EU

Regulation 1107/2006 establishes the rights of disabled persons and persons with reduced mobility when travelling by air (see EC, 2006). However, it is Regulation 261/2004 of the European Parliament and of the Council of 11 February 2004, establishing common rules on compensation and assistance to passengers in the event of denied boarding and of cancellation or long delay of flights (see EC, 2004), that is particularly noteworthy. This regulation applies to all flights departing/arriving from/at an airport located within the EU if the airline has a licence issued by an authority in a member state. Whereas MC99 provides for compensation for passengers depending upon their individual circumstances, Regulation 261/2004 standardises entitlements without regard to individuals' circumstances.

IATA tested its conviction that because all member countries and the EU itself are signatories to MC99, Regulation 261/2004 violates Article 29 of MC99, which claims exclusive jurisdiction. IATA also argued that Regulation 261/2004 was disproportionate because liability may arise even in extraordinary circumstances. In comparison, MC99 absolves liability for compensation if delays are caused by factors outside their control. The Court of Justice of the European Union (CJEU) upheld the legality of Regulation 261/2004. Its argument, in a nutshell, was that there are two types of damage resulting from delays, one of which is legitimately the concern of the EU in providing for standardised and immediate compensation, and the other type which requires an assessment of damage on a case-by-case basis, and which is the preserve of MC99. The CJEU argued that these types of delay should be considered in sequence, and that Regulation 261/2004 complements MC99 in substance and legally (Prassl, 2014).

Regulation 261/2004 specifies that, in the event of cancellation of a flight or denied boarding, the airline shall offer the passenger the choice between being rerouted or reimbursed. Where rerouting is chosen, the airline's duty of care (phone call, refreshments and meals, accommodation, transport to the place of accommodation) is prescribed, as it is in the case of delays to flights. The level of care for delays depends upon duration of the delay (in hours) and the distance of the flight (in kilometres). In addition, Regulation 261/2004 specifies the level of compensation for lost, damaged or delayed baggage, with the caveat that airlines shall not be liable if they have taken all reasonable measures to avoid the damages or it was impossible to take such measures.

The CJEU has made several significant interpretations about Regulation 261/2004. In 2008, the court decided that a technical error with an aircraft does not constitute an extraordinary circumstance unless it could be attributed to events that, by their nature or origin, are not inherent in the normal exercise of the activity of the air carrier concerned and are beyond its actual control. In another ruling handed down the following year, the so-called Sturgeon case, it was decided that a passenger might be entitled to compensation if a delayed flight resulted in their arrival at the final destination later than three hours after the scheduled time. In such lengthy delays, the court took the view that a lengthy delay could be regarded as equivalent to a cancellation of a flight for the purpose of awarding compensation.

Further controversy arose about the European Commission's (EC) interpretation of Regulation 261/2004 when the majority of European airspace was closed in April 2010 as a result of the cloud of ash that blanketed Europe after Eyjafjallajökull volcano in Iceland began erupting on 20 March 2010. More than 100,000 flights and 10 million passengers were disrupted during the period of airspace closure, and an additional 7,000 flights were affected in May when the ash cloud drifted back over parts of Europe, and the net losses suffered by the airline industry alone have been estimated to be US$2.2 billion (Henry and Gardner, 2012). Meteorological events, including volcanic ash clouds, fall within the definition of extraordinary events, and thus the airlines were exempted from paying compensation. However, the EC issued advice that all other rights, including duty of care, would apply. Also, the EC argued that carriers were responsible for getting passengers to their final destination, even if it meant using other modes of transport.

In 2012, the EC proposed amendments to Regulation 261/2004 to accommodate the interpretations of the CJEU (Prassl, 2014) and to address key problems identified in a thorough study of the effectiveness of the regulation (Steer Davies Gleave, 2010). Key among these were the lack of consistent compliance by air carriers, ineffective enforcement by member states, inadequate mechanisms in several member states for passengers to obtain redress from carriers, and continuing lack of clarity on such matters as long delays and cancellations, including missed connections due to delays. The EC subjected four options to an impact assessment, including the costs of compliance, and concluded in favour of reaching a balance between stronger enforcement via national enforcement bodies (NEBs) and economic incentives, including an increase in the threshold determining that compensation for delays should commence only after a delay of five hours. The legislative process to adopt the revision of (EC) 261/2004 was still ongoing in June 2016 when the EC issued new guidelines aimed at clarifying existing rules.

The EC periodically reports summary statistics about the number of complaints registered with the individual NEBs. For example, over the period between 2010 and 2012, inclusive, 201,879 complaints were lodged under Regulation 261/2004, with 91,276 occurring in 2010 following major disruptions resulting from the volcanic ash cloud (EC, 2014). Less than 1 per cent of all flights were delayed by more than two hours, and airlines would have been responsible for providing care and assistance on 1.2 per cent of flights, including the statistics for 2010. The financial impact of Regulation 261/2004 on a typical airline was estimated to lie between 0.6 and 1.8 per cent of turnover, depending on the proportion of entitled passengers that claim compensation, but for some airlines the impact could rise as high as 5 per cent of sales revenue (EC, 2014). If airlines were successful in passing all of the costs to the consumer, Regulation 261/2004 would have added between €1 and €3 per one-way ticket during the reporting period. In an earlier study carried out for the EC, it was found, however, that there was only one complaint registered with a NEB in every 800 passengers who would be eligible for a remedy under Regulation 261/2004 (Steer Davies Gleave, 2010).

As is the case in the US, EU legislation mandates that at all times, the purchaser must be presented with the final air fare, including applicable taxes and charges, and those surcharges and fees that the customer is obligated to pay. Furthermore, the purchaser must be shown a breakdown between the fare, taxes, airport charges, and any other surcharges and fees. The regulations also stipulate that any optional price supplements must be communicated in a clear, transparent and unambiguous way at the beginning of the booking process. Passengers also must be informed about the identity of the carrier at the time of purchase.

In addition, the EU has considered how best to deal with situations when airlines cease operations. Notably, it:

> would appear that with every holiday season and every airline insolvency consumer watchdogs reiterate their call for the introduction of an aviation bankruptcy regime to help stranded passengers return safely and have their air fares refunded if an air carrier has to cease operations due to financial difficulties.
>
> *(Steppler and Vogler, 2012: 359)*

Reference is made in such debates to the Package Travel Directive – Council Directive 90/314/EEC of 13 June 1990 (see EEC, 1990) that provides protection for purchasers of package travel, package holiday and package tour products through mechanisms to ensure service delivery by charter air operators (Pantazi, 2010). The question has arisen whether a similar mechanism is required for scheduled airlines.

The facts are that 96 scheduled airlines were declared insolvent in the EU between 2000 and 2010, with a peak of 14 in 2004 and again in 2008 (Steer Davies Gleave, 2011). It is important to recognise that it is not insolvency that causes the inconvenience and hardship for passengers; rather, it is the cessation of service (Steppler and Vogler, 2012). This can arise for reasons other than insolvency, including sanctions applied by safety regulators. What is more, the regulations relating to the issue of operating licences within the EU provide scope for action whenever regulators observe an airline in financial distress (Pantazi, 2010). Considering these arguments, the EU has not yet been convinced of the need to introduce a regulation to cover financial insolvency of scheduled airlines.

## Understanding passengers' complaints

### What is known about complaints?

Normally, complaints about service levels are made directly to an airline or to its agent, and in some cases to airports. This information is not generally available to governments, let alone to the public. However, in a study conducted for the EC, consultants estimated that airlines registered in the EU received a million complaints in 2008 (Steer Davies Gleave, 2010). Three hundred thousand of these were deemed to be about matters covered by Regulation 261/2004 out of a total population of 572 million passengers. Thus, the complaint rate to airlines about delays, cancellations, denied boarding and baggage was about 5.2 per 10,000 passengers. In contrast, the NEBs received 28,000 complaints during the same period, implying that for every official complaint registered in accordance with Regulation 261/2004, there were almost 11 complaints lodged with airlines.

It does appear that the rate of lodging official complaints in the EU is significantly higher than in the US. There is no consistent reporting of statistics about complaints on a global basis, but some information was made available in 2013 when ICAO convened its sixth air transport conference. China reported to the conference that only 1,000 of its 320 million passengers in 2012 registered an official complaint. Singapore noted a sharp rise in official complaints after the commencement of services by low cost carriers, but public education programmes about airline services resulted in this rate dropping to 1.5 per 100,000 passengers by 2012. Chile reported that 4,510 claims were lodged in that country in 2012 out of 15 million trips.

Considering the importance attached to complaints by regulators, it is disappointing to find there is a paucity of factual data, and that analysis of regulatory and industry performance (e.g. EC, 2014; Steer Davies Gleave, 2010) does not take advantage of published research about complaints. As noted above, this body of research has its origins in the consumer movement in the US in the 1970s. The FTC, Office of Consumer Affairs (OCA), National Science Foundation, and Marketing Science Institute provided support to convene an annual conference addressing consumer dissatisfaction and complaining behaviour, beginning in 1976 (Hunt, 1991). The papers are made available in a specialised publication, the *Journal of Consumer Satisfaction, Dissatisfaction and Complaining Behavior*. Although this provided a focal point for researchers, the field widened, and relevant papers can be found in a broad cross-section of journals specialising in consumer research, management, economics, law and public policy. The sections below will highlight some of the important conclusions that can be drawn from this work.

## What causes consumers to be dissatisfied?

In the 1970s, the motivation for research into consumer satisfaction was to understand what led to complaints. As explained by one of the pioneers in this field, "While we applaud positive disconfirmations, they do not require consumer protection" (Hunt, 1991: 109). Disconfirmation in this context was understood to be the source of dissatisfaction – a comparison of what the consumer got from a purchase experience as opposed to what was expected. Researchers' understanding of dissatisfaction evolved in subsequent work and definitions of the concept abound in the literature. A recent paper on the subject in an airline context described satisfaction in terms of pleasurable fulfilment of a consumption goal that involves both cognition and emotional reactions, and manifests itself as well in an overall customer attitude towards a service provider (Baker, 2013).

Turning to some applied research, Suzuki (2000) found that switching rates from passengers who had experienced a delayed flight were higher than for passengers without any delay experience. But an important question for both regulators and airlines is how much of a delay is considered acceptable by passengers. Wittmer and Laesser (2010) focused specifically on business travellers and found that a delay of up to 30 minutes was tolerable. But when account was taken of the frequency of travel, passengers became increasingly dissatisfied with delays.

Ferrer et al. (2012) confirmed the negative impact of delays on passenger behaviour, but they added insights that multiple delays have a greater negative impact than a single event, the marginal impact of additional delays is negative and convex, and that passengers tend not to forget delay experiences. An interesting finding was that there was no significant difference in reactions to delays by both members and non-members of FFPs, but the latter are more likely to experience multiple delays, and hence end up being more dissatisfied, and are more likely to switch to another airline. Another possible explanation, backed up by research findings (Chow, 2015), is that an increase in expectations about on-time performance results in an increase in complaints – setting high standards of service is a double-edged sword. Indeed, there is evidence that the level of importance attached to service levels increase across the board with frequency of travel (Curtis et al., 2012). Yet another explanation is that frequent travellers are rewarded with privileges, but this raises expectations, and "when customers face service failure or feel dissatis-fied, their privilege status may provide cues for their expectations toward complaint handling" (Chiou et al., 2009: 469).

Considering the growing popularity and increasing frequency of air travel, it is perhaps not surprising to find that consumers raise the bar – that dissatisfaction can increase even when a product or service improves. Lapré and Tsikriktsis (2006) posited that customer dissatisfaction follows a U-shaped learning curve based on experience. Their application of this theory led them to conclude that, out of the 10 largest airlines in the US in the period 1987 to 1998, airlines with focused marketing strategies learned faster how to respond to changing passenger expecta-tions, a good example being Southwest Airlines. A later study confirmed the lower propensity to complain by Southwest Airlines' passengers, even when controlling for the influence of service quality. In that study, it was speculated that this behaviour could be explained by price-based expectations of service quality, lack of information about how to complain to the DOT, or quali-tative differences in front-line customer service between airlines (Wittman, 2014).

Steven et al. (2012) provide yet another explanation about the tendency for complaints to increase despite improvements to service. Their argument was that there are diminishing returns to quality so that there is a non-linear relationship between satisfaction and service levels illustrated by the findings that:

> increasing on-time performance leads to fewer complaints, but that the level of complaints bottoms at around an 80% on-time rate. Similarly, increasing the number of lost bags increases the number of complaints, but at a decreasing rate, tapering off at about 15 lost bags per 100,000 passengers.
>
> *(Steven et al., 2012: 749–750)*

These results emphasise the need to consider price whenever assessing satisfaction levels. Notably, a recent study found that "Price and service quality are found to be the antecedents of satisfaction, suggesting that affordable ticket prices and good service will lead passengers to be more satisfied" (Calisir et al., 2016: 216). Thus, although this study found that service quality exerts the stronger impact on satisfaction, price remains part of the equation in assessing value for money. This confirmed an earlier finding that "perceived value plays an important role in affecting a customer's satisfaction and future behavioral intentions in the airline service context" (Chen, 2008: 716).

### What happens when a customer is dissatisfied?

The literature on this subject classifies responses to dissatisfaction as: voice, exit and retaliation. Voice is the initial reaction when consumers make a decision whether to complain or remain silent, and if they complain whether a choice is made to do this with the seller and/or to a third party. Exit involves switching to a rival firm for repeat purchases, or it can result in less consumption of that particular product/service in the future. Retaliation usually takes the form of negative WOM, but it can involve more extreme forms of behaviour.

Regulators focus on the voice phase, although economists would argue that exit and retaliation are important if competition policy is to work. That is, the risk of losing customers and gaining a bad reputation is a discipline on those sellers who consistently fail to deliver satisfactory service. What is important to make the market function properly is to ensure that consumers perceive they have choices. The evidence is that such choices result in a greater propensity to take complaints directly to sellers rather than to a public authority, and they are more likely to switch to a rival when dissatisfied (Kolodinsky, 1995).

Researchers have found that enhancing customer service (on-time performance, mishandled baggage and overbooking) results in higher levels of satisfaction, and this translates into improved airline profitability (Dresner and Xu, 1995). This finding has been confirmed repeatedly in subsequent research. Suzuki (2000), for example, found that improved on-time performance positively affects an airline's market share. Sim et al. (2010) showed, for the period between 1990 and 2006 in the US, that the number of complaints registered with the DOT is a lead indicator of an airline's return on sales. Thus, competition policy, by providing consumers with options, is a powerful discipline on those firms that disappoint their consumers. Not surprisingly, Steven et al. (2012) found that increasing market concentration moderates the impact of customer satisfaction, as reflected in complaints to the DOT, and airline profitability. Their conclusion was that all airlines "both big and small, benefit by operating in less competitive markets in terms of increasing their profitability without having to concomitantly increase customer satisfaction" (Steven et al., 2012: 752).

As noted, the most common way consumers retaliate when they experience unsatisfactory service is to engage in negative WOM. It is a well-established fact that information provided by a friend or family member tends to be highly trusted, and hence WOM exerts a significant impact on a firm's reputation. WOM is increasingly important in marketing because of the growing popularity of "social networks (Facebook, LinkedIn, Google+), content communities (e.g. YouTube, Pinterest), blogs (e.g. WordPress), microblogs (Twitter), and various other electronic means of sharing communication" (Lang and Hyde, 2013: 1). Of course, WOM can be positive as well as negative, and the challenge for airlines is to ensure, even when there is a service level failure, that any ensuing WOM is turned to their advantage. To a large extent, this hinges on the way firms deal with dissatisfied customers, although the challenge is to encourage consumers to voice their concerns. Complaints therefore can be considered as an opportunity for a firm to learn about how to satisfy customers.

Observing that only 5 to 10 per cent of dissatisfied customers choose to complain following a service-level failure, Bamford and Xystouri (2005) documented the reasons why consumers do not complain. First, some customers do not complain because they believe nothing will result from their action. A second reason is that the customers do not wish to be involved in confronting the person responsible for the failure. Some customers are simply not sure about their rights and about the obligations of the firm. Finally, the time and cost involved in complaining might simply not justify the effort.

A good deal of research has gone into the search for different attitudes about complaining based on personal differences such as gender, age and education, as well as whether cultural differences exist. Notably, Blodgett et al. (2006) found that differences in complaining behaviour were far more influenced by policies on return of goods than on cultural differences. This topic remains a fertile area of research, and in contrast another study found that "consumers from collectivist nations tend to refrain from verbal responses for fear of losing face, but they are more likely to tell family members and friends about a bad service" (Kim and Lee, 2009: 350). A more recent study concluded that "there are no global consumers" – Germans are more critical of differential treatment than US consumers (Mayser and von Wangenheim, 2013). Of course, the likelihood that a customer will complain increases when there is a reward for doing so. Jacoby and Jaccard (1981) observed that firms with reputations for liberal return policies were more likely to receive complaints.

Folkes (1984) described a body of research known as attribution theory, which posits that consumers make assessments about the causes of product/service failures and the resulting attributions influence responses. For example, consumers consider whether the cause of service level failure is relatively stable over time or whether it fluctuates, and then they decide who is to blame. It is also important to know whether consumers believe the underlying cause of the fault is capable of being controlled. In the context of the airline industry, it is notable that researchers have found that:

> customers who perceive a failure to be highly controllable are more likely to exhibit low post-recovery satisfaction and mitigate their feelings toward the positive relationship between the service recovery process and recovery satisfaction than those who perceive the failure to be less controllable.
>
> *(Nikbin et al., 2014: 829)*

Folkes (1984) added the insight that consumers are not free of biases when they carry out attribution analysis and they sometimes place more weight on particular causes. As a result, perceptions about fault are not always aligned with the facts. What is more, airline "management should not expect equally high levels of recovery satisfaction in response to excellent redress for stable and controllable service failures" (Nikbin et al., 2014: 831).

## Responding to dissatisfied consumers

### *Managing complaints*

Steer Davies Gleave (2010), in a consulting study undertaken for the EC, observed that most of the airlines they examined dealt with passenger complaints through a department responsible for customer relations. Typically, a complaint is registered in the airline's database and then is dealt with by a handler who assesses the case, including the possible need for escalation to more senior management or the legal team. Then the passenger is sent a summary response containing, when applicable, an offer of compensation. On those occasions when a passenger is not satisfied with the outcome, the process can go through further iterations. Apart from noting that some airlines contract complaint handling to specialists, while others use artificial intelligence software to automate responses to be sent to those queries and complaints that do not require individual attention, this study generated no additional insights into the way airlines manage complaints.

A well-understood research finding is that emotions are a strong driver of complaint behaviour, and that a focus on objective responses is likely to result in less satisfaction with the process (Chebat et al., 2004). In that case, psychological compensation addressing anger, anxiety and resignation should be the first priority. Subsequent research about airline passengers found that a prompt response to a complaint by the most senior, responsible person accompanied by an offer of compensation leads to the most satisfaction with the complaint handling process (Bamford and Xystouri, 2005).

Justice theory has been found to be a useful way to understand consumer perceptions about complaint handling, with a distinction made between interactional, procedural and distributive justice. Personal interaction between the consumer and representatives of the firm are known to be very important in service industries. Thus, the theory suggests that a customer's overall satisfaction will be influenced by whether they believe that they have been dealt with fairly by the people representing the firm. Separately, consumers consider whether the policies and procedures applied by the firm are appropriate. Finally, consumers then judge whether the outcome, including any compensation, is acceptable.

In research applying these concepts, it has been found that all three dimensions of justice have a significant, positive influence on customer satisfaction, but distributive justice is the best way to encourage repeat purchases, whereas interactional justice has the most significant impact on WOM (Lin et al., 2011). This research also found that the combinations of distributive justice with procedural justice, and of distributive justice with interactional justice have significant impacts on customer satisfaction, WOM and intention to repeat purchasing.

Similar research findings by Gelbrich et al. (2015) led these authors to recommend a four-step approach in dealing with service-level failures. First, it is important to acknowledge the distress of the consumer in a sympathetic and caring manner. Second, an apology should be made, followed by a third step in trying to fix the problem, including offering a substitute service. Only after these steps have been taken should compensation be offered. Interestingly, these authors suggested that compensation worth 70 to 80 per cent of the loss is generally optimal to achieve a balance between satisfying the consumer and optimising the outcome from the firm's point of view.

Roschk and Gelbrich (2014) found that compensation is more effective when it is tailored to the type of complaint. For example, monetary compensation is appropriate when the customer complains about a financial loss, but if the complaint focuses on a service-level failure, the firm should offer to re-perform the service. Furthermore, if a complainant emphasises that they were not paid sufficient attention, then it would be better to recognise that psychological factors such as status and self-esteem have been threatened.

Surprisingly, there is relatively little published work to guide practitioners on the optimal level of compensation, and attention is therefore drawn to the findings of Gelbrich et al. (2015). Recognising that some consumers will reject any solution to continue using the service (e.g. rebooking on another flight), these authors found that, in such cases, the highest incremental effect of compensation on satisfaction lies in the range of 60 to 120 per cent of the price paid. When a consumer accepts a service solution, the initial compensation, even if it is only partial in nature, has the best return in terms of customer satisfaction. Notably, Gelbrich et al. (2015) demonstrated a methodology for determining the optimal amount of compensation. Costantino et al. (2013) also designed a model to assess which elements of service quality can be of greatest help to airlines to retain passengers.

## Promoting long-term commitment to the brand

As noted, researchers have found that satisfied customers tend to become repeat customers. The evidence is that they are also likely to complain less and engage in favourable WOM, and "are willing to pay more for the benefits they receive and are more likely to be tolerant of an increase in price" (Baker, 2013: 70). The airline industry has been a leader in adopting marketing practices designed to encourage repeat business. For example, Rust et al. (1995) describe how United Airlines became aware through analysis of complaints data and proprietary survey results that its most frequent business travellers were the least satisfied and most frustrated with air travel. The company then invested US$400 million to upgrade seats, food, lounges and boarding procedures. United also enticed these travellers with additional benefits under its FFP.

United Airlines has engaged in researching its customers since the 1950s, and introduced the first FFP in 1972. When the domestic airlines in the US were deregulated in 1978, the FFP quickly evolved into a rewards scheme based on mileage flown, and it has generally been described as a loyalty programme because of its role in attracting repeat business. Researchers have tended to equate repeat purchasing with loyalty, but this interpretation is open to serious objection. There can be no argument about the power of an FFP as an incentive, but it is questionable whether it leads to a long-term commitment to a brand. One researcher concluded that "Many IT-driven airline loyalty programmes remain, however, crude attempts to increase short-term sales without adding to the quality of the long-term relationship between an airline and its customers" (Bejou and Palmer, 1998: 7).

Researchers are well aware that a definition of loyalty based simply on the frequency of purchase is deficient because many customers buy the same brand simply because they do not have a choice, or out of habit. For example, "A longer relationship may allow not only for the service provider to empathise with its customers, but customers to empathise with the problems faced by the provider in trying to deliver consistently high standards of service" (Bejou and Palmer, 1998: 16). Loyalty, properly understood, involves a commitment to a brand, and the evidence is that long-term relationships tend to increase profitability (Costantino et al., 2013).

What is important in the context of this chapter is that it is possible to turn a dissatisfied customer into a loyal one, but success hinges first on learning from the customer about the perceived failure in service delivery. There is an extensive literature on complaint handling, and it is not surprising that Steer Davies Gleave (2010) found that airlines tend to manage complaints in a customer relations department. This brings the account back to modern management practices such as CRM. A point on which to end this discussion is to note that effective use of CRM encourages an airline to maximise the number of complaints it receives. If the complaints are handled well, there is less incentive for a passenger to make contact with a regulatory body or a court/tribunal. This possibility suggests a fruitful line of future research.

## Conclusion

The research cited in this chapter suggests several arguments that explain why the number of complaints could increase even when service levels improve. Some of the factors to consider include: the influence of increased incentives to complain; diminishing rates of increase in satisfaction relative to improvements in service; increasing expectations with growing experience of travel; and negative publicity about airlines affecting their credibility and leading consumers to be less tolerant of service level failures. While these findings might provide little comfort to management, they nevertheless enlighten debates about complaining behaviour.

This chapter has made reference to two policy debates that had different outcomes. One resulted in the introduction of the so-called tarmac delay rule in the US. The other involved demands for enhanced protection for passengers from airline bankruptcies, and in that case the policymakers decided a new regulation was not necessary. Both were the subject of much discussion in the media and strong measures were advocated by consumer activists.

What the cases illustrate is that policymakers and regulators can, in the field of passenger protection, be put in the position where there are powerful political pressures to do something. In this situation, it is important to have recourse to facts about the nature and extent of the problem, and about the alternative courses of action, including competition policy. In a systematic approach to policy formulation involving, for example, a regulatory impact assessment, consideration would also be given to the practicability of proposed measures and assessments of the costs and benefits to all parties. Considering the proliferation of demands for passenger rights, further research documenting factual information about passenger complaints and illustrating how to evaluate passenger protection measures would be beneficial.

The airline industry has its share of pioneers in management thinking. FFPs are arguably the best-known example of a mechanism to lock customers into repeat purchasing. This chapter has pointed out that a more sustainable approach in a highly competitive environment is to ensure customers remain loyal. In this context, relationship management takes centre stage in handling complaints. Those airlines that embrace such approaches to management aim to strengthen commitment to the brand and they encourage their passengers to tell them when they are not satisfied. Further documentation of these modern airline approaches to handling complaints and managing relationships would be of value both to airline managers and policymakers.

## References

Agbonifoh, E.A. and Edoreh, P.E. (1993). Consumer awareness and complaining behaviour, *European Journal of Marketing*, 27, 43–49.

Akamavi, R.K., Mohamed, E., Pellmann, K. and Xu, Y. (2015). Key determinants of passenger loyalty in the low-cost airline business, *Tourism Management*, 46, 528–545.

Baker, D.Mc.A. (2013). Service quality and customer satisfaction in the airline industry: a comparison between legacy airlines and low-cost airlines, *American Journal of Tourism Research*, 2(1), 67–77.

Bamford, D. and Xystouri, T. (2005). A case study of service failure and recovery within an international airline, *Managing Service Quality*, 15(3), 306–322.

Bejou, D. and Palmer, A. (1998). Service failure and loyalty: an exploratory empirical study of airline customers, *Journal of Services Marketing*, 12(1), 7–22.

Berg, D.A. (2010). DOT's new deplaning rule: a recipe for consumer disruption, not protection, *Air and Space Law*, 23(1), 1.

Blodgett, J., Hill, D. and Bakir, A. (2006). Cross-cultural complaining behavior? An alternative explanation, *Journal of Consumer Satisfaction, Dissatisfaction & Complaining Behavior*, 19, 103–117.

Boudreaux, D.J. and DiLorenzo, T.J. (1993). The protectionist roots of antitrust, *The Austrian Review of Economics*, 6(2), 81–96.

Bureau of Transportation Statistics (2016). *Air carrier statistics database (T-100 data bank)*. Online. Available at: www.transtats.bts.gov/DatabaseInfo.asp?DB_ID=111 (accessed 12 June 2017).

Calisir, N., Basak, E. and Calisir, F. (2016). Key drivers of passenger loyalty: a case of Frankfurt–Istanbul flights, *Journal of Air Transport Management*, 53, 211–217.

Chang, Y.-H. and Cheng, C.H. (2007). Analyzing the strategies of LCCs and FSCs in Southeast Asia, *Aerlines Magazine e-zine edition*, 36, 1–6.

Chebat, J.-C., Davidow, M. and Codjovi, I. (2004). Silent voices: why some dissatisfied consumers fail to complain, *Journal of Service Research*, 7(4), 328–342.

Chen, C.-F. (2008). Investigating structural relationships between service quality, perceived value, satisfaction, and behavioral intentions for air passengers: evidence from Taiwan, *Transportation Research Part A: Policy and Practice*, 42, 709–717.

Chiou, W.-B., Chang, M.-H. and Yang, C.-C. (2009). Customers' expectations of complaint handling by airline service: privilege status and reasonability of demands from a social learning perspective, *Psychological Reports*, 104, 468–472.

Chow, C.K.W. (2015). On-time performance, passenger expectations and satisfaction in the Chinese airline industry, *Journal of Air Transport Management*, 47, 39–47.

Cohen, L. (2010). Warne lecture: is it time for another round of consumer protection? The lessons of twentieth-century U.S. history, *Journal of Consumer Affairs*, 44(1), 234–246.

Costantino, F., Di Gravio, G. and Tronci, M. (2013). Return on quality: simulating customer retention in a flight firming project, *Journal of Air Transport Management*, 27(1), 20–24.

Crandall, R.W. and Winston, C. (2003). Does antitrust policy improve consumer welfare? Assessing the evidence, *Journal of Economic Perspectives*, 17(4), 3–26.

Curtis, T., Rhoades, D.L. and Waguespack Jr., B.P. (2012). Satisfaction with airline service quality: familiarity breeds contempt, *International Journal of Aviation Management*, 1(4), 242–256.

DOT (Department of Transportation) (2016a). *About us: aviation enforcement and proceedings*. Online. Available at: www.transportation.gov/airconsumer/about-us (accessed 24 October 2016).

DOT (Department of Transportation) (2016b). *Air Travel Consumer Report*. Online. Available at: www.transportation.gov/airconsumer/air-travel-consumer-report (accessed 10 May 2016).

Dresner, M. and Xu, K. (1995). Customer service customer satisfaction and corporate performance in the service sector, *Journal of Business Logistics*, 16(1), 23–40.

EC (European Commission) (2004). *Regulation 261/2004 of the European Parliament and of the Council of 11 February 2004 Establishing Common Rules on Compensation and Assistance to Passengers in the Event of Denied Boarding and of Cancellation or Long Delay of Flights*, Brussels, EC.

EC (European Commission) (2006). *Regulation (EC) No 1107/2006 of the European Parliament and of the Council of 5 July 2006 Concerning the Rights of Disabled Persons and Persons with Reduced Mobility when Travelling by Air*, Brussels, EC.

EC (European Commission) (2014). *Complaint Handling and Enforcement by Member States of the Air Passenger Rights Regulations*, European Commission Staff Working Document, 7.5.2014, SWD(2014) 156 final, Brussels, EC.

EEC (European Economic Community) (1990). *Council Directive 90/314/EEC of 13 June 1990 on Package Travel, Package Holidays and Package Tours*, Brussels, EEC.

Ferrer, J.C., Rocha e Oliveira, P. and Parasuraman, A. (2012). The behavioral consequences of repeated flight delays, *Journal of Air Transport Management*, 20, 35–38.

Folkes, V.A. (1984). Consumer reactions to product failure: an attributional approach, *Journal of Consumer Research*, 10(4), 398–409.

Gelbrich, K., Gäthke, J. and Grégoire, Y. (2015). How much compensation should a firm offer for a flawed service? An examination of the nonlinear effects of compensation on satisfaction, *Journal of Service Research*, 18, 107–123.

Harris, C.P. (1978). What price consumerism? *European Journal of Marketing*, 12(4), 299–305.

Henry, J. and Gardner, M. (2012). New tarmac delay rule and the volcanic ash cloud over European airspace: one year later, *Journal of Air Law & Commerce*, 76(4), 633–660.

Huffman, M. (2010). Bridging the divide? Theories for integrating competition law and consumer protection, *European Competition Journal*, 6(1), 7–45.

Hunt, K. (1991). Consumer satisfaction, dissatisfaction, and complaining behaviour, *Journal of Social Issues*, 47(1), 107–117.

IATA (International Air Transport Association) (2013). *A proposal for a set of high-level, non-prescriptive core principles on consumer protection*. Presented at the 38th Session of the Assembly of ICAO, Montreal, September–October.

IATA (International Air Transport Association) (2016). *Changing the debate*. Online. Available at: www.iata.org/policy/consumer-pax-rights/consumer-protection/Pages/changing-debate.aspx (accessed 17 October 2016).

ICAO (International Civil Aviation Organisation) (2008). *Policy and Guidance Material on the Regulation of International Air Transport*, ICAO Doc. 9587, 3rd edition, Montreal, ICAO.

ICAO (International Civil Aviation Organisation) (2013). *Effectiveness of consumer protection regulations*. Presented at the ICAO Worldwide Air Transport Conference Sixth Meeting, Montreal, March.

ICAO (International Civil Aviation Organisation) (2015). *ICAO Core Principles on Consumer Protection*, Attachment to State Letter Ref.: SP38/1-15/60 issued 31 July 2015, Montreal, ICAO.

Jacoby, J. and Jaccard, J. (1981). The sources, meaning, and validity of consumer complaint behaviour: a psychological analysis, *Journal of Retailing*, 57(3), 4–25.

Kahn, A.E. (2002). The deregulatory tar baby: the precarious balance between regulation and deregulation, 1970–2000 and henceforward, *Journal of Regulatory Economics*, 21, 35–56.

Kaynak, E. (1985). Some thoughts on consumerism in developed and less developed countries, *International Marketing Review*, 2(2), 15–31.

Kim, Y.K. and Lee, H.R. (2009). Passenger complaints under irregular airline conditions: cross-cultural study, *Journal of Air Transport Management*, 15(6), 350–353.

Kolodinsky, J. (1995). Usefulness of economics in explaining consumer complaints, *Journal of Consumer Affairs*, 29(1), 29–54.

Kuo, T.C., Kremer, O., Phuong, N.T. and Hsu, C.-W. (2016). Motivations and barriers for corporate social responsibility reporting: evidence from the airline industry, *Journal of Air Transport Management*, 57, 184–195.

Lang, B. and Hyde, K.F. (2013). Word of mouth: what we know and what we have yet to learn, *Journal of Consumer Satisfaction, Dissatisfaction & Complaining Behavior*, 26, 1–13.

Lapré, M.A. and Tsikriktsis, N. (2006). Organizational learning curves for customer dissatisfaction: heterogeneity across airlines, *Management Science*, 52(3), 352–366.

Levine, M.E. (2006). Regulation, the market, and interest group cohesion: why airlines were not reregulated, *New York University Law and Economics Working Papers*, 80.

Lin, H.-H., Wang, Y.-S. and Chang, L.-K. (2011). Consumer responses to online retailer's service recovery after a service failure: a perspective of justice theory, *Managing Service Quality*, 21(5), 511–534.

Martin-Castilla, J.I. and Rodriguez-Ruiz, Ó. (2008). EFQM model: knowledge governance and competitive advantage, *Journal of Intellectual Capital*, 9(1), 133–156.

Mayser, S. and von Wangenheim, F. (2013). Perceived fairness of differential customer treatment: consumers' understanding of distributive justice really matters, *Journal of Service Research*, 16, 99–113.

Nikbin, D., Marimuthu, M., Hyun, S.S. and Ismail, I. (2014). Effects of stability and controllability attribution on service recovery evaluation in the context of the airline industry, *Journal of Travel and Tourism Marketing*, 31(7), 817–834.

Pantazi, T. (2010). Airline bankruptcy and consumer protection in the European Union, *Air & Space Law*, 35(6), 409–421.

Pappalardo, J.K. (2012). Product literacy and the economics of consumer protection policy, *Journal of Consumer Affairs*, 46(2), 319–332.

Prassl, J. (2014). Reforming air passenger rights in the European Union, *Air & Space Law*, 39(1), 59–81.

Ramsay, I. (2006). Consumer law, regulatory capitalism and the 'New Learning' in regulation, *Sydney Law Review*, 28(9), 9–35.

Roschk, H. and Gelbrich, K. (2014). Identifying appropriate compensation types for service failures: a meta-analytic and experimental analysis, *Journal of Service Research*, 17, 195–211.

Rust, R.T., Zahorik, A.J. and Keiningham, T.L. (1995). Return on quality: making service quality financially accountable, *Journal of Marketing*, 59(2), 58–70.

Sim, K.L., Sang, C.J. and Killough, L.N. (2010). Service quality, service recovery, and financial performance: an analysis of the US airline industry. In: P.M. Epstein and J.Y. Lee (eds). *Advances in Management Accounting*, Volume 18, Bingley, Emerald.

SITA (2016). *2016 Air Transport Industry Insights, the Baggage Report*, Geneva, SITA, in association with Air Transport World.

Staroňová, K. (2010). Regulatory impact assessment: formal institutionalization and practice, *Journal of Public Policy*, 30(1), 117–136.

Steer Davies Gleave (2010). *Evaluation of Regulation 261/2004. Final Report February 2010*, report prepared for the European Commission Directorate-General Energy and Transport, DM28 5/70, Brussels, Steer Davies Gleave.

Steer Davies Gleave (2011). *Impact Assessment of Passenger Protection in the Event of Airline Insolvency. Final Report March 2011*, report prepared for the European Commission DG MOVE DM24, Brussels, Steer Davies Gleave.

Steppler, U. and Vogler, R. (2012). Airline insolvency protection: a justified form of relief or the next level of 'consumerism'? *Air & Space Law*, 37(4/5), 359–368.

Steven, A.B., Dong, Y. and Dresner, M. (2012). Linkages between customer service, customer satisfaction and performance in the airline industry: investigation of non-linearities and moderating effects, *Transportation Research Part E: Logistics and Transportation Review*, 48(4), 743–754.

Suzuki, Y. (2000). The relationship between on-time performance and airline market share: a new approach, *Transportation Research E: Logistics and Transportation Review*, 36(2), 139–154.

Svetiev, Y. (2013). How consumer law travels, *Journal of Consumer Policy*, 36(3), 209–230.

van Boom, H.W. (2011). Price intransparency, consumer decision making and European consumer law, *Journal of Consumer Policy*, 34, 359–376.

Waguespack, B.P. and Rhoades, D.L. (2014). Twenty-five years of measuring airline service quality or why is airline service quality only good when times are bad? *Research in Transportation Business & Management*, 10, 33–39.

Wittman, M.D. (2014). Are low-cost carrier passengers less likely to complain about service quality? *Journal of Air Transport Management*, 35, 64–71.

Wittmer, A. and Laesser, C. (2010). The perception of time in air transport: what delay is accepted by air travelers? *Journal of Air Transport Studies*, 1(1), 48–61.

# 24

# Low cost carrier implications for human resource management

*Geraint Harvey and Peter Turnbull*

## Introduction

Human resources play a critical role in air transport. The number of people directly employed in the air transport sector stands at around 10 million people, with a further 63 million jobs supported by aviation (ATAG, 2016). Moreover, people play a vital role in airline operations as the productivity of staff and/or the customer service performance of staff offers the airline a competitive advantage. As former airline CEO and aviation scholar Rigas Doganis succinctly put it, "labour is the key" to airline success (Doganis, 2006: 101). Consequently, effective human resource management (HRM) is crucial. This chapter documents the importance of HRM with reference to several critical incidents in the civil aviation industry. It begins with civil aviation liberalisation (see also Chapters 6 and 7) and focuses specifically, but not exclusively, on the low cost model – an airline business model (see also Chapter 8) developed by Southwest Airlines in the United States (US) and adopted (and adapted) to a greater or lesser extent by low cost carriers (LCCs) around the world. The chapter discusses the human resources (HR) practices associated with the low cost model and the impact of competition from these airlines on the HRM strategies of traditional full service or legacy carriers. The chapter proceeds chronologically and considers the influence of industry crises that followed: (i) the terrorist attacks in the US on 11 September 2001; and (ii) the global financial crisis. Recent HRM initiatives are documented, and the chapter ends with a discussion of what is the most enduring, distinctive and arguably the most successful HRM strategy in civil aviation.

## LCCs and HRM

Prior to liberalisation, air transport was organised according to bilateral air service agreements between governments that specified the routes that airlines could fly and the tariffs they could charge. Price competition was limited, at best, under these agreements and entry into the industry was highly restricted. With the advent of liberalisation and increased competition (see Chapters 6 and 7), in particular price competition, civil aviation became a far more dynamic but also more volatile industry. Unburdened by historical commitments to the workforce, the new entrant LCCs achieved cost savings through employment contracts whose terms and conditions were inferior to those of their full service or legacy airline competitors – cost savings that the airline could then pass onto the customer. Although there were differences between the new European LCCs in terms of their HRM strategies – and these differences have become more pronounced in recent times – there were common HRM practices that distinguished them from the legacy airlines. Most notably, these are lower starting salaries and a more compressed salary scale, a higher proportion of variable pay, more intense work schedules (rosters), precarious employment contracts, and a preference for direct communication (individual employee voice), combined with an aversion to collective representation (indirect voice via a trade union or professional association).

In the years immediately after liberalisation, staff at LCCs received markedly different remuneration to their counterparts at the legacy airlines (Harvey and Turnbull, 2010), while also working more intensively due to lower crew numbers and higher utilisation (Doganis, 2006). A reduced complement of staff in the cabin was possible because the LCCs did not have a meal service, nor a cabin differentiated by class of service. LCCs offered passengers little in the way of the complementary comforts provided by their legacy counterparts, although extras could be purchased for an additional charge. These and other add-ons (e.g. ground transport to/from the secondary airports preferred by LCCs to the main centres of population) provided an ancillary revenue stream for the LCCs. By unbundling the different components of air travel, LCCs not only turn the flight experience into a commodity for the passenger, with payment for all the different elements of the flight (e.g. seat choice, checked-in baggage, in-flight food and drinks); they also change the nature and expectations of work for staff (e.g. a significant component of pay for cabin crew is based on in-flight sales performance). Most LCCs use some form of variable pay for cabin crew, which often comprises more than half the employee's monthly pay (Harvey and Turnbull, 2012). Although the difference between LCC and legacy airline labour costs has narrowed, largely as a result of cost-cutting by the legacy airlines (Harvey and Turnbull, 2010), the difference between LCCs and legacy airlines in terms of employee productivity remains stark. Data from airline financial statements for 2015 illustrate the sheer size of this particular performance gap: the net profit per employee at Ryanair (€90,413) was more than six times that of Lufthansa (€14,202).

The low cost model is synonymous with various forms of subcontracting and the increased use of agency or temporary workers, whereby direct employees are replaced by (bogus) self-employed workers (see Jorens et al., 2015) and other staff hired on more precarious employment contracts (e.g. fixed-term or seasonal contracts). British Airways had been unsuccessful previously in implementing a similar system as part of its virtual airline plan (the Business Efficiency Programme, proposed in the mid-1990s), whereby the airline would retain only core functions and even operate aircraft supplied and staffed under wet lease arrangements with other airlines. Following the proposals, members of the British Airline Pilots Association (BALPA) threatened to strike in 1996, while their cabin crew colleagues, who were members of the British Airlines Stewards and Stewardesses Association (BASSA), took industrial action in the following year.

LCCs have used subcontracting in order first to outsource non-essential functions and then more recently to outsource core functions in order to allow market forces to reduce the cost of these functions. Whereas easyJet pioneered the approach to subcontracting non-specialist functions (Sull, 1999), Ryanair have outsourced cabin crew work to employment agencies and flight crew work to self-employed pilots (Harvey and Turnbull, 2012, 2014). Although precarious work contracts are not the preserve of LCCs, a sizeable proportion of the workforce at these airlines are employed on short-term (seasonal or temporary) contracts, and many are recruited through an agency rather than being directly employed by the airline. At the airport, almost all ground services (e.g. ground handling, fuelling, check-in) are subcontracted to third parties (see Harvey and Turnbull, 2012, 2014).

With regard to the employee voice, an important dimension of an airline's strategy for enhancing employee performance and productivity is its relationship, or lack thereof, with trade unions that represent workers in the industry. In the United Kingdom (UK), many airlines formally recognise trade unions for the purposes of collective bargaining – the process through which the terms and conditions of work are determined. However, easyJet initially operated on a non-union basis (pilots and then cabin crew voted for union representation under the recognition procedure introduced by the Employment Relations Act, 1999), and management at some LCCs, most notably Ryanair, have vehemently opposed trade union participation in the decision-making processes of the airline (see Gunnigle and O'Sullivan, 2009; Harvey and Turnbull, 2015). Compared to Ryanair, most other LCCs have taken a less antagonistic but nonetheless antipathetic approach to trade unions (Harvey and Turnbull, 2012).

## Industry crises and HRM

When LCCs first entered the European market, the response of legacy airlines was essentially studied neglect because the newcomers rarely competed head-on with legacy airlines (i.e. flights to/from the same airports, even when advertised as the same destination), which had little direct impact on passenger numbers at the legacy airlines. Where competition existed, for example on routes between Stansted, Luton, Gatwick and Heathrow Airports in London and those serving Barcelona (Barcelona, Girona and Reus), the LCCs generated new markets rather than cannibalising those of the legacy airlines, initially at least (Harvey and Turnbull, 2014). As the low-fares model took hold, and with LCCs increasingly competing head-on with national (flag) airlines and capturing a greater share of the market, several legacy airlines introduced their own LCCs. British Airways, for example, created Go, KLM introduced Buzz, and SAS set up Snowflake. One effect of these new start-ups, however, was to take some traffic away from the legacy airline's own short-haul network, rather than new entrants such as Ryanair and easyJet. Moreover, the success of airlines such as Go served to legitimise the new low cost market: with the British Airways brand behind it, and cafetière coffee and a free newspaper on board, Go appealed to many of the high(er)-value customers of British Airways travelling on short business trips within Europe, as well as the more typical low cost customers (tourists and those visiting friends and relatives), and was widely regarded as the low cost airline for the middle classes. Go was eventually sold to easyJet and Buzz to Ryanair. Snowflake only operated for two years, with SAS then deciding instead to offer a no-fills (Snowflake equivalent) service in a section of the economy-class cabin on its existing short-haul routes.

The scale of growth of the LCCs in the new millennium and their unfettered success after the civil aviation industry crisis that followed the 9/11 terrorist attacks on the US altered the competitive strategy, and subsequently the HRM strategy, of many legacy airlines. Following considerable growth in demand for air transport in the early years of the 1990s, demand decreased significantly from 1995 onwards, and had not recovered when the aftermath of the terrorist attacks exacerbated what had been a very difficult period for many airlines. In the wake of the 9/11 crisis, the true extent of the competitive threat facing legacy airlines from the LCCs came into sharper focus. At the turn of the millennium, LCCs accounted for only 5 per cent of the intra-European market, but they weathered the storm wrought by the crisis of 2001–2002 far better than their legacy counterparts. In the last quarter of 2001, the passenger traffic carried by the European LCCs easyJet, Ryanair and Go increased by around 30 per cent.

The industry crisis that followed 9/11 compounded the difficulties faced by legacy airlines, many of which pursued radical cost saving initiatives in 2001–2002. In seeking cost savings, labour is an obvious target for airline management because of the proportion and pliancy of labour costs. For most legacy (full service) airlines, labour typically accounts for around one-third of total operating costs (see Chapter 11 for a discussion about airline costs). Pilots are especially well paid (around £90,000 per annum on average, which, according to the Office of National Statistics, puts them among the highest paid workers in the UK), but most flight crew start their career with training debts of around £100,000 (Tovey, 2014). LCCs typically expect their first officers to pay for type-rate training, adding another £20,000 plus to the pilot's initial training debts. Airlines can, of course, make some significant savings; for example, deals can be negotiated with (secondary) airports to reduce or subsidise landing charges, bulk purchasing aircraft may attract a reduction from aircraft manufacturers, and airlines might negotiate advantageous fuel hedge contracts. But most operating costs are (quasi-)fixed, at least in the short term. Labour costs, in contrast, are more malleable, and it is hardly surprising that airline cost-cutting initiatives invariably focus on labour costs (see Harvey and Turnbull, 2009).

However, seeking concessions from staff is a precarious business for airline management for a number of reasons. First, the workforce offers an airline a competitive advantage not only when they are cheap and highly productive, but also when they provide care and attention to passengers. This is often central to the business model of the airline, most notably airlines such as Emirates, Qatar and Singapore Airlines (the top three airlines, according to the Skytrax World Airline Awards 2016). Airline management must be mindful of the detrimental impact that a labour cost-reduction policy might have on employees and their willingness to provide excellent customer service.

Second, the cost of industrial sanction imposed by workers can be catastrophic for the airline; for example, the dispute that resulted in strike action by ground services workers that erupted at Sabena, the Belgian flag carrier, following 9/11 contributed to the demise of the airline. The service offered by the airline is perishable. In other words, airlines cannot stockpile seats on cancelled flights for use on another occasion – if a flight is cancelled, then the revenue from ticket sales is lost. Flight cancellations have an immediate and direct impact on an airline's performance, and so industrial action taken by airline employees can be highly detrimental to the company's reputation and profitability. Industrial action by pilots employed by Lufthansa and Air France in 2014, for example, cost the airlines an estimated €174 million and €500 million, respectively. The strike action organised by Unite the Union at British Airways in 2010 cost the airline an estimated £150 million (Goodley, 2016). The threat alone of industrial action can have a negative impact on airline profitability, as passengers who are concerned about whether their flight will be cancelled book their tickets with other airlines. In this context, the cooperation and the consent of the workforce are paramount: disgruntled staff are bad for customer service, while disruptive staff are disastrous for the bottom line.

Third, the nature of air transport demand complicates negotiations between airline management and staff. The cyclical nature of demand (see Chapter 1) often leads to the expectations of management and labour being out of sync with respect to current and future market conditions. A common response to unfavourable economic conditions among airlines has been to control costs more tightly, and employees are often expected to make concessions such as accepting a pay freeze or pay cuts, or the suspension of allowances such as staff travel (see Harvey and Turnbull, 2009; Turnbull and Harvey, 2001). When demand increases, the response of airline management is cautious, and there is rarely a swift reinstatement of the benefits that were conceded because managers anticipate the next downturn in an increasingly competitive environment. The perception of front-line staff, who handle more and more passengers, is of a business in rude health, and they consequently anticipate improvements in terms and conditions to reflect the evident prosperity of the airline. This mismatch between the expectations of staff and the caution of management can be highly problematic, particularly at the peak of the business cycle when business appears to be booming, but where airline management foresee or face falling demand (e.g. a decline in advance bookings).

For the LCCs around the world, the pro-cyclical demand of the business cycle is exacerbated by shorter-term seasonal (cyclical) variation in demand. Passengers visiting friends and relatives and leisure travellers remain an important customer base of LCCs. Consequently, the difference between peak demand in the summer months and the demand-trough in the winter is more pronounced for LCCs than it is for legacy airlines.

While the consequences of 9/11 were highly detrimental for legacy airlines, the crisis also served as an opportunity to introduce significant cost-reduction measures that led to accusations of opportunism from many aviation unions (Harvey and Turnbull, 2002: 19). However, according to the Director General and CEO of IATA at the time, "Even before September 11th this industry was ill prepared to weather even a mild regular economic cycle" (Jeanniot, 2002, cited in Harvey and Turnbull, 2002: 20). Post-crisis cost-reduction measures invariably focused on labour.

Analysis of airlines' response to the crisis revealed that many airlines across the globe, especially in liberal market economies such as the US and UK, moved quickly to reduce labour costs by offering voluntary redundancy to (and imposing compulsory redundancy on) staff, alongside voluntary and compulsory furlough (i.e. the requirement that staff take unpaid leave). In Europe and Asia–Pacific, cost-reduction initiatives also impacted severely on more junior and temporary workers, as there was widespread non-renewal of temporary contracts and probationary staff not being transferred onto full-time contracts. These measures taken in response to the crisis, whether they reflected necessity or opportunism, were to have a profound impact on employment relations at many airlines. As noted by von Nordenflycht (2001) at the time, the response to the crisis served to increase tensions between labour and management, lower trust between both parties, and provided the backdrop for future conflict.

By 2008, LCCs were responsible for almost 30 per cent of the US domestic market and around 40 per cent of the intra-European market. It is in this context of increasing LCC market share that civil aviation was once again plunged into turmoil following the global financial crisis that eclipsed the problems encountered after 9/11. Airline revenue fell by 7 per cent in the crisis that followed 9/11, but this figure was dwarfed by plummeting revenues in the wake of the financial crisis when revenue fell by 15 per cent in 2009. The operating losses of the world's top 150 airlines totalled US$15 billion in 2009, compared with profits of US$29 billion in 2007 (see also Chapter 1). Several airlines ceased trading, and many more responded with cost-reduction strategies that once again directly impacted on labour, with staff-reduction programmes alongside leave of absence (furloughs) and a reduction in training. Data from studies conducted in 2001 and 2009 suggest an increased incidence of redundancy (voluntary and compulsory) in the latter period, despite the opposition of trade unions to compulsory redundancy (Harvey and Turnbull, 2010: 16). The global financial crisis impacted on the success of the principal European LCCs in terms of passengers carried, but these airlines have recovered more quickly. Immediately prior to the most recent financial crisis (2007–2008), all the largest (top 10) network airlines were profitable, while all but one of the top 10 LCCs was making money (Dunn, 2011). In 2008, seven of the top 10 network airlines lost money, compared to just three of the top 10 LCCs. A year later, nine of the top 10 network airlines were in the red, compared to just two of the leading LCCs.

## Contemporary HRM strategies

By 2013, LCCs carried more than half of the domestic passengers in Spain, the Netherlands and Italy, and more than half of the international traffic originating in Latvia, Slovakia, Lithuania, Poland, Hungary and Spain (see Harvey and Turnbull, 2014: 14). In the decade to May 2014, European LCCs grew at an average of 14 per cent per annum, whereas legacy airlines grew by only 1 per cent per annum (OAG, 2014). In a single European aviation market, there are far greater opportunities for social dumping – "a strategy geared towards the lowering of wage or social standards for the sake of enhanced competitiveness" (Bernaciak, 2012: 6) – because airlines can readily take advantage of the competition between workers in different geographical regions. As previously noted, subcontracting and the use of agency workers are central to the HRM innovations made by the LCCs; however, the extent of use of these policies has varied between LCCs. For example, Ryanair was found guilty of social dumping by French courts in 2014 for paying less than 11 per cent of the requisite 45 per cent social cost for its staff based in the country.

Aside from increasing numbers of people in the industry working for the LCCs, the success of the LCCs has further impacted on employment within the industry, primarily in two ways. First, the increased competitive pressure exerted by the LCCs on legacy airlines is manifest in renewed efforts to replicate elements of the low cost model. Whereas abortive attempts were made by several airlines in the late 1990s to replicate the low cost model via a subsidiary (e.g. British Airways' Go and KLM's Buzz), more recent ventures by Lufthansa (Germanwings) and Air France-KLM (Transavia) have been more successful, especially in terms of reducing labour costs within the airline. Cabin crew at Germanwings, for example, are paid around 40 per cent less than their colleagues in the Lufthansa mainline operation and experience a much slower progression up the pay scale (Harvey and Turnbull, 2014: 17). Alternatively, British Airways has pioneered an approach whereby a new workforce has been created inside the airline, with new staff hired on inferior terms and conditions of employment. Alongside its Euro and Worldwide Fleets, the airline now has a third, Mixed Fleet. Unlike the physical separation of Germanwings from Lufthansa mainline, British Airways Mixed Fleet operates both short-haul (European) and long-haul (intercontinental) flights from London Heathrow.

The second development is a consequence of the diminishing returns from the low cost model. This is manifest both in terms of longer and thinner (i.e. lower-demand) routes as the LCCs seek out new markets that are more costly to service, and the (inevitable) limits to continually cutting labour costs: at some point, the low motivation of poorly paid and insecure staff will result in a decline in (even basic) service quality that will outweigh any savings from lower unit labour costs. It comes as no surprise, then, that LCCs such as easyJet now differentiate their service in terms of the tariff, with FLEXI fares that include allocated seating, speedy boarding and one piece of hold luggage. Consequently, if the options for continuous cost reduction diminish, the only financial alternative is to grow revenue. This can be achieved by adding value (e.g. offering ancillary products and services such as travel insurance, car hire, hotel accommodation, surface transport, on-board and online gambling, and in-flight sales) and/or targeting different passenger groups, especially those with more disposable income. Ryanair, for example, earned around 20 per cent of its revenue from ancillary products and services in 2013, including excess baggage charges, which is higher than other LCCs (e.g. 11 per cent at Norwegian Air Shuttle) (Harvey and Turnbull, 2014: 18).[1]

No LCC has ever survived a full economic cycle on a long-haul (intercontinental) route. However, new market opportunities are being created through the negotiation of open skies agreements with non-European Union (EU) countries, most notably the US. With the commission of a European sovereign state (an Air Operator's Certificate), European LCCs are now able to adopt and adapt the maritime practice of Flags of Convenience (FoC) and Crews of Convenience (CoC) as a way of redefining employment relationships, exerting control over labour and extracting surplus value. The clearest example of this strategy – the creation of Norwegian Air International, a subsidiary of Norwegian Air Shuttle – is now a cause célèbre on both sides of the Atlantic.

These developments explain why the business strategies of LCCs are evolving (e.g. facilitating transfers, entering alliances, acquiring other airlines) (see Chapters 8 and 9) and why the experience of work for aircrew will differ not only between legacy and LCCs, but also between different legacy and low cost operators. For example, LCCs such as easyJet, with a denser route network and access to more and higher-value passengers at primary airports, will have different expectations of staff and a more stable roster throughout the year (i.e. less variation between summer and winter schedules). Based on OAG data for 2011, a comparison between the lowest monthly flight capacity expressed as a percentage of the highest monthly flight capacity illustrates significant differences within the low cost group of airlines (e.g. easyJet 74.6 per cent, Ryanair 66.6 per cent and Vueling 51.5 per cent) and between LCCs and legacy airlines (e.g. BA 91.5 per cent and Lufthansa 89.9 per cent). This means that staff at the LCCs will have a shorter and more intensive workload, flying the majority of their annual flight time allowance in the summer months, certainly when compared to their counterparts at the legacy airlines. While easyJet and Vueling target higher-value passengers and primary airports, the self-styled ultra LCCs (Ryanair and Wizz Air) will no doubt continue to reduce labour costs, and staff will find themselves working right up to the maximum flight and duty time during the busy summer schedule, with enforced lay-offs or unpaid leave becoming the norm during the winter when aircraft are grounded. Ryanair, for example, now flex the fleet between winter and summer schedules, and typically ground between 60 and 80 aircraft each winter, principally because the carrier no longer makes a profit during the winter and relies on summer profits to offset winter losses.

It is clear that the continued success of the LCCs, through a strategy of increasingly direct competition with legacy airlines at primary airports for the same passenger groups, will also impact on staff at the legacy airlines. easyJet already poses a direct competitive challenge to many legacy airlines as the company has invested heavily in frequent services to/from primary airports whilst maintaining a low cost operating base. In some EU member states, easyJet is now the benchmark used by management calling for a reduction in legacy labour costs, but in other member states it is an employer of choice for many aspiring cabin crew, including many staff who work for British Airways Mixed Fleet. Direct competition from Ryanair is rather more challenging. When legacy airlines with a much higher (legacy) cost base face social dumping by an ultra LCC the pressure on revenue and staff costs can be considerable.

The churn created by low cost competition for legacy airline staff is not confined to the low cost version of the main brand (e.g. staff employed by British Airways Mixed Fleet, Iberia Express, Germanwings and Transavia). A combination of more fuel-efficient aircraft and open skies agreements with neighbouring countries has enabled LCCs to extend the geographic reach of their route network to many of the attractive and lucrative long-haul destinations traditionally served by legacy airlines. As of March 2017, the Norwegian Group, for example, offers flights to Boston, Florida, Gaudeloupe, Los Angeles, Matinique, New York, San Francisco and San Juan. From a multi-base network, LCCs can retain the cost advantages of their original business model on these routes.

Thus far, the focus has been on what is commonly understood to be low road HRM, highlighting some of the dangers inherent in the low road approach in civil aviation. The most recent examples include the protracted consideration by the US Department of Transport of

Norwegian Airlines' application for an air operator's licence, due to vehement opposition by North American aviation unions. The recent innovations by the European legacy airlines to operate what staff regard as mainline services via a low cost subsidiary led to industrial action and significant costs at both Lufthansa and Air France. In 2014, British Airways experienced disquiet in its Mixed Fleet and narrowly avoided industrial action, after a ballot that returned 95 per cent in favour of industrial sanctions. Had the action been taken, then the airline might have encountered similar losses to those experienced in 2010 when Unite the Union coordinated industrial action among cabin crew, and the airline estimated the cost of the action at £7 million per day. The situation at Ryanair is very different but no less problematic. As a non-union airline, strike action against the Irish carrier is unlikely, though not inconceivable. As unions press for representation at Ryanair, a succession of legal challenges have been launched in respect of workers' terms and conditions of employment, especially on the part of staff hired via an agency (who now constitute the vast majority of Ryanair's workforce). Such disquiet casts doubt on the sustainability of the low road employment model in civil aviation.

## Southwest Airlines and HRM

In documenting the changes to HRM in civil aviation since the liberalisation of the industry, and implying that it has been nothing but deteriorating terms and conditions of employment and simmering discontent, it is pertinent to consider an approach to HRM that delivers for both the airline and its workforce. The theory of strategic HRM predicts that a low cost business model is predicated on a "low road" approach to people management (Jackson et al., 2014: 9), but Southwest Airlines does not conform: as the pioneer LCC and one of the most successful global airlines over the past 40 years, it also manages staff with a high road alternative.

The low cost operating model developed by Southwest Airlines has, to a greater or lesser extent, been replicated by LCCs around the world. Far less influential has been the airline's distinctive HRM strategy, and no LCC has successfully replicated the airline's high road approach to HRM and industrial relations, despite the fact that the company's people strategy is at the heart of its sustained competitive advantage. Southwest Airlines is now the largest US domestic carrier, with a market share of over 70 per cent of the top 100 city pairs and around 25 per cent of the total market. It has recorded 40 years of consecutive profitability, with an average profit margin of just under 9 per cent over the period between 1999 and 2008. This success has been achieved in no small part due to the FUN-loving attitude of its staff who are keen to demonstrate their servant's heart[2] to provide passengers with a novel flight experience. The employment relations system adopted by the airline is exemplified by the former CEO, Herb Kelleher, who encapsulated the airline's approach towards staff in the following statement: "You put your employees first. If you truly treat your employees that way, they will treat your customers well, your customers will come back, and that's what makes your shareholders happy" (Herb Kelleher, cited in McDermott et al., 2013: 306). Treating staff well includes industry-leading pay and benefits. In 2016, Southwest Airlines invested US$100 million in staff development, engaging staff in around 2 million hours of training. The airline's University for People provides training and career development to help employees learn and grow.

Southwest Airlines is the most highly unionised airline in America – union density currently stands at around 83 per cent – and unions are treated as business partners, not third parties. To illustrate how opportunities to participate in decision-making (e.g. on pay and benefits) can directly enhance the performance of the organisation, consider the process of collective bargaining and how this might affect customer service (e.g. delays caused by strikes or other forms of industrial action) or passengers' perceptions of the reliability of a particular airline (e.g. adversarial contract negotiations reported in the media that might lead to future flight cancellations if the parties cannot reach an amicable settlement). Southwest Airlines leads the way in timely contract negotiations in the US through its partnership approach with trade unions. In its 40-year history, the airline has only ever experienced one strike (Gittell et al., 2004). Conversely, US industry data indicate that efforts by airlines to avoid unions are not likely to produce a sustained improvement in either service quality or airline financial performance.

## Conclusion

HRM is extremely important to the success of airlines in the liberalised era of civil aviation, wherein competition between airlines is far greater than it was previously. First, workers can provide airlines with a productivity and/or service advantage. For example, the productivity advantage achieved by Ryanair through its intensive utilisation of staff is significant, while staff at airlines that compete on service quality, such as Emirates, Qatar and Singapore Airlines, are the source of the customer service competitive advantage. Second, labour costs comprise a sizeable proportion of airline operating costs, and as these are pliable, then airline management might more easily reduce labour costs than other operating costs, such as fuel and landing charges. Whereas labour costs are pliable, there are risks attached to reducing the cost of labour. For the airline that competes on service quality, cost-reduction initiatives have the potential to antagonise staff, resulting in a diminished propensity to care for the customer. Antagonising staff is treacherous for all airlines because the airline product is perishable, and industrial action by employees can have a severe and immediate impact on profitability if flights are cancelled.

In contrast to the legacy airlines, the European LCCs that emerged as a result of liberalisation introduced a system of HRM marked by inferior terms and conditions of employment (comparatively lower pay and a higher variable component), more intensive working, precarious employment contracts, and reduced options for employee voice. Due to the success of Ryanair and easyJet that is directly linked to a cost advantage secured via HRM, especially in the wake of two industry crises, the low cost model of HRM has been highly influential and legacy airlines have adopted and adapted elements of the low road approach. However, it is important to note that the (low road) degradation of employee terms and conditions of work are not inevitable in order for airlines to compete in the contemporary civil aviation industry. It is clear that the most successful and sustainable HRM strategy in the industry – that of Southwest Airlines – is one that is based on attractive terms and conditions, investment in employee development, and respect for the democratic rights of employees, as demonstrated by extensive direct and indirect voice mechanisms. Sustainable competitive advantage through HRM is the ultimate goal for airline management, and the evidence to date indicates that this goal is achievable via the high road to HRM.

## Notes

1 In 2015, around one-quarter of Ryanair's revenue (25 per cent, €1.5 billion) came from ancillary charges.
2 The three values promoted by Southwest Airlines are the servant's heart, warrior spirit and FUN-loving attitude (www.southwest.com/html/about-southwest/careers/culture.html).

## References

ATAG (Air Transport Action Group) (2016). *Aviation: Benefits Beyond Borders*, Geneva, ATAG.
Bernaciak, M. (2012). *Social Dumping: Political Catchphrase or Threat to Labour Standards?* Working Paper 2012.06, Brussels, European Trade Union Institute.
Doganis, R. (2006). *The Airline Business*, London, Routledge.

Dunn, G. (2011). Low-cost carriers: growth expectations, *Airline Business*, 18 April.

Gittell, J.H., von Nordenflycht, A. and Kochan, T. (2004). Mutual gains or zero sum? Labor relations and firm performance in the airline industry, *Industrial & Labor Relations Review*, 57(2), 163–180.

Goodley, S. (2016) British Airways cabin crew vote for industrial action but no strike, *The Guardian*, 17 August.

Gunnigle, P. and O'Sullivan, M. (2009). Bearing all the hallmarks of oppression: union avoidance in Europe's largest low cost airline, *Labor Studies Journal*, 34(2), 252–270.

Harvey, G. and Turnbull, P. (2002). *Contesting the Crisis: Aviation Industrial Relations and Trade Union Strategies After 11 September*, London, International Transport Workers' Federation.

Harvey, G. and Turnbull, P. (2009). *The Impact of the Financial Crisis on Labour in the Civil Aviation Industry*, Geneva, International Labour Office.

Harvey, G. and Turnbull, P. (2010). *Contesting the Financial Crisis*, London, International Transport Workers' Federation.

Harvey, G. and Turnbull, P. (2012). *The Development of the Low Cost Model in the European Civil Aviation Industry*, Brussels, European Transport Workers' Federation.

Harvey, G. and Turnbull, P. (2014). *Evolution of the Labour Market in the Airline Industry Due to the Development of the Low Fares Airlines (LFAs)*, Brussels, European Transport Workers' Federation.

Harvey, G. and Turnbull, P. (2015). Can labor arrest the Sky Pirates? International trade unionism in the European civil aviation industry, *Labor History*, 56(3), 308–326.

Jackson, S.E., Schuler, R.S. and Jiang, K. (2014). An aspirational framework for strategic human resource management, *The Academy of Management Annals*, 8(1), 1–56.

Jorens, Y., Gillis, D., Valcke, L. and De Coninck, J. (2015). *Atypical Forms of Employment in the Aviation Sector*, Brussels, European Social Dialogue, European Commission.

McDermott, A.M., Conway, E., Rousseau, D.M. and Flood, P.C. (2013). Promoting effective psychological contracts through leadership: the missing link between HR strategy and performance, *Human Resource Management*, 52, 289–310.

OAG (2014). *OAG FACTS: May 2014*. Online. Available at: http://aerolatinnews.com/wp-content/uploads/2014/04/OAG_Global_Market_Analysis_Report_May14.pdf (accessed 12 June 2017).

Sull, D. (1999). Case study: easyJet's $500 million gamble, *European Management Journal*, 17(1), 20–38.

Tovey, A. (2014). Want to be a pilot? Count the cost first, *The Telegraph*, 12 April.

Turnbull, P. and Harvey, G. (2001). *The Impact of 11 September on the Civil Aviation Industry: Social and Labour Effects*, Working Paper No. 182, Geneva, International Labour Office.

von Nordenflycht, A. (2001) *Alternative Approaches to Airline Labor Relations*, Cambridge, MA, MIT Press.

# Air transport and climate change

*Stefan Gössling*

## Introduction

Environmental impacts of aviation have been highlighted for decades (Fabian, 1974, 1978; Johnston, 1971; Schumann, 1990; Schumann and Wurzel, 1994). With the expansion of air traffic, environmental consequences of aviation received growing attention, in particular in the United States (US) and Europe. Today, aviation's contribution to climate change is considered the sector's most important environmental impact. This chapter provides a brief overview of the sector's environmental impacts (see also Chapters 17 and 18), though its main focus is a discussion of air travel's contribution to emissions of greenhouse gases and policy responses to address the situation.

## Air transport and the environment

Janić (1999), in a summary of aviation's impacts on the environment, discussed aircraft noise, air quality, ozone depletion, climate change, loss of land, water and air pollution, and waste generation (see also Chapters 17 and 18, and Daley, 2010). As shown in Table 25.1, environmental impacts of aviation include noise from operations and testing, with, in particular, residential areas adjacent to airports being exposed to the sound of engines during take-off, landing and taxing, often even during the night. Sonic booms related to military flight can be a noise-related impact in some areas. A local environmental aspect of aviation is air quality, which may be affected by emissions from aircraft, airport operations, or access traffic. Airport infrastructure causes the loss of land, contributes to soil erosion, and affects water tables, as well as biodiversity. Water and soil pollution can be a result of contaminated run-off. Waste generation contributes to landfills, sometimes containing toxic substances. Accidents and incidents can involve dangerous goods, toxic substances, as well as fuel dumping in emergency situations.

With regard to land use, protests against the expansion of airports accompanied growth in aviation, and may have peaked in the 1970s and 1980s, when physical clashes between opponents and authorities sometimes involved considerable numbers of protestors and police. For example, in Frankfurt, Germany, protests against Startbahn West involved 10,000 demonstrators and resulted in the death of two policemen in 1984 (Frankfurter Rundschau, 2014).

*Table 25.1* Environmental impacts of aviation

| Environmental issue | Areas of concern |
|---|---|
| Aircraft noise | Aircraft operations |
| | Engine testing |
| | Airport sources |
| | Sonic boom |
| Local air quality | Aircraft engine emissions |
| | Emissions from airport operations |
| | Emissions from airport access traffic |
| | Emissions from other airport sources |
| Airport infrastructure construction | Loss of land |
| | Soil erosion |
| | Impacts on water tables, river courses and field drainage |
| | Impacts on flora and fauna |
| Water and soil pollution | Pollution due to contaminated run-off from airports |
| | Pollution due to leakage from storage tanks |
| Waste generation | Airport waste |
| | Waste generated in-flight |
| | Toxic materials from aircraft servicing and maintenance |
| Aircraft accidents/incidents | Accidents/incidents involving dangerous cargo |
| | Other environmental problems due to aircraft accidents |
| | Fuel dumping |
| Climate change | Long-lived greenhouse gases |
| | Short-lived greenhouse gases |

Source: Adapted from Janić (1999) (based on Crayston, 1992; Morrissette, 1996).

Airport extensions continue to be relevant in developing countries, as well as in developed economies: London and Copenhagen are examples of cities that seek to expand their airports (e.g. BBC, 2016; UK Government, 2016). Protest against such plans continues, though the argument against new runways is now largely based on aviation's contribution to climate change (e.g. Plane Stupid, 2016).

Aircraft-related noise can be an annoyance, and it is now widely acknowledged that noise has serious health effects, including sleep deprivation, general stress and hypertension (Franssen et al., 2004; Jarup et al., 2008; Rosenlund et al., 2001). Stansfeld et al. (2005) found, for instance, that children exposed to chronic aircraft noise faced reading comprehension problems and recognition memory impairment. Governments, often as a result of public pressure, have forced airports to apply different types of noise management procedures, ranging from noise abatement to limits on the total noise allowed (Lu, 2009). For example, the Federal Aviation Administration (FAA) in the US was given authority to impose aircraft noise standards in 1968 (NoiseQuest, 2016). Since then, standards have subsequently improved, and night flight restrictions, night quotas, noise charges and penalties have been introduced in a range of countries (Lu, 2009).

Problems related to changes in atmospheric physics and chemistry (see Table 25.2) received attention in the 1970s, when processes of stratospheric ozone depletion, and specifically the role of nitrogen oxides ($NO_x$), became increasingly scrutinised out of concerns that supersonic flights would interfere with atmosphere physics and chemistry (Crutzen, 1972; Johnston, 1971). Contrails and aviation-induced cirrus clouds became a focus of research in the early 1990s (Schumann and Wurzel, 1994), based on first assessments of fuel use distribution and emissions in the global atmosphere (Nüßer and Schmitt, 1990). Research also began to focus on sulphur

*Table 25.2* Contribution of aviation to changes in atmosphere physics and chemistry

| Gas | Impact |
| --- | --- |
| $CO_2$ | Contribution to global warming |
| $H_2O$ | Cirrus and contrails contribute to warming |
| | Affects physical and chemical processes at flight altitude |
| $NO_x$ | Ozone generation in higher troposphere |
| | Ozone depletion in the lower troposphere |
| | Affects physical and chemical processes at flight altitude |
| $SO_2$ | Sulphuric acid can act as condensation nuclei |
| | Sulphuric acid-aerosols change albedo |
| | Affects physical and chemical processes at flight altitude |
| HC, CO | Affects physical and chemical processes at flight altitude |
| Soot | Acts as condensation nuclei |
| | Increases warming |
| | Affects physical and chemical processes at flight altitude |

*Source*: Arnold et al. (1992), Lee et al. (1996) and Schumann and Wurzel (1994).

dioxide ($SO_2$), hydrocarbons (HC) and carbon monoxide (CO), while the role of soot was studied in particular in the context of its importance as cloud condensation nuclei (Kärcher et al., 1996, 1998).

The discussion shows that concerns about air transport and its environmental consequences evolved with the overall scale of the activity (see Figure 25.1). Notably, all of these issues continue to be relevant. From today's viewpoint, it may, however, be argued that aviation's main environmental impact is climate change, as the sector is characterised by significant and growing emissions of greenhouse gases (Bows and Anderson, 2007). Climate change interferes with ecosystem functioning, potentially jeopardising food production, and bringing with it the risk of extreme events at large regional scales (IPCC, 2014a). If short-term efforts to keep emissions within safe guardrails – defined as stabilisation of the climate system at a maximum of 2°C compared to pre-industrial levels (UNFCCC, 2016) – are unsuccessful, a high-temperature future posing wide-ranging threats to human survival and well-being are unavoidable (Anderson and Peters, 2016). Aviation is crucial in this context, because its contribution to global warming includes both carbon dioxide ($CO_2$) and short-lived greenhouse gases (Lee, 2009). The sector's strong growth is in stark contrast to mitigation objectives, and given the anticipated decline in emissions from other economic

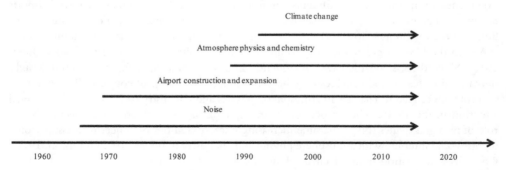

*Figure 25.1* Emerging environmental issues in the context of aviation

*Source*: Author.

sectors, aviation's role will become increasingly crucial (IPCC, 2014b). In light of this, the focus of the following sections is on aviation's contribution to climate change, the sector's responses, and the efficiency of global policy processes in addressing mitigation.

## Climate change

The importance of greenhouse gases has been recognised for more than a century, with Arrhenius (1896) publishing a first calculation of global warming related to a potential doubling of atmospheric concentrations of $CO_2$ from anthropogenic sources. However, it was not until the 1950s that Gilbert Plass reconsidered the importance of $CO_2$ for global warming (Plass, 1956). The phenomenon was studied more systemically only by the 1970s (Matthews et al., 1971; US National Research Council, 1979). Finally, in 1988, the Intergovernmental Panel on Climate Change (IPCC) was founded to report in intervals on the state of climate change science. Every five to seven years, the IPCC publishes three reports focusing on: (i) physical aspects of the climate system; (ii) aspects of climate change vulnerability and its outcomes; and (iii) options to mitigating the impacts of climate change. A specific report on climate change and aviation was published in 1999 (IPCC, 1999).

Aviation is of particular importance for climate change because of interrelated environmental, social, economic and political reasons. The sector is generally considered central to national economies, but it also contributes disproportionately to climate change because of specific effects of emissions at flight altitude in the upper troposphere and lower stratosphere (Lee, 2009). Equally relevant is the sector's catering to an elite of air travellers, and the unequal social distribution of air travel and associated emissions (Gössling et al., 2009a). Politically, aviation's emissions are addressed outside the United Nations Framework Convention on Climate Change (UNFCCC); for instance, responsibility to addressing mitigation in the sector was transferred to the International Civil Aviation Organisation (ICAO) in 1997. This has caused an impasse on mitigation, and the presentation of insufficient solutions to deal with the sector's contribution to climate change. These aspects are discussed in more detail in the following sections.

## *Aviation's contribution to climate change*

The contribution of human activities to climate change is measured on the basis of the so-called basket of six, including the long-lived greenhouse gases carbon dioxide ($CO_2$), methane ($CH_4$), nitrous oxide ($N_2O$), hydrofluorocarbons (HFCs), perfluorocarbons (PFCs) and sulphur hexafluoride ($SF_6$). Aviation has specific importance for climate change, however, because a large share of emissions is emitted at flight altitude (i.e. in the upper troposphere and lower stratosphere), where they interact differently with atmosphere physics and chemistry than emissions released at the earth's surface. This leads to higher levels of radiative forcing (and hence warming), defined by the IPCC as:

> The strength of drivers is quantified as Radiative Forcing (RF) in units watts per square meter (W/m²) [. . .]. RF is the change in energy flux caused by a driver and is calculated at the tropopause or at the top of the atmosphere.
>
> *(IPCC, 2014b)*

As a result of differences in the lifetime of greenhouse gases, the impacts of short-lived and long-lived gases are not directly comparable. Long-lived gases include $CO_2$, and to calculate the contribution made by this gas to the aviation RF it is necessary to consider the accumulated emissions from the sector since its inception (Lee, 2009). For short-lived gases, forcings can be calculated on the basis of one-year pertubations, with the exception of $CH_4$ and its slightly longer lifetime. To quantify aviation RF, it is consequently necessary to look backward in time in order to calculate the sector's accumulated effect over time (Lee, 2009). An important aspect of aviation is the non-comparability of long-term and short-term effects (Forster et al., 2006; Fuglestvedt et al., 2003), which would be of importance in the assessment of the impact of individual trips made by air, and hence mitigation policy.

The current contribution of RF from aviation has been summarised as follows (Lee, 2009: 33):

- $CO_2$ results in a positive RF (warming);
- $NO_x$ results in the formation of tropospheric $O_3$ via atmospheric chemistry, with a positive RF (warming);
- $NO_x$ results in the destruction of ambient $CH_4$ via atmospheric chemistry, with a negative RF (cooling);
- Sulphate particles arising from sulphur in the fuel result in a negative direct RF (cooling);
- Soot particles result in a direct positive RF (warming);
- Persistent linear contrails may form that result in both positive and negative RF but overall cause a positive RF effect (warming);
- The formation of aircraft-induced cirrus cloud from spreading contrails results in both positive and negative RF effects but overall is considered to cause a positive RF effect (warming);
- Particles emitted from aircraft engines may act as cloud condensation nuclei and seed cirrus cloud formation, which can either increase or decrease the number of ice particles and impact on both the albedo and the emissivity of cirrus clouds. This effect may result in either positive or negative RF effects (warming/cooling) and the sign is rather uncertain.

Overall, civil aviation is believed to contribute about 3 per cent to emissions of total anthropogenic $CO_2$ emissions, though its contribution to RF is larger, in the range of 1.3 to 14.0 per cent (Lee et al., 2009). Industry has consistently argued, with reference to $CO_2$, that the sector's contribution to climate change is small (ICAO, 2016b).

## Growth in aviation

Fuel use in civil aviation has grown rapidly since the 1960s, even though there is also a considerable share of fuel use attributed to the military that is rarely discussed. The Magazine *Forbes* (2008) suggested, for instance, that the US Department of Defense is the "single-largest consumer of fuel in the world," with more than two-thirds of overall fuel demand being jet fuel. Worldwide, civil aviation counted 3,700 aircraft in the global commercial fleet in 1970, and 9,100 by 1990 (Airbus, 2014; Boeing, 2014). By 2010, this number again doubled to 21,000, with even greater growth in revenue passenger kilometres (RPKs). RPKs increased nearly ninefold between 1970 and 2010 (Airbus, 2014), indicating a growing average capacity of aircraft as well as longer average distances flown. It is estimated that by 2030, there will be approximately 40,000 aircraft accounting for more than 10,000 billion RPKs per annum (Boeing, 2014). Continued growth after 2030 is expected: long-term scenarios suggest that air travel will quadruple between 2005 and 2050 (IEA, 2009; see also ICAO, 2016c; Owen et al., 2010) (see also Chapter 19).

Even though a wide range of technological solutions have been advocated by airlines and aviation organisations, including air traffic management (see Chapter 4), new air frames, engine technology innovations, or biofuels (see Chapter 17), these have not resulted in absolute emission reductions; on the contrary, emissions from the sector have consistently grown (Peeters et al., 2016). In this context, it is important to distinguish annual relative efficiency gains and absolute emission growth, which are often confused or used interchangeably by airlines, airline organisations and aviation advocates: while relative efficiency gains per passenger kilometre (PKM) are often presented as an indicator of progress on climate change mitigation, only a decline in absolute emissions would actually represent such progress. With regard to relative fuel efficiencies, consumption per PKM has declined since the 1960s, by some 70 per cent (Peeters et al., 2016). However, much of this progress was made in the early decades of aviation, and year-on-year savings have consistently declined, as the physical limits of flight are reached. It is thus questionable whether efficiency gains of 2 per cent per year can be maintained up to 2020, or even to 2050, as envisaged by industry (ICAO, 2016a, 2016c). Peeters and Middel (2007) expect fuel efficiency gains to decline to under 1 per cent per year in the 2020s, and there is no evidence that year-on-year gains in the order of 2 per cent have actually been achieved prior to 2015 (Peeters et al., 2016). In contrast, absolute emissions from the sector have consistently grown, and are anticipated to continue to grow at about 3.5 per cent per year, as passenger growth is expected to be close to 5 per cent per year over the next two decades (Airbus, 2015; Boeing, 2015).

## Individual contributions to climate change

A key argument of the aviation industry has been that aviation's contribution to emissions is negligible, at about 1 to 2 per cent of total anthropogenic emissions (ICAO, 2016a, 2016c). As outlined, this perspective not only omits non-$CO_2$ effects from aviation; it also conceals that a large share of air travel is the result of the activities of a small share of humanity. Suggestions by, for instance, IATA (2016) that there are more than 3.5 billion travellers per year have contributed to a public understanding that large parts of the global population participate in flying. However, the figure refers to individual flights (i.e. there are at least two flights involved in any business or leisure trip, and many travellers also use connecting flights). Furthermore, individual travellers are known to participate in hundreds of flights per year. This leads to a concentration of flight activity, with a small minority of people accounting for a large share of emissions from aviation. Studies have shown that business travellers can be constantly on the move, covering hundreds of thousands of kilometres per year (Gössling et al., 2009a). As an example, Hillary Clinton reportedly travelled more than 1.5 million kilometres by air in her time as Secretary of State (*The Atlantic*, 2013). Even a single flight, for instance from Europe to Australia, can exceed sustainable average emissions per person per year (Eijgelaar et al., 2010). Individual contributions to climate change are thus key to understanding the sector's importance, particularly given the expansion of aeromobile lifestyles on a global scale, and the propensity of Generation Y to fly frequently (Gössling and Stavrinidi, 2015).

This insight is also related to the question of air travel demand. For instance, low cost carriers (LCCs) offering flights for a few euros will induce, rather than meet, an existing demand. Business travellers are known to participate in additional flights to maintain their frequent flyer status (Gössling and Nilsson, 2010) or to reduce the cost of trips (*The Economist*, 2013). Is it reflecting real demand if people decide to fly between continents over the weekend for shopping? Economists would assume that any demand is real, though a function of cost. Sociological viewpoints include aviation's growing relevance in connecting distant relations (Hall, 2005), as well as its role in social status generation (Gössling and Stavrinidi, 2015). The discussion of what constitutes necessary air travel is likely to become increasingly relevant in the context of climate change: any tonne of $CO_2$, a recent paper suggested, leads to the loss of three square metres of the Arctic (Notz and Stroeve, 2016). A transcontinental flight consequently causes the loss of up to 10 square metres of ice. Emerging perspectives such as this put greater emphasis on travel motives and may also have importance for the expansion of airports, which are currently based on growth models that do not question travel motives (e.g. CPH, 2014).

## An 'inaction timeline': ICAO

Article 2 of the Kyoto Protocol (ratified in 1997) assigns responsibility for limiting and reducing greenhouse gas emissions from international aviation to ICAO. Domestic flight emissions are covered in national greenhouse gas inventories, but these account for only a minor share of overall aviation-related emissions. ICAO has consequently been in charge of addressing emissions from international aviation for almost two decades. Yet this has had no implications for mitigation (see Figure 25.2). Until 2001, ICAO did not even address emissions, and its first political statements on the issue only emphasised the organisation's opposition to fuel taxes, a closed Emissions Trading Scheme (ETS) for aviation, or emission standards, which could have served as environmental benchmarks between airlines. In 2004, ICAO also imposed a three-year moratorium on charges, which the organisation had discussed as a possible alternative to taxes, instead endorsing inclusion of aviation in existing emission trading schemes. This decision was recalled in 2007, and ICAO now favoured non-binding, aspirational targets, to be formulated by a newly founded Group on International Aviation and Climate Change (GIACC). GIACC later recommended an aspirational global fuel efficiency target of 2 per cent per annum to 2020, a timeline later extended to 2050. To achieve this goal, new technology, market-based measures, and alternative fuels were proposed. These efficiency targets were neither binding nor scientifically realistic (Peeters et al., 2016). Yet in 2010, ICAO adopted a new goal, again aspirational, to achieve carbon-neutral growth from 2020 onwards.

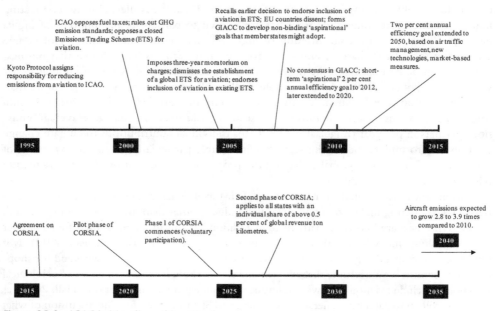

*Figure 25.2* ICAO's 'timeline of inaction'

Source: Adapted from Scott et al. (2012), expanded based on ICAO (2016a, 2016c).

Essentially, the scheme (CNG2020) implies that aviation continues to grow unabated until 2020; by then, market-based measures will ensure carbon-neutral growth, including the off-setting of emissions from the sector's anticipated continued growth by measures carried out in other sectors (ICAO, 2016a).

More recently, plans by the European Union (EU) to integrate aviation in the EU ETS (EC, 2016) increased pressure on ICAO to define and bring into action measures addressing the sector's emission growth. Following the UNFCCC's Paris Agreement in 2015, ICAO presented a newly developed framework for a Carbon Offsetting and Reduction Scheme for International Aviation (CORSIA) to achieve: a short-term efficiency improvement goal of 1.5 per cent per annum; a mid-term goal to stabilise net $CO_2$ emissions at the 2020 level through carbon-neutral growth; and a long-term goal to halve aviation $CO_2$ emissions by 2050 when compared with 2005 levels (ICAO, 2016a).

To achieve these goals, market-based measures would be implemented from 2021 onwards in various steps, including a pilot phase from 2021 to 2023, a first phase from 2024 and 2026, and a second phase from 2027 to 2035 (ICAO, 2016a). The first phase applies to "States that have volunteered to participate in the scheme," and the second phase:

> to all States that have an individual share of international aviation activities in RTKs in year 2018 above 0.5 per cent of total RTKs or whose cumulative share in the list of States from the highest to the lowest amount of RTKs reaches 90 per cent of total RTKs, except Least Developed Countries (LDCs), Small Island Developing States (SIDS) and Landlocked Developing Countries (LLDCs) unless they volunteer to participate in this phase.
>
> *(ICAO, 2016a)*

No calculation is provided that would illustrate the share of emissions covered by the scheme, which addresses only those emissions exceeding those of the base year 2020. Industry also highlighted the need to only implement one measure that would simultaneously protect against the implementation of any other measures: "A single mechanism will obviate the need for existing and new economic measures to be applied to international aviation emissions on a regional or national basis," and if remaining the sole measure would be manageable at cost increases of US$0.57 to US$9.16 (ICAO, 2016b: 3). The future cost imposed by CORSIA is considered manageable because it constitutes an insignificant deterrent to air traffic growth. In other words, the design is accepted because it does not have tangible implications for aviation. A notable issue with CORSIA is that the non-$CO_2$ effects from aviation are ignored. Such a situation was anticipated almost two decades ago, when Lee and Sausen (2000) outlined that open emission trading could increase aviation's contribution to global warming if $CO_2$ credits were exchanged without consideration of non-$CO_2$ effects (Lee and Sausen, 2000).

In summary, CORSIA is of such complexity that few people (and perhaps none) would understand its implications for mitigation; it seems clear, however, that the system will not contribute to carbon-neutral growth. The inefficiency of the scheme is also evident in the fact that baseline emissions will remain unaddressed for decades to come, with the overall outcome of massive growth in aviation: ICAO (2016c) anticipates that absolute emissions from air traffic will grow by a factor of 2.8 to 3.9 between 2010 and 2040. This is a considerable problem in a situation where the cumulative effect of greenhouse gas emissions determines the future degree of warming, and highlights the failure of CORSIA to address all emissions from the sector (including non-$CO_2$ emissions), while suggesting offsetting including forestry projects as the favoured solution; for instance, projects that provide no long-term guarantee for mitigation (Gössling et al., 2007). Figure 25.2 illustrates this impasse.

## *Discourses and unaccountability: the example of SAS*

For decades, mitigation in aviation has been characterised by unaccountability and implausibility: highly optimistic assumptions regarding annual efficiency gains, nonbinding targets, a missing discussion of growth in absolute emissions (and focus on the discussion of relative efficiency gains), omission of non-$CO_2$ emissions, generic solutions (fleet renewal, biofuels, air traffic management), and the absence of milestones against which to measure progress on emission reductions (Peeters et al., 2016). The implication of this situation is that there is a belief in the wider public that emission growth in aviation will be resolved, and that there is no personal responsibility for emissions (Gössling et al., 2009b). Even more important is that at the same time, discourses of aviation's economic and social importance have been maintained and fostered, with ICAO highlighting the importance of air travel over decades: "in 1988 the number of passengers carried yearly by the world's airlines approximated one fifth of the world's population" (cited in Nüßer and Schmitt, 1990). As outlined, this perspective omits highly skewed distributions in air travel participation (Gössling et al., 2009a).

An example of the role of discourses in shaping ignorance (Proctor and Schiebinger, 2008; see also Burns and Cowlishaw, 2014) is Scandinavian Airlines (SAS), an airline widely considered to be leading global sustainability efforts in aviation (Lynes and Dredge, 2006). SAS published environmental reports for over 20 years (SAS, 1996). Lynes and Andrachuk (2008) suggest that engagement in CSR comes at least in part out of feelings of a national responsibility, which may be particularly true in Sweden: "As flag carriers of the country in which they are based, national carriers have a certain responsibility to uphold a positive image for their country," and "SAS has been identified as a leader in environmental commitment by its suppliers and other airlines as well as by representatives of international organisations such as the Air Transport Action Group (ATAG) and the International Air Transportation Association (IATA)" (Lynes and Andrachuk, 2008: 382). The airline embraced the triple bottom line (i.e. considering economic, social and environmental goals) in its 2000 environmental report, and has, according to Lynes and Andrachuk (2008), considered the integration of environmental issues in decision-making as a win–win situation, including benefits such as long-term stability, financial savings as a result of eco-efficiencies, competitive advantage, good corporate citizenship, and hence public image, as well as the delay or avoidance of regulatory action. In particular, the last aspect may be of importance, as the following discussion suggests.

In response to an increasingly negative public image of aviation as a major contributor to climate change after the publication of the fourth climate change assessment report (IPCC, 2007), SAS suggested growing confidence in its achievements and future opportunities of technology innovation. In 2010, SAS rhetorically asked: "Can you fly with a clear environmental consciousness? Yes, you can!" The importance of this claim was that the airline addressed the morality of flying in the context of climate change, relieving individuals of their personal accountability for emissions from air travel. The brochure informed about "Truths and myths about the environmental impact of air travel," suggesting that flying is not a climatically relevant sector, contributing only 2 to 3 per cent to global emissions of $CO_2$, with most growth coming from developing countries. It highlighted that the SAS Group is environmentally aware, seeking to constantly develop new solutions to mitigate its contribution to climate change. It also assured that in the longer-term future, SAS would reduce its climate impact to zero. This general perspective is embedded in a range of misleading claims. As an example, the brochure suggests:

> Air travel currently accounts for 2–3% of the world's total carbon dioxide emissions. In Denmark, domestic air transport accounts for 0.4% of total $CO_2$ emissions. In Norway,

which ranks second worldwide in terms of domestic air travel per capita in the EU, air transport represents less than 2%, while in Sweden, is it less than 1%.

*(SAS, 2010: 8)*

In comparing global emission shares (including international flights) with national emission shares (only including domestic flights), SAS discursively minimised the contribution made by air travel to climate change. A proper comparison would include all flights (domestic and international) by Scandinavian citizens, revealing a fundamentally different situation. For example, in Sweden, international aviation accounted for 4.1 megatonnes of $CO_2$ in 2005–2006, while national emissions amounted to 52.5 megatonnes of $CO_2$ (including a 1 per cent share of domestic aviation emissions). Consequently, the share of aviation in national emissions (defined as emissions by Swedish citizens) is approximately eight times higher than the figure published by SAS would suggest. Notably, this excludes additional warming effects related to emissions released at flight altitude.

The image presented in the 2010 brochure can also be compared to SAS's actual achievements in reducing its impact on climate change. In 2016, the airline was rated among the least efficient in the world, with 99 airlines performing better than SAS (and 23 worse), as revealed by the Atmosfair Airline Index (Atmosfair, 2016), which compares airlines on the basis of their actual performance. SAS's 2015 sustainability report (SAS, 2015) carries the headline. "It should be possible to fly with no fossil fuel $CO_2$ emissions by 2050," outlining that the group's 2015 environmental goal is to "reduce flight $CO_2$ emissions by 20% in 2015 compared with 2005," while the 2020 goal is to "reduce relative $CO_2$ flight emissions by 20% in 2020 compared with 2010." Hence, mitigation efforts were focused on absolute emissions up to 2015, to then be replaced with a relative mitigation goal (i.e. efficiencies per PKM or RPK). SAS acknowledges that it did not meet the targets set by itself: "SAS reduced its absolute $CO_2$ flight emissions by 14.0% and relative emissions per passenger kilometer by 18.3% in 2015 compared with 2005." Data provided in the report also reveal that fuel use increased from 2012–2013 to 2013–2014, and that absolute emissions in 2014–2015 were higher than in 2012–2013, while emissions per PKM were higher in 2014–2015 than in 2013–2014. There is consequently no clear trend of emission reductions over this period with regard to either relative or absolute emissions, and a major share of emission reductions claimed in the report must have been achieved in earlier years. Non-$CO_2$ emissions are not mentioned.

While SAS must thus be considered a business using discursive strategies to present itself as responsible, the airline is in reality highly inefficient, encouraging people to fly. This mirrors the situation in aviation on a global scale, as Peeters et al. (2016: 40) conclude:

Under these prevailing conditions an understanding of aviation as a sector soon-to-become-sustainable has been, and continues to be, successfully perpetuated. Ultimately, this would constitute a form of propaganda in which emotional responses to aviation, for instance framed as the sector's social and economic benefits, are fuelled by pseudo-rational information – myths – to generate a widely held understanding of, and continuing faith in a looming future of sustainable aviation, and, ultimately, 'zero emission flight'.

Compounding this situation is that many governments have framed environmental problems as consumer responsibilities, as exemplified by the nudge perspectives of the Obama and Cameron administrations (*The Independent*, 2010). In consequence, it is not surprising that virtually all of the critique that has been directed at airlines has been coming from environmental groups, not consumers (Mayer et al., 2014). In an apparent contradiction, some governments have decided to expand airports, for instance in the United Kingdom (UK) and Denmark. At the same time, tax exemptions on fuel constitute a subsidy that is worth hundreds of millions to airlines, if compared to the taxation of gasoline. This calculation is based on the assumption that civil aviation currently emits about one gigatonne of $CO_2$ per year (extrapolation based on Dessens et al., 2014). Only a share of this is domestic aviation, which may be taxed at modest levels. In comparison to gasoline for cars, which is taxed in Europe at levels ranging between US$0.90 and 1.16 per litre, and at a minimum of US$0.10 per litre in Mexico (Sterner, 2012), a rough estimate would suggest that fuel tax exemptions are worth US$30 million to US$300 million per year to airlines. Notably, even comparably high fuel taxes for gasoline do not cover the actual cost of (auto)mobility to society (Becker et al., 2012).

Not only does it thus become increasingly difficult for the public to judge the claims made by airlines and aviation organisations; it is equally impossible for politicians to judge the different strategies presented by ICAO, which also contain aspirational and voluntary goals, as well as complex sets of exemptions. Yet ICAO's strategy has been widely accepted, as it removes the burden of having to make environmentally responsible decisions (to fly less) or to take action against the powerful aviation industry (governance). The difficulty of introducing even modest legislation in the context of climate change became evident when international flights to the EU were to be covered by the EU ETS: considerable resistance to the scheme caused an impasse (EC, 2016). To create an image of responsibility, many airlines have also begun to introduce pro bono initiatives, associating themselves with charity goals. As an example, easyJet collects donations from travellers during flights, allowing the airline to highlight their pro-social activities at no cost. In partnership with UNICEF, the airline claims that: "Together, we have raised over £8 million for children" (easyJet, 2016), with the discursive implication that any measure curbing air travel would reduce donations to children in need.

## Conclusion

This chapter discussed various environmental aspects of aviation, and their current importance. Many of the issues that became increasingly important with the growth of air travel, including noise, land use needs for airport construction and expansion, or climate change, continue to be of relevance. On a global scale, climate change is now the most relevant issue facing the sector, and has been the focus of this chapter.

Aviation's contribution to climate change is often presented as negligible by industry, but this ignores non-$CO_2$ effects, and the global distribution of air travel as an activity in which only a comparably small share of the global population participates. Given observed and projected growth of the sector in comparison to the limited opportunities to minimise its emissions through technical innovation, there is consensus that the sector's contribution to climate change will continue to grow rapidly: ICAO (2016c) anticipates emission growth by up to a factor of four between 2010 and 2040. This is a development in stark contrast to pledges to stabilise warming at levels not dangerously interfering with the climate system (UNFCCC, 2016).

Politically, ICAO has been responsible for decades to initiate and implement processes that would lead to a decline in absolute emissions from aviation. However, as shown in this chapter, the organisation has a track record of inaction. ICAO's current perspective is that aviation should be allowed to continue to grow in emissions until 2020. After that, the share of additional growth would be addressed. Not only does this justify unabated growth until 2020, it also means that emissions in the order of one gigatonne of $CO_2$ will be released by the sector for decades to come. Of the additional growth, only a share will be addressed on the basis of measures including offsetting, essentially from 2027 onwards. The efficiency of these measures to contribute to actual reductions in emissions is consequently questionable, and there is considerable risk that aviation's contribution to climate change will continue to grow unabated. In conclusion, aviation is the sector in which climate governance has failed, and continues to fail, with potentially significant repercussions for the achievement of a 2°C maximum global warming scenario.

# References

Airbus (2014). *Global Market Forecast 2014–2033*, Toulouse, Airbus.

Airbus (2015). *Global Market Forecast 2015–2034*, Toulouse, Airbus.

Anderson, K. and Peters, G. (2016). The trouble with negative emissions, *Science*, 354(6309), 182–183.

Arnold, F., Scheid, J., Stilp, T., Schlager, H. and Reinhardt, M.E. (1992). Measurements of jet aircraft emissions at cruise altitude I: the odd nitrogen gases NO, NO2, $HNO_2$ and $HNO_3$, *Geophysical Research Letters*, 19(24), 2421–2424.

Arrhenius, S. (1896). On the influence of carbonic acid in the air upon the temperature of the ground, *London, Edinburgh, and Dublin Philosophical Magazine and Journal of Science*, 41(5), 237–275.

Atmosfair (2016). *Atmosfair Airline Index 2016*. Online. Available at: www.atmosfair.de/documents/ 10184/882239/AAI_EN_Broschüre_2016_final.pdf/c33b01ee-9ae7-4ee8-afab-8011f4f6be0a (accessed 25 December 2016).

BBC (2016). *Third runway at Heathrow cleared for takeoff by ministers*. Online. Available at: www.bbc.com/ news/business-37760187 (accessed 28 December 2016).

Becker, U.J., Becker, T. and Gerlach, J. (2012). *The true costs of automobility: external costs of cars. Overview on existing estimates in EU-27*. Online. Available at: www.greens-efa.eu/fileadmin/dam/Documents/ Studies/Costs_of_cars/The_true_costs_of_cars_EN.pdf (accessed 28 December 2016).

Boeing (2014). *Current Market Outlook 2014–2033*, Seattle, WA, Boeing.

Boeing (2015). *Current Market Outlook 2015–2034*, Seattle, WA, Boeing.

Bows, A. and Anderson, K.L. (2007). Policy clash: can projected aviation growth be reconciled with the UK government's 60% carbon-reduction target? *Transport Policy*, 14(2), 103–110.

Burns, P.M. and Cowlishaw, C. (2014). Climate change discourses: how UK airlines communicate their case to the public, *Journal of Sustainable Tourism*, 22(5), 740–767.

CPH (Copenhagen Airport) (2014). *Copenhagen Airport must be able to handle 40 million passengers annually*. Online. Available at: www.cph.dk/en/about-cph/press/news/20141/1/expanding-cph/ (accessed 22 December 2016).

Crayston, J. (1992). *ICAO Group Identifies Environmental Problems Associated with Civil Aviation*, ICAO Journal, Montreal, ICAO.

Crutzen, P.J. (1972). SST's: a threat to the earth's ozone shield, *Ambio*, 41–51.

Daley, B. (2010). *Air Transport and the Environment*, London, Routledge.

Dessens, O., Köhler, M.O., Rogers, H.L., Jones, R.L. and Pyle, J.A. (2014). Aviation and climate change, *Transport Policy*, 34, 14–20.

easyJet (2016). *Our Change for Good partnership with UNICEF*. Online. Available at: www.easyjet.com/en/ unicef (accessed 27 December 2016).

EC (European Commission) (2016). *Reducing emissions from aviation*. Online. Available at: http://ec.europa. eu/clima/policies/transport/aviation_en (accessed 28 December 2016).

Eijgelaar, E., Thaper, C. and Peeters, P. (2010). Antarctic cruise tourism: the paradoxes of ambassadorship, 'last chance tourism' and greenhouse gas emissions, *Journal of Sustainable Tourism*, 18(3), 337–354.

Fabian, P. (1974) *Residence Time of Aircraft Exhaust Contaminants in the Stratosphere*, CIAP Contract No. 05–30027, Washington, DC, US Department of Transportation.

Fabian, P. (1978). Ozone increase from Concorde operations? *Nature*, 272, 306–307.

*Forbes* (2008). *The world's biggest fuel consumer*. Online. Available at: www.forbes.com/2008/06/05/mileage-military-vehicles-tech-logistics08-cz_ph_0605fuel.html (accessed 28 December 2016).

Forster, P.M.D.F., Shine, K.P. and Stuber, N. (2006). It is premature to include non-$CO_2$ effects of aviation in emission trading schemes, *Atmospheric Environment*, 40(6), 1117–1121.

Frankfurter Rundschau (2014). *Von Polizisten niedergeknüppelt*. Online. Available at: www.fr-online.de/ flughafen-frankfurt/30-jahre-startbahn-west-von-polizisten-niedergeknueppelt,2641734,26814946. html (accessed 22 December 2016).

Franssen, E.A., van Wiechen, C.M., Nagelkerke, N.J. and Lebret, E. (2004). Aircraft noise around a large international airport and its impact on general health and medication use, *Journal of Occupational and Environmental Medicine*, 61, 405–413.

Fuglestvedt, J.S., Berntsen, T.K., Godal, O., Sausen, R., Shine, K.P. and Skodvin, T. (2003). Metrics of climate change: assessing radiative forcing and emission indices, *Climatic Change*, 58(3), 267–331.

Gössling, S. and Nilsson, J.H. (2010). Frequent flyer programmes and the reproduction of mobility, *Environment and Planning A*, 42, 241–252.

Gössling, S. and Stavrinidi, I. (2015). Social networking, mobility, and the rise of liquid identities, *Mobilities*, 11(5), 723–743.

Gössling, S., Broderick, J., Upham, P., Peeters, P., Strasdas, W., Ceron, J.-P., et al. (2007). Voluntary carbon offsetting schemes for aviation: efficiency and credibility, *Journal of Sustainable Tourism*, 15(3), 223–248.

Gössling, S., Ceron, J.-P., Dubois, G. and Hall, C.M. (2009a). Hypermobile travellers. In: S. Gössling and P. Upham (eds). *Climate Change and Aviation: Issues, Challenges and Solutions*, London, Earthscan.

Gössling, S., Haglund, L., Källgren, H., Revahl, M. and Hultman, J. (2009b). Swedish air travellers and voluntary carbon offsets: towards the co-creation of environmental value? *Current Issues in Tourism*, 12(1), 1–19.

Hall, C.M. (2005). *Tourism: Rethinking the Social Science of Mobility*. Upper Saddle River, NJ, Pearson Education.

IATA (International Air Transport Association) (2016). *Annual Review 2016*. Online. Available at: www.iata.org/publications/Pages/annual-review.aspx (accessed 28 December 2016).

ICAO (International Civil Aviation Organisation) (2016a). *What is CORSIA and how does it work?* Online. Available at: www.icao.int/environmental-protection/Pages/A39_CORSIA_FAQ2.aspx (accessed 23 December 2016).

ICAO (International Civil Aviation Organisation) (2016b). *High-level meeting on a global market-based measure scheme, Montreal 11–13 May 2016, ICAO HLM-GMBM-WP/12*. Online. Available at: www.icao.int/Meetings/HLM-MBM/Documents/HLM_GMBM_IATA_WP12_en.pdf (accessed 23 December 2016).

ICAO (International Civil Aviation Organisation) (2016c). *Why ICAO decided to develop a global MBM scheme for international aviation*. Online. Available at: www.icao.int/environmental-protection/Pages/A39_CORSIA_FAQ1.aspx (accessed 28 December 2016).

IEA (International Energy Agency) (2009). *World Energy Outlook 2009*, Paris, IEA.

IPCC (Intergovernmental Panel on Climate Change) (1999). *Aviation and the Global Atmosphere*, New York, IPCC.

IPCC (Intergovernmental Panel on Climate Change) (2007). Summary for Policymakers. In: *Climate Change 2007: The Physical Science Basis. Contribution of Working Group I to the Fourth Assessment Report of the Intergovernmental Panel on Climate Change* [S.D. Solomon, M. Qin, Z. Manning, M. Chen, K.B. Marquis, M.T. Averyt and H.L. Miller (eds)], Cambridge, Cambridge University Press.

IPCC (Intergovernmental Panel on Climate Change) (2014a). *Climate Change 2014: Synthesis Report. Contribution of Working Groups I, II and III to the Fifth Assessment Report of the Intergovernmental Panel on Climate Change* [Core writing team, R.K. Pachauri and L.A. Meyer (eds)], Geneva, IPCC.

IPCC (Intergovernmental Panel on Climate Change) (2014b). Annex II: Glossary [K.J. Mach, S. Planton and C. von Stechow (eds)]. In: *Climate Change 2014: Synthesis Report. Contribution of Working Groups I, II and III to the Fifth Assessment Report of the Intergovernmental Panel on Climate Change* [Core writing team, R.K. Pachauri and L.A. Meyer (eds)], Geneva, IPCC.

Janić, M. (1999). Aviation and externalities: the accomplishments and problems, *Transportation Research Part D: Transport and Environment*, 4(3), 159–180.

Jarup, L., Dudley, M.-L., Babisch, W., Houthuijs, D., Swart, W., Pershagen, G., et al. (2008). Hypertension and exposure to noise near airports (HYENA), *Environmental Health Perspectives*, 116, 329–333.

Johnston, H. (1971). Reduction of stratospheric ozone by nitrogen oxide catalysts from supersonic transport exhaust, *Science*, 173(3996), 517–522.

Kärcher, B., Peter, T., Biermann, U.M. and Schumann, U. (1996). The initial composition of jet condensation trails, *Journal of the Atmospheric Sciences*, 53(21), 3066–3083.

Kärcher, B., Busen, R., Petzold, A., Schröder, F.P., Schumann, U. and Jensen, E.J. (1998). Physicochemistry of aircraft-generated liquid aerosols, soot, and ice particles. 2: comparison with observations and sensitivity studies, *Journal of Geophysical Research*, 103, 17129–17147.

Lee, D.S. (2009). Aviation and climate change: the science. In: S. Gössling and P. Upham (eds). *Climate Change and Aviation: Issues, Challenges and Solutions*, London, Earthscan.

Lee, D.S. and Sausen, R. (2000). New directions: assessing the real impact of $CO_2$ emissions trading by the aviation industry, *Atmospheric Environment*, 34(29), 5337–5338.

Lee, D.S., Fahey, D.W., Forster, P.M., Newton, P.J., Wit, R.C.N., Lim, L.L., et al. (2009). Aviation and global climate change in the 21st century, *Atmospheric Environment*, 43(22), 3520–3537.

Lee, S.H., Le Dilosquer, M., Singh, R. and Rycroft, M.J. (1996). Further considerations of engine emissions from subsonic aircraft at cruise altitude, *Atmospheric Environment*, 30(22), 3689–3695.

Lu, C. (2009). Aviation and economic development: the implications of environmental costs on different airline business models and flight networks. In: S. Gössling and P. Upham (eds). *Climate Change and Aviation: Issues, Challenges and Solutions*, London, Earthscan.

Lynes, J.K. and Andrachuk, M. (2008). Motivations for social and environmental responsibility: a case study of Scandinavian Airlines, *Journal of International Management*, 14, 377–390.

Lynes, J.K. and Dredge, D. (2006). Going green: motivations for environmental commitment in the airline industry – a case study of Scandinavian Airlines, *Journal of Sustainable Tourism*, 14(2), 116–138.

Matthews, W., Kellogg, W. and Robinson, G. (eds) (1971). *Man's Impact on the Climate: Study of Critical Environmental Problems (SCEP) Report*, Cambridge, MA, MIT Press.

Mayer, R., Ryley, T. and Gillingwater, D. (2014). The role of green marketing: insights from three airline case studies, *Journal of Sustainable Mobility*, 1(2), 46–72.

Morrissette, S.E. (1996). A survey of environmental issues in the civilian aviation industry, *Journal of Air Transport World Wide*, 1, 22–38.

NoiseQuest (2016). *Noise basics and metrics*. Online. Available at: www.noisequest.psu.edu (accessed 22 December 2016).

Notz, D. and Stroeve, J. (2016). Observed Arctic sea-ice loss directly follows anthropogenic $CO_2$ emission, *Science*, 354(6313), 747–750.

Nüßer, H.G. and Schmitt, A. (1990). The global distribution of air traffic at high altitudes, related fuel consumption and trends. In: U. Schumann (ed.). *Air Traffic and the Environment: Background, Tendencies and Potential Global Atmospheric Effects*, Berlin, Springer Berlin Heidelberg.

Owen, B., Lee, D.S. and Lim, L. (2010). Flying into the future: aviation emissions scenarios to 2050, *Environmental Science & Technology*, 44(7), 2255–2260.

Peeters, P.M. and Middel, J. (2007). Historical and future development of air transport fuel efficiency. In: R. Sausen, A. Blum, D.S. Lee and C. Brüning (eds). *Proceedings of an International Conference on Transport, Atmosphere and Climate (TAC)*, Oberpfaffenhoven, DLR Institut für Physik der Atmosphäre.

Peeters, P., Higham, J., Kutzner, D., Cohen, S. and Gössling, S. (2016). Are technology myths stalling aviation climate policy? *Transportation Research Part D: Transport and Environment*, 44, 30–42.

Plane Stupid (2016). *Protesters blockade mock runway outside Parliament to oppose airport expansion*. Online. Available at: www.planestupid.com (accessed 22 December 2016).

Plass, G.N. (1956). Effect of carbon dioxide variations on climate, *American Journal of Physics*, 24, 376–387.

Proctor, R. and Schiebinger, L.L. (eds) (2008). *Agnotology: The Making and Unmaking of Ignorance*, Redwood City, CA, Stanford University Press.

Rosenlund, M., Berglind, N., Pershagen, G., Järup, L. and Bluhm, G. (2001). Increased prevalence of hypertension in a population exposed to aircraft noise, *Occupational and Environmental Medicine*, 58(12), 769–773.

SAS (Scandinavian Airlines) (1996). *Environmental Report 1995*, Stockholm, SAS.

SAS (Scandinavian Airlines) (2010). *Can I fly with a clear environmental consciousness?* Online. Available at: www.flysas.com/upload/International/SKI/travel_info/SAS_Environment_folder.pdf (accessed 25 December 2016).

SAS (Scandinavian Airlines) (2015). *SAS Sustainability Report November 2014–October 2015*. Online. Available at: www.sasgroup.net/en/wp-content/uploads/sites/2/2016/02/SAS-Group-Sustainability-Report-2014_2015-English.pdf (accessed 25 December 2016).

Schumann, U. (ed.) (1990). *Air Traffic and the Environment: Background, Tendencies and Potential Global Atmospheric Effects. Proceedings of a DLR International Colloquium, Bonn, Germany, November 15/16, 1990*, Berlin, Springer Berlin Heidelberg.

Schumann, U. and Wurzel, D. (eds) (1994). *Impact of Emissions from Aircraft and Spacecraft upon the Atmosphere. Proceedings of an International Scientific Colloquium on the Impact of Emissions from Aircraft and Spacecraft upon the Atmosphere*, Cologne, DLR (German Aerospace Centre).

Scott, D., Hall, C.M. and Gössling, S. (2012). *Tourism and Climate Change: Impacts, Mitigation and Adaptation*, London, Routledge.

Stansfeld, S.A., Berglund, B., Clark, C., Lopez-Barrio, I., Fischer, P., Öhrström, E., et al. (2005). Aircraft and road traffic noise and children's cognition and health: a cross-national study, *The Lancet*, 365(9475), 1942–1949.

Sterner, T. (2012). Distributional effects of taxing transport fuel, *Energy Policy*, 41, 75–83.

*The Atlantic* (2013). *Hillary Clinton traveled 956,733 miles during her time as Secretary of State*. Online. Available at: www.theatlantic.com/politics/archive/2013/01/hillary-clinton-traveled-956-733-miles-during-her-time-as-secretary-of-state/272656/ (accessed 28 December 2016).

*The Economist* (2013). *Around the world in cheaper ways*. Online. Available at: www.economist.com/blogs/gulliver/2013/11/fuel-dumping (accessed 26 December 2016).

*The Independent* (2010). *First Obama, now Cameron embraces 'nudge theory'*. Online. Available at: www.independent.co.uk/news/uk/politics/first-obama-now-cameron-embraces-nudge-theory-2050127.html (accessed 28 December 2016).

UK Government (2016). *Government decides on new runway at Heathrow*. Online. Available at: www.gov.uk/government/news/government-decides-on-new-runway-at-heathrow (accessed 22 December 2016).

UNFCCC (United Nations Framework Convention on Climate Change) (2016). *The Paris Agreement*. Online. Available at: http://unfccc.int/paris_agreement/items/9485.php (accessed 26 December 2016).

US National Research Council (1979). *Report of an Ad Hoc Study Group on Carbon Dioxide and Climate*, Washington, DC, National Academies Press.

# Index

Abdelghany, K.F. 253
Aberdeen Airport 55
Abrate, G. 198
Abu Dhabi Airports Company 231
Accenture 337–338
acceptable means of compliance (AMC) 61, 62
accidents 402–403
accounting rate of return (ARR) 177
Acharya, A. 355
ACI Europe 156, 196, 229, 230
activity factors 314
additive manufacturing 90
Adler, N. 172, 192, 198
advanced remote tower (ART) 78n4
advertising: airport marketing 223, 227, 228;
    consumer protection 377, 378, 380; sold by
    airlines 210; sponsorship 214–216; sustainability
    and corporate social responsibility 286
Aena Aeropuertos 129
Aer Lingus 24n8, 24n9, 130, 284
Aeromexico 98, 99, 114–115
AeroSpace and Defence Industries Association of
    Europe (ASD) 78n2
aerotropolis concept 123, 132, 133
Africa: age of fleet 176; air cargo 30, 32, 34;
    airport economic performance 196; average
    trips per passenger 314; cross-regional
    ownership 99; fares 112; fleet composition
    84; global network carriers 102; growth in air
    transport demand 314; low cost airports 159;
    market concentration 104; market openness
    109; passenger numbers 13; proportion of world
    airports in 49
Agbonifoh, E.A. 376
Ageeva, Y. 243
Agtmael, A.W.V. 319
Aigle Azur 99
Air Asia 365
Air Berlin 99, 130
Air Canada: deregulation 95; market share 24n8;
    Rouge 101, 105n4; Star Alliance 98, 100
air cargo 4, 29–47, 51, 124, 126; airport
    competition 157–158; airport marketing 221,

223; Asia 21; Brussels Airport 164; business
    models 42–43; categories of goods 39–40;
    China 324; commercial aerospace industry
    86–87; costs 172–173; current state of industry
    35–37; demand forecasts 317; development of
    industry 30–31; diversification 146; emerging
    markets 326–327; growth potential 37–38;
    low cost carriers 130; market analysis 31–35;
    Prestwick Airport 57; regulatory obstacles
    44–45; Saudi Arabia 118; security 357–358;
    service provision 40–41; see also freight tonne
    kilometres
Air Cargo or Mail Carrier Certificate (ACC3) 358
Air China 22, 43, 44, 110, 146
Air France 24n1, 104, 113, 125, 140; air cargo
    43; consolidation 18; cross-regional ownership
    99; KLM merger 24n9, 148–149, 165; labour
    costs 25n12; market share 24n8; price-fixing 45;
    SkyTeam 98, 100, 102, 181; strikes 19, 395, 399;
    Transavia 397; US dollar denominations 24n11
Air Liberalisation Index (ALI) 108–109
air mail 30, 31–32, 35, 82
Air Marshal Service 347–348
Air Mauritius 365
air navigation service providers (ANSPs) 2, 4, 60,
    263; alliances 64–65; business models 65–66;
    certification 61, 63; common support services
    68; COOPANS 78n3; EACCC 74; free route
    airspace 71; liberalisation 133; performance
    scheme 78; safety issues 77; throughput
    maximisation 272, 274–275
air navigation services (ANS) 60, 61, 65
Air New Zealand: corporate social responsibility
    279; joint ventures 100; partnerships 150;
    privatisation 140; Star Alliance 98
air quality 51, 298, 301, 304, 402–403
Air Serbia 99, 146
air service agreements (ASAs) 20, 183n13, 392;
    emerging markets 321; Indonesia 115–116;
    Kenya 111; Mexico 113–114, 120n1; Saudi
    Arabia 118
Air Service Agreements Projector (ASAP) 113,
    114, 118

Air Seychelles 99
air traffic control (ATC) 51, 65, 158; free route
    airspace 71; main functions 263; remote tower
    services 68–69; rule changes 273, 275; runway
    capacity 265; strikes 19; technology 67
air traffic flow management (ATFM) 65, 66,
    72–74, 75, 273
air traffic management (ATM) 4, 60–80, 87;
    business models 65–66; environmental issues
    74–76; Europe 19, 20; functional airspace
    blocks 63–65; institutional and regulatory
    framework 61–62; network issues 72–74;
    new technologies and concepts 66–71; safety
    challenges 76–77; throughput maximisation
    272, 275
Air Traffic Safety Electronic Personnel (ATSEP) 77
air traffic services (ATS) 65, 67, 68, 264
Air Transat 24n8, 286
Air Transport Action Group (ATAG) 3, 74, 88, 410
Air Transport Research Society (ATRS) 196, 197
Air Transport World (ATW) 16
AirAsia 22, 25n14, 116, 117
AirAsia X 21, 101, 105, 130
AirBridgeCargo 43, 44
Airbus 82; A350 83; A320 91; A350 101; A330
    101; A319 130; A320 130; A380 145, 146;
    A319 208; A320 208; A321 208; A320 239;
    A330 239; A320 264; air cargo 37, 41; average
    trips per passenger 314; 'aviation megacities'
    50; backlog orders 13, 16, 89; demand
    forecasts 317; emerging markets 108, 109, 327;
    technological developments 342
aircraft: air cargo 31, 35, 41; backlog orders 13,
    89; buy or lease decision 178; capital structure
    177–178; commercial aerospace industry 5,
    81–91; drivers of demand 315; economics 172;
    emissions reductions 280–281; First World War
    52; fleet planning 335; increased size of 54;
    investment 176–177; maintenance 336–337,
    339–340; noise 75–76, 282; number of 2; seat
    capacity 273; separation requirements 263–264;
    technological developments 331, 332, 342;
    Turkish Airlines 19; US carriers 17
aircraft-based augmentation system (ABAS) 70
aircraft, crew, maintenance and insurance
    (ACMI) 43
aircraft recovery 250–252, 253
aircraft routing 244–246, 247, 249–250, 251, 252
aircraft routing model (ARM) 240, 244–246, 248
Airline Quality Rating (AQR) 366, 368
airline recovery 247, 250–254
airline reservation systems (ARSs) 332, 337
airlines: air cargo 40–41, 43; airport marketing
    221; alliances 96–103; business models 96,
    122–135, 139, 150; capacity planning and
    management 6, 238–258, 272, 275; consumer
    protection and complaints 373–374, 377–389;

deregulation 94–96, 154; economics and
    finance 6, 171–188; emerging markets 108;
    fleet composition 85; fleet developments 84–85;
    global industry 4, 11–28; growth in passenger
    numbers 12; Indonesia 116; interaction with
    airports 190; marketing 6, 206–219, 387;
    number of 2; profitability 179–182; service
    quality 7, 362–372; slot coordination 270;
    strategy 5, 87–88, 139–153; sustainability and
    corporate social responsibility 6–7, 277–296,
    376; technology 7, 331–343; vertical integration
    165–166
airlines-within-airlines 101; see also carrier-within-
    a-carrier strategies
airport cities 123, 132, 163
Airport Cooperative Research Program (ACRP)
    226, 319
Airport World 3
airports 4, 48–59; air cargo 33, 37–38, 40, 45;
    air traffic management 63; Asia 21; business
    models 122, 123, 125–126, 129, 131–132;
    capacity planning and management 6, 259–276;
    changing patterns of ownership 53–56; charges
    19, 189–190, 193–194, 272, 275; China 22;
    demand 175, 183n5, 189–190; discrete choice
    models 318; EACCC 74; economics and
    finance 6, 189–205; emerging markets 119;
    environmental issues 75–76, 297, 298–301,
    303–305, 306–307; facilities 262–263, 268–270;
    growth of the industry 51–53; Indonesia
    115; infrastructure investment 87, 132–133;
    Kenya 112; low cost carriers 127; marketing 6,
    220–237; Mexico 113; number of 2; operations
    support systems 334, 339; profitability
    56–58; protests against airport expansion
    402–403; remote tower services 69; security
    345–346; SESAR 67, 68; strategy 6, 154–170;
    sustainability and corporate social responsibility
    7, 297–310; Turkish Airlines 19; uneven
    distribution of 49–50
Airports Company South Africa 231
Airports Council International (ACI) 3, 56–57,
    226–227, 298; demand forecasts 319, 327;
    environmental issues 300, 304; security
    351–352; see also ACI Europe
airspace 19–20
airspace management (ASM) 65
AirTran 24n6, 141–142, 147, 148, 151
Akartunali, K. 255
Alamdari, F. 318
Alaska Airlines 17, 24n6, 103, 141–142, 148
Alaska Airport 45
Albania 64
Albers, S. 141
Alekseev, K.P.G. 324
Alexander, D.W. 35, 37, 317
Alitalia 24n8, 99, 100, 181, 284

all-business-class airlines 123
All Nippon Airways 23, 44, 100, 126, 144
Allaz, C. 39–40
Allegiant Airlines 17, 105
Alliance Airlines 99
alliances 24n7, 96–103, 122, 140, 155, 180–181; air traffic management 64–65; airports 164, 165–166, 167; antitrust immunity 105n1, 183n14; deregulation 104–105; hybrid LCCs 130; market share 24n8; route expansion 88; strategic 147, 149; United States 17–18; see also joint ventures; partnerships
Alqeed, M.A. 364
Amadeus Altea 342
Amazon 31, 87
American Airlines 103, 125, 141–142; air cargo 43; ancillary revenues 17; automated booking system 332; capacity growth 16; employee well-being and engagement 283; fares 209; frequent flyer programme 180, 368; joint ventures 18, 100; LGBT employees 283; market share 24n8; merger 24n6, 148, 181; Oneworld 98, 100; premium economy cabins 207–208; profit 16; sponsorship 214, 215; sustainability and corporate social responsibility 280; UNICEF Change for Good programme 284
Amsterdam Schiphol 17, 145, 165, 261; branding 231, 232; low cost terminal 160; market power 158, 192; non-aeronautical revenues 195–196; security 346; SkyTeam 98; website and mobile innovations 229
ANA 22, 282, 284
Anchorage International Airport 38, 45
ancillary revenues 17, 123, 130–131, 209–210, 212–213, 393, 397, 400n1
Andrachuk, M. 410
Andriuslaitis, R.J. 157
Ansoff Matrix 143–144, 161
antitrust: air cargo 29, 35, 45; immunity 17, 23, 100, 105n1, 126, 181, 183n14; Sherman Antitrust Act 374
Appold, S. 195
approach procedures with vertical guidance (APV) 71
apps 213–214, 228–229, 338–339
Araghi, Y. 286–287
Arblaster, M. 193
Argentina 50, 166, 320
Argüello, M.F. 251
Arrhenius, S. 405
Arvis, J.F. 88
ASA Liberalisation Index (ALI) 321
Asia: air cargo 30, 32, 38, 43, 45; air traffic management 60, 77; commercial aerospace industry 81; deregulation 103; fleet composition 84, 86; global network carriers 102; growth in air transport demand 109, 262, 272, 313–314,

359; high-speed rail 182; low cost carriers 101, 105, 140; passenger numbers 12; profitability of airlines 20–23; proportion of world airports in 49
Asia-Pacific: air cargo 32, 34, 37, 38, 45–46; airport economic performance 196; average trips per passenger 314; cost-reduction initiatives 396; cross-regional ownership 99; CWCs 144; fleet composition 86; growth in air transport demand 14, 314; market concentration 104; passenger numbers 12–13; profitability of airlines 20–23
Asiana 22, 23, 44, 284, 289
ASL Aviation Group 99
Assaf, A. 197, 198
Association of Southeast Asian Nations (ASEAN) 20–21, 25n15, 116, 117
Athens International Airport 130
Atlanta 17, 49, 56, 147, 261, 264, 272
Atmosfair Airline Index 286–287, 411
attribution theory 386
Australasia 49, 140
Australia: air cargo 30, 35; air transport demand 315; airports 50, 166, 196, 198; Australia-EU open skies market 130; brand perception 368; Capital Express 145; charter services 124; demand models 318; deregulation 94, 95, 96, 103; economic regulation 193; foreign ownership restrictions 97; market concentration 105; Qantas/Emirates agreement 150; service quality 365; tourism 149; traffic growth 272
Austria 35, 64, 78n3
Austrian Airlines 24n8, 24n9, 99, 181
automatic dependent surveillance-broadcast (ADS-B) 70–71, 75
available seat kilometres (ASKs) 147–148
aviation marketing 221–224
'aviation megacities' 50
Aviation Week 342
awards 226–227, 363–364
Azuk 99
Azul 99, 101

Badanik, B. 161
Baek, J. 316
Bahamas 229
Baikgaki, O.A. 324
Baker, D.Mc.A. 387
Bamford, D. 385
Bangkok 261
Bangladesh 320
Banister, D. 278
banking 177
bankruptcies 128, 131, 179; air cargo 36; Alitalia 181; consumer protection 382, 388; United States 17; see also liquidation

Barbot, C. 225
Barcelona 130, 394
barcodes 342
bargaining power 157, 158
Barnhart, C. 240, 241–242, 244
Barros, C. 197, 198
Başar, G. 318
Basso, L. 189
Bates, J. 231, 232–233
Batik Air 116
Beckers, T. 191
behavioural assessment 350, 351
Behavioural Modelling for Security in Airports
  (BEMOSA) 353
Behrens, C. 174
Beijing 49, 165, 272
Beijing Airport 261
Bejou, D. 388
Bel, G. 88, 192, 193
Belanger, N. 240
Belgium 40, 64, 358
belly carriers 21, 41, 42, 43, 45, 86, 126
Ben Gurion International Airport 355
benchmarking 141–142, 223, 255
Benda, P. 344, 354
Benders, J.F. 246–247, 250
Berg, D.A. 379
Berge, M.E. 242
Beria, P. 225
Berlin Brandenburg 159
Berlin Schoenefeld 269
Berlin Tegel 266
Bernaciak, M. 397
Berrittella, M. 172
Bhadra, D. 317
Bhat, C. 318
Bieger, T. 315
bilateral air services agreements (BASAs) 115–116,
  118, 183n13, 392
Bilotkach, V. 125, 174, 192, 193
biodiversity 305, 402
biofuels 89, 281
biometric security measures 341, 342, 350, 351,
  352, 354–355
Birmingham Airport 55, 56, 165, 166, 233,
  301–302
Birney, Z. 355
Bisaillon, S. 254
Bish, E.K. 242
Bjelicic, B. 177
Black, W.R. 278
Blodgett, J. 385
Bloningen, B. 88
Boeing: B747 41, 54; B707 82; B777 82; B747
  82–83; B737 86; B777 91; B737 130; B777
  208; B737 208, 264; air cargo 31, 37, 41;
  aircraft data 90; Asia-Pacific region 14, 22;

backlog orders 13, 16, 89; B787 Dreamliner
  35, 83, 85, 101, 207–208; emerging markets
  109; open skies agreements 20; technological
  developments 342
Bogota 261
Bolfing, A. 352
Bolivia 50
Bombardier 83, 89–90
Bordeaux 131, 160
Borealis 64–65
Bork, A. 226
Bosnia and Herzegovina 64
Bottasso, A. 196
Bourjade, S. 178
Bowen, J. 20
brand commitment 387–388, 389
Brander, J.A. 178
branding 231–233, 234, 339, 368–369
Branson, Richard 286
Brazil 110, 119; air transport demand 315,
  319–324; airports 50, 56, 197; demand models
  318; deregulation 94, 103; foreign ownership
  restrictions 97
Brenneman, G. 216
Brexit 14, 24n1, 38, 128
BRIC economies 110, 119
Bristol Airport 56
British Airports Authority (BAA) 54–55, 56, 129,
  164–165, 166, 231
British Airways 102, 125, 140; air cargo 44;
  Amadeus Altea system 342; apprenticeships
  284–285; Birmingham Airport 166; charitable
  partnerships 284, 287; flight capacity 398;
  franchising 150; Go 141, 394, 397; IAG
  24n9; market share 24n8; Mixed Fleet 397,
  399; Oneworld 98, 100, 181; price-fixing
  45; revenue accounting 341; strikes 395;
  subcontracting 393; sustainability and corporate
  social responsibility 277
Brons, M. 316
Brooks, N. 350
Brueckner, J.K. 182n3
Brüggen, A. 172, 179
Brunei 95
Brussels Airlines 24n8, 24n9, 164, 181
Brussels Airport 56, 127, 164, 167, 266, 346
Bryan, V. 368
Buck, S. 142
Buckley, R. 286
Budapest Airport 131, 165, 167
buffer times 247
Buhalis, D. 332
Bulgaria 64, 320
bundling 209, 210
Burghouwt, G. 194
Burns, P.M. 290
Bush, H. 156, 193

business class 207
business models 5, 105; air cargo 40, 42–43; air
    navigation service providers 65–66; airlines
    85, 96, 122–135, 139, 140–142, 150; demand
    forecasts 317; environmental issues 307
business strategy *see* strategy
business travel: all-business-class airlines 123,
    128; climate change 407; complaints 387–388;
    delays 383; elasticity of demand 316–317;
    growth in passenger numbers 12; London
    City Airport 160; loyalty schemes 130;
    non-aeronautical revenues 195; passenger
    segmentation 13; premium economy cabins
    207; price elasticity of demand 175; Saudi
    Arabia 118; value of time 183n6
Button, K. 96, 347
buyers 157
Buzz 127, 394, 397

C-trip 213
cabotage 125
Calisir, N. 384
call centres 211–212, 334, 339
Canada: airports 50; deregulation 94, 95, 96,
    103; foreign ownership restrictions 97; joint
    ventures 100; low cost carriers 105; MALIAT
    95; market concentration 104, 105; mergers and
    acquisitions 172; security 344, 346, 347, 350
Canadian Airlines International 98
cancellations 20, 252, 379, 381, 383, 395
capacity: air cargo 21, 33, 39, 42, 43; air traffic
    management 63, 73; airlines 6, 238–258;
    airports 6, 259–276, 298; capacity discipline
    103; disruption management 247–254;
    economic regulation 191; environmental
    300–301; Europe 18; fleet assignment models
    240–247; growth 12, 16; low cost carriers 398;
    route development 221; SESAR 67
capacity utilisation indices (CUIs) 261, 267
capital 172, 177–178, 199
Capital Express 145
carbon dioxide ($CO_2$) emissions 280–281,
    304; air cargo 35; air traffic management
    74–76; charging 315; climate change 404–406,
    407–408, 409, 410–411, 412; compensation
    300; free route airspace 71; reductions in 89;
    SESAR 67; tax exemptions 412
Carbon Offsetting and Reduction Scheme for
    International Aviation (CORSIA) 75, 408, 409
carbon-offsetting schemes 281, 288, 290–291,
    300, 412
cargo *see* air cargo
Cargolux 38, 39, 40, 43, 44, 126
Caribbean: airport branding 231; average trips per
    passenger 314; charter services 124; growth in
    air transport demand 314; proportion of world
    airports in 49; Southwest-AirTran merger 147

Carney, M. 155
carrier-within-a-carrier (CWC) strategies 141,
    144; *see also* airlines-within-airlines
Carter, D.A. 178
Castillo-Manzano, J. 195, 333
Castro, R. 233
Cathay Pacific: air cargo 21, 40, 43, 44; fuel
    hedging 16; fuel surcharge 22; Oneworld 98;
    UNICEF Change for Good programme 284
Caves, D.W. 172
Cavusoglu, H. 357
Cayley, George 1, 2
Cebu Pacific 22, 101
Central America: air cargo 34; low cost airports
    159; market openness 109; passenger numbers
    13; proportion of world airports in 49
central flow management unit (CFMU) 72
Centre for Aviation (CAPA) 3, 116
Chan, E.W. 356–357
Chang, Y.-H. 376
Changi Airport 48, 117, 162; air cargo 38;
    branding 231, 232–233; low cost terminal 160,
    166; online shopping 229; retail 226; smart
    cards 342
Changi Airport Group (CAG) 226
Chao, C. 195
charitable partnerships 284, 287, 412
charter services 124, 125, 142–143; air cargo
    33, 40–41, 42; Brussels Airport 164; business
    models 127–128; consumer protection 382
check-in procedures 23
Chen, C. 195
Chen, C.-F. 384
Chen, F.-Y. 281
Chen, H. 110
Chen, S.C. 180
Cheng, C.H. 376
Chi, J. 316
Chi-Lok, A. 198
Chicago 17, 165, 261
Chicago Convention 60, 61, 358
Chile 95, 97, 103, 320, 383
China: air cargo 30, 32, 35, 37, 45; air traffic
    management 77; air transport demand 315,
    319–324, 325, 327; airline industry 22–23;
    airport capacity 272; airports 50, 159, 198;
    aviation market 14; BeiDou Navigation Satellite
    system 70; complaints 383; deregulation 94,
    103, 181–182; economic growth 36; flight
    numbers 25n17; foreign ownership restrictions
    97; frequent flyer programmes 180; fuel
    hedging 22; growth 109; high-speed rail 174;
    investment in British airports 55; liberalisation
    110; pilots 22; sustainability and corporate social
    responsibility 277
China Airlines 43, 44
China Eastern 22, 43, 44, 99, 110

China Southern 22, 43, 44, 110
China's Commercial Aircraft Corporation (COMAC) 89–90
Chinese Taipei 266, 320
Chiou, W.-B. 384
Choi, K. 173
Choo, Y. 193
Chua, C. 179
Chung, Y.-S. 195
cirrus cloud formation 75, 403, 404, 406
CitiExpress 150
Civil Aeronautics Board (CAB) 94
Civil Air Navigation Services Organisation (CANSO) 76, 78n2
Civil Aviation Authority (CAA) 54, 190, 305
climate change 8, 51, 279–280, 281, 307, 402–416; airport sustainability and corporate social responsibility 290, 298, 299, 300, 305; aviation's contribution to 405–406, 412–413; discourses and unaccountability 410–412; ICAO 'timeline of inaction' 408–409; individual contributions to 407–408
Cline, R.C. 109–110
Clinton, Hillary 407
Clougherty, J.A. 182
Cobham, Alan 52
code-share agreements 102–103, 105n5, 130, 140, 149, 150
Coles, T. 284, 290, 291
collaboration 223–224, 233, 306; see also alliances; partnerships
Collaborative Action for Renovation of Air Transport Systems (CARATS) 66
Colombia 30, 50, 97, 320
Columbia University 319, 320
Comair 99
commercial aerospace industry 5, 81–92
commercial decision support systems 335–336
commercial sector marketing 225–226, 234
commercialisation 125, 129, 155, 156, 167, 221; consequences of 57; emerging markets 119; liberalisation 123; strategic growth 164; United Kingdom 54
Committee on Aircraft Noise (CAN) 298
common support services 68, 78
communications: airline marketing 214–216; airport marketing 227–231, 234; sustainability and corporate social responsibility 286–287, 292, 306
communications, navigation and surveillance (CNS) 65, 66, 78
community investments 307
community involvement 214, 283–284, 285, 289, 299
community opposition 302, 303, 304
compensation 20, 25n13; complaints 386, 387; consumer protection 375, 377, 378–379, 380,

381; environmental impacts of airports 299, 300, 303, 307
competition 129, 374; air cargo 33, 45; airports 57, 154, 156–159, 167, 198, 220; alliances 98, 104–105; business models 122; consolidation 23; consumer protection 375; customer satisfaction 385; deregulation 104, 139–140, 182; domestic 182; emerging markets 110, 119, 120; Europe 20; evolutionary economics 122; Indonesia 116–117; joint ventures 100, 101; Kenya 112–113; market power 179, 180; Mexico 114; non-price 179, 180, 182; price 392; regulation 133; Saudi Arabia 118, 119; seat allocation 176; strategy 139
competitive advantage: airports 155–156, 160, 163, 167; alliances 181; human resource management 400; labour 395; Southwest Airlines 399; sustainability and corporate social responsibility 277
complaints 7–8, 373–374, 375–377, 389; customer management systems 340; European Union 381–382; responding to 386–387; understanding 382–386; United States 378
composite materials 81, 83
Computer-Assisted Passenger Prescreening System (CAPPSII) 352
computer reservation systems (CRSs) 124, 211, 332, 337
concentric diversification 161, 163–164
Concorde 82
condensation trails (contrails) 75, 403, 404, 406
conferences 226
congestion 195, 261, 273; air cargo 33; congestion pricing 190; technological developments 332, 342
Congo 30
connectivity, on-board 90, 146, 228–229, 340
connectivity, route 142, 221
consolidation 16–17, 23, 100, 103–104, 155; air cargo 43, 45–46; commercial aerospace industry 83; Europe 18; market power 179; service quality 368; United States 24n6; see also mergers and acquisitions
consumers: airport marketing 226–233; consumer protection 7–8, 373–391; consumerism movement 375; see also customer satisfaction
Conti, M. 196
Continental 141–142; air cargo 43; merger 24n6, 148, 181; SkyTeam 98
continuous descent operations (CDOs) 76
contrails 75, 403, 404, 406
convergence 123, 129–131, 133, 141
COOPANS 64–65, 78n3
Copenhagen Airport 56, 195–196, 220, 228, 229, 403
Copenhagen Economics 156
Cordeau, J.-F. 244, 246, 247–248

corporate social responsibility (CSR): airlines 6–7, 277–296, 376; airports 7, 234, 301–303, 306–307; communication and publicity 286–287; criticism and greenwash 290–291; definitions of 278–279; drivers for 303; economic dimension 284–285; environmental dimension 279–282, 304; reporting 287–290; SAS 410; social dimension 282–284; sponsorship 214
corporate societal marketing (CSM) 286
corporate sustainability (CS) 277–296; *see also* sustainability
Coshall, J. 318
cost-benefit analysis 347–349
cost leadership strategy 159, 160
Costantino, F. 387
costs: air cargo 39, 43, 172–173; air traffic management 66–67; aircraft 172; airports 52, 57, 131, 175, 196–197, 298; alliances 103; cost competitiveness 179–180; crew 244; disruption management 244, 248, 252; economic regulation 192; efficiencies 23; environmental issues 307; fleet assignment models 240, 246; fuel 86, 171, 178–179, 182, 244; labour 19, 25n12, 394–395, 396, 397, 398, 400; low cost carriers 127; low cost terminals 131; seat allocation 176; security 353, 359; stage length 179; sustainability and corporate social responsibility 306; terrorism 345
Coughlin, C. 345
Court of Justice of the European Union (CJEU) 380–381
Cowlishaw, C. 290
Cowper-Smith, A. 282, 283, 284, 289
Craig, S. 198
Cranfield University 2
credit card companies 17, 24
crew pairing model (CPM) 244–245, 246
crew planning 334, 336
crew recovery 250, 252–253
crew scheduling 244–245, 247–248, 249–250
Crews of Convenience (CoC) 398
crises 394–396
crisis management 73
Cristea, A. 88
Croatia 64, 78n3
Cronin, J.J. 363
cross-selling 24
crowdsourcing 228
cultural differences 385–386
Curi, C. 198
currency issues 19, 22, 57–58
Curtis, T. 365
CUSS 342
customer management systems 334, 340
customer relationship management (CRM) 141, 210, 232, 368, 376; complaints 388, 389; technology 333, 338

customer satisfaction 180, 383; airport marketing 229, 230, 232; complaints 386–387; service quality 363, 364–366, 367–368, 369, 376, 385
cybersecurity 67, 77
Cyprus 64
Czech Airlines 99
Czech Republic 64, 94, 320
Czerny, A. 189

Daft, J. 141
Dahlsrud, A. 301
Daley, B. 279–280
D'Alfonso, T. 195
Dallas/Fort Worth (DFW) 17, 162, 231, 260
Dantas, T.M. 318
Darnton, G. 286
data 76, 90
data analytics 209, 210, 215–216, 230
data envelopment analysis (DEA) 199
data privacy 341
Daw, O.D. 324
de Grosbois, D. 282, 283, 284, 289
De Havilland Comet 82
de Neufville, R. 160
De Vany, A. 173
De Wit, J.G. 143
de Wit, W. 194
debt 17
deceptive advertising 377, 378, 380
decibels (dB) 75–76
decision support systems 334, 335–337
declared capacity 265–266
delays 175, 195, 198; air traffic management 73; compensation 20; complaints 383–384; consumer protection 377, 380–381, 388; disruption management 247, 248–250, 251–252; tolerable 265
Delhi Airport 21, 229, 261
Delta Air Lines 103, 125, 141–142; air cargo 43; ancillary revenues 17; automated booking system 332; banking partnership 17; capacity growth 16; cross-regional ownership 99; domestic market 17; equity partnerships 23; fares 209; joint ventures 18, 100; market share 24n8; merger 24n6, 148, 181; partnerships 150; premium cabins 207; SkyTeam 98, 100, 181; sponsorship 215; US-Mexico ASA 113–114
Delta Automated Travel Account System (DATAS) 332
demand 7, 313–330; airports 57–58, 183n5, 189–190, 231, 262–263, 274; capacity management 238, 239, 265, 274; commercial aerospace industry 86, 90–91; cyclical nature of 14, 395–396; deregulation 96; drivers of 173–175, 314–315, 322–327; dynamic scheduling 242–243; elasticity of 173, 175,

194, 316–317, 322–324, 347; emerging markets
319–327; firm-specific 180; fleet assignment
models 241, 242; forecasts 259; growth in 11,
272, 273, 313–314, 327; induced 407; models
and forecasts 317–319; sustainability and
corporate social responsibility 306; terrorism
impact on 345
Dempsey, P.S. 125
Denmark 64, 78n3, 410, 411–412
Dennis, N. 194–195
Department of Transportation (DOT) 114, 183n6,
398–399; complaints 384, 385; consumer
protection 378–380; families flying together
208–209; joint ventures 100, 101; service
quality 366, 367
departure control systems 339
departure management (DMAN) 76
deregulation 2, 93, 103, 104–105, 122, 124–125,
154, 181–182; air cargo 31, 44–45; airlines
94–96; airport marketing 221; alliances 97;
competition pressures 139–140; franchising
149–150; growth in passenger numbers 12;
low cost carriers 159; market power 179, 180;
mature markets 5; mergers and acquisitions 172;
see also liberalisation; privatisation
Desaulniers, G. 252
Dessart, L. 339
Detroit 17, 261
Deutsche Post 35, 43
DHL 29, 31, 35, 40, 43–44, 45, 126
Dieke, P. 197, 198
differentiation: airlines 23, 123, 130–131, 133,
139, 141, 142–143; airports 159–160, 163,
167, 231, 233; fares 209; low cost carriers 397;
service quality 362; technology 341
digital marketing 227, 228; see also Internet;
social media
direct marketing 227
Directorate-General for Mobility and Transport
(DG MOVE) 78n2
disabilities 283, 377, 378, 380
discount airport schemes 224–225, 233–234
discount cash flow (DCF) 177
discount fares 175–176
discrete choice models 318
discrimination 377, 378
diseconomies of scale 197
disruption management 238, 244, 247–254
disruption recovery 243, 247
distance 174
distribution 209, 210, 211–214, 331, 333
diversification: airlines 129–130, 143–144, 146;
airports 156, 161, 162, 163, 198
diversity 283, 285, 306
divestiture 161, 166, 167
Doganis, Rigas 2, 392
Dolnicar, S. 180

domestic markets 16–17; airlines-within-airlines
101; airport incentive schemes 224; alliances
97; competition 182; deregulation 96; elasticity
of demand 316–317; emerging markets 110,
321–322, 324–326; greenhouse gas emissions
408; Indonesia 115, 116; Kenya 112; low cost
carriers 104, 105; Saudi Arabia 118; Southwest
Airlines 399; tax exemptions 412; United States
17, 313
Domingues, S. 358
Doucouliagos, H. 316
Douglas DC-3 82
Dovica, I. 248–249
drones 31, 46, 67
Drukair Royal Bhutan Airlines 366
Drumwright, M.E. 286
dual-till approach 191, 192
Dubai 21, 49, 102, 146, 229, 261; aerotropolis
concept 132; air cargo 32, 38; airport
infrastructure 159; branding 231; code-share
agreements 106n8; Emirates 147; market
development 145; Qantas/Emirates agreement
150; runway capacity 266; World Central
Airport 19, 38
Dubbs, C. 89
Dublin Airport 197, 266
Dumas, J. 241
Dunbar, M. 247, 248, 249–250
Düsseldorf 266, 271
duty of care 381
dwell time 194, 195, 200
dynamic scheduling 242–243

e-commerce 87, 334, 338, 340; air cargo 33, 37,
39, 46; airline marketing 206
e-tickets 212, 333, 337, 342
East Midlands Airport 53–54, 55, 56
Eastern Europe 12, 60
easyGroup 146
easyJet 18, 24n1, 104, 394, 398, 400; bases
157; business model 127, 130; diversification
146; fuel hedging 15–16; labour costs 25n12;
non-unionisation 394; optional extras 141;
point-to-point network structure 96; service
differentiation 397; subcontracting 393;
sustainability and corporate social responsibility
280–281, 285, 286, 290; UNICEF Change
for Good programme 284, 412; US dollar
denominations 25n11
Eccles, R.G. 288, 290
ecolabels 286–287
economic growth: air cargo 37; airports 50, 297;
China 22, 36; commercial aerospace industry
85, 88–89; decrease in 105; emerging markets
108; energy consumption 304–305; Kenya 111;
mature markets 93; see also growth
economic impact 11, 50

economic sustainability 284–285, 288
economics: airlines 6, 171–188; airports 6,
    189–205; cyclical nature of economic activity
    14, 23
economies of density 97, 103, 142, 172–173,
    181, 238
economies of scale 172; Africa 112; air cargo 35,
    43; airports 193, 196–197; low cost carriers 238;
    overinvestment 177–178
economies of scope 97, 354
economy class 207, 208
Edinburgh Airport 55, 165
Edoreh, P.E. 376
efficiency 173, 180, 368; airports 196–199, 200;
    deregulation 181; economic regulation 192;
    SESAR 67
Eggenberg, N. 248, 251
Egypt 64, 320
EgyptAir 119
Eilbirt, H. 286
elasticity of demand 173, 175, 194, 316–317,
    322–324, 347
electronic tickets 212, 333, 337, 342
Elias, B. 358
Embraer 13, 83, 89–90, 239
Embrey-Riddle Aeronautical University 1–2
Emerging Market Global Players (EMGP)
    319, 320
emerging markets: air transport demand 319–327;
    commercial aerospace industry 84, 85; definitions
    of 319; liberalisation 5, 108–121
Emirates 16, 98–99, 113; air cargo 35, 38, 43,
    44; code-share agreements 106n8; Flydubai
    129; free Wi-Fi 146; global network 102; hub
    airports 126; market development 145; organic
    growth 147–148; passenger care 395, 400; profit
    15; revenue accounting 341; sponsorship 214;
    strategic agreement with Qantas 150
emissions 280–281, 299, 402–404; climate
    change 298, 307, 404–406, 410–411, 412–413;
    compensation 300; GRI framework 288;
    growth in 406–407, 409, 412; technological
    developments 75–76, 332; see also carbon
    dioxide emissions
Emissions Trading Scheme (ETS) 75, 280, 304,
    408, 409, 412
employee well-being and engagement 282–283,
    287, 289, 399
Enders, N. 346
energy 303, 304–305
Enerjet 105
engagement marketing 228, 234
entry barriers 12, 17, 124
environmental issues 54, 402–403, 412; air traffic
    management 74–76; airline sustainability and
    corporate social responsibility 278, 279–282,
    286, 288, 289, 291; airports 58, 297, 298–301;

303–305, 306–307; commercial aerospace
    industry 81, 89; financial performance 285; fleet
    purchasing behaviour 254; greenwash 290–291,
    292; SESAR 67; technological developments
    332; see also climate change; emissions;
    sustainability
Eos 128
equality 283
equity partnerships 23
Erbetta, F. 198
Errunza, V.R. 319
Estonia 64
Ethiopian Airlines 112
Etihad Airways 16, 23, 98; air cargo 43, 44; code-
    share agreements 130; cross-regional ownership
    99; family-friendly services 146; global network
    102; growth 148; hub airports 126; partnerships
    150; premium cabins 207; sponsorship 214
Europe: air cargo 30, 32, 34, 38, 44–45; air
    traffic management 60, 77; air traffic share
    109; airport branding 231; airport charges 275;
    airport economics and finance 192, 193, 196,
    198; airport incentive schemes 225; airport
    industry 49, 56; airport marketing 229; airport
    ownership 155; airport revenues 50–51; airport
    strategy 166; average trips per passenger 314;
    charter carriers 128, 143; consolidation 23;
    cost-reduction initiatives 396; cross-regional
    ownership 99; deregulation 122, 124–125;
    fleet composition 84, 86; franchising 149–150;
    free route airspace 71–72; Galileo system 70;
    growth in air transport demand 262, 272,
    313–314; high-speed rail 182; low cost airports
    159; low cost carriers 101, 140, 396; market
    concentration 103–104; market dominance
    162; mergers and acquisitions 148–149, 172,
    181; noise restrictions 282; passenger numbers
    12, 13; privatisation 129; profitability of
    airlines 18–20, 24n2; public transit 268; Route
    Development Funds 225; runway capacity
    267; security 350, 358; slot coordination 259,
    265, 270, 274; see also European Commission;
    European Union
European aeronautical information system database
    (EAD) 74
European Air Traffic Control Harmonisation and
    Integration Programme (EATCHIP) 63
European Air Traffic Management Standards
    Coordination Group (EASCG) 62, 78n2
European Aviation Crisis Coordination Cell
    (EACCC) 74
European Aviation Safety Agency (EASA) 61–62,
    63, 69–70, 77, 78n2
European Centre for Cyber Security in Aviation
    (ECCSA) 77
European Commission (EC): air traffic
    management 61; airports 57, 197; complaints

383; consumer protection 381; corporate social responsibility 278–279, 301; EACCC 74; functional airspace blocks 63; grey literature 3; liberalisation 124; mergers and acquisitions 148–149; Road Feeder Services 40; SESAR Joint Undertaking 67
European Committee for Electrotechnical Standardisation (CENELEC) 62, 78n2
European Committee for Standardisation (CEN) 62, 78n2
European Common Aviation Area (ECAA) 125
European Defence Agency (EDA) 78n2
European Federation of Quality Management (EFQM) 376
European Organisation for Civil Aviation Equipment (EUROCAE) 62, 78n2
European Organisation for the Safety of Air Navigation (EUROCONTROL) 61, 62, 67, 78n2; demand forecasts 259, 318; EATCHIP 63; environmental issues 298; income elasticity of demand 316; network management 72, 74
European Regional Airlines Association (ERAA) 129
European Telecommunications Standards Institute (ETSI) 62, 78n2
European Union (EU): air cargo 31; air traffic management 61, 66–67, 78; airports 51; Australia-EU open skies market 130; Brexit 14; complaints 383; consumer protection 374, 375, 378, 380–382; deregulation 95, 96, 103; Emissions Trading Scheme 75, 280, 304, 409, 412; fines 45; foreign ownership restrictions 97; free route airspace 71; grey literature 3; Indonesia's agreement with 116; information security 77; international networks 104; joint ventures 100; liberalisation 129; low cost carriers 105; MALIAT 95; market concentration 105; mergers and acquisitions 148–149; regulation 150; remotely piloted aircraft systems 70; security 346, 353, 358; Single European Sky 19–20, 31, 60, 62–63, 67–68, 74; slot coordination 265, 270, 274
Eurowings 101, 105
EVA Air 44
evolutionary economics 122
Exeter Airport 56
exhibitions 226
Expedia 213
explosion detection systems (EDS) 349–350, 351, 354
exports 37, 40
express air cargo 31–32

Facebook 215, 228, 230, 385
Fageda, X. 88, 192, 193, 364
family-friendly services 146, 208–209

fares 96, 123–124, 194, 209–211; Africa 112; consumer protection 382; hub airports 125; increases in 103; Indonesia 116; joint ventures 100, 101, 105; low cost carriers 127; operational support systems 337; Saudi Arabia 118; see also prices
Farmaki, A. 131
Fastjet 112–113
Federal Aviation Authority (FAA) 90, 209; airports 56; minimum seat size 208; noise standards 403; passenger terminal size 269; practical capacity 265; runway capacity 264; safety issues 25n16; security 350; separation requirements 264
Federal Trade Commission (FTC) 380, 383
FedEx 29, 31, 35, 40–41, 43–44, 45, 172–173
Fenclova, E. 284
Ferrer, J.C. 383
Ferrovial 55, 166
Fichert, F. 224, 225
finance 6, 176–179, 182, 192; see also economics
financial control 334, 335, 340–341
financial performance 285, 367–368
Financial Times Stock Exchange (FTSE) 319, 320
Finland 64
Finnair 24n8, 284
Firefly 144
First Choice 143
first class 207
First World War 30, 52, 82, 332
Five Forces model 156–157
Five Forty Aviation 112
flag carriers 124, 140; Asia 21; business models 122; emerging markets 108; Indonesia 116; Kenya 112; Saudi Arabia 119; see also legacy carriers
Flags of Convenience (FoC) 398
Flanagan, Maurice 214
fleet assignment (FA) 238, 239, 240–247, 254
fleet assignment models (FAMs) 239, 240–247
fleet composition 84, 85–86, 172
fleet planning 334, 335
fleet size 238
flexible use of airspace 74
Flight Airline Business 3
flight management systems 334, 339
flight numbers 2, 67, 260
flight planning 73, 334, 336
Fly Too 105
Fly540 112
Flybe 280–281, 285, 286, 287, 290
Flydubai 105, 129
Flynas 118, 119
focus strategies 159, 160, 162
Folkes, V.A. 386
Ford Airlines 30
Ford Motor Company 30

forecasts 13, 259; air cargo 37; aircraft requirements 41; airport master plans 262–263; demand 317–319, 327
foreign direct investment (FDI) 88, 322–327
foreign ownership restrictions 97, 116, 181, 183n13
Forsyth, P. 95, 164, 280, 285
four P's 6, 206–216
France: aeronautical science 1; air cargo 30; airports 50; functional airspace blocks 64; strikes 19
franchising 147, 149–150
Franke, M. 333, 341
Frankfurt International Airport 17, 132, 145, 261, 269; capacity utilisation 271; market power 158; protests against airport expansion 402; QR codes 229; security 346; Star Alliance 98
Fraport 165, 233, 342
Freathy, P. 195, 226
free route airspace (FRA) 64, 71–72
freight see air cargo
freight forwarders 41–44, 45, 157–158, 221, 223
freight tonne kilometres (FTKs) 21, 32, 34, 35–38, 317, 321–322, 324, 326–327
Frelinger, D.R. 349
frequency 238, 315
frequent flyer programmes (FFPs) 24, 126, 140, 210, 388, 389; alliances 149; credit card companies 17; delays 384; drivers of demand 315; hybrid airlines 141; induced demand 407; low cost carriers 130; loyalty 368; non-price competition 180; operations support systems 339; passenger segmentation 13; technology 338; Virgin Australia 150; see also loyalty schemes
Frey, B.S. 346, 348
Friedman, M. 285, 303
Frontier 105, 208
Froyland, G. 248
Fu, X. 193
fuel 171, 182; air cargo 33, 36–37; Asia 22; biofuels 89, 281; commercial aerospace industry 85, 86; emerging markets 110; free route airspace 71; growth in fuel use 406; hedging 15–16, 22, 23–24, 24n3, 171, 178–179, 290; prices 140, 315; tax exemptions 412; technological developments 332
fuel efficiency 83, 89, 171, 180, 254, 407, 408
Fuerst, F. 195
Fuhr, J. 191
full service network carriers (FSNCs) 23, 103, 104, 122, 125; airport cities 132; business models 123, 125–131, 133, 140, 141–142, 150; franchising 150; hub airports 123, 126; mergers and acquisitions 148; non-aeronautical revenues 194–195; revenue management 126; service quality 362; strategies 143, 144; sustainability and corporate social responsibility 285

functional airspace blocks (FABs) 63–65, 71
Fung, M. 197, 198

Galileo system 70
Gallet, C.A. 316
game theory 176
Gardiner, J. 223
Garuda 21, 22, 116, 117
Gatwick Airport 50, 54, 164–165, 261, 272; environmental issues 305; low cost carriers 130, 394; QR codes 229; rebranding 233; runway capacity 266; selling of 55
Gelbrich, K. 387
Gemini Air Cargo 36
gender inequality 283
general air freight 31–32
generic fleet assignment model (GFAM) 241–242
Geneva 266
geo-economic drivers of demand 314–315
German Institute for Experimental Aviation (DVL) 1–2
Germanwings 397
Germany: aeronautical science 1; air cargo 30, 35; airport capacity utilisation 271; airport industry 50, 52; charter carriers 143; DFS 133; functional airspace blocks 64; open skies agreements 94; protests against airport expansion 402
Geuens, M. 195
Gibson, W.E. 176–177, 183n10
Gillen, D.W. 96, 172, 195, 198, 316, 317, 347, 351, 357–358
Gitto, L. 172
Givoni, M. 282
Glasgow Airport 55
Global Air Navigation Plan (GANP) 66, 71
global distribution systems (GDSs) 18, 130, 211–213, 333, 334, 337, 338
global financial crisis (GFC) 173, 263, 396; air cargo 29, 36; airport strategy 142, 148, 156; finance after the 177
global market-based measure (GMBM) 75
Global Navigation Satellite System (GNSS) 70
global network carriers 102, 113
Global Positioning System (GPS) 31, 70, 273
Global Reporting Initiative (GRI) 287–289, 302, 306
global value chains (GVCs) 31, 34, 36
globalisation 33, 104, 105, 149, 359
Globalnaya Navigazionnaya Sputnikovaya Sistema (GLONASS) 70
Go 141, 394, 397
Goetz, A. 125
Gol 99
Goldstein, A. 109
Gonzalez-Savignat, M. 174
Google+ 230, 385
Gopalan, R. 240

Gorjidooz, J. 196, 198
Gössling, S. 280, 281, 286, 291
governance 68, 289
Graduate School of Aerospace and Mechanical
    Engineering, Paris 1–2
Graham, A.: airport branding 231; airport
    economics and finance 194–195, 199; airport
    marketing 220–221, 224; airport strategy
    155–156, 159, 160, 162; drivers of demand
    315; income elasticity of demand 316; route
    development 222, 223
gravity models 174, 317
Greece 64, 197, 315, 320
greenhouse gases 280, 307, 404, 405–406,
    408–409; see also carbon dioxide emissions
greenwash 290–291, 292
grey literature 3
Griffin, T. 222
Grosche, T. 317
gross domestic product (GDP) 11, 88; air cargo
    37; Asia 12, 20; China 36; demand forecasts
    317; demand influenced by 14, 174; emerging
    markets 109, 119, 320–321, 322–326; Europe
    18, 19; growth 13; Indonesia 115; Kenya 111;
    Mexico 113; Saudi Arabia 118
ground-based augmentation system (GBAS) 70
ground handling 158
Group on International Aviation and Climate
    Change (GIACC) 408
growth 4, 11–12, 14, 261–262, 272; air cargo
    33, 37–38; air transport demand 313–314,
    327; airport industry 51–53, 161–167; airport
    performance 222; Brexit 14; climate change
    409; emerging markets 109, 119, 320–322;
    environmental issues 74, 303, 307; fuel use 406;
    Indonesia 115; mature markets 93; mergers and
    acquisitions 148; Mexico 113; organic 147–148,
    162–164; strategies 143–146; see also economic
    growth
Grubb, H. 318
Guberinic, S. 250
Gulf Air 146, 214
Gulf Cooperation Council (GCC) 117
Guzhva, V.S. 315
GVK Chhatrapati Shivaji International Airport 229

Haase, K. 253
Hainan Airlines 284
Halpern, N.: airport branding 231; airport
    marketing 220–221, 224, 228; airport strategy
    155–156, 162; route development 222, 223;
    social media 229–231
Hamad International Airport 48
Hamburg 266
Hanaoka, S. 20
Hane, C.A. 240
Hansen, M. 179

Hansman, R.J. 333
Haouari, M. 245–246
Harteveldt, H. 337, 338
Hartsfield-Jackson Atlanta International Airport 56
Hawaiian Airlines 18, 141–142, 148
Hazledine, T. 317
Heathrow Airport 50, 53, 54, 145, 164–165, 261;
    air cargo 38, 45; alliances 103; BA Mixed Fleet
    397; capacity utilisation 272; environmental
    issues 300, 305, 306; investors 56; joint ventures
    17; low cost carriers 130; market power
    158; noise 304; Oneworld 98; retail 57; runway
    capacity 264, 266, 267; slot trading 271; third
    runway 52, 272, 304; waste 305; website and
    mobile innovations 229
hedging 15–16, 22, 23–24, 24n3, 171, 178–179, 290
Helsinki 266
Herfindahl-Hirschman Index (HHI) 103–104,
    106n9, 109; Indonesia 116–117; Kenya 112;
    Mexico 114; Saudi Arabia 119
Hess, S. 318
high-speed rail (HSR) 174, 182
HNA Group 99, 149
Hong, C. 197, 198
Hong Kong 32, 37, 365
Hong Kong Airlines 146
Hong Kong International Airport 132, 165, 228,
    231, 264, 272
Hong, Y. 178–179
Hopperstad, C.A. 242
horizontal integration 161, 164–165
Hoskisson, R.E. 319
Hotelling, Harold 123, 129
Hsu, C. 195
Hu, Q. 177, 183n9
Hu, Y. 324
hub-and-spoke networks 96, 122, 125, 140;
    Cargolux 38; demand 173; economies of
    density 97, 238; network development 239
hubs 49–50, 96, 123, 125–126, 131, 273;
    airport cities 132; branding 232; charges 193;
    commercial aerospace industry 84; competition
    158; Gulf 16, 18; hub carrier failure 167;
    secondary 88; vulnerability 155, 167–168
Huffman, M. 374
human resource management (HRM) 8, 392–401
human resources (HR) 334, 335, 340
humanitarian air cargo 30, 31
Humphreys, I. 220
Hungary 64, 105, 320, 397
Hunt, K. 383
Huschelrath, K. 103
hybrid airlines 130, 140, 141, 142, 150

Iberia 24n8, 24n9, 100, 102, 181
IBM 24n4, 332
Iceland 105

Icelandair 24n8, 128
Icelandic volcanic eruption 73, 381–382
IdeaworksCompany 17, 209–210
in-flight entertainment (IFE) 90, 207, 334, 340
incentive schemes 224–225, 233–234
Incheon International Airport 23, 38, 132, 165, 231
incomes: growth in passenger numbers 12; income
    elasticity of demand 316, 322–324
increasing returns to scale (IRS) 197
India 14, 110; air cargo 30; air transport demand
    315, 319–323, 327; airports 50, 56; deregulation
    94, 103; foreign ownership restrictions 97;
    infrastructure constraints 21; safety issues 25n16;
    service quality 365
Indonesia 320; air cargo 32; airports 21, 50;
    foreign ownership restrictions 97; liberalisation
    115–117, 119; safety issues 22, 25n16
industrial action 19, 73, 393, 395, 399–400
industry rivalry 157
information and communications technologies
    (ICTs) 331, 333–335, 341–342
information management 334–335
information security 77
information technology (IT) 174, 337; airline
    marketing 209, 210; alliances 103; cost
    efficiencies 23; infrastructure 335, 340; see also
    Internet; technology
infrastructure: Africa 109; air cargo 33, 45; air
    traffic management 65, 66–67, 68; airports 51,
    53–54, 57, 131, 132–133, 159, 161, 197; Asia
    21; commercial aerospace industry 85, 87–88;
    environmental issues 307, 402–403; Europe
    19, 20; IT 334, 335, 340; pre-financing 192;
    resistance to development 262, 274, 302;
    SESAR 67
innovation 24, 46; airports 163; commercial
    aerospace industry 82, 89, 90–91; product
    development 145–146; technological 331–332,
    340, 343
Inoue, Y. 285
insolvency 382; see also bankruptcies
Instagram 215, 230
instrument flight rules (IFR) 266–267
instrument landing systems (ILSs) 71, 273
integration strategies 161, 164–166, 167
intelligence 76, 224, 230, 233, 331, 334, 351
Intergovernmental Panel on Climate Change
    (IPCC) 298, 405
Interjet 114, 120n1
International Air Transport Association (IATA) 3,
    105, 110; air cargo 32–33, 36, 358; airports 156;
    Asia 20; average trips per passenger 313–314;
    brand perception 368; carbon-offsetting
    schemes 281; consumer protection 373, 377,
    380; income elasticity of demand 316; New
    Distribution Capability 210, 213, 338, 362, 369;
    passenger numbers 407; passenger survey report

13; return on invested capital 15; SAS 410;
    security 351–352; self-service technologies 333;
    service quality 368, 369; slot coordination 259,
    265, 270–271, 274, 336
International Airlines Group (IAG) 24n1, 24n9,
    99, 102, 104; consolidation 18; labour costs
    25n12; profit 15, 16; US dollar denominations
    24n11
International Civil Aviation Organisation (ICAO)
    3; air cargo 358; air traffic management 61–62;
    airport master plans 262, 274; climate change
    405, 408–409, 412; consumer protection 373,
    377; demand forecasts 317, 319; Global Air
    Navigation Plan 66, 71; global market-based
    measure 75; GNSS standard 70; noise 297–298;
    passenger numbers 410; passenger traffic 11;
    safety issues 21–22, 25n16, 117; security 77,
    345; separation requirements 264
International Consumer Protection Enforcement
    Network (ICPEN) 375
International Monetary Fund (IMF) 19, 22, 319
International Organisation for Standardisation
    (ISO) 62, 287, 289, 306
Internet 212, 331, 333; airport marketing 227;
    low cost carriers 127; on-board connectivity 90,
    146; see also social media; websites
Internet booking engines (IBEs) 337, 338
Internet of Things (IoT) 342
InterVISTAS 316, 324
investment: aircraft 176–177; airports 45, 51,
    55, 87, 132–133; capacity 275; community
    307; emerging markets 319; environmental
    management 301; pre-financing 192;
    technology 342–343
Iran 320
Ireland 64, 78n3
ISO 14001 standard 289, 306
ISO 26000 standard 289
Israel 97, 320
Istanbul 18, 38, 165, 261, 264
Italy: air cargo 30; airport charges 19; airport
    economics and finance 198; airport incentive
    schemes 225; functional airspace blocks 64; low
    cost carriers 397; open skies agreements 94
itineraries 253–254, 318
itinerary-based fleet assignment model (IFAM) 241
Ito, H. 14, 315, 345

Jaccard, J. 386
Jackson, B.A. 344, 348–349, 356, 358
Jacobs, T. 241
Jacobson, S. 349–350
Jacoby, J. 386
Jain, A. 354–355
Jakarta 21
JamboJet 112
Janić, M. 299, 402

Japan: air cargo 30, 32, 37, 45; airline industry 23; airports 197; banking 177; BASA with Indonesia 115–116; foreign ownership restrictions 97; joint ventures 100; open skies agreements 20; pilots 22
Japan Air Lines (JAL) 22, 23, 282, 284, 289
Jarach, D. 220
Jarrah, A. 250, 251
Jazeera Airways 130
JD Powers 363–364
Jean, D.A. 148
Jet Airways 99
JetBlue 103, 141–142, 148; free Wi-Fi 146; point-to-point network structure 96; pricing 211; sponsorship 215
Jetstar 22, 25n14, 101, 105, 141, 144, 211
Jiang, H. 180, 242
Jin Air 101, 144
Jin, Y. 178
jobs 2, 88, 111, 284–285, 392
John F. Kennedy (JFK) International Airport 17, 45, 50, 54, 160, 261
Johnson, E.L. 243
Joint Authorities for Rulemaking on Unmanned Systems (JARUS) 69
joint ventures (JVs) 23, 96–97, 99–101, 105, 155, 181; airports 125–126, 161; Mexico 114; United States 17–18; see also alliances
Jomo Kenyatta International Airport (JKIA) 111
Jones, O.C. 225
Jordan 64, 366
Jorge-Calderon, J.D. 199, 314
Jorion, P. 178
*Journal of Air Transport Management* (JATM) 3
journals 3, 383
just in time (JIT) production 31, 39–40
justice theory 387

Kahn, Alfred 379
Kang, L. 243
Karamanos, G. 232
Karp, A. 206
Kasarda, J. 132, 195
Kasprzychi, T. 355
Kayak 213
Kee, J. 317
Kelleher, Herb 399
Keller, K.L. 286
Kennedy, John F. 375
Kenya 97, 111–113, 119
Kenya Airways 99, 112, 113
Kim, Y.K. 385–386
Kirschenbaum, A.A. 353
KLM 24n1, 104, 113, 125; air cargo 43; Air France merger 24n9, 148–149, 165; alliances 126; antitrust immunity 183n14; Buzz 394, 397; consolidation 18; cross-regional ownership 99;

joint ventures 100; labour costs 25n12; market share 24n8; price-fixing 45; SkyTeam 98, 100, 102, 181; strikes 19; US dollar denominations 24n11
Klophaus, R. 224, 225
Klose, L. 172, 179
Knowles, J. 352
Koo, T.R. 141
Koopmans, C. 171
Korea 319, 320; air cargo 32, 35; foreign ownership restrictions 97; service quality 365
Korean Air 22–23; air cargo 21, 37, 43, 44, 45; cross-regional ownership 99; JinAir 144; SkyTeam 98
Kotler, P. 286
Kramer, L. 220
Kuala Lumpur 20, 25n14, 38, 130, 132, 160
Kutlu, L. 198
Kyrgyzstan 109–110

La Compagnie 128
labour costs 19, 25n12, 394–395, 396, 397, 398, 400
Laesser, C. 383
Laker Airways 130
Lakew, P.A. 37, 172–173
Lall, A. 195
LAN Colombia 284
Lan Peru 284
Lan, S. 248
Langley, Samuel 1
Lapré, M.A. 384
Las Vegas McCarran 342
LATAM 99, 150–151
Latin America: age of fleet 176; air cargo 32, 34; airport branding 231; airport economic performance 196; average trips per passenger 314; cross-regional ownership 99; fleet composition 84, 86; growth in air transport demand 314; low cost airports 159; market concentration 104; Southwest-AirTran merger 147; see also South America
LaTourrette, T. 356, 358
Latvia 64, 397
Laurino, A. 225
Lazarev, J. 175
leasing 178, 183n10
Lee, D. 14, 315, 345
Lee, D.S. 409
Lee, H.R. 385–386
Lee, S. 285
leg-based fleet assignment model (LFAM) 240, 241–242
legacy carriers 96, 394, 398; Europe 20; fares 209; human resource management 393; industrial action 399; joint ventures 100; labour costs 395; overinvestment 177–178; premium cabins 207; United States 173; see also flag carriers

legislation: air cargo 30, 31; air traffic management 61–62; airports 54, 55; carbon emissions 304; consumer protection 374, 375, 381–382; environmental 298; Indonesia 115, 117; minimum seat size 208; *see also* regulation
Lei, Z. 142, 195
Leick, R. 126, 130
LeighFisher 156, 195–196
Leonardo da Vinci 1
lesbian, gay, bisexual and transgender (LGBT) people 283, 291
Lettovsky, L. 253
Levine, M.E. 379
Levitt, T. 285
Lewis, T.R. 178
Li, M.Z.F. 176
Li, P. 132
Li, Y. 180
liberalisation 2, 124–125, 129, 139, 154, 181–182, 315; air cargo 29, 31, 33, 44–45; air navigation service providers 133; air traffic management 65; airport marketing 221; Asia 20; commercial aerospace industry 85, 87; demand forecasts 317; emerging markets 5, 108–121, 321; Europe 12; low cost carriers 159, 392–393, 400; mature markets 5, 93–107; mergers and acquisitions 172; *see also* deregulation; privatisation
Liebert, V. 192, 198, 199
Lieshout, R. 171
Lilienthal, Otto 1
Lim, S.H. 178–179
Lin, L. 197, 198
Lin, Y. 195
Lin, Z. 197, 199
Líneas Aéreas Privadas Argentinas (LAPA) 166
LinkedIn 230, 385
Lion Air 21, 101, 116, 117
liquid scanners 354
liquidation 161, 166–167, 168, 179; *see also* bankruptcies
Lisbon 266
List, G.F. 254
Lithuania 64, 397
Littlechild, S. 193
Littlewood, K. 176
Liu, Y. 180
load factors 103, 313; air cargo 33–34, 35, 45; business models 124, 125, 128; cost competitiveness 179
local economic development 284–285
locational factors 314–315
Loganair 150
logos 231, 232
Lohatepanot, M. 240
Lohmann, G. 130, 141, 144, 148, 233
London 50, 128; airport capacity 272; airport economics and finance 190, 192; airport

expansion 403; discrete choice models 318; low cost carriers 130, 394; *see also* Gatwick Airport; Heathrow Airport; Stansted Airport
London City Airport 56, 160, 301
López-Valpuesta, L. 333
Los Angeles International Airport 17, 103, 231, 232
low cost airports 160
low cost carriers (LCCs) 23, 159, 313; air cargo 21; aircraft capabilities 81; airport marketing 224, 227; airports 167, 263; Asia 21; Brussels Airport 164; business models 104, 122–123, 127–131, 133, 140–142, 150; buy or lease decision 178; charitable partnerships 284; code-share agreements 102–103, 105n5, 130; competition 180; deregulation 95; Europe 18; finance 177; growth of 12, 104, 154–155; human resource management 8, 392–401; Indonesia 116, 117; induced demand 407; joint ventures 100; Kenya 112–113; local economic development 285; long-haul flights 101, 105, 130–131, 398; market concentration 104; Mexico 114; non-aeronautical revenues 194–195; operational flexibility 157; passenger segmentation 13; point-to-point network structure 96, 127, 238; Saudi Arabia 118; seasonal grounding of aircraft 143; secondary airport subsidies 225; service quality 362, 365; short-haul flights 85–86; slimline seats 208; strategies 143, 144; sustainability and corporate social responsibility 285, 291; technological developments 333; ticket distribution 212; ultra-low cost carriers 105, 398; United States 16, 148; websites 337
low cost long haul (LCLH) 130–131
low cost terminals (LCTs) 131, 132, 159, 160, 161
loyalty 180, 227, 389; brand 368–369, 388; crowdsourcing 228; operations support systems 334; service quality 363, 364, 366, 367, 368; social media 339
loyalty schemes 130, 162, 229, 338, 340, 376, 388; *see also* frequent flyer programmes
Lufthansa 24n9, 104, 125; air cargo 30, 31, 40, 43, 44; barcodes 342; consolidation 18; employee productivity 393; Eurowings 101; flight capacity 398; fuel costs 171; Germanwings 397; joint ventures 100, 125–126; labour costs 25n12; market share 24n8; Munich Airport 166; premium economy cabins 207; profit 15; Star Alliance 98, 100, 181; strikes 19, 395, 399; sustainability and corporate social responsibility 280; Turkish Airlines competition with 102, 106n7; US dollar denominations 24n11
Luton Airport 50, 55, 128, 394
Luxembourg 40, 45, 64
Lynden Pindling International 229
Lynes, J.K. 410

Macário, R. 358
Mackie, P.J. 183n6
Madrid 17, 158
Maertens, S. 158, 192
Maher, S.J. 248, 254
maintenance management 334, 339–340
maintenance planning 334, 336–337
Malaysia 20, 97, 320, 365
Malaysian Airlines 20, 22, 25n14, 97, 144
Malév Airlines 131
Malina, R. 225
Malindi Airways 25n14
Malinowski, H. 230
Malta 64, 94
Manchester Airport 55, 228, 263, 266, 300, 305
Manchester Airports Group (MAG) 55, 300, 302
Manila 21
Mantin, B. 179
Marazzo, M. 324
market concentration 103–104, 105, 106n9, 109;
    airports 260–261, 274; customer satisfaction
    385; Indonesia 116–117; Kenya 112; Saudi
    Arabia 119
market development 143–144, 145, 161, 162, 163
market dominance 162, 164
market entry 103, 119, 122, 124, 146
market penetration 143–144, 161, 162
market power: airlines 179, 180–181, 182, 238;
    airports 158, 190, 192, 193
market pressures 57–58, 84–85
market share 123, 129; alliances 24n8, 98, 181;
    Herfindahl-Hirschman Index 106n9, 109;
    market penetration 144, 162; Southwest
    Airlines 399
marketing: air cargo 42; airlines 6, 24, 206–219,
    387; airports 6, 162, 163, 220–237; alliances 98,
    140, 149, 181; social media 24; sustainability
    and corporate social responsibility 286
Marques, R. 198
Marseille 160
Martin-Domingo, L. 229
Martin, J.C. 196, 229
Martin, S.C. 221
Mason, A. 318
Mason, K.J. 318
master plans 262–263, 274, 299
Matsumoto, H. 317
Mauritius 97, 320
maximum take-off mass (MTOM) 264
MaxJet 128
Mayer, R. 286, 290, 291
McCarthy, P. 197, 198
Medard, C.P. 253
Melbourne 160
Meng, Q. 242
merchandising 210, 212, 337, 338, 343n1
Mercier, A. 246, 248

mergers and acquisitions 126, 155; air cargo 43;
    airline economics and finance 172, 180–181;
    airline strategy 142, 147, 148–149, 150–151;
    airports 164, 167; see also consolidation
Meridiana 99
Merkert, R. 35, 37, 317
Merrill Lynch 21
meta search websites 213
metal neutral joint ventures (MNJVs) 99–101,
    102, 105
Metz, D. 315
Mew, K. 155
Mexico: air cargo 30; air transport demand
    319–322; airports 50; ASA with the US
    113–114, 120n1; liberalisation 103, 113–115,
    119; security 346
Mexico City 261
MGM Grand Air 128
Microsoft 213
Middel, J. 407
middle class 12, 13, 93, 111, 115, 375
Middle East: air cargo 32, 34, 38; air traffic
    management 60, 77; airport branding 231;
    average trips per passenger 314; commercial
    aerospace industry 81; fleet composition 84,
    86; global network carriers 102; growth in air
    transport demand 109, 272, 314; hub airports
    126; low cost airports 159; market concentration
    104; market development 145; premium
    cabins 207; proportion of world airports in 49;
    sponsorship 214; state subsidies 57
Mifsud, P. 100
Milan Malpensa 131
Minervini, F. 172
Minneapolis 17
Mint 141
Mitsubishi 89–90
mobile technology 213–214, 227, 228–229, 334,
    338–339, 342
models 317–319
Mongolfier brothers 1
Mongolia 95
Morley, C.L. 149
Morrell, P.S. 176–177, 183n10
Morrison, S.A. 175
Morrison, W. 96, 199
Morrison, W.G. 347, 351, 357–358
Mouawad, J. 368
MSCI 319, 320
Mueller, J. 192, 347–348
Muller, K. 103
multi-airport groups 164
Multilateral Agreement on the Liberalisation of
    Air Transportation (MALIAT) 94–95
Mumbai 21
Munich Airport 48, 131, 166, 261, 266; capacity
    utilisation 271; joint venture 125–126; layout

267–268; market power 158; non-aeronautical facilities 163; passenger terminals 269; security 346
Murphy, P.E. 286

Nader, Ralph 375
Nafchi, M.Z. 366
Narita International Airport 160
Nas Air 118
Nash equilibrium 176
national supervisory authorities (NSAs) 61
net present value (NPV) 176–177
Netherlands: air cargo 35, 40; functional airspace blocks 64; low cost carriers 397; open skies agreements 94, 183n14; security 346
network design 42
network management 72–74
Network Operations Plan (NOP) 74
network planning 334, 335
New Distribution Capability (NDC) 210, 213, 338, 362, 369
new entrants 157, 158–159
New York 17, 50, 54, 128
New York La Guardia 50, 261, 272
New Zealand: airport economic performance 196; Capital Express 145; deregulation 94, 95, 96, 103; drones 31; foreign ownership restrictions 97; MALIAT 95; sustainability and corporate social responsibility 277
Newark 17, 50, 128
newspapers 30
Next Generation Air Transportation System (NextGen) 66, 87, 273
Nice 229, 266
niche strategy 159, 162–163
Niemeier, H.-M. 160, 193, 199
Nigeria 320, 365, 366
Nikbin, D. 386
Nile Air 119
9/11 terrorist attacks 14, 16, 173, 174, 315, 344–345, 350, 394, 396
Niskala, J. 220
Nissen, R. 253
Njegovan, N. 315, 317
Njoya, E.T. 160
noise 51, 54, 198, 402–404; airline sustainability and corporate social responsibility 279, 281–282, 288; airport sustainability and corporate social responsibility 297–298, 299, 301, 303–304; capacity planning and management 259; compensation 300; technological developments 75–76, 332, 342
Nok Air 146
non-flyers 315
non-governmental organisations (NGOs) 299
North America: air cargo 30, 32, 34; air traffic share 109; airport economic performance

196, 199; airport marketing 226–227; average trips per passenger 314; commercial aerospace industry 81; fleet composition 84; global network carriers 102; growth in air transport demand 272, 313–314; low cost carriers 101; market concentration 103–104; market dominance 162; passenger numbers 12, 13; profits 24n2; proportion of world airports in 49; see also Canada; Mexico; United States
Northwest: alliances 126; antitrust immunity 183n14; joint ventures 100; merger 24n6, 181; SkyTeam 98
Norway 35, 64, 351, 410–411
Norwegian Air 24n1, 101, 105, 398–399; bases 157; free Wi-Fi 146; long-haul flights 130; US dollar denominations 24n11

OAG 260, 332, 398
Oceania 49
O'Connell, F. 195, 226
oil prices 171, 173, 298; air cargo 29, 36–37; demand forecasts 317; hedging 15–16, 178–179; see also fuel
oligopoly 125
Oman 320
Oman Air 271
on-time performance 13
Oneworld 24n7, 98–99, 100, 102, 105, 140; destinations 126; market share 24n8, 181; price-fixing 45; United States 17
online brand communities (OBCs) 339
online reservation systems 143
online travel agencies (OTAs) 212–213, 337–338
Ontario 162
Ontario Teachers' Pension Plan (OTPP) 56
open skies agreements 23, 397; air cargo 44–45; alliances 149; antitrust immunity 100, 183n14; ASEAN 117; Asia 20, 21; Canada 95; low cost carriers 398; United States 94
operational support systems 334, 337–340
operations control systems 334, 339
operations decision support systems 336–337
operations management 238, 300–301
optimum pricing 190
Orbitz 213
organic growth 147–148, 162–164
Organisation for Economic Co-operation and Development (OECD) 305, 319
Organisation of the Petroleum Exporting Countries (OPEC) 36
organisational culture 76
origin-destination fleet assignment model (ODFAM) 241–242
original equipment manufacturers (OEMs) 84
Oslo 266
Oswald, N. 232
Ottawa International Airport 230

Oum, T.H. 173, 175, 178, 192, 196, 197
outsourcing 65, 173, 198, 393
overcapacity 33, 140
overinvestment 177–178, 183n9
ownership: air cargo 45; air traffic management 65; airports 51, 55–56, 58, 131, 155, 191, 197–198; buy or lease decision 178; cross-regional 99; foreign ownership restrictions 97; *see also* privatisation
ozone depletion 403, 404

Paat-Dahlstrom, E. 89
Pagiavlas, N. 315
Pagliari, R. 150
Pakistan 320
Palma de Mallorca 266
Palmer, A. 388
Papadakos, N. 244, 246, 247
Papatheodorou, A. 131
Paraguay 50
Paris 130
Paris Charles de Gaulle 128, 158, 261, 346
Park, S.-Y. 285
Parket, I.R. 286
partnerships: air cargo 43, 45; airports and airlines 133; charitable 284, 287, 412; equity 23; frequent flyer programmes 140; *see also* alliances; collaboration
passenger mix model (PMM) 241
passenger numbers 11, 12, 13, 88, 331; China 22; Emirates 147; Indonesia 115; Kenya 111; Mexico 113; misrepresentation of 407, 410; Prestwick Airport 57; Saudi Arabia 118; Turkish Airlines 18
passenger recovery 250, 253–254
passenger segmentation 12–13
passenger terminals 268–270
Paternoster, J. 232
Pathomsiri, S. 198
Peach 144
Peeters, P. 407, 411
Pels, E. 174, 175, 182n3, 318
People Express 130
Perelman, S. 196, 197
performance: air traffic management 61–62, 63, 78; airports 196–199, 200, 222; common support services 68; economic regulation 192; productivity 173; reporting 341; SERVPERF 363; sustainability and corporate social responsibility 285
performance-based navigation (PBN) 66–67, 71
Perng, S.W. 195
Perry, A. 143
Persico, N. 352
personal selling 222, 223, 224, 227, 233
Perth 266
Peru 97, 320
Petersen, J.D. 254

Peterson, J. 358
Philadelphia 17
Philippines 25n16, 97, 319–323
Philippines Airlines 146
Philpott, D. 356
Pidgeon, J. 355
pilots 22, 393, 395
Pinterest 230, 385
Pita, J.P. 240
Plass, Gilbert 405
point-to-point network structure 101, 102–103, 122, 125; airport competition 157; Changi Airport 166; low cost carriers 96, 127, 238; regional airlines 128
Polak, J.W. 318
Poland 64, 94, 320, 397
Polar Air Cargo 40, 43, 44
political sustainability 301
Polk, A. 125, 192
pollution 259, 279–280, 299, 304, 305, 402–403
Poole, R.W. Jr. 347, 348, 350–351
Porter, K. 129
Porter, M.E. 139, 156–157, 159, 160, 162
Portugal 64, 94, 318
Post Office Department (POD) 30
practical capacity 265, 266–267
pre-financing 192
PreCheck programme 348
Precision Air 112, 113
premium airlines 128
premium cabins 207
premium economy cabins 207–208
premium pricing 35
Prentice, B.E. 344, 346, 348
Prestwick Airport 54, 57
price-cap/incentive regulation 191, 192, 193
price elasticity of demand 173, 175, 194, 316–317, 347
Priceline 213
prices: air cargo 35; airline marketing 209–211; airport charges 19, 189–190, 193–194, 272, 275; airport marketing 223, 224; alliances 97, 181; Asia 21; competition 392; consumer protection 377, 382; deregulation 125; drivers of demand 174, 175, 315; economic regulation 192; fleet assignment models 241; influence on ticket purchases 13; liberalisation 87; New Distribution Capability 369; price controls 94; price discrimination 126, 175–176, 183n7, 275; price-fixing 45, 101; revenue management 336; route development 221; *see also* fares
privatisation 2, 95, 140; air cargo 45; air traffic management 77; airports 51, 54–56, 58, 123, 129, 155, 164, 167, 191, 197–198; emerging markets 119; Kenya 111; Mexico 114; revenue management 126; security 346; *see also* deregulation; liberalisation

procurement 284, 340–341
product 206–209
product development 143–144, 145–146, 161, 163
productivity 17, 19, 173, 198, 343, 393, 400
profiling of passengers 357
profit/profitability 2, 11, 14–23, 103, 374; air cargo 43; airlines 179–182; airports 56–58, 196, 197; alliances 98; capacity management 244; corporate social responsibility 285; customer satisfaction 385; decision support systems 335–336; economic regulation 192; service quality 364, 369; Southwest Airlines 399; technology 343
Programmed Airline Reservation System (PARS) 332
promotion 214–216, 223, 227, 228, 229
protectionism 33, 95, 108, 113, 118, 124
public-private partnerships (PPPs) 133; air traffic management 65; airports 55, 56, 129; Indonesia 116; SESAR Joint Undertaking 67
public relations 215, 227, 228, 286
public sector marketing 221, 224, 234

Qantas: air cargo 43; aircraft 82; airports 166; Amadeus Altea system 342; code-share agreements 106n8; Jetstar 141, 144; joint ventures 100; Oneworld 98, 99; privatisation 95; profit 15; strategic agreement with Emirates 150; UNICEF Change for Good programme 284
Qatar 55, 320
Qatar Airways 16, 113; air cargo 44; cross-regional ownership 99; equity partnerships 23; global network 102; growth 147, 148; hub airports 126; market development 145; passenger care 395, 400
quick release (QR) codes 228, 229

radiative forcing (RF) 75, 405–406
radio frequency identification (RFID) 342, 354
Radio Technical Commission for Aeronautics (RTCA) 62
rail transport 174, 182, 272, 315
random checks 351
Rao, V.K. 179
rate of return (ROR)/cost plus regulation 191, 193
recession 14; see also global financial crisis
reduced vertical separation minima (RVSM) 74
Regent Air 128
regional airlines 123, 128–129
Regmi, U.K. 231
regulation 2, 124, 133, 150, 183n13; air cargo 33, 44–45; air traffic management 61–62, 77; airports 51, 57, 155, 167, 191–193, 199; commercial aerospace industry 85, 87; consumer protection 374–375, 377, 378–382, 388–389; emerging markets 108, 120;

environmental 280, 303, 305, 307; Europe 20; Indonesia 116, 117; remotely piloted aircraft systems 69–70; see also deregulation; legislation
Rekiel, J. 346
remote tower services 68–69
remotely piloted aircraft systems (RPASs) 69–70, 78n5
Rendeiro, R. 198
reporting: performance measurement 341; sustainability and corporate social responsibility 287–290, 292, 302
required navigational performance (RNP) 71
research and development (R&D) 163, 230
retail 123, 132, 158, 175, 269; airport marketing 225–226, 228, 232, 234; airports 57; online shopping 229
retrenchment strategies 161, 166–167
return on invested capital (ROIC) 15, 196
revenue management (RM) 126, 175–176, 209; airline pricing 210, 211; decision support systems 334, 336; fleet assignment 239, 242–243; low cost carriers 127
revenue passenger kilometres (RPKs) 20, 108, 259, 313–314, 317, 321–322, 324–326, 406
revenue passenger miles (RPMs) 103
revenue tonne kilometres (RTKs) 313–314, 321–322, 409
revenues 15, 24, 142; aeronautical 193–194; air cargo 21, 35, 36, 43; airports 50, 57, 158, 163, 190–191, 193–196, 200, 232; alliances 24n7, 98, 103; ancillary 17, 123, 130–131, 209–210, 212–213, 393, 397, 400n1; customer satisfaction 232; diversification 156; Europe 20; fleet assignment models 241–242; global financial crisis 396; information management 334; low cost carriers 397; mergers and acquisitions 148; non-aeronautical 57, 129, 132, 155, 158, 161, 163, 190, 194–196, 225–226; revenue accounting 340–341; US carriers 17
Rexing, B. 240
Rhoades, D.L. 373
Rietveld, P. 282
Rigby, C. 279
risk: airports 156, 160, 192; concentric diversification 163; diversification 167; emerging markets 319; environmental issues 307; risk-based security 349–352, 358, 359; risk-sharing arrangements 224; security cost-benefit analysis 348–349
Road Feeder Services (RFS) 40
robust planning 247
Romania 64, 320
Rome Fiumicino 158
Roschk, H. 387
Rosenberger, J. 243, 251, 252
Rosskopf, M. 254
Rouge 101, 105n4

route churn 157
route development 221–224, 225, 233–234, 239, 303
Route Development Funds (RDFs) 225
Royal Aeronautical Society 1
Royal Jordanian 365
runways 53, 54; capacity 259, 264–267, 272, 274; paved 49, 50, 52
Russia 110, 119; air cargo 32; air transport demand 319–322, 325; airports 50; deregulation 103; GLONASS 70
Rust, R.T. 387
Ryanair 18, 24n1, 104, 131, 394, 398; ancillary revenues 397, 400n1; bases 157, 167; business model 127, 130; charity claims 291; customer experience 24n10; employee productivity 393, 400; extra charges 362; fuel 16, 171; long-haul flights 130; Mexico 114; non-unionisation 394, 399; point-to-point network structure 96; profit 15; seasonal grounding of aircraft 143, 398; service quality 367; slimline seats 208; social dumping 397; subcontracting 393; US dollar denominations 24n11
Ryerson, M.S. 224–225

Sabena 149, 164, 395
SABRE 213, 332, 338, 341
Safair 99
SafariLink 112
safety: air traffic management 60, 66, 76–77; Asia 21–22; drivers of demand 174, 315; EASA 61–62, 63, 69–70, 77, 78n2; efficiency 180; Indonesia 25n16, 117; network management 72–73; remotely piloted aircraft systems 69; sustainability and corporate social responsibility 306
Saha, M. 286
salaries 393, 395, 397
Salazar-Gonzalez, J. 246
sales planning 332, 334, 336
sales promotions 227, 228, 229
Sama 118
Samagaio, A. 318
Samoa 95
Samuelson, P.A. 345
San Diego 261, 266–267, 272
San Francisco 17, 229, 261, 318
Sandler, T. 346
Sao Paulo 48, 261
SAS (Scandinavian Airlines): climate change 410–411; Snowflake 394; Star Alliance 98; sustainability and corporate social responsibility 277, 282, 283, 286, 287, 289
satellite applications 70–71, 78
satellite-based augmentation system (SBAS) 70
Saudi Arabia 117–119, 315
Saudi Arabian Airlines 118, 119

SaudiGulf Airlines 119
Sausen, R. 409
Sawhney, N. 253
scanners 354
scenario analysis 318, 319, 327
schedule generation (SG) 238, 239, 240, 241, 243
schedule recovery 250, 251–252
scheduling 243–244, 254; crew 244–245, 247–248, 249–250; decision support systems 334, 335–336; disruption management 247; drivers of demand 315; maintenance management 339–340; operational support systems 337
Schlumberger, C.E. 112
Schuckert, M. 230
Schulte-Strathaus, U. 20
Schumpeter, Joseph 122
Schwaninger, A. 352
Scoot 101, 141, 144
Scotland 54, 55, 150
Scotti, D. 198
screening 348, 349–352, 353; layered 356–357; non-passenger 357–358; technology 354
seating: capacity 272, 273, 275; marketing 206–209; revenue management 336; seat allocation 176
Second World War 30–31, 53, 82, 332
secondary airports 88, 127, 154–155, 157, 159, 167–168, 225
security 7, 51, 54, 58, 140, 344–361; air cargo 33; biometric 341, 342, 350, 351, 352, 354–355; cost-benefit analysis 347–349; drivers of demand 174, 315; human factor 352–354; impact on non-aeronautical revenue 195, 196; information 77; layered screening 356–357; non-passenger 357–358; as public good 345–347; risk-based 349–352, 358, 359; SESAR 67; supplier buying power 158; technology 354–355
Seelhorst, M. 180
segmentation 12–13
Seixas, J.M. 324
self-service technologies (SSTs) 333
Senegal 35
Sentence, A. 156
Seoul 38, 195–196
separation requirements 263–264, 265
Serebrisky, T. 196, 197
service quality 7, 123–124, 362–372, 376, 379, 385; airport branding 232; airports 57, 175, 198; complaints 384; consumer protection 373; customer retention 387; defining the concept 362–363; drivers of demand 315; emerging markets 119; low cost carriers 397; managerial implications 368–369; non-price competition 180; passenger care 395, 400; popular press awards 363–364; research on 363–367
service-related drivers of demand 314, 315
SERVPERF 363, 364, 365
SERVQUAL 363, 364, 365, 368

SESAR Deployment Manager (SDM) 78n2
SESAR Joint Undertaking (SJU) 67, 78n2
Sgouridis, S. 281
Shanghai 45, 165, 261, 272, 325
shareholders 285, 302, 303
Shaw, S. 139
Shepherd, B. 37, 88
Sherali, H.D. 240
shipping 40
shocks 315
SilverJet 128
Sim, K.L. 385
Sinclair, K. 254
Singapore 20, 25n14, 320; air cargo 32, 37, 38;
    capacity 261; complaints 383; foreign ownership
    restrictions 97; investment in British airports 55;
    MALIAT 95; safety issues 22; Scoot 101, 144;
    see also Changi Airport
Singapore Airlines 25n14, 117; air cargo 21, 43,
    44; Capital Express 145; charitable partnerships
    284; market development 145; partnerships 150;
    passenger care 395, 400; premium economy
    cabins 207; price-fixing 45; Scoot 141; smart
    cards 342; sponsorship 214; Star Alliance 98
single aviation markets (SAMs) 95
Single European Sky (SES) 19–20, 31, 60, 62–63,
    67–68, 74
Single European Sky ATM Research (SESAR) 62,
    63, 66, 67–68, 76, 273
single-till approach 191–192
SITA 342
Skorupski, J. 354
Skouloudis, A. 302
Skyscanner 213
SkyTeam 24n7, 98, 100, 102, 105, 140; air cargo
    126; destinations 126; market share 24n8, 181;
    price-fixing 45; United States 17
SkyTrax 363–364
SkyWest 141–142, 148
slot coordination 259, 265, 270–271, 273,
    274, 336
Slovak Republic 64
Slovakia 397
Slovenia 64, 320
smart cards 342
smartphones 213, 228–229, 338; see also mobile
    technology
Smith, Adam 374
Smith, B. 243
Smith, C.R. 332
Snowflake 394
social dumping 397, 398
social engagement 282–284, 287, 288, 291
social equity 299
social marketing 221, 224, 234
social media: airline marketing 24, 209, 214,
    215–216, 338–339; airport marketing 223, 227,

228, 229–231; branding 232; innovations 340;
    word of mouth 385; see also Internet
Soshkin, M. 84
Soumis, F. 241, 248, 253
South Africa 30, 56, 319–324
South America: air cargo 30, 34; airports 49, 196;
    mergers and acquisitions 150–151; passenger
    numbers 13; see also Latin America
Southampton Airport 54, 55
Southwest Airlines 103, 104, 140, 141–142;
    ancillary revenues 17; baggage fees 210; business
    model 127; complaints 384; employee well-
    being and engagement 283, 287, 399; fuel
    hedging 179; human resource management
    399–400; merger 24n6, 147, 148, 151; organic
    growth 147; service quality 376; short-haul
    flights 85–86; sponsorship 215; sustainability and
    corporate social responsibility 277, 282, 285, 287
Spain: air cargo 35; airports 19, 129, 198;
    functional airspace blocks 64; low cost
    carriers 397
Spasojevic, B. 221
specialisation 122, 123, 125–129, 131, 133, 161
speed 33, 34, 39
Spiller, P.T. 182n3
Spirit 103, 105, 362, 367
Spohr, Carsten 19
sponsorship 214–216, 223
SPOT programme 348
Spreen, W.E. 83
Sriwijaya Air 116
stage length 173, 179
stakeholder engagement 167, 223–224, 279, 302,
    306–307
Stambaugh, C. 229
standards 62
Stansfeld, S.A. 403
Stansted Airport 50, 54, 159, 164–165, 194;
    charges 194; environmental issues 305; low cost
    carriers 130, 394; runway capacity 266; selling
    of 55; website and mobile innovations 229
Star Alliance 24n7, 98, 100, 102, 105, 140; Altea
    DCS 342; destinations 126; market share 24n8,
    181; price-fixing 45; United States 17
Starkie, D. 156, 193, 194, 197
state ownership 191, 303
Steer Davies Gleave 271, 386, 388
Steppler, U. 382
Steurer, R. 302
Steven, A.B. 384, 385
Stewart, M. 347–348
Stockholm Arlanda Airport 304
Stojković, M. 253
strategic planning 143, 144, 156, 161, 263, 269, 274
strategy: air cargo 42, 43; airlines 5, 87–88,
    139–153; airports 6, 154–170, 233; customer
    satisfaction 376; low cost carriers 398

strikes 19, 73, 393, 395, 399–400
Sturm, R.R. 178
Stuttgart 266
subcontracting 65, 393, 397
subnetwork fleet assignment model (SFAM) 241–242
substitutes 157, 158
suppliers 157, 158
supply chains: air cargo 33, 34–35, 37, 39, 41; airports 165; commercial aerospace industry 91; global airline industry 23; value chains 88
surface transport 40
sustainability: airlines 6–7, 277–296; airports 7, 297–310; commercial aerospace industry 81, 89; communication and publicity 286–287; criticism and greenwash 290–291; definitions of 278, 299–300; drivers for 303; economic dimension 284–285; environmental dimension 279–282; reporting 287–290; social dimension 282–284; see also environmental issues
Sustainable Framework for Aviation 299
Suzuki, Y. 383, 385
Swan, W. 172
Sweden: ACR 133; air cargo 35; air transport demand 315; carbon emissions 411; COOPANS 78n3; corporate social responsibility 410; functional airspace blocks 64; remote tower services 68
Swiss Air 24n8, 24n9, 113, 149, 181, 342
Switzerland 19, 64
Sydney 130, 161–162, 261
system-wide information management (SWIM) 65–66, 68, 75

Taipei 266, 320
Taiwan: air cargo 32, 35, 37, 45; foreign ownership restrictions 97; open skies agreements 20; service quality 365
Talluri, K.T. 240
Tampa 269
Tan, A.K.-J. 116
Tanzania 113
TAP Portugal 99, 211
taxes 347, 382
taxiways 267
Taylor, S.A. 363
technicians 22
technology 7, 101, 331–343; air cargo 30, 31, 46, 327; air traffic control 263, 273, 275; air traffic management 63, 66–71, 77, 78; airline marketing 206, 213–214, 216; airport developments 54; airport marketing 226, 227; commercial aerospace industry 81, 82, 89, 90, 91; cost efficiencies 23; emissions reductions 75–76, 280; Second World War 53; security 354–355, 359; US carriers 17; see also information technology; Internet; mobile technology

Ted 141
Ted Stevens Anchorage International Airport 38
Teodorović, D. 250
terminal control airspace (TCA) 263–264
terrorism 14, 105, 315; air cargo 33; Kenya 111; security issues 344–361; Turkey 102; see also 9/11 terrorist attacks
Thai Airways 21, 98
Thailand 14, 320; air cargo 35; foreign ownership restrictions 97; safety issues 22, 25n16; service quality 365
Thelle, M.H. 156, 157, 158, 220, 221
Thengvall, B.G. 250–251
Thomas Cook Airlines 101, 286
Thomson 128, 143
threat image projection (TIP) 354
3D printing 90
throughput maximisation 272–273, 274–275
ticket distribution channels 211–214
time-series models 317, 318
TNT 43
Todd, P.E. 352
Tok, Y.C.A. 37
Tomer, J.F. 298
Tonga 95
Topping, P. 226
Toronto Pearson Airport 163, 231, 233, 342
Torres, E. 195
total factor productivity (TFP) 173, 198
total journey time 174
tour operators 124, 143, 221
tourism 11–12, 24, 124, 133, 158; airport marketing 220, 223–224, 231; business models 122; charter services 142, 143; demand forecasts 317; emerging markets 120; Kenya 111; Mexico 113; pricing 209; Route Development Funds 225; strategic alliances 149
Tovar, B. 198
trade 11, 24, 105; air cargo 29, 40; fall in 36; growth in passenger numbers 12; liberalisation 104
trade unions 23, 394, 396, 399–400
training 353, 354, 395
Trans World Airlines 332
Transavia 397
transhipment 37–38
Transportation Research 3
Transportation Security Administration (TSA) 350, 354, 356
travel agents 131, 212–213, 332, 337–338
travel banks 224
travel management companies (TMCs) 213
Travel Norwich International 165
travel supermarket concept 132, 133
Travelocity 213
Treanor, S. 178
Treat, A. 358
Tretheway, M.W. 157, 220

triple bottom line 278, 279
Troester, J. 338
trusted traveller programmes (TTPs) 348, 351, 356–357
Tsekeris, T. 197
Tsikriktsis, N. 179, 384
TUI 101, 128, 143
Tunisia 64
Tupolev 82
Turkey 159, 319–324, 365, 366
Turkish Airlines 101, 102, 106n7; free Wi-Fi 146; growth 18–19; market share 24n8; sustainability and corporate social responsibility 282
turnaround 161
Turner, S.P. 179
Twitter 215, 216, 228, 230, 385
two-sided platforms 190

Uchronski, P. 354
Uganda 366
Ukraine 320
ultra-low cost carriers 105, 398
unbundling 209, 211
uncertainty 154, 254, 327, 336
UNICEF Change for Good programme 284, 287, 412
unions 23, 394, 396, 399–400
United Aircraft Corporation (UAC) 89–90
United Airlines 103, 125; air cargo 43; ancillary revenues 17; Apollo reservation system 332; capacity growth 16; community involvement 283; complaints 387–388; cross-regional ownership 99; fares 209; frequent flyer programme 17, 388; joint ventures 18, 100; LGBT employees 291; market share 24n8; merger 24n6, 181; Mexico 114; premium cabins 207; pricing 211; slimline seats 208; sponsorship 215; Star Alliance 98, 100; Ted 141
United Arab Emirates 105, 320
United Kingdom (UK): aeronautical science 1; air cargo 30, 31; air transport demand 315; airport charges 19; airport economics and finance 190, 191, 192, 196, 197; airport expansion 411–412; airport industry 52, 53–57; airport marketing 220; airport strategy 164–165; aviation market 14; Brexit 14, 24n1, 38; charter carriers 143; demand forecasts and models 317, 318; drones 31; elasticity of demand 316, 317; environmental issues 305; functional airspace blocks 64; green belt 308n1; number of airports 50; passenger segmentation 13; peak hour traffic 269; PPPs 133; price controls 94; privatisation 129; sustainability and corporate social responsibility 290, 299; trade unions 394
United Nations (UN) 31, 89, 307, 375
United Nations Conference on Trade and Development (UNCATD) 319

United Nations Environment Programme (UNEP) 298
United Nations Framework Convention on Climate Change (UNFCCC) 405, 409
United Nations World Tourism Organisation (UNWTO) 12–13
United States (US): aeronautical revenues 193; aeronautical science 1; air cargo 29, 30, 31, 35, 38, 44–45; air traffic management 77; air transport demand 14, 315; airport construction 52; airport economics and finance 198; airport incentive schemes 224–225; airport strategy 166; antitrust immunity 100, 181; aviation market 14; banking 177; business models 125; charter carriers 128; commercial aerospace industry 83; complaints 383, 384; consolidation 23, 103, 104; consumer protection 374–375, 378–380; demand models 318; deregulation 94–95, 96, 103, 122, 124; disruptions 247; domestic traffic 313; economic regulation 191–192; fares 209; foreign ownership restrictions 97; franchising 149–150; fuel use 406; GPS 70; international networks 104; joint ventures 100; low cost airports 159; low cost carriers 105, 396; market concentration 105; mergers and acquisitions 24n6, 148, 172, 181; Mexico ASA 113–114, 120n1; noise restrictions 282; number of airports 49, 50; productivity 173; profitability of airlines 16–18; runway capacity 264, 266–267; seating 206–207; security 344, 346, 347–348, 350; service quality 366, 367; Southwest Airlines 399; sponsorship 214, 215; sustainability and corporate social responsibility 277; tourism 124; traffic growth 262; Transportation Research Board 3
University of Michigan 1–2
University of Westminster 2
Unmanned Aircraft System traffic management (UTM) 69
Unmanned Aircraft Systems (UASs) 62, 69, 78n5
Upham, P. 278, 299
UPS 35, 40, 43, 44, 45, 172–173
urbanisation 13, 33, 93, 115
US Airways 24n6, 181
user-preferred routes (UPRs) 71
Uzbekistan 35

Valdes, V. 315
Value Alliance 130
value chains 88
value of travel time savings (VTTS) 183n6
Van Marrewijk, M. 279
Vancouver International Airport 48
Vantage Airport Group 233
Vasigh, B. 196, 198
Veisten, K. 351
Venezuela 320

vertical integration 43, 161, 165–166
VHF omnidirectional ranges (VORs) 71
VietJet 21
Vietnam 35, 320
Virgin America 24n6, 151, 368
Virgin Atlantic 18, 101, 105n6, 151; air cargo 43; code-share agreements 99, 102; joint ventures 181; market share 24n8; sustainability and corporate social responsibility 280–281, 286, 290
Virgin Australia 99, 100, 130, 149, 150, 151
Virgin Group 146
Viscusi, W.K. 348
visual flight rules (VFR) 266–267
VivaAerobus 114
Vogel, H.-A. 197–198
Vogler, R. 382
Volaris 114, 120n1, 211
Voltes-Dorta, A. 196
von Nordenflycht, A. 396
von Wartburg, M. 183n6
Vueling 24n9, 181, 398

Wadud, Z. 315
Waguespack, B.P. 373
Wang, J.-H.E. 179
Wang, X. 242
Wanke, P. 197
war 14, 30; see also First World War; Second World War
Warburg, V. 242
Warsaw 266
Washington 17
waste 280, 282, 303, 305, 402–403
water use 280, 303, 305
Waters II, W.G. 183n6
Wattanacharoensil, W. 230
Weatherill, J. 225
websites 212, 213, 337; airport marketing 223, 227, 228–229; service quality 366, 367; sponsorship 215; see also Internet; social media
Wei, G. 253
Weide, O. 247, 248
weighted average cost of capital (WACC) 196
Weisskopf, N. 112
Wells, E. 223–224
Wensveen, J. 126, 130
WestJet 96, 101, 105
Wheatcroft, S. 290

White, L.J. 172
Whyte, R. 130, 144
Wi-Fi 146, 209, 340
Wiltshire, J. 156
Winston, C. 175
Wittman, M. 103
Wittmer, A. 383
Wizz Air 24n1, 96, 105, 131, 211, 398
Wojahn, O.W. 177
Wolters, M. 318
Wong, S. 350
word of mouth (WOM) 385, 387
WordPress 385
World Bank 112, 301, 319
World Business Council for Sustainable Development (WBCSD) 278, 282–283
World Commission on Environment and Development (WCED) 278
World Meteorological Organisation (WMO) 298
World Trade Organisation (WTO) 104, 108, 113, 114, 118, 321
WOW Air 101, 105, 126
Wright brothers 1, 30, 51–52, 82, 331–332

X-ray screening 352
Xia, Z.Y. 132
Xystouri, T. 385

Yan, S. 241, 251
Yang, D.H. 251
Yang, H. 193
Yang, X. 324
Yao, S. 324
Yarrow, G. 194
Yayla-Kullu, H.M. 368
Yemen 358
Yoshida, Y. 197
YouTube 230, 385
Yu, C. 173, 197
Yu, M. 198

Zhang, A. 110, 177, 182, 183n9, 189, 198
Zhang, Y. 174, 175, 180, 317
Zhao, Q. 198
Zink, K.J. 279
Zoom Airlines 130
Zuidberg, J. 143, 172, 179
Zurich Airport 48, 167, 220, 269, 304, 342, 346